NOTES,

EXPLANATORY AND PRACTICAL,

ON THE [redacted]

EPISTLES OF PAUL

TO THE

EPHESIANS, PHILIPPIANS, AND COLOSSIANS.

BY ALBERT BARNES.

NEW YORK:
HARPER & BROTHERS, PUBLISHERS
329 & 331 PEARL STREET,
FRANKLIN SQUARE.
1854.

[redacted]

INTRODUCTION.

§ 1. *The Situation of Ephesus, and the Character of its People.*

This epistle purports to have been written to the "Saints in Ephesus, and to the faithful in Christ Jesus," though, as we shall see, the fact of its having been directed to the church at Ephesus has been called in question. Assuming now that it was sent to Ephesus, it is of importance to have a general view of the situation of that city, of the character of its people, and of the time and manner in which the gospel was introduced there, in order to a correct understanding of the epistle. Ephesus was a celebrated city of Ionia in Asia Minor, and was about 40 miles south of Smyrna, and near the mouth of the river Cayster. The river, though inferior in beauty to the Meander which flows south of it, waters a fertile vale of the ancient Ionia. Ionia was the most beautiful and fertile part of Asia Minor; was settled almost wholly by Greek colonies; and embosomed Pergamos, Smyrna, Ephesus, and Miletus. See Travels of Anacharsis, i. 91. 208; vi. 192. 97, 98. The climate of Ionia is represented as remarkably mild, and the air as pure and sweet, and this region became early celebrated for every thing that constitutes softness and effeminacy in life. Its people were distinguished for amiableness and refinement of manners, and also for luxury, for music and dancing, and for the seductive arts that lead to vicious indulgence. Numerous festivals occupied them at home, or attracted them to neighbouring cities, where the men appeared in magnificent habits, and the women in all the elegance of female ornament, and with all the desire of pleasure.—*Anachar.*

Ephesus was not, like Smyrna, distinguished for commercial advantages. The consequence has been that, not having such advantage, it has fallen into total ruin, while Smyrna has retained some degree of its ancient importance. It was in a rich region of country, and seems to have risen into importance mainly because it became the favourite resort of foreigners in the worship of Diana, and owed its celebrity to its temple more than to any thing else. This city was once, however, the most splendid city in Asia Minor. Stephens, the geographer, gives it the title of *Epiphanestate*, or "Most Illustrious;" Pliny styles it "The Ornament of Asia." In Roman times it was the metropolis of Asia, and unquestionably rose to a degree of splendour that was surpassed by few, if any, oriental cities.

That for which the city was most celebrated was the Temple of Diana. This temple was 425 feet in length, and 220 in breadth. It was encompassed by 127 pillars, each 60 feet in height, which were presented by as many kings. Some of those pillars, it is said, are yet to be seen in the mosque of St. Sophia at Constantinople, having been removed there when the church of St. Sophia was erected. These, however, were the pillars that constituted a part of the temple after it had been burned and was repaired, though it is probable that the same pillars were retained in the second temple which had constituted the glory of the first. All the provinces of Asia Minor contributed to the erection of this splendid temple, and two hundred years were consumed in building it. This temple was set on fire by a man named Herostratus, who, when put to the torture, confessed that his only motive was to immortalize his name. The general assembly of the states of Ionia passed a decree to devote his name to oblivion; but the fact of the decree has only served to perpetuate it. Cicer. de Nat. Deor. 2. 27. Plutarch, Life of Alex. Comp. Anachar. vi. 189. The whole of the edifice was consumed except the four walls and some of the columns. It was, however, rebuilt, with the same magnificence as before, and was regarded as one of the wonders of the world. It is now in utter ruin. After the temple had been repeatedly pillaged by the barbarians, Justinian removed the columns to adorn the church of St. Sophia at Constantinople. The place where it stood can now be identified certainly, if at all, only by the marshy spot on which it was erected, and by the prodigious arches raised above as a foundation. The vaults formed by them compose a sort of labyrinth, and the water is knee-deep beneath. There is not an apartment entire; but thick walls, shafts of columns, and fragments of every kind, are scattered around in confusion. Ency. Geog. ii. 273, 274.

In the reign of Tiberius, Ephesus was greatly damaged by an earthquake; but it was repaired and embellished by the emperor. In the war between Mithridates and the Romans, Ephesus took part with the former, and massacred the Romans who dwelt in it. Sylla severely punished this cruelty; but Ephesus was afterwards treated with lenity, and enjoyed its own laws, with other privileges. About the end of the eleventh century, it was seized by a pirate named Tangripermes, but he was routed by John Ducas, the Greek Admiral, in a bloody battle. Theodorus Lascarus, a Greek, made himself master of it in 1206. The Mohammedans recovered it in 1283. In the year 1401, Tamerlane employed a whole month in plundering the city and the neighbouring country. Shortly after the city was set on fire, and was mostly burnt in a combat between the Turkish governor and the Tartars. In 1405, it was taken by Mahomet I., and has continued since that time in the possession of the Turks. *Calmet.*

There is now a small and mean village, named Ayasaluk, near the site of the ancient town, consisting of a few cottages, which is all that now represents this city of ancient splendour. Dr. Chavolla says, "the inhabitants are a few Greek peasants, living in extreme wretchedness, dependence, and insensibility; the representatives of an illustrious people, and inhabiting the wreck of their greatness—some in the substructions of the glorious edifices which they raised—some beneath the vaults of the stadium, once the crowded scene of their diversions—and some by the abrupt precipice in the sepulchres which received their ashes. Its streets are obscured and overgrown. A herd of goats was driven to it for shelter from the sun at noon, and a noisy flight of crows from the quarries seemed to insult its silence. We heard the partridge call in the area of the theatre and the stadium. The glorious pomp of its heathen worship is no longer numbered; and Christianity, which was here nursed by apostles, and fostered by general councils, until it increased to fulness of stature, barely lingers on in an existence hardly visible." Travels, p.

131. Oxford, 1775. A very full and interesting description of Ephesus, as it appeared in 1739, may be seen in Pococke's Travels, vol. ii. Part ii. pp. 45—53, ed. Lond. 1745. Several ruins are described by him, but they have mostly now disappeared. The Temple of Diana was on the western side of the plain on which the city was built, and the site is now in the midst of a morass which renders access difficult. The ruins of several theatres and other buildings are described by Pococke.

In the year 1821, Mr. Fisk, the American Missionary, visited the ruins of Ephesus, of which he has given the following account. "We sent back our horses to Aisaluck, and set out on foot to survey the ruins of Ephesus. The ground was covered with high grass or grain, and a very heavy dew rendered the walking rather unpleasant. On the east side of the hill, we found nothing worthy of notice; no appearance of having been occupied for buildings. On the north side was the circus or stadium. Its length from east to west is forty rods or one stadium. The north or lower side was supported by arches which still remain. The area where the races used to be performed, is now a field of wheat. At the west end was the gate. The walls adjoining it are still standing, and are of considerable height and strength. North of the stadium, and separated only by a street, is a large square, inclined with fallen walls, and filled with the ruins of various edifices. A street running north and south divides this square in the centre. West of the stadium is an elevation of ground, level at the top, with an immense pedestal in the centre of it. What building stood there it is not easy to say. Between this and the stadium was a street passing from the great plain north of Ephesus, into the midst of the city.

"I found on the plains of Ephesus some Greek peasants, men and women, employed in pulling up tares and weeds from the wheat. I ascertained, however, that they all belonged to villages at a distance, and came there to labour. Tournefort says, that when he was at Ephesus, there were thirty or forty Greek families there. Chandler found only ten or twelve individuals. Now no human being lives in Ephesus; and in Aisaluck, which may be considered as Ephesus under another name, though not on precisely the same spot of ground, there are merely a few miserable Turkish huts.

"The plain of Ephesus is now very unhealthy, owing to the fogs and mists which almost continually rest upon it. The land, however, is rich, and the surrounding country is both fertile and healthy. The adjacent hills would furnish many delightful situations for villages, if the difficulties were removed which are thrown in the way by a despotic government, oppressive agas, and wandering banditti." Missionary Herald for 1821, p. 319.

The following cuts represent—the first, a general view of the ruins of Ephesus, and the second, from the Pictorial Bible, a view of one part of that city.

General View of the Ruins at Ephesus

Ephesus.

§ 2. *The Introduction of the Gospel at Ephesus.*

It is admitted by all that the gospel was introduced into Ephesus by the apostle Paul. He first preached there when on his way from Corinth to Jerusalem, about the year 54. Acts xviii. 19. On this visit he went into the synagogue, as was his usual custom, and preached to his own countrymen, but he does not appear to have preached publicly to the heathen. He was requested to remain longer with them, but he said he must by all means be in Jerusalem at the approaching feast—probably the passover. Acts xviii. 21. He promised, however, to visit them again if possible, and sailed from Ephesus to Jerusalem. Two persons had gone with Paul from Corinth—Priscilla and Aquila—whom he appears to have left at Ephesus, or who at any rate soon returned there. Acts xviii. 18. 26. During the absence of Paul, there came to Ephesus a certain Jew, born in Alexandria, named Apollos, an eloquent man, and mighty in the Scriptures, who had received the baptism of John, and who taught the doctrine that John had taught. Acts xviii. 24. 25. What was the precise nature of that doctrine it is difficult now to understand. It seems to have been in substance that repentance was necessary, that baptism was to be performed, and that the Messiah was about to appear. This doctrine Apollos had embraced with zeal, was ready to defend it, and was in just the state of mind to welcome the news that the Messiah had come. This zealous and talented man, Priscilla and Aquila instructed more fully in the doctrines of the Christian religion, and communicated to him the views which they had received from Paul. Acts xviii. 26. Paul having gone to Jerusalem as he purposed, returned again to Asia Minor, and taking Phrygia and Galatia in his way, revisited Ephesus, and remained there about three years. Acts xviii. 23; xix. 1, seq. It was during this time that the church was founded, which afterwards became so prominent, and to which this epistle was written. The principal events in the life of Paul there were, (1.) his baptizing the twelve persons whom he found there, who were disciples of John. Notes, Acts xix. 1—7. (2.) Paul went into the synagogue there, and engaged in an earnest discussion with the Jews, about three months, respecting the Messiah. Acts xix. 8—10. (3.) When many of the Jews opposed him, he left the synagogue, and obtained a place to preach in, in the school-room of a man by the name of Tyrannus. In this place he continued to preach without molestation for two years, and proclaimed the gospel so that a large portion of the inhabitants had an opportunity of hearing it. (4.) The cause of religion was greatly promoted by the miracles which Paul wrought. Acts xix. 11—17. (5.) Paul remained there until his preaching excited great commotion, and he was at last driven away by the tumult which was excited by Demetrius. Acts xix. 23—41. At this time the gospel had secured such a hold on the people that there was danger that the temple of Diana would be forsaken, and that all who were dependent on the worship of Diana for a livelihood would be thrown out of employment. It is not probable that Paul visited Ephesus after this, unless it was after his first imprisonment at Rome. See Intro. to II. Timothy. On his way from Macedonia to Jerusalem he came to Miletus, and sent for the elders of Ephesus, and gave them his deeply affecting parting address, expecting to see them no more. Acts xx. 16, seq.

Paul remained longer at Ephesus than he did at any other one place preaching the gospel. He seems to have set himself deliberately to work to establish a church there, which would ultimately overthrow idolatry. Several reasons may have led him to depart so far from his usual plan, by labouring so long in one place. One may have been that this was the principal seat of idolatry then in the world. The evident aim of Paul in his ministry was, to reach the centres of influence and power. Hence he mainly sought to preach the gospel in large cities, and thus it was that Antioch, and Ephesus, and Corinth, and Athens, and Philippi, and Rome, shared so largely in his labours. Not ashamed of the gospel any where, he yet sought mainly that its power should be felt where wealth, and earning, and genius, and talent were concentrated. The very places, therefore, where the most magnificent temples were erected to the gods, and where the worship of idols was celebrated with the most splendour and pomp, and where that worship was defended most strongly by the civil arm, were those in which the apostles sought first to preach the gospel. Ephesus, therefore, as the most splendid seat of idolatry at that time in the whole Pagan world, particularly attracted the attention of the apostle, and hence it was that he was willing to spend so large a part of his public life in that place. It may have been for this reason that John afterwards made it his permanent abode, and spent so many years there as the minister of the church which had been founded by Paul. See § 3. Another reason why Paul sought Ephesus as a field of labour may have been, that it was at that time not only the principal seat of idolatry, but was a place of great importance in the civil affairs of the Roman empire. It was the residence of the Roman Proconsul, and the seat of the courts of justice in Asia Minor, and consequently was a place to which there would be attracted a great amount of learning and talent. *Macknight.* The apostle, therefore, seems to have been anxious that the full power of the gospel should be tried there, and that Ephesus should become as important as a centre of influence in the Christian world, as it had been in Paganism and in civil affairs.

§ 3. *Notices of the History of the Church at Ephesus.*

The church at Ephesus was one of the seven churches of Asia, and the first one mentioned to which John was directed to address an epistle from Patmos. Rev. ii. 1—7. Little is said of it in the New Testament from the time when Paul left it until the book of Revelation was written. The *tradition* is, that Timothy was a minister at Ephesus, and was succeeded by the apostle John; but whether John came there while Timothy was living, or not until his removal or death, even *tradition* does not inform us. In the subscription to the sacred epistle to Timothy, it is said of Timothy that he was "ordained the first Bishop of the church of the Ephesians;" but this is of no authority whatever. All that can be with certainty learned about the residence of Timothy at Ephesus, is what the Apostle Paul says of him in his first epistle to Timothy. Ch. i. 3. "As I besought thee to abide still at Ephesus, when I went into Macedonia, that thou mightest charge some that they teach no other doctrine." From this it would appear that the residence of Timothy at Ephesus was a *temporary arrangement*, designed to secure a result which Paul wished particularly to secure, and to avoid an evil which he had reason to dread would follow from his own absence. That it was a temporary arrangement, is apparent from the fact that Paul soon after desired him to come to Rome, 2 Tim. iv. 9. 11. The second epistle of Paul to Timothy was written but a few years after the first. According to Lardner, the first was written in the year 56, and the second in the year 62; according to Hug, the first was written in the year 59, and the second in the year 61; according to the Editor of the Polyglott Bible, the first was written A. D. 65, and the second A. D. 66. According to either calculation the time of the residence of Timothy in Ephesus was brief. There is not the slightest evidence from the New Testament that he was a permanent Bishop of Ephesus, or indeed that he was a Bishop at all in the modern sense of the term. Those who may be disposed to look further into this matter, and to examine the relation which Timothy sustained to the church of Ephesus, and the claim which is sometimes set up for his having sustained the office of *a Bishop*, may find an examination in the Review of Bishop Onderdonk's Tract on Episcopacy, published in the Quarterly Christian Spectator in March 1834, and March 1835, and republished in 1843 under the title of "The Organization and Government of the Apostolic Church," pp. 99—107.

Whatever was the relation which he sustained to the church in Ephesus, it is agreed on all hands that John the apostle spent there a considerable portion of his life. At what time he went to Ephesus, or why he did it, is not now known. The common opinion is, that he remained at or near Jerusalem for some fifteen years after the crucifixion of the Lord Jesus, during which time he had the special charge of Mary the mother of the Saviour; that he then preached the gospel to the Parthians and the Indians, and that he then returned and went to Ephesus, in or near which he spent his latter days, and in which, at a very advanced age, he died. It was from Ephesus that, under the Emperor Domitian, A. D. 95, he was banished to the island of Patmos, from which he returned A. D. 97, on the accession of Nerva to the crown, who recalled all who had been banished. John is supposed at that time to have been about ninety years of age. He is said to have died at Ephesus in the third year of Trajan, A. D. 100, aged about ninety-four years. For a full and interesting biography of the Apostle John, the reader may consult the "Lives of the Apostles," by David Francis Bacon, pp. 307—376.

Of the subsequent history of the church at Ephesus, little is known, and it would not be necessary to dwell upon it in order to an exposition of the epistle before us. It is sufficient to remark, that the "candlestick is removed out of its place," (Rev. ii. 5,) and that all the splendour of the temple of Diana, all the pomp of her worship, and all the glory of the Christian church there, have alike faded away.

§ 4. *The time and place of writing the Epistle.*

It has never been denied that the Apostle Paul was the author of this epistle, though it has been made a question whether it were written to the Ephesians or to the Laodiceans. See § 5. Dr. Paley (*Horæ Paulinæ*) has shown that there is conclusive internal proof that this epistle was written by Paul. This argument is derived from the style, and is carried out by a comparison of this epistle with the other undoubted writings of the apostle. The historical evidence on this point also is undisputed.

It is generally supposed, and indeed the evidence seems to be clear, that this epistle was written during the imprisonment of the apostle at Rome; but whether it was during his first or his second imprisonment, is not certain. Paul was held in custody for some two years in Cesarea, (Acts xxiv. 27,) but there is no evidence that during that time, he addressed any epistle to the churches which he had planted. That this was written when he was a prisoner, is apparent from the epistle itself. "The two years in which Paul was imprisoned at Cesarea," says Wall, as quoted by Lardner, "seem to have been the most inactive part of St. Paul's life. There is no account of any proceedings or disputations, or of any epistles written in this space." This may have arisen, Lardner supposes, from the fact that the Jews made such an opposition that the Roman governor would not allow him to have any intercourse with the people at large, or procure any intelligence from the churches abroad. But when he was at Rome, he had more liberty. He was allowed to dwell in his own hired house, (Acts xxviii. 30,) and had permission to address all who came to him, and to communicate freely with his friends abroad. It was during this period that he wrote at least four of his epistles—to the Ephesians, the Philippians, the Colossians, and Philemon. Grotius, as quoted by Lardner, says of these epistles, that though all Paul's epistles are excellent, yet he most admires those written by him when a prisoner at Rome. Of the epistle to the Ephesians, he says it surpasses all human eloquence—rerum sublimitatem adæquans verbis sublimioribus, quam ulla unquam habuit lingua humana—describing the sublimity of the things by corresponding words more sublime than are found elsewhere in human language. The evidence that it was written when Paul was a prisoner, is found in the epistle itself. Thus in ch. iii. 1, he says, "I Paul, the prisoner of Jesus Christ—ὁ δέσωιος τοῦ χριστοῦ—for you Gentiles." So he alludes to his afflictions in ch. iii. 13. "I desire that ye faint not at my tribulations for you." In ch. iv. 1, he calls himself the "prisoner of the Lord," or in the margin, "in the Lord"—ὁ δέσμιος ἐν κυρίω. And in ch. vi. 19, 20, there is an allusion which seems to settle the inquiry beyond dispute, and to prove that it was written while he was at Rome. He there says that he was an "ambassador *in bonds*"—ἐν ἁλύσει—*in chains, manacles, or shackles;* and yet he desires (ver. 19, 20) that they would pray for him, that utterance might be given him to open his mouth boldly to make known the mystery of the gospel, that he might speak boldly, as he ought to speak. Now this is a remarkable circumstance. A man in custody, in bonds or chains, and that too for being an "ambassador," and yet asking the aid of their prayers, that in these circumstances he might have grace to be a bold preacher of the gospel. If he was in prison this could not well be. If he was under a strict prohibition it could not well be. The circumstances of the case tally exactly with the statement in the last chapter of the Acts of the Apostles, that Paul was in custody in Rome; that he was permitted to "dwell by himself with a soldier that kept him," (ver. 16;) that he was permitted to call the Jews together, and to debate with them freely, (vs. 17—28;) and that Paul dwelt in his own hired house for two years, and "received all that came in with him, preaching the kingdom of God," &c. (vs. 30, 31.) So exactly do these circumstances correspond, that I have no doubt that was the time when the epistle was written. And so unusual is such a train of circumstances—so unlikely would it be to occur to a man to *forge* such a coincidence, that it furnishes a striking proof that the epistle was written, as it purports to be, by Paul. An impostor would not have thought of inventing such a coincidence. If it had occurred to him to make *any* such allusion, the place and time would have been more distinctly mentioned, and not have been left as a mere incidental allusion. The Apostle Paul is supposed to have been at Rome as a prisoner twice, (Comp. Intro. to 2 Tim.,) and to have suffered martyrdom there about A. D. 65 or 66. If the epistle to the Ephesians was written during his second imprisonment at Rome, as is commonly supposed, then it must have been somewhere between the years 63 and 65. Lardner and Hug suppose that it was written April 61; Macknight supposes it was in 60 or 61; the Editor of the Polyglott Bible places it at 64. The exact time when it was written cannot now be ascertained, and is not material.

§ 5. *To whom was the Epistle written?*

The epistle purports to have been written to the Ephesians—"to the saints which are at Ephesus,"—i. 1. But the opinion that it was written to the Ephesians, has been called in question by many expositors. Dr. Paley (*Hor. Paul.*) supposes that it was written to the Laodiceans. Wetstein also maintained the same opinion. This opinion was expressly stated also by Marcion, a "heretic" of the second century. Michaelis (Intro.) supposes that it was a "circular epistle,' addressed not to any church in particular, but intended for the Ephesians, Laodiceans, and some other churches of Asia Minor. He supposes that the apostle had several copies taken; that he made it intentionally of a very general character, so as to suit all; that he affixed with his own hand the subscription, ch. vi. 24, to each copy—"Grace be with all them that love our Lord Jesus Christ in sincerity;" that at the beginning of the epistle the name was inserted of the particular church to which it was to be sent—as "to the church in Ephesus"—"in Laodicea," &c. When the several works composing the New Testament were collected into a volume, he supposes that it so happened, that the copy of this epistle which was used, was one obtained from Ephesus, containing a direction to the saints there. This is also the opinion of Archbishop Usher and Koppe. It does not comport with the design of these Notes, to go into an extended examination of this question; and after all that has been written on it, and the different opinions which have been entertained, it certainly does not become any one to be very confident. It is not a question of great importance, as it involves no point of doctrine or duty; but those who wish to see it discussed at length, can be satisfied by referring to Paley's *Horæ Paulinæ;* to Michaelis' Intro., vol. iv. ch. xx., and to the Prolegomena of Koppe. The arguments which are alleged to prove that it was addressed to the church at Laodicea, or at least *not* to the church at Ephesus, are summarily the following:—(1.) The testimony of Marcion, a heretic of the second century, who affirms that it was sent to the church in Laodicea, and that instead of the reading (ch. i. 1) "in Ephesus," in the copy which he had it was "in Laodicea." But the opinion of Marcion is now regarded as of little weight. It is admitted that he was in the habit of altering the Greek text to suit his own views. (2.) The principal objection to the opinion that it was written to the church at Ephesus, is found in certain internal marks, and particularly in the want of any allusion to the fact that Paul had ever been there, or to any thing that particularly related to the church there. This difficulty comprises several particulars. (*a*) Paul spent nearly three years in Ephesus, and was engaged there in deeply interesting transactions and occurrences. He had founded the church, ordained its elders, taught them the doctrines which they held, and had at last been persecuted there and driven away. If the epistle was written to them, it is remarkable that there is in the epistle no allusion to any one of these facts or circumstances. This is the more remarkable, as it was his usual custom to allude to the events which had occurred in the churches which he had founded, (see the epistles to the Corinthians and Philippians,) and as on two other occasions at least he makes direct allusion to these transactions at Ephesus. See Acts xx. 18—35, 1 Cor. xv. 32. (*b*) In the other epistles which Paul wrote, it was his custom to salute a large number of persons by name; but in this epistle there is no salutation of any kind. There is a general invocation of "peace to the brethren," (ch. vi. 23,) but no mention of an individual by name. There is not even an allusion to the "elders" whom, with so much affection, he had addressed at Miletus, (Acts xx.,) and to whom he had given so solemn a charge. This is the more remarkable, as in this place he had spent three years in preaching the gospel, and must have been acquainted with all the leading members in the church. To the church at Rome, which he had never visited when he wrote his epistle to the Romans, he sends a large number of salutations, (ch. xvi.); to the church at Ephesus, where he had spent a longer time than in any other place, he sends none. (*c*) The name of Timothy does not occur in the epistle. This is remarkable, because Paul had left him there with a special charge, (1 Tim. i. 3,) and if he was still there, it is singular that no allusion is made to him, and no salutation sent to him. If he had left Ephesus, and had gone to Rome to meet Paul as he requested, (2 Tim. iv. 9,) it is remarkable that Paul did not join his name with his own in sending the epistle to the church, or at least allude to the fact that he had arrived. This is the more remarkable, because in the Epistles to the Philippians, Colossians, and 1 and 2 Thessalonians, the name of Timothy is joined with that of Paul at the commencement of the epistle. (*d*) Paul speaks of the persons to whom this epistle was sent, as if he had not been with them, or at least in a manner which is hardly conceivable, on the supposition that he had been the founder of the church. Thus in ch. i. 15, 16, he says, "Wherefore also after I *heard* of your faith in Christ Jesus," &c. But this circumstance is not conclusive. Paul may have been told of the *continuance* of their faith, and of their *growing* love and zeal, and he may have alluded to that in this passage. (*e*) Another circumstance on which some reliance has been placed, is the statement in ch. iii. 1, 2. "For this cause, I Paul, the prisoner of Jesus Christ for you Gentiles, if ye have heard of the dispensation of the grace of God which is given to you-ward," &c. It is argued (see Michaelis) that this is not language which would have been employed by one who had founded the church, and with whom they were all acquainted. He would not have spoken in a manner implying any doubt whether they had ever *heard* of him and his labours in the ministry on account of the Gentiles. Such are the considerations relied on to show that the epistle could not have been written to the Ephesians.

On the other hand there is proof of a very strong character that it was written to them. That proof is the following:

1. The common reading in ch. i. 1, "To the saints which are in Ephesus." It is true, as we have seen, that this reading has been called in question. Mill says that it is omitted by Basil, (Lib. 2. *Adversus Eunomium*,) as he says, "on the testimony of the fathers and of ancient copies." Griesbach marks it with the sign *om.*, denoting that it was omitted by some, but that in his judgment it is to be retained. It is found in the Vulgate, the Syriac, the Arabic, and the Ethiopic in Walton's Polyglott. Rosenmüller remarks that "most of the ancient codices, and all the ancient versions, retain the word." To my mind this fact is conclusive. The testimony of Marcion is admitted to be of almost no authority: and as to the testimony of Basil, it is only one against the testimony of all the ancients, and is at best negative in its character. See the passage from Basil, quoted in Hug's Introduction.

2. A slight circumstance may be adverted to as throwing light incidentally on this question. This epistle was sent by Tychicus. Ch. vi. 21. The Epistle to the Colossians was also sent from Rome by the same messenger. Col. iv. 7. Now there is a strong improbability in the opinion held by Michaelis, Koppe and others, that this was a *circular* letter, sent to the churches at large, or that different copies were prepared, and the name Ephesus inserted in one, and Laodicea in another, &c. The improbability is this, that the apostle would at the same time send such a circular letter to several of the churches, and a *special* letter to the church at Colosse. What claim had *that* church to special notice? What pre-eminence had it over the church at Ephesus? And why should he send them a letter bearing so strong a resemblance to that addressed to the other churches, when the same letter would have suited the church at Colosse as well as the one which was actually sent to them; for there is a nearer resemblance between these two epistles, than any other two portions of the Bible. Besides, in 2 Tim. iv. 12, Paul says that he had sent "Tychicus *to Ephesus*;" and what is more natural than that at that time he sent this epistle by him?

3. There is the utter want of evidence from MSS. or versions, that this epistle was sent to Laodicea, or to any other church, except Ephesus. Not a MS. has been found having the name *Laodicea* in ver. i. 1.; and not one which omits the words "in Ephesus." If it had been sent to another church, or if it had been a circular letter addressed to no particular church, it is scarcely credible that this could have occurred.

These considerations make it plain to me that this epistle was addressed, as it purports to have been, to the church in Ephesus. I confess myself wholly unable, however, to explain the remarkable circumstances that Paul does not refer to his former residence there; that he alludes to none of his troubles or his triumphs; that he makes no mention of the "elders," and salutes no one by name; and that throughout he addresses them as if they were to him personally unknown. In this respect it is unlike all the other epistles which he ever wrote, and all which we should have expected from a man in such circumstances. May it not be accounted for from *this very fact*, that an attempt to specify individuals where so many were known, would protract the epistle to an unreasonable length? There is, indeed, one supposition suggested by Dr. Macknight, which may possibly explain to some extent the remarkable circumstances above referred to. It is, that a direction may have been given by Paul to Tychicus, by whom he sent the letter, to send a copy of it to the Laodiceans, with an order to them to communicate it to the Colossians. In such a case every thing local would be designedly omitted, and the epistle would be of as general a character as possible. This is, however, mere conjecture, and does not remove the whole of the difficulty.

§ 6. *The object for which the epistle was written.*

Very various opinions have been formed in regard to the design for which this epistle was written. Macknight supposes that it was with reference to the Eleusinian mysteries, and to various religious rites in the Temple of Diana, and that Paul intended particularly to state the "mysteries" of the gospel in contradistinction from them. But there is no clear evidence that the apostle had any such object, and it is not necessary to go into an explanation of those mysteries in order to an understanding of the epistle. The epistle is such as might be addressed to any Christians, though there are allusions to customs which then prevailed, and to opinions then held, which it is desirable to understand in order to a just view of it. That there were Jews and Judaizing Christians in Ephesus, may be learned from the epistle itself. That there were those there who supposed that the Jews were to have a more elevated rank than the Gentiles, may also be learned from the epistle; and one object was to show that all true Christians, whether of Jewish or Heathen origin, were on a level, and were entitled to the same privileges. That there was the prevalence of a false and dangerous philosophy there, may also be learned from the epistle; and that there were those who attempted to cause divisions, and who had violated the unity of the faith, may also be learned from it.

The epistle is divided into two parts—I. The doctrinal part, ch. i.—iii.; and, II. The practical part, or the application, ch. iv.—vi.

I. The doctrinal part comprises the following topics.

(1.) Praise to God for the revelation of his eternal counsels of recovering mercy. Ch. i. 3—14.

(2.) A prayer of the apostle, expressing his earnest desire that the Ephesians might avail themselves fully of all the advantages of this eternal purpose of mercy. Ch. i. 15—23.

(3.) The doctrine of the native character of man, as being dead in sins, illustrated by the past lives of the Ephesians. Ch. ii. 1—3.

(4.) The doctrine of regeneration by the grace of God, and the advantages of it. Ch. ii. 5—7.

(5.) The doctrine of salvation by grace alone without respect to our own works. Ch. ii. 8, 9.

(6.) The privilege of being thus admitted to the fellowship of the saints. Ch. ii. 11—22.

(7.) A full statement of the doctrine that God meant to admit the Gentiles to the privileges of his people, and to break down the barriers between the Gentiles and the Jews. Ch. iii. 1—12.

(8.) The apostle prays earnestly that they might avail themselves fully of this doctrine, and be able to appreciate fully the advantages which it was intended to confer; and with this prayer he closes the doctrinal part of the epistle. Ch. iii. 13—21.

II. The practical part of the epistle embraces the following topics, viz.

(1.) Exhortation to unity, drawn from the consideration that there was one God, one faith, &c. Ch. iv. 1—16.

(2.) An exhortation to a holy life *in general*, from the fact that they differed from other Gentiles. Ch. iv. 17—24.

(3.) Exhortation to exhibit *particular* virtues—*specifying* what was required by their religion, and what they should avoid—particularly to avoid the vices of anger, lying, licentiousness, and intemperance. Ch. iv. 25—32. Ch. v. 1—20.

(4.) The duties of husbands and wives. Ch. v. 21—33.

(5.) The duties of parents and children. Ch. vi. 1—3.

(6.) The duties of masters and servants. Ch. vi. 4—9.

(7.) An exhortation to fidelity in the Christian warfare. Ch. vi. 10—20.

(8.) Conclusion. Ch. vi. 21—24.

The style of this epistle is exceedingly animated. The apostle is cheered by the intelligence which he had received of their deportment in the gospel, and is warmed by the grandeur of his principal theme—the eternal purposes of divine mercy. Into the discussion of that subject he throws his whole soul, and there is probably no part of Paul's writings where there is more ardour, elevation, and *soul* evinced, than in this epistle. The great doctrine of predestination he approaches as a most important and vital doctrine; states it freely and fully, and urges it as the basis of the Christian's hope, and the foundation of eternal gratitude and praise. Perhaps nowhere is there a better illustration of the power of that doctrine to elevate the soul and fill it with grand conceptions of the character of God, and to excite grateful emotions, than in this epistle; and the Christian, therefore, may study it as a portion of the sacred writings eminently fitted to excite his gratitude, and to fill him with adoring views of God.

THE EPISTLE OF

PAUL THE APOSTLE TO THE EPHESIANS.

CHAPTER I.

PAUL, an apostle of Jesus Christ by the will of God, to the saints[a] which are at Ephesus,[b] and to the faithful[c] in Christ Jesus:

a Ro. 1. 7. b Ac. ch. 19, 20. c Col. 1. 2.

ANALYSIS OF THE CHAPTER.

(1.) The salutation. Vs. 1, 2.

(2.) The doctrine of predestination, and its bearing and design. Vs. 3—14.

(*a*) It is the foundation of praise to God, and is a source of gratitude. Ver. 3.

(*b*) Christians have been chosen before the foundation of the world. Ver. 4.

(*c*) The object was that they should be holy and blameless. Ver. 4.

(*d*) They were predestinated to be the children of God. Ver. 5.

(*e*) The cause of this was the good pleasure of God, or he did it according to the purpose of his will. Ver. 5.

(*f*) The object of this was his own glory. Ver. 6.

(3.) The benefits of the plan of predestination to those who are thus chosen. Vs. 7—14.

(*a*) They have redemption and the forgiveness of sins. Vs. 7, 8.

(*b*) They are made acquainted with the mystery of the divine will. Vs. 9, 10.

(*c*) They have obtained an inheritance in Christ. Ver. 11.

(*d*) The object of this was the praise of the glory of God. Ver. 12.

(*e*) As the result of this, or in the execution of this purpose, they were sealed with the Holy Spirit of promise. Vs. 13, 14.

(4.) An earnest prayer that they might have a full understanding of the great and glorious plan of redemption. Vs. 15—23.

(*a*) Paul says that he had been informed of their faith. Ver. 15.

(*b*) He always remembered them in his prayers. Ver. 16.

(*c*) His especial desire was that they might see the glory of the Lord Jesus, whom God had exalted to his own right hand in heaven Vs. 17—23.

1. *Paul, an apostle.* See Notes on Rom. i. 1. ¶ *By the will of God.* See Notes on 1 Cor. i. 1. ¶ *To the saints.* A name often given to Christians because they are holy. See Notes on 1 Cor. i. 2. ¶ *In Ephesus.* See the Introduction, § 1. 5. ¶ *And to the faithful in Christ Jesus.* This evidently refers to others than to those who were in Ephesus, and it is clear that Paul expected that this epistle would be read by others. He gives it a *general* character, as if he supposed that it might be transcribed, and become the property of the church at large. It was not uncommon for him thus to give a general character to the epis-

2 Grace [a] *be* to you, and peace, from God our Father, and *from* the Lord Jesus Christ.

3 Blessed [b] *be* the God and Father of our Lord Jesus Christ, who hath blessed us with all spiritual blessings in heavenly [1] *places* in Christ:

a Ga. 1. 3; Ti. 1. 4. b 2 Co. 1. 3; 1 Pe. 1. 3.

1 or, *things*. He. 9. 23.

tles which he addressed to particular churches, and so to write that others than those to whom they were particularly directed, might feel that they were addressed to them. Thus the first epistle to the Corinthians was addressed to "the church of God in Corinth—with all that in every place call upon the name of Christ Jesus our Lord." The second epistle to the Corinthians in like manner was addressed to "the church of God which is at Corinth, with all the saints which are in all Achaia." Perhaps, in the epistle before us, the apostle referred particularly to the churches of Asia Minor which he had not visited, but there is no reason for confining the address to them. All who are "faithful in Christ Jesus" may regard the epistle as addressed by the Holy Spirit to them, and may feel that they are as much interested in the doctrines, promises, and duties set forth in this epistle, as were the ancient Christians of Ephesus. The word "faithful" here is not used in the sense of *trust-worthy*, or in the sense of *fidelity*, as it is often employed, but in the sense of *believing*, or *having faith* in the Lord Jesus. The apostle addresses those who were firm in the faith—another name for true Christians. The epistle contains great doctrines about the divine purposes and decrees in which they, as Christians, were particularly concerned; important "mysteries," (ver. 9,) of importance for them to understand, and which the apostle proceeds to communicate to them as such. The fact that the letter was designed to be published, shows that he was not unwilling that those high doctrines should be made known to the world at large; still they pertained particularly to the church, and they are doctrines which should be particularly addressed to the church. They are rather fitted to comfort the hearts of *Christians*, than to bring *sinners* to repentance. These doctrines may be addressed to the *church* with more prospect of securing a happy effect than to the world. In the church they will excite gratitude, and produce the hope which results from assured promises and eternal purposes; in the minds of sinners they may arouse envy, and hatred, and opposition to God.

2. *Grace to you*, &c. See Notes, Rom. i. 7.

3. *Blessed* be *the God and Father of our Lord Jesus Christ.* This commences a sentence which continues to the close of ver. 12. The length of the periods in the writings of Paul, is one cause of the obscurity of his style, and renders an explanation often difficult. The meaning of this phrase is, that God has laid a foundation for gratitude for what he has done. The ground or reason of the praise here referred to, is that which is stated in the following verses. The leading thing on which the apostle dwells is God's eternal purpose—his everlasting counsel in regard to the salvation of man. Paul breaks out into the exclamation that God is worthy of praise for such a plan, and that his eternal purposes, now manifest to men, give exalted views of the character and glory of God. Most persons suppose the contrary. They feel that the plans of God are dark, and stern, and forbidding, and such

as to render his character any thing but amiable. They speak of him when he is referred to as a sovereign, as if he were tyrannical and unjust, and they never connect the idea of that which is amiable and lovely with the doctrine of eternal purposes. There is no doctrine that is usually so unpopular; none that is so much reproached; none that is so much abused. There is none that men desire so much to disbelieve or avoid; none that they are so unwilling to have preached; and none that they are so reluctant to find in the Scriptures. Even many Christians turn away from it with dread; or if they *tolerate* it, they yet feel that there is something about it that is peculiarly dark and forbidding. Not so felt Paul. He felt that it laid the foundation for eternal praise; that it presented glorious views of God; that it was the ground of confidence and hope; and that it was desirable that Christians should dwell upon it, and praise God for it. Let us feel, therefore, as we enter upon the exposition of this chapter, that God is to be praised for ALL his plans, and that it is *possible* for Christians to have such views of the doctrine of *eternal predestination* as to give them most elevated conceptions of the glory of the divine character. And let us also be *willing* to know the truth. Let us approach word after word, and phrase after phrase, and verse after verse, in this chapter, willing to know *all* that God teaches; to believe all that he has revealed; and ready to say, 'Blessed be the God and Father of our Lord Jesus Christ for all that he has done.' ¶ *Who hath blessed us.* Who does Paul mean here by "*us?*" Does he mean all the world? This cannot be, for all the world are not thus blessed with *all* spiritual blessings. Does he mean *nations?* For the same reason this cannot be. Does he mean the Gentiles in contradistinction from the Jews? Why then does he use the word *us*, including himself, who was a Jew? Does he mean to say that they were blessed with external privileges, and that this was the only object of the eternal purposes of God? This cannot be, for he speaks of "spiritual blessings;" he speaks of the persons referred to as having "redemption" and "the forgiveness of sins;" as having "obtained an inheritance," and as being sealed with the "Holy Spirit of promise." These appertain not to nations, or to external privileges, or the mere offers of the gospel, but to true Christians; to persons who have been redeemed. The persons referred to by the word "*us*," are those who are mentioned in ver. 1, as "*saints*"—ἁγίοις—*holy;* and "faithful"—πιστοῖς—*believing*, or *believers*. This observation is important, because it shows that the plan or decree of God had reference to individuals, and not merely to nations. Many have supposed (see Whitby, Dr. A. Clarke, Bloomfield and others) that the apostle here refers to the *Gentiles*, and that his object is to show that they were now admitted to the same privileges as the ancient Jews, and that the whole doctrine of predestination here referred to, has relation to that fact. But, I would ask, were there no *Jews* in the church at Ephesus? See Acts xviii. 20. 24; xix. 1—8. The matter of fact seems to have been, that Paul was uncommonly successful there among his own countrymen, and that his chief difficulty there arose, not from the Jews, but from the influence of the heathen. Acts xix. 24. Besides, what evidence is there that the apostle speaks in this chapter peculiarly of the Gentiles, or that he was writing to that portion of the church at Ephesus which was of Gentile origin? And if he was, why did he name himself among them as one

4 According as he hath chosen [a] us in him before the foundation of the world that we should be holy, [b] and without blame before him in love:

a 1 Pe. 1. 2.

b Lu. 1. 75; Col. 1. 22.

---

on whom this blessing had been bestowed? The fact is, that this is a mere supposition, resorted to without evidence, and in the face of every fair principle of interpretation, to avoid an unpleasant doctrine. Nothing can be clearer than that Paul meant to write to *Christians as such;* to speak of privileges which they enjoyed as peculiar to themselves; and that he had no particular reference to *nations*, and did not design merely to refer to external privileges. ¶ *With all spiritual blessings.* Pardon, peace, redemption, adoption, the earnest of the Spirit, &c., referred to in the following verses —blessings which *individual Christians* enjoy, and not external privileges conferred on nations. ¶ *In heavenly* places *in Christ.* The word *places* is here understood, and is not in the original. It may mean heavenly *places*, or heavenly *things.* The word *places* does not express the best sense. The idea seems to be, that God has blessed us in Christ in regard to heavenly subjects or matters. In ver. 20, the word "places" seems to be inserted with more propriety. The same phrase occurs again in ch. ii. 6; iii. 10; and it is remarkable that it should occur in the same elliptical form four times in this one epistle, and, I believe, in no other part of the writings of Paul. Our translators have in each instance supplied the word "places," as denoting the rank or station of Christians, of the angels, and of the Saviour, to each of whom it is applied. The phrase probably means, in things pertaining to heaven; fitted to prepare us for heaven; and tending toward heaven. It probably refers here to every thing that was heavenly in its nature, or that had relation to heaven, whether gifts or graces. As the apostle is speaking, however, of the mass of Christians on whom these things had been bestowed, I rather suppose that he refers to what are called Christian graces, than to the extraordinary endowments bestowed on the few. The sense is, that *in* Christ; i. e. through Christ, or by means of him, God had bestowed all spiritual blessings that were fitted to prepare for heaven—such as pardon, adoption, the illumination of the Spirit, &c.

4. *According as.* The importance of this verse will render proper a somewhat minute examination of the words and phrases of which it is composed. The general sense of the passage is, that these blessings pertaining to heaven were bestowed upon Christians in accordance with an eternal purpose. They were not conferred by chance or hap-hazard. They were the result of intention and design on the part of God. Their value was greatly enhanced from the fact that God had designed from all eternity to bestow them, and that they come to us as the result of his everlasting plan. It was not a recent plan; it was not an after-thought; it was not by mere chance; it was not by caprice; it was the fruit of an eternal counsel. Those blessings had all the value, and all the assurance of *permanency*, which must result from that fact. The phrase "according as"—καθὼς—implies that these blessings were in conformity with that eternal plan, and have flowed to us as the expression of that plan. They are limited by

that purpose, for it marks and measures all. It was *as* God had chosen that it should be, and had appointed in his eternal purpose. ¶ *He hath chosen us.* The word "*us*" here shows that the apostle had reference to individuals, and not to communities. It includes Paul himself as one of the "chosen," and those whom he addressed—the mingled Gentile and Jewish converts in Ephesus. That it must refer to individuals is clear. Of no *community* as such can it be said that it was "chosen in Christ before the foundation of the world to be holy." It is not true of the Gentile world as such, nor of any one of the nations making up the Gentile world. The word rendered here "hath chosen"—ἐξελέξατο—is from a word meaning *to lay out together*, (Passow,) to choose out, to select. It has the idea of making a choice or selection among different objects or things. It is applied to things, as in Luke x. 42. Mary "*hath chosen* that good part;"—she has made a choice, or selection of it, or has shown a *preference* for it. 1 Cor. i. 27. "God hath chosen the foolish things of the world;" he has *preferred* to make use of them among all the conceivable things which might have been employed "to confound the wise." Comp. Acts i. 2. 24; vi. 5; xv. 22. 25. It denotes *to choose out*, with the accessary idea of kindness or favour. Mark xiii. 20. "For the elect's sake whom *he hath chosen*, he hath shortened the days." John xiii. 18. "I know whom I have chosen." Acts xiii. 17. "The God of this people of Israel *chose* our fathers;" that is, selected them from the nations to accomplish important purposes. This is evidently the sense of the word in the passage before us. It means to make a selection or choice with the idea of favour or love, and with a view to impart important benefits on those whom he chose. The idea of making some *distinction* between them and others, is essential to a correct understanding of the passage—since there can be no choice where no such distinction is made. He who chooses one out of many things makes a difference, or evinces a preference—no matter what the ground or reason of his doing it may be. Whether this refers to communities and nations, or to individuals, still it is true that a distinction is made, or a preference given of one over another. It may be added, that so far as *justice* is concerned, it makes no difference whether it refers to nations or to individuals. If there is injustice in choosing an *individual* to favour, there cannot be less in choosing *a nation*—for a nation is nothing but a collection of individuals. Every objection which has ever been made to the doctrine of election as it relates to individuals, will apply with equal force to the choice of a nation to peculiar privileges. If a distinction is made, it may be made with as much propriety in respect to individuals as to nations. ¶ *In him.* In Christ. The choice was not without reference to any means of saving them; it was not a mere purpose to bring a certain number to heaven; it was with reference to the mediation of the Redeemer, and his work. It was a purpose that they should be saved *by* him, and share the benefits of the atonement. The whole choice and purpose of salvation had reference to him, and *out* of him no one was chosen to life, and no one out of him will be saved. ¶ *Before the foundation of the world.* This is a very important phrase in determining the time when the choice was made. It was not an *afterthought*. It was not commenced in time. The purpose was far back in the ages of eternity. But what is the meaning of the phrase "before the foundation of the world?" Dr. Clarke supposes that it means "from the commencement *of the religious system of the Jews*, which," says he, "the phrase sometimes means." *Such* principles of interpretation are they compelled to resort to who endeavour to show that this refers to a national election to privileges, and who deny that it refers to individuals. On such principles the Bible may be made to signify any thing and every thing. Dr. Chandler, who also supposes that it refers to nations, admits, however, that the word "foundation" means the beginning of any thing; and that the phrase here means, "before the world began." There is scarcely any phrase in the New Testament which is more clear in its signification than this. The word rendered "foundation"—καταβολή—means properly a laying down, a founding, a foundation—as where the foundation of a building is laid—and the phrase "before the foundation of the world" clearly means before the world was made, or before the work of creation. See Matt. xiii. 35; xxv. 34. Luke xi. 50. Heb. ix. 26. Rev. xiii. 8, in all which places the phrase "the foundation of the world" means the beginning of human affairs; the beginning of the world; the beginning of history, &c. Thus in John xvii. 24, the Lord Jesus says, "thou lovedst me before the foundation of the world," i. e. from eternity, or before the work of creation commenced. Thus Peter says (1 Epis. i. 20) of the Saviour, "who verily was fore-ordained before the foundation of the world." It was the purpose of God before the worlds were made, to send him to save lost men. Comp. Rev. xvii. 8. Nothing can be clearer than that the phrase before us must refer to a purpose that was formed before the world was made. It is not a temporary arrangement; it has not grown up under the influence of vacillating purposes; it is not a plan newly formed, or changed with each coming generation, or variable like the plans of men. It has all the importance, dignity, and assurances of stability which necessarily result from a purpose that has been eternal in the mind of God. It may be observed here, (1.) that if the plan was formed "before the foundation of the world," all objections to the doctrine of an *eternal* plan are removed. If the plan was formed *before* the world, no matter whether a moment, an hour, a year, or millions of years, the plan is equally fixed, and the event equally necessary. All the objections which will lie against an *eternal* plan, will lie against a plan formed a day or an hour before the event. The one interferes with our freedom of action as much as the other. (2.) If the plan was formed "before the foundation of the world," it *was eternal*. God has no new plan. He forms no new schemes. He is not changing and vacillating. If we can ascertain what is the plan of God at any time, we can ascertain what his eternal plan was with reference to the event. It has always been the same—for "he is of ONE MIND, and who can turn him?" Job xxiii. 13. In reference to the plans and purposes of the Most High, there is nothing better settled than that WHAT HE ACTUALLY DOES, HE ALWAYS MEANT TO DO—which is the doctrine of eternal decrees—*and the whole of it.* ¶ *That we should be holy.* Paul proceeds to state the *object* for which God had chosen his people. It is not merely that they should enter into heaven. It is not that they may live in sin. It is not that they may flatter themselves that they are safe, and then live as they please. The tendency among men has always been to abuse the doctrine of predestination and elec-

5 Having predestinated[a] us unto the adoption[b] of children by Jesus Christ to himself, according to the good pleasure[c] of his will,

a Ro. 8. 29, 30. b Jno. 1. 12. c Lu. 12. 32.

tion; to lead men to say that if all things are fixed there is no need of effort; that if God has an eternal plan, no matter how men live, they will be saved if he has elected them, and that at all events they cannot change that plan, and they may as well enjoy life by indulgence in sin. The apostle Paul held no such view of the doctrine of predestination. In his apprehension it is a doctrine fitted to excite the gratitude of Christians, and the whole tendency and design of the doctrine, according to him, is to make men holy, and without blame before God in love. ¶ *And without blame before him in love.* The expression "in love," is probably to be taken in connection with the following verse, and should be rendered '*In love,* having predestinated us unto the adoption of children.' It is all to be traced to the love of God. (1.) It was love for us which prompted to it. (2.) It is the highest expression of love *to be* ordained to eternal life—for what higher love could God show us? (3.) It is love on his part, because we had no claim to it, and had not deserved it. If this be the correct view, then the doctrine of predestination is not inconsistent with the highest moral excellence in the divine character, and should never be represented as the offspring of partiality and injustice. Then too we should give thanks that "God *has, in love,* predestinated us to the adoption of children by Jesus Christ, according to the good pleasure of his will."

5. *Having predestinated us.* On the meaning of the word here used, see Notes on Rom. i. 4; viii. 29. The word used (προορίζω) means properly *to set bounds before;* and then to *pre-determine.* There is the essential idea of setting bounds or limits, and of doing this beforehand. It is not that God determined to do it when it was actually done, but that he intended to do it beforehand. No language could express this more clearly, and I suppose this interpretation is generally admitted. Even by those who deny the doctrine of particular election, it is not denied that the word here used means to *pre-determine;* and they maintain that the sense is, that God had predetermined to admit the Gentiles to the privileges of his people. Admitting then that the meaning is to predestinate in the proper sense, the only question is, *who* are predestinated? To whom does the expression apply? Is it to nations, or to individuals? In reply to this, in addition to the remarks already made, I would observe, (1.) that there is no specification of *nations* here as such, no mention of the Gentiles in contradistinction from the Jews. (2.) those referred to were those included in the word "*us,*" among whom Paul was one—but Paul was not a heathen. (3.) The same objection will lie against the doctrine of predestinating *nations* which will lie against predestinating *individuals.* (4.) Nations are made up of individuals, and the pre-determination must have had some reference to individuals. What is a nation but a collection of individuals? There is no such abstract being or thing as a nation; and if there was any purpose in regard to a nation, it must have had some reference to the individuals composing it. He that would act on the ocean, must act on the drops of water that make up the ocean; for besides the

collection of drops of water there is no ocean. He that would remove a mountain, must act on the particles of matter that compose that mountain; for there is no such thing as an abstract mountain. Perhaps there was never a greater illusion than to suppose that all difficulty is removed in regard to the doctrine of election and predestination, by saying that it refers to *nations*. What difficulty is lessened? What is gained by it? How does it make God appear more amiable and good? Does it render him less *partial* to suppose that he has made a difference among nations, than to suppose he has made a difference among individuals? Does it remove any difficulty about the offer of salvation, to suppose that he has granted the knowledge of his truth to some *nations*, and withheld it from others? The truth is, that all the reasoning which has been founded on this supposition, has been merely throwing dust in the eyes. If there is *any* well-founded objection to the doctrine of decrees or predestination, it is to the doctrine *at all*, alike in regard to nations and individuals, and there are just the same difficulties in the one case as in the other. But there is no real difficulty in either. Who could worship or honour a God who had no plan, or purpose, or intention in what he did? Who can believe that the universe was formed and is governed without design? Who can doubt that what God *does* he always meant to do? When, therefore, he converts and saves a soul, it is clear that he always intended to do it. He has no new plan. It is not an after-thought. It is not the work of chance. If I can find out any thing that God has *done*, I have the most certain conviction that he *always meant* to do it—and this is all that is intended by the doctrine of election or predestination. What God does, he always meant to do. What he permits, he always meant to permit. I may add further, that if it is right to *do* it, it was right to *intend* to do it. If there is no injustice or partiality in the act itself, there is no injustice or partiality in the intention to perform it. If it is right to save a soul, it was always right to intend to save it. If it is right to condemn a sinner to wo, it was right to intend to do it. Let us then look *at the thing itself*, and if that is not wrong, we should not blame the purpose to do it, however long it has been cherished. ¶ *Unto the adoption*, &c. See Notes, John i. 12. Rom. viii. 15. ¶ *According to the good pleasure of his will.* The word rendered "good pleasure"—(ἐνδοκία)—means *a being well pleased;* delight in any thing, favour, good-will. Luke ii. 14. Phil. i. 15. Comp. Luke xii. 32. Then it denotes purpose, or will, the idea of benevolence being included. *Robinson*. Rosenmüller renders the phrase, "from his most benignant decree." The evident object of the apostle is to state why God chose the heirs of salvation. It was done as it seemed good to him in the circumstances of the case. It was not that man had any control over him, or that man was consulted in the determination, or that it was based on the good works of man, real or foreseen. But we are not to suppose that there were no good reasons for what he has thus done. Convicts are frequently pardoned by an executive. He does it according to his own will, or as seems good in his sight. He is to be the judge, and no one has a right to control him in doing it. It may *seem* to be entirely arbitrary. The executive may not have communicated the reasons why he did it, either to those who are pardoned, or to the other prisoners, or to any one else. But we are not to infer that there was no *reason* for

6 To the praise[a] of the glory of his grace, wherein he hath made us accepted[b] in the Beloved:

a 1 Pe. 2. 9. b 1 Pe. 2. 5.

doing it. If he is a wise magistrate, and worthy of his station, it is to be presumed that there were reasons which, if known, would be satisfactory to all. But those reasons he is under no obligations to make known. Indeed, it might be improper that they should be known. Of that he is the best judge. Meantime, however, we may see what would be the effect in those who were not forgiven. It would excite, very likely, their hatred, and they would charge him with partiality or with tyranny. But they should remember that whoever might be pardoned, and on whatever ground it might be done, they could not complain. They would suffer no more than they deserve. But what if, when the act of pardon was made known to one part, it was offered to the others also on certain plain and easy conditions? Suppose it should appear that while the executive meant, for wise but concealed reasons, to forgive a part, he had also determined to offer forgiveness to all. And suppose that they were in fact disposed in the highest degree to neglect it, and that no inducements or arguments could prevail on them to accept of it. Who then could blame the executive? Now this is about the case in regard to God, and the doctrine of election. All men were guilty and condemned. For wise reasons, which God has not communicated to us, he determined to bring a portion at least of the human race to salvation. This he did not intend to leave to chance and hap-hazard. He saw that all would of themselves reject the offer, and that unless some efficient means were used, the blood of the atonement would be shed in vain. He did not make known to men who they were that he meant to save, nor the reason why *they* particularly were to be brought to heaven. Meantime he meant to make the offer universal; to make the terms as easy as possible, and thus to take away every ground of complaint. If men *will not* accept of pardon; if they prefer their sins; if nothing can induce them to come and be saved, why should they complain? If the doors of a prison are open, and the chains of the prisoners are knocked off, and they *will not* come out, why should they complain that others are in fact *willing* to come out and be saved? Let it be borne in mind that the purposes of God correspond exactly to *facts* as they actually occur, and much of the difficulty is taken away. If in the *facts* there is no just ground of complaint, there can be none, because it was the *intention of God that the facts should be so.*

6. *To the praise of the glory of his grace.* This is a Hebraism, and means the same as "to his glorious grace." The object was to excite thanksgiving for his glorious grace manifested in electing love. The real tendency of the doctrine in minds that are properly affected, is not to excite opposition to God, or to lead to the charge of partiality, tyranny, or severity; it is to excite thankfulness and praise. In accordance with this, Paul introduced the statement (ver. 3) by saying that God was to be regarded as "blessed" for forming and executing this plan. The meaning is, that the doctrine of predestination and election lays the foundation of adoring gratitude and praise. This will appear plain by a few considerations.

7 In whom [a] we have redemption through his blood, the forgive-

a He. 9. 12; 1 Pe. 1. 18, 19.

(1.) It is the only foundation of hope for man. If he were left to himself, all the race would reject the offers of mercy and would perish. History, experience, and the Bible alike demonstrate this. (2.) All the joys which any of the human race have, are to be traced to the purpose of God to bestow them. Man has no power of originating any of them, and if God had not intended to confer them, none of them would have been possessed. (3.) All these favours are conferred on those who had no claim on God. The Chrisatin who is pardoned had no claim on God for pardon; he who is admitted to heaven could urge no claim for such a privilege and honour; he who enjoys comfort and peace in the hour of death, enjoys it only through the glorious grace of God. (4.) *All* that is done by election is fitted to excite praise. Election is to life, and pardon, and holiness, and heaven. But why should not a man praise God for these things? God chooses men to be holy, not sinful; to be happy, not miserable; to be pure, not impure; to be saved, not to be lost. For these things he should be praised. He should be praised that he has not left the whole race to wander away and die. Had he chosen but one to eternal life, that one should praise him, and all the holy universe should join in the praise. Should he now see it to be consistent to choose but one of the fallen spirits, and to make him pure, and to readmit him to heaven, that one spirit would have occasion for eternal thanks, and all heaven might join in his praises. How much more is praise due to him, when the number chosen is not one, or a few, but when millions which no man can number, shall be found to be chosen to life. Rev. vii. 9. (5.) The doctrine of predestination to life has added no pang of sorrow to any one of the human race. It has made millions happy who would not otherwise have been, but not one miserable. It is not a choice to sorrow, it is a choice to joy and peace. (6.) No one has a right to complain of it. Those who are chosen assuredly should not complain of the grace which has made them what they are, and which is the foundation of all their hopes. And they who are *not* chosen, have no right to complain; for (*a*) they have no claim to life. (*b*) They are *in fact* unwilling to come. They have no desire to be Christians and to be saved. Nothing can induce them to forsake their sins and come to the Saviour. Why then should they complain if others are *in fact* willing to be saved? Why should a man complain for being left to take his own course, and to walk in his own way? Mysterious, therefore, as is the doctrine of predestination; and fearful and inscrutable as it is in some of its aspects, yet, in a just view of it, it is fitted to excite the highest expressions of thanksgiving, and to exalt God in the apprehension of man. He who has been redeemed and saved by the love of God; who has been pardoned and made pure by mercy; on whom the eye of compassion has been tenderly fixed, and for whom the Son of God has died, has abundant cause for thanksgiving and praise. ¶ *Wherein he hath made us accepted.* Has regarded us as the objects of favour and complacency. ¶ *In the Beloved.* In the Lord Jesus Christ, the well-beloved Son of God. Notes, Matt. iii. 17. He has chosen us in him, and it is through him that these mercies have been conferred on us.

7. *In whom we have redemption.*

ness of sins, according to the riches of his grace;

8 Wherein he hath abounded toward us in all wisdom and prudence;

9 Having made known unto

On the meaning of the word here rendered redemption—(ἀπολύτρωσις)—See Notes on Rom. iii. 24. The word here, as there, denotes that deliverance from sin and from the evil consequences of sin, which has been procured by the atonement made by the Lord Jesus Christ. This verse is one of the passages which prove conclusively that the apostle here does not refer to *nations* and to *national privileges.* Of what *nation* could it be said that it had "redemption through the blood of Jesus, even the forgiveness of sins?" ¶ *Through his blood.* By means of the atonement which he has made. See this phrase fully explained in the Notes on Rom. iii. 25. ¶ *The forgiveness of sins.* We obtain through his blood, or through the atonement which he has made, the forgiveness of sins. We are not to suppose that this is *all* the benefit which we receive from his death, or that this is *all* that constitutes redemption. It is the main, and perhaps the most important thing. But we also obtain the hope of heaven, the influences of the Holy Spirit, grace to guide us and to support us in trial, peace in death, and perhaps many more benefits. Still *forgiveness* is so prominent and important, that the apostle has mentioned that as if it were all. ¶ *According to the riches of his grace.* According to his rich grace. See a similar phrase explained in the Notes on Rom. ii. 4. The word *riches,* in the form in which it is used here, occurs also in several other places in this epistle. Ch. i. 18; ii. 7; iii. 8. 16. It is what Paley (*Horæ Paul.*) calls "a *cant* phrase," and occurs often in the writings of Paul. See Rom. ii. 4; ix. 23; xi. 12. 33. Phil. iv 19. Col. i. 27; ii. 2. It is not found in any of the other writings of the New Testament, except once in a sense somewhat similar, in James (ii. 5), "Hath not God chosen the poor of this world *rich* in faith," and Dr. Paley from this fact has constructed an argument to prove that this epistle was written by Paul. It is peculiar to him, and marks his style in a manner which cannot be mistaken. An impostor, or a forger of the epistle, would not have thought of introducing it, and yet it is just such a phrase as would naturally be used by Paul.

8. *Wherein he hath abounded.* Which he has liberally manifested to us. This grace has not been stinted and confined, but has been liberal and abundant. ¶ *In all wisdom.* That is, he has evinced great wisdom in the plan of salvation; wisdom in so saving men as to secure the honour of his own law, and in devising a scheme that was eminently adapted to save men. See Notes on 1 Cor. i. 24. ¶ *And prudence.* The word here used (φρονήσις) means understanding, thinking, prudence. The meaning here is, that, so to speak, God had evinced great *intelligence* in the plan of salvation. There was ample proof of *mind* and of *thought.* It was adapted to the end in view. It was far-seeing; skilfully arranged; and carefully formed. The sense of the whole is, that there was a wise design running through the whole plan, and abounding in it in an eminent degree.

9. *Having made known to us the mystery of his will.* The word *mystery* (μυστήριον) means literally something into which one must be *initiated* before it is fully known (from μυέω, to initiate, to instruct);

us the mystery of his will, according to his good pleasure which he hath [a] purposed in himself:

a 2 Ti. 1. 9.

10 That in the dispensation of the fulness of times, he might gather together in one all things in

and then any thing which is concealed or hidden. We commonly use the word to denote that which is above our comprehension or unintelligible. But this is never the meaning of the word in the New Testament. It means there some doctrine or fact which has been concealed, or which has not before been fully revealed, or which has been set forth only by figures and symbols. When the doctrine is made known, it may be as clear and plain as any other. Such was the doctrine that God meant to call the Gentiles, which was long concealed, at least in part, and which was not fully made known until the Saviour came, and which had been till that time *a mystery—a concealed truth*—though when it was revealed, there was nothing incomprehensible in it. Thus in Col. i. 26, "The mystery which hath been hid from ages and from generations, but now is made manifest to his saints." So it was in regard to the doctrine of election. It was a mystery until it was made known by the actual conversion of those whom God had chosen. So in regard to the incarnation of the Redeemer; the atonement; the whole plan of salvation. Over all these great points there was a veil thrown, and men did not understand them until God revealed them. When they were revealed, the mystery was removed, and men were able to see clearly the manifestation of the will of God. ¶ *Which he hath purposed in himself.* Without foreign aid or counsel. His purposes originated in his own mind, and were concealed until he chose to make them known. See 2 Tim. i. 9.

10. *That in the dispensation.* The word here rendered 'dispensation,' οἰκονομία, means properly *the management of household affairs.* Then it means stewardship or administration; a dispensation or arrangement of things: a scheme or plan. The meaning here is, that this plan was formed in order (εἰς) or *unto* this end, that in the full arrangement of times, or in the arrangements completing the filling up of the times, God might gather together in one all things. Tindal renders it, "to have it declared when the time was full come," &c. ¶ *The fulness of times.* When the times were fully completed; when all the periods should have passed by which he had prescribed, or judged necessary to the completion of the object. The period referred to here is that when all things shall be gathered together in the Redeemer at the winding up of human affairs, or the consummation of all things. The arrangement was made with reference to that, and embraced all things which conduced to that. The plan stretched from before 'the foundation of the world' to the period when all times should be completed; and of course all the events occurring in that intermediate period were embraced in the plan. ¶ *He might gather together in one.* The word here used —ἀνακεφαλαιόω—means literally, to sum up, to recapitulate, as an orator does at the close of his discourse. It is from κεφαλή, the head; or κεφάλαιον, the sum, the chief thing, the main point. In the New Testament, the word means to collect under one head, or to comprehend several things under one. Rom. xiii. 9. "It is *briefly comprehended*, i. e.

Christ, both which are in [1] heaven and which are on earth: *even* in him,

[1] *the heavens.*

summed up under this one precept," sc., *love.* In the passage before us, it means that God would sum up, or comprehend all things in heaven and earth through the Christian dispensation; he would make one empire, under one head, with common feelings, and under the same laws. The reference is to the unity which will hereafter exist in the kingdom of God, when all his friends on earth and in heaven shall be united, and all shall have a common head. Now there is alienation. The earth has been separated from other worlds by rebellion. It has gone off into apostasy and sin. It refuses to acknowledge the Great Head to which other worlds are subject, and the object is to restore it to its proper place, so that there shall be one great and united kingdom. ¶ *All things.* τὰ παντά. It is remarkable that Paul has here used a word which is in the neuter gender. It is not all *persons,* all angels, or all men, or all the elect, but all *things.* Bloomfield and others suppose that *persons* are meant, and that the phrase is used for τοὺς πάντες. But it seems to me that Paul did not use this word without design. All *things* are placed under Christ, (ver. 22. Matt. xxviii. 18,) and the design of God is to restore harmony in the universe. Sin has produced disorder not only in *mind,* but in *matter.* The world is disarranged. The effects of transgression are seen everywhere; and the object of the plan of redemption is to put things on their pristine footing, and restore them as they were at first. Every thing is, therefore, put under the Lord Jesus, and all things are to be brought under his control, so as to constitute one vast harmonious empire. The amount of the declaration here is, that there is hereafter to be one kingdom, in which there shall be no jar or alienation; that the now separated kingdoms of heaven and earth shall be united under one head, and that henceforward all shall be harmony and love. The things which are to be united in Christ, are those which are "in heaven and which are on earth." Nothing is said of *hell.* Of course this passage cannot teach the doctrine of universal salvation, since there is *one* world which is not to have a part in this ultimate union. ¶ *In Christ.* By means of Christ, or under him, as the great head and king. He is to be the great agent in effecting this, and he is to preside over this united kingdom. In accordance with this view the heavenly inhabitants, the angels as well as the redeemed, are uniformly represented as uniting in the same worship, and as acknowledging the Redeemer as their common head and king. Rev. v. 9, 10, 11, 12. ¶ *Both which are in heaven.* Marg. as in Gr., *in the heavens.* Many different opinions have been formed of the meaning of this expression. Some suppose it to mean the saints in heaven, who died before the coming of the Saviour; and some that it refers to the Jews, designated as *the heavenly people,* in contradistinction from the Gentiles, as having nothing divine and heavenly in them, and as being of the *earth.* The more simple and obvious interpretation is, however, without doubt, the correct one, and this is to suppose that it refers to the holy inhabitants of other worlds. The object of the plan of salvation is to produce a harmony between them and the redeemed on earth, or to produce out of all, one great and united kingdom. In doing this, it is not necessary to suppose that any change is to be produced in the inhabitants

11 In whom also we have obtained an inheritance, [a] being pre-

[a] Ac. 20. 32.

of heaven. All the change is to occur among those on earth, and the object is to make out of all, one harmonious and glorious empire. ¶ *And which are on earth.* The redeemed on earth. The object is to bring them into harmony with the inhabitants of heaven. This is the great object proposed by the plan of salvation. It is to found one glorious and eternal kingdom, that shall comprehend all holy beings on earth and all in heaven. There is now discord and disunion. Man is separated from God, and from all holy beings. Between him and every holy being there is by nature discord and alienation. Unrenewed man has no sympathy with the feelings and work of the angels; no love for their employment; no desire to be associated with them. Nothing can be more unlike than the customs, feelings, laws, and habits which prevail on earth, from those which prevail in heaven. But the object of the plan of salvation is to restore harmony to those alienated communities, and produce eternal concord and love. Learn hence, (1.) The greatness and glory of the plan of salvation. It is no trifling undertaking to *reconcile worlds*, and of such discordant materials to found one great and glorious and eternal empire. (2.) The reason of the interest which angels feel in the plan of redemption. 1 Peter i. 12. They are deeply concerned in the redemption of those who, with them, are to constitute that great kingdom which is to be eternal. Without envy at the happiness of others; without any feeling that the accession of others will diminish *their* felicity or glory, they wait to hail the coming of others, and rejoice to receive even one who comes to be united to their number. (3.) This plan was worthy of the efforts of the Son of God. To restore harmony in heaven and earth; to prevent the evils of alienation and discord; to rear one immense and glorious kingdom, was an object worthy the incarnation of the Son of God. (4.) The glory of the Redeemer. He is to be exalted as the Head of this united and ever-glorious kingdom, and all the redeemed on earth and the angelic hosts shall acknowledge him as their common Sovereign and Head. (5.) This is the greatest and most important enterprise on earth. It should engage every heart, and enlist the powers of every soul. It should be the earnest desire of all to swell the numbers of those who shall constitute this united and ever-glorious kingdom, and to bring as many as possible of the human race into union with the holy inhabitants of the other world.

11. *In whom also we have obtained an inheritance.* We who are Christians. Most commentators suppose that by the word "*we*" the Jews particularly are intended, and that it stands in contradistinction from "ye," as referring to the Gentiles, in ver. 13. This construction, they suppose, is demanded by the nature of the passage. The meaning may then be, that the Jews who were believers had *first* obtained a part in the plan of redemption, as the offer was first made to them, and then that the same favour was conferred also on the Gentiles. Or it may refer to those who had been first converted, without particular reference to the fact that they were Jews; and the reference may be to the apostle and his fellow-labourers. This seems to me to be the correct interpretation. '*We* the ministers of religion first believed, and have

destinated according to the purpose of him who worketh all things after the counsel of his own will;

obtained an inheritance in the hopes of Christians, that we should be to the praise of God's glory; and *you* also, after hearing the word of truth, believed.' Ver. 13. The word which is rendered "obtained our inheritance"—κληρόω—means literally *to acquire by lot*, and then to obtain, to receive. Here it means that they had received the favour of being to the praise of his glory for having first trusted in the Lord Jesus. ¶ *Being predestinated.* Ver. 5. ¶ *According to the purpose.* On the meaning of the word *purpose*, see Notes, Rom. viii. 28. ¶ *Of him who worketh all things.* Of God, the universal agent. The affirmation here is not merely that God accomplishes the designs of salvation according to the counsel of his own will, but that *he does everything.* His agency is not confined to one thing, or to one class of objects. Every object and event is under his control, and is in accordance with his eternal plan. The word rendered *worketh*—ἐνεργέω—means to work, to be active, to produce. Eph. i. 20. Gal. ii. 8. Phil. ii. 13. A universal agency is ascribed to him. "The same God which *worketh* all in all." 1 Cor. xii. 6. He has an agency in causing the emotions of our hearts. "God, who worketh in you both to will and to do of his good pleasure." Phil. ii. 13. He has an agency in distributing to men their various allotments and endowments. "All these worketh that one and the self-same Spirit, dividing to every man severally as he will." 1 Cor. xii. 11. The agency of God is seen everywhere. Every leaf, flower, rose-bud, spire of grass; every sunbeam, and every flash of lightning; every cataract and every torrent, all declare his agency; and there is not an object that we see that does not bespeak the control of an All-present God. It would be impossible to affirm more explicitly that God's agency is universal, than Paul does in the passage before us. He does not attempt to prove it. It is one of those points on which he does not deem it necessary to pause and reason, but which may be regarded as a conceded point in the discussion of other topics, and which may be employed without hesitation in their illustration. Paul does not state the *mode* in which this is done. He affirms merely the fact. He does not say that he *compels* men, or that he overbears them by mere physical force. His agency he affirms to be universal; but it is undoubtedly in accordance with the nature of the object, and with the laws which he has impressed on them. His agency in the work of creation was absolute and entire; for there was nothing to act on, and no established laws to be observed. Over the mineral kingdom his control must also be entire, yet in accordance with the laws which he has impressed on matter. The crystal and the snow are formed by his agency; but it is in accordance with the laws which he has been pleased to appoint. So in the vegetable world his agency is everywhere seen; but the lily and the rose blossom in accordance with uniform laws, and not in an arbitrary manner. So in the animal kingdom. God gives sensibility to the nerve, and excitability and power to the muscle. He causes the lungs to heave, and the arteries and veins to bear the blood along the channels of life; but it is not in an arbitrary manner. It is in accordance with the laws which he has ordained and he never disregards in his agency over these kingdoms. So in his government of mind. He "works" everywhere.

12 That we should be to the praise of his glory who first trusted in Christ.

¹ or, *hoped.*

But he does it in accordance with the laws of mind. His agency is not exactly of the same kind on the rose-bud that it is on the diamond, nor on the nerve that it is on the rose-bud, nor on the heart and will that it is on the nerve. In all these things he consults the laws which he has impressed on them; and as he chooses that the nerve should be affected in accordance with its laws and properties, so it is with mind. God does not violate its laws. Mind is free. It is influenced by truth and motives. It has a sense of right and wrong. And there is no more reason to suppose that God disregards these laws of mind in controlling the intellect and the heart, than there is that he disregards the laws of crystallization in the formation of the ice, or of gravitation in the movements of the heavenly bodies. The general doctrine is, that God works in all things, and controls all; but that *his agency everywhere is in accordance with the laws and nature of that part of his kingdom where it is exerted.* By this simple principle we may secure the two great points which it is desirable to secure on this subject, (1.) the doctrine of the universal agency of God; and (2.) the doctrine of the freedom and responsibility of man. ¶ *After the counsel of his own will.* Not by consulting his creatures, or conforming to their views, but by his own views of what is proper and right. We are not to suppose that this is by *mere* will, as if it were arbitrary, or that he determines anything without good reason. The meaning is, that his purpose is determined by what *he* views to be right, and without consulting his creatures or conforming to their views. His dealings often seem to us to be arbitrary. We are incapable of perceiving the reasons of what he does. He makes those his friends who we should have supposed would have been the last to have become Christians. He leaves those who seem to us to be on the borders of the kingdom, and they remain unmoved and unaffected. But we are not thence to suppose that he is arbitrary. In every instance, we are to believe that there is a good reason for what he does, and one which we may be permitted yet to see, and in which we shall wholly acquiesce. The phrase "counsel of his own will" is remarkable. It is designed to express in the strongest manner the fact that it is not by human counsel or advice. The word "counsel"—βουλή—means *a council* or *senate;* then a determination, purpose, or decree. See Rob. Lex. Here it means that his determination was formed by his own will, and not by human reasoning. Still, his will in the case may not have been arbitrary. When it is said of man that he forms his own purposes, and acts according to his own will, we are not to infer that he acts without reason. He may have the highest and best reasons for what he does, but he does not choose to make them known to others, or to consult others. So it may be of God, and so we should presume it to be. It may be added, that we ought to have such confidence in him as to believe that he will do all things well. The best possible evidence that anything is done in perfect wisdom and goodness, is the fact that God does it. When we have ascertained that, we should be satisfied that all is right.

12. *That we should be to the praise of his glory.* Should be the occasion or the means of celebrating

13 In whom ye also *trusted*, after that ye heard [a] the word of truth, the gospel of your salvation: in whom also, after that ye believed, ye were sealed [b] with that holy Spirit of promise,

a Ro. 10. 17. *b* 2 Co. 1. 22.

---

his glory; or that praise should be ascribed to him as the result of our salvation. ¶ *Who first trusted in Christ.* Marg., *hoped.* This is in accordance with the original. The foundation of their *hope* was the Saviour. Some suppose that the apostle here refers to the Jews who were converted before the gospel was preached extensively to the Gentiles. The reason for this opinion is, that in the following verse he contrasts those to whom he here refers with others whom he was addressing. But it may be that by the word "we" in vs. 11, 12, he refers to himself and to his fellow-labourers who had *first* hoped in the Saviour, and had then gone and proclaimed the message to others. See Notes on ver. 11. They *first* believed, and then preached to others; and they also believed, and became partakers of the same privileges.

13. *In whom ye also* trusted. This stands in contrast with those who had *first* embraced the gospel.—¶ *Heard the word of truth.* The gospel; called the *word* or message of truth, the word of God, &c. See Rom. x. 17. The phrase 'the word of truth' means 'the true word or message.' It was a message unmixed with Jewish traditions or Gentile philosophy. ¶ *The gospel of your salvation.* The gospel bringing salvation to you. ¶ *In whom also.* In the Lord Jesus. A little different translation of this verse will convey more clearly its meaning. 'In whom also, ye, having heard the word of truth (the gospel of your salvation), in whom having also believed, ye were sealed,' &c. The sealing was the result of believing, and that was the result of hearing the gospel. Comp. Rom. x. 14, 15. ¶ *Ye were sealed.* On the meaning of the word *seal*, see Notes on John iii. 33; vi. 27. On the phrase 'ye were sealed,' see Notes on 2 Cor. i. 22. ¶ *With that holy Spirit of promise.* With the Holy Spirit that was promised. See John xvi. 7—11. 13; xv. 26; xiv. 16, 17. It is not improbable, I think, that the apostle here refers particularly to the occurrence of which we have a record in Acts xix. 1—6. Paul, it is there said, having passed through the upper provinces of Asia Minor, came to Ephesus. He found certain persons who were the disciples of John, and he asked them if they had received the Holy Ghost since they "believed," ver. 2. They replied that they had not heard whether there was any Holy Ghost, and that they had been baptized unto John's baptism. Paul taught them the true nature of the baptism of John; explained to them the christian system; and they were baptized in the name of the Lord Jesus, and "the Holy Ghost came upon them, and they spake with tongues, and prophesied." They were thus sealed by the Holy Spirit of promise, '*after* they had believed' (Eph. i. 13); they had the full evidence of the favour of God in the descent of the promised Holy Spirit, and in his miraculous influences. If this be the true interpretation, it constitutes a striking coincidence between the epistle and the Acts, of such a nature as constitute the arguments in Paley's *Horæ Paulinæ* (though he has not referred to this), which shows that the epistle was not forged. The circumstance is such that it would not have been alluded to in this manner by one who should forge the epistle; and the mention of it in the epistle is so slight, that

14 Which is the earnest [a] of our inheritance, until the redemption [b] of the purchased [c] possession, unto the [d] praise of his glory.

a 2 Co. 5. 5. b Ro. 8. 23. c Ac. 20. 28. d ver. 6, 12.

15 Wherefore I also, after I heard of your faith in the Lord Jesus, and love unto all the saints,

16 Cease not to give thanks for you, making mention of you in my prayers;

no one, from the account there, would think of forging the account in the Acts. The coincidence is just such as would occur on the supposition that the transaction actually occurred, and that both the Acts and the epistle are genuine. At the same time, there *is* a sealing of the Holy Spirit which is common to all Christians. See the Notes referred to on 2 Cor. i. 22.

14. *Which is the earnest of our inheritance.* On the meaning of this, see Notes on 2 Cor. i. 22. ¶ *Until the redemption.* See Notes on Rom. viii. 23. The meaning here is, we have the Holy Spirit as the pledge that that shall be ours, and the Holy Spirit will be imparted to us until we enter on that inheritance. ¶ *Of the purchased possession.* Heaven, purchased for us by the death of the Redeemer. The word here used—περιποίησις—occurs in the following places in the New Testament: 1 Thess. v. 9, rendered "to *obtain* salvation;" 2 Thess. ii. 14, "to the *obtaining* of the glory of the Lord;" Heb. x. 39, "to the *saving* of the soul;" 1 Pet. ii. 9, "a *peculiar* people;" literally, a people of *acquirement* to himself; and in the passage before us. It properly means, an acquisition, an obtaining, a laying up. Here it means, the complete deliverance from sin, and the eternal salvation *acquired* for us by Christ. The influence of the Holy Spirit, renewing and sanctifying us, comforting us in trials, and sustaining us in afflictions, is the pledge that the redemption is yet to be wholly ours. ¶ *Unto the praise of his glory.* See ver. 6.

15. *Wherefore I also, after I heard of your faith in the Lord Jesus.* This is one of the passages usually relied on by those who suppose that this epistle was not written to the Ephesians. The argument is, that he writes to them as if they were strangers to him, and that it is not language such as would be used in addressing a people among whom he had spent three years. See the Intro. § 5. But this inference is not conclusive. Paul had been some years absent from Ephesus when this epistle was written. In the difficult communication in those times between distant places, it is not to be supposed that he would hear often from them. Perhaps he had heard nothing after the time when he bade farewell to the elders of Ephesus at Miletus (Acts xx.), until the time here referred to. It would be, therefore, a matter of great interest with him to hear from them; and when in some way intelligence was brought to him at Rome of a very gratifying character about their growth in piety, he says that his anxiety was relieved, and that he did not cease to give thanks for what he had heard, and to commend them to God in prayer.

16. *Cease not to give thanks for you.* In the prosperity of the church at Ephesus he could not but feel the deepest interest, and their welfare he never forgot. ¶ *Making mention of you in my prayers.* Paul was far distant from them, and expected to see them no more. But he had faith in prayer, and he sought that they might advance in knowledge and in grace. What was the

17 That the God [a] of our Lord Jesus Christ, the Father of glory, may give unto you the Spirit of wisdom [b] and revelation [1] in the knowledge of him:

a Jno. 20. 17. *b* Col. 1. 9.
1 or, *for the acknowledgment.*

18 The eyes [c] of your understanding being enlightened; that ye may know what is the hope [d] of his calling, and what the riches [e] of the glory of his inheritance in the saints,

c Is. 42. 7. *d* c. 4. 4. *e* c. 3. 16.

---

particular subject of his prayers, he mentions in the following verses.

17. *That the God of our Lord Jesus Christ.* The God who has sent the Lord Jesus into the world, and appointed him as the Mediator between himself and man. The particular reason why Paul here speaks of him as 'the God of the Lord Jesus' is, that he prays that they might be further acquainted with the Redeemer, and be enlightened in regard to the great work which he came to do. ¶ *The Father of glory.* The glorious Father, that is, the Father who is worthy to be praised and honoured. ¶ *May give unto you the Spirit of wisdom.* May make you wise to understand the great doctrines of the religion of the Redeemer. ¶ *And revelation.* That is, revealing to you more and more of the character of the Redeemer, and of the nature and results of his work. It is probable here that by the word 'Spirit' the apostle refers to the Holy Spirit as the author of all wisdom, and the revealer of all truth. His prayer is, that God would grant to them the Holy Spirit to make them wise, and to reveal his will to them. ¶ *In the knowledge of him.* Marg. *for the acknowledgment.* That is, in order that you may more fully acknowledge him, or know him more intimately and thoroughly. They had already made high attainments (ver. 15), but Paul felt that they might make still higher; and the idea here is, that however far Christians may have advanced in knowledge and in love, there is an unfathomed depth of knowledge which they may still explore, and which they should be exhorted still to attempt to fathom. How far was Paul from supposing that the Ephesians had attained to perfection!

18. *The eyes of your understanding being enlightened.* The *construction* here in the Greek is, probably, 'that he may give you (δώη, ver. 17) the Spirit of wisdom, &c.—eyes of the understanding enlightened,' &c. Or the phrase, 'the eyes of your understanding being enlightened,' may be in the accusative absolute, which Koppe and Bloomfield prefer. The phrase, 'the eyes of the understanding,' is a figure that is common in all languages. Thus Philo says, 'What the eye is to the body, that is the mind to the soul.' Comp. Matth. vi. 22. The eye is the instrument by which we see; and in like manner the understanding is that by which we perceive truth. The idea here is, that Paul not only wished their *hearts* to be right, but he wished their *understanding* to be right also. Religion has much to do in enlightening the mind. Indeed, its effect there is not less striking and decisive than it is on the heart. The understanding has been blinded by sin. The views which men entertain of themselves and of God are narrow and wrong. The understanding is enfeebled and perverted by the practice of sin. It is limited in its operations by the necessity of the case, and by the impossibility of fully comprehending the great truths which pertain to the divine administration. One of the

19 And what *is* the exceeding greatness of his power [a] to usward who believe, according to the working [1] of his mighty power,

a Ps. 110. 3.

1 *the might of his power.*

first effects of true religion is on the understanding. It enlarges its views of truth; gives it more exalted conceptions of God; corrects its errors; raises it up towards the great Fountain of love. And nowhere is the effect of the true religion more apparent than in shedding light on the intellect of the world, and restoring the weak and perverted mind to a just view of the proportion of things, and to the true knowledge of God. ¶ *That ye may know what is the hope of his calling.* What is the full import of that hope to which he has called and invited you by his Spirit and his promises. The meaning here is, that it would be an inestimable privilege to be made fully acquainted with the benefits of the christian hope, and to be permitted to understand fully what Christians have a right to expect in the world of glory. This is the *first* thing which the apostle desires they should fully understand. ¶ *And what the riches of the glory of his inheritance.* This is the *second* thing which Paul wishes them to understand. There is a force in this language which can be found perhaps nowhere else than in the writings of Paul. His mind is full, and language is burdened and borne down under the weight of his thoughts. See Notes on 2 Cor. iv. 17. On the word "riches" here used, see Notes on ver. 7. The phrase 'riches of glory' means *glorious wealth;* or, as we would say, 'how rich and glorious!' The meaning is, that there is an abundance—an infinitude of wealth. It is not such a possession as man may be heir to in this world, which is always limited from the necessity of the case, and which cannot be enjoyed long; it is infinite and inexhaustible. Comp. Notes, Rom. ii. 4. The "inheritance" here referred to is eternal life. Notes, Rom. viii. 17. ¶ *In the saints.* Among the saints. Note, 1 Cor. i. 2.

19. *And what is the exceeding greatness of his power.* On the language here used, comp. Notes on 2 Cor. iv. 17. There is much emphasis and energy of expression here, as if the apostle were labouring under the greatness of his theme, and wanted words to express the magnitude of his conception. This is the *third* thing which he was particularly desirous they should know—that they should be fully acquainted with the *power* of God in the salvation of men. He refers not merely to the power which he *had* evinced in their salvation, but also to what the gospel was *able* to accomplish, and which they *might* yet experience. The "power" referred to here as exercised towards believers does not refer to one thing merely. It is the whole *series* of the acts of power towards Christians which results from the work of the Redeemer. There was power exerted in their conversion. There would be power exerted in keeping them. There would be power in raising them up from the dead, and exalting them with Christ to heaven. The religion which they professed was a religion of *power.* In all the forms and stages of it the power of God was manifested towards them, and would be until they reached their final inheritance. ¶ *To us-ward.* Towards us, or in relation to us. ¶ *Who believe.* Who are Christians. ¶ *According to the working of his mighty power.* Marg., *The might of his power.* This should be taken with the clause in the following verse, "which he wrought in Christ;" and the meaning is, that the power which

20 Which he wrought in Christ, when he [a] raised him from the dead, and set *him* at his own right hand in the heavenly *places*,

21 Far [b] above all principality, and power, and might, and dominion, and every name that is named, not only in this world, but also in that which is to come;

a Ac. 2. 24, 33.

b Ph. 2. 9. Col. 2. 10.

God has exerted in us is in accordance with the power which was shown in raising up the Lord Jesus. It was the proper result of that, and was power of a similar kind. The same power is requisite to convert a sinner which is demanded in raising the dead. Neither will be accomplished but by omnipotence (see Notes, ch. ii. 5); and the apostle wished that they should be fully apprised of this fact, and of the vast *power* which God had put forth in raising them up from the death of sin. To illustrate this sentiment is one of his designs in the following verses; and hence he goes on to show that men before their conversion were "dead in trespasses and sins;" that they had no spiritual life; that they were the "children of wrath;" that they were raised up from their death in sin by the same power which raised the Lord Jesus from the grave, and that they were wholly saved by grace. Ch. ii. 1—10. In order to set this idea of the *power* which God had put forth in their regeneration in the strongest light, he goes into a magnificent description of the resurrection and exaltation of the Lord Jesus, and shows now that was connected with the renewing of Christians. God had set him over all things. He had put all things under his feet, and had made principalities and dominions everywhere subject to him. In this whole passage (ch. i. 19—23; ii. 1—10), the *main thing* to be illustrated is the POWER which God has shown in renewing and saving his people; and the leading sentiment is, that the SAME power is evinced in that which was required to raise up the Lord Jesus from the dead, and to exalt him over the universe.

20. *Which he wrought in Christ.* Which he exerted in relation to the Lord Jesus when he was dead. The *power* which was then exerted was as great as that of creation. It was imparting life to a cold and "mangled" frame. It was to open again the arteries and veins, and teach the heart to beat and the lungs to heave. It was to diffuse vital warmth through the rigid muscles, and to communicate to the body the active functions of life. It is impossible to conceive of a more direct exertion of *power* than in raising up the dead; and there is no more striking illustration of the nature of conversion than such a resurrection. ¶ *And set* him *at his own right hand.* The idea is, that great *power* was displayed by this, and that a similar exhibition is made when man is renewed and exalted to the high honour of being made an heir of God. On the *fact* that Jesus was received to the right hand of God, see Notes on Mark xvi. 19. Comp. Notes on Acts ii. 33. ¶ *In the heavenly* places. See Notes on ver. 3. The phrase here evidently means in heaven itself.

21. *Far above all principality.* The general sense in this verse is, that the Lord Jesus was exalted to the highest conceivable dignity and honour. Comp. Phil. ii. 9. Col. ii. 10. In this beautiful and most important passage, the apostle labours for words to convey the greatness of his conceptions, and uses those which denote the highest conceivable dignity and glory. The *main* idea is, that God had manifested great *power* in thus exalting the Lord Jesus

22 And hath put [a] all *things* under his feet, and gave him *to* be the head over all *things* to the church,

a Ps. 8. 6. Mat. 28. 18.

and that similar power was exhibited in raising up the sinner from the death of sin to the life and honour of believing. The work of religion throughout was a work of power; a work of exalting and honouring *the dead*, whether dead in sin or in the grave; and Christians ought to know the extent and glory of the power thus put forth in their salvation. The word rendered 'far above'—ὑπεράνω—is a compound word, meaning *high above*, or greatly exalted. He was not merely *above* the ranks of the heavenly beings, as the head; he was not one of their own rank, placed by office a little above them, but he was infinitely exalted over them, as of different rank and dignity. How could this be if he were a mere man; or if he were an angel? The word rendered '*principality*'—ἀρχή—means properly, *the beginning;* and then the first, the first place, power, dominion, pre-eminence, rulers, magistrates, &c. It may refer here to any rank and power, whether among men or angels, and the sense is, that Christ is exalted above all. ¶ *And power.* It is not easy to distinguish between the exact meaning of the words which the apostle here uses. The general idea is, that Christ is elevated above all ranks of creatures however exalted, and by whatever name they may be known. As in this he refers to the 'world that is to come,' as well as this world, it is clear that there is a reference here to the ranks of the angels, and probably he means to allude to the prevailing opinion among the Jews, that the angels are of different orders. Some of the Jewish Rabbies reckon four, others ten orders of angels, and they presume to give them names according to their different ranks and power. But all this is evidently the result of mere fancy. The Scriptures hint in several places at a difference of rank among the angels, but the sacred writers do not go into detail. It may be added that there is no improbability in such a subordination, but it is rather to be presumed to be true. The creatures of God are not made alike; and difference of degree and rank, as far as our observation extends, everywhere prevails. On this verse comp. Notes on Rom. viii. 38. ¶ *Dominion.* Gr. *Lordship.* ¶ *And every name that is named.* Every creature of every rank. ¶ *Not only in this world.* Not only above all kings, and princes, and rulers of every grade and rank on earth. ¶ *But also in that which is to come.* This refers undoubtedly to heaven. The meaning is, that he is supreme over all.

22. *And hath put all* things *under his feet.* See Notes on 1 Cor. xv. 27. ¶ *And gave him* to be *the head over all* things. Appointed him to be the supreme ruler. ¶ *To the church.* With reference to the church, or for its benefit and welfare. See Notes on John xvii. 2. The universe is under his control and direction for the welfare of his people. (1.) All the elements—the physical works of God—the winds and waves—the seas and rivers—all are under him, and all are to be made tributary to the welfare of the church. (2.) Earthly kings and rulers; kingdoms and nations are under his control. Thus far Christ has controlled all the wicked rulers of the earth, and they have not been able to destroy that church which he redeemed with his own blood. (3.) Angels in heaven, with all their ranks and orders, are under his con-

23 Which is his body, [a] the fulness of him that filleth all in all.

a 1 Co. 12. 12. Col. 1. 18, 24.

trol with reference to the church. See Notes on Heb. i. 14. Comp. Matt. xxvi. 53. (4.) Fallen angels are under his control, and shall not be able to injure or destroy the church. See Notes on Matt. xvi. 18. The church, therefore, is safe. All the great powers of heaven, earth, and hell, are made subject to its Head and King; and no weapon that is formed against it shall prosper.

23. *Which is his body.* This comparison of the church with *a person* or body, of which the Lord Jesus is the head, is not uncommon in the New Testament. Comp. Notes on 1 Cor. xi. 3; xii. 27. Eph. iv. 15, 16. ¶ *The fulness of him.* The word here rendered *fulness*—πλήρωμα—means properly, that with which any thing is filled; the filling up; the contents. Notes, Rom. xi. 12. The exact idea here, however, is not very clear, and interpreters have been by no means united in their opinions of the meaning. It seems probable that the sense is, that the church is the *completion* or *filling up* of his power and glory. It is that without which his dominion would not be complete. He has control over the angels and over distant worlds, but his dominion would not be complete without the control over his church, and that is so glorious, that it *fills up* the honour of the universal dominion, and makes his empire complete. According to Rosenmüller, the word *fulness* here means a *great number* or multitude: a multitude, says he, which, not confined to its own territory, spreads afar, and fills various regions. Koppe also regards it as synonymous with *multitude* or *many*, and supposes it to mean *all* the dominion of the Redeemer over the body—the church. He proposes to translate the whole verse, 'He has made him the Head over his church, that he might rule it as his own body—the whole wide state of his universal kingdom.' "This," says Calvin (*in loc.*), "is the highest honour of the church, that the Son of God regards himself as in a certain sense imperfect unless he is joined to us." The church constitutes the *complete body* of the Redeemer. A body is complete when it has all its members and limbs in proper proportions, and those members might be said to be the *completion*, or the filling-up, or the *fulness* — πλήρωμα — of the body or the person. This language would not, indeed, be such as would usually be adopted to express the idea now; but this is evidently the sense in which Paul uses it here. The meaning is, that the church sustains the same relation to Christ which the body does to the head. It helps to form the entire person. There is a close and necessary union. The one is not complete without the other. And one is dependant on the other. When the body has all its members in due proportion, and is in sound and vigorous health, the whole person then is complete and entire. So it is to be in the kingdom of the Redeemer. He is the head; and that redeemed Church is the body, the fulness, the completion, the filling-up of the entire empire over which he presides, and which he rules. On the meaning of the word *fulness*—πλήρωμα—the reader may consult Storr's Opus cula, vol. 1, pp. 144—187, particularly pp. 169—183. Storr understands the word in the sense of full or abundant mercy, and supposes that it refers to the great benignity which *God* has shown to his people, and renders it, "The great benignity of him who filleth all things with good, as

he called Jesus from the dead to life and placed him in heaven, so even you, sprung from the heathen, who were dead in sin on account of your many offences in which you formerly lived, &c.—hath he called to life by Christ." This verse, therefore, he would connect with the following chapter, and he regards it all as designed to illustrate the great power and goodness of God. Mr. Locke renders it, "Which is his body, which is completed by him alone," and supposes it means, that Christ is the head, who perfects the church by supplying all things to all its members which they need. Chandler gives an interpretation in accordance with that which I have first suggested, as meaning that the church is the full 'complement' of the body of Christ; and refers to Ælian and Dionysius Halicarnassus, who use the word 'fulness' or πλήρωμα as referring to the rowers of a ship. Thus also we say that the ship's crew is its 'complement,' or that a ship or an army has its *complement* of men; that is, the ranks are filled up or complete. In like manner, the church will be the filling-up, or the complement, of the great kingdom of the Redeemer—that which will give *completion* or perfectness to his universal dominion. ¶ *Of him.* Of the Redeemer. ¶ *That filleth all in all.* That fills all things, or who pervades all things. See Notes, 1 Cor. xii. 6; xv. 28. Comp. Col. iii. 11. The idea is, that there is no place where he is not, and which he does not fill; and that he is the source of all the holy and happy influences that are abroad in the works of God. It would not be easy to conceive of an expression more certainly denoting omnipresence and universal agency than this; and if it refers to the Lord Jesus, as seems to be indisputable, the passage teaches not only his supremacy, but demonstrates his universal agency, and his omnipresence—things that pertain only to God. From this passage we may observe, (1.) That just views of the exaltation of the Redeemer are to be obtained only by the influence of the Spirit of God on the heart. Vs. 17—19. Man, by nature, has no just conceptions of the Saviour, and has no desire to have. It is only as the knowledge of that great doctrine is imparted to the mind by the Spirit of God, that we have any practical and saving acquaintance with such an exaltation. The Christian sees him, by faith, exalted to the right hand of God, and cheerfully commits himself and his all to him, and feels that all his interests are safe in his hands. (2.) It is very desirable to have such views of an exalted Saviour. So Paul felt when he earnestly prayed that God would give such views to the Ephesians, vs. 17—20. It was desirable in order that they might have a right understanding of their privileges; in order that they might know the extent of the power which had been manifested in their redemption; in order that they might commit their souls with confidence to him. In my conscious weakness and helplessness; when I am borne down by the labours and exposed to the temptations of life; when I contemplate approaching sickness and death, I desire to feel that that Saviour to whom I have committed my all is exalted far above principalities and powers, and every name that is named. When the church is persecuted and opposed; when hosts of enemies rise up against it and threaten its peace and safety, I rejoice to feel assured the Redeemer and Head of the church is over all, and that he has power to subdue all her foes and his. (3.) The church is safe. Her great Head is on the throne of the universe, and no weapon that is formed against her can prosper. He has defended it hitherto

CHAPTER II.

AND you [a] *hath he quickened,* who were dead in trespasses and sins;

a Jno. 5. 24. Col. 2. 13.

---

in all times of persecution, and the past is a pledge that he will continue to protect it to the end of the world. (4.) Let *us* commit our souls to this exalted Redeemer. Such a Redeemer we need—one who has all power in heaven and earth. Such a religion we need—that can restore the dead to life. Such hope and confidence we need as he can give—such peace and calmness as shall result from unwavering confidence in him who filleth all in all.

CHAPTER II.

ANALYSIS.

This chapter is closely connected in sense with the preceding, and should not have been separated from it. The great object is to illustrate the subject which was commenced in the previous chapter (ver. 19)—the greatness of the POWER of God, evinced in the salvation of his people. The *great* manifestation of his power had been in raising up the Lord Jesus from the dead. That had been connected with and followed by *their* resurrection from the death of sin; and the one had involved the exercise of a power similar to the other. In the illustration of this main idea, the apostle observes (ver. 1) that God had quickened those who had been dead in trespasses and sins, and proceeds (vs. 2, 3) to show the condition in which they were before their conversion. He then observes (vs. 4—7), that God of his infinite mercy, when they were dead in sin, had quickened them together with Christ, and had raised them up to sit with him in heavenly places. He then states that this was not by human power, but was the work of divine power, and that they were the workmanship of God, vs. 8—10. The remainder of the chapter (vs. 11—22) is occupied with a statement of the *privileges* resulting from the mercy of God in calling them into his kingdom. The apostle endeavours to impress their minds strongly with a sense of the mercy and love and power of God in thus calling them to himself. He reminds them of their former condition when Gentiles, as being without God, and that they were now brought nigh by the blood of Christ (vs. 11—13); he states that this had been done by one great Mediator, who came to break down the wall of partition between the Jews and Gentiles, and who had now made both one (vs. 14—18); and he compares them now to a temple raised for God, and to constitute the place of his dwelling on the earth. Vs. 19—22. By all these considerations he endeavours to impress their minds with a sense of obligation, and to lead them to devote themselves to that God who had raised them from the dead, and had breathed into them the breath of immortal life.

1. *And you* hath he quickened. The words 'hath he quickened,' or *made to live,* are supplied, but not improperly, by our translators. The object of the apostle is to show the great power which God had evinced towards the people (ch. i. 19); and to show that this was put forth in connexion with the resurrection of the Lord Jesus, and his exaltation to the right hand of God in heaven. See Notes on Rom. vi. 4—11. Comp. Col. ii. 12, 13; iii. 1. The words 'hath he quickened' mean, hath he made alive, or made to live. John v. 21. Rom. iv. 17. 1 Cor. xv. 36. ¶ *Who were dead in trespasses and sins.* On the meaning of the word

2 Wherein[a] in time past ye walked according to the course

a Ac. 19. 35.

dead, see Notes on Rom. v. 12; vi. 2. It is affirmed here of those to whom Paul wrote at Ephesus, that before they were converted they were 'dead in sins.' There is not anywhere a more explicit proof of depravity than this, and no stronger language can be used. They were *dead* in relation to that to which they afterwards became alive—*i. e.*, to holiness. Of course, this does not mean that they were in all respects dead. It does not mean that they had no animal life, or that they did not breathe, and walk, and act. Nor can it mean that they had no living intellect or mental powers, which would not have been true. Nor does it settle any question as to their ability or power while in that state. It simply affirms a fact—that in relation to real spiritual life they were, in consequence of sin, like a dead man in regard to the objects which are around him. A corpse is insensible. It sees not, and hears not, and feels not. The sound of music, and the voice of friendship and of alarm, do not arouse it. The rose and the lily breathe forth their fragrance around it, but the corpse perceives it not. The world is busy and active around it, but it is unconscious of it all. It sees no beauty in the landscape; hears not the voice of a friend; looks not upon the glorious sun and stars; and is unaffected by the running stream and the rolling ocean. So with the sinner in regard to the spiritual and eternal world. He sees no beauty in religion; he hears not the call of God; he is unaffected by the dying love of the Saviour; and he has no interest in eternal realities. In all these he feels no more concern, and sees no more beauty, than a dead man does in the world around him. Such is, *in fact*, the condition of a sinful world. There *is*, indeed, life, and energy, and motion. There are vast plans and projects, and the world is intensely active. But in regard to religion, all is dead. The sinner sees no beauty there; and no human power can arouse him to act for God, any more than human power can rouse the sleeping dead, or open the sightless eye-balls on the light of day. The same power is needed in the conversion of a sinner which is needed in raising the dead; and one and the other alike demonstrate the omnipotence of him who can do it.

2. *Wherein.* In which sins, or in the practice of which transgressions. ¶ *Ye walked.* You lived, life being often compared to a journey or a race. Note, Rom. vi. 4. ¶ *According to the course of this world.* In conformity with the customs and manners of the world at large. The word here rendered *world*—αἰῶν—means properly *age*, but is often used to denote the present world, with its cares, temptations, and desires; and here denotes particularly the men of this world. The meaning is, that they had lived formerly as other men lived, and the idea is strongly conveyed that the course of the men of this world is to walk in trespasses and sins. The sense is, that there was by nature no difference between them and others, and that all the difference which now existed had been made by grace. ¶ *According to the prince of the power of the air.* See ch. vi. 12. Comp. Notes on 2 Cor. iv. 4. There can be no doubt that Satan is here intended, and that Paul means to say that they were under his control as their leader and prince. The phrase, 'the prince of the power,' may mean either 'the powerful prince,' or it may mean that this prince had power over the air, and lived and reigned there particularly. The word 'prince'

of this world, according to the prince [a] of the power of the air, the spirit that now worketh in the children [b] of disobedience:

a c. 6. 12. b Col. 3. 6.

ἄρχοντα—*Archon*, means one first in authority and power, and is then applied to any one who has the preeminence or rule. It is applied to Satan, or the chief of the fallen angels, as where he is called 'the prince—ἄρχων—of the devils,' Matth. ix. 34; xii. 24. Mark iii. 22. Luke xi. 15; 'the prince of this world,' John xii. 31; xiv. 30; xvi. 11. But *why* he is here called the prince having power *over the air*, it is not easy to determine. Robinson (*Lex.*) supposes it to be because he is lord of the powers of the air; that is, of the demons who dwell and rule in the atmosphere. So Doddridge supposes that it means that he controls the fallen spirits who are permitted to range the regions of the atmosphere. It is generally admitted that the apostle here refers to the prevailing opinions both among the Jews and heathen, that the air was thickly peopled with spirits or demons. That this was a current opinion, may be seen fully proved in Wetstein. Comp. Bloomfield, Grotius, and particularly Koppe. Why the region of the *air* was supposed to be the dwelling-place of such spirits, is now unknown. The opinion may have been either that such spirits *dwelt* in the air, or that they had control over it, according to the later Jewish belief. Cocceius and some others explain the word *air* here as meaning the same as *darkness*, as in profane writers. It is evident to my mind that Paul does not speak of this as a mere tradition, opinion, or vagary of the fancy, or as a superstitious belief; but that he refers to it as a thing which he regarded as true. In this opinion I see no absurdity that should make it impossible to believe it. For, (1.) the Scriptures abundantly teach that there are fallen, wicked spirits; and the existence of fallen angels is no more improbable than the existence of fallen men. (2.) The Bible teaches that they have much to do with this world. They tempted man; they inflicted disease in the time of the Saviour; they are represented as alluring and deceiving the race. (3.) They must have *some* locality—some part of the universe where they dwell. That they were not confined down to hell in the time of the Redeemer, is clear from the New Testament; for they are often represented as having afflicted and tortured men. (4.) Why is there any improbability in the belief that their residence should have been in the regions of the air? That while they were suffered to be on earth to tempt and afflict men, they should have been permitted peculiarly to occupy these regions? Who can tell what may be in the invisible world, and what spirits may be permitted to fill up the vast space that now composes the universe? And who can tell what control may have been given to such fallen spirits over the regions of the atmosphere—over clouds, and storms, and pestilential air? *Men* have control over the earth, and pervert and abuse the powers of nature to their own ruin and the ruin of each other. The elements they employ for the purposes of ruin and of temptation. Fruit and grain they convert to poison; minerals, to the destruction caused by war. In itself considered, there is nothing more improbable that spirits of darkness may have had control over the regions of the air, than that fallen man has over the earth; and no more improbability that that power has been abused to ruin men, than that the power of men is abused to destroy each other. No one can

3 Among whom also we [a] all had our conversation in times past in the lusts of our flesh, fulfilling the [1] desires of the flesh and of the mind; and were by nature [b] the children of wrath, even as others.

a 1 Pe. 4. 3. [1] *wills.* *b* Ps. 51. 5.

prove that the sentiment here referred to by Paul is *not* true; and no one can show how the doctrine that fallen spirits may do mischief in any part of the works of God, is any more improbable than that wicked *men* should do the same thing. The word '*power*' here—'power of the air'—I regard as synonymous with *dominion* or *rule;* 'a prince having dominion or rule over the air.'— ¶ *The spirit that now worketh.* That still lives, and whose energy for evil is still seen and felt among the wicked. Paul here means undoubtedly to teach that there *was* such a spirit, and that he was still active in controlling men. ¶ *The children of disobedience.* The wicked. Col. iii. 6.

3. *We all had our conversation.* See Notes on 2 Cor. i. 12. Comp. 1 Pet. iv. 3. ¶ *In the lusts of our flesh.* Living to gratify the flesh, or the propensities of a corrupt nature. It is observable here that the apostle changes the form of the address from "*ye*" to "*we*," thus including himself with others, and saying that this was true of *all* before their conversion. He means undoubtedly to say, that whatever might have been the place of their birth, or the differences of religion under which they had been trained, they were substantially alike by nature. It was a characteristic of all that they lived to fulfil the desires of the flesh and of the mind. The *design* of the apostle in thus grouping himself with them was, to show that he did not claim to be any better by nature than they were, and that all which any of them had of value was to be traced to the grace of God. There is much delicacy here on the part of the apostle. His object was to remind them of the former grossness of their life, and their exposure to the wrath of God. Yet he does not do it harshly. He includes himself in their number. He says that what he affirms of them was substantially true of himself—of all—that they were under condemnation, and exposed to the divine wrath. ¶ *Fulfilling the desires of the flesh and of the mind.* Marg. as in Greek, *wills.* Complying with the wishes of a depraved nature. The 'will of the flesh' is that to which the flesh, or the unrenewed nature of man, prompts; and Paul says that all had been engaged in fulfilling those fleshly propensities. This was clearly true of the heathen, and it was no less true of the unconverted Jew that he lived for himself, and sought to gratify the purposes of a depraved nature, though it might manifest itself in a way different from the heathen. The 'will of the mind' referred to here relates to the wicked *thoughts* and *purposes* of the unrenewed nature—the sins which relate rather to the *intellect* than to the gross passions. Such, for instance, are the sins of pride, envy, ambition, covetousness, &c.; and Paul means to say, that before conversion they lived to gratify these propensities, and to accomplish these desires of the soul. ¶ *And were by nature.* φύσει. By birth, or before we were converted. By conversion and adoption they became the children of God; before that, they were all the children of wrath. This is, I think, the fair meaning of this important declaration. It does not affirm *when* they began to be such, or that they were such as soon as

4 But God, who is rich in mercy, for his great love wherewith he loved us,

they were born, or that they were such before they became moral agents, or that they became such in virtue of their connection with Adam —whatever may be the truth on these points; but it affirms that before they were renewed, they were the children of wrath. So far as *this* text is concerned, this might have been true at their very birth; but it does not directly and certainly prove that. It proves that at no time before their conversion were they the children of God, but that their whole condition before that was one of exposure to wrath. Comp. Rom. ii. 14. 27. 1 Cor. xi. 14. Gal. ii. 15. Some men are born Jews, and some heathen; some free, and some slaves; some white, and some black; some are born to poverty, and some to wealth; some are the children of kings, and some of beggars; but, whatever their rank or condition, they are born exposed to wrath, or in a situation which would render them liable to wrath. But *why* this is, the apostle does not say. Whether for their own sins or for the sins of another; whether by a corrupted soul or by imputed guilt; whether they act as moral agents as soon as born, or at a certain period of childhood, Paul does not say. ¶ *The children of wrath.* Exposed to wrath, or liable to wrath. They did not by nature inherit holiness; they inherited that which would subject them to wrath. The meaning has been well expressed by Doddridge, who refers it "to the original apostasy and corruption, in consequence of which men do, according to the course of nature, fall early into personal guilt, and so become obnoxious to the divine displeasure." Many modern expositors have supposed that this has no reference to any original tendency of our fallen nature to sin, or to native corruption, but that it refers to the *habit* of sin, or to the fact of their having been the slaves of appetite and passion. I admit that the direct and immediate sense of the passage is that they were, when without the gospel, and before they were renewed, the children of wrath; but still the fair interpretation is, that they were born to that state, and that that condition was the regular result of their native depravity; and I do not know a more strong or positive declaration that can be made to show that men are by nature destitute of holiness, and exposed to perdition. ¶ *Even as others.* That is, 'do not suppose that you stand alone, or that you are the worst of the species. You are indeed, by nature, the children of wrath; but not you alone. All others were the same. You have a common inheritance with them. I do not mean to charge you with being the worst of sinners, or as being alone transgressors. It is the common lot of man—the sad, gloomy inheritance to which we all are born.' The Greek is, οἱ λοιποὶ — '*the remainder*, or *the* others,'—including all. Comp. Notes on Rom. v. 19. This doctrine that men without the gospel are the children of wrath, Paul had fully defended in Rom. i., ii., iii. No truth, perhaps, is more frequently stated in the Bible; none is more fearful and awful in its character. What a declaration, that we 'are by nature the children of wrath!' Who should not inquire what it means? Who should not make an effort to escape from the wrath to come, and become a child of glory and an heir of life?

4. *But God, who is rich in mercy.* On the use of the word *rich* by Paul, see Notes on ch. i. 7. It is a beautiful expression. 'God is *rich*

5 Even[a] when we were dead in sins, hath quickened us together with Christ, (by[1] grace[b] ye are saved;)

6 And hath raised[c] *us* up together, and made *us* sit together in heavenly *places* in Christ Jesus;

a Ro. 5. 6, 8, 10. [1] *by whose.* *b* Ro. 3. 24.

c Col. 2. 12.

in mercy;' overflowing, abundant. Mercy is the riches or the wealth of God. Men are often rich in gold, and silver, and diamonds, and they pride themselves in these possessions; but God is *rich in mercy.* In that he abounds; and he is so rich in it that he is willing to impart it to others; so rich that he can make all blessed. ¶ *For his great love.* That is, his great love was the reason why he had compassion upon us. It is not that we had any claim or deserved his favour; but it is, that God had for man original and eternal love, and that love led to the gift of a Saviour, and to the bestowment of salvation.

5. *Even when we were dead in sins.* Notes, ver. 1. Comp. Rom. v. 8. The construction here is, 'God, who is rich in mercy, on account of the great love which he bare unto us, even being dead in sin, hath quickened us,' &c. It does not mean that he quickened us when we were dead in sin, but that he loved us then, and made provision for our salvation. It was love to the children of wrath; love to those who had no love to return to him; love to the alienated and the lost. That is true love—the sincerest and the purest benevolence—love, not like that of men, but such only as God bestows. Man loves his friend, his benefactor, his kindred—God loves his foes, and seeks to do them good. ¶ *Hath quickened us.* Hath made us alive. See ver. 1. ¶ *Together with Christ.* In connection with him; or in virtue of his being raised up from the grave. The meaning is, that there was such a connection between Christ and those whom the Father had given to him, that his resurrection from the grave involved their resurrection to spiritual life. It was like raising up the head and the members—the whole body together. Comp. Notes on Rom. vi. 5. Everywhere in the New Testament, the close connection of the believer with Christ is affirmed. We are crucified with him. We die with him. We rise with him. We live with him. We reign with him. We are joint heirs with him. We share his sufferings on earth (1 Pet. iv. 13), and we share his glory with him on his throne. Rev. iii. 21. ¶ *By grace ye are saved.* Marg., *by whose.* See Notes on Rom. iii. 24. Paul's mind was full of the subject of salvation by grace, and he throws it in here, even in an argument, as a point which he would never have them lose sight of The subject before him was one eminently adapted to bring this truth to mind, and though, in the train of his arguments, he had no time now to dwell on it, yet he would not suffer any opportunity to pass without referring to it.

6. *And hath raised* us *up together.* That is, we are raised from the death of sin to the life of religion, in connection with the resurrection of Jesus, and in virtue of that. So close is the connection between him and his people, that his resurrection made theirs certain. Comp. Col. ii. 12. Notes, Rom. vi. 5. ¶ *And made* us *sit together.* Together with him. That is, we share his honours. So close is our connection with him, that we shall partake of his glory, and in some measure do now. Comp. Notes on Matt. xix. 28, and Rom. viii. 17. ¶ *In heavenly* places. See Notes on ch. i. 3.

7 That in the ages to come he might shew the exceeding riches of his grace, in *his* kindness [a] toward us through Christ Jesus.

8 For by grace [b] are ye saved through faith; [c] and that not [d] of yourselves; *it is* the gift of God:

a Tit. 3. 4.

b 2 Ti. 1. 9. c Ro. 4. 16. d Jno. 6. 44. 65.

The meaning is, that he has gone to the heavenly world as our Head and Representative. His entrance there is a pledge that we shall also enter there. Even here we have the anticipation of glory, and are admitted to exalted honours, as if we sat in heavenly places, in virtue of our connection with him. ¶ *In Christ Jesus.* It is in connection with him that we are thus exalted, and thus filled with joy and peace. The meaning of the whole is, 'We are united to Christ. We die with him, and live with him. We share his sufferings, and we share his joys. We become dead to the world in virtue of his death; we become alive unto God in virtue of his resurrection. On earth we are exalted to honour, peace, and hope, in virtue of his resurrection; in heaven we shall share his glory and partake of his triumphs.'

7. *That in the ages to come.* In all future times. The sense is, that the riches of divine grace, and the divine benignity, would be shown in the conversion of Christians and their salvation, to all future times. Such was his love to those who were lost, that it would be an everlasting monument of his mercy, a perpetual and unchanging proof that he was good. The sense is, we are raised up with Christ, and are made to partake of his honour and glory in order that others may forever be impressed with a sense of the divine goodness and mercy to us. ¶ *The exceeding riches of his grace.* The *abounding*, *overflowing* riches of grace. Comp. Notes, ch. i. 7. This is Paul's favourite expression — an expression so beautiful and so full of meaning that it will bear often to be repeated. We may learn from this verse, (1.) That one object of the conversion and salvation of sinners, is to furnish a *proof* of the mercy and goodness of God. (2.) Another object is, that their conversion may be an *encouragement* to others. The fact that such sinners as the Ephesians had been, were pardoned and saved, affords encouragement also to others to come and lay hold on life. And so of all other sinners who are saved. Their conversion is a standing encouragement to all others to come in like manner; and now the history of the church for more than eighteen hundred years furnishes all the encouragement which we could desire. (3.) The conversion of *great* sinners is a special proof of the divine benignity. So Paul argues in the case before us; and so he often argued from his own case. Comp. Notes on 1 Tim. i. 16. (4.) Heaven, the home of the redeemed, will exhibit the most impressive proof of the goodness of God that the universe furnishes. There will be a countless host who were once polluted and lost; who were dead in sins; who were under the power of Satan, and who have been saved by the riches of the divine grace—a host now happy and pure, and free from sin, sorrow, and death—the living and eternal monuments of the grace of God.

8. *For by grace are ye saved.* By mere favour. It is not by your own merit; it is not because you have any claim. This is a favourite doctrine with Paul, as it is with all who love the Lord Jesus in sincerity. Comp. Notes on Rom. i. 7; iii. 24. ¶ *Through faith.* Grace bestowed

9 Not of works, lest any man should boast.

10 For we are his workmanship, created in Christ Jesus unto

through faith, or in connection with believing. See Notes on Rom. i. 17; iv. 16. ¶ *And that not of yourselves.* That is, salvation does not proceed from yourselves. The word rendered *that*—τοῦτο—is in the neuter gender, and the word *faith*—πίστις—is in the feminine. The word "that," therefore, does not refer particularly to faith, as being the gift of God, but to *the salvation by grace* of which he had been speaking. This is the interpretation of the passage which is the most obvious, and which is now generally conceded to be the true one. See Bloomfield. Many critics, however, as Doddridge, Beza, Piscator, and Chrysostom, maintain that the word '*that*' (τοῦτο) refers to '*faith*' (πίστις); and Doddridge maintains that such a use is common in the New Testament. As a matter of *grammar* this opinion is certainly doubtful, if not untenable; but as a matter of *theology* it is a question of very little importance. Whether this passage proves it or not, it is certainly true that faith is the gift of God. It exists in the mind only when the Holy Ghost produces it there, and is, in common with every other Christian excellence, to be traced to his agency on the heart. This opinion, however, does not militate at all with the doctrine that man himself *believes.* It is not God that *believes* for him, for that is impossible. It is *his own mind* that actually believes, or that exercises faith. See Notes on Rom. iv. 3. In the same manner *repentance* is to be traced to God. It is one of the fruits of the operation of the Holy Spirit on the soul. But the Holy Ghost does not *repent* for us. It is *our own mind* that repents; our own heart that feels; our own eyes that weep —and without this there can be no true repentance. No one can repent for another; and God neither can nor ought to repent for us. He has done no wrong, and if repentance is ever exercised, therefore, it must be exercised by our own minds. So of faith. God cannot believe for us. *We* must believe, or *we* shall be damned. Still this does not conflict at all with the opinion, that if we exercise faith, the inclination to do it is to be traced to the agency of God on the heart. I would not contend, therefore, about the grammatical construction of this passage, with respect to the point of the theology contained in it; still it accords better with the obvious grammatical construction, and with the design of the passage to understand the word "that" as referring not to *faith* only, but to *salvation by grace.* So Calvin understands it, and so it is understood by Storr, Locke, Clarke, Koppe, Grotius, and others. ¶ *It is the gift of God.* Salvation by grace is his gift. It is not of merit; it is wholly by favour.

9. *Not of works.* See Notes on Rom. iii. 20. 27.

10. *For we are his workmanship.* We are his *making*—ποίημα. That is, we are *created* or *formed* by him, not only in the general sense in which all things are made by him, but in that peculiar sense which is denoted by the new creation. See Notes on 2 Cor. v. 17. Whatever of peace, or hope, or purity we have, has been produced by his agency on the soul. There cannot be conceived to be a stronger expression to denote the agency of God in the conversion of men, or the fact that salvation is wholly of grace. ¶ *Created in Christ Jesus.* On the word created, see Notes on 2 Cor. v. 17. ¶ *Unto good works.* With reference to a holy life; or, the design for which we have been created in Christ is, that we should lead a holy

good works, which [a] God hath before [1] ordained that we should walk in them.

11 Wherefore remember, that ye *being* in time past Gentiles in the flesh, who are called Uncircumcision by that which is called the Circumcision in the flesh made by hands;

a c. 1. 4. [1] or, *prepared.*

life. The primary object was not to bring us to heaven. It was that we should be *holy.* Paul held perhaps more firmly than any other man, to the position that men are saved by the mere grace of God, and by a divine agency on the soul; but it is certain that no man ever held more firmly that men must lead holy lives, or they could have no evidence that they were the children of God. ¶ *Which God hath before ordained.* Marg., *prepared.* The word here used means to *prepare beforehand*, then to predestinate, or appoint before. The proper meaning of this passage is, 'to which (οἷς) good works God has predestinated us, or appointed us beforehand, that we should walk in them.' The word here used—προετοιμάζω—occurs in the New Testament nowhere else except in Rom. ix. 23, where it is rendered 'had afore prepared.' It involves the idea of a previous determination, or an arrangement beforehand for securing a certain result. The previous preparation here referred to was, the divine intention; and the meaning is, that God had predetermined that we should lead holy lives. It accords, therefore, with the declaration in ch. i. 4, that he had chosen his people before the foundation of the world, that they should be holy. See Notes on that verse. ¶ *That we should walk in them.* That we should live holy lives. The word *walk* is often used in the Scriptures to denote the course of life. Notes on Rom. vi. 4.

11. *Wherefore remember.* The design of this evidently is, to excite a sense of gratitude in their bosoms for that mercy which had called them from the errors and sins of their former lives, to the privileges of Christians. It is a good thing for Christians to '*remember*' what they were. No faculty of the mind can be better employed to produce humility, penitence, gratitude, and love, than the *memory.* It is well to recall the recollection of our former sins; to dwell upon our hardness of heart, our alienation, and our unbelief; and to remember our wanderings and our guilt, until the heart be affected, and we are made to feel. The converted Ephesians had much guilt to recollect and to mourn over in their former life; and so have all who are converted to the Christian faith. ¶ *That ye being in time past.* Formerly—(ποτε.) ¶ *Gentiles in the flesh.* You were Gentiles *in the flesh*, i. e. under the dominion of the flesh, subject to the control of carnal appetites and pleasures. ¶ *Who are called Uncircumcision.* That is, who are called 'the uncircumcised.' This was a term similar to that which we use when we speak of 'the unbaptized.' It meant that they were without the pale of the people of God; that they enjoyed none of the ordinances and privileges of the true religion; and was commonly a term of reproach. Comp. Judges xiv. 3; xv. 18. 1 Sam. xiv. 6; xvii. 26; xxxi. 4. Ezek. xxxi. 18. ¶ *By that which is called the Circumcision.* By those who are circumcised, i. e. by the Jews. ¶ *In the flesh made by hands.* In contradistinction from the circumcision of the heart. See Notes on Rom. ii. 28, 29. They had externally adopted the rites of the true religion, though it did not follow that

12 That at that time ye were without Christ, being aliens from the commonwealth of Israel, and strangers from the covenants of promise, having no hope, and without God in the world:

---

they had the circumcision of the heart, or that they were the true children of God.

12. *Ye were without Christ.* You were without the knowledge of the Messiah. You had not heard of him; of course you had not embraced him. You were living without any of the hopes and consolations which you now have, from having embraced him. The object of the apostle is to remind them of the deplorable condition in which they were by nature; and nothing would better express it than to say they were "without Christ," or that they had no knowledge of a Saviour. They knew of no atonement for sin. They had no assurance of pardon. They had no well-founded hope of eternal life. They were in a state of darkness and condemnation, from which nothing but a knowledge of Christ could deliver them. All Christians may in like manner be reminded of the fact that, before their conversion, they were "without Christ." Though they had heard of him, and were constantly under the instruction which reminded them of him, yet they were without any true knowledge of him, and without any of the hopes which result from having embraced him. Many were infidels. Many were scoffers. Many were profane, sensual, corrupt. Many rejected Christ with scorn; many, by simple neglect. *All* were without any true knowledge of him; all were destitute of the peace and hope which result from a saving acquaintance with him. We may add, that there is no more affecting description of the state of man by nature than to say, he is without a Saviour. Sad would be the condition of the world without a Redeemer—sad *is* the state of that portion of mankind who reject him. Reader, are *you* without Christ? ¶ *Being aliens from the commonwealth of Israel.* This is the second characteristic of their state before their conversion to Christianity. This means more than that they were not *Jews.* It means that they were strangers to that *polity*—πολιτεία—or arrangement by which the worship of the true God had been kept up in the world, and of course were strangers to the true religion. The arrangements for the public worship of JEHOVAH were made among the Jews. They had his law, his temple, his Sabbaths, and the ordinances of his religion. See Notes on Rom. iii. 2. To all these the heathens had been strangers, and of course they were deprived of all the privileges which resulted from having the true religion. The word here rendered *commonwealth*—πολιτεία—means properly citizenship, or the right of citizenship, and then a community, or state. It means here that arrangement or organization by which the worship of the true God was maintained. The word *aliens*—ἀπηλλοτριωμένοι—here means merely that they were *strangers to.* It does not denote, of necessity, that they were *hostile* to it; but that they were ignorant of it, and were, therefore, deprived of the benefits which they might have derived from it, if they had been acquainted with it. ¶ *And strangers.* This word—ξένος—means properly a guest, or a stranger, who is hospitably entertained; then a foreigner, or one from a distant country; and here means that they did not belong to the community where the covenants of promise were enjoyed; that is, they were strangers to the privileges of the people of God. ¶ *The cove-*

nants of promise. See Notes on Rom. ix. 4. The covenants of promise were those various arrangements which God made with his people, by which he promised them future blessings, and especially by which he promised that the Messiah should come. To be in possession of them was regarded as a high honour and privilege; and Paul refers to it here to show that, though the Ephesians had been by nature without these, yet they had now been brought to enjoy all the benefits of them. On the word covenant, see Notes on Gal. iii. 15. It may be remarked, that Walton (Polyglott) and Rosenmüller unite the word '*promise*' here with the word '*hope*'—*having no hope of the promise.* But the more obvious and usual interpretation is that in our common version, meaning that they were not by nature favoured with the covenants made with Abraham, Isaac, Jacob, &c., by which there was a promise of future blessings under the Messiah. ¶ *Having no hope.* The apostle does not mean to affirm that they did not cherish *any* hope, for this is scarcely true of any man; but that they were without any proper ground of hope. It is true of perhaps nearly all men that they cherish *some* hope of future happiness. But the ground on which they do this is not well understood by themselves, nor do they in general regard it as a matter worth particular inquiry. Some rely on morality; some on forms of religion; some on the doctrine of universal salvation; all who are impenitent believe that they do not *deserve* eternal death, and expect to be saved by *justice.* Such hopes, however, must be unfounded. No hope of life in a future world can be founded on a proper basis which does not rest on some promise of God, or some assurance that he will save us; and these hopes, therefore, which men take up they know not why, are delusive and vain. ¶ *And without God in the world.* Gr. ἄθεοι—*atheists;* that is, those who had no knowledge of the true God. This is the last specification of their miserable condition before they were converted; and it is an appropiate crowning of the climax. What an expression! To be without God—without God in his own world, and where he is all around us! To have no evidence of his favour, no assurance of his love, no hope of dwelling with him! The meaning, as applied to the heathen Ephesians, was, that they had no knowledge of the true God. This was true of the heathen, and in an important sense also it is true of all impenitent sinners, and was once true of all who are now Christians. They had no God. They did not worship him, or love him, or serve him, or seek his favours, or act with reference to him and his glory. Nothing can be a more appropriate and striking description of a sinner now than to say that he is 'without God in the world.' He lives, and feels, and acts, as if there were no God. He neither worships him in secret, nor in his family, nor in public. He acts with no reference to his will. He puts no confidence in his promises, and fears not when he threatens; and were it announced to him that there *is no God,* it would produce no change in his plan of life, or in his emotions. The announcement that the emperor of China, or the king of Siam, or the sultan of Constantinople, was dead, would produce *some* emotion, and *might* change some of his commercial arrangements; but the announcement that there is no God would interfere with none of his plans, and demand no change of life. And, if so, what is man in this beautiful world without a God? A traveller to eternity without a God! Standing over the grave without a God! An immortal

13 But now, in Christ Jesus, ye who sometimes were far off, are made nigh by the blood [a] of Christ.

a He. 9. 12.

14 For he [b] is our peace, who hath made both [c] one, and hath broken down the middle wall of partition *between us;*

b Mi. 5. 5. c Jno. 10. 16. Ga. 3. 28.

being without a God! A man—fallen, sunk, ruined, with no God to praise, to love, to confide in; with no altar, no sacrifice, no worship, no hope; with no Father in trial, no counsellor in perplexity, no support in death! Such is the state of man by nature. Such are the effects of sin.

13. *But now in Christ Jesus.* By the coming and atonement of the Lord Jesus, and by the gospel which he preached. ¶ *Ye who sometimes were afar off.* Who were *formerly*—ποτὲ. Tindal translates it, *a whyle agoo.* The phrase *afar off*—μακρὰν—means that they were formerly far off from God and his people. The expression is derived from the custom of speaking among the Hebrews. God was supposed to reside in the temple. It was a privilege to be near the temple. Those who were remote from Jerusalem and the temple were regarded as far off from God, and hence as peculiarly irreligious and wicked. See Notes on Isa. lvii. 19. ¶ *Are made nigh.* Are admitted to the favour of God, and permitted to approach him as his worshippers. ¶ *By the blood of Christ.* The Jews came near to the mercy-seat on which the symbol of the divine presence rested (Notes on Rom. iii. 25), by the blood that was offered in sacrifice; that is, the High Priest approached that mercy-seat with blood and sprinkled it before God. Now we are permitted to approach him with the blood of the atonement. The shedding of that blood has prepared the way by which Gentiles as well as Jews may approach God, and it is by that offering that we are led to seek God.

14. *For he is our peace.* There is evident allusion here to Isa. lvii. 19. See Notes on that verse. The *peace* here referred to is that by which a *union* in worship and in feeling has been produced between the Jews and the Gentiles. Formerly they were alienated and separate. They had different objects of worship; different religious rites different views and feelings. The Jews regarded the Gentiles with hatred, and the Gentiles the Jews with scorn. Now, says the apostle, they are at peace. They worship the same God. They have the same Saviour. They depend on the same atonement. They have the same hope. They look forward to the same heaven. They belong to the same redeemed family. Reconciliation has not only taken place with God, but with each other. *The best way to produce peace between alienated minds is to bring them to the same Saviour.* That will do more to silence contentions, and to heal alienations, than any or all other means. Bring men around the same cross; fill them with love to the same Redeemer, and give them the same hope of heaven, and you put a period to alienation and strife. The love of Christ is so absorbing, and the dependence in his blood so entire, that they will lay aside these alienations, and cease their contentions. The work of the atonement is thus designed not only to produce peace with God, but peace between alienated and contending minds. The feeling that we are redeemed by the same blood, and that we have the same Saviour, will unite the rich and the poor, the bond and the free

15 Having abolished [a] in his flesh the enmity, *even* the law of commandments *contained* in ordinances; for to make in himself of twain one new man, *so* making peace;

a Col. 2. 14.

the high and the low, in the ties of brotherhood, and make them feel that they are one. This great work of the atonement is thus designed to produce peace in alienated minds everywhere, and to diffuse abroad the feeling of universal brotherhood. ¶ *Who hath made both one.* Both Gentiles and Jews. He has united them in one society. ¶ *Having broken down the middle wall.* There is an allusion here undoubtedly to the wall of partition in the temple by which the court of the Gentiles was separated from that of the Jews. See Notes and the plan of the temple, in Matt. xxi. 12. The idea here is, that that was now broken down, and that the Gentiles had the same access to the temple as the Jews. The sense is, that in virtue of the sacrifice of the Redeemer they were admitted to the same privileges and hopes.

15. *Having abolished.* Having brought to naught, or put an end to it—καταργήσας. ¶ *In his flesh.* By the sacrifice of his body on the cross. It was not by instruction merely; it was not by communicating the knowledge of God; it was not as a teacher; it was not by the mere exertion of power; it was by his flesh—his human nature—and this can mean only that he did it by his sacrifice of himself. It is such language as is appropriate to the doctrine of the atonement—not indeed teaching it directly—but still such as one would use who believed that doctrine, and such as no other one would employ. Who would now say of a moral teacher that he accomplished an important result by *his flesh?* Who would say of a man that was instrumental in reconciling his contending neighbours, that he did it *by his flesh?* Who would say of Dr. Priestley that he established Unitarianism *in his flesh?* No man would have ever used this language who did not believe that Jesus died as a sacrifice for sin. ¶ *The enmity.* Between the Jew and the Gentile. Tindal renders this, "the cause of hatred, that is to say, the law of commandments contained in the law written." This is expressive of the true sense. The idea is, that the ceremonial law of the Jews, on which they so much prided themselves, was the cause of the hostility existing between them. That made them different people, and laid the foundation for the alienation which existed between them. They had different laws; different institutions; a different religion. The Jews looked upon themselves as the favourites of Heaven, and as in possession of the knowledge of the only way of salvation; the Gentiles regarded their laws with contempt, and looked upon the peculiar institutions with scorn. When Christ came, and abolished by his death their peculiar ceremonial laws, of course the cause of this alienation ceased. ¶ Even *the law of commandments.* The law of positive commandments. This does not refer to the *moral* law, which was not the cause of the alienation, and which was not abolished by the death of Christ, but to the laws commanding sacrifices, festivals, fasts, &c., which constituted the peculiarity of the Jewish system. These were the occasion of the enmity between the Jews and the Gentiles, and these were abolished by the great sacrifice which the Redeemer made; and of course when that was made, the purpose for which these laws were instituted was ac-

16 And that he might reconcile [a] both unto God in one body by the cross, having slain the enmity [1] thereby;

17 And came and preached peace to you [b] which were afar off and to them that were nigh.

18 For through [c] him we both

a Col. 1. 20-22. [1] or, *in himself.* b Ac. 2. 39. c Jno. 14. 6. 1 Pe. 3. 18.

complished, and they ceased to be of value and to be binding. ¶ Contained *in ordinances.* In the Mosaic commandments. The word *ordinance* means, decree, edict, law. Luke ii. 1. Acts xvi. 4; xvii. 7. Col. ii. 14. ¶ *For to make in himself.* By virtue of his death, or under him as the head. ¶ *Of twain one new man.* Of the two—Jews and Gentiles—one new spiritual person; that they might be united. The idea is, that as two persons who had been at enmity, might become reconciled and be one in aim and pursuit, so it was in the effect of the work of Christ on the Jews and Gentiles. When they were converted they would be united and harmonious.

16. *And that he might reconcile both unto God.* This was another of the effects of the work of redemption, and indeed the main effect. It was not merely to make them harmonious, but it was that both, who had been alienated from God, should be reconciled to *him.* This was a different effect from that of producing peace between themselves, though in some sense the one grew out of the other. They who are reconciled to God will be at peace with each other. They will feel that they are of the same family, and are all brethren. On the subject of reconciliation, see Notes on 2 Cor. v. 18. ¶ *In one body.* One spiritual personage—the church. See Notes on ch. i. 23. ¶ *By the cross.* By the atonement which he made on the cross. See Col. i. 20. Comp. Notes on Rom. iii. 25. It is by the atonement only that men ever become reconciled to God. ¶ *Having slain the enmity.* Not only the enmity between Jews and Gentiles, but the enmity between the sinner and God. He has by that death removed all the obstacles to reconciliation on the part of God and on the part of man. It is made efficacious in removing the enmity of the sinner against God, and producing peace. ¶ *Thereby.* Marg., *in himself.* The meaning is, in his cross, or by means of his cross.

17. *And came and preached peace.* That is, the system of religion which he proclaimed, was adapted to produce peace with God. This he preached personally to those who "were nigh," that is, the Jews; to those were "afar off"—the Gentiles—he preached it by his apostles. He was the author of the system which proclaimed salvation to both. The word *peace* here refers to reconciliation with God. ¶ *To you which were afar off,* &c. See Notes on ver. 13. Comp. Notes on Acts ii. 39.

18. *For through him.* That is, he has secured this result that we have access to God. This he did by his death—reconciling us to God; by the doctrines which he taught—acquainting us with God; and by his intercession in heaven—by which our "prayers gain acceptance" with him. ¶ *We both have access.* Both Jews and Gentiles. See Notes on Rom. v. 2. We are permitted to approach God through him, or in his name. The Greek word here—προσαγωγή—relates properly to the introduction to, or audience which we are permitted to have with a prince or other person of high rank. This must be effected through an officer of court to whom the duty is intrusted. *Rosenmüller,* Alt. und neu. Morgenland, in loc. ¶ *By one Spirit.*

have access by one Spirit unto the Father.

19 Now therefore ye are no more strangers and foreigners, but fellow-citizens [a] with the saints, and of the household [b] of God;

20 And are built [c] upon the [d]

a He. 12. 22, 23. b c. 3. 15.
c 1 Co. 3. 9, 10. d Mat. 16. 18. Re. 21. 14.

By the aid of the same Spirit—the Holy Ghost. See Notes, 1 Cor. xii. 4. ¶ *Unto the Father.* We are permitted to come and address God as our Father. See Notes on Rom. viii. 15. 26.

19. *Now therefore ye are no more strangers and foreigners.* You are reckoned with the people of God. You are entitled to their privileges, and are not to be regarded as outcasts and aliens. The meaning is, that they belonged to the same community—the same family—as the people of God. The word rendered *strangers*—ξένοι—means *foreigners in a state,* as opposed to citizens. The word rendered *foreigners*—πάροικοι—means *guests in a private family,* as opposed to the members of the family. *Rosenmüller.* Strangers and such as proposed to reside for a short time in Athens, were permitted to reside in the city, and to pursue their business undisturbed, but they could perform no public duty; they had no voice in the public deliberations, and they had no part in the management of the state. They could only look on as spectators, without mingling in the scenes of state, or interfering in any way in the affairs of the government. They were bound humbly to submit to all the enactments of the citizens, and observe all the laws and usages of the republic. It was not even allowed them to transact any business in their own name, but they were bound to choose from among the citizens one to whose care they committed themselves as a patron, and whose duty it was to guard them against all injustice and wrong. Potter's Gr. Ant. 1. 55. Proselytes, who united themselves to the Jews, were also called in the Jewish writings, *strangers.* All foreigners were regarded as 'strangers,' and Jews only were supposed to have near access to God. But now, says the apostle, this distinction is taken away, and the believing heathen, as well as the Jew, has the right of citizenship in the New Jerusalem, and one, as well as another, is a member of the family of God. *Burder,* Ros. Alt. u. neu. Morgenland, in loc. The meaning here is, that they had not come to *sojourn* merely as guests or foreigners, but were a part of the family itself, and entitled to all the privileges and hopes which others had. ¶ *But fellow-citizens with the saints.* Belonging to the same community with the people of God. ¶ *And of the household of God.* Of the same family. Entitled to the same privileges, and regarded by him as his children See ch. iii. 15.

20. *And are built upon the foundation.* The comparison of the church with a building, is common in the Scriptures. Comp. Notes on 1 Cor. iii. 9, 10. The comparison was probably taken from the temple, and as that was an edifice of great beauty, expense, and sacredness, it was natural to compare the church with it. Besides, the temple was the sacred place where God dwelt on the earth; and as the church was the place where he delighted now to abide, it became natural to speak of his church as the temple, or the residence of God. See Notes on Isa. liv. 11, 12. That building, says Paul, was permanently founded, and was rising with great beauty of proportion, and with great majesty and splendour. ¶ *Of the apostles.* The

foundation of the apostles and prophets, Jesus Christ himself being the chief[a] corner-*stone;*

21 In whom all the building

a Is. 28. 16.

doctrines which they taught are the basis on which the church rests. It is *possible* that Paul referred here to a splendid edifice, particularly because the Ephesians were distinguished for their skill in architecture, and because the celebrated temple of Diana was among them. An allusion to a building, however, as an illustration of the church, occurs several times in his other epistles, and was an allusion which would be everywhere understood. ¶ *And prophets.* The prophets of the Old Testament, using the word, probably, to denote the Old Testament in general. That is, the doctrines of divine revelation, whether communicated by prophets or apostles, were laid at the foundation of the Christian church. It was not founded on philosophy, or tradition, or on human laws, or on a venerable antiquity, but on the great truths which God had revealed. Paul does not say that it was founded on *Peter*, as the Papists do, but on the prophets and apostles in general. If Peter had been the 'vicegerent of Christ,' and the head of the church, it is incredible that his brother Paul should not have given him some honourable notice in this place. Why did he not allude to so important a fact? Would one who believed it have omitted it? Would a Papist now omit it? Learn here, (1.) That no reliance is to be placed on philosophy as a basis of religious doctrine. (2.) That the traditions of men have no authority in the church and constitute no part of the foundation. (3.) That nothing is to be regarded as a fundamental part of the Christian system, or as binding on the conscience, which cannot be found in the 'prophets and apostles;' that is, as it means here, in the Holy Scriptures. No decrees of councils; no ordinances of synods; no 'standard' of doctrines; no creed or confession, is to be urged as authority in forming the opinions of men. They may be valuable for some purposes, but not for this; they may be referred to as interesting parts of history, but not to form the faith of Christians; they may be used in the church to *express* its belief, but not to *form* it. What is based on the authority of apostles and prophets is true, and always true, and only true; what may be found elsewhere, may be valuable and true, or not, but, at any rate, is not to be used to control the faith of men. ¶ *Jesus Christ himself being the chief corner*-stone. See Notes on Isa. xxviii. 16. Rom. ix. 33. The corner-stone is the most important in the building. (1.) Because the edifice rests mainly on the corner-stones. If they are small, and unstable, and settle down, the whole building is insecure; and hence care is taken to place a large stone firmly at each corner of an edifice. (2.) Because it occupies a conspicuous and honourable place If documents or valuable articles are deposited at the foundation of a building it is within the corner-stone. The Lord Jesus is called the 'corner-stone,' because the whole edifice rests on him, or he occupies a place relatively as important as the corner-stone of an edifice. Were it not for him, the edifice could not be sustained for a moment. Neither prophets nor apostles alone could sustain it. See Notes on 1 Cor. iii. 11. Comp. 1 Pet. ii. 6.

21. *In whom.* That is, *by* whom, or *upon* whom. It was in connection with him, or by being reared on him as a foundation. ¶ *All the*

fitly framed together, groweth unto an holy [a] temple in the Lord:

22 In whom ye also are builded [b] together for an habitation of God through the Spirit.

a 1 Co. 3. 17. 2 Co. 6. 16.

b 1 Pe. 2. 4, 5.

---

building. The whole church of Christ. ¶ *Fitly framed together.* The word here used means *to joint together*, as a carpenter does the frame-work of a building. The materials are accurately and carefully united by mortices and tenons, so that the building shall be firm. Different materials may be used, and different kinds of timber may be employed, but one part shall be worked into another, so as to constitute a durable and beautiful edifice. So in the church. The different materials of the Jews and Gentiles; the people of various nations, though heretofore separated and discordant, become now united, and form an harmonious society. They believe the same doctrines; worship the same God; practise the same holiness, and look forward to the same heaven. ¶ *Groweth unto an holy temple in the Lord.* See Notes on 1 Cor. iii. 17. 2 Cor. vi. 16.

22. *In whom.* In Christ, or on Christ, as the solid and precious foundation. ¶ *Ye also are builded together.* You are built *into* that, or constitute a part of it. You are not merely *added* to it, but you constitute *a part* of the building. ¶ *For an habitation of God.* For the indwelling, or the dwelling-place, of God. Formerly he dwelt in the temple. Now he dwells in the church, and in the hearts of his people. See Notes on 2 Cor. vi. 16.

REMARKS.

1. We were by nature dead in sin. Ver. 1. We had no spiritual life. We were insensible to the calls of God, to the beauty of religion, to the claims of the Creator. We were like corpses in the tomb in reference to the gay and busy and happy world around them.—There we should have remained, had not the grace of God given us life, just as the dead will remain in their graves for ever, unless God shall raise them up. How humble should we be at the remembrance of this fact! how grateful that God has not left us to sleep that sleep of death for ever!

2. Parents should feel deep solicitude for their children. Ver. 3. They, in common with all others, are "children of wrath." They have a nature prone to evil; and that nature will develope itself in evil for ever, unless it is changed—just as the young thorn-bush will be a thorn-bush, and will put forth thorns, and not roses; and the Bohon Upas will be a Bohon Upas, and not an olive or an orange; and as the lion will be a lion, and the panther a panther, and not a lamb, a kid, or a gazelle. They will act out their nature, unless they are changed; and they will not be changed, but by the grace of God. I do not mean that their nature is in every sense like that of the lion or the asp; but I mean that they will be as certainly *wicked*, if unrenewed, as the lion will be ferocious, and the asp poisonous. And if so, what deep anxiety should parents feel for the salvation of their children! How solicitous should they be that, by the grace of God, the evil propensities of their nature may be eradicated, and that they become the adopted children of God!

3. The salvation of sinners involves all the exercise of power that is put forth in the resurrection of the dead. Ver. 5. It is not a work to be performed by man; it is not a work of angelic might. None can

impart spiritual life to the soul but he who gave it life at first. On that great Source of life we are dependant for our resurrection from spiritual death; and to God we must look for the grace by which we are to live.—It is true that though we are by nature "dead in sins," we are not in all respects like the dead. Let not this doctrine be abused to make us secure in sin, or to prevent effort. The dead in the grave are dead in all respects. We by nature are dead only in sin. We are active in other things; and indeed the powers of man are not less active than they would be if he were holy. But it is a tremendous activity for evil, and for evil only. The dead in their graves hear nothing, see nothing, and feel nothing. Sinners hear, and see, and feel; but they hear not God, and they see not his glory, any more than if they were dead. To the dead in the grave, no command could with propriety be addressed; on them, no entreaty could be urged to rise to life. But the sinner may be commanded and entreated; for he *has* power, though it is misdirected; and what is needful is, that he should put forth his power in a proper manner. While, therefore, we admit, with deep humiliation, that we, our children and friends, are by nature dead in sin, let us not abuse this doctrine as though we could be required to do nothing. It is with us wilful death. It is death because we do not choose to live. It is a voluntary closing our eyes, and stopping our ears, *as if* we were dead; and it is a voluntary remaining in this state, when we have all the requisite power to put forth the energies of life. Let a sinner be as active in the service of God as he is in the service of the Devil and the world, and he would be an eminent Christian. Indeed, all that is required is, that the misdirected and abused energy of this world should be employed in the service of the Creator. Then all would be well.

4. Let us remember our former course of life. Vs. 11, 12. Nothing is more profitable for a Christian than to sit down and reflect on his former life—on his childhood, with its numerous follies and vanities; on his youth, with its errors, and passions, and sins; and on the ingratitude and faults of riper years. Had God left us in that state, what would be now our condition? Had he cut us off, where had been our abode? Should he now treat us as we deserve, what would be our doom? When the Christian is in danger of becoming proud and self-confident, let him REMEMBER what he was. Let him take some period of his life—some year, some month, or even some one day—and think it all over, and he will find enough to humble him. These are the uses which should be made of the past. (1.) It should make us humble. If a man had before his mind a vivid sense of all the past in his own life, he would never be lifted up with pride. (2.) It should make us grateful. God cut off the companions of my childhood—why did he spare me? He cut down many of the associates of my youth in their sins—why did he preserve me? He has suffered many to live on in their sins, and they are in 'the broad road'—why am I not with them, treading the path to death and hell? (3.) The recollection of the past should lead us to devote ourselves to God. Professing Christian, '*remember*' how much of thy life is gone to waste. *Remember* thy days of folly and vanity. *Remember* the injury thou hast done by an evil example. *Remember* how many have been corrupted by thy conversation; perverted by thy opinions; led into sin by thy example; perhaps ruined in body and soul for ever by the errors and follies of

thy past life. And then REMEMBER how much thou dost owe to God, and how solemnly thou art bound to endeavour to repair the evils of thy life, and to save *at least as many* as thou hast ruined.

5. Sinners are by nature without any well-founded hope of salvation. Ver. 12. They are living without Christ, having no belief in him, and no hope of salvation through him. They are 'aliens' from all the privileges of the friends of God. They have no 'hope.' They have no well-founded expectation of happiness beyond the grave. They have a dim and shadowy expectation that *possibly* they may be happy; but it is founded on no evidence of the divine favour, and no promise of God. *They could not tell on what it is founded, if they were asked*; and what is such a hope worth? These false and delusive hopes do not sustain the soul in trial; they flee away in death. And what a description is this! In a world like this, to be without hope! Subject to trial; exposed to death; and yet destitute of any well-founded prospect of happiness beyond the tomb! They are 'without God' also. They worship no God; they confide in none. They have no altar in their families; no place of secret prayer. They form their plans with no reference to the will of God; they desire not to please him. There are multitudes who are living just as if there were no God. Their plans, their lives, their conversation, would not be different if they had the assurance that there was no God. All that they have ever asked of God, or that they would now ask of him, is, *that he would let them alone*. There are multitudes whose plans would be in no respect different, if it were announced to them that there was no God in heaven. The only effect might be to produce a more hearty merriment, and a deeper plunge into sin. What a world! How strange that in God's own world it should thus be! How sad the view of a world of atheists—a race that is endeavouring to feel that the universe is without a Father and a God! How wicked the plans which can be accomplished only by labouring to forget that there is a God; and how melancholy that state of the soul in which happiness can be found only in proportion as it believes that the universe is without a Creator, and moves on without the superintending care of a God!

6. The gospel produces peace. Vs. 14—17. (1.) It produces peace in the heart of the individual, reconciling him to God. (2.) It produces peace and harmony between different ranks and classes and complexions of men, causing them to love each other, and removing their alienations and antipathies. The best way of producing friendship between nations and tribes of men; between those of different complexions, pursuits, and laws, is to preach to them the gospel. The best way to produce harmony between the oppressor and the oppressed, is to preach to both of them the gospel of peace, and make them feel that they have a common Saviour. (3.) It is fitted to produce peace among the nations. Let it spread, and wars will cease right and justice will universally prevail, and harmony and concord will spread over the world. See Notes on Isa. ii. 4.

7. Let us rejoice in the privileges which we now have as Christians. We have access to the Father. Ver. 18. None are so poor, so ignorant, so down-trodden that they may not come to God. In all times of affliction, poverty, and oppression, we may approach the Father of mercies. Chains may bind the body, but no chain can fetter the soul in its intercourse with God. We may be thrown into a dungeon, but communion with God may be maintained there. We may

be cast out and despised by men, but we may come at once unto God, and he will not cast us away. Further. We are not now strangers and foreigners. We belong to the family of God. We are fellow-citizens with the saints. Ver. 19. We are participants of the hope of the redeemed, and we share their honours and their joys. It is right that true Christians should rejoice, and their joy is of such a character that no man can take it from them.

8. Let us make our appeal on all doctrines and duties to the Bible—to the prophets and the apostles. Ver. 20. On them and their doctrine we can build. On them the church is reared. It is not on the opinion of philosophers and lawgivers; not on creeds, symbols, traditions, and the decisions of councils; it is on the authority of the inspired book of God. The church is in its most healthy state when it appeals for its doctrines most directly to the Bible. Individual Christians grow most in grace when they appeal most to this 'book of books.' The church is in great danger of error when it goes off from this pure 'standard' and makes its appeal to other standards—to creeds and symbols of doctrine. "The Bible is the religion of Protestants;" and the church will be kept pure from error, and will advance in holiness, just as this is made the great principle which shall always govern and control it. If a doctrine is not found in the 'apostles and prophets'—in some part of the Bible, it is not to be imposed on the conscience. It may, or may not be true; it may, or may not be fitted to edify a people; but it is not to be an article of faith, or imposed on the consciences of men.

9. Let us evince always special regard for the Lord Jesus. Ver. 20. He is the precious corner-stone on which the whole spiritual temple is reared. On him the church rests. How important, then, that the church should have correct views of the Redeemer! How important that the true doctrine respecting his divine nature; his atonement; his incarnation; his resurrection, should be maintained. It is not a matter of indifference whether he be God or man; whether he died as an atoning sacrifice or as a martyr; whether he be the equal of God, or whether he be an archangel. Everything depends on the view which is held of that Redeemer—and as men entertain different opinions about him, they go off into different systems as wide from each other as the poles. Everything in the welfare of the church, and in the individual peace of its members, depends on proper views of the Lord Jesus.

10. The church is designed as the place of the special residence of the Holy Spirit on earth. Vs. 21, 22. It is the beautiful temple where he dwells; the edifice which is reared for his abode. How holy should that church be; how pure should be each Christian to be an appropriate habitation for such a guest! Holy should be the heart where that Spirit dwells With what anxious care should we cherish the presence of such a guest; with what solicitude should we guard our conduct that we may not grieve him away! How anxious we are so to live that we may not grieve away our friends from our dwellings! Should an illustrious guest become an inmate in our abode, how anxious should we be to do all that we can to please him, and to retain him with us! How much more anxious should we be to secure the indwelling of the eternal Spirit! How desirous that he should make our hearts and the church his constant abode!

CHAPTER III.

ANALYSIS.

This chapter consists properly of three parts:—

I. A statement that the Gentiles were to be made partakers of the gospel, and that the work of proclaiming this was especially intrusted to Paul. Vs. 1—12. In illustrating this, Paul observes.

(1.) That he was the prisoner of Jesus Christ in behalf of the Gentiles. Ver. 1. He was in bonds for maintaining that the gospel was to be preached to the Gentiles, and for endeavouring to convey it to them.

(2.) He reminds them all of the fact that he was called by special revelation to make known this truth, and to convey to the Gentiles this gospel — supposing that they had heard of the manner of his conversion. Vs. 2, 3.

(3.) He refers them to what he had said before in few words on this point as proof of his acquaintance with this great plan of the gospel. Vs. 3, 4.

(4.) He speaks of this great truth as a 'mystery' — the 'mystery of Christ;' the great and important truth which was concealed until Christ came, and which was fully made known by him. Vs. 4, 5, 6. This had been hidden for ages. But now it had been fully revealed by the Spirit of God to the apostles and prophets in the Christian church that the great wall of partition was to be broken down, and the gospel proclaimed alike to all.

(5.) The apostle says, that to him especially was this office committed to proclaim among the Gentiles the unsearchable riches of Christ. Vs. 8, 9.

(6.) The *design* of this was to illustrate, in view of all worlds, the great wisdom of God in the plan of salvation. Vs. 10—12. It was intended to show to other intelligent beings the glory of the divine perfections, and to make manifestations of the divine character which could be perceived nowhere else.

II. Paul expresses an earnest wish that they should comprehend the glory of this plan of salvation. Vs. 13—19. Particularly he desires them not to faint on account of his afflictions in their behalf; declares that he bows his knees in prayer before the Great Father of the redeemed family, that God would be pleased to strengthen them, and enlighten them, and give them clear views of the glorious plan.

III. The chapter concludes with an ascription of praise to God, in view of the great goodness which he had manifested, and of the glory of the plan of salvation. Vs. 20, 21.

1. *For this cause.* On account of preaching this doctrine; that is, the doctrine that the gospel was to be proclaimed to the Gentiles. ¶ *I Paul, the prisoner of Jesus Christ.* A prisoner in the service of the Lord Jesus; or made a prisoner in his cause. Not a prisoner for crime, or debt, or as a captive in war, but a captive in the service of the Redeemer. This proves that at the time of writing this, Paul was in bonds, and there can be no question that he was in Rome. This would be more correctly rendered, 'For this cause I, Paul, am the prisoner,' &c. So Tindal renders it, "For this cause I, Paul, the servant of Jesus, am in bonds." So also Locke, Rosenmüller, Doddridge, Whitby, Koppe, and others understand it. By this construction the abruptness now manifest in our common version is avoided. ¶ *For you Gentiles.* Made a prisoner at Rome on your behalf, because I maintained that the gospel was to be preached to the Gentiles. See Acts xxii. 21—23. He was taken first to Cesarea, and then to Rome. The cause of his impris-

CHAPTER III.

FOR this cause I Paul, the prisoner of Jesus Christ for you Gentiles,

2 (If ye have heard of the dispensation [a] of the grace [b] of God, which is given me to you-ward:

3 How that by revelation [c] he made known unto me the mys-

a Col. 1. 25. b Ro. 12. 3. c Ga. 1. 12.

onment and of all his difficulties was, that he maintained that the gospel was to be preached to the Gentiles; that when the Jews rejected it God rejected them; and that he was specially called to carry the message of salvation to the heathen world.

2. *If ye have heard.* Εἴγε. "*If at least, if indeed, if so be,* spoken of what is taken for granted." *Robinson.* Comp. 2 Cor. v. 3. Gal. iii. 4. Eph. iv. 21. Col. i. 23, for the use of the particle. The particle here is not designed to express a doubt whether they had heard of it or not, for he takes it for granted that they had. Doddridge renders it, 'since I well know you have heard,' &c. He had informed them of his being called to be the minister to the Gentiles (ver. 3), but still there was a possibility that they had not received the letter containing the information, and he goes, therefore, into another statement on the subject, that they might fully comprehend it. Hence this long parenthetical sentence—one of the longest that occurs in the writings of Paul, and expressed under the impulse of a mind full of the subject; so full, as we would say, that he did not know what to say first. Hence it is exceedingly difficult to understand the exact state of mind in which he was. It seems to me that the whole of this long statement grew out of the incidental mention (ver. 1) of the fact that he was a prisoner for the Gentiles. Instantly he seems to have reflected that they would be grieved at the intelligence that he was suffering on their account. He goes, therefore, into this long account, to show them how it happened; that it was by the appointment of God; that it was in the evolving of a great and glorious mystery; that it was in a cause adapted to promote, in an eminent degree, the glory of God; that it was according to an eternal purpose; and he, therefore (ver. 13), says, that he desires that they would not "faint" or be unduly distressed on account of his sufferings for them, since his sufferings were designed to promote their "glory." *He* was comforted in the belief that he was making known the glorious and eternal plan of God, and in the belief that it was for the welfare of mankind; and he, therefore, entreated them also not to be troubled inordinately at his sufferings. ¶ *The dispensation.* Gr. *economy;* rendered *stewardship,* Luke xvi. 2, 3, 4; and *dispensation,* Eph. i. 10; iii. 2. Col. i. 25. See Notes on ch. i. 10. It means here that this arrangement was made that he should be the apostle to the Gentiles. In the assignment of the different parts of the work of preaching the gospel, the office had been committed to him of making it known to the heathen. ¶ *Of the grace of God.* In the arrangements of his grace. ¶ *Which is given me to you-ward.* Toward you who are Gentiles. Not to the Ephesians particularly, but to the nations at large. See Notes on Gal. ii. 7.

3. *How that by revelation.* See Notes on Gal. i. 12. He refers to the revelation which was made to him when he was called to the apostolic office, that the gospel was to be preached to the Gentiles, and that he was converted for the special pur-

tery; as I wrote afore [1] in few words,

4 Whereby, when ye read, ye may understand my knowledge in the [a] mystery of Christ;

5 Which in other ages was not [b] made known unto the sons of men, as it is now revealed unto the holy apostles and prophets by the Spirit;

[1] or, *a little before.* [a] c. 1. 9.

[b] Mat. 13. 17. Ro. 16. 25. 1 Pe. 1. 10-12.

pose of carrying it to them. See Acts ix. 15; xxii. 21. ¶ *Unto me the mystery.* The hitherto concealed truth that the gospel was to be preached to the Gentiles. See Notes, ch. i. 9, on the meaning of the word *mystery.* ¶ *As I wrote afore in few words.* Marg., *a little before.* To what this refers commentators are not agreed. Bloomfield, Doddridge, Rosenmüller, Erasmus, Grotius, Locke, and others, suppose that he refers to what he had written in the two previous chapters respecting the plan of God to call the Gentiles to his kingdom. Calvin supposes that he refers to some former epistle which he had written to them, but which is now lost. He remarks in regard to this, 'If the solicitude of Paul be rightly considered; if his vigilance and assiduity; if his zeal and studious habits; if his kindness and promptitude in assisting his brethren, it is easy to suppose that he wrote many epistles publicly and privately to this place and to that place. But those only which the Lord saw necessary to the welfare of his church has he taken care to have preserved.' In this opinion there is nothing in itself improbable (Comp. Introduction to Isaiah, § 5, (1.)), but it may be doubted whether Paul here refers to any such epistle. The addition which he makes, 'whereby, when ye read,' &c., seems rather to imply that he refers to what he had just written.

4. *Whereby, when ye read.* By the bare reading of which you may understand the view which I entertain of the plan of salvation, and the knowledge which I have of God's method of saving men, particularly of his intention in regard to the salvation of the Gentiles. ¶ *In the mystery of Christ.* This does not refer to any thing *mysterious* in the person of Christ; or the union of the divine and human nature in him; or to any thing difficult of apprehension in the work of the atonement. It means the hitherto concealed doctrine that through the Messiah, the Gentiles were to be received to the same privileges as the Jews, and that the plan of salvation was to be made equally free for all. This great truth had been hitherto concealed, or but partially understood, and Paul says that he was appointed to make it known to the world. His *knowledge* on the subject, he says, could be understood by what he had said, and from that they could judge whether he was qualified to state and defend the doctrines of the gospel. Paul evidently supposed that the knowledge which he had on that subject was of eminent value; that it was possessed by few; that it was important to understand it. Hence he dwells upon it. He speaks of the glory of that truth. He traces it back to the counsels of God. He shows that it entered into his eternal plans; and he evidently felt that the truth which he had communicated in the former part of this epistle, was among the most important that could come before the mind.

5. *Which in other ages.* The great purposes of God in regard to the salvation of mankind were not revealed. See Notes on Rom. xvi. 25. ¶ *And prophets.* Those who exercised the office of a prophet or

6 That the Gentiles should be fellow-heirs, and of the same body, and partakers of his promise in Christ by the gospel;

7 Whereof I was made a minister, according to the gift of the grace of God given unto me by the effectual [a] working of his power.

8 Unto me, who am less [b] than the least of all saints, is this grace given, that I should preach among

a Is. 43. 13. c. 1. 19. b 1 Co. 15. 9.

---

inspired teacher in the Christian church. See Notes on 1 Cor. xii. 1. ¶ *By the Spirit.* This proves that those who exercised the office of prophet in the Christian church were inspired. They were persons endowed in this manner for the purpose of imparting to the newly formed churches the doctrines of the Christian system. There is no evidence that this was designed to be a permanent order of men in the church. They were necessary for settling the church on a permanent basis, in the absence of a full written revelation, and when the apostles were away. When the volume of revelation was finished, and the doctrines of the gospel were fully understood, the functions of the office ceased.

6. *That the Gentiles should be fellow-heirs.* Fellow-heirs with the ancient people of God—the Jews—and entitled to the same privileges. See Notes on Rom. viii. 17, and Eph. ii. 13—18.

7. *Whereof I was made a minister.* See Notes on ver. 2. ¶ *According to the gift of the grace of God.* It was not by my own seeking or merit; it was a free gift. ¶ *Of the grace of God.* The sentiment is, that throughout it was a mere matter of grace that he was called into the ministry, and that so important an office was intrusted to him as that of bearing the gospel to the Gentiles. ¶ *By the effectual working of his power.* Not by any native inclination which *I* had to the gospel, and not by any power which I have put forth. It is by 'the *energy* of his power.' Comp. Notes, Gal. ii. 8. Locke understands this of the energy or power which God put forth in converting the Gentiles under his ministry. But it seems to me that it refers rather to the power which God put forth in the conversion of Paul himself, and putting him into the ministry. This is clear from the following verse. The meaning is, that such was his opposition to the gospel by nature, that nothing but the 'energy of God' could overcome it, and that his conversion was to be traced to that alone.

8. *Unto me, who am less than the least of all saints.* This is one of the class of expressions peculiar to Paul. The ordinary terms of language do not express the idea which he wishes to convey, and a word is therefore *coined* to convey an idea more emphatically. Comp. Notes on 2 Cor. iv. 17. The word here used—ἐλαχιστότερος—does not occur elsewhere in the New Testament. It is a comparative made from the superlative. Similar expressions are found, however, in later Greek writers. See Bloomfield and Rosenmüller for examples. The word means here, 'who am *incomparably* the least of all the saints; or who am not worthy to be reckoned among the saints.' It is expressive of the deep sense which he had of the sinfulness of his past life; of his guilt in persecuting the church and the Saviour; and perhaps of his sense of his low attainments in piety. See Notes on 1 Cor. xv. 9. Paul never could forget the guilt of his former life; never forget the time when he was engaged in persecuting the

the Gentiles the unsearchable riches[a] of Christ;

9 And to make all *men* see, what *is* the fellowship of the mystery,[b] which from the beginning of the world hath been hid

a Co. 1. 27.

b ver. 4, 5. 1 Ti. 3. 16.

church of God. ¶ *The unsearchable riches of Christ.* On the word *riches*, as used by Paul, see Notes on ch. i. 7. The word rendered *unsearchable*, ἀνεξιχνίαστον, occurs but once elsewhere in the New Testament (Rom. xi. 33), where it is rendered *past finding out.* See Notes on that verse. It means that which cannot be *traced out*, or explored; which is inscrutable, or incomprehensible. The meaning here is, that there was a *sufficiency* in Christ which could not be traced out or explored. It was wholly incomprehensible. The fulness of the riches in him could not be appreciated. There is no more emphatic expression in the New Testament than this. It shows that the heart of the apostle was full of admiration of the sufficiency and glory that was in the Saviour; that he wanted words to express it; and that he considered it the highest honour to be permitted to tell the world that there *were* such riches in the Redeemer.

9. *And to make all* men *see.* In order that the whole human family might see the glory of God in the plan of salvation. Hitherto the revelation of his character and plans had been confined to the Jews. Now it was his design that all the race should be made acquainted with it. ¶ *What* is *the fellowship of the mystery.* Instead of *fellowship* here—κοινωνία—most MSS. and versions read οἰκονομία—*dispensation.* See Mill. This reading is adopted by Griesbach, Tittman, Rosenmüller, Koppe, and is regarded by most critics as being the genuine reading. The mistake might easily have been made by a transcriber. The meaning then would be, 'to enlighten all in respect to the dispensation of this mystery;' that is, to cause all to understand the manner in which this great truth of the plan of salvation is communicated to men. If the word *fellowship* is to be retained, it means that this doctrine, or secret counsel of God, was now *common* to all believers. It was not to be confined to any class or rank of men. Locke renders it, "and to make all men perceive how this mystery comes now to be communicated to the world." Archbishop Whately (Errors of Romanism, ch. ii. § 1) renders it, "the common participation of the mystery;" that is, of truths formerly unknown, and which could not be known by man's unaided powers, but which were now laid open by the gracious dispensation of Divine Providence; no longer concealed, or confined to a few, but to be partaken of by all. The allusion, according to him, is to the mysteries of the ancient pagan religions; and he supposes that the apostle designs to contrast those 'mysteries' with Christianity. In those 'mysteries' there was a distinction between the initiated and uninitiated. There was a revelation to some of the worshippers, of certain holy secrets from which others were excluded. There were in some of the mysteries, as the Eleusinian, *great* and *lesser* doctrines, in which different persons were initiated. In strong contrast with these, the 'great mystery' in Christianity was made known to all. It was concealed from none, and there was no distinction made among those who were initiated. No truths which God had revealed were held back from any part, but there was a common participation by all. Christianity has no hidden truths for a part only of its friends; it has no

in God, who created all things by [a] Jesus Christ:

10 To the intent that now unto the principalities and powers in

a Ps. 33. 6. Jno. 1. 3. Co. 1. 16. He. 1. 2.

'*reserved*' doctrines; it has no truths to be intrusted only to a sacred priesthood. Its doctrines are to be published to the wide world, and every follower of Christ is to be a partaker of all the benefits of the truths which Christ has revealed. It is difficult to determine which is the true reading, and it is not very important. The general sense is, that Paul felt himself called into the ministry in order that all men might understand now that salvation was free for all—a truth that had been concealed for ages. Bearing this great truth, he felt that he had a message of incalculable value to mankind, and he was desirous to go and proclaim it to the wide world. On the word *mystery*, see Notes, ch. i. 9. ¶ *Hath been hid in God.* With God. It has been concealed in his bosom. The plan was formed, but it had not before been made known. ¶ *Who created all things.* This is plain enough; but it is not quite so plain why the declaration is introduced in this place. Locke and Rosenmüller suppose that it refers to the new creation, and that the sense is, that God frames and manages this new creation wholly by Jesus Christ. But the expression contains a truth of larger import, and naturally conveys the idea that *all* things were made by God, and that this was only a part of his great and universal agency. The meaning is, that God formed all things, and that this purpose of extending salvation to the world was a part of his great plan, and was under his control. ¶ *By Jesus Christ.* As this stands in our common Greek text, as well as in our English version, there is a striking resemblance between the passage and that in Col. i. 15, 16. But the phrase is wanting in the Vulgate, the Syriac, the Coptic, and in several of the ancient MSS. Mill remarks that it was probably inserted here by some transcriber from the parallel passage in Col. i. 16; and it is rejected as an interpolation by Griesbach. It is not *very* material whether it be retained in this place or not, as the same sentiment is elsewhere abundantly taught. See John i. 3; Col. i. 16; Heb. i. 2. If it is to be retained, the sentiment is that the Son of God—the second person of the Trinity—was the great and immediate agent in the creation of the universe.

10. *To the intent.* Greek, '*that*'—Ἵνα. The sense is, that it was with this design, or that this was the purpose for which all things were made. One grand purpose in the creation of the universe was, that the wisdom of God might be clearly shown by the church. It was not enough to evince it by the formation of the sun, the stars, the earth, the seas, the mountains, the floods. It was not enough to show it by the creation of intelligent beings, the formation of immortal minds on earth, and the various ranks of the angelic world. There were views of the divine character which could be obtained only in connection with the redemption of the world. Hence the universe was created, and man was made upon the earth, not merely to illustrate the divine perfections in the work of creation, but in a still more illustrious manner in the work of redemption. And hence the deep interest which the angelic hosts have ever evinced in the salvation of man. ¶ *That now.* The word *now*—νῦν—is wanting in the Vulgate, Syriac, and Arabic; and is omitted by many of the Fathers. See Koppe. If it is to be retained, it means that this

heavenly *places* might be known, by the church, the manifold wisdom [a] of God,

11 According to the eternal [b] purpose which he purposed in Christ Jesus our Lord:

a Ro. 11. 33. 1 Co. 2. 7.

b c. 1. 9.

display is to be made under the gospel. 'Now, since the Messiah is come; now, under the christian dispensation, this revelation is to be made to distant worlds.' ¶ *Unto the principalities and powers.* To the angelic hosts—the intelligent beings that surround the throne of God. See Notes on ch. i. 21. ¶ *By the church.* By the incarnation of the Redeemer to save it; by the mercy shown to it; by the wise arrangement made to recover his people from the fall; and by all the graces and beauties which that redeemed church will evince on earth and in heaven.—¶ *The manifold wisdom of God.* Literally, *much-variegated.* It means the *greatly-diversified* wisdom. It does not mean merely that there was *great* wisdom, but that the wisdom shown was diversified and varied; like changing, variegated colours. There was a "beautiful and well-ordered variety of dispensations" towards that church, all of which tended to evince the wisdom of God. It is like a landscape, or a panoramic view passing before the mind, with a great variety of phases and aspects, all tending to excite admiration. In the redemption of the church, there is not merely one form or one phase of wisdom. It is wisdom, ever-varying, ever-beautiful. There was wisdom manifested when the plan was formed; wisdom in the selection of the Redeemer; wisdom in the incarnation; wisdom in the atonement; wisdom in the means of renewing the heart, and sanctifying the soul; wisdom in the various dispensations by which the church is sanctified, guided, and brought to glory. The wisdom thus shown is like the ever-varying beauty of changing clouds, when the sun is reflected on them at evening. Each aspect is full of beauty. One bright cloud differs in appearance from others; yet all tend to fill the mind with elevated views of God.

11. *According to the eternal purpose.* See Note ch. i. 4. Literally, 'the purpose of ages,' or of eternity. Locke, Chandler, and Whitby render this, 'according to that disposition or arrangement of the ages which he made in Jesus Christ, or through him.' The object of such an interpretation seems to be to avoid the doctrine that God had a purpose or plan in the salvation of men, and hence such expositors suppose it refers to the arrangement of the *ages* of the world by which the plan of redemption was introduced. On the word here rendered *purpose*—πρόθεσις—see Notes on Rom. viii. 28. Comp. Eph. i. 11. It is rendered *shewbread*—'the bread of *setting before*,' Matt. xii. 4. Mark ii. 26. Luke vi. 4. Heb. ix. 2; *purpose*, Acts xi. 23; xxvii. 13. Rom. viii. 28; ix. 11. Eph. i. 11; iii. 11. 2 Tim. i. 9; iii. 10. It does not occur elsewhere in the New Testament. In most of these cases it refers to the *purpose* or *intention* of God; in not a single case does it mean *arrangement* or *disposition* in any sense like that of making an arrangement of *ages* or periods of the world; and the interpretation proposed by Whitby, Locke, Clarke, and others, is wholly at variance with the settled use of the word. The word rendered *eternal*—αἰώνων—*may* mean ages; but it also most usually means eternity. See ver. 9. Here it *may* mean 'the purpose of *ages*;' i. e. the purpose formed in past ages; but the word is most commonly used in the New Testament in the sense of

12 In whom we have boldness[a] and access with confidence by the faith of him.

a He. 4. 16.

13 Wherefore I desire that ye faint not at my tribulations for you, which[b] is your glory.

b 2 Co. 1. 6.

ever, and *for ever*. Comp. the following places, where it is so rendered in our common version, and beyond a doubt correctly. Matt. vi. 13; xxi. 19. Mark iii. 29; xi. 14. Luke i. 33. 55. John iv. 14; vi. 51. 58; viii. 35; xiv. 16. Rom. i. 25; ix. 5; xi. 36; xvi. 27. 2 Cor. ix. 9; xi. 31. Gal. i. 5. The fair meaning of the passage here is, that God had formed a plan which was *eternal* in reference to the salvation of men; that that plan had reference to the Lord Jesus; and that it was now executed by the gospel. It is impossible to get away from the idea that God has *a plan*. It is too often affirmed in the Scriptures, and is too consonant with our reason, to be disputed. It is as *undesirable* as it is impossible to escape from that idea. Who could respect or honour an intelligent being that had no plan, no purpose, no intention, and that did all things by caprice and hap-hazard? If God has any plan, it must be eternal. He has no *new* schemes; he has no intentions which he did not always have. ¶ *Which he purposed.* Literally, 'which he *made*.' ¶ *In Christ Jesus.* With reference to him; or which were to be executed through him. The eternal plan had respect to him, and was to be executed by his coming and work.

12. *We have boldness.* The word here used—παῤῥησίαν—means, properly, boldness of speaking. 2 Cor. vii. 4. John vii. 26. Acts iv. 13. 29. 31. Here it seems to mean 'freedom of utterance;' and the idea is, that we may come to God now in prayer with confidence through the Lord Jesus. See Heb. iv. 16. ¶ *And access.* See Notes ch. ii. 18. ¶ *By the faith of him.* By faith in him. The sense is, that we may now come confidently and boldly to the throne of grace for mercy in the name of the Redeemer. Boldness is not rashness; and faith is not presumption; but we may come without hesitating, and with an assurance that our prayers will be heard.

13. *Wherefore I desire that ye faint not.* The connection here is this. Paul was then a prisoner at Rome. He had been made such in consequence of his efforts to diffuse the Christian religion among the Gentiles. See Notes on ver. 1. His zeal in this cause, and the opinions which he held on this subject, had roused the wrath of the Jews, and led to all the calamities which he was now suffering. Of that the Ephesians, he supposes, were aware. It was natural that they should be distressed at his sufferings, for all his privations were endured on their account. But here he tells them not to be troubled and disheartened. He was indeed suffering; but he was reconciled to it, and they should be also, since it was promoting their welfare. The word rendered "faint"—ἐκκακεω—means literally, to turn out a coward, or to lose one's courage; then to be faint-hearted, &c. Notes, 2 Cor. iv. 1. It is rendered *faint* in Luke xviii. 1. 2 Cor. iv. 1. 16. Eph. iii. 13, and *weary* in Gal. vi. 9. 2 Thess. iii. 13. It does not elsewhere occur. It is rendered here by Locke *dismayed*. Koppe supposes it means that they should not suppose that the Christian religion was vain and false because he was suffering so much from his countrymen on account of it. But it rather means that they might be in danger of being discouraged by the fact that *he* was enduring so much. They might become disheartened in their

14 For this cause I bow my knees unto the Father of our Lord Jesus Christ,

15 Of whom the whole family in heaven and earth is named,

---

attachment to a system of religion which exposed its friends to such calamities. Paul tells them that this ought not to follow. They were to be profited by all *his* sufferings, and they should, therefore, hold fast to a religion which was attended with so many benefits to *them*—though *he* should suffer. ¶ ***Which is your glory.*** Which tends to your honour and welfare. You have occasion to rejoice that you have a friend who is willing thus to suffer for you; you have occasion to rejoice in all the benefits which will result to you from his trials in your behalf.

14. *For this cause.* Some suppose that this is a resumption of what he had commenced saying in ver. 1, but which had been interrupted by a long parenthesis. So Bloomfield explains it. But it seems to me more probable that he refers to what immediately precedes. 'Wherefore, that the great work may be carried on, and that the purposes of these my sufferings may be answered in your benefit and glory, I bow my knees to God, and pray to him.' ¶ *I bow my knees.* I pray. The usual, and the proper posture of prayer is to kneel. Comp. 2 Chron. vi. 13. Dan. vi. 10. Luke xxii. 21. Acts vii. 60; ix. 40; xx. 26; xxi. 5. It is a posture which indicates reverence, and should, therefore, be assumed when we come before God. It has been an unhappy thing that the custom of kneeling in public worship has ever been departed from in the Christian churches. ¶ *Unto the Father of our Lord Jesus Christ.* To whom, undoubtedly, prayer should ordinarily be addressed. But this does not make it improper to address the Lord Jesus in prayer. See Notes on Acts i. 24; vii. 59, 60.

15. *Of whom the whole family.* This expression 'of whom,' may refer either to 'the Father,' or to the Lord Jesus. Commentators have been divided in opinion in regard to it. Bloomfield, Chandler, Erasmus, Koppe, and some others, refer it to the Father. Locke, Doddridge, Calvin, and some others, refer it to the Lord Jesus. This is the more natural interpretation. The whole 'family of God,' means all his children; and the idea is, that they all bear the same name, derived from the Redeemer; all are Christians. No matter where they are, in heaven or in earth; no matter from what nation they are converted, whether Jews or Gentiles, they all have one name, and one Redeemer, and all belong to one family. See ch. iv. 4—6. ¶ *In heaven.* Spirits of just men made perfect. It does not properly refer to angels, for he is not speaking of them, but of the family of the redeemed. If the phrase 'in heaven,' could *ever* be taken to denote the Jews as contradistinguished from the Gentiles, I should think that this was one of the places. Many expositors have supposed that it is frequently so used in this epistle, but I see no clear evidence of it, and no instance where it seems very probable, unless this should be one. And it is not necessary here, for it may mean *all* the redeemed, whether in heaven or earth, though the connection would seem rather to have suggested a reference to the Jews and the Gentiles. An expression similar to this occurs in Col. i. 20. "To reconcile all things to himself, whether they be things in earth, or things in heaven." The passage before us is one that is commonly explained by a reference to Jewish

16 That he would grant you according to the riches [a] of his glory, to be [b] strengthened with might by his Spirit in the inner man; [c]

a Ph. 4. 19. *b* c. 6. 10. Col. 1. 11. *c* Ro. 7. 22.

17 That Christ may dwell [d] in your hearts by faith; that ye, being [e] rooted and grounded in love,

18 May be able to comprehend

d Jno. 14. 23. c. 2. 22. *e* Co. 2. 7.

---

opinions. The Jews were accustomed to call the angels in heaven God's *upper family*, and his people on earth his *lower family*. See the passages cited from the Rabbinical writers in Wetstein. ¶ *Is named.* This means substantially the same as *is.* They are all of one family. They all have one father, and are all of one community. The expression is taken from the custom in a family, where all bear the name of the *head* of the family; and the meaning is, that all in heaven and on earth are united under one head, and constitute one community. It does not mean that all are *called* by the same name, or that the name *Christian* is given to the angels, but that they all pertain to the same community, and constitute the same great and glorious brotherhood. Part are in heaven, near his throne; part in distant worlds; part are angels of light; part redeemed and happy spirits; part are in the church on earth; but they are all united as one family, and have one head and Father. This glorious family will yet be gathered together in heaven, and will encompass the throne of their common Father rejoicing.

16. *According to the riches of his glory.* According to the glorious abundance of his mercy. See Phil. iv. 19. Out of those stores of rich grace which can never be exhausted. The word *riches,* so often used by Paul, denotes *abundance*, and the idea here is, that his grace was inexhaustible and ample for all their wants. ¶ *To be strengthened with might.* To be powerfully strengthened. That is, to give you abundant strength to bear trials; to perform your duties; to glorify his name. ¶ *In the inner man.* In the heart, the mind, the soul. See Notes on Rom. vii. 22. The *body* needs to be strengthened every day. In like manner the soul needs constant supplies of grace. Piety needs to be constantly invigorated, or it withers and decays. Every Christian needs grace given each day to enable him to bear trials, to resist temptation, to discharge his duty, to live a life of faith.

17. *That Christ may dwell in your hearts by faith.* See Notes, ch. ii. 22. Expressions like this often occur in the Scriptures, where God is said to dwell in us, and we are said to be the temples of the Holy Ghost. See Notes on John xiv. 23. 1 Cor. vi. 19. ¶ *That ye being rooted.* Firmly established—as a tree is whose roots strike deep, and extend afar. The meaning is, that his love should be as firm in our hearts, as a tree is in the soil, whose roots strike deep into the earth. ¶ *And grounded.* τεθεμελιωμένοι—*founded*—as a building is on a foundation. The word is taken from architecture where a firm foundation is laid, and the meaning is, that he wished them to be as firm in the love of Christ, as a building is that rests on a solid basis. ¶ *In love* In love to the Redeemer—perhaps also in love to each other—and to all. Love was the great principle of the true religion, and the apostle wished that they might be fully settled in that.

18. *May be able to comprehend with all saints.* That all others

with all saints, what *is* the breadth, and length, and depth, and height;

19 And to know the love of Christ, which passeth knowledge.

with you may be able to understand this. It was his desire that others, as well as they, might appreciate the wonders of redemption. ¶ *What* is *the breadth, and length*, &c. It has been doubted to what this refers. Locke says it refers to the mystery of calling the Gentiles as well as the Jews. Chandler supposes there is an allusion in all this to the temple at Ephesus. It was one of the wonders of the world—exciting admiration by its length, and height, and dimensions in every way, as well as by its extraordinary riches and splendour. In allusion to this, the object of so much admiration and pride to the Ephesians, he supposes that Paul desires that they should become fully acquainted with the extent and beauty of the spiritual temple. But I do not see that there is clear evidence that there is allusion here to the temple at Ephesus. It seems rather to be the language of a heart that was full of the subject, and impressed with its greatness; and the words are employed to denote the *dimensions* of that love, and are similar to what would be meant if he had said, 'that you may know how *large*, or how *great* is that love.' The apostle evidently meant to express the strongest sense of the greatness of the love of the Redeemer, and to show in the most emphatic manner how much he wished that they should fully understand it. On the phrase 'depth and height,' comp. Notes on Rom. viii. 39.

19. *And to know the love of Christ.* The love of Christ towards us; the immensity of redeeming love. It is not merely the love which he showed for the Gentiles in calling them into his kingdom, which is here referred to; it is the love which is shown for the lost world in giving himself to die. This love is often referred to in the New Testament, and is declared to surpass all other which has ever been evinced. See Notes on Rom. v. 7, 8. John xv. 13. To know this; to feel this; to have a lively sense of it, is one of the highest privileges of the Christian. Nothing will so much excite gratitude in our hearts; nothing will prompt us so much to a life of self-denial; nothing will make us so benevolent and so dead to the world. See Notes on 2 Cor. v. 14. ¶ *Which passeth knowledge.* There *seems* to be a slight contradiction here in expressing a wish to know what cannot be known, or in a desire that they should understand that which cannot be understood. But it is the language of a man whose heart was full to overflowing. He had a deep sense of the love of Christ, and he expressed a wish that they should understand it. Suddenly he has such an apprehension of it, that he says it is indeed infinite. No one can attain to a full view of it. It had no limit. It was unlike any thing which had ever been evinced before. It was love which led the Son of God to become incarnate; to leave the heavens; to be a man of sorrows; to be reviled and persecuted; to be put to death in the most shameful manner—ON A CROSS. Who could understand that? Where else had there been any thing like that? What was there with which to compare it? What was there by which it could be illustrated? And how could it be fully understood? Yet *something* of it might be seen, known, felt; and the apostle desired that as far as possible they should understand that great love which the Lord Jesus had manifested for a dying world. ¶ *That ye might be filled with all the fulness of God.* What an ex-

that ye might be filled with all the fulness [a] of God.

20 Now [b] unto him that is able to do exceeding abundantly above all that we ask or think, according to the power that worketh in *us*,

21 Unto him *be* glory in the church by Christ Jesus, throughout all ages, world without end. Amen.

a Jno. 1. 6.
b Ro. 16. 25. He. 13. 20, 21. Jude 24.

pression! How rich and glorious! Who can comprehend all that it implies? Let us inquire into its meaning. There *may* be here in these verses an allusion to the *temple.* The apostle had spoken of their being founded in love, and of surveying the length, and breadth, and depth, and height of that love, as of a vast and splendid edifice, and he now desires that those whom he addressed might be pervaded or filled with the indwelling of God. The language here is cumulative, and is full of meaning and richness. (1.) They were to be *full of God.* That is, he would dwell in them. (2.) They were to be filled with *the fulness of God*—τὸ πλήρωμα τὸυ θεὸυ. On the word rendered *fulness,* see Notes on ch. i. 10. 23. It is a favourite word with Paul. Thus he speaks of the *fulness* of the Gentiles, Rom. xi. 25; the *fulness* of time, Gal. iv. 4; the *fulness* of him that filleth all in all, Eph. i. 23; the *fulness* of Christ, Eph. iv. 13; the *fulness* of the Godhead in Christ, Col. i. 19; ii. 9. It means here, 'that you may have the richest measures of divine consolation and of the divine presence; that you may partake of the entire enjoyment of God in the most ample measure in which he bestows his favours on his people.' (3.) It was to be with *all* the fulness of God; not with partial and stinted measures of his gracious presence, but with *all* which he ever bestows. Religion is not a name. It is not a matter of form. It is not a trifle. It is the richest, best gift of God to man. It ennobles our nature. It more clearly teaches us our true dignity than all the profound discoveries which men can make in science; for none of them will ever fill us with the fulness of God. Religion is spiritual, elevating, pure, Godlike. We dwell with God; walk with God; live with God; commune with God; are like God. We become partakers of the divine nature (2 Pet. i. 4); in rank we are associated with angels; in happiness and purity we are associated with God!

20. *Now unto him.* It is not uncommon for Paul to utter an ascription of praise in the midst of an argument. See Rom. ix. 5; xi. 36. Gal. i. 5. Here his mind is full of the subject; and in view of the fact that God communicates to his people such blessings—that they may become filled with all his fulness, he desires that praise should be given to him. ¶ *That is able to do.* See Notes, Rom. xvi. 25. ¶ *Exceeding abundantly.* The compound word here used occurs only in this place, and in 1 Thess. iii. 10; v. 13. It means, to an extent which we cannot express. ¶ *Above all that we ask or think.* More than all that we can desire in our prayers; more than all that we can conceive. See Notes on 1 Cor. ii. 9. ¶ *According to the power that worketh in us.* The exertion of that same power can accomplish for us more than we can now conceive.

21. *Unto him be glory.* See Notes, Rom. xvi. 27. ¶ *In the church.* Or, *by* the church. Ver. 10. The church was to be the instrument by which the glory of God would be shown; and it was *by* the church

that his praise would be celebrated. ¶ *Throughout all ages, world without end.* There is a richness and amplification of language here which shows that his heart was full of the subject, and that it was difficult to find words to express his conceptions. It means, in the strongest sense, FOR EVER. It is one of "the apostle's self-invented phrases" (***Bloomfield***); and Blackwall says that no version can fully express the meaning. It is literally, 'Unto all generations of the age of ages,' or 'unto all the generations of the eternity of eternities, or the eternity of ages.' It is the language of a heart FULL of the love of God, and desiring that he might be praised without ceasing for ever and ever.

REMARKS.

1. It is a great and glorious truth that the offers of the gospel are made to us, who are by nature Gentiles; and that those offers are confined to no class or condition of men—to no nation or tribe. Vs. 1—6. This truth had been concealed for ages. The Jews regarded themselves as a peculiar people, and as exclusively the favourites of Heaven. The great effort has been made everywhere to show that there was a favoured class of men—a class whom God regarded with peculiar affection, on account of their birth, or rank, or nation, or wealth, or complexion. In one nation, there has been a distinction of *caste* carefully kept up from age to age, and sustained by all the power of the priesthood and the laws; and it has been held that that one class was the favourite of Heaven, and that every other was overlooked or despised. In another nation, it has been held that the services of an illustrious ancestry made a difference among men, and that this fact was to be regarded, even in religion. In another, complexion has made a difference; and the feeling has insensibly grown up that one class were the favourites of Heaven, because they had a skin not coloured like others, and that those not thus favoured might be doomed to hopeless toil and servitude. In another, the attempt is made to create such a distinction by wealth; and it is felt that the rich are the favourites of Heaven. In all these cases, there is the secret feeling that in virtue of rank, or blood, or property, one class are the objects of divine interest, more than others; and that the same plan of salvation is not needed for them which is required for the poor, for the ignorant, and for the slave. The gospel regards all men as on a level; offers the same salvation to all; and offers it on the same terms. This is one of its glories; and for this we should love it. It meets man as he is—as everywhere a fallen and a ruined being—and provides a plan adapted to raise *all* to the glories of the same heaven.

2. Humility becomes us. Ver. 8. Paul felt that he was the least of all saints. He remembered his former life. He recalled the time when he persecuted the church. He felt that he was not worthy to be enrolled in that society which he had so greatly injured. If Paul was humble, who should not be? Who, since his time, has equalled his ardour, his zeal, his attainments in the divine life? Yet the remembrance of his former life served always to keep him humble, and operated as a check on all the tendencies to pride in his bosom. So it should be with us—with all Christians. There has been enough in our past lives to make us humble, if we would recall it, and to make us feel that we are not worthy to be enrolled among the saints. One has been an infidel; one licentious; one intemperate; one rash, revengeful, passionate; one has been proud and ambitious; one has been false, dishonest, faithless; all have

had hearts opposed to God, alienated from good, and prone to evil; and there is not a Christian in the world who will not find enough in his past life to make him humble, if he will examine himself—enough to make him feel that he deserves not even the lowest place among the saints. So we shall feel if we look over our lives *since* we made a profession of religion. The painful conviction will come over our souls, that we have lived so far from God, and done so little in his cause, that we are not worthy of the lowest place among the blessed.

3. It is a privilege to preach the gospel. Ver. 8. So Paul felt. It was an honour of which he felt that he was by no means worthy. It was proof of the favour of God towards him that he was permitted to do it. It *is* a privilege—an honour—to preach the gospel, anywhere, and to any class of men. It is an honour to be permitted to preach in christian lands; it is an honour to preach among the heathen. It is an honour far above that of conquerors; and he who does it will win a brighter and more glorious crown than he who goes forth to obtain glory by dethroning kings, and laying nations waste. The warrior goes with the sword in one hand, and the torch in the other. His path is marked with blood, and with smouldering ruins. He treads among the slain; and the music of his march is made up of dying groans, and the shrieks of widows and orphans. Yet he is honoured, and his name is blazoned abroad; he is crowned with the laurel, and triumphal arches are reared, and monuments are erected to perpetuate his fame. The man who carries the gospel goes for a different purpose. He is the minister of peace. He goes to tell of salvation. He fires no city; lays waste no field; robs no one of a home, no wife of a husband, no child of a father, no sister of a brother;—he goes to elevate the intellect, to mould the heart to virtue, to establish schools and colleges; to promote temperance, industry, and chastity; to wipe away tears, and to tell of heaven. *His* course is marked by intelligence and order; by peace and purity; by the joy of the domestic circle, and the happiness of a virtuous fire-side; by consolation on the bed of pain, and by the hope of heaven that cheers the dying. Who would not rather be a preacher of the gospel than a blood-stained warrior? Who would not rather have the wreath that shall encircle the brows of Paul, and Schwartz, and Martin, and Brainerd, than the laurels of Alexander and Cæsar?

4. There is ample fulness in the plan of salvation by the Redeemer. Ver. 8. In Christ there is unsearchable riches. None can understand the fulness that there is in him; none can exhaust it. Millions, and hundreds of millions, have been saved by the fulness of his merits; and still those merits are as ample as ever. The sun in the heavens has shone for six thousand years, and has shed light and comfort on countless millions; but his beams are not exhausted or diminished in splendour. To-day, while I write—this beautiful, calm, sweet day—(June 24, 1840) his beams are as bright, as rich, as full, as they were when they were shed on Eden. So of the Sun of righteousness. Millions have been enlightened by his beams; but to-day they are as full, and rich, and glorious, as they were when the first ray from that sun reached the benighted mind of a penitent sinner. And that fulness is not *to be* exhausted. No matter how many partake of his abundance; no matter how many darkened minds are enlightened; no matter though nation after nation comes and partakes of his fulness, yet there is no approach to ex-

haustion. The sun in the heavens may waste his fires and burn out, and become a dark orb, diffusing horror over a cold and cheerless world; but not so with the Sun of righteousness. That will shine on in glory for ever and ever; and the last penitent sinner on earth who comes to partake of the riches of the grace of Christ shall find it as full and free as did the first who sought pardon through his blood. Oh, the UNSEARCHABLE RICHES of Christ! Who can understand this? Who can grow weary in its contemplation?

5. There is no good reason why any sinner should be lost. Ver. 8. If the merits of the Saviour were limited; if his arm were a feeble human arm; if he died only for a part, and if his merit were already well-nigh exhausted, we might begin to despair. But it is not so. The riches of his grace are unbounded and inexhaustible. And why then does the sinner die? I can answer. He dies like the man who expires of thirst while fountains bubble and streams flow all around him; like him who is starving amidst trees loaded with fruit; like him who is dying of fever in the midst of medicines that would at once restore him; like him who holds his breath and dies while the balmy air of heaven—pure, full, and free—floats all around him. If a man thus dies, who is to blame? If a man goes down to hell from lands where the gospel is preached, whose is the fault? It is not because the merits of Christ are limited; it is not because they are exhausted.

6. The church is designed to accomplish a most important purpose in the manifestation of the divine glory and perfections. Ver. 10. It is by that that his great wisdom is shown. It is by that entirely that his *mercy* is displayed. Ch. ii. 7. His power is shown in the creation and support of the worlds; his goodness in the works of creation and Providence; his truth in his promises and threatenings; his greatness and majesty are everywhere displayed in the universe which he has brought into being. His mercy is shown in the church; and there alone. Angels in heaven not having sinned, have had no occasion for its exercise; and angels that are fallen have had no offer of pardon. Throughout the wide universe there has been, so far as we know, no exercise of mercy but in the church. Hence the interest which the angelic beings feel in the work of redemption. Hence they desire to look into these things, and to see more of the heighth and depth and length and breadth of the love of God evinced in the work of redemption. Hence the church is to be honoured for ever as the means of making known to distant worlds the way in which God shows mercy to rebellious creatures. It is honour enough for one world thus to be the sole means of making known to the universe one of the attributes of God; and while other worlds may contain more proofs of his power and greatness, it is enough for ours that it shows to distant worlds how he can exercise compassion.

7. All tribulation and affliction may be intended to do some good, and may benefit others. Ver. 13. Paul felt that *his* sufferings were for the "glory"—the welfare and honour of the Gentiles in whose cause he was suffering. He was then a prisoner at Rome. He was permitted no longer to go abroad from land to land to preach the gospel. How natural would it have been for him to be desponding, and to feel that he was leading a useless life. But he did not feel thus. He felt that in some way he might be doing good. He was suffering in a good cause, and his trials had been brought on him by the appointment of God. He

gave himself to writing letters; he talked with all who would come to him (Acts xxviii. 30, 31), and he expected to accomplish something by his example in his sufferings. The sick, the afflicted, and the imprisoned often feel that they are useless. They are laid aside from public and active life, and they feel that they are living in vain. But it is not so. The long imprisonment of John Bunyan—so mysterious to him and to his friends—was the means of producing the Pilgrim's Progress, now translated into more than twenty languages, and already blessed to the salvation of thousands. The meekness, and patience, and kindness of a Christian on a bed of pain, may do more for the honour of religion than he could do in a life of health. It shows the sustaining power of the gospel; and this is much. It is *worth* much suffering to show to a world what the gospel can do in supporting the soul in times of trial; and he who is imprisoned or persecuted; he who lies month after month or year after year on a bed of languishing, may do more for the honour of religion than by many years of active life.

8. There is but one family among the friends of God. Ver. 15. They all have one Father, and all are brethren. In heaven and on earth they belong to the same family, and worship the same God. Let Christians, therefore, first love one another. Let them lay aside all contention and strife. Let them feel that they are brethren—that though they belong to different denominations, and are called by different names, yet they belong to the same family, and are united under the same glorious head. Let them, secondly, realize how highly they are honoured. They belong to the same family as the angels of light and the spirits of just men made perfect. It is an honour to belong to such a family; an honour to be a Christian. Oh, if we saw this in its true light, how much more honourable would it be to belong to this "family" than to belong to the families of the great on earth, and to have our names enrolled with nobles and with kings!

9. Let us seek to know more of the love of Christ in our redemption—to understand more of the extent of that love which he evinced for us. Vs. 16—19. It is worth our study. It will reward our efforts. There are few Christians—if there are any—who understand the richness and fulness of the gospel of Christ; few who have such elevated views as they might have and should have of the glory of that gospel. It is wonderful that they who profess to love the Lord Jesus do not study that system more, and desire more to know the heighth, and depth, and length, and breadth of the love of Christ. True, it passes knowledge. We cannot hope fully to fathom it in this world. But we may know more of it than we do. We may aspire to being filled with all the fulness of God. We may long for it; pant for it; strive for it; pray for it—and we shall not strive in vain. Though we shall not attain all we wish; though there will be an infinity beyond what we can understand in this world, yet there will be enough attained to reward all our efforts, and to fill us with love and joy and peace. The love of God our Saviour is indeed an illimitable ocean; but we may see enough of it in this world to lead us to adore and praise God with overflowing hearts.

CHAPTER IV.

ANALYSIS OF THE CHAPTER.

This chapter is the commencement of the *practical* part of the epistle, and is made up, like the remaining chapters, of various exhortations. It is in accordance with the usual habit of Paul to conduct an *argument* in his epistles, and then to enforce various practical duties, either growing out of the argument which he had maintained, or, more commonly, adapted to some particular state of things in the church to which he wrote. The points of exhortation in this chapter are, in general, the following:

I. An exhortation to *unity.* Vs. 1—6. He entreats them to walk worthy of their vocation (ver. 1); shows them how it could be done, or what he meant; and that, in order to that, they should show meekness and kindness (ver. 3), and particularly exhorts them to unity (ver. 3); for they had one God, one Saviour, one baptism, one religion. Vs. 4—6.

II. He shows them that God had made ample provision for his people, that they might be sound in the faith, and in unity of life and of doctrine, and need not be driven about with every wind of opinion. Vs. 7—16. He assures them that to every Christian is given grace in the Redeemer adapted to his circumstances (ver. 7); that the Lord Jesus ascended to heaven to obtain gifts for his people (vs. 8—10); that he had given apostles, prophets, and evangelists, for the very purpose of imparting instruction, and confirming them in the faith of the gospel (vs. 11, 12); that this was in order that they might attain to the highest elevation in christian knowledge and piety (ver. 13); and particularly that they might not be driven to and fro, and carried about with every wind of doctrine. Vs. 14—16.

III. Having these arrangements made for their knowledge and piety, he exhorts them not to live as the heathen around them lived, but to show that they were under a better influence. Vs. 17—24. Their understanding was darkened, and they were alienated from the life of God, or true religion (ver. 18); they were past feeling, and were given over to every form of sensuality. Ver. 19. The Ephesians, however, had been taught a different thing (vs. 20, 21), and the apostle exhorts them to lay aside everything pertaining to their former course of life, and to become wholly conformed to the principles of the new man. Vs. 22—24.

IV. He exhorts them to perform particular christian duties, and to put away certain evils, of which they and all others were in danger. Vs. 25—32. In particular, he entreats them to avoid lying (ver. 25); anger (ver. 26); theft (ver. 28); corrupt and corrupting conversation (ver. 29); grieving the Holy Spirit (ver. 30); bitterness, evil-speaking, and malice (ver. 31); and entreats them to manifest in their intercourse with each other a spirit of kindness and forgiveness. Ver. 32.

1. *I, therefore.* In view of the great and glorious truths which God has revealed, and of the grace which he has manifested towards you who are Gentiles. See the previous chapters. The sense of the word 'therefore'—οὖν—in this place, is, 'Such being your exalted privileges; since God has done so much for you; since he has revealed for you such a glorious system; since he has bestowed on you the honour of calling you into his kingdom, and making you partakers of his mercy, I entreat you to live in accordance with these elevated privileges, and to show your sense of his goodness by devoting your all to his service.' The force of the word "*I*," they would all feel. It was the appeal and ex-

CHAPTER IV.

I THEREFORE, the prisoner [1] of the Lord,) beseech you that ye walk [a] worthy of the vocation wherewith ye are called.

[1] or, *in.*

[a] Col. 1. 10.

hortation of the founder of their church—of their spiritual father—of one who had endured much for them, and who was now in bonds on account of his devotion to the welfare of the Gentile world.—¶ *The prisoner of the Lord.* Marg., *in.* It means, that he was now a prisoner, or in confinement *in the cause* of the Lord; and he regarded himself as having been made a prisoner because the Lord had so willed and ordered it. He did not feel particularly that he was the prisoner of Nero; he was bound and kept because the *Lord* willed it, and because it was in his service. See Notes on ch. iii. 1. ¶ *Beseech you that ye walk worthy.* That you live as becomes those who have been called in this manner into the kingdom of God. The word *walk* is often used to denote *life*, *conduct*, &c. See Notes on Rom. iv. 12; vi. 4. 2 Cor. v. 7. ¶ *Of the vocation.* Of the *calling*—της κλήσεως. This word properly means *a call*, or *an invitation*—as to a banquet. Hence it means that divine invitation or calling by which Christians are introduced into the privileges of the gospel. The word is translated *calling* in Rom. xi. 29. 1 Cor. i. 26; vii. 20. Eph. i. 18; iv. 1. 4. Phil. iii. 14. 2 Thess. i. 11. 2 Tim. i. 9. Heb. iii. 1. 2 Pet. i. 10. It does not elsewhere occur. The sense of the word, and the agency employed in calling us, are well expressed in the Westminster Shorter Catechism. "Effectual calling is the work of God's Spirit, whereby convincing us of our sin and misery, enlightening our minds in the knowledge of Christ, and renewing our wills, he doth persuade and enable us to embrace Jesus Christ freely offered to us in the gospel." This *calling* or *vocation* is through the agency of the Holy Spirit, and is his appropriate work on the human heart. It consists essentially in influencing the mind to turn to God, or to enter into his kingdom. It is the exertion of *so much* influence on the mind as is necessary to secure the turning of the sinner to God. In this all Christians are agreed, though there have been almost endless disputes about the actual influence exerted, and the mode in which the Spirit acts on the mind. Some suppose it is by "moral suasion;" some by physical power; some by an act of creation; some by inclining the mind to exert its proper powers in a right way, and to turn to God. What is the precise agency employed perhaps we are not to expect to be able to decide. See John iii. 8. The great, the essential point is held, if it be maintained that it is by the agency of the Holy Spirit that the result is secured—and this I suppose to be held by all evangelical Christians. But though it is by the agency of the Holy Spirit, we are not to suppose that it is without the employment of *means.* It is not literally like the act of creation. It is preceded and attended with *means* adapted to the end; means which are almost as various as the individuals who are *called* into the kingdom of God. Among those means are the following. (1.) *Preaching.* Probably more are called into the kingdom by this means than any other. It is "God's great ordinance for the salvation of men." It is eminently fitted for it. The *pulpit* has higher advantages for acting on the mind than any other means of affecting men. The truths that are dispensed; the sacredness of the place; the peace and quietness of the sanctuary; and the appeals to the reason, the conscience, and the heart —all are fitted to affect men, and to bring them to reflection. The Spirit makes use of the word preached, but in a great variety of ways. Sometimes many are impressed simultaneously; sometimes the same truth affects one mind while others are unmoved; and sometimes truth reaches the heart of a sinner which he has heard a hundred times before, without being interested. The Spirit acts with sovereign power, and by laws which have never yet been traced out. (2.) The events of Providence are used to call men into his kingdom. God appeals to men by laying them on a bed of pain, or by requiring them to follow a friend in the still and mournful procession to the grave. They feel that they must die, and they are led to ask the question whether they are prepared. Much fewer are affected in this way than we should suppose would be the case; but still there are many, in the aggregate, who can trace their hope of heaven to a fit of sickness, or to the death of a friend. (3.) Conversation is one of the means by which sinners are called into the kingdom of God. In some states of mind, where the Spirit has prepared the soul like mellow ground prepared for the seed, a few moments' conversation, or a single remark, will do more to arrest the attention than much preaching. (4.) Reading is often the means of calling men into the kingdom. The Bible is the great means—and if we can get men to read that, we have very cheering indications that they will be converted. The profligate Earl of Rochester was awakened and led to the Saviour by reading a chapter in Isaiah. And who can estimate the number of those who have been converted by reading Baxter's Call to the Unconverted; Alleine's Alarm; the Dairyman's Daughter; or the Shepherd of Salisbury Plain? He does good who places a good book in the way of a sinner. That mother or sister is doing good, and making the conversion of a son or brother *probable*, who puts a Bible in his chest when he goes to sea, or in his trunk when he goes on a journey. Never should a son be allowed to go from home without one. The time will come when, far away from home, he will read it. He will read it when his mind is pensive and tender, and the Spirit may bear the truth to his heart for his conversion. (5.) The Spirit calls men into the kingdom of Christ by presiding over, and directing in some unseen manner their own reflections, or the operations of their own minds. In some way unknown to us, he turns the thoughts to the past life; recalls forgotten deeds and plans; makes long past sins rise to remembrance; and overwhelms the mind with conscious guilt from the memory of crime. He holds this power over the soul; and it is among the most mighty and mysterious of all the influences that he has on the heart. *Sometimes*—a man can hardly tell how—the mind will be pensive, sad, melancholy; then conscious of guilt; then alarmed at the future. Often, by sudden transitions, it will be changed from the gay to the grave, and from the pleasant to the sad; and often, unexpectedly to himself, and by associations which he cannot trace out, the sinner will find himself reflecting on death, judgment, and eternity. It is the Spirit of God that leads the mind along. It is not by force; not by the violation of its laws, but in accordance with those laws, that the mind is thus led along

2 With all lowliness [a] and meekness, with long-suffering, forbearing one another in love;

a Mat. 11. 29.

to the eternal world. In such ways, and by such means, are men "*called*" into the kingdom of God. To 'walk worthy of that calling,' is to live as becomes a Christian, an heir of glory; to live as Christ did. It is, (1.) To bear our religion with us to all places, companies, employments. Not merely to be a Christian on the Sabbath, and at the communion table, and in our own land, but every day, and everywhere, and in any land where we may be placed. We are to *live* religion, and not merely to *profess* it. We are to be Christians in the counting-room, as well as in the closet; on the farm as well as at the communion table; among strangers, and in a foreign land, as well as in our own country and in the sanctuary. (2.) It is to do nothing inconsistent with the most elevated Christian character. In temper, feeling, plan, we are to give expression to no emotion, and use no language, and perform no deed, that shall be inconsistent with the most elevated Christian character. (3.) It is to do *right always:* to be just to all; to tell the simple truth; to defraud no one; to maintain a correct standard of morals; to be known to be honest. There *is* a correct standard of character and conduct; and a Christian should be a man so living, that we may always know *exactly where to find him.* He should so live, that we shall have no doubts that, however others may act, we shall find *him* to be the unflinching advocate of temperance, chastity, honesty, and of every good work—of every plan that is really fitted to alleviate human woe, and benefit a dying world. (4.) It is to live as one should who expects soon to be *in heaven.* Such a man will feel that the earth is not his home; that he is a stranger and a pilgrim here; that riches, honours, and pleasures are of comparatively little importance; that he ought to watch and pray, and that he ought to be holy. A man who feels that he may die at any moment, will watch and pray. A man who realizes that *to-morrow* he may be in heaven, will feel that he ought to be holy. He who begins a day on earth, feeling that at its close he *may* be among the angels of God, and the spirits of just men made perfect; that before its close he *may* have seen the Saviour glorified, and the burning throne of God, will feel the importance of living a holy life, and of being wholly devoted to the service of God. Pure should be the eyes that are soon to look on the throne of God; pure the hands that are soon to strike the harps of praise in heaven; pure the feet that are to walk the 'golden streets above.'

2. *With all lowliness.* Humility. See Notes on Acts xx. 19, where the same Greek word is used. Comp. also the following places, where the same Greek word occurs: Phil. ii. 3, "in *lowliness* of mind, let each esteem other better than themselves;" Col. ii. 18, "in a voluntary *humility;*" Col. ii. 23; iii. 12. 1 Pet. v. 5. The word does not elsewhere occur in the New Testament. The idea is, that humility of mind becomes those who are "called" (ver 1), and that we walk worthy of that calling when we evince it. ¶ *And meekness.* See Notes on Matt. v. 5. Meekness relates to the manner in which we receive injuries. We are to bear them patiently, and not to retaliate, or seek revenge. The meaning here is, that we adorn the gospel when we show its power in enabling us to bear injuries without anger or a desire of revenge, or with a mild and forgiving spirit.

See 2 Cor. x. 1. Gal. v 23; vi. 1. 2 Tim. ii. 25. Titus iii. 2; where the same Greek word occurs. ¶ *With long-suffering*, &c. Bearing patiently with the foibles, faults, and infirmities of others. See Notes on 1 Cor. xiii. 4. The virtue here required is that which is to be manifested in our manner of receiving the provocations which we meet with from our brethren. No virtue, perhaps, is more frequently demanded in our intercourse with others. We do not go far with any fellow-traveller on the journey of life, before we find there is great occasion for its exercise. He has a temperament different from our own. He may be sanguine, or choleric, or melancholy; while we may be just the reverse. He has peculiarities of taste, and habits, and disposition, which differ much from ours. He has his own plans and purposes of life, and his own way and time of doing things. He may be naturally irritable, or he may have been so trained that his modes of speech and conduct differ much from ours. Neighbours have occasion to remark this in their neighbours; friends in their friends; kindred in their kindred; one church-member in another. A husband and wife — such is the imperfection of human nature—can find enough in each other to embitter life, if they choose to magnify imperfections, and to become irritated at trifles; and there is no friendship that may not be marred in this way, if we will allow it. Hence, if we would have life move on smoothly, we must learn to bear and forbear. We must indulge the friend that we love in the little peculiarities of saying and doing things which may be important to him, but which may be of little moment to us. Like children, we must suffer each one to build his play-house in his own way, and not quarrel with him because he does not think our way the best. All usefulness, and all comfort, may be prevented by an unkind, a sour, a crabbed temper of mind—a mind that can bear with no difference of opinion or temperament. A spirit of fault-finding; an unsatisfied temper; a constant irritability; little inequalities in the look, the temper, or the manner; a brow cloudy and dissatisfied — your husband or your wife cannot tell why — will more than neutralize all the good you can do, and render life anything but a blessing. It is in such gentle and quiet virtues as meekness and forbearance, that the happiness and usefulness of life consist, far more than in brilliant eloquence, in splendid talent, or illustrious deeds that shall send the name to future times. It is the bubbling spring which flows gently; the little rivulet which glides through the meadow, and which runs along day and night by the farm-house, that is useful, rather than the swollen flood or the roaring cataract. Niagara excites our wonder; and we stand amazed at the power and greatness of God there, as he 'pours it from his hollow hand.' But one Niagara is enough for a continent or a world; while that same world needs thousands and tens of thousands of silver fountains, and gently flowing rivulets, that shall water every farm, and every meadow, and every garden, and that shall flow on, every day and every night, with their gentle and quiet beauty. So with the acts of our lives. It is not by great deeds only, like those of Howard — not by great sufferings only, like those of the martyrs—that good is to be done; it is by the daily and quiet virtues of life—the christian temper, the meek forbearance, the spirit of forgiveness in the husband, the wife, the father, the mother, the brother, the sister, the friend, the neighbour—that good is to be done; and in this all may be useful.

3 Endeavouring to keep the unity of the Spirit in the bond of peace.

4 *There is* one body and one Spirit, even as ye are called in one hope of your calling;

3. *The unity of the Spirit.* A united spirit, or oneness of spirit. This does not refer to the fact that there is one Holy Spirit; but it refers to unity of affection, of confidence, of love. It means that Christians should be united in temper and affection, and not be split up into factions and parties. It may be implied here, as is undoubtedly true, that such a unity would be produced only by the Holy Spirit; and that, as there was but one Spirit which had acted on their hearts to renew them, they ought to evince the same feelings and views. There was occasion among the Ephesians for this exhortation; for they were composed of Jews and Gentiles, and there might be danger of divisions and strifes, as there had been in other churches. There is *always* occasion for such an exhortation; for (1.) *unity* of feeling is eminently desirable to honour the gospel (see Notes on John xvii. 21); and (2.) there is always danger of discord where men are brought together in one society. There are so many different tastes and habits; there is such a variety of intellect and feeling; the modes of education have been so various, and the temperament may be so different, that there is constant danger of division. Hence the subject is so often dwelt on in the Scriptures (see Notes on 1 Cor. ii. seq.), and hence there is so much need of caution and of care in the churches. ¶ *In the bond of peace.* This was to be by the cultivation of that peaceful temper which binds all together. The American Indians usually spoke of peace as a 'chain of friendship' which was to be kept bright. The meaning here is, that they should be bound or united together in the sentiments and affections of peace. It is not mere *external* unity; it is not a mere unity of creed; it is not a mere unity in the forms of public worship; it is such as the Holy Spirit produces in the hearts of Christians, when he fills them all with the same love, and joy, and peace in believing. The following verses contain the reasons for this.

4. There is *one body.* One church—for so the word *body* means here—denoting the body of Christ. See Notes on Rom. xii. 5. Comp. Notes on Eph. i. 23. The meaning here is, that as there is really but one church on earth, there ought to be unity. The church is, at present, divided into many denominations. It has different forms of worship, and different rites and ceremonies. It embraces those of different complexions and ranks in life, and it cannot be denied that there are often unhappy contentions and jealousies in different parts of that church. Still, there is but one—"one holy, catholic (i. e., *universal*) church;" and that church should feel that it is one. Christ did not come to redeem and save different churches, and to give them a different place in heaven. He did not come to save the Episcopal communion merely, or the Presbyterian or the Methodist communions only; nor did he leave the world to fit up for them different mansions in heaven. He did not come to save merely the black man, or the red, or the white man; nor did he leave the world to set up for them separate mansions in the skies. He came that he might collect into one community a multitude of every complexion, and from every land, and unite them in one great brotherhood on earth, and ultimately assemble them in the same heaven. The church is one

Every sincere Christian is a brother in that church, and has an equal right with all others to its privileges. Being one by the design of the Saviour, they should be one in feeling; and every Christian, no matter what his rank, should be ready to hail every other Christian as a fellow-heir of heaven. ¶ *One Spirit.* The Holy Spirit. There is one and the self-same Spirit that dwells in the church. The same Spirit has awakened all; enlightened all; convicted all; converted all. Wherever they may be, and whoever, yet there has been substantially the same work of the Spirit on the heart of every Christian. There are circumstantial differences arising from diversities of temperament, disposition, and education; there may be a difference in the depth and power of his operations on the soul; there may be a difference in the degree of conviction for sin and in the evidence of conversion, but still there are the same operations on the heart essentially, produced by the same Spirit. See Notes on 1 Cor. xii. 6—11. All the gifts of prayer, and of preaching; all the zeal, the ardour, the love, the self-denial in the church, are produced by the same Spirit. There should be, therefore, *unity.* The church is united in the agency by which it is saved; it should be united in the feelings which influence its members. ¶ *Even as ye are called.* See ver. 1. The sense is, 'there is one body and one spirit, *in like manner* as there is one hope resulting from your calling.' The same notion of *oneness* is found in relation to each of these things. ¶ *In one hope of your calling.* In one hope *resulting from* your being called into his kingdom. On the meaning of the word *hope*, see Notes on ch. ii. 12. The meaning here is, that Christians have the same hope, and they should therefore be one. They are looking forward to the same heaven; they hope for the same happiness beyond the grave. It is not as on earth among the people of the world, where there is a variety of hopes—where one hopes for pleasure, and another for honour, and another for gain; but there is the prospect of the same inexhaustible joy. This *hope* is fitted to promote union. There is no rivalry—for there is enough for all. *Hope* on earth does not always produce union and harmony. Two men hope to obtain the same office; two students hope to obtain the same honour in college; two rivals hope to obtain the same hand in marriage—and the consequence is jealousy, contention, and strife. The reason is, that but *one* can obtain the object. Not so with the crown of life—with the rewards of heaven. All may obtain *that* crown; all may share those rewards. How *can* Christians contend in an angry manner with each other, when the hope of dwelling in the same heaven swells their bosoms and animates their hearts?

5. *One Lord.* This evidently refers to the Lord Jesus. The "Spirit" is mentioned in the previous verse; the Father in the verse following. On the application of the word "Lord" to the Saviour, see Notes on Acts i. 24. The argument here is, that there ought to be *unity* among Christians, because they have one Lord and Saviour. They have not different Saviours adapted to different classes; not one for the Jew and another for the Greek; not one for the rich and another for the poor; not one for the bond and another for the free. There is but one. He belongs in common to all as their Saviour; and he has a right to rule over one as much as over another. There is no better way of promoting unity among Christians than by reminding them that they have the same Saviour. And when jealousies and heart-burnings arise; or when

5 One Lord, one faith, one baptism,

6 One God and Father of all,

they are disposed to contend about trifles; when they magnify unimportant matters until they are in danger of rending the church asunder, let them feel that they have one Lord and Saviour, and they will lay aside their contentions and be one again. Let two men who have never seen each other before, meet in a distant land, and feel that they have the same Redeemer, and their hearts will mingle into one. They are not aliens, but friends. A cord of sympathy is struck more tender than that which binds them to country or home; and though of different nations, complexions, or habits, they will feel that they are one. Why should contentions ever arise between those who have the same Redeemer? ¶ *One faith.* The same belief. That is, either the belief of the same doctrines, or faith of the same nature in the heart. The word may be taken in either sense. I see no reason why it should not include *both* here, or be used in the widest sense. If so used, it means that Christians should be united because they hold the same great doctrines; and also, because they have the same confidence in the Redeemer in their hearts. They hold the same system as distinguished from Judaism, Paganism, Mohammedanism, Deism; and they should, therefore, be one. They have the same trust in Christ, as a living, practical principle—and they should, therefore, be one. They may differ in other attachments; in temperament; in pursuit; in professions in life—but they have a common faith—and they should be ONE. ¶ *One baptism.* This does not affirm that there is one *mode* of baptism, but it refers to *the thing itself.* They are all baptized in the name of the same Father, Saviour, Sanctifier. They have all in this manner been consecrated unto God, and devoted to his service. Whether by immersion, or by pouring, or by sprinkling, they have all been baptized with water; whether it is done in adult years, or in infancy, the same solemn act has been performed on all—the act of consecration to the Father, the Son, and the Holy Ghost. This passage cannot be adduced to prove that only one *mode* of baptism is lawful, unless it can be shown that the thing referred to here was the *mode* and not *the thing itself;* and unless it can be proved that Paul meant to build his argument for the *unity* of Christians on the fact that the same *form* was used in their baptism. But this is evidently not the point of his argument. The argument is, that there was really but *one baptism*—not that there was but one *mode* of baptism. I could not use this argument in this form, 'Christians should be one because they have been all baptised *by sprinkling;*' and yet the argument would be just as forcible as to use it in this form, 'Christians should be one because they have all been baptised by *immersion.*' There is one *baptism,* not one *mode* of baptism; and no man has a right to *assume* that there can be but one mode, and then apply this passage to that The *essential thing* in the argument before us is, that there has been a consecration to the Father, the Son, and the Holy Ghost, by the application of water. Thus understood, the argument is one that will be *felt* by all who have been devoted to God by baptism. They have taken the same vows upon them. They have consecrated themselves to the same God. They have made the same solemn profession of religion. Water has been applied to one and all as the emblem of the purifying influences of the Holy Spirit; and having been thus initiated in a solemn

who *is* above all, and through all, and in you all.

7 But unto every one of us is

---

manner into the same profession of religion, they should be one.

6. *One God.* The same God; therefore there should be unity. Were there *many* gods to be worshipped, there could be no more hope of unity than there is among the worshippers of Mammon and Bacchus, and the various other idols that men set up. Men who have different pursuits, and different objects of supreme affection, can be expected to have no union. Men who worship many gods, cannot hope to be united. Their affections are directed to different objects, and there is no harmony or sympathy of feeling. But where there is one supreme object of attachment, there may be expected to be unity. The children of a family that are devoted to a parent, will be united among themselves; and the fact that all Christians have the same great object of worship, should constitute a strong bond of union among themselves—a chain always kept bright. ¶ *The Father of all.* One God who is the Father of all; that is, who is a common Father to all who believe. That this refers to the Father, in contradistinction from the Son and the Holy Spirit, seems evident. The Spirit and the Son are mentioned in the previous verses. But the fact that the "Father of all" is mentioned as "God," does not prove that the Spirit and the Son are not also endowed with divine attributes. That question is to be determined by the attributes ascribed to the Son and the Holy Spirit in other places. All sincere Christians worship *one* God, and *but* one. But they suppose that this one God subsists as Father, Son, and Holy Ghost, united in a mysterious manner, and constituting THE one God, and that there is no other God. That the Father is divine, they all hold, as Paul affirms here; that the Son and the Holy Spirit are also divine, they also hold. See Notes on John i. Heb. i. Phil. ii. 6. Rom. ix. 5. The meaning here is, that God is the common Father of *all* his people—of the rich and the poor; the bond and the free; the learned and the unlearned. He is no respecter of persons. Nothing would tend more to overcome the prejudices of colour, rank, and wealth, than to feel that we all have one Father; and that we are all equally the objects of his favour. Comp. Notes on Acts xvii. 26. ¶ *Who is above all.* Who is supreme; who presides over all things. ¶ *And through all.* He pervades universal nature, and his agency is seen everywhere. ¶ *And in you all.* There is no one in whose heart he does not dwell. You are his temple; and he abides in you. See ch. ii. 22. Notes, 1 Cor. vi. 19. The argument here is, that as the same God dwelt in every heart, they ought to be one. See this argument beautifully expressed in the Saviour's prayer, John xvii. 21. Comp. John xiv. 23.

7. *But unto every one of us.* Every Christian. ¶ *Is given grace.* The favour of God; meaning here, that God had bestowed upon each sincere Christian the means of living as he ought to do, and had in his gospel made ample provision that they might walk worthy of their vocation. What *are* the endowments thus given, the apostle states in the following verses. The *grace* referred to here, most probably means *the gracious influences of the Holy Spirit*, or his operations on the heart in connection with the use of the means which God has appointed. ¶ *According to the measure of the gift of Christ.* Grace is bestowed

given grace according to the measure [a] of the gift of Christ.

a Ro. 12. 3.

8 Wherefore he saith, [b] When

b Ps. 68. 18.

upon all true Christians, and all have enough to enable them to live a life of holiness. Yet we are taught here, (1.) That it is a *gift*. It is *bestowed* on us. It is not what is originated by ourselves. (2.) It is by a certain *measure*. It is not unlimited, and without rule. There is a wise adaptation; an imparting it by a certain rule. The same grace is not given to all, but to all is given enough to enable them to live as they ought to live. (3.) That measure is the gift of Christ, or what is given in Christ. It comes through him. It is what he has purchased; what he has obtained by his merits. All have enough for the purposes for which God has called them into his kingdom; but there are not the same endowments conferred on all. Some have grace given them to qualify them for the ministry; some to be apostles; some to be martyrs; some to make them eminent as public benefactors. All this has been obtained by Christ; and one should not complain that another has more distinguished endowments than he has. Comp. Notes on Rom. xii. 3. John i. 16.

8. *Wherefore he saith.* The word "he" is not in the original; and it may mean 'the Scripture saith,' or 'God saith.' The *point* of the argument here is, that Christ, when he ascended to heaven, obtained certain *gifts* for men, and that those gifts are bestowed upon his people in accordance with this. To *prove* that, he adduces this passage from Ps. lxviii. 18. Much perplexity has been felt in regard to the *principle* on which Paul quotes this Psalm, and applies it to the ascension of the Redeemer. The Psalm seems to have been composed on the occasion of removing the ark of the covenant from Kirjath-jearim to Mount Zion. 2 Sam. vi. 1, seq. It is a song of triumph, celebrating the victories of JEHOVAH, and particularly the victories which had been achieved when the *ark* was at the head of the army. It *appears* to have no relation to the Messiah; nor would it probably occur to any one on reading it, that it referred to his ascension, unless it had been so quoted by the apostle. Great difficulty has been felt, therefore, in determining on what principle Paul applied it to the ascension of the Redeemer. Some have supposed that the Psalm had a primary reference to the Messiah; some that it referred to him in only a secondary sense; some that it is applied to him by way of 'accommodation,' and some that he merely uses the words as adapted to express his idea, as a man adopts words which are familiar to him, and which will express his thoughts, though not meaning to say that the words had any such reference originally. Storr supposes that the words were used by the Ephesian Christians in their *hymns*, and that Paul quoted them as containing a sentiment which was admitted among them. This is *possible;* but it is mere conjecture. It has been also supposed that the tabernacle was a type of Christ; and that the whole Psalm, therefore, having original reference to the tabernacle, might be applied to Christ as the antitype. But this is both conjectural and fanciful. On the various modes adopted to account for the difficulty, the reader may consult Rosenmüller *in loc*. To me it seems plain that the Psalm had original reference to the bringing up the ark to Mount Zion, and is a triumphal song. In the song or

he ascended up on high, he led [1] captivity captive, and gave gifts unto men.

[1] or, *a multitude of captives.*

Psalm, the poet shows why God was to be praised—on account of his greatness, and his benignity to men. Vs. 1—6. He then recounts the doings of God in former times—particularly his conducting his people through the wilderness, and the fact that his enemies were discomfited before him. Vs. 7—12. All this refers to the God, the symbols of whose presence were on the tabernacle, and accompanying the ark. He then speaks of the various fortunes that had befallen the ark of the covenant. It had lain among the pots, ver. 13, yet it had formerly been white as snow when God scattered kings by it. Ver. 14. He then speaks of the hill of God—the Mount Zion to which the ark was about to be removed, and says that it is an "high hill"—'high as the hills of Bashan,' the hill where God desired to dwell for ever. Ver. 16. God is then introduced as ascending that hill, encompassed with thousands of angels, as in Mount Sinai; and the poet says that, in doing it, he had triumphed over his enemies, and had led captivity captive. Ver. 18. The fact that the ark of God thus ascended the hill of Zion, the place of rest; that it was to remain there as its permanent abode, no more to be carried about at the head of armies; was the proof of its triumph. It had made everything captive. It had subdued every foe; and its ascent there would be the means of obtaining invaluable gifts for men. Mercy and truth would go forth from that mountain; and the true religion would spread abroad, even to the rebellious, as the results of the triumph of God, whose symbol was over the tabernacle and the ark. The placing the ark there was the proof of permanent victory, and would be connected with most important benefits to men. The 'ascending on high,' therefore, in the Psalm, refers, as it seems to me, to the ascent of the symbol of the Divine Presence accompanying the ark on Mount Zion, or to the placing it 'on high' above all its foes. The remainder of the Psalm corresponds with this view. This ascent of the ark on Mount Zion; this evidence of its triumph over all the foes of God; this permanent residence of the ark there; and this fact that its being established there would be followed with the bestowment of invaluable gifts to men, might be regarded as a **BEAUTIFUL EMBLEM** of the ascension of the Redeemer to heaven. There were strong points of resemblance. He also ascended on high. His ascent was the proof of victory over his foes. He went there for a permanent abode. And his ascension was connected with the bestowment of important blessings to men. It is as such emblematic language, I suppose, that the apostle makes the quotation. It did not originally refer to this; but the events were so similar in many points, that the one would suggest the other, and the same language would describe both. It was language familiar to the apostle; language that would aptly express his thoughts, and language that was not improbably applied to the ascension of the Redeemer by Christians at that time. The phrase, therefore, 'he saith'—λέγει—or 'it saith,' or 'the Scripture saith,' means, 'it is said;' or, 'this language will properly express the fact under consideration, to wit, that there is grace given to each one of us, or that the means are furnished by the Redeemer for us to lead holy lives.' ¶ ***When he ascended up on high.*** To heaven. The Psalm is, 'Thou hast ascended on high.' Comp. Eph. i 22, 23.

9 (Now that he ascended, what is it but that he also descended first into the lower parts of the earth?

10 He that descended is the same also that ascended up far above all heavens, that he might [1] fill all things.)

[1] or, *fulfil.*

¶ *He led captivity captive.* The meaning of this in the Psalm is, that he triumphed over his foes. The margin is, '*a multitude of captives.*' But this, I think, is not quite the idea. It is language derived from a conqueror, who not only makes captives, but who makes captives of those who were then prisoners, and who conducts them as a part of his triumphal procession. He not only subdues his enemy, but he leads his captives in triumph. The allusion is to the public triumphs of conquerors, especially as celebrated among the Romans, in which captives were led in chains (Tacitus, Ann. xii. 38), and to the custom in such triumphs of distributing presents among the soldiers. Comp. also Judges v. 30, where it appears that this was also an early custom in other nations. *Burder*, in Ros. Alt. u. neu. Morgenland, *in loc.* When Christ ascended to heaven, he triumphed over all his foes. It was a complete victory over the malice of the great enemy of God, and over those who had sought his life. But he did more. He rescued those who were the captives of Satan, and led them in triumph. Man was held by Satan as a prisoner. His chains were around him. Christ rescued the captive prisoner, and designed to make him a part of his triumphal procession into heaven, that thus the victory might be complete—triumphing not only over the great foe himself, but swelling his procession with the attending hosts of those who *had been* the captives of Satan, now rescued and redeemed. ¶ *And gave gifts unto men.* Such as he specifies in ver. 11.

9. *Now that he ascended.* That is, it is affirmed in the Psalm that he *ascended*—"Thou hast ascended on high." This implies that there must have been a previous *descent;* or, as applicable to the Messiah, '*it is a truth* that he previously descended.' It is by no means certain that Paul meant to say that the *word* 'ascended' demonstrated that there must have been a previous descent; but he probably means that in the case of Christ there was, *in fact*, a descent into the lower parts of the earth first. The language here used will appropriately express his descent to earth. ¶ *Into the lower parts of the earth.* To the lowest state of humiliation. This seems to be the fair meaning of the words. Heaven stands opposed to earth. One is above; the other is beneath. From the one, Christ descended to the other; and he came not only *to* the earth, but he stooped to the most humble condition of humanity here. See Phil. ii. 6—8. Comp. Notes on Isa. xliv. 23. Some have understood this of the grave; others of the region of departed spirits; but these interpretations do not seem to be necessary. It is the *earth itself* that stands in contrast with the heavens; and the idea is, that the Redeemer descended from his lofty eminence in heaven, and became a man of humble rank and condition. Comp. Ps. cxxxix. 15.

10. *He that descended is the same also that ascended.* The same Redeemer came down from God, and returned to him. It was not a different being, but the same. ¶ *Far above all heavens.* See Notes on ch. i. 20—23. Comp. Heb. vii. 26. He is gone above the visible heavens, and has ascended into the highest abodes of bliss. See Notes

11 And [a] he gave some, apostles; and some, prophets; and some, evangelists; and some, pastors and teachers:

a 1 Co. 12. 28.

12 For the perfecting of the saints, for the work of the ministry, for the edifying of the body of Christ:

---

on 2 Cor. xii. 2. ¶ *That he might fill all things.* Marg., *fulfil.* The meaning is, "that he might fill all things by his influence, and direct and overrule all by his wisdom and power." *Doddridge.* See Notes on ch. i. 23.

11. *And he gave some, apostles.* He gave some to be apostles. The *object* here is to show that he has made ample provision for the extension and edification of his church. On the meaning of the word *apostles*, and on their appointment by the Saviour, see Notes on Matt. x. 1. ¶ *And some, prophets.* He appointed some to be prophets. See Notes on Rom. xii. 7. 1 Cor. xii. 28; xiv. 1. ¶ *And some, evangelists.* See Notes on Acts xxi. 8. Comp. 2 Tim. iv. 5. The word does not elsewhere occur in the New Testament. What was the precise office of the evangelist in the primitive church, it is now impossible to determine. The evangelist *may* have been one whose main business was *preaching*, and who was not particularly engaged in the *government* of the church. The word properly means 'a messenger of good tidings;' and Robinson (Lex.) supposes that it denotes a minister of the gospel who was not located in any place, but who travelled as a missionary to preach the gospel, and to found churches. The word is so used now by many Christians; but it cannot be proved that it is so used in the New Testament. An explanation of the words which here occur may be found in Neander on the Primitive Church, in the Biblical Repository, vol. iv. p. 258, seq. The office was distinct from that of the *pastor*, the *teacher*, and the *prophet*; and was manifestly an office in which *preaching* was the main thing. ¶ *And some pastors.* Literally *shepherds*—ποιμένας. Comp. Matt. ix. 36; xxv. 32; xxvi. 31. Mark vi. 34; xiv. 27. Luke ii. 8. 15. 18. 20. John x. 2. 11, 12. 14. 16, where it is rendered *shepherd*, and *shepherds;* also Heb. xiii. 20. 1 Pet. ii. 25. In Matt. xxvi. 31. Mark xiv. 27. Heb. xiii. 20. 1 Pet. ii. 25, it is applied to the Lord Jesus as the *great shepherd* of the flock—the church. It is rendered *pastors* only in the place before us. The word is given to ministers of the gospel with obvious propriety, and with great beauty. They are to exercise the same watchfulness and care over the people of their charge which a shepherd does over his flock. Comp. Notes on John xxi. 15, 16. The meaning here is, that Christ exercised a special care for his church by appointing *pastors* who would watch over it as a shepherd does over his flock. ¶ *And teachers.* See Notes on Rom. xii. 7.

12. *For the perfecting of the saints.* On the meaning of the word here rendered *perfecting*—καταρτισμὸν—see Notes on 2 Cor. xiii. 9. It properly refers to *the restoring of anything to its place;* then putting in order, making complete, &c. Here it means that these various officers were appointed in order that everything in the church might be well arranged, or put into its proper place; or that the church might be *complete.* It is that Christians may have every possible advantage for becoming complete in love, and knowledge, and order. ¶ *For the work of the ministry.* All these are engaged in the work of the *ministry*, though in

13 Till we all come [1] in the unity [a] of the faith, and of the knowledge of the Son of God, unto a perfect [b] man, unto the measure of the [2] stature of the fulness of Christ:

[1] or, *into*. [a] Co. 2. 2. [b] 1 Co. 14. 20. [2] or, *age*.

different departments. Together they constituted THE *ministry* by which Christ meant to establish and edify the church. All these offices had an existence at that time, and all were proper; though it is clear that they were not all designed to be permanent. The apostolic office was of course to cease with the death of those who were *the witnesses* of the life and doctrines of Jesus (comp. Notes on 1 Cor. ix. 1); the office of *prophets* was to cease with the cessation of inspiration; and in like manner it is possible that the office of teacher or evangelist might be suspended, as circumstances might demand. But is it not clear from this that Christ did not appoint *merely* three orders of clergy to be permanent in the church? Here are *five* orders enumerated, and in 1 Cor. xii. 28, there are *eight* mentioned; and how can it be demonstrated that the Saviour intended that there should be *three* only, and that they should be permanent? The presumption is rather that he meant that there should be but one permanent order of ministers, though the departments of their labour might be varied according to circumstances, and though there might be helpers, as occasion should demand. In founding churches among the heathen, and in instructing and governing them there, there is need of reviving nearly all the offices of teacher, helper, evangelist, &c., which Paul has enumerated as actually existing in his time. ¶ *For the edifying.* For building it up; that is, in the knowledge of the truth, and in piety. See Notes on Rom. xiv. 19. ¶ *The body of Christ.* The church. See Notes on ch. i. 23.

13. *Till we all come.* Till all Christians arrive at a state of complete unity, and to entire perfection ¶ *In the unity of the faith.* Marg *into.* The meaning is, till we all hold the same truths, and have the same confidence in the Son of God. See Notes on John xvii. 21—23. ¶ *And of the knowledge of the Son of God.* That they might attain to the same practical acquaintance with the Son of God, and might thus come to the maturity of Christian piety. See Notes on ch. iii. 19. ¶ *Unto a perfect man.* Unto a complete man. This figure is obvious. The apostle compares their condition then to a state of childhood. The perfect man here refers to the man *grown up*—the man of mature life. He says that Christ had appointed pastors and teachers that the infant church might be conducted to *maturity;* or become strong—like a man. He does not refer to the doctrine of *sinless perfection* — but to the state of manhood as compared with that of childhood—a state of strength, vigour, wisdom, when the full growth should be attained. See 1 Cor. xiv. 20. ¶ *Unto the measure of the stature.* Marg. or *age.* The word *stature* expresses the idea. It refers to the growth of a man. The stature to be attained to was that of Christ. He was the standard—not in size, not in age, but in moral character. The measure to be reached was Christ; or we are to grow till we become like him. ¶ *Of the fulness of Christ.* See Notes on ch. i. 23. The phrase 'the measure of the fulness,' means, probably, the 'full measure'—by a form of construction that is common in the Hebrew writings, where two nouns are so used that one is to be rendered as an adjective—as *trees of greatness*

14 That we *henceforth* be no more children, tossed to and fro, and carried [a] about with every wind of doctrine, by the sleight of men, *and* cunning craftiness, whereby they lie in wait to deceive;

a Ja. 1. 6.

—meaning great trees. Here it means, that they should so advance in piety and knowledge as to become wholly like him.

14. *That we* henceforth *be no more children.* In some respects Christians *are* to be like children. They are to be docile, gentle, mild, and free from ambition, pride, and haughtiness. See Notes on Matt. xviii. 2, 3. But children have other characteristics besides simplicity and docility. They are often changeable (Matt. xi. 17); they are credulous, and are influenced easily by others, and led astray. In these respects, Paul exhorts the Ephesians to be no longer children, but urges them to put on the characteristics of manhood; and especially to put on the *firmness* in religious opinion which became maturity of life. ¶ *Tossed to and fro.* κλυδωνιζόμενοι. This word is taken from waves or billows that are constantly tossed about—in all ages an image of instability of character and purpose. ¶ *And carried about with every wind of doctrine.* With no firmness; no settled course; no helm. The idea is that of a vessel on the restless ocean, that is tossed about with every varying wind, and that has no settled line of sailing. So many persons are in regard to religious doctrines. They have no fixed views and principles. They hold no doctrines that are settled in their minds by careful and patient examination, and the consequence is, that they yield to every new opinion, and submit to the guidance of every new teacher. The *doctrine* taught here is, that we should have settled religious opinions. We should carefully examine what is truth, and having found it, should adhere to it, and not yield on the coming of every new teacher. We should not, indeed, close our minds against conviction. We should be open to argument, and be willing to follow *the truth* wherever it will lead us. But this state of mind is not inconsistent with having settled opinions, and with being firm in holding them until we are convinced that we are wrong. No man can be useful who has not settled principles. No one who has not such principles can inspire confidence or be happy, and the first aim of every young convert should be to acquire settled views of the truth, and to become firmly grounded in the *doctrines* of the gospel. ¶ *By the sleight of men.* The cunning, skill, *trickery* of men. The word used here—κυβεία—is from a word (κύβος) meaning a cube, a die, and properly means a game at dice. Hence it means game, gambling; and then any thing that turns out by mere chance or haphazard—as a game at dice does. It *may* possibly also denote the trick or fraud that is sometimes used in such games; but it seems rather to denote a man's forming his religious opinions by *the throw of a die;* or, in other words, it describes a man whose opinions seem to be the result of mere chance. Any thing like casting a die, or like opening the Bible at random to determine a point of duty or doctrine, may come under the description of the apostle here, and would all be opposed to the true mode, that by calm examination of the Bible, and by prayer. A man who forms his religious principles by chance, can *unform* them in the same way; and

15 But, [1] speaking the truth [a] in love, may grow up into him in all things, which is the head, [b] *even* Christ:

[1] or, *being sincere.* a 2 Co. 4. 2.

b Co. 1. 18, 19.

he who has determined his faith by one cast of the die, will be likely to throw them into another form by another. The phrase '*the sleight of* men,' therefore, I would render 'by the mere chance of men, or as you may happen to find men, one holding this opinion, and the next that, and allowing yourself to be influenced by them without any settled principles.' ¶ *Cunning craftiness.* Deceit, trick, art. See 2 Cor. xii. 16. Luke xx. 23. 1 Cor. iii. 19. Notes, 2 Cor. iv. 2; xi. 3. ¶ *Whereby they lie in wait to deceive.* Literally, 'Unto the method of deceit;' that is, in the usual way of deceit. Doddridge, "In every method of deceit." This is the true idea. The meaning is, that men would use plausible pretences, and would, if possible, deceive the professed friends of Christ. Against such we should be on our guard; and not by their arts should our opinions be formed, but by the word of God.

15. *But speaking the truth in love.* Marg., *being sincere.* The translation in the text is correct—literally, *truthing in love*—ἀληθεύοντες. Two things are here to be noted. (1.) The truth is *to be spoken*—the simple, unvarnished truth. This is the way to avoid error, and this is the way to preserve others from error. In opposition to all trick, and art, and cunning, and fraud, and deception, Christians are to speak the simple truth, and nothing but the truth. Every statement which they make should be unvarnished truth; every promise which they make should be true; every representation which they make of the sentiments of others should be simple truth. *Truth is the representation of things as they are;* and there is no virtue that is more valuable in a Christian than the love of simple truth. (2.) The second thing is, that the truth should be spoken *in love.* There *are* other ways of speaking truth. It is sometimes spoken in a harsh, crabbed, sour manner, which does nothing but disgust and offend. When we state truth to others, it should be with love to their souls, and with a sincere desire to do them good. When we admonish a brother of his faults, it should not be in a harsh and unfeeling manner, but in love. Where a minister pronounces the awful truth of God about depravity, death, the judgment, and future woe, it should be in love. It should not be done in a harsh and repulsive manner; it should not be done as if he rejoiced that men were in danger of hell, or as if he would like to pass the final sentence; it should not be with indifference, or in a tone of superiority. And in like manner, if we go to convince one who is in error, we should approach him in love. We should not dogmatize, or denounce, or deal out anathemas. Such things only repel. *He has done about half his work in convincing another of* ERROR *who has first convinced him that he* LOVES *him;* and if he does not do that, he may argue to the hour of his death and make no progress in convincing him. ¶ *May grow up into him.* Into Christ; that is, to the stature of a complete man in him. ¶ *Which is the head.* Notes, ch. i. 22. 1 Cor. xi. 3.

16. *From whom the whole body.* The church, compared with the human body. The idea is, that as the *head* in the human frame conveys vital influences, vigour, motion, &c., to every part of the body; so Christ is the source of life, and vigour, and

16 From whom [a] the whole body fitly joined together, and compacted by that which every joint supplieth, according to the

[a] Jno. 15. 5.

energy, and increase, to the church. The sense is, 'The whole human body is admirably arranged for growth and vigour. Every member and joint contributes to its healthful and harmonious action. One part lends vigour and beauty to another, so that the whole is finely proportioned and admirably sustained. All depend on the head with reference to the most important functions of life, and all derive their vigour from that. So it is in the church. It is as well arranged for growth and vigour as the body is. It is as beautifully organized in its various members and officers as the body is. Everything is designed to be in its proper place, and nothing by the divine arrangement is wanting in its organization, to its perfection. Its officers and its members are, in their places, what the various parts of the body are with reference to the human frame. The church depends on Christ, as the head, to sustain, invigorate, and guide it, as the body is dependant on the head.' See this figure carried out to greater length in 1 Cor. xii. 12—26. ¶ *Fitly joined together.* The body, whose members are properly united so as to produce the most beauty and vigour. Each member is in the best place, and is properly united to the other members. Let any one read Paley's Natural Theology, or any work on anatomy, and he will find innumerable instances of the truth of this remark; not only in the proper adjustment and placing of the members, but in the manner in which it is united to the other parts of the body. The foot, for instance, is in its proper place. It should not be where the head or the hand is. The eye is in its proper place. It should not be in the knee or the heel. The mouth, the tongue, the teeth, the lungs, the heart, are in their proper places. No other places would answer the purpose so well. The brain is in its proper place. Anywhere else in the body, it would be subject to compressions and injuries which would soon destroy life. And these parts are as admirably united to the other parts of the body, as they are admirably located. Let any one examine, for instance, the tendons, nerves, muscles, and bones, by which the *foot* is secured to the body, and by which easy and graceful motion is obtained, and he will be satisfied of the wisdom by which the body is 'joined together.' How far the *knowledge* of the apostle extended on this point, we have not the means of ascertaining; but all the investigations of anatomists only serve to give increased beauty and force to the general terms which he uses here. All that he says here of the human frame is strictly accurate, and is such language as may be used by an anatomist now. The *word* which is here used (συναρμολογέω) means properly to sew together; to fit together; to unite; to make one. It is applied often to musicians, who produce *harmony* of various parts of music. *Passow.* The idea of harmony, or appropriate union, is that in the word. ¶ *And compacted.* συμβιβαζόμενον. Tindal renders this, 'knit together in every joint.' The word properly means, to make to come together; to join or knit together. It means here that the different parts of the body are *united* and sustained in this manner. ¶ *By that which every joint supplieth.* Literally, 'through every joint of supply;' that is, which affords or ministers mutual aid. The word *joint* here—αφή—(from ἅπτω, to fit)

effectual working in the measure of every part, maketh increase of the body unto the edifying of itself in love.

—means anything which *binds, fastens, secures;* and does not refer to the *joint* in the sense in which we commonly use it, as denoting *the articulation* of the limbs, or the joining of two or more bones; but rather that which *unites* or *fastens* together the different parts of the frame—the blood-vessels, cords, tendons, and muscles. The meaning is, that every such *means of connecting one part of the body with another* ministers nourishment, and that thus the body is sustained. One part is dependant on another; one part derives nourishment from another; and thus all become mutually useful as contributing to the support and harmony of the whole. Thus it furnishes an illustration of the *connection* in the members of the church, and of the aid which one can render to another. ¶ *According to the effectual working.* Gr., 'According to the energy in the measure of each one part.' Tindal, "According to the operation as every part has its measure." The meaning is, that each part contributes to the production of the whole result, or *labours* for this. This is in proportion to the 'measure' of each part; that is, in proportion to its power. Every part labours to produce the great result. No one is idle; none is useless. But none are overtaxed or overworked. The support demanded and furnished by every part is in exact proportion to its strength. This is a beautiful account of the anatomy of the human frame. (1.) Nothing is useless. Every part contributes to the general result—the health, and beauty, and vigor of the system. Not a muscle is useless; not a nerve, not an artery, not a vein. All are employed, and all have an important place, and all contribute *something* to the health and beauty of the whole. So numerous are the blood-vessels, that you cannot perforate the skin anywhere without piercing one; so numerous are the pores of the skin, that a grain of sand will cover thousands of them; so minute the ramifications of the nerves, that wherever the point of a needle penetrates, we feel it; and so numerous the absorbents, that millions of them are employed in taking up the chyme of the food, and conveying it to the veins. And yet all are employed—all are useful —all minister life and strength to the whole. (2.) None are overtaxed. They all work according to the 'measure' of their strength. Nothing is required of the minutest nerve or blood-vessel which it is not fitted to perform; and it will work on for years without exhaustion or decay. So of the church. There is no member so obscure and feeble that he may not contribute something to the welfare of the whole; and no one is required to labour beyond his strength in order to secure the great object. Each one *in his place*, and labouring as he should there, will contribute to the general strength and welfare; *out of his place*—like nerves and arteries out of their place, and crossing and recrossing others—he will only embarrass the whole, and disarrange the harmony of the system. ¶ *Maketh increase of the body.* The body grows in this manner. ¶ *Unto the edifying of itself.* To building itself up—that is, it grows up to a complete stature. ¶ *In love.* In mutual harmony. This refers to the *body*. The meaning is, that it seems to be made on the principle of *love*. There is no jar, no collision, no disturbance of one part with another. A great number of parts, composed of different substances, and with different functions—bones, and nerves, and

17 This I say therefore, and testify in the Lord, that ye henceforth walk not as other Gentiles walk, in the vanity of their mind.

muscles, and blood-vessels—are united in one, and live together without collision; and so it should be in the church. Learn, hence, (1.) That no member of the church need be useless, any more than a minute nerve or blood-vessel in the body need be useless. No matter how obscure the individual may be, he may contribute to the harmony and vigour of the whole. (2.) Every member of the church should contribute something to the prosperity of the whole. He should no more be idle and unemployed than a nerve or a blood-vessel should be in the human system. What would be the effect if the minutest nerves and arteries of the body should refuse to perform their office? Languor, disease, and death. So it is in the church. The obscurest member may do *something* to destroy the healthful action of the church, and to make its piety languish and die. (3.) There should be *union* in the church. It is made up of materials which differ much from each other, as the body is made up of bones, and nerves, and muscles. Yet, in the body these are united; and so it should be in the church. There need be no more jarring in the church than in the body; and a jar in the church produces the same effect as would be produced in the body if the nerves and muscles should resist the action of each other, or as if one should be out of its place, and impede the healthful functions of the other. (4.) Every member in the church should keep his place, just as every bone, and nerve, and muscle in the human frame should. Every member of the body should be in its right position; the heart, the lungs, the eye, the tongue, should occupy their right place; and every nerve in the system should be laid down just where it is designed to be. If so, all is well. If not so, all is deformity, or disorder, just as it is often in the church.

17. *This I say, therefore, and testify in the Lord.* I bear witness in the name of the Lord Jesus, or ministering by his authority. The object of this is, to exhort them to walk worthy of their high calling, and to adorn the doctrine of the Saviour. With this view, he reminds them of what they were before they were converted, and of the manner in which the heathen around them lived. ¶ *That ye henceforth walk not.* That you do not henceforth *live*—the christian life being often in the Scriptures compared to a journey. ¶ *As other Gentiles walk.* This shows that probably the mass of converts in the church at Ephesus were from among the heathen, and Paul regarded them as Gentile converts. Or it may be that he here addressed himself more particularly to that portion of the church, as especially needing his admonition and care. ¶ *In the vanity of their mind.* In the way of folly, or in mental folly. What he means by this, he specifies in the following verses. The word 'vanity' in the Scriptures means more than mere *emptiness.* It denotes moral wrong, being applied usually to those who worshipped *vain* idols, and then those who were alienated from the *true* God.

18. *Having the understanding darkened.* That is, because they were alienated from the true God, and particularly because of "the blindness of their hearts." The apostle does not say that this was a 'judicial' darkening of the understanding; or that they might not have perceived the truth; or that they had no ability to understand it. He speaks of a simple and well-known fact—a fact that is seen now

18 Having the understanding[a] darkened, being alienated from the life of God through the ignorance that is in them, because of the [1] blindness of their heart;

[a] Ac. 26. 18.

[1] or, *hardness.*

as well as then—that the understanding becomes darkened by indulgence in sin. A man who is intemperate, has no just views of the government of the appetites. A man who is unchaste, has no perception of the loveliness of purity. A man who is avaricious or covetous, has no just views of the beauty of benevolence. A man who indulges in low vices, will weaken his mental powers, and render himself incapable of intellectual effort. Indulgence in vice destroys the intellect as well as the body, and unfits a man to appreciate the truth of a proposition in morals, or in mathematics, or the beauty of a poem, as well as the truth and beauty of religion. Nothing is more obvious than that indulgence in sin weakens the mental powers, and renders them unfit for high intellectual effort. This is seen all over the heathen world now—in the stolid, stupid mind; the perverted moral sense; the incapacity for profound or protracted mental effort, as really as it was among the heathens to whom Paul preached. The missionary who goes among the heathen has almost to create an *intellect* as well as a *conscience*, before the gospel will make an impression. It is seen, too, in all the intellect of the bar, the senate, the pulpit, and the medical profession, that is ruined by intemperance, and in the intellect of multitudes of young men wasted by licentiousness and drunkenness. I know that under the influence of ambition and stimulating drinks, the intellect may seem to put forth unnatural efforts, and to glow with an intensity nowhere else seen. But it *soon burns out*—and the wastes of such an intellect become soon like the hardened scoriæ of the volcano, or the cinders of the over-heated furnace. Learn hence, that if a man wishes to be blessed with a clear understanding, he should be a *good man.* He who wishes a mind well balanced and clear, should fear and love God; and had Christianity done no other good on earth than to elevate the *intellect* of mankind, it would have been the richest blessing which has ever been vouchsafed to the race. It follows, too, that as man has debased his *understanding* by sin, it is needful to make an exertion to elevate it again; and hence a large part of the efforts to save men must consist in patient *instruction.* Hence the necessity of *schools* at missionary stations. ¶ *Being alienated.* See Notes on ch. ii. 12. ¶ *From the life of God.* From a life *like* that of God, or a life of which he is the source and author. The meaning is, that they lived a life which was *unlike* God, or which he could not approve. Of the truth of this in regard to the heathen everywhere, there can be no doubt. See Notes on Rom. i. ¶ *Through the ignorance that is in them.* The ignorance of the true God, and of what constituted virtue. Comp. Notes on Rom. i. 20—23. ¶ *Because of the blindness of their hearts.* Marg. *hardness.* Hardness is a better word. It is a better translation of the Greek; and it better accords with the design of the apostle. Here the reason is stated why they lived and acted as they did, and why the *understanding* was blinded. It is not that God has enfeebled the human intellect by a judicial sentence on account of the sin of Adam, and made it incapable

19 Who being past feeling, have [a] given themselves over unto lasciviousness, to work all uncleanness with greediness.

20 But ye have not so learned Christ;

21 If so be that ye have heard him, and have been taught by him, as the truth is in Jesus;

22 That ye put [b] off, concerning the former conversation, the old [c] man, which is corrupt according to the deceitful lusts;

a Ro. 1. 24, 26. b Co. 3. 8, 9. c Ro. 6. 6.

of perceiving the truth. It is not that there is any deficiency or incapacity of natural powers. It is not that the truths of religion are so exalted that man has no natural ability to understand them, for they may be as well understood as any other truths. See Notes on 1 Cor. i. 14. The simple reason is, "*the hardness* OF THE HEART." That is the solution given by an inspired apostle, and that is enough. A man who has a blind and hard heart sees no beauty in truth, and feels not its force, and is insensible to all its appeals. Learn, then, (1.) That men are to blame for the blindness of their understanding. Whatever proceeds from a *wicked heart* they are responsible for. But for mere *inferiority of intellect* they would not be to blame. (2.) They are under obligation to repent and love God. If it was required of them to enlarge their intellects, or create additional faculties of mind, they could not be bound to do it. But where the whole thing required is to have a *better heart*, they may be held responsible. (3.) The way to elevate the understandings of mankind is to purify the heart. The approach must be made through the affections. Let men *feel* right towards God, and they will soon *think* right; let the heart be pure, and the understanding will be clear.

19. *Who being past feeling.* Wholly hardened in sin. There is a *total want* of all emotion on moral subjects. This is an accurate description of the state of a sinner. He has no *feeling*, no *emotion*. He often gives an intellectual assent to the truth, but it is without *emotion* of any kind. The heart is insensible as the hard rock. ¶ *Have given themselves over.* They have done it voluntarily. In Rom. i. 24, it is said that "*God* gave them up." There is no inconsistency. Whatever was the agency of God in it, they preferred it. Comp. Notes on Rom. i. 21. ¶ *Unto lasciviousness.* See Notes on Rom. i. 24—26.

20. *But ye have not so learned Christ.* You have been taught a different thing by Christ; you have been taught that his religion requires you to abandon such a course of life.

21. *If so be that ye have heard him.* If you have listened attentively to his instructions, and learned the true nature of his religion. There may be a slight and delicate *doubt* implied here whether they had attentively listened to his instructions. Doddridge, however, renders it, "Seeing ye have heard him." Comp. Notes on ch. iii. 2. ¶ *And have been taught by him.* By his Spirit, or by the ministers whom he had appointed. ¶ *As the truth is in Jesus.* If you have learned the true nature of his religion as he himself taught it. What the truth was which the Lord Jesus taught, or what his principles implied, the apostle proceeds to state in the following verses.

22. *That ye put off.* That you lay aside, or renounce. The manner in which the apostle states these duties, renders it not improbable that there had been some instruction among them of a contrary character,

23 And be renewed [a] in the spirit of your mind;

a Ro. 12. 2.

24 And that ye put on the new man, which after God is created [b]

b Ga. 6 15. c. 2. 10.

and that it is possible there had been some teachers there who had not enforced, as they should have done, the duties of practical religion. ¶ *Concerning the former conversation.* The word *conversation* here means *conduct*—as it commonly does in the Bible. See Notes, 2 Cor. i. 12. The meaning here is, 'with respect to your former conduct or habits of life, lay aside all that pertained to a corrupt and fallen nature. You are not to lay *every thing* aside that formerly pertained to you. Your dress, and manners, and modes of speech and intercourse, might have been in many respects correct. But every thing that proceeded from sin; every habit, and custom, and mode of speech and of conduct that was the result of depravity, is to be laid aside. The peculiar characteristics of an unconverted man you are to put off, and are to assume those which are the proper fruits of a renewed heart. ¶ *The old man.* See Notes on Rom. vi. 6. ¶ *Which is corrupt according to the deceitful lusts.* The meaning is, (1.) That the unrenewed man is not under the direction of reason and sound sense, but is controlled by his *passions* and *desires.* The word *lusts,* has a more limited signification with us than the original word. That word we now confine to one class of sensual appetites; but the original word denotes any passion or propensity of the heart. It may include avarice, ambition, the love of pleasure, or of gratification in any way; and the meaning here is, that the heart is by nature under the control of such desires. (2.) Those passions are deceitful. They lead us astray. They plunge us into ruin. All the passions and pleasures of the world are illusive. They promise more than they perform; and they leave their deluded votaries to disappointment, and to tears. Nothing is more "deceitful" than the promised pleasures of this world; and all who yield to them find at last that they "flatter but to betray."

23. *And be renewed.* That is, it is necessary that a man who has been following these should become a new man. See Notes on John iii. 3, seq. Comp. Notes on 2 Cor. iv. 16. The word here used—ἀνανεόω—does not occur elsewhere in the New Testament; but it has the same meaning as the word used in 2 Cor. iv. 16, and Col. iii. 10. It means to make new, and is descriptive of the work of regeneration. This was addressed to the church, and to those whom Paul regarded as Christians; and we may learn from this, (1.) That it is necessary that man should be *renewed* in order to be saved. (2.) That it is proper to exhort Christians to be renewed. They need renovated strength every day. (3.) That it is a matter of *obligation* to be renewed. Men are *bound* thus to be renovated. And (4.) That they have sufficient natural ability to change from the condition of the old to that of the *new* man, or they could not be exhorted to it. ¶ *In the spirit of your mind.* In your temper; your heart; your nature.

24. *And that ye put on the new man.* The new man refers to the renovated nature. This is called, in other places, the 'new creature, or the new creation" (see Notes on 2 Cor. v. 17), and refers to the condition after the heart is changed. The change is so great, that there is no impropriety in speaking of one who has experienced it as 'a new man.' He has new feelings, princi

in righteousness and [1] true holiness.

[1] or, *holiness of truth.* Jno. 17. 17.

25 Wherefore putting away lying, speak every man truth [a]

[a] Zec. 8. 16.

ples, and desires. He has laid aside his old principles and practices, and, in everything that pertains to moral character, he is new. His body is indeed the same; the intellectual structure of his mind the same; but there has been a change in his principles and feelings which make him, in all the great purposes of life, a new being. Learn, that regeneration is not a trifling change. It is not a mere change of relations, or of the outward condition. It is not merely being brought from the world into the church, and being baptized, though by the most holy hands; it is much more. None of these things would make proper the declaration, 'he is a new man.' Regeneration by the Spirit of God *does.* ¶ *After God.* κατὰ Θεὸν. In respect to God. The idea is, evidently, that man is so renewed as to become *like God*, or the divine image is restored to the soul. In the parallel passage in Colossians (iii. 9), the idea is expressed more fully, "renewed in knowledge after *the image* of him that created him." Man, by regeneration, is restored to the lost image of God. Comp. Gen. i. 26. ¶ *Is created.* A word that is often used to denote the new birth, from its strong resemblance to the first act of creation. See it explained in the Notes on 2 Cor. v. 17. ¶ *In righteousness.* That is, the renewed man is made to resemble God in righteousness. This *proves* that man, when he was made, was righteous; or that righteousness constituted a part of the image of God in which he was created. The object of the work of redemption is to restore to man the lost image of God, or to bring him back to the condition in which he was before he fell. ¶ *And true holiness.* Marg. as in Greek, *holiness of truth*—standing in contrast with 'lusts of deceit' (*Greek*), in ver. 22. *Holiness* properly refers to purity towards God, and *righteousness* to integrity towards men; but it is not certain that this distinction is observed here. The general idea is, that the renovated man is made an upright and a pious man; and that, therefore, he should avoid the vices which are practised by the heathen, and which the apostle proceeds to specify. This phrase also proves that, when man was created, he was a *holy* being.

25. *Wherefore putting away lying.* It may seem strange that the apostle should seriously exhort Christians to put away *lying*, implying that they were in the habit of indulging in falsehood. But we are to remember, (1.) that lying is the universal vice of the heathen world. Among the ancient heathens, as among the moderns, it was almost universally practised. It has been remarked by a distinguished jurist who had spent much time in India, that he would not believe a Hindoo on his oath. The same testimony is borne by almost all the missionaries, of the character of heathens everywhere. No confidence can be placed in their statements; and, where there is the slightest temptation to falsehood, they practise it without remorse. (2.) The Ephesians had been recently converted, and were, to a great extent, ignorant of the requirements of the gospel. A *conscience* has to be *created* when heathens are converted, and it is long before they see the evils of many things which appear to us to be palpably wrong. (3.) The effects of former habits abide long, often, after a man is converted. He who has been in the habit of profane swear-

with his neighbour: for we[a] are members one of another.

26 Be ye angry and sin not; let[b] not the sun go down upon your wrath:

a Ro. 12. 5.

b Ec. 7. 9.

ing, finds it difficult to avoid it; and he who has been all his life practising deception, will find himself tempted to practise it still. It was for reasons such as these, probably, that the apostle exhorted the Ephesians to put away *lying*, and to speak the truth only. Nor is the exhortation now inappropriate to Christians, and there are many classes to whom it would now be proper—such as the following: (1.) He who is in the habit of concealing the defects of an article in trade, or of commending it for more than its real value—*let him put away lying*. (2. He, or she, who instructs a servant to say that they are not at home, when they are at home; or that they are sick, when they are not sick; or that they are engaged, when they are not engaged—*let them put away lying*. (3.) He that is in the habit of giving a colouring to his narratives; of conveying a false impression by the introduction or the suppression of circumstances that are important to the right understanding of an account—*let him put away lying*. (4.) He that is at no pains to ascertain the exact truth in regard to any facts that may affect his neighbour; that catches up flying rumours without investigating them, and that circulates them as undoubted truth, though they may seriously affect the character and peace of another—*let him put away lying*. (5.) He that is in the habit of making promises only to disregard them—*let him put away lying*. The community is full of falsehoods of that kind, and they are not *all* confined to the people of the world. Nothing is more important in a community than simple *truth*—and yet, it is to be feared that nothing is more habitually disregarded. No professing Christian can do any good who has not an unimpeachable character for integrity and truth—and yet who can lay his hand on his breast and say before God that he is in all cases a man that speaks the simple and unvarnished TRUTH? ¶ *For we are members one of another*. We belong to one body—the church—which is the body of Christ. See Notes Rom. v. 12. The idea is, that falsehood tends to loosen the bonds of brotherhood. In the *human body* harmony is observed. The eye never deceives the hand, nor the hand the foot, nor the heart the lungs. The whole move harmoniously *as if* the one could put the utmost confidence in the other—and falsehood in the church is as ruinous to its interests as it would be to the body if one member was perpetually practising a deception on another.

26. *Be ye angry and sin not*. It has been remarked that the direction here is conformable to the usage of the Pythagoreans, who were bound, when there were any differences among them, to furnish some token of reconciliation before the sun set. *Burder*, in Ros. Alt. u. neu. Morgenland, *in loc*. It is implied here (1.) that there *may* be anger without sin; and (2.) that there is special danger in *all* cases where there is anger that it will be accompanied with sin. *Anger* is a passion too common to need any description. It is an excitement or agitation of mind of more or less violence, produced by the reception of a real or supposed injury, and attended commonly with a desire or purpose of revenge. The desire of revenge, however, is not essential to the existence of the passion, though it is probably always

attended with a disposition to express displeasure, to chide, rebuke, or punish. Comp. Mark iii. 5. To a great extent the sudden excitement on the reception of an injury is involuntary, and consequently innocent. Anger is excited when a horse kicks us; when a serpent hisses; when we dash our foot against a stone—and so when a man raises his hand to strike us. The *object*, or *final cause* of implanting this passion in the mind of man is, to rouse him to an immediate defence of himself when suddenly attacked, and before his reason would have time to suggest the proper means of defence. It prompts at once to self-protection; and when that is done its proper office ceases. If persevered in, it becomes sinful malignity, or revenge —always wrong. Anger may be excited against a *thing* as well as a *person;* as well against an *act* as *a man.* We are suddenly excited by a wrong *thing*, without any malignancy against the *man;* we may wish to rebuke or chide *that*, without injuring *him.* Anger is sinful in the following circumstances. (1.) When it is excited without any sufficient cause—when we are in no danger, and do not need it for a protection. We should be safe without it. (2.) When it transcends the cause, if any cause really exists. All that is beyond the necessity of immediate self-protection, is apart from its design, and is wrong. (3.) When it is against *the person* rather than the *offence.* The object is not to injure another; it is to protect ourselves. (4.) When it is attended with the desire of *revenge.* That is always wrong. Rom. xii. 17. 19. (5.) When it is cherished, and heightened by reflection. And (6.) When there is an unforgiving spirit; a determination to exact the utmost satisfaction for the injury which has been done. If men were perfectly holy, that sudden *arousing of the mind* in danger, or on the reception of an injury, which would serve to prompt us to save ourselves from danger, would exist, and would be an important principle of our nature. As it is now, it is violent; excessive; incontrollable; persevered in — and is almost always wrong. If men were holy, this excitement of the mind would obey the first injunctions of *reason*, and be wholly under its control; as it is now, it seldom obeys reason at all—and is wholly wrong. Moreover, if *all* men were holy; if there were none *disposed* to do an injury, it would exist only in the form of a sudden arousing of the mind against immediate danger—which would all be right. Now, it is excited not only in view of *physical* dangers, but in view of the *wrongs* done by others—and hence it terminates on the *person* and not the *thing*, and becomes often wholly evil. ¶ *Let not the sun go down* Do not cherish anger. Do not sleep upon it. Do not harbour a purpose of revenge; do not cherish ill-will against another. *When the sun sets on a man's anger, he may be sure it is wrong.* The meaning of the whole of this verse then is, '*If* you be angry, which may be the case, and which may be unavoidable, see that the sudden excitement does not become sin. Do not let it overleap its proper bounds; do not cherish it; do not let it remain in your bosom even to the setting of the sun. Though the sun be sinking in the west, let not the passion linger in the bosom, but let his last rays find you always peaceful and calm.'

27. *Neither give place to the devil.* This has respect probably to the exhortation in the former verse. 'Do not yield to the suggestions and temptations of Satan, who would take every opportunity to persuade you to cherish unkind and angry feelings, and to keep up a spirit of resentment among brethren.'

27 Neither [a] give place to the devil.

a Ja. 4. 7.

28 Let him that stole steal no more: but rather let [b] him labour,

b Ac. 20. 35.

Many of our feelings, when we suppose we are merely defending our rights, and securing what is our own, are produced by the temptations of the devil. The heart is deceitful; and seldom more deceitful in any case than when a man is attempting to vindicate himself from injuries done to his person and reputation. The devil is always busy when we are angry, and in some way, if possible, will lead us into sin; and the best way to avoid his wiles is to curb the temper, and restrain even sudden anger. No man sins by *restraining* his anger: no man is certain that he will *not* who indulges it for a moment.

28. *Let him that stole steal no more.* Theft, like lying, was, and is, almost a universal vice among the heathen. The practice of pilfering prevails in, probably, every pagan community, and no property is safe which is not guarded, or so locked up as to be inaccessible. Hence, as the Christian converts at Ephesus had been long addicted to it, there was danger that they would fall into it again; and hence the necessity of special cautions on that head. We are not to suppose that *pilfering* was a common vice in the church, but the cautions on this point proceed on the principle that, where a man has been long in the habit of a particular sin, he is in great danger of falling into it again. Hence we caution the man who has been intemperate against the least indulgence in intoxicating drinks; we exhort him not to touch that which would be so strong a temptation to him. The object of the apostle was to show that the gospel requires holy living in all its friends, and to entreat Christians at Ephesus in a special manner to avoid the vices of the surrounding heathen. ¶ *But rather let him labour.* Let him seek the means of living in an honest manner, by his own industry, rather than by wronging others. ¶ *Working with* his *hands.* Pursuing some honest employment. Paul was not ashamed to labour with '*his* own hands' (Acts xx. 35); and no man is dishonoured by labour. God made man for toil (Gen. ii. 15); and employment is essential to the happiness of the race. No man, who is *able* to support himself, has a *right* to depend on others. See Notes on Rom. xii. 11. ¶ *That he may have to give to him that needeth.* Marg., *distribute.* Not merely that he may have the means of support, but that he may have it in his power to aid others. The reason and propriety of this is obvious. The human race is one great brotherhood. A considerable part *cannot* labour to support themselves. They are too old, or too young; or they are crippled, or feeble, or laid on beds of sickness. If others do not divide with them the avails of their labours, they will perish. We are required to labour in order that we may have the privilege of contributing to their comfort. Learn from this verse, (1.) That every Christian should have some calling, business, or profession, by which he may support himself. The Saviour was a carpenter; Paul a tentmaker; and no man is disgraced by being able to build a house or to construct a tent. (2.) Christianity promotes industry. It is rare that an idle man becomes a Christian; but if he does, religion makes him industrious just in proportion as it has influence over his mind. To talk of a *lazy Christian*, is about the same as to talk of burning water or freezing fire. (3.) Christians should

working with *his* hands the thing which is good, that he may have to [1] give to him that needeth.

[1] or, *distribute.*

29 Let [a] no corrupt communication proceed out of your mouth, but that which is good [1] to the use

a Co. 4. 6. [1] or, *to edify profitably.*

---

have some *useful* and *honest* employment. They should work "*that which is good.*" They should not pursue an employment which will necessarily injure others. No man has a right to place a nuisance under the window of his neighbour; nor has he any *more* right to pursue an employment that shall lead his neighbour into sin or ruin him. An *honest* employment benefits everybody. A good farmer is a benefit to his neighbourhood and country; and a good shoemaker, blacksmith, weaver, cabinetmaker, watchmaker, machinist, is a blessing to the community. He injures no one; he benefits all. How is it with the distiller, and the vender of alcoholic drinks? He benefits no one; he injures every body. Every quart of intoxicating drink that is taken from his house does evil somewhere—evil, and only evil, and that continually. No one is made better, or richer; no one is made more moral or industrious; no one is helped on the way to heaven by it. Thousands are helped on the way to hell by it, who are already in the path; and thousands are *induced* to walk in the way to death who, *but* for that distillery, store, or tavern, might have walked in the way to heaven. Is this then 'working that WHICH IS GOOD?' Would Paul have done it? Would Jesus do it? Strange, that by a professing Christian it was ever done! See a striking instance of the way in which the Ephesian Christians acted when they were first converted, in the Acts of the Apostles, ch. xix. 19. Comp. Notes on that place. (4.) The main business of a Christian is not *to make money*, and to become rich. It is that he may have the means of benefiting others. Beyond what he needs for himself, his poor, and sick, and aged, and afflicted brother and friend has a claim on his earnings—and they should be liberally bestowed. (5.) We should labour *in order* that we may have the means of doing good to others. It should be just as much a matter of plan and purpose to do this, as it is to labour *in order* to buy a coat, or to build a house, or to live comfortably, or to have the means of a decent burial. Yet how few are those who have any such end in view, or who pursue their daily toil definitely, *that they may have something to give away!* The world will be soon converted when all Christians make that the purpose of life. See Notes on Rom. xii. 11.

29. *Let no corrupt communication proceed.* See Notes on 1 Cor. xv. 33. The word rendered *corrupt* (σαπρὸς) means *bad, decayed, rotten*, and is applied to putrid vegetable or animal substances. Then it is applied to a tree that is of a useless character, that produces no good fruit. Matt. vii. 17. Then it is used in a moral sense, as our word 'corrupt' is, to denote that which is depraved, evil, contaminating, and may denote here any thing that is obscene, offensive, or that tends to corrupt others. The importance of this admonition will be appreciated when it is remembered, (1.) that such obscene and filthy conversation prevailed everywhere, and does still among the heathen. So general is this, that at almost every missionary station it has been found that the common conversation is so corrupt and defiling, that missionaries have felt it necessary to send their chil-

of edifying, that it may minister grace unto the hearers.

30 And grieve [a] not the holy Spirit of God, whereby ye are

a Is. 63. 10.

dren home to be educated, in order to secure them from the contaminating influence of those around them. (2.) Those who have had the misfortune to be familiar with the common conversation of the lower classes in any community, and especially with the conversation of young men, will see the importance of this admonition. Scarcely any thing can be conceived more corrupt or corrupting, than that which often prevails among young men—and even young men in the academies and colleges of this land. (3.) Its importance will be seen from the *influence* of such corrupt communications. "The passage of an impure thought through the mind leaves pollution behind it;" the expression of such a thought deepens the pollution on the soul, and corrupts others. It is like retaining an offensive carcase above ground, to pollute the air, and to diffuse pestilence and death, which should at once be buried out of sight. A Christian should be PURE in his conversation. His Master was pure. His God is pure. The heaven to which he goes is pure. The religion which he professes is pure. NEVER should he indulge himself in an obscene allusion; never should he retail anecdotes of an obscene character, or smile when they are retailed by others. Never should he indulge in a jest having a double meaning; never should he listen to a song of this character. If those with whom he associates have not sufficient respect for themselves and him to abstain from such corrupt and corrupting allusions, *he should at once leave them.* ¶ *But that which is good to the use of edifying.* Marg., *to edify profitably.* Greek, 'to useful edification;' that is, adapted to instruct, counsel, and comfort others; to promote their intelligence and purity. Speech is an invaluable gift; a blessing of inestimable worth. We may *so* speak as *always* to do good to others. We may give them some information which they have not; impart some consolation which they need; elicit some truth by friendly discussion which we did not know before, or recall by friendly admonition those who are in danger of going astray. He who talks for the mere sake of talking will say many foolish things; he whose great aim in life is to benefit others, will not be likely to say that which he will have occasion to regret. Comp. Matt. xii. 36. Eccl. v. 2. Prov. x. 19. James i. 19.

30. *And grieve not the holy Spirit of God.* This is addressed to *Christians*, and it proves that it is possible for them to grieve the Holy Spirit. The word here used—λυπεῖτε—means properly to afflict with sorrow; to make sad or sorrowful. It is rendered to make sorry, or sorrowful, Matt. xiv. 9; xvii. 23; xviii. 31; xix. 22; xxvi. 22. 37. Mark xiv. 19. John xvi. 20. 2 Cor. ii. 2; vi. 10; vii. 8, 9. 11. 1 Thess. iv. 13. It is rendered *grieved*, Mark x. 22. John xxi. 17. Rom. xiv. 15. 2 Cor. ii. 4, 5. Eph. iv. 20: and once, '*in heaviness*,' 1 Pet. i. 6. The verb does not elsewhere occur in the New Testament. The common meaning is, to treat others so as to cause grief. We are not to suppose that the Holy Spirit literally endures *grief*, or *pain*, at the conduct of men. The language is such as is fitted to describe what *men* endure, and is applied to him to denote that kind of conduct which is *fitted* to cause grief; and the meaning here is, 'do not pursue such a course as is *fitted*, in its own nature, to pain the bene-

sealed [a] unto the day of redemption.

31 Let all bitterness, [b] and wrath, and anger, and clamour, and [c] evil-speaking, be put away from you, with all malice:

32 And be ye kind one to another, tender-hearted, forgiving [d]

a c.1. 13, 14. b Co. 3. 8. c Ti. 3. 2. d Mar. 11. 25, 26.

---

volent heart of a holy being. Do not act towards the Holy Spirit in a manner which would produce pain in the bosom of a friend who loves you. There is a course of conduct which will drive that Spirit from the mind *as if* he were grieved and pained—as a course of ingratitude and sin would pain the heart of an earthly friend, and cause him to leave you.' If asked what that conduct is, we may reply, (1.) Open and gross sins. They are particularly referred to here; and the meaning of Paul is, that theft, falsehood, anger, and kindred vices, would grieve the Holy Spirit, and cause him to depart. (2.) Anger, in all its forms. Nothing is more fitted to drive away all serious and tender impressions from the mind, than the indulgence of anger. (3.) Licentious thoughts and desires. The Spirit of God is pure, and he dwells not in a soul that is filled with corrupt imaginings. (4.) Ingratitude. *We* feel ingratitude more than almost anything else; and why should we suppose that the Holy Spirit would not feel it also? (4.) Neglect. The Spirit of God is grieved by that. Often he prompts us to pray; he disposes the mind to seriousness, to the perusal of the Bible, to tenderness and penitence. We neglect those favoured moments of our piety, and lose those happy seasons for becoming like God. (5.) Resistance. Christians often resist the Holy Ghost. He would lead them to be dead to the world; yet they drive on their plans of gain. He would teach them the folly of fashion and vanity; yet they deck themselves in the gayest apparel. He would keep them from the splendid party, the theatre, and the ball-room; yet they go there. All that is needful for a Christian to do in order to be eminent in piety, is to yield to the gentle influences which would draw him to prayer and to heaven. ¶ *Whereby ye are sealed.* See Notes on 2 Cor. i. 22. ¶ *Unto the day of redemption.* See Notes on ch. i. 14.

31. *Let all bitterness.* See Notes on ver. 2 of this chapter. ¶ *And wrath.* The word here does not differ essentially from anger. ¶ *Anger.* See Note on ver. 26. All cherished, unreasonable anger. ¶ *And clamour.* Noise, disorder, high words; such as men use in a brawl, or when they are excited. Christians are to be calm and serious. Harsh contentions and strifes; hoarse brawls and tumults, are to be unknown among them. ¶ *And evil-speaking.* Slander, backbiting, angry expressions, tale-bearing, reproaches, &c. ¶ *With all malice.* Rather, 'with all *evil*'—κακίᾳ. Every kind and sort of evil is to be put away, and you are to manifest only that which is good.

32. *And be ye kind one to another.* Benignant, mild, courteous, *polite*—χρηστοὶ. 1 Pet. iii. 8. Christianity produces true courteousness, or politeness. It does not make one rough, crabbed, sour; nor does it dispose its followers to violate the proper rules of social intercourse. The secret of true politeness is *benevolence*, or a desire to make others happy; and a Christian *should* be the most polite of men. There is no religion in a sour, misanthropic temper; none in rudeness, stiffness, and repulsiveness; none in violating the rules of good-breeding.

one another, even as God for Christ's sake hath forgiven you.

There is a hollow-hearted politeness, indeed, which the Christian is not to aim at or copy. His politeness is to be based on *kindness.* Col. iii. 12. His courtesy is to be the result of love, good-will, and a desire of the happiness of all others; and this will prompt to the kind of conduct that will render his intercourse with others agreeable and profitable.— ¶ *Tender-hearted.* Having a heart disposed to pity and compassion, and especially disposed to show kindness to the faults of erring brethren; for so the connection demands. ¶ *Forgiving one another.* See Notes on Matt. vi. 12. ¶ *As God for Christ's sake hath forgiven you.* As God, on account of what Christ has suffered and done, has pardoned you. He has done it, (1.) *freely*—without merit on our part—when we were confessedly in the wrong. (2.) *Fully;* he has forgiven *every* offence. (3.) *Liberally;* he has forgiven *many* offences, for our sins have been innumerable. This is to be the rule which we are to observe in forgiving others. We are to do it *freely, fully, liberally.* The forgiveness is to be entire, cordial, constant. We are not to *rake up* old offences, and charge them again upon them; we are to treat them as though they had not offended, for *so* God treats us. Learn, (1.) That the forgiveness of an offending brother is a DUTY which we are not at liberty to neglect. (2.) The peace and happiness of the church depend on it. All are liable to offend their brethren, as all are liable to offend God; all need forgiveness of one another, as we all need it of God. (3.) There is no danger of carrying it too far. Let the rule be observed—'*As God has forgiven you,* so *do you forgive others.*' Let a man recollect his own sins and follies; let him look over his life, and see how often he has offended God; let him remember that *all* has been forgiven; and then, fresh with this feeling, let him go and meet an offending brother, and say, 'My brother, I forgive you. I do it frankly, fully, wholly. So Christ has forgiven me; so I forgive you. The offence shall be no more remembered. It shall not be referred to in our intercourse to harrow up your feelings; it shall not diminish my love for you; it shall not prevent my uniting with you in doing good. Christ treats me, a poor sinner, as a friend; and *so* I will treat you.'

CHAPTER V.

ANALYSIS OF THE CHAPTER.

This chapter is a continuation of the practical exhortations commenced in ch. iv. It comprises the following points, or subjects:

1. The exhortation to be followers of God, and to walk in love. Vs. 1, 2.

2. The duty of avoiding the impure practices of the surrounding heathen, and of wholly breaking off from the vices in which even they themselves had indulged, before their conversion to Christianity. Vs. 3—17.

3. The apostle cautions them particularly against the use of wine, and the revelry which attends its use, and exhorts them rather to engage in the exercises to which the Holy Spirit would prompt them, and to the services of praise and thanksgiving. Vs. 18—20.

4. He exhorts them to mutual subjection; and particularly enjoins on wives the duty of being subject to their husbands. Vs. 21—24.

5. The chapter closes with a statement of the duty of husbands to love their wives, illustrated by that which Christ showed for the church. Vs. 25—33.

CHAPTER V.

BE ye therefore followers of God, as dear children;

2 And walk in love, [a] as Christ also hath loved us, and hath given himself for us, an offering and a

a Jno. 13. 34.

1. *Be ye therefore followers of God.* Gr., 'Be *imitators*—μιμηταὶ—of God.' The idea is not that they were to be the friends of God, or numbered among his followers, but that they were to *imitate* him in the particular thing under consideration. The word 'therefore'—ὀυν—connects this with the previous chapter, where he had been exhorting them to kindness, and to a spirit of forgiveness, and he here entreats them to imitate God, who was always kind and ready to forgive. Comp. Matt. v. 44—47. As he forgives us (ch. iv. 32), we should be ready to forgive others; as he has borne with our faults, we should bear with theirs; as he is ever ready to hear our cry when we ask for mercy, we should be ready to hear others when they desire to be forgiven; and as he is never weary with doing us good, we should never be weary in benefiting them. ¶ *As dear children.* The meaning is, 'as those children which are beloved follow the example of a father, so we, who are beloved of God, should follow his example.' What a simple rule this is! And how much contention and strife would be avoided if it were followed! If every Christian who is angry, unforgiving, and unkind, would just ask himself the question, 'How does God treat me?' it would save all the trouble and heart-burning which ever exists in the church.

2. *And walk in love.* That is, let your lives be characterized by love; let that be evinced in all your deportment and conversation. See Notes on John xiii. 34. ¶ *As Christ also hath loved us.* We are to evince the same love for one another which he has done for us. He showed *his* love by giving himself to die for us, and we should evince similar love to one another. 1 John iii. 16. ¶ *And hath given himself for us.* This is evidently added by the apostle to show what he meant by saying that Christ loved us, and what we ought to do to evince our love for each other. The strength of *his* love was so great that he was willing to give himself up to death on our account; our love for our brethren should be such that we would be willing to do the same thing for them. 1 John iii. 16. ¶ *An offering.* The word here used—προσφορά—means properly that which is *offered to God*—in any way, or whatever it may be. It is, however, in the Scriptures, commonly used to denote an offering without blood—a thank-offering—and thus is distinguished from a sacrifice or a bloody oblation. The word occurs only in Acts xxi. 26; xxiv. 17. Rom. xv. 16. Eph. v. 2. Heb. x. 5. 8. 10. 14. 18. It means here that he regarded himself as an offering to God. ¶ *And a sacrifice.* θυσίαν. Christ is here expressly called a *Sacrifice*—the usual word in the Scriptures to denote a proper sacrifice. A sacrifice was an offering made to God by killing an animal and burning it on an altar, designed to make atonement for sin. It always implied the *killing* of the animal as an acknowledgment of the sinner that *he* deserved to die. It was the giving up of *life*, which was supposed to reside in the *blood* (see Notes on Rom. iii. 25), and hence it was necessary that *blood* should be shed. Christ was such a sacrifice; and his love was shown in his being willing that his blood should be shed to save men. ¶ *For a sweet-smelling savour.* See Notes

sacrifice to God for a [a] sweet-smelling savour.

3 But fornication, [b] and all uncleanness, or covetousness, let it

a Le. 1. 9.

b 1 Co. 6. 18. 1 Th. 4. 3.

on 2 Cor. ii. 15, where the word *savour* is explained. The meaning here is, that the offering which Christ made of himself to God, was like the grateful and pleasant smell of *incense*, that is, it was acceptable to him. It was an exhibition of benevolence with which he was pleased, and it gave him the opportunity of evincing his own benevolence in the salvation of men. The meaning of this in the connection here is, that the offering which Christ made was one of *love.* So, says Paul, do you love one another. Christ sacrificed himself by *love*, and that sacrifice was acceptable to God. So do you show love one to another. Sacrifice every thing which opposes it, and it will be acceptable to God. He will approve all which is designed to promote love, as he approved the sacrifice which was made, under the influence of love, by his Son.

3. *But fornication.* A *common* vice among the heathen then as it is now, and one into which they were in special danger of falling. See Notes on Rom. i. 29. 1 Cor. vi. 18. ¶ *And all uncleanness.* Impurity of life. See Notes on Rom. i. 24. Comp. Rom. vi. 19. Gal. v. 19. Eph. iv. 19. Col. iii. 5. ¶ *Or covetousness.* The *connection* in which this word is found is remarkable. It is associated with the lowest and most debasing vices, and this, as well as those vices, was not once to be *named* among them. What was Paul's estimate then of covetousness? He considered it as an odious and abominable vice; a vice to be regarded in the same light as the most gross sin, and as wholly to be abhorred by all who bore the Christian name. See ver. 5. The covetous man, according to Paul, is to be ranked with the sensual, and with idolaters (ver. 5), and with those who are entirely excluded from the kingdom of God. Is this the estimate in which the vice is held now? Is it the view which professing Christians take of it? Do we not feel that there is a *great* difference between a covetous man and a man of impure and licentious life? Why is this? Because, (1.) it is so common; (2.) because it is found among those who make pretensions to refinement and even religion; (3.) because it is not so easy to define what is covetousness, as it is to define impurity of life; and (4.) because the public conscience is seared, and the mind blinded to the low and grovelling character of the sin. Yet is not the view of Paul the right view? Who is a covetous man? A man who, in the pursuit of gold, neglects his soul, his intellect, and his heart. A man who, in this insatiable pursuit, is regardless of justice, truth, charity, faith, prayer, peace, comfort, usefulness, conscience; and who shall say that there is *any* vice more debasing or degrading than this? The time *may* come, therefore, when the covetous man will be regarded as deserving the same rank in the public estimation with the most vicious, and when TO COVET will be considered as much opposed to the spirit of the gospel as any of the vices here named. When that time shall come, the world's conversion will probably be not a distant event. ¶ *Let it not be once named among you.* That is let it not exist; let there be no occasion for mentioning such a thing among you; let it be wholly unknown. This cannot mean that it is wrong to *mention* these vices for the purpose of rebuking them, or cautioning those in danger of com-

not be once named [a] among you, as becometh saints;

4 Neither filthiness, nor foolish talking, nor jesting, which [b] are

a c. 5. 12.

b Ro. 1. 28.

mitting them—for Paul himself in this manner mentions them here, and frequently elsewhere—but that they should not *exist* among them. ¶ *As becometh saints.* As befits the character of Christians, who are regarded as holy. Literally, 'as becometh *holy ones*'—ἁγίοις.

4. *Neither filthiness.* That is, obscene, or indecent conversation. Literally, that which is shameful, or deformed—αἰσχρότης. The word does not elsewhere occur in the New Testament. ¶ *Nor foolish talking.* This word—μωρολογία—does not occur elsewhere in the New Testament. It means that kind of talk which is insipid, senseless, stupid, foolish; which is not fitted to instruct, edify, profit—the idle *chit-chat* which is so common in the world. The meaning is, that Christians should aim to have their conversation sensible, serious, sincere—remembering the words of the Lord Jesus, "that every idle word that men shall speak, they shall give account thereof in the day of judgment." Matt. xii. 36. ¶ *Nor jesting.* εὐτραπελία. This word occurs also nowhere else in the New Testament. It properly means, that which is *well-turned* (εὖ—*well*, and τρεπω—*to turn*); and then that which is sportive, refined, courteous; and then *urbanity, humour, wit;* and then *jesting, levity*—which is evidently the meaning here. The apostle would not forbid courteousness, or refinement of manners (comp. 1 Pet. iii. 8), and the reference, therefore, must be to that which is light and trifling in conversation; to that which is known among us as jesting. It may be observed, (1.) that *courteousness* is not forbidden in the Scriptures, but is positively required. 1 Pet. iii. 8. (2.) *Cheerfulness* is not forbidden—for if any thing can make cheerful, it is the hope of heaven. (3.) *Pleasantry* cannot be forbidden. I mean that quiet and gentle humour that arises from good-nature, and that makes one good-natured in spite of himself. Such are many of the poems of Cowper, and many of the essays of Addison in the "Spectator"—a benevolent humour which disposes us to smile, but not to be malignant; to be good-natured, but not to inspire levity. But levity and jesting, though often manifested by ministers and other Christians, are as inconsistent with true dignity as with the gospel. Where were they seen in the conversation of the Redeemer? Where in the writings of Paul? ¶ *Which are not convenient.* That is, which are not *fit* or *proper;* which do not become the character of Christians. Notes, Rom. i. 28. Christians should be grave and serious—though cheerful and pleasant. They should feel that they have great interests at stake, and that the world has too. They are redeemed—not to make sport; purchased with precious blood—for other purposes than to make men laugh. They are soon to be in heaven—and a man who has any impressive sense of that will habitually feel that he has much else to do than to make men laugh. The true course of life is midway between moroseness and levity; sourness and lightness; harshness and jesting. Be benevolent, kind, cheerful, bland, courteous, but serious. Be solemn, thoughtful, deeply impressed with the presence of God and with eternal things, but pleasant, affable, and benignant. Think not a smile sinful; but think not levity and jesting harmless. ¶ *But rather giving of*

not convenient; but rather giving of thanks.

5 For this ye know, that [a] no whoremonger, nor unclean person, nor covetous man, who [b] is an idolater, hath any inheritance

a He. 13. 4. Re. 22. 15.

b Co. 3. 5.

thanks. Thanks to God, or praises, are more becoming Christians than jesting. The idea here seems to be, that such employment would be far more appropriate to the character of Christians, than idle, trifling, and indelicate conversation. Instead, therefore, of meeting together for low wit and jesting; for singing songs, and for the vulgar discourse which often attends such 'gatherings' of friends, Paul would have them come together for the purpose of praising God, and engaging in his service. Men are social in their nature; and if they do not assemble for good purposes, they will for bad ones. It is much more appropriate to the character of Christians to come together to sing praises to God, than to sing songs; to pray than to jest; to converse of the things of redemption than to tell anecdotes; and to devote the time to a contemplation of the world to come, than to trifles and nonsense.

5. *For this know.* Be assured of this. The object here is, to deter from indulgence in those vices by the solemn assurance that no one who committed them could possibly be saved. ¶ *Nor unclean person.* No one of corrupt and licentious life can be saved. See Rev. xxii. 15. ¶ *Nor covetous man, who is an idolater.* That is, he bestows on money the affections due to God. See Col. iii. 5. To worship money is as real idolatry as to worship a block of stone. If this be so, what an idolatrous world is this! How many idolaters are there in professedly Christian lands! How many, it is to be feared, in the church itself! And since *every* covetous man is certainly to be excluded from the kingdom of God, how anxious should we be to examine our hearts, and to know whether this sin may not lie at our door! ¶ *Hath any inheritance*, &c. Such an one shall never enter heaven. This settles the inquiry about the final destiny of a large portion of the world; and this solemn sentence our conscience and all our views of heaven approve. Let us learn hence, (1.) that heaven will be *pure.* (2.) That it will be a *desirable* place—for who would wish to live always with the licentious and the impure? (3.) It is right to reprove these vices and to preach against them. Shall we not be allowed to preach against those sins which will certainly exclude men from heaven? (4.) A large part of the world is exposed to the wrath of God. What numbers are covetous! What multitudes are licentious! In how many places is licentiousness openly and unblushingly practised! In how many more places in secret! And in how many more is the *heart* polluted, while the external conduct is moral; the soul *corrupt*, while the individual moves in respectable society! (5.) What a world of shame will hell be! How dishonourable and disgraceful to be damned forever, and to linger on in eternal fires, because the man was TOO POLLUTED to be admitted into pure society! Here, perhaps, he moved in fashionable life, and was rich, and honoured, and flattered; there he will be sent down to hell because his whole soul was corrupt, and because God would not suffer heaven to be contaminated by his presence! (6.) What a doom awaits the *covetous* man! He, like the sensualist, is to be excluded from the

in the kingdom of Christ and of God.

6 Let no man deceive [a] you with vain words: for because of these things cometh the wrath of God upon the children of [1] disobedience.

7 Be not ye therefore partakers with them.

8 For [b] ye were sometimes darkness, but now *are ye* light [c] in the Lord: walk as children [d] of light;

a Je. 29. 8, 9. [1] or, *unbelief*. *b* c. 2. 11, 12. *c* 1 Th. 5. 5. *d* Jno. 12. 36.

kingdom of God. And what is to be his doom? Will he have a place apart from the common damned—a golden palace and a bed of down in hell? No. It will be no small part of his aggravation that he will be doomed to spend an eternity with those in comparison with whom on earth, perhaps, he thought himself to be pure as an angel of light. (7.) With this multitude of the licentious and the covetous, will sink to hell *all* who are not renewed and sanctified. What a prospect for the gay, the fashionable, the moral, the amiable, and the lovely, who have no religion! For all the impenitent and the unbelieving, there is but one home in eternity. Hell is less terrible from its penal fires and its smoke of torment, than from its being made up of the profane, the sensual, and the vile; and its supremest horrors arise from its being the place where shall be gathered all the corrupt and unholy dwellers in a fallen world; all who are so impure that they cannot be admitted into heaven. Why then will the refined, the moral, and the amiable not be persuaded to seek the society of a pure heaven? to be prepared for the world where holy beings dwell?

6. *Let no man deceive you.* Let no one by artful pleas persuade you that there will be no danger from practising these vices. We may suppose that they would be under strong temptations to mingle in the gay and festive scenes where these vices were not frowned on, or where they were practised; or that they might be tempted to commit them by some of the plausible arguments which were then used for their indulgence. Many of their friends may have been in these circles; and they would endeavour to convince them that such were the customs which had been long practised, and that there could be no harm still in their indulgence. Not a few philosophers endeavoured, as is well known, to defend some of these practices, and even practised them themselves. See Notes on Rom. i. It required, therefore, all the authority of an apostle to convince them, that however plausible were the arguments in defence of them, they certainly exposed those who practised them to the wrath of God. ¶ *For because of these things cometh the wrath of God.* See Notes on Rom. i. 18; ii. 8, 9. ¶ *Upon the children of disobedience.* See Notes on Matt. i. 1. Rom. ii. 8.

7. *Be not ye therefore partakers with them.* Since these things displease God and expose to his wrath, avoid them.

8. *For ye were sometimes darkness.* See Notes on ch. ii. 11, 12. 1 Cor. vi. 11. The meaning here is, that they were themselves formerly sunk in the same ignorance, and practised the same abominations. ¶ *But now* are ye *light in the Lord.* Light is the emblem of happiness, knowledge, holiness. The meaning is, that they had been enlightened by the Lord to see the evil of these practices, and that they ought, therefore, to forsake them. ¶ *Walk as*

9 (For the fruit [a] of the Spirit *is* in all goodness and righteousness and truth;)

10 Proving [b] what is acceptable unto the Lord.

11 And have [c] no fellowship with the unfruitful works of darkness, but rather reprove [d] *them*.

12 For it is a shame even to speak of those things which are done of them in secret.

a Ga. 5. 22, &c. b Ro. 12. 2. c 1 Co. 5. 9, 11. d 1 Ti. 5. 20.

children of light. See Notes on Matt. i. 1, on the use of the word *son*, or *children*. The meaning here is, that they should live as became those who had been enlightened to see the evil of sin, and the beauty of virtue and religion. Comp. John xii. 36, where the same phrase occurs.

9. *For the fruit of the Spirit.* That is, since the Holy Spirit through the gospel produces goodness, righteousness, and truth, see that you exhibit these in your lives, and thus show that you are the children of light. On the fruits of the Spirit, see Notes on Gal. v. 22, 23. ¶ *Is in all goodness.* Is seen in producing all kinds of goodness. He who is not *good* is not a Christian.

10. *Proving what is acceptable unto the Lord.* That is, 'Walk as children of light (ver. 8), thus showing what is acceptable to the Lord.' Rosenmüller supposes that the participle is used here instead of the imperative. The meaning is, that by so living you will make a fair trial of what is acceptable to the Lord. The result on your happiness in this life and the next, will be such as to show that such a course is pleasing in his sight. Dr. Chandler, however, renders it as meaning that by this course they would show that they discerned and approved of what was acceptable to the Lord. See Notes on Rom. xii. 2, where a similar form of expression occurs.

11. *And have no fellowship.* See the sentiment here expressed fully explained in the Notes on 2 Cor. vi. 14—18. ¶ *The unfruitful works.* The deeds of darkness that produce no *benefit* to the body or the soul. The word *unfruitful* is here used in contrast with the 'fruit of the Spirit,' ver. 9. ¶ *But rather reprove* them. By your life, your conversation, and all your influence. This is the business of Christians. Their lives should be a standing rebuke of a sinful world, and they should be ever ready to express their disapprobation of its wickedness in every form.

12. *For it is a shame even to speak* &c. Comp. Notes, Rom. i. 24—32 It is still a shame to speak of the practices of the heathen. Missionaries tell us that they *cannot* describe the images on the car of Juggernaut, or tell us what is done in the idol temples. All over the world the same thing is true. The cheek of modesty and virtue would be suffused with shame at the very mention of what is done by the worshippers of idols; and the same is true of what is done by multitudes in Christian lands, who are not worshippers of idols. Their deeds cannot be described in the circles of the refined and the delicate; they cannot be told in the presence of mothers and sisters. Is there not emphasis here in the words 'even to SPEAK of these things?' If the apostle would not allow them to *name* those things, or to *speak* of them, is it wise or safe for Christians now to be familiar with the accounts of those practices of pollution, and for ministers to portray them in the pulpit, and for the friends of 'moral reform' to describe them before the world? The very *naming* of those abomi-

13 But all things that are [1] reproved are made manifest [a] by the light: for whatsoever doth make manifest is light.

14 Wherefore [2] he saith, [b] Awake

[1] or, *discovered.* a Jno. 3. 20, 21.

[2] or, *it.* b Is. 60. 1.

nations often produces improper associations in the mind; the description creates polluting images before the imagination; the exhibition of pictures, even for the purpose of condemning them, defiles the soul. There are some vices which, from the corruptions of the human heart, cannot be safely described, and it is to be feared that, under the plea of faithfulness, many have done evil by exciting improper feelings, where they should have only alluded to the crime, and then spoken in thunder. Paul did not *describe* these vices, he denounced them; he did not dwell upon them long enough for the imagination to find employment, and to corrupt the soul. He mentioned the vice—and then he mentioned the wrath of God; he alluded to the sin, and then he spoke of the exclusion from heaven. Comp. Notes on 1 Cor. vi. 18. ¶ *Which are done of them in secret.* Many have supposed that there is an allusion here to the "*mysteries*" which were celebrated in Greece, usually at night, and far from the public eye. Many of these were indeed impure and abominable, but there is no necessity for supposing that there is such an allusion here. The reference may be to the vices which were secretly practised then as now; the abominations which flee from the eye of day, and which are performed far from the public gaze.

13. *But all things that are reproved.* Marg., *discovered.* The word here used properly means proved, demonstrated, reproved, or convicted (see Notes on John xvi. 8); but it seems here to be used in the sense of disclosed, or discovered. The sense is, that *its true nature is demonstrated;* that is, it is made known. ¶ *Are made manifest by the light.* The sense is, 'light is the means of seeing what things are. We discern their form, nature, appearance, by it. So it is with the gospel—the light of the world. It enables us to see the true nature of actions. They are done in darkness, and are like objects *in* the dark. Their form and nature cannot then be known; but, when the light shines, we see what they are.' Comp. Notes on John iii. 20, 21. ¶ *For whatsoever doth make manifest is light.* 'Anything which will show the real form and nature of an object, deserves to be called *light.*' Of the *truth* of this, no one can doubt. The meaning in this connection is, that that system which discloses the true nature of what is done by the heathen, deserves to be considered as *light;* and that the gospel which does this, should be regarded as a system of light and truth. It discloses their odiousness and vileness, and it stands thus in strong contrast with all the false and abominable systems which have upheld or produced those vices.

14. *Wherefore he saith.* Marg., or *it.* Διὸ λέγει. The meaning may be, either that the Lord says, or the Scripture. Much difficulty has been experienced in endeavouring to ascertain *where* this is said. It is agreed on all hands that it is not found, in so many words, in the Old Testament. Some have supposed that the allusion is to Isa. xxvi. 19, "Thy dead men shall live—awake and sing, ye that dwell in the dust, for thy dew is as the dew of herbs," &c. But the objections to this are obvious and conclusive. (1.) This is *not* a quotation of that place, nor has it a *resemblance* to it, except in

thou that sleepest, and arise from the dead, and Christ shall give thee light.

---

the word "awake." (2.) The passage in Isaiah refers to a different matter, and has a different sense altogether. See Notes on the passage. To make it refer to those to whom the gospel comes, is most forced and unnatural. Others have supposed that the reference is to Isa. lx. 1—3, "Arise, shine; for thy light is come," &c. But the objection to this is not less decisive. (1.) It is *not* a quotation of that passage, and the resemblance is very remote, if it can be seen at all. (2.) *That* is addressed to the church, calling on her to let her light shine; *this*, to awake and arise from the dead, with the assurance that Christ would give them light. The exhortation here is to Christians, to *avoid the vices of the heathen around them;* the exhortation in Isaiah is to the church, to *rejoice* and *exult* in view of the fact that the day of triumph had come, and that the heathen were to be converted, and to come in multitudes and devote themselves to God. In the *design* of the two passages there is no resemblance. Some have supposed that the words are taken from some book among the Hebrews which is now lost. Epiphanius supposed that it was a quotation from a prophecy of Elijah; Syncellus and Euthalius, from some writing of Jeremiah; Hippolytus, from the writing of some now unknown prophet. Jerome supposed it was taken from some apocryphal writings. Grotius supposes that it refers to the word *light* in ver. 13, and that the sense is, 'That light says; that is, that a man who is pervaded by that light, let him so say to another.' Heumann, and after him Storr, Michaelis, and Jenning (Jewish Ant. ii. 252), suppose that the reference is to a song or hymn that was sung by the early Christians, beginning in this manner, and that the meaning is, 'Wherefore, as it is said in the hymns which we sing,

'Awake, thou that sleepest;
Arise from the dead;
Christ shall give thee light.'

Others have supposed that there is an allusion to a sentiment which prevailed among the Jews, respecting the significancy of blowing the trumpet on the first day of the month, or the feast of the new moon. Maimonides conjectures that that call of the trumpet, especially in the month Tisri, in which the great day of atonement occurred, was designed to signify a special call to repentance; meaning, 'You who sleep, arouse from your slumbers; search and try yourselves; think on your Creator, repent, and attend to the salvation of the soul.' *Burder*, in Ros. Alt. u. neu. Morgenland, *in loc.* But all this is evidently conjecture. I see no evidence that Paul meant to make a quotation at all. Why may we not suppose that he speaks as an inspired man, and that he means to say, simply, that God *now* gives this command, or that God now speaks in this way? The sense then would be, 'Be separate from sinners. Come out from among the heathen. Do not mingle with their abominations; do not name them. You are the children of light; and God says to you, awake from false security, rouse from the death of sin, and Christ shall enlighten you.' Whatever be the origin of the sentiment in this verse, it is worthy of inspiration, and accords with all that is elsewhere said in the Scriptures. ¶ *Awake thou that sleepest.* Arouse from a state of slumber and false security. *Sleep* and *death* are striking representations of the state in which men are by nature. In *sleep* we are, though living, insensible to any danger that may be near; we are unconscious of what may be going on around us; we hear not the voice of our friends; we see not the beauty of the grove or the landscape; we are forgetful of our real character and condition. So with the sinner. It is as if his faculties were locked in a deep slumber. He hears not when God calls; he has no sense of danger; he is insensible to the beauties and glories of the heavenly world; he is forgetful of his true character and condition. To see all this, he must be first awakened; and hence this solemn command is addressed to man. He must rouse from this condition, or he cannot be saved. But can he awaken himself? Is it not the work of God to awaken a sinner? Can he rouse himself to a sense of his condition and danger? How do we do in other things? The man that is sleeping on the verge of a dangerous precipice we would approach, and say, 'Awake, you are in danger.' The child that is sleeping quietly in its bed, while the flames are bursting into the room, we would rouse, and say, 'Awake, or you will perish.' Why not use the same language to the sinner slumbering on the verge of ruin, in a deep sleep, while the flames of wrath are kindling around him? We have no difficulty in calling on sleepers elsewhere to awake when in danger; how can we have any difficulty when speaking to the sinner? ¶ *And arise from the dead.* The state of the sinner is often compared to death. See Notes on ch. ii. 1. Men are by nature dead in sins; yet they must rouse from this condition, or they will perish. How singular, it may be said, to call upon the dead to rise! How *could* they raise themselves up? Yet God speaks thus to men, and commands them to rise from the death of sin. Learn, then, (1.) That men are not dead in sin in any such sense that they are not moral agents, or responsible. (2.) That they are not dead in any such sense that they have no power of any kind. (3.) That it is right to call on sinners to arouse from their condition, and live. (4.) That they must put forth their efforts as if they were to *begin* the work themselves, without waiting for God to do it for them. *They* are to awake; *they* are to arise. It is not God who is to awake; it is not Christ who is to arise. It is *the sinner* who is to awake from his slumber, and arise from the state of death; nor is he to wait for God to do the work for him. ¶ *And Christ shall give thee light.* Christ is the light of the world. See Notes on John i. 4. 9; viii. 12. Heb. i. 3. The idea here is, that if they will use all the powers with which God has endowed them, and arouse from their spiritual slumber, and make an appropriate effort for salvation, then they may expect that Christ will shine upon them, and bless them in their efforts. This is just the promise that we need, and it is *all* that we need. All that man can ask is, that if he will make efforts to be saved, God will bless those efforts, so that they shall not be in vain. Faculties of mind have been given us to be employed in securing our salvation; and if we will employ them as they were intended to be employed, we may look for the divine aid; if not, we cannot expect it. "God helps those who help themselves;" and they who will make no effort for their salvation must perish, as they who will make no effort to provide food must starve. This command was indeed addressed at first to Christians; but it involves a principle which is applicable to all. Indeed, the *language* here is rather descriptive of the condition of impenitent sinners, than of Christians. In a far more important sense they

15 See then that ye walk [a] circumspectly, not as fools, but as wise,

16 Redeeming the time, because the days are evil. [b]

a Co. 4. 5.

b Ps. 37. 19.

are "asleep," and are "dead;" and with the more earnestness, therefore, should they be entreated to awake, and to rise from the dead, that Christ may give them light.

15. *See then that ye walk circumspectly.* Carefully, anxiously, solicitous lest you fall into sin. The word rendered 'circumspectly'—ἀκριβῶς—means *diligently*, and the idea here is, that they were to take special pains to guard against the temptations around them, and to live as they ought to. ¶ *Not as fools, but as wise.* Not as the people of this world live, indulging in foolish pleasures and desires, but as those who have been taught to understand heavenly wisdom, and who have been made truly wise.

16. *Redeeming the time.* The word here rendered *redeeming*, means *to purchase; to buy up* from the possession or power of any one; and then to redeem, to set free—as from service or bondage. Notes, Gal. iii. 13. Here it means, to rescue or recover our time from waste; to improve it for great and important purposes. ¶ *Because the days are evil.* Because the times in which you live are evil. There are many allurements and temptations that would lead you away from the proper improvement of time, and that would draw you into sin. Such were those that would tempt them to go to places of sinful indulgence and revelry, where their time would be wasted, and worse than wasted. As these temptations abounded, they ought therefore to be more especially on their guard against a sinful and unprofitable waste of time. This exhortation may be addressed to all, and is applicable to all periods. The sentiment is, that we ought to be solicitous to improve our time to some useful purpose, because *there are, in an evil world, so many temptations to waste it.* Time is given us for most valuable purposes. There are things enough to be done to occupy it all, and no one need have it hang heavy on his hands. He that has a soul to be saved from eternal death, need not have one idle moment. He that has a heaven to win, has enough to do to occupy all his time. Man has just enough given him to accomplish all the purposes which God designs, and God has not given him more than enough. They redeem their time who employ it (1.) in gaining useful knowledge; (2.) in doing good to others; (3.) in employing it for the purpose of an honest livelihood for themselves and families; (4.) in prayer and self-examination to make the heart better; (5.) in seeking salvation, and in endeavouring to do the will of God. They are to redeem time from all that would waste and destroy it—like recovering marshes and fens to make them rich meadows and vineyards. There is *time* enough wasted by each sinner to secure the salvation of the soul; time enough wasted to do all that is needful to be done to spread religion around the world, and to save the race. We should still endeavour to redeem our time for the same reasons which are suggested by the apostle—because the days are evil. There are evil influences abroad; allurements and vices that would waste time, and from which we should endeavour to rescue it. There are evil influences tending to waste time (1.) in the allurements to pleasure and amusement in every place, and especially in cities; (2.) in the temptations to novel-reading, con-

17 Wherefore be ye not unwise, but understanding what [a] the will of the Lord *is*.

a Jno. 7. 17.

18 And be not drunk [b] with wine, wherein is excess; but be filled with the Spirit;

b Lu. 21. 34.

suming the precious hours of probation to no valuable purpose; (3.) in the temptations of ambition, *most* of the time spent for which is wholly thrown away, for few gain the prize, and when gained, it is all a bauble, not worth the effort; (4.) in dissipation—for who can estimate the amount of valuable time that is worse than thrown away in the places of revelry and dissipation; (5.) in wild and visionary plans—temptations to which abound in all lands, and pre-eminently in our own; (6.) and in luxurious indulgence—in dressing, and eating, and drinking.

17. *Be ye not unwise.* Be not fools in the employment of your time, and in your manner of life. Show true wisdom by endeavouring to understand what the will of the Lord is, and then doing it.

18. *And be not drunk with wine.* A danger to which they were exposed, and a vice to which those around them were much addicted. Comp. Notes on Luke xxi. 34. It is not improbable that in this verse there is an allusion to the orgies of Bacchus, or to the festivals celebrated in honour of that heathen god. He was 'the god of wine,' and during those festivals, men and women regarded it as an acceptable act of worship to become intoxicated, and with wild songs and cries to run through streets, and fields, and vineyards. To these things the apostle opposes psalms, and hymns, and spiritual songs, as much more appropriate modes of devotion, and would have the Christian worship stand out in strong contrast with the wild and dissolute habits of the heathen. Plato says, that while those abominable ceremonies in the worship of Bacchus continued, it was difficult to find in all Attica a single sober man. *Rosenmüller*, Alt. u. neu. Morgenland, *in loc.* On the subject of *wine*, and the wines used by the ancients, see Notes on John ii. 10, 11. We may learn from this verse (1.) that it was not uncommon in those times to become intoxicated on wine; and (2.) that it was positively forbidden. *All* intoxication is prohibited in the Scriptures—no matter by what means it is produced. There is, *in fact*, but one thing that produces intoxication. It is *alcohol*—the poisonous substance produced by fermentation. This substance is neither created nor changed, increased nor diminished, by distillation. It exists in the cider, the beer, and the wine, after they are fermented, and the whole process of distillation consists in driving it off by heat, and collecting it in a concentrated form, and so that it may be preserved. But distilling does not *make* it, nor change it. Alcohol is precisely the same thing in the wine that it is in the brandy after it is distilled; in the cider or the beer that it is in the whisky or the rum; and why is it right to become intoxicated on it in one form rather than in another? Since therefore there is danger of intoxication in the use of wine, as well as in the use of ardent spirits, why should we not abstain from one as well as the other? How can a man prove that it is *right* for him to drink alcohol in the form of wine, and that it is *wrong* for me to drink it in the form of brandy or rum? ¶ *Wherein is excess.* There has been much difference of opinion about the word here rendered *excess*—ἀσωτία. It occurs only in two other places in the New Testament, where it is

19 Speaking to yourselves in [a] psalms and hymns, and spiritual

a Co. 3. 16.

rendered *riot*. Tit. i. 6. 1 Pet. iv. 4. The *adjective* occurs once (Luke xv. 13), where it is rendered *riotous*. The word (derived, according to *Passow*, from α, and σώζω—*to save, deliver*) means that which is unsafe, not to be recovered; lost beyond recovery; then that which is abandoned to sensuality and lust; dissoluteness, debauchery, revelry. The meaning here is, that all this follows the use of wine. Is it proper then for Christians to be in the habit of drinking it? "Wine is so frequently the cause of this, by the ungrateful abuse of the bounty of Providence in giving it, that the enormity is represented by a very strong and beautiful *figure*, as contained in the *very liquor*." *Doddridge*. ¶ *But be filled with the Spirit*. The Holy Spirit. How much more appropriate to Christians than to be filled with the spirit of intoxication and revelry! Let Christians, when about to indulge in a glass of wine, think of this admonition. Let them remember that their bodies should be the temple of the Holy Ghost, rather than a receptacle for intoxicating drinks. Was any man ever made a better Christian by the use of wine? Was any minister ever better fitted to counsel an anxious sinner, or to pray, or to preach the gospel, by the use of intoxicating drinks? Let the history of wine-drinking and intemperate clergymen answer.

19. *Speaking to yourselves*. Speaking among yourselves, that is, endeavouring to edify one another, and to promote purity of heart by songs of praise. This has the force of a command, and it is a matter of obligation on Christians. From the beginning, praise was an important part of public worship, and is designed to be to the end of the world. See Notes on 1 Cor. xiv. 15. Nothing is more clear than that it was practised by the Saviour himself and the apostles (see Matt. xxvi. 30), and by the primitive church, as well as by the great body of Christians in all ages. ¶ *In psalms*. The Psalms of David were sung by the Jews at the temple, and by the early Christians (Notes Matt. xxvi. 30), and the singing of those Psalms has constituted a delightful part of public worship in all ages. They speak the language of devotion at all times, and a large part of them are as well fitted to the services of the sanctuary now as they were when first composed. ¶ *And hymns*. It is not easy to determine precisely what is the difference in the meaning of the words here used, or to designate the kind of compositions which were used in the early churches. A *hymn* is properly a song or ode in honour of God. Among the heathen it was a song in honour of some deity. With us now it denotes a short poem, composed for religious service, and sung in praise to God. Such brief poems were common among the heathen, and it was natural that Christians should early introduce and adopt them. Whether any of them were composed by the apostles it is impossible now to determine, though the presumption is very strong that if they had been they would have been preserved with as much care as their epistles, or as the Psalms. One thing is proved clearly by this passage, that there were other compositions used in the praise of God than the Psalms of David; and if it was right then to make use of such compositions, it is now. They were not merely "Psalms" that were sung, but there were *hymns* and *odes*. ¶ *Spiritual songs*. Spiritual *odes* —ᾠδαῖς. Odes or songs relating to spiritual things in contradistinction

songs, singing [a] and making melody in your [b] heart to the Lord;

a Ps. 147. 7. b Ps. 57. 7, 8.

from those which were sung in places of festivity and revelry. An *ode* is properly a short poem or song adapted to be set to music, or to be sung; a lyric poem. In what way these were sung, it is now vain to conjecture. Whether with or without instrumental accompaniments; whether by a choir or by the assembly; whether by an individual only, or whether they were by responses, it is not possible to decide from anything in the New Testament. It is probable that it would be done in the most simple manner possible. Yet as music constituted so important a part of the worship of the temple, it is evident that the early Christians would be by no means indifferent to the nature of the music which they had in their churches. And as it was so important a part of the worship of the heathen gods, and contributed so much to maintain the influence of heathenism, it is not unlikely that the early Christians would feel the importance of making *their* music attractive, and of making it tributary to the support of religion. If there is attractive music at the banquet, and in the theatre, contributing to the maintenance of amusements where God is forgotten, assuredly the music of the sanctuary should not be such as to disgust those of pure and refined taste. ¶ *Singing.* ᾄδοντες. The prevailing character of music in the worship of God should be *vocal.* If instruments are employed, they should be so subordinate that the service may be characterized as *singing.* ¶ *And making melody. Melody* is an agreeable succession of sounds; a succession so regulated and modulated as to please the ear. It differs from *harmony*, inasmuch as melody is an agreeable succession of sounds by a single voice; harmony consists in the accordance of different sounds. It is not certain, however, that the apostle here had reference to what is properly called *melody.* The word which he uses — ψάλλω — means to touch, twitch, pluck — as the hair, the beard; and then to twitch a string — to *twang* it—as the string of a bow, and then the string of an instrument of music. It is most frequently used in the sense of touching or playing a lyre, or a harp; and then it denotes to make music in general, to sing — perhaps usually with the idea of being accompanied with a lyre or harp. It is used, in the New Testament, only in Rom. v. 19. 1 Cor. xiv. 15, where it is translated *sing;* in James v. 13, where it is rendered *sing psalms*, and in the place before us. The idea here is, that of singing in the heart, or praising God from the heart. The psalms, and hymns, and songs were to be sung so that the heart should be engaged, and not so as to be *mere music*, or a mere external performance. On the phrase 'in the heart,' see Notes on 1 Cor. xiv. 15. ¶ *To the Lord.* In praise of the Lord, or addressed to him. Singing, as here meant, is a direct and solemn act of worship, and should be considered such as really as prayer. In singing we should regard ourselves as speaking directly to God, and the words, therefore, should be spoken with a solemnity and awe becoming such a direct address to the great Jehovah. So Pliny says of the early Christians, *Carmenque Christo quasi Deo dicere secum invicem* — 'and they sang among themselves hymns to Christ as God.' If this be the true nature and design of public psalmody, then it follows (1.) that all should regard it as an act of solemn worship in which they should engage—in *heart* at least, if

20 Giving thanks [a] always for all things unto God and the Father

a Is. 63. 7

they cannot themselves sing. (2.) Public psalmody should not be intrusted wholly to the light and gay; to the trifling and careless part of a congregation. (3.) They who conduct this part of public worship ought to be pious. The leader *ought* to be a Christian; and they who join in it *ought* also to give their hearts to the Redeemer. Perhaps it would not be proper to say absolutely that no one who is not a professor of religion should take part in the exercises of a choir in a church; but there can be no error in saying that such persons *ought* to give themselves to Christ, and to sing from the heart. Their voices would be none the less sweet; their music no less pure and beautiful; nor could their own pleasure in the service be lessened. A choir of sweet singers in a church—united in the same praises here—*ought* to be prepared to join in the same praises around the throne of God.

20. *Giving thanks always.* This is probably designed to be connected with the preceding verse, and to denote that the proper subject of psalms and hymns is thanksgiving and praise. This is indeed always the main design, and should be so regarded; and this part of worship should be so conducted as to keep up in the heart a lively sense of the mercy and goodness of God. ¶ *For all things.* ὑπὲρ πάντων—for all *things*, or all *persons*. Dr. Barrow supposes that the meaning here is, that they were to give thanks for *all persons*, and to regard themselves as under obligations to give thanks for the mercies bestowed upon *the human race*, in accordance with the idea expressed in the Liturgy of the Episcopal church, "We, thine unworthy servants, do give thee most humble and hearty thanks for thy goodness and loving-kindness to us, and to all men." This idea is beautiful; and it accords with the requirements of the Scriptures elsewhere. 1 Tim. ii. 1. "I exhort, therefore, that first of all, supplications, prayers, intercessions, and *giving of thanks*, be made for all men." Such is the duty of Christians; and I see no departure from the fair meaning of the words here, in supposing that the apostle may have designed to express such an idea. The sense, according to this, would be, that we are to praise God for his general mercy to mankind; for all the happiness which mortals are permitted to enjoy; for the love of God to mankind in creation, in providence, and in redemption—just as a grateful child will give thanks for all the kindness shown to his brothers and sisters. One obvious effect of this would be to overcome *selfishness*, and to make us rejoice in the happiness of others as well as in our own. Another effect would be to make us feel a deeper interest in the condition of our fellow creatures. Another would be to elevate and enlarge our conceptions of the goodness of God—directing the mind to all the favours which he has bestowed on the race. Man has much for which to be grateful; and the duty of acknowledging the mercy of God to the race should not be forgotten. We are often prone so to magnify our calamities, and to contemplate the woes of the race, that we overlook the occasions for gratitude; and we should, therefore, look upon the *mercies* which we enjoy as well as the miseries which we endure, that our hearts may be right. He who looks only on his trials will soon find his mind soured and complaining; he who endeavours to find how many occasions for gratitude he has will soon

in the name of our Lord Jesus Christ;

21 Submitting yourselves one to another in the fear of God.

22 Wives, [a] submit yourselves unto your own husbands, as unto the Lord.

a 1 Pe. 3. 1, &c. Col. 3. 18, &c.

---

find the burden of his sorrows alleviated, and his mind tranquil and calm. Yet, if the words here are to be taken as in our translation, "for all things," they are full of force and beauty. At the close of life, and in heaven, we shall see occasion to bless God for *all* his dealings with us. We shall see that we have not suffered one pang too much, or been required to perform one duty too severe. We shall see that all our afflictions, as well as our mercies, were designed for our good, and were needful for us. Why then should we not bless God in the furnace as well as in the palace; on a bed of pain as well as on a bed of down; in want as well as when sitting down at the splendid banquet? God knows what is best for us; and the way in which he leads us, mysterious though it seem to be now, will yet be seen to have been full of goodness and mercy. ¶ *Unto God and the Father.* Or, 'to God, even the Father.' It cannot mean to God as distinguished from the Father, or first to God and then to the Father, as if the Father were distinct from God. The meaning is, that thanks are to be given specially to God the Father—the great Author of all mercies, and the source of all blessings. ¶ *In the name of our Lord Jesus Christ.* That is, through his mediation, or trusting in him. See Notes on John xiv. 13. The meaning is, that we are *always* to approach God through the mediation of the Lord Jesus. When we ask for mercy, it is to be on his account, or through his merits; when we plead for strength and grace to support us in trial, it is to be in dependence on him; and when we give thanks, it is to be through him, and because it is through his intervention that we receive all blessings, and by his merits that even the gratitude of beings so sinful as we are can be accepted.

21. *Submitting yourselves one to another.* Maintaining due subordination in the various relations of life. This general principle of religion, the apostle proceeds now to illustrate in reference to wives (vs. 22—24); to children (ch. vi. 1—3); and to servants, ch. vi. 5—8. At the same time that he enforces this duty of submission, however, he enjoins on others to use their authority in a proper manner, and gives solemn injunctions that there should be no abuse of power. Particularly he enjoins on husbands the duty of loving their wives with all tenderness (vs. 25—33); on fathers, the duty of treating their children so that they might easily obey them (ch. vi. 4); and on masters, the duty of treating their servants with kindness, remembering that they have a Master also in heaven. Ch. vi. 9. The general meaning here is, that Christianity does not break up the relations of life, and produce disorder, lawlessness, and insubordination; but that it will confirm every proper authority, and make every just yoke lighter. Infidelity is always disorganizing; Christianity, never.

22. *Wives, submit yourselves unto your own husbands.* On this passage, comp. Notes on 1 Cor. xi. 3—9. The *duty* of the submission of the wife to her husband is everywhere enjoined in the Scriptures. See 1 Pet. iii. 1. Col. iii. 18. Titus ii. 5. While Christianity designed

to elevate the character of the wife, and to make her a fit companion of an intelligent and pious husband, it did not intend to destroy all subordination and authority. Man, by the fact that he was first created; that the woman was taken from him; that he is better qualified for ruling than she is, is evidently designed to be at the head of the little community that constitutes a family. In many other things, woman may be his equal; in loveliness, and grace, and beauty, and tenderness, and gentleness, she is far his superior; but these are not the qualities adapted for government. Their place is in another sphere; and *there*, man should be as cautious about invading her prerogative, or abridging her liberty, as *she* should be about invading the prerogative that belongs to him. In every family there should be a head —some one who is to be looked up to as the counsellor and the ruler; some one to whom all should be subordinate. God has given that prerogative to man; and no family prospers where that arrangement is violated. Within proper metes and limits, therefore, it is the duty of the wife to obey, or to submit herself to her husband. Those limits are such as the following: 1. In domestic arrangements, the husband is to be regarded as the head of the family; and he has a right to direct as to the style of living, the expenses of the family, the clothing, &c. 2. In regard to the laws which are to regulate the family, he is the head. It is his to say what is to be done; in what way the children are to employ themselves, and to give directions in regard to their education, &c. 3. In business matters, the wife is to submit to the husband. She may counsel with him, if he chooses; but the affairs of business and property are under his control, and must be left at his disposal. 4. In everything, except that which relates to *conscience* and *religion*, he has authority. But there his authority ceases. He has no right to require her to commit an act of dishonesty, to connive at wrong-doing, to visit a place of amusement which her conscience tells her is wrong, nor has he a right to interfere with the proper discharge of her religious duties. He has no right to forbid her to go to church at the proper and usual time, or to make a profession of religion when she pleases. He has no right to forbid her endeavouring to exercise a religious influence over her children, or to endeavour to lead them to God. She is bound to obey God, rather than *any* man (see Notes on Acts iv. 19); and when even a husband interferes in such cases, and attempts to control her, he steps beyond his proper bounds, and invades the prerogative of God and his authority ceases to be binding. It ought to be said, however that in order to justify her acting independently in such a case, the following things are proper: (1.) It should be *really* a case of conscience —a case where the Lord has plainly required her to do what she proposes to do—and not a mere matter of whim, fancy, or caprice. (2.) When a husband makes opposition to the course which a wife wishes to pursue in religious duties, it should lead her to re-examine the matter, to pray much over it, and to see whether she cannot, with a good conscience, comply with his wishes. (3.) If she is convinced that she is right, she should still endeavour to see whether it is not *possible* to win him to her views, and to persuade him to accord with her. See 1 Pet. iii. 1. It is *possible* that, if she does right, he may be *persuaded* to do right also. (4.) If she is constrained, however, to differ from him, it should be with mildness and gentleness. There should be no reproach, and no contention. She should simply state

23 For the husband is the head of the wife, even as Christ is the head of the church: and he is the Saviour of the body.

24 Therefore as the church is subject unto Christ, so *let* the wives *be* to their own husbands in every thing.

25 Husbands, love your wives, even as Christ also loved the church, and gave himself for it;

---

her reasons, and leave the event to God. (5.) She should, *after* this, be a better wife, and put forth more and more effort to make her husband and family happy. She should show that the effect of her religion has been to make her love her husband and children more; to make her more and more attentive to her domestic duties, and more and more kind in affliction. By a *life* of pure religion, she should aim to secure what she could not by her entreaties—his consent that she should live as she thinks she ought to, and walk to heaven in the path in which she believes that her Lord calls her. While, however, it is to be conceded that the husband has *authority* over the wife, and a *right* to command in all cases that do not pertain to the conscience, it should be remarked, (1.) That *his* command should be reasonable and proper. (2.) He has no right to require anything wrong, or contrary to the will of God. (3.) WHERE COMMANDS BEGIN *in this relation*, HAPPINESS USUALLY ENDS; and the moment a husband *requires* a wife to do anything, it is usually a signal of departing or departed affection and peace. When there are proper feelings in both parties in this relation, there will be no occasion either to command or to obey. There should be such mutual love and confidence, that the known *wish* of the husband should be a law to the wife; and that the known desires of the wife should be the rule which he would approve. A perfect government is that where the known wish of the lawgiver is a sufficient rule to the subject. Such is the government of heaven; and a family on earth should approximate as nearly as possible to that. ¶ *As unto the Lord.* As you would to the Lord, because the Lord requires it, and has given to the husband this authority.

23. *For the husband is the head of the wife.* See Notes on 1 Cor. xi. 3. ¶ *As Christ is the head of the church.* As Christ rules over the church, and has a right to direct and control it. ¶ *And he is the Saviour of the body.* That is, of the church, represented as *his body.* See Notes, ch. i. 23. The idea here seems to be, that as Christ gave himself to save his body, the church; as he practised self-denial, and made it an object of intense solicitude to preserve that church, so ought the husband to manifest a similar solicitude to make his wife happy, and to save her from want, affliction, and pain. He ought to regard himself as her natural protector; as bound to anticipate and provide for her wants; as under obligation to comfort her in trial, even as Christ does the church. What a beautiful illustration of the spirit which a husband should manifest is the care which Christ has shown for his "bride," the church! See Notes on vs. 25—29.

24. *In every thing.* In every thing which is not contrary to the will of God. See Notes on ver. 23.

25. *Husbands, love your wives.* The duty of the wife is to obey; the right of the husband is to command. But the apostle would guard against the abuse of that right by enjoining the manifestation of such a spirit on the husband as would secure obedi-

26 That he might sanctify and cleanse it with the washing [a] of water by the word:

a Ti. 3. 5.

ence on the part of the wife. He proceeds, therefore, to show, that the husband, in all his intercourse with the wife, should manifest the same spirit which the Lord Jesus did towards the church; or, in other words, he holds up the conduct of the Redeemer towards the church, as the model for a husband to imitate. If a husband wished a rule that would be short, simple, clear, and efficacious, about the manner in which he should regard and treat his wife, he could not find a better one than that here suggested. ¶ *Even as Christ loved the church.* This was the strongest love that has ever been evinced in this world. It follows, that a husband is in no danger of loving his wife too much, provided she be not loved more than God. We are to make the love which Christ had for the church the model. ¶ *And gave himself for it.* Gave himself to die to redeem it. The meaning here is, that husbands are to imitate the Redeemer in this respect. As he gave himself to suffer on the cross to save the church, so we are to be willing to deny ourselves, and to bear toil and trial, that we may promote the happiness of the wife. It is the duty of the husband to toil for her support; to provide for her wants; to deny himself of rest and ease, if necessary, in order to attend on her in sickness; to go before her in danger; to defend her if she is in peril; and to be ready to die to save her. Why should he not be? If they are shipwrecked, and there is a single plank on which safety can be secured, should he not be willing to place her on that, and see *her* safe at all hazards to himself? But there may be more implied in this than that a man s to toil, and even to lay down his life for the welfare of his wife. Christ laid down his life to *save* the church; and a husband should feel that it should be one great object of his life to promote the salvation of his wife. He is bound so to live as not to interfere with her salvation, but so as to promote it in every way possible. He is to furnish her all the *facilities* that she may need, to enable her to attend on the worship of God; and to throw no obstacles in her way. He is to set her the example; to counsel her if she needs counsel, and to make the path of salvation as easy for her as possible. If a husband has the spirit and self-denial of the Saviour, he will regard no sacrifice too great if he may promote the salvation of his family.

26. *That he might sanctify.* The great object of the Redeemer was to purify and save the church. The meaning here is, that a husband is to manifest similar love towards his wife, and a similar desire that she should be prepared to 'walk before him in white.' ¶ *And cleanse it with the washing of water.* In all this there is an allusion doubtless to the various methods of purifying and cleansing those who were about to be married, and who were to be united to monarchs as their brides. In some instances this previous preparation continued for twelve months. The means of purification were various, but consisted usually in the use of costly unguents. See Esther ii. 12. "Six months with oil of myrrh, and six months with sweet odours, and with other things for the purifying of women." Comp. Ps. xlv. 13, 14. Ezek. xvi. 7—14. As such a virgin was purified and prepared for her husband by washing and by anointing, so the church is to be prepared for Christ. It is to be

27 That he might present [a] it to himself a glorious church, not having spot, [b] or wrinkle, or any such thing; but that it should be holy and without blemish.

28 So ought men to love their wives as their own bodies; he

a Jude 24. b Ca. 4. 7.

made pure and holy. Outwardly there is to be the application of water—the symbol of purity; and within there is to be holiness of heart. See Notes on 2 Cor. xi. 2, where Paul says of the Corinthians, "I have espoused you to one husband, that I may present you as a chaste virgin to Christ." ¶ *By the word.* There has been much diversity of opinion respecting the meaning of this. Probably the sense of the expression is, that all this was to be accomplished by the instrumentality of the truth—the word of God. By that truth they were to be sanctified (John xvii. 17); and in accordance with that the whole work from the commencement to the close was to be accomplished. It was not by external ceremonies, and not by any miraculous power on the heart, but by the faithful application of truth to the heart.

27. *That he may present it to himself.* In the last day, when he shall receive the church as his spouse to heaven. Rev. xxi. 9. Perhaps the word *prepare* would better express the sense here than *present*—that he may prepare it for himself as a holy church. Tindal renders it, 'to make it unto himself.' ¶ *A glorious church.* A church full of honour, splendour, beauty. The idea of *shining*, or of being *bright*, would convey the sense here. Probably there is still here an allusion to a bride 'adorned for her husband' (Rev. xxi. 2; comp. Ps. xlv. 9—14); and the idea is, that the church will be worthy of the love of the bridegroom, to whom it will then be presented. ¶ *Not having spot.* Not having a stain, a defect, or any impurity—still retaining the allusion to a bride, and to the care taken to remove every blemish. ¶ *Or wrinkle.* In the vigour and beauty of youth; like a bride in whom there is no wrinkle of age. ¶ *Or any such thing.* Nothing to deform, disfigure, or offend. To this beautiful illustration of the final glory of the church, the apostle was led by the mention of the relation of the husband and the wife. It shows, (1.) The tendency of the thoughts of Paul. He delighted to allow the associations in his mind, no matter what the subject was, to draw him along to the Redeemer. (2.) The passage here shows us what the church will yet be. There will be a period in its history when there shall not be any imperfection; when there shall be neither spot, nor wrinkle, nor any such thing. In heaven all will be pure. On earth we are preparing for that world of purity; and it cannot be denied that here there is much that is imperfect and impure. But in that future world, where the church shall be presented to Christ, clothed in the robes of salvation, there shall not be one unholy member; one deceiver or hypocrite; one covetous or avaricious man; one that shall pain the hearts of the friends of purity by an unholy life. And in all the millions that shall be gathered there out of every land, and people, and tongue, and age, there shall be no envy, malice, backbiting, pride, vanity, worldliness; there shall be no annoying and vexing conflict in the heart with evil passions, '*nor any such thing.*' How different from the church as it now is; and how we should pant for that blessed world!

28. *So ought men to love their wives, as their own bodies.* Because

that loveth his wife loveth himself.

29 For no man ever yet hated his own flesh; but nourisheth and cherisheth it; even as the Lord the church:

30 For we are members [a] of

[a] 1 Co. 12. 27.

they are one flesh. Ver. 31. This is the subject on which Paul had been speaking, and from which he had been diverted by the allusion to the glorified church. The doctrine here is, that a husband should have the same care for the comfort of his wife which he has for himself. He should regard her as one with himself; and as he protects his own body from cold and hunger, and, when sick and suffering, endeavours to restore it to health, so he should regard and treat her. ¶ *He that loveth his wife, loveth himself.* (1.) Because she is one with him, and their interests are identified. (2.) Because, by this, he really promotes his own welfare, as much as he does when he takes care of his own body. A man's kindness to his wife will be more than repaid by the happiness which she imparts; and all the real solicitude which he shows to make her happy, will come to more than it costs. If a man wishes to promote his own happiness in the most effectual way, he had better begin by showing kindness to his wife.

29. *For no man ever yet hated his own flesh.* This is urged as an argument why a man should love his wife and show kindness to her. As no man disregards the happiness of his own body, or himself, so he should show equal care to promote the happiness of his wife. A sentiment similar to this is found in the classic writers. Thus Curtius (lib. vii.) says, *Corporibus nostris quæ utique non odimus*—'We do not hate those things that pertain to our own bodies.' So Seneca (Epis. 14), *Fateor insitam nobis esse corporis nostri charitatem*—'I confess that there is implanted in us the love of our own body.' The word *nourisheth* here means properly to bring up, as e. g., children. The sense here is, that he provides for it, and guards it from exposure and want. The word *cherisheth*—θάλπει—means properly *to warm;* and may mean here that he defends it from cold by clothing—and the two expressions denote that he provides food and raiment for the body. So he is to do for his wife; and in like manner the Lord Jesus regards the church, and ministers to its spiritual necessities. But this should not be spiritualized too far. The *general* idea is all that we want—that Christ has a tender concern for the wants of the church, as a man has for his own body, and that the husband should show a similar regard for his wife.

30. *For we are members of his body.* Of the body of Christ. See Notes on 1 Cor. xi. 3; xii. 27. John xv. 1—6, and Eph. i. 23. The idea here is, that there is a close and intimate union between the Christian and the Saviour—a union *so* intimate that they may be spoken of as *one.* ¶ *Of his flesh, and of his bones.* There is an allusion here evidently to the language which Adam used respecting Eve. "This is now bone of my bones, and flesh of my flesh.' Gen. ii. 23. It is language which is employed to denote the closeness of the marriage relation, and which Paul applies to the connection between Christ and his people. Of course, it cannot be understood *literally.* It is not true literally that our bones are a part of the bones of Christ, or our flesh of his flesh; nor should language ever be used that would imply a miraculous union. It is not a physical union, but a union

his body, of his flesh, and of his bones.

31 For [a] this cause shall a man leave his father and mother, and shall be joined unto his wife, and they two [b] shall be one flesh.

32 This is a great mystery:

a Ge. 2. 24. b 1 Co. 6. 16.

---

of attachment; of feeling; of love. If we avoid the notion of a *physical* union, however, it is scarcely possible to use too strong language in describing the union of believers with the Lord Jesus. The Scriptures make use of language which is stronger than that employed to describe any other connection; and there is no union of affection so powerful as that which binds the Christian to the Saviour. So strong is it, that he is willing for it to forsake father, mother, and home; to leave his country, and to abandon his possessions; to go to distant lands and dwell among barbarians to make the Redeemer known; or to go to the cross or the stake from simple love to the Saviour. Account for it as men may, there has been manifested on earth nowhere else so strong an attachment as that which binds the Christian to the cross. It is stronger love than that which a man has for his own flesh and bones; for it makes him willing that his flesh should be consumed by fire, or his bones broken on the wheel rather than deny him. Can the infidel account for this strength of attachment on any other principle than that it has a divine origin?

31. *For this cause.* Ἀντὶ τούτου. This verse is a quotation from Gen. ii. 24, and contains the account of the institution of marriage. The meaning of the phrase rendered 'for this cause' is, 'answerably to this;' or corresponding to this—that is, to what Paul had just said of the union of believers and the Redeemer. On the meaning of this verse, see Notes on Matt. xix. 4. There is no evidence that the marriage connection was originally designed to symbolize or typify this union, but it may be used to illustrate that connection, and to show the strength of the attachment between the Redeemer and his people. The comparison should be confined, however, strictly to the use made of it in the New Testament.

32. *This is a great mystery.* The Latin Vulgate translates this, *sacramentum hoc magnum est*—'this is a great *sacrament*'—and this is the proof, I suppose, and the only proof adduced by the Papists that marriage is *a sacrament*. But the original here conveys no such idea. The word *mystery*—μυστήριον—means something which is concealed, hidden, before unknown; something into which one must be *initiated* or instructed before he can understand it. It does not mean that it is *incomprehensible* when it is disclosed, but that hitherto it has been kept secret. When disclosed it may be as intelligible as any other truth. See the word explained in the Notes on ch. i. 9. Here it means, simply, that there was much about the union of the Redeemer with his people, resembling the marriage connection, which was not obvious, except to those who were instructed; which was obscure to those who were not initiated; which they did not understand who had not been *taught*. It does not mean that no one could understand it, but that it pertained to the class of truths into which it was necessary for one to be *initiated* in order to comprehend them. The truth that was so great a mystery was, that the eternal Son of God should form such an union with

but I speak concerning Christ and the church.

33 Nevertheless, let every one of you in particular, so love his wife even as himself; and the wife *see* that she reverence *her* husband.

---

men; that he should take them into a connection with himself, implying an ardour of attachment, and a strength of affection superior to even that which exists in the marriage relation. This was a great and profound truth, to understand which, it was necessary to receive instruction. No one would have understood it without a revelation; no one understands it now except they who are taught of God. ¶ *But I speak concerning Christ and the Church.* This, it seems to me, is an explicit disclaimer of any intention to be understood as affirming that the marriage contract was designed to be a *type* of the union of the Redeemer and his people. The apostle says expressly, that his remarks do not refer to *marriage at all* when he speaks of the mystery. They refer *solely* to the union of the Redeemer and his people. How strange and unwarranted, therefore, are all the comments of expositors on this passage designed to explain marriage as *a mysterious type* of the union of Christ and the church! If men would allow the apostle to speak for himself, and not force on him sentiments which he expressly disclaims, the world would be saved from such insipid allegories as Macknight and others have derived from this passage. The Bible is a book of sense; and the time will come, it is hoped, when, freed from all such allegorizing expositions, it will commend itself to the good sense of mankind. Marriage is an important, a holy, a noble, a pure institution, altogether worthy of God; but it does not thence follow that marriage was designed to be a type of the union between Christ and the church, and it is certain that the apostle Paul meant to teach no such thing.

33. *Nevertheless.* The apostle here resumes the subject which he had been discussing in vs. 21—29, and says that it was the duty of every man to love his wife as he did himself. This was the main topic, from which he had been diverted by the discussion respecting the love which the Redeemer had shown for his church. ¶ *And the wife* see *that she reverence* her *husband.* The word '*see*' is supplied by our translators. The meaning is, that it was the especial duty of the wife to show respect for her husband as the head of the family, and as set over her in the Lord. See Notes on vs. 22, 23. The word rendered *reverence*, is that which usually denotes *fear*—φοβῆται. She is to *fear*; i. e. to honour, respect, obey the will of her husband. It is, of course, not implied that it is not also her duty to love her husband, but that there should be no usurping of authority; no disregard of the arrangement which God has made; and that order and peace should be secured in a family by regarding the husband as the source of law.

From what is here said of the duties of husband and wife we may remark,

(1.) That the happiness of society depends on just views of the marriage relation. It is true the world over, that the views which prevail in regard to this relation, determine every thing in reference to all other relations of life, and to all other sources of enjoyment.

(2.) God designed that woman should occupy a subordinate, though an important place in the relations of social life. *This* arrangement is never disregarded without evils which cannot be corrected until the original intention is secured. No imaginary good that can come out of the violation of the original design; no benefits which females, individual or associated, can confer on mankind by disregarding this arrangement, can be a compensation for the evil that is done, nor can the evil be remedied unless woman occupies the place which God designed she should fill. *There* nothing else can supply her place; and when she is absent from that situation—no matter what good she may be doing elsewhere—there is a silent evil reigning, which can be removed only by her return. It is not hers to fight battles, or to command armies and navies, or to control kingdoms, or to make laws. Nor is it hers to go forward as a public leader even in enterprises of benevolence, or in associations designed to act on the public mind. Her empire is the domestic circle; her first influence is there; and in connection with that, in such scenes as she can engage in without trenching on the prerogative of man, or neglecting the duty which she owes to her own family.

(3.) It is not best that there should be the open exercise of authority in a family. When *commands* begin in the relation of husband and wife, *happiness* flies; and the moment a husband is *disposed to* COMMAND his wife, or is *under a necessity* of doing it, that moment he may bid adieu to domestic peace and joy.

(4.) A wife, therefore, should never give her husband *occasion* to command her to do any thing, or to forbid any thing. His known wish, except in cases of conscience, should be law to her. The moment she can ascertain what his will is, that moment ought to settle her mind as to what is to be done.

(5.) A husband should never *wish* or *expect* any thing that it may not be perfectly proper for a wife to render. He, too, should consult *her* wishes; and when he understands what they are, he should regard what she prefers as the very thing which he would command. The known wish and preference of a wife, unless there be something wrong in it, should be allowed to influence his mind, and be that which he directs in the family.

(6.) There is no danger that a husband will love a wife too much, provided his love be subordinate to the love of God. The command is, to love her as Christ loved the church. What love has ever been like that? How can a husband exceed it? What did not Christ endure to redeem the church? So should a husband be willing to deny himself to promote the happiness of his wife; to watch by her in sickness, and, if need be, to peril health and life to promote her welfare. Doing this, he will not go beyond what Christ did for the church. He should remember that she has a special claim of justice on him. For him she has left her father's home, forsaken the friends of her youth, endowed him with whatever property she may have, sunk her name in his, confided her honour, her character, and her happiness, to his virtue; and the least that he can do for her is to *love* her, and strive to make her happy. This was what she asked when she consented to become his; and a husband's love is what she still asks to sustain and cheer her in the trials of life. If she has not this, whither shall she go for comfort?

(7.) We may see, then, the guilt of those husbands who withhold their affections from their wives, and forsake those to whom they had solemnly pledged themselves at the altar; those who neglect to provide for their wants, or to minister to them in sickness; and those who become the victims of intemperance, and leave their wives to tears. There is much, much guilt of this kind on earth. There are many, many broken vows. There are many, many hearts made to bleed. There is many a pure and virtuous woman who was once the object of tender affection, now, by no fault of hers, forsaken, abused, broken-hearted, by the brutal conduct of a husband.

(8.) Wives should manifest such a character as to be worthy of love. They owe this to their husbands. They demand the confidence and affection of man; and they should show that they are worthy of that confidence and affection. It is not possible to love that which is unlovely, nor to force affection where it is undeserved; and, as a wife expects that a husband will love her more than he does any other earthly being, it is but right that she should evince such a spirit as shall make that proper. A wife may easily alienate the affections of her partner in life. If she is irritable and fault-finding; if none of his ways please her; if she takes no interest in his plans, and in what he does; if she forsakes her home when she should be there, and seeks happiness abroad; or if, at home, she never greets him with a smile; if she is wasteful of his earnings, and extravagant in her habits, it will be impossible to prevent the effects of such a course of life on his mind. And when a wife perceives the slightest evidence of alienated affection in her husband, she should inquire at once whether she has not given occasion for it, and exhibited such a spirit as tended inevitably to produce such a result.

(9.) To secure mutual love, therefore, it is necessary that there should be mutual kindness, and mutual *loveliness* of character. Whatever is seen to be offensive or painful, should be at once abandoned. All the little peculiarities of temper and modes of speech that are observed to give pain, should be forsaken; and, while one party should endeavour to tolerate them, and *not* to be offended, the other should make it a matter of conscience to remove them.

(10.) The great secret of conjugal happiness is in the cultivation of a proper temper. It is not so much in the great and trying scenes of life that the strength of virtue is tested; it is in the events that are constantly occurring; the manifestation of kindness in the things that are happening every moment; the gentleness that flows along every day, like the stream that winds through the meadow and around the farm-house, noiseless but useful, diffusing fertility by day and by night. Great deeds rarely occur. The happiness of life depends little on them, but mainly on the little acts of kindness in life. We need them everywhere; we need them always. And eminently in the marriage relation there is need of gentleness and love, returning each morning, beaming in the eye, and dwelling in the heart through the livelong day.

CHAPTER VI.

ANALYSIS OF THE CHAPTER.

This chapter comprises the following subjects: (1.) An exhortation to children to obey their parents, with a promise of the blessing that would follow from obedience. Vs. 1—3. (2.) An exhortation to fathers to manifest such a character that children could properly obey them, and to train them up in a proper manner. Ver. 4. (3.) The duty of servants. Vs. 5—8. (4.) The duty of masters towards their servants. Ver. 9. (5.) An exhortation to put on the whole armour of God, with a description of the christian soldier, and of the christian

CHAPTER VI.

CHILDREN, [a] obey your parents in the Lord: for this is right.

a Pr. 23. 22. Co. 3. 20, &c.

panoply. Vs. 10—17. (6.) The duty of prayer, and especially of prayer for the apostle himself, that he might be enabled to speak with boldness in the cause of his Master. Vs. 18—20. (7.) In the conclusion (vs. 21—24), he informs them that if they wished to make any inquiries about his condition, Tychicus, who conveyed this letter, could acquaint them with his circumstances; and then closes the epistle with the usual benedictions.

1. *Children.* τέκνα. This word usually signifies those who are young; but it is here used, evidently, to denote those who were under the care and government of their parents, or those who were not of age. ¶ *Obey your parents.* This is the first great duty which God has enjoined on children. It is, to do what their parents command them to do. The God of nature indicates that this is duty; for he has impressed it on the minds of all in every age; and the Author of revelation confirms it. It is particularly important, (1.) Because the good order of a family, and hence of the community, depends on it; no community or family being prosperous where there is not due subordination in the household. (2.) Because the welfare of the child depends on it; it being of the highest importance that a child should be early taught obedience to *law*, as no one can be prosperous or happy who is not thus obedient. (3.) Because the child is not competent, as yet, to *reason* on what is right, or qualified to direct himself; and, while that is the case, he must be subject to the *will* of some other person. (4.) Because the parent, by his age and experience, is to be presumed to be qualified to direct and guide a child. The love which God has implanted in the heart of a parent for a child secures, in general, the administration of this domestic government in such a way as not to injure the child. A father will not, unless under strong passion or the excitement of intoxication, abuse his authority. He loves the child too much. He desires his welfare; and the placing of the child under the authority of the parent is about the same thing in regard to the welfare of the child, as it would be to endow the child at once with all the wisdom and experience of the parent himself. (5.) It is important, because the family government is designed to be an imitation of the government of God. The government of God is what a perfect family government would be; and to accustom a child to be obedient to a parent, is designed to be one method of leading him to be obedient to God. No child that is disobedient to a parent will be obedient to God; and that child that is most obedient to a father and mother will be most likely to become a Christian, and an heir of heaven. And it may be observed, in general, that no disobedient child is virtuous, prosperous, or happy. Every one foresees the ruin of such a child; and most of the cases of crime that lead to the penitentiary, or the gallows, commence by disobedience to parents. ¶ *In the Lord.* That is, as far as their commandments agree with those of God, and no farther. No parent can have a right to require a child to steal, or lie, or cheat, or assist him in committing murder, or in doing any other wrong thing. No parent has a right to forbid a child to pray, to read the Bible, to

2 Honour[a] thy father and mother, (which is the first commandment with promise,)

3 That it may be well with thee, and thou mayest live long on the earth.

a Ex. 20. 12.

worship God, or to make a profession of religion. The duties and rights of children in such cases are similar to those of wives (see Notes on ch. v. 22); and, in all cases, God is to be obeyed rather than man. When a parent, however, is opposed to a child; when he expresses an unwillingness that a child should attend a particular church, or make a profession of religion, such opposition should in all cases be a sufficient reason for the child to pause and re-examine the subject. He should pray much, and think much, and inquire much, before, in any case, he acts contrary to the will of a father or mother; and, when he *does* do it, he should state to them, with great gentleness and kindness, that he believes he *ought* to love and serve God. ¶ *For this is right.* It is right, (1.) because it is so appointed by God as a duty; (2.) because children owe a debt of gratitude to their parents for what they have done for them; (3.) because it will be for the good of the children themselves, and for the welfare of society.

2. *Honour thy father and mother.* See Ex. xx. 12. Comp. Notes on Matt. xv. 4. ¶ *Which is the first commandment with promise.* With a promise annexed to it. The promise was, that their days should be long in the land which the Lord their God would give them. It is not to be supposed that the observance of the four first commandments would not be attended with a blessing, but no particular blessing is promised. It is true, indeed, that there is a *general declaration* annexed to the second commandment, that God would show mercy to thousands of generations of them that loved him and that kept his commandments. But that is rather a declaration in regard to *all* the commands of God than a promise annexed to that specific commandment. It is an assurance that obedience to the law of God would be followed with blessings to a thousand generations, and is given in view of the first and second commandments together, because they related particularly to the honour that was due to God. But the promise in the fifth commandment is a *special* promise. It does not relate to obedience to God in general, but it is a particular assurance that they who honour their parents shall have a particular blessing as the result of that obedience.

3. *That it may be well with thee* This is found in the fifth commandment as recorded in Deut. v. 16. The whole commandment as there recorded is, "Honour thy father and thy mother, as the Lord thy God hath commanded thee; that thy days may be prolonged, and that it may go well with thee in the land which the Lord thy God giveth thee." The meaning here is, that they would be more happy, useful, and virtuous if they obeyed their parents than if they disobeyed them. ¶ *And thou mayest live long on the earth.* In the commandment as recorded in Ex. xx. 12, the promise is, 'that thy days may be long upon the land which the Lord thy God giveth thee.' This referred to the promised land—the land of Canaan. The meaning doubtless, is, that there would be a special providence, securing to those who were obedient to parents length of days. Long life was regarded as a great blessing; and this blessing was promised. The apostle here gives to the promise a more general form, and says that obedi-

4 And ye fathers, provoke not your children to wrath: but bring them up in the nurture and admonition of the Lord.

---

ence to parents was connected at all times with long life. We may remark here (1.) that long life *is* a blessing. It affords a longer space to prepare for eternity; it enables a man to be more useful; and it furnishes a longer opportunity to study the works of God on earth. It is not improper to desire it; and we should make use of all the means in our power to lengthen out our days, and to preserve and protract our lives. (2.) It is still true that obedience to parents is conducive to length of life, and that those who are most obedient in early life, other things being equal, have the best prospect of living long. This occurs because (*a*) obedient children are saved from the vices and crimes which shorten life. No parent will command his child to be a drunkard, a gambler, a spendthrift, a pirate, or a murderer. But these vices and crimes, resulting in most cases from disobedience to parents, all shorten life; and they who early commit them are certain of an early grave. No child who disobeys a parent can have any *security* that he will not fall a victim to such vices and crimes. (*b*) Obedience to parents is connected with virtuous habits that are conducive to long life. It will make a child industrious, temperate, sober; it will lead him to restrain and govern his wild passions; it will lead him to form habits of self-government which will in future life save him from the snares of vice and temptation. (*c*) Many a life is lost early by disobeying a parent. A child disobeys a father and goes into a dram-shop; or he goes to sea; or he becomes the companion of the wicked—and he may be wrecked at sea, or his character on land may be wrecked for ever. Of disobedient children there is perhaps not one in a hundred that ever reaches an honoured old age. (*d*) We may still believe that God, in his providence, will watch over those who are obedient to a father and mother. If he regards a falling sparrow (Matt. x. 29), he will not be unmindful of an obedient child; if he numbers the hairs of the head (Matt. x. 30), he will not be regardless of the little boy that honours him by obeying a father and mother.

4. *And ye fathers.* A command addressed particularly to *fathers*, because they are at the head of the family, and its government is especially committed to them. The object of the apostle here is, to show parents that their commands should be such that they can be easily obeyed, or such as are entirely reasonable and proper. If children are required to *obey*, it is but reasonable that the commands of the parent should be such that they can be obeyed, or such that the child shall not be discouraged in his attempt to obey. This statement is in accordance with what he had said (ch. v. 22—25) of the relation of husband and wife. It was the duty of the wife to obey—but it was the corresponding duty of the husband to manifest such a character that it would be pleasant to yield obedience—so to love her, that his known *wish* would be *law* to her. In like manner it is the duty of children to obey a parent; but it is the duty of a parent to exhibit such a character, and to maintain such a government, that it would be proper for the child to obey; to command nothing that is unreasonable or improper, but to train up his children in the ways of virtue and pure religion. ¶ *Provoke not your children to wrath.* That is, by unreasonable commands; by needless severity; by the manifesta

tion of anger. So govern them, and so punish them—if punishment is necessary—that they shall not lose their confidence in you, but shall love you. The apostle here has hit on the very danger to which parents are most exposed in the government of their children. It is that of souring their temper; of making them feel that the parent is under the influence of anger, and that it is right for them to be so too. This is done (1.) when the commands of a parent are unreasonable and severe. The spirit of a child then becomes irritated, and he is "discouraged." Col. iii. 21. (2.) When a parent is evidently *excited* when he punishes a child. The child then feels (*a*) that if his *father* is angry, it is not wrong for him to be angry; and (*b*) the very fact of anger in a parent kindles anger in his bosom—just as it does when two men are contending. If he submits in the case, it is only because the parent is the *strongest*, not because he is *right*, and the child cherishes *anger*, while he yields to *power*. There is no principle of parental government more important than that a father should command his own temper when he inflicts punishment. He should punish a child not because he is *angry*, but because it is *right;* not because it has become a matter of *personal contest*, but because God requires that he should do it, and the welfare of the child demands it. The moment when a child sees that a parent punishes him under the influence of anger, that moment the child will be likely to be angry too—and his anger will be as proper as that of the parent. And yet, how often is punishment inflicted in this manner! And how often does the child feel that the parent punished him simply because he was the *strongest*, not because it was *right;* and how often is the mind of a child left with a strong conviction that wrong has been done him by the punishment which he has received, rather than with repentance for the wrong that he has himself done. ¶ *But bring them up.* Place them under such discipline and instruction that they shall become acquainted with the Lord. ¶ *In the nurture.* ἐν παιδείᾳ. The word here used means *training of a child;* hence education, instruction, discipline. Here it means that they are to train up their children in such a manner as the Lord approves; that is, they are to educate them for virtue and religion. ¶ *And admonition.* The word here used—νουθεσία—means, literally, *a putting in mind*, then warning, admonition, instruction. The sense here is, that they were to put them in mind of the Lord—of his existence, perfections, law, and claims on their hearts and lives. This command is positive, and is in accordance with all the requirements of the Bible on the subject. No one can doubt that the Bible enjoins on parents the duty of endeavouring to train up their children in the ways of religion, and of making it the grand purpose of this life to prepare them for heaven. It has been often objected that children should be left on religious subjects to form their own opinions when they are able to judge for themselves. Infidels and irreligious men always oppose or neglect the duty here enjoined; and the plea commonly is, that to teach religion to children is to make them prejudiced; to destroy their independence of mind; and to prevent their judging as impartially on so important a subject as they ought to. In reply to this, and in defence of the requirements of the Bible on the subject, we may remark, (1.) That to suffer a child to grow up without any instruction in religion, is about the same as to suffer a garden to lie without any culture. Such a gar-

5 Servants,[a] be obedient to them that are *your* masters according to the flesh, with fear and trembling, in singleness of your heart, as unto Christ.

a 1 Pe. 2. 18, &c.

den would soon be overrun with weeds, and briars, and thorns—but not sooner, or more certainly, than the mind of a child would. (2.) Men *do* instruct their children in a great many things, and why should they not in religion? They teach them how to behave in company; the art of farming; the way to make or use tools; how to make money; how to avoid the arts of the cunning seducer. But why should it not be said that all this tends to destroy their independence, and to make them prejudiced? Why not leave their minds open and free, and suffer them to form their own judgments about farming and the mechanic arts when their minds are matured? (3.) Men *do* inculcate their own sentiments in religion. An infidel is not usually *very* anxious to conceal his views from his children. Men teach by example; by incidental remarks; by the *neglect* of that which they regard as of no value. A man who does not pray, is teaching his children not to pray; he who neglects the public worship of God, is teaching his children to neglect it; he who does not read the Bible, is teaching his children not to read it. Such is the constitution of things, that it is impossible for a parent *not* to inculcate his own religious views on his children. Since this is so, all that the Bible requires is, that his instructions should be RIGHT. (4.) To inculcate the truths of religion is *not* to make the mind narrow, prejudiced, and indisposed to perceive the truth. Religion makes the mind candid, conscientious, open to conviction, ready to follow the truth. Superstition, bigotry, infidelity, and *all* error and falsehood, make the mind narrow and prejudiced. (5.) If a man does not teach his children *truth*, others will teach them *error*. The young skeptic that the child meets in the street; the artful infidel; the hater of God; the unprincipled stranger, *will* teach the child. But is it not better for a parent to teach his child the *truth* than for a stranger to teach him *error?* (6.) Religion is the most important of all subjects, and *therefore* it is of most importance that children on that subject should be taught TRUTH. Of whom can God so properly require this as of a parent? If it be asked *in what way* a parent is to bring up his children in the nurture and admonition of the Lord, I answer, 1. By directly inculcating the doctrines and duties of religion—just as he does any thing else that he regards as of value. 2. By placing them in the Sabbath-school, where he may have a guarantee that they will be taught the truth. 3. By *conducting* them—not merely *sending* them—to the sanctuary, that they may be taught in the house of God. 4. By example—all teaching being valueless without that. 5. By prayer for the divine aid in his efforts, and for the salvation of their souls. These duties are plain, simple, easy to be performed, and are such as a man *knows* he ought to perform. If neglected, and the soul of the child be lost, a parent has a most fearful account to render to God.

5. *Servants.* Οἱ δοῦλοι. The word here used denotes one who is bound to render service to another, whether that service be free or voluntary, and may denote, therefore, either a slave, or one who binds himself to render service to another. It is often used in these senses in the New Tes-

tament, just as it is elsewhere. It cannot be demonstrated that the word here necessarily means *slaves;* though, if slavery existed among those to whom this epistle was written—as there can be little doubt that it did—it is a word which would apply to those in this condition. Comp. Notes on 1 Cor. vii. 21. Gal. iii. 28. On the general subject of slavery, and the Scripture doctrine in regard to it, See Notes on Isa. lviii. 6. Whether the persons here referred to were slaves, or were those who had bound themselves to render a voluntary servitude, the directions here given were equally appropriate. It was not the design of the Christian religion to produce a rude sundering of the ties which bind man to man, but to teach all to perform their duties aright *in* the relations in which Christianity found them, and gradually to modify the customs of society, and to produce ultimately the universal prevalence of that which is right. ¶ *Be obedient to them.* This is the uniform direction in the New Testament. See 1 Pet. ii. 18. 1 Tim. vi. 1—3. Notes, 1 Cor. vii. 21. The idea is, that they were to show in that relation the excellence of the religion which they professed. If they could be made free, they were to prefer that condition to a state of bondage (1 Cor. vii. 21), but while the relation remained, they were to be kind, gentle, and obedient, as became Christians. In the parallel place in Colossians (iii. 22), it is said that they were to obey their masters "in all things." But evidently this is to be understood with the limitations implied in the case of wives and children (see Notes on ch. v. 24; vi. 1), and a master would have no right to command that which was morally wrong. ¶ *According to the flesh.* This is designed, evidently, to limit the obligation to obedience. The meaning is, that they had control over *the body, the flesh.* They had the power to command the service which the body could render; but they were not lords of the spirit. The soul acknowledged God as its Lord, and to the Lord they were to be subject in a higher sense than to their masters. ¶ *With fear and trembling.* With reverence and with a dread of offending them. They have authority and power over you, and you should be afraid to incur their displeasure. Whatever might be true about the propriety of slavery, and whatever might be the duty of the master about setting the slave free, it would be more to the honour of religion for the servant to perform his task with a willing mind, than to be contumacious and rebellious. He could do more for the honour of religion by patiently submitting to even what he felt to be wrong, than by being punished for what would be regarded as rebellion. It may be added here, that it was presumed that servants then could *read.* These directions were addressed to *them,* not to their masters. Of what use would be directions like these addressed to American slaves—scarce any of whom can read? ¶ *In singleness of your heart.* With a simple, sincere desire to do what ought to be done. ¶ *As unto Christ.* Feeling that by rendering proper service to your masters, you are in fact serving the Lord, and that you are doing that which will be well-pleasing to him. See Notes on 1 Cor. vii. 22. Fidelity, in whatever situation we may be in life, is acceptable service to the Lord. A Christian may as acceptably serve the Lord Jesus in the condition of a servant, as if he were a minister of the gospel, or a king on a throne. Besides, it will greatly lighten the burdens of such a situation, and make the toils of an humble condition easy, to remember that we are then ***serving the Lord.***

6 Not with eye-service, as men-pleasers; but as the servants of Christ, doing the will of God from the heart;

7 With good-will doing service, as to the Lord, and not to men;

---

6. *Not with eye-service.* That is, not with service rendered only under the eye of the master, or when his eye is fixed on you. The apostle has here adverted to one of the evils of involuntary servitude as it exists everywhere. It is, that the slave will usually obey only when the eye of the master is upon him. The freeman who agrees to labour for stipulated wages may be trusted when the master is out of sight; but not the slave. Hence the necessity where there are slaves of having 'drivers' who shall attend them, and who shall compel them to work. This evil it is impossible to avoid, except where true religion prevails—and the extensive prevalence of true religion would set the slave at liberty. Yet as long as the relation exists, the apostle would enjoin on the servant the duty of performing his work conscientiously, as rendering service to the Lord. This direction, moreover, is one of great importance to all who are employed in the service of others. They are bound to perform their duty with as much fidelity as though the eye of the employer was always upon them, remembering that though the eye of man may be turned away, that of God never is. ¶ *As men-pleasers.* As if it were the main object to please men. The object should be rather to please and honour God. ¶ *But as the servants of Christ.* See Notes on 1 Cor. vii. 22. ¶ *Doing the will of God from the heart.* That is, God requires industry, fidelity, conscientiousness, submission, and obedience in that rank of life. We render acceptable service to God when, from regard to his will, we perform the services which are demanded of us in the situation in life where we may be placed, however humble that may be.

7. *As to the Lord, and not to men.* That is, he should regard his lot in life as having been ordered by Divine Providence for some wise and good purpose; and until he may be permitted to enjoy his liberty in a quiet and peaceable manner (Notes, 1 Cor. vii. 21), he should perform his duties with fidelity, and feel that he was rendering acceptable service to God. This would reconcile him to much of the hardships of his lot. The feeling that *God* has ordered the circumstances of our lives, and that he has some wise and good ends to answer by it, makes us contented there; though we may feel that our fellow-man may be doing us injustice. It was this principle that made the martyrs so patient under the wrongs done them by men; and this may make even a slave patient and submissive under the wrongs of a master. But let not a master think, because a pious slave shows this spirit, that, therefore, the slave feels that the master is right in withholding his freedom; nor let him suppose, because religion requires the slave to be submissive and obedient, that, therefore, it approves of what the master does. It does this no more than it sanctioned the conduct of Nero and Mary, because religion required the martyrs to be unresisting, and to allow themselves to be led to the stake. A conscientious slave may find happiness in submitting to God, and doing his will, just as a conscientious martyr may. But this does not sanction the wrong, either of the slave-owner or of the persecutor.

8 Knowing that whatsoever good thing any man doeth, the same shall he receive of the Lord, whether *he be* bond or free.

9 And ye masters, do the same things unto them, [1] forbearing threatening: knowing that [2] your

[1] *moderating.*
[2] some read, *both your and their.*

8. *Knowing that whatsoever good thing.* Whatever a man does that is right, for that he shall be appropriately rewarded. No matter what his rank in life, if he discharges his duty to God and man, he will be accepted. A man in a state of servitude may so live as to honour God; and, so living, he should not be greatly solicitous about his condition. A master may fail to render suitable recompense to a slave. But, if the servant is faithful to God, he will recompense him in the future world. It is in this way that religion would make the evils of life tolerable, by teaching those who are oppressed to bear their trials in a patient spirit, and to look forward to the future world of reward. Religion does not approve of slavery. It is the friend of human rights. If it had full influence on earth, it would restore every man to freedom, and impart to each one his rights. Christianity nowhere requires its friends to make or to own a slave. No one under the proper influence of religion ever yet made a man a slave; there is no one under its proper influence who would not desire that all should be free; and just in proportion as true religion spreads over the world, will universal freedom be its attendant. But Christianity would lighten the evils of slavery even while it exists, and would comfort those who are doomed to so hard a lot, by assuring them that there they may render acceptable service to God, and that they soon will be admitted to a world where galling servitude will be known no more. If they may not have freedom here, they may have contentment; if they feel that wrong is done them by men, they may feel that right will be done them by God; if their masters do not reward them for their services here, God will; and if they may not enjoy liberty here, they will soon be received into the world of perfect freedom—*heaven.*

9. *And ye masters.* The object of this is, to secure for servants a proper treatment. It is evident, from this, that there *were* in the christian church those who were *masters;* and the most obvious interpretation is, that they were the owners of slaves. Some such persons would be converted, as such are now. Paul did not say that they could not be Christians. He did not say that they should be excluded at once from the communion. He did not hold them up to reproach, or use harsh and severe language in regard to them. He taught them their duty towards those who were under them, and laid down principles which, if followed, would lead ultimately to universal freedom. ¶ *Do the same things unto them.* τὰ αὐτὰ. The 'same things,' here, seem to refer to what he had said in the previous verses. They were, to evince towards their servants the same spirit which he had required servants to evince towards them—the same kindness, fidelity, and respect for the will of God. He had required servants to act conscientiously; to remember that the eye of God was upon them, and that in that condition in life they were to regard themselves as serving God, and as mainly answerable to him. The same things the apostle would have masters feel. They were to be faithful, conscientious, just, true to the interests of their servants, and to re-

Master also is in heaven; neither is there respect[a] of persons with him.

a Ro. 2. 11.

member that they were responsible to God. They were not to take advantage of their power to oppress them, to punish them unreasonably, or to suppose that they were freed from responsibility in regard to the manner in which they treated them. In the corresponding passage in Colossians (iv. 1), this is, "Masters, give unto your servants that which is just and equal." See Note on that place. ¶ *Forbearing threatening.* Marg., *moderating.* The Greek word means, to *relax, loosen;* and then, to *omit, cease from.* This is evidently the meaning here. The sense is, that they were to be kind, affectionate, just. It does not mean that they were to remit punishment where it was deserved; but the object is to guard against that to which they were so much exposed in their condition—a fretful, dissatisfied temper; a disposition to govern by terror rather than by love. Where this unhappy state of society exists, it would be worth the trial of those who sustain the relation of masters, to see whether it would not be *possible* to govern their servants, as the apostle here advises, by the exercise of *love.* Might not kindness, and confidence, and the fear of the Lord, be substituted for threats and stripes?—¶ *Knowing that your Master also is in heaven.* Marg., "Some read, *both your and their.*" Many MSS. have this reading. See Mill. The sense is not materially affected, further than, according to the margin, the effect would be to make the master and the servant feel that, in a most important sense, they were on an equality. According to the common reading, the sense is, that masters should remember that they were responsible to God, and this fact should be allowed to influence them in a proper manner. This it would do in two ways. (1.) By the fact that injustice towards their servants would then be punished as it deserved—since there was no respect of persons with God. (2.) It would lead them to act towards their servants as they would desire God to treat them. Nothing would be better adapted to do this than the feeling that they had a common Master, and that they were soon to stand at his bar. ¶ *Neither is there respect of persons with him.* See this expression explained in the Notes on Rom. ii. 11. The meaning here is, that God would not be influenced in the distribution of rewards and punishments, by a regard to the rank or condition of the master or the slave. He would show no favour to the one because he was a master; he would withhold none from the other because he was a slave. He would treat both according to their character. In this world they occupied different ranks and conditions; at his bar they would be called to answer before the same Judge. It follows from this, (1.) that a slave is not to be regarded as a "chattel," or a "thing," or as "property." He is a man; a redeemed man; an immortal man. He is one for whom Christ died. But Christ did not die for "chattels" and "things." (2.) The master and the servant in their great interests are on a level. Both are sinners; both will soon die; both will moulder back in the same manner to dust; both will stand at the tribunal of God; both will give up their account. The one will not be admitted to heaven because he is a master; nor will the other be thrust down to hell because he is a slave. If both are Christians, they will be admitted to a heaven where the distinctions of rank and colour are unknown. If

10 Finally, my brethren, be strong in the Lord, and in the power of his might.

11 Put on the whole armour[a] of God, that ye may be able to

a Ro. 13. 12. 2 Co. 6. 7.

---

the master is not a Christian and the servant is, he who has regarded himself as superior to the servant in this life, will see *him* ascend to heaven while he himself will be thrust down to hell. (3.) Considerations like these will, if they have their proper influence, produce two effects. (*a*) They will lighten the yoke of slavery while it continues, and while it may be difficult to remove it at once. If the master and the slave were both Christians, even if the relation continued, it would be rather a relation of mutual confidence. The master would become the protector, the teacher, the guide, the friend; the servant would become the faithful helper—rendering service to one whom he loved, and to whom he felt himself bound by the obligations of gratitude and affection. (*b*) But this state of feeling would soon lead to emancipation. There is something shocking to the feelings of all, and monstrous to a Christian, in the idea of holding *a Christian brother* in bondage. So long as the slave is regarded as a "chattel" or a mere piece of "property," like a horse, so long men endeavour to content themselves with the feeling that he may be held in bondage. But the moment it is felt that he is *a Christian brother*—a redeemed fellow-traveller to eternity, a joint heir of life—that moment a Christian should feel that there is something that violates all the principles of his religion in holding him AS A SLAVE; in making a "chattel" of that for which Christ died, and in buying and selling, like a horse, an ox, or an ass, a child of God, and an heir of life. Accordingly, the prevalence of Christianity soon did away the evil of slavery in the Roman empire; and if it prevailed in its purity, it would soon banish it from the face of the earth.

10. *Finally, my brethren, be strong in the Lord.* Paul had now stated to the Ephesians the duties which they were to perform. He had considered the various relations of life which they sustained, and the obligations resulting from them. He was not unaware that in the discharge of their duties they would need strength from above. He knew that they had great and mighty foes, and that to meet them, they needed to be clothed in the panoply of the Christian soldier. He closes, therefore, by exhorting them to put on all the strength which they could to meet the enemies with which they had to contend; and in the commencement of his exhortation he reminds them that it was only by the strength of the Lord that they could hope for victory. To be 'strong in the Lord,' is, (1.) to be strong or courageous in his cause; (2.) to feel that *he* is our strength, and to rely on him and his promises.

11. *Put on the whole armour of God.* The whole description here is derived from the weapons of an ancient soldier. The various parts of those weapons—constituting the 'whole panoply'—are specified in vs. 14—17. The word rendered 'whole armour' (πανοπλίαν, *panoply*), means *complete armour*, offensive and defensive. See Luke xi. 22 Notes, Rom. xiii. 12. 2 Cor. vi. 7. 'The armour of *God*' is not that which God wears, but that which he has provided for the Christian soldier. The meaning here is, (1.) that we are not to provide in our warfare such weapons as men employ in their contests, but such as

stand against the wiles of the devil.

12 For we wrestle not against [1] flesh and blood, but against prin-

[1] *blood and flesh.*

God provides; that we are to renounce the weapons which are carnal, and put on such as God has directed for the achievement of the victory. (2.) We are to put on the '*whole* armour.' We are not to go armed partly with what God has appointed, and partly with such weapons as men use; nor are we to put on *a part* of the armour only, but the *whole* of it. A man needs *all* that armour if he is about to fight the battles of the Lord; and if he lacks *one* of the weapons which God has appointed, defeat may be the consequence. ¶ *That ye may be able to stand.* The foes are so numerous and mighty, that unless clothed with the divine armour, victory will be impossible. ¶ *Against the wiles of the devil.* The word rendered '*wiles*' (μεθοδεία), means properly that which is traced out with *method;* that which is *methodized*; and then that which is well laid—art, skill, cunning. It occurs in the New Testament only in Eph. iv. 14, and in this place. It is appropriately here rendered *wiles*, meaning cunning devices, arts, attempts to delude and destroy us. The wiles *of the devil* are the various arts and stratagems which he employs to drag souls down to perdition. We can more easily encounter open force than we can cunning; and we need the weapons of Christian armour to meet the attempts to draw us into a snare, as much as to meet open force. The idea here is, that Satan does not carry on an open warfare. He does not meet the Christian soldier face to face. He advances covertly; makes his approaches in darkness; employs cunning rather than power, and seeks rather to delude and betray than to vanquish by mere force. Hence the necessity of being *constantly* armed to meet him whenever the attack is made. A man who has to contend with a visible enemy, may feel safe if he only prepares to meet him in the open field. But far different is the case if the enemy is invisible; if he steals upon us slyly and stealthily; if he practises war only by ambushes and by surprises. Such is the foe that *we* have to contend with—and almost all the Christian struggle is a warfare against stratagems and wiles. Satan does not openly appear. He approaches us not in repulsive forms, but comes to recommend some plausible doctrine, to lay before us some temptation that shall not immediately repel us. He presents the world in an alluring aspect; invites us to pleasures that seem to be harmless, and leads us in indulgence until we have gone so far that we cannot retreat.

12. *For we wrestle.* Gr., 'The wrestling to us;' or, 'There is not to us a wrestling with flesh and blood.' There is undoubtedly here an allusion to the ancient games of Greece, a part of the exercises in which consisted in wrestling. See Notes on 1 Cor. ix. 25—27. The Greek word here used—πάλη—denotes a *wrestling;* and then a struggle, fight, combat. Here it refers to the struggle or combat which the Christian is to maintain—the christian warfare. ¶ *Not with flesh and blood.* Not with men. See Notes on Gal. i. 16. The apostle does not mean to say that Christians had no enemies among men that opposed them, for they were exposed often to fiery persecution; nor that they had nothing to contend with in the carnal and corrupt propensities of their nature, which was true of them then as it is now; but that their main

cipalities,[a] against powers, against the rulers of the darkness of this world, against [2] spiritual wickedness in [3] high *places*.

a Ro. 8. 38.

[1] or, *wicked spirits*. [2] or, *heavenly*, as c. 1. 3.

controversy was with the invisible spirits of wickedness that sought to destroy them. They were the source and origin of all their spiritual conflicts, and with them the warfare was to be maintained. ¶ *But against principalities.* There can be no doubt whatever that the apostle alludes here to evil spirits. Like good angels, they were regarded as divided into ranks and orders, and were supposed to be under the control of one mighty leader. See Notes on ch. i. 21. It is probable that the allusion here is to the ranks and orders which they sustained before their fall, something like which they may still retain. The word *principalities* refers to principal rulers, or chieftains. ¶ *Powers.* Those who had power, or to whom the name of *powers* was given. Milton represents Satan as addressing the fallen angels in similar language:

"Thrones, dominations, princedoms, virtues, powers."

¶ *Against the rulers of the darkness of this world.* The rulers that preside over the regions of ignorance and sin with which the earth abounds. Comp. Notes on ch. ii. 2. *Darkness* is an emblem of ignorance, misery, and sin; and no description could be more accurate than that of representing these malignant spirits as ruling over a dark world. The earth—dark, and wretched, and ignorant, and sinful—is just such a dominion as they would choose, or as they would cause; and the degradation and woe of the heathen world are just such as foul and malignant spirits would delight in. It is a wide and a powerful empire. It has been consolidated by ages. It is sustained by all the authority of law; by all the omnipotence of the perverted religious principle; by all the reverence for antiquity; by all the power of selfish, corrupt, and base passions. No empire has been so extended, or has continued so long, as that empire of darkness; and nothing on earth is so difficult to destroy. Yet the apostle says that it was on *that* kingdom they were to make war. Against that, the kingdom of the Redeemer was to be set up; and that was to be overcome by the spiritual weapons which he specifies. When he speaks of the christian warfare here, he refers to the contest with the powers of this dark kingdom. He regards each and every Christian as a soldier to wage war on it in whatever way he could, and wherever he could attack it. The contest, therefore, was not primarily with *men*, or with the internal corrupt propensities of the soul; it was with this vast and dark kingdom that had been set up over mankind. I do not regard this passage, therefore, as having a primary reference to the struggle which a Christian maintains with his own corrupt propensities. It is a warfare on a large scale with the entire kingdom of darkness over the world. Yet in *maintaining* the warfare, the struggle will be with such portions of that kingdom as we come in contact with, and will actually relate (1.) to our own sinful propensities—which are a part of the kingdom of darkness; (2.) with the evil passions of others—their pride, ambition, and spirit of revenge—which are also a part of that kingdom; (3.) with the evil customs, laws, opinions, employments, pleasures of the world—which are also a part of that dark kingdom; (4.) with error, superstition, false doctrine—which are also a part of that kingdom; and (5.) with the wickedness of the heathen world—the sins

13 Wherefore take unto you the whole armour of God, that ye may be able to withstand in the evil day, and, having done [1] all, to stand.

[1] or, *overcome.*

14 Stand therefore, having your loins girt [a] about with truth, and having on the breast-plate of righteousness;

[a] Is. 11. 5.

of benighted nations—also a part of that kingdom. Wherever we come in contact with evil—whether in our own hearts or elsewhere—there we are to make war. ¶ *Against spiritual wickedness.* Marg. 'or *wicked spirits.*' Literally, 'The spiritual things of wickedness;' but the allusion is undoubtedly to evil spirits, and to their influences on earth. ¶ *In high* places. ἐν τοῖς ἐπουρανίοις—'in celestial, or heavenly places.' The same phrase occurs in ch. i. 3; ii. 6, where it is translated, 'in heavenly places.' The word (ἐπουράνιος) is used of those that dwell in heaven, Matt. xviii. 35. Phil. ii. 10; of those who come from heaven, 1 Cor. xv. 48. Phil. iii. 21; of the heavenly bodies, the sun, moon, and stars. 1 Cor. xv. 40. Then the neuter plural of the word is used to denote the heavens; and then the *lower* heavens, the sky, the air, represented as the seat of evil spirits. Notes, ch. ii. 2. This is the allusion here. The evil spirits are supposed to occupy the lofty regions of the air, and thence to exert a baleful influence on the affairs of man. What was the origin of this opinion it is not needful here to inquire. No one can *prove*, however, that it is incorrect. It is against such spirits, and all their malignant influences, that Christians are called to contend. In whatever way their power is put forth—whether in the prevalence of vice and error; of superstition and magic arts; of infidelity, atheism, or antinomianism; of evil customs and laws; of pernicious fashions and opinions, or in the corruptions of our own hearts, we are to make war on all these forms of evil, and never to yield in the conflict.

13. *In the evil day.* The day of temptation; the day when you are violently assaulted. ¶ *And having done all, to stand.* Marg. 'or *overcome.*' The Greek word means, to work out, effect, or produce; and then to work up, to make an end of, to vanquish. *Robinson*, Lex. The idea seems to be, that they were to overcome or vanquish all their foes, and *thus* to stand firm. The whole language here is taken from war; and the idea is, that every foe was to be subdued—no matter how numerous or formidable they might be. Safety and triumph could be looked for only when every enemy was slain.

14. *Stand therefore.* Resist every attack—as a soldier does in battle. In what way they were to do this, and how they were to be armed, the apostle proceeds to specify; and in doing it, gives a description of the ancient armour of a soldier. ¶ *Having your loins girt about.* The *girdle*, or *sash*, was always with the ancients an important part of their dress, in war as well as in peace. They wore loose, flowing robes; and it became necessary to gird them up when they travelled, or ran, or laboured. The girdle was often highly ornamented, and was the place where they carried their money, their sword, their pipe, their writing instruments, &c. See Notes on Matt. v. 38—41. The 'girdle' seems sometimes to have been a cincture of iron or steel, and designed to keep every part of the armour in its place, and to gird the soldier on every side. The following figure will give an idea of part of the armour of an ancient soldier.

Grecian Warrior.

Occasionally he was entirely encased in mail, as in the following figure.

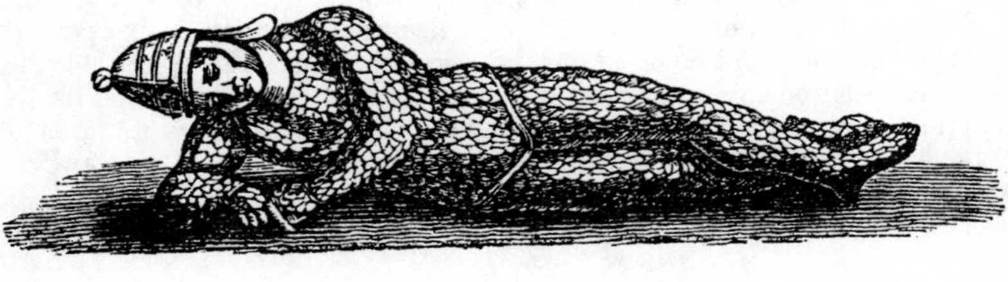

¶ *With truth.* It may not be easy to determine with entire accuracy the resemblance between the parts of the armour specified in this description, and the things with which they are compared, or to determine precisely why he compared *truth* to a girdle, and *righteousness* to a breast-plate, rather than why he should have chosen a different order, and compared righteousness to a girdle, &c. Perhaps in themselves there may have been no special reason for this arrangement, but the object may have been merely to specify the different parts of the armour of a soldier, and to compare them with the weapons which Christians were to use, though the comparison should be made somewhat at random. In some of the cases, however, we can see a particular significancy in the comparisons which are made; and it may not be improper to make suggestions of that kind as we go along. The idea here may be, that as the girdle was the bracer up, or support of the body, so truth is fitted to brace us up, and to gird us for constancy and firmness. The girdle kept all the parts of the armour in their proper place, and preserved firmness and consistency in the dress; and so truth might serve to give consistency and firmness to our conduct. "Great," says Grotius, "is the laxity of falsehood; truth binds the man." Truth preserves a man from those lax views of morals, of duty and of religion, which leave him exposed to every assault. It makes the soul sincere, firm, constant, and always on its guard. A man who has no consistent views of truth, is just the man for the adversary successfully to assail. ¶ *And having on the breast-plate.* The word here rendered 'breast-plate' (θώραξ) denoted the *cuirass*, Lat., *lorica*, or coat of mail; i. e. the armour that covered the body from the neck to the thighs, and consisted of two parts, one covering the front and the other the back. It was made of rings, or in the form of scales, or of plates, so fastened together that they would be flexible, and yet guard the body from a sword, spear, or arrow. It is referred to in the Scriptures as a *coat of mail* (1 Sam. xvii. 5); an *habergeon* (Neh. iv. 16); or as a *breast-plate.* We are told that Goliath's coat of mail weighed five thousand shekels of brass, or nearly one hundred and sixty pounds. It was often formed of plates of brass, laid one upon another, like the scales of a fish. The cuts on the following page will give an idea of this ancient piece of armour. ¶ *Of righteousness.* Integrity, holiness, purity of life, sincerity of piety. The breast-plate defended the vital parts of the body; and the idea here may be that integrity of life, and righteousness of character, is as necessary to defend us from the assaults of Satan, as the coat of mail was to preserve the heart from the arrows of an enemy It was the incorruptible integrity of Job, and, in a higher sense, of the Redeemer himself, that saved them from the temptations of the devil. And it is as true now that no one can successfully meet the power of temptation unless he is righteous, as that a soldier could not defend himself against a foe without such a coat of mail. A want of integrity will leave a man exposed to the assaults of the enemy, just as a man would be whose coat of mail was defective, or some part of which was wanting. The king of Israel was smitten by an arrow sent from a bow, drawn at a venture, "between the joints of his harness" or the 'breast-plate' (margin), 1 Kings xxii. 34; and many a man who thinks he has on the *christian* armour is smitten in the same manner. There is some defect of character; some want of incorruptible integrity; some point that is unguarded—and *that*

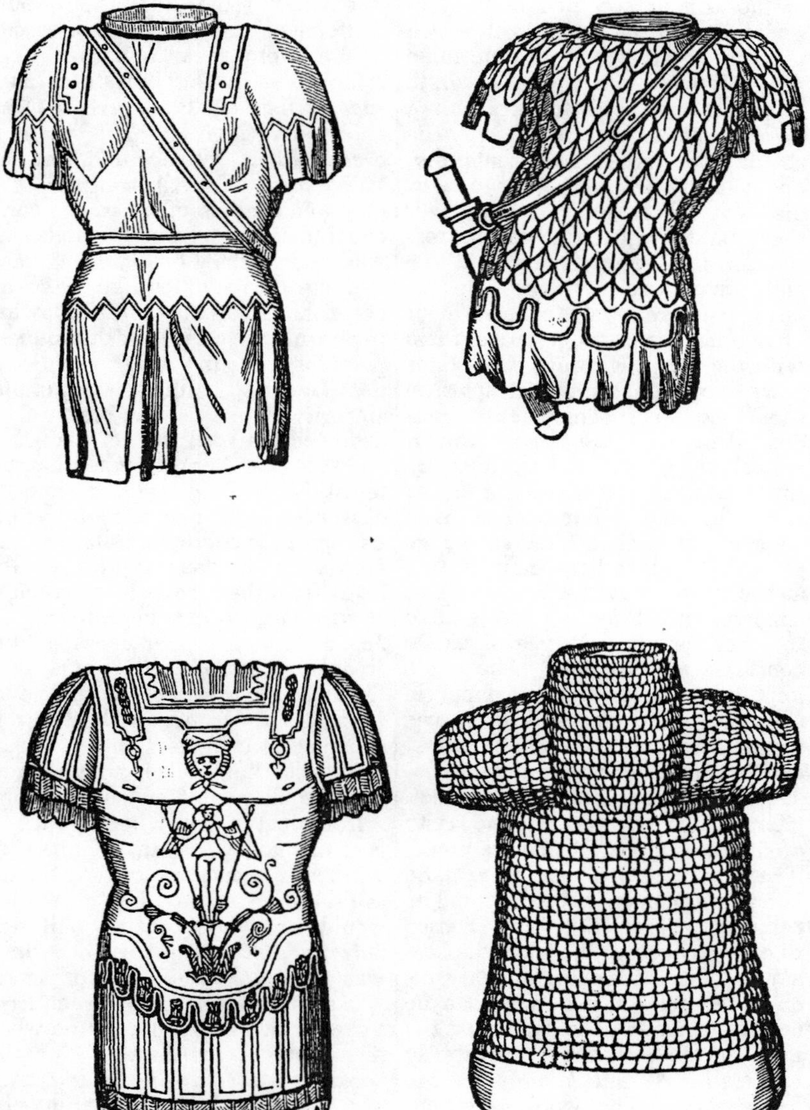

Cuirasses, or Coats of Ma

15 And your feet [a] shod with the preparation of the gospel of peace;

a Ca. 7. 1.

will be sure to be the point of attack by the foe. So David was tempted to commit the enormous crimes that stain his memory, and Peter to deny his Lord. So Judas was assailed, for the want of the armour of righteousness, through his avarice; and so, by some want of incorruptible integrity in a single point, many a minister of the gospel has been assailed and has fallen. It may be added here, that we need a righteousness which God alone can give; the righteousness of God our Saviour, to make us perfectly invulnerable to all the arrows of the foe.

15. *And your feet shod.* There is undoubtedly an allusion here to what was worn by the ancient soldier to guard his feet. The Greek is, literally, 'having underbound the feet;' that is, having bound on the shoes, or sandals, or whatever was worn by the ancient soldier. The protection of the feet and ancles consisted of two parts. (1.) The sandals, or shoes, which were probably made so as to cover the foot, and which often were fitted with nails, or armed with spikes, to make the hold firm in the ground; or (2.) with *greaves* that were fitted to the legs, and designed to defend them from any danger. These *greaves*, or boots (1 Sam. xvii. 6), were made of brass, and were in almost universal use among the Greeks and Romans. See the figure of the 'Grecian warrior' on page 144. ¶ *With the preparation.* Prepared with the gospel of peace. The sense is, that the christian soldier is to be prepared with the gospel of peace to meet attacks similar to those against which the ancient soldier designed to guard himself by the sandals or greaves which he wore. The word rendered *preparation*—(ἑτοιμασία)—means properly readiness, fitness for, alacrity; and the idea, according to Robinson (*Lex.*), is, that they were to be ever ready to go forth to preach the gospel. Taylor (Fragments to Calmet's Dic., No. 219) supposes that it means, "Your feet shod with the preparation of the gospel; not iron, not steel—but patient investigation, calm inquiry, assiduous, laborious, lasting; or with *firm footing* in the gospel of peace." Locke supposes it to mean, 'with a readiness to walk in the gospel of peace.' Doddridge supposes that the allusion is to *greaves*, and the spirit recommended is that peaceful and benevolent temper recommended in the gospel, and which, like the boots worn by soldiers, would bear them safe through many obstructions and trials that might be opposed to them, as a soldier might encounter sharp-pointed thorns that would oppose his progress. It is difficult to determine the exact meaning; and perhaps all expositors have erred in endeavouring to explain the reference of these parts of armour by some particular thing in the gospel. The apostle figured to himself a soldier, clad in the usual manner. Christians were to resemble him. One part of his dress or preparation consisted in the covering and defence of the foot. It was to preserve the foot from danger, and to secure the facility of his march, and perhaps to make him firm in battle. Christians were to have the principles of the gospel of peace—the peaceful and pure gospel—to facilitate them; to aid them in their marches; to make them firm in the day of conflict with their foes. They were not to be furnished with carnal weapons, but with the peaceful gospel of the Redeemer; and, sustained by this, they were to go on in their march through

16 Above all, taking the shield of faith, [a] wherewith ye shall be able to quench all the fiery darts of the wicked.

a 1 Jno. 5. 4.

---

the world. The principles of the gospel were to do for them what the greaves and iron-spiked sandals did for the soldier—to make them ready for the march, to make them firm in their foot-tread, and to be a part of their defence against their foes.

16. *Above all.* 'Επὶ πᾶσιν. Not *above all* in point of importance or value, but *over* all, as a soldier holds his shield to defend himself. It constitutes a protection over every part of his body, as it can be turned in every direction. The idea is, that as the shield covered or protected the other parts of the armour, so faith had a similar importance in the christian virtues. ¶ *The shield.* Note, Isa. xxi. 9. The shield was usually made of light wood, or a rim of brass, and covered with several folds or thicknesses of stout hide, which was preserved by frequent anointing. It was held by the left arm, and was secured by straps, through which the arm passed, as may be seen in the annexed cut. The outer surface

Greek Warrior.

of the shield was made more or less rounding from the centre to the edge, and was polished smooth, or anointed with oil, so that arrows or darts would glance off, or rebound. ¶ *Of faith.* On the nature of faith, see Notes on Mark xvi. 16. Faith here is made to occupy a more important place than either of the other christian graces. It bears, to the whole christian character, the same relation which the shield does to the other parts of the armour of a soldier. It protects all, and is indispensable to the security of all, as is the case with the shield. The shield was an ingenious device by which blows and arrows might be parried off, and the whole body defended. It could be made to protect the head, or the heart, or thrown behind to meet an attack there. As long as the soldier had his shield, he felt secure; and as long as a Christian has faith, he is safe. It comes to his aid in every attack that is made on him, no matter from what quarter; it is the defence and guardian of every other christian grace; and it secures the protection which the Christian needs in the whole of the spiritual war. ¶ *Wherewith ye shall be able to quench all the fiery darts of the wicked.* Or, rather, 'of the WICKED ONE—τοῦ πονηροῦ. The allusion is undoubtedly to the great enemy of the people of God, called, by way of eminence, THE *wicked one*. Comp. 2 Thess. iii. 3. Mr. Locke renders this, "Wherein you may receive, and so render ineffectual," &c. There seems a little incongruity in the idea of *quenching* darts by *a shield.* But the word *quench*, here, means only that they would be *put out* by being thrown *against* the shield, as a candle would by being thrown against anything. The *fiery darts* that were used in war were small, slender pieces of cane, which were filled with combustible materials, and set on fire; or darts around which some combustible material was wound, and which were set on fire, and then shot *slowly* against a

a, *b*, *c*, Egyptian Helmets, worn by Warriors; *d*, *e*, Caps of Egyptian Soldiers; *f*, *g*, Persian Helmets; *h*, *i*, *k*, Syrian; *l*, *m*, *n*, *o*, Phrygian; *p*, *q*, Dacian.

17 And take the helmet [a] of salvation, and the sword [b] of the Spirit, which is the word of God:

[a] Is. 59. 17. [b] He. 4. 12.

foe. The object was to make the arrow fasten in the body, and increase the danger by the burning; or, more frequently, those darts were thrown against ships, forts, tents, &c., with an intention to set them on fire. They were in common use among the ancients. Arrian (Expe. Alex. 11) mentions the πυρφορα βελη, the fire-bearing weapons; Thucydides (ii. c. 75), the πυρφοροι όϊστοι, the fire-bearing arrows; and Livy refers to similar weapons as in common use in war. Lib. xxi. c. 8. By the 'fiery darts of the wicked,' Paul here refers, probably, to the temptations of the great adversary, which are like fiery darts; or those furious suggestions of evil, and excitements to sin, which he may throw into the mind like fiery darts. They are—blasphemous thoughts, unbelief, sudden temptation to do wrong, or thoughts that wound and torment the soul. In regard to them, we may observe, (1.) that they come suddenly, like arrows sped from a bow; (2.) they come from unexpected quarters, like arrows shot suddenly from an enemy in ambush; (3.) they pierce, and penetrate, and torment the soul, as arrows would that are on fire; (4.) they set the soul on fire, and enkindle the worst passions, as fiery darts do a ship or camp against which they are sent. The only way to meet them is by the 'shield of faith;' by confidence in God, and by relying on his gracious promises and aid. It is not by our own strength; and, if we have not faith in God, we are wholly defenceless. We should have a shield that we can turn in any direction, on which we may receive the arrow, and by which it may be put out.

17 *And take the helmet.* The helmet was a cap made of thick leather, or brass, fitted to the head, and was usually crowned with a plume, or crest, as an ornament. Its use was to guard the head from a blow by a sword, or war-club, or battle-axe. The cuts on the preceding page will show its usual form. It may be seen, also, in the figure of the 'Grecian warrior,' on p. 144. ¶ *Of salvation.* That is, *of the hope of salvation;* for so it is expressed in the parallel place in 1 Thess. v. 8. The idea is, that a well-founded hope of salvation will preserve us in the day of spiritual conflict, and will guard us from the blows which an enemy would strike. The helmet defended the head, a vital part; and so the hope of salvation will defend the soul, and keep it from the blows of the enemy. A soldier would not fight well without a hope of victory. A Christian could not contend with his foes, without the hope of final salvation; but, sustained by this, what has he to dread? ¶ *And the sword.* The sword was an essential part of the armour of an ancient soldier. His other weapons were the bow, the spear, or the battle-axe. But, without a sword, no soldier would have regarded himself as well armed. The ancient sword was short, and usually two-edged, and resembled very much a dagger, as may be seen in the annexed engraving, representing Roman swords. ¶ *Of the Spirit.* Which the Holy Spirit furnishes; the truth which he has revealed. ¶ *Which is the word of God.* What God has spoken—his truth and promises. See Notes on Heb. iv. 12. It was with this weapon that the Saviour met the tempter in the wilderness. Matt. iv. It is only by this that Satan can now be

Roman Swords.

met. Error and falsehood will not put back temptation; nor can we hope for victory, unless we are armed with truth. Learn, hence, (1.) That we should study the Bible, that we may understand what the truth is. (2.) We should have texts of Scripture at command, as the Saviour did, to meet the various forms of temptation. (3.) We should not depend on our own reason, or rely on our own wisdom. A single text of Scripture is better to meet a temptation, than all the philosophy which the world contains. The tempter can reason, and reason plausibly too. But he cannot resist a direct and positive command of the Almighty. Had Eve adhered simply to the word of God, and urged his command, without attempting to *reason* about it, she would have been safe. The Saviour (Matt. iv. 4. 7. 10) met the tempter with the word of God, and he was foiled. So *we* shall be safe if we adhere to the simple declarations of the Bible, and oppose a temptation by a positive command of God. But, the moment we leave that, and begin to parley with sin, that moment we are gone. It is as if a man should throw away his sword, and use his naked hands only in meeting an adversary. Hence, (4.) we may see the importance of training up the young in the accurate study of the Bible. There is nothing which will furnish a better security to them in future life, when temptation comes upon them, than to have a pertinent text of Scripture at command. Temptation often assails us so suddenly that it checks all *reasoning*; but a text of Scripture will suffice to drive the tempter from us.

18 Praying always [a] with all prayer and supplication in the Spirit, and watching [b] thereunto with all perseverance and supplication for all saints;

a Lu. 18. 1.

b Mat. 26. 41.

18. *Praying always.* It would be well for the soldier who goes forth to battle, to pray—to pray for victory; or to pray that he may be prepared for death, should he fall. But soldiers do not often feel the necessity of this. To the Christian soldier, however, it is indispensable. Prayer crowns all lawful efforts with success, and gives a victory when nothing else would. No matter how complete the armour; no matter how skilled we may be in the science of war; no matter how courageous we may be, we may be certain that without prayer we shall be defeated. God alone can give the victory; and when the Christian soldier goes forth armed completely for the spiritual conflict, if he looks to God by prayer, he may be sure of a triumph. This prayer is not to be intermitted. It is to be *always.* In every temptation and spiritual conflict we are to pray. See Notes on Luke xviii. 1. ¶ *With all prayer and supplication.* With all kinds of prayer; prayer in the closet, the family, the social meeting, the great assembly; prayer at the usual hours, prayer when we are specially tempted, and when we feel just like praying (see Notes, Matt. vi. 6); prayer in the form of supplication for ourselves, and in the form of intercession for others. This is, after all, the great weapon of our spiritual armour, and by this we may hope to prevail.

"Restraining prayer, we cease to fight;
Prayer makes the Christian armour bright,
And Satan trembles when he sees,
The meanest saint upon his knees."

¶ *In the Spirit.* By the aid of the Holy Spirit; or perhaps it may mean that it is not to be prayer of form merely, but when the spirit and the heart accompany it. The former idea seems, however, to be the correct one. ¶ *And watching thereunto.* Watching for opportunities to pray; watching for the spirit of prayer; watching against all those things which would hinder prayer. See Notes, Matt. xxvi. 38. 41. Comp. 1 Pet. iv. 7. ¶ *With all perseverance.* Never becoming discouraged and disheartened. Comp. Notes, Luke xviii. 1. ¶ *And supplication for all saints.* For all Christians. We should do this (1.) because they are our brethren—though they may have a different skin, language, or name. (2.) Because, like us, they have hearts prone to evil, and need, with us, the grace of God. (3.) Because nothing tends so much to make us love others and to forget their faults, as to pray for them. (4.) Because the condition of the church is always such that it greatly needs the grace of God. Many Christians have backslidden; many are cold or lukewarm; many are in error; many are conformed to the world; and we should pray that they may become more holy and may devote themselves more to God. (5.) Because each day many a Christian is subjected to some peculiar temptation or trial, and though he may be unknown to us, yet our prayers may benefit him. (6.) Because each day and each night many Christians die. We may reflect each night as we lie down to rest, that while we sleep, some Christians are kept awake by the prospect of death, and are now passing through the dark valley; and each morning we may reflect that *to-day* some Christian will die, and we should remember them before God. (7.) Because *we* shall soon die, and it will be a comfort to

19 And for[a] me, that utterance may be given unto me, that I may open my mouth boldly, to make known the mystery of the gospel,

20 For which I am an ambassador in bonds; [1] that [2] therein I may speak boldly, as I ought [a] to speak.

a 2 Th. 3. 1.

[1] or, *a chain.* [2] or, *thereof.* *a* Is. 58. 1.

us if we can remember then that *we* have often prayed for dying saints, and if we may feel that they are praying for us.

19. *And for me.* Paul was then a prisoner at Rome. He specially needed the prayers of Christians, (1.) that he might be sustained in his afflictions; and (2.) that he might be able to manifest the spirit which he ought, and to do good as he had opportunity. Learn hence that we should pray for the prisoner, the captive, the man in chains, the slave. There are in *this* land constantly not far from ten thousand prisoners—husbands, fathers, sons, brothers; or wives, mothers, daughters. True, they are the children of *crime*, but they are also the children of sorrow; and in either case or both they need our prayers. There are in this land not far from three millions of slaves—and they need our prayers. They are the children of misfortune and of many wrongs; they are sunk in ignorance and want and wo; they are subjected to trials, and exposed to temptations to the lowest vices. But many of them, we trust, love the Redeemer; and whether they do or do not, they need an interest in the prayers of Christians. ¶ *That utterance may be given unto me.* Paul, though a prisoner, was permitted to preach the gospel. See Notes, Acts xxviii. 30, 31. ¶ *That I may open my mouth boldly.* He was in Rome. He was almost alone. He was surrounded by multitudes of the wicked. He was exposed to death. Yet he desired to speak boldly in the name of the Lord Jesus, and to invite sinners to repentance. A Christian in chains, and surrounded by the wicked, *may* speak boldly, and *may* have hope of success—for Paul was not an unsuccessful preacher even when a captive at Rome. See Notes on Phil. iv. 22. ¶ *The mystery of the gospel.* Notes, ch. i. 9.

20. *For which I am an ambassador in bonds.* In chains (see the margin); or in confinement. There is something peculiarly touching in this. He was *an ambassador*—sent to proclaim peace to a lost world. But he was now in chains. An ambassador is a sacred character. No greater affront can be given to a nation than to put its ambassadors to death, or even to throw them into prison. But Paul says here that the unusual spectacle was witnessed of an ambassador seized, bound, confined, imprisoned; an ambassador who ought to have the privileges conceded to all such men, and to be permitted to go everywhere publishing the terms of mercy and salvation. See the word ambassador explained in the Notes on 2 Cor. v. 20. ¶ *That therein.* Marg. or *thereof.* Gr., ἐν ἀυτῷ—*in it;* that is, says Rosenmüller, in the gospel. It means, that in speaking the gospel he might be bold. ¶ *I may speak boldly.* Openly, plainly, without fear. See Notes on Acts iv. 13; ix. 27; xiii. 46; xiv. 3; xviii. 26; xix. 8; xxvi. 26. ¶ *As I ought to speak.* Whether in bonds or at large. Paul felt that the gospel ought always to be spoken with plainness, and without the fear of man. It is remarkable that he did not ask them to pray that he might be released. *Why* he did not we do not know; but perhaps the desire of release did not lie so near his heart as

21 But that ye also may know my affairs, *and* how I do, Tychicus,[a] a beloved brother and faithful minister in the Lord, shall make known to you all things:

22 Whom[b] I have sent unto you for the same purpose, that ye might know our affairs, and *that* he might comfort your hearts.

23 Peace[c] *be* to the brethren, and love with faith, from God the Father, and the Lord Jesus Christ.

24 Grace *be* with all them that

a Ac. 20. 4. *b* Co. 4. 7, 8.

c 1 Pe. 5. 14.

the duty of speaking the gospel with boldness. It may be of much more importance that we perform our duty aright when we are afflicted, or are in trouble, than that we should be released.

21. *But that ye may know my affairs.* May understand my condition, my feelings, and in what I am engaged. To them it could not but be a subject of deep interest. ¶ *And how I do.* Gr., 'What I do;' that is, how I am employed. ¶ *Tychicus.* Tychicus was of the province of Asia, in Asia Minor, of which Ephesus was the capital. See Acts xx. 4. It is not improbable that he was of Ephesus, and that he was well known to the church there. He also carried the letter to the Colossians (Col. iv. 7), and probably the Second Epistle to Timothy. 2 Tim. iv. 12. Paul also proposed to send him to Crete to succeed Titus. Tit. iii. 12. He was high in the confidence of Paul, but it is not known when he was converted, or why he was now at Rome. The Greeks speak of him as one of the seventy disciples, and make him bishop of Colophon, in the province of Asia.

22. *Whom I have sent unto you.* The churches where Paul had preached, would feel a great interest in his welfare. He was a prisoner at Rome, and it was doubtful what the result would be. In this situation, he felt it proper to despatch a special messenger to give information about his condition; to state what was doing in Rome; to ask the prayers of the churches; and to administer consolation to them in their various trials. The same sentiment in regard to the embassy of Tychicus, is expressed in the Epistle to the Colossians. Ch. iv. 7, 8. No small part of the consolation which he would impart to them would be found in these invaluable letters which he bore to them from the apostle.

23. *Peace* be *to the brethren.* The epistle is closed with the usual salutations. The expression '*peace to you,*' was the common form of salutation in the East (Notes, Matt. x. 13. Luke xxiv. 36. Rom. xv. 33. Comp. Gal. vi. 16. 1 Pet. v. 14. 3 John 14), and is still the '*salam*' which is used—the word *salam* meaning *peace.* ¶ *And love with faith.* Love united with faith; not only desiring that they might have faith, but the faith which worked by love. ¶ *From God the Father and the Lord Jesus Christ.* The Father and the Son are regarded as equally the author of peace and love. Comp. Notes on 2 Cor. xiii. 14.

24. *Grace* be, &c. Note, Rom. xvi. 20. ¶ *That love our Lord Jesus Christ.* See Notes on 1 Cor. xvi. 22. ¶ *In sincerity.* Marg. *with incorruption.* With a pure heart; without dissembling; without hypocrisy. There could not be a more appropriate close of the epistle than such a wish; there will be nothing more needful for us when we come to the close of life than the consciousness that we love the Lord Jesus Christ IN SINCERITY. To writer and reader may this be

love our Lord Jesus Christ [1] in sincerity. Amen.

Written from Rome unto the Ephesians by Tychicus.

[1] or, *with incorruption.*

equally the inestimable consolation then! Better, far better then will be the evidence of such sincere love, than all the wealth which toil can gain, all the honours which the world can bestow—than the most splendid mansion, or the widest fame.

The subscription to this epistle, like those affixed to the other epistles, is of no authority, but in this instance there is every reason to believe that it is correct. Comp. Notes at the end of the Epistle to the Romans and 1 Corinthians.

THE

EPISTLE TO THE PHILIPPIANS.

INTRODUCTION.

§ 1. *The situation of Philippi.*

PHILIPPI is mentioned in the New Testament only in the following places and connections. In Acts xvi. 11, 12, it is said that Paul and his fellow-travellers "loosed from Troas, came with a straight course to Samothracia and Neapolis, and from thence to Philippi." It was at this time that the "Lord opened the heart of Lydia to attend to the things which were spoken by Paul," and that the jailer was converted under such interesting circumstances. In Acts xx. 1—6, it appears that Paul again visited Philippi after he had been to Athens and Corinth, and when on his way to Judea. From Philippi he went to Troas. In 1 Thess. ii. 2, Paul alludes to the shameful treatment which he had received at Philippi, and to the fact, that having been treated in that manner at Philippi, he had passed to Thessalonica, and preached the gospel there.

Philippi received its name from Philip, the father of Alexander the Great. Before his time, its history is unknown. It is said that it was founded on the site of an old Thasian settlement, and that its former name was Crenides, from the circumstance of its being surrounded by numerous rivulets and springs descending from the neighbouring mountains (from *κρήνη—krene, a spring*). The city was also called Dathos, or Datos—Δατος. Notes, Acts xvi. 12. The Thasians, who inhabited the island of Thasus, lying off the coast in the Ægean sea, had been attracted to the place by the valuable mines of gold and silver which were found in that region. It was a city of Macedonia, to the north-east of Amphipolis, and nearly east of Thessalonica. It was not far from the borders of Thrace. It was about fifteen or twenty miles from the Ægean sea, in the neighbourhood of Mount Pangæus, and had a small river or stream running near it which emptied into the Ægean sea. Of the *size* of the city when the gospel was preached there by Paul, we have no information.

This city was originally within the limits of Thrace. Philip of Macedon having turned his attention to Thrace, the situation of Crenides and Mount Pangæus naturally attracted his notice. Accordingly he invaded this country; expelled the feeble Cotys from his throne, and then proceeded to found a new city, on the site of the old Thasian colony, which he called after his own name, *Philippi*. *Anthon*, Class. Dic. When Macedonia became subject to the Romans, the advantages attending the situation of Philippi induced that people to send a colony there, and it became one of the most flourishing cities of the empire. Comp. Acts xvi. 12. Pliny, iv. 10. There is a medal of this city with the following inscription. Col. Jul. Aug. Phil; from which it appears that there was a colony sent there by Julius Cæsar. *Michaelis.* The city derived considerable importance from the fact that it was a principal thoroughfare from Asia to Europe, as the great leading road from one continent to the other was in the vicinity. This road is described at length by Appian, De Bell. Civ. L. iv. c. 105, 106.

This city is celebrated in history from the fact that it was here that a great victory—deciding the fate of the Roman empire—was obtained by Octavianus (afterwards Augustus Cæsar) and Antony over the forces of Brutus and Cassius, by which the republican party was completely subdued. In this battle, Cassius, who was hard pressed and defeated by Antony, and who supposed that every thing was lost, slew himself in despair. Brutus deplored his loss with tears of the sincerest sorrow, calling him "the last of the Romans.' After an interval of twenty days, Brutus hazarded a second battle. Where he himself fought in person he was successful; but the army everywhere else gave way, and the battle terminated in the entire defeat of the republican party. Brutus escaped with a few friends; passed a night in a cave, and seeing that all was irretrievably lost, ordered Strato, one of his attendants, to kill him. Strato for a long time refused; but seeing Brutus resolute, he turned away his face, and held his sword, and Brutus fell upon it. The city of Philippi is often mentioned by the Byzantine writers in history. Its ruins still retain the name of *Filibah.* Two American missionaries visited these ruins in May, 1834. They saw the remains of what might have been the forum or market-place, where Paul and Silas were beaten (Acts xvi. 19); and also the fragments of a splendid palace. The road by which Paul went from Neapolis to Philippi, they think is the same that is now travelled, as it is cut through the most difficult passes in the mountains. It is still paved throughout.

§ 2. *The establishment of the church in Philippi.*

Philippi was the first place in Europe where the gospel was preached; and this fact invests the place with more interest and importance than it derives from the battle fought there. The gospel was first preached here, in very interesting circumstances, by Paul and Silas. Paul had been called by a remarkable vision (Acts xvi. 9) to go into Macedonia, and the first place where he preached was Philippi—having made his way, as his custom was, directly to the capital. The first person to whom he preached was Lydia, a seller of purple, from Thyatira, in Asia Minor. She was converted, and received Paul and Silas into her house, and entertained them hospitably. In consequence of Paul's casting out an evil spirit from a "damsel possessed of a spirit of divination," by which the hope of gain by those who kept her in their employ was destroyed, the populace was excited, and Paul and Silas were thrown into the inner prison, and their feet were made fast in the stocks. Here, at midnight, God interposed in a remarkable manner. An earthquake shook the prison; their bonds were loosened; the doors of the prison were thrown open, and their keeper, who before had treated them with peculiar severity, was converted, and all his family were baptized. It was in such solemn circumstances that the gospel was first introduced into Europe. After the tumult, and the conversion of the jailer, Paul was honourably released, and soon left the city, Acts xvi. 40. He subsequently visited Macedonia before his imprisonment at Rome, and doubtless went to Philippi (Acts. xx. 1, 2). It is supposed, that after his first imprisonment at Rome, he was released and again visited the churches which he had founded. In this epistle (ch. i. 25, 26; ii. 24) he expresses a confident hope that he would be released, and would be permitted to see them again; and there is a probability that his wishes in regard to this were accomplished. See Intro. to 2 Timothy.

§ 3. *The time when the epistle was written.*

It is evident that this epistle was written from Rome. This appears, (1.) because it was composed when Paul was in 'bonds' (ch. i. 13, 14); (2.) because circumstances are suggested, such as to leave no doubt that the imprisonment was at Rome. Thus, in ch. i. 13, he says that his 'bonds were manifested *in all the palace;*' a phrase which would naturally suggest the idea of the Roman capitol; and, in ch. iv. 22, he says, "All the saints salute you, chiefly they that *are of Cæsar's household.*" It is further evident that it was after he had been imprisoned for a considerable time, and, probably, not long before his release. This appears from the following circumstances: (1.) The apostle had been a prisoner so long in Rome, that the character which he had manifested in his trials had contributed considerably to the success of the gospel. Ch. i. 12—14. His bonds, he says, were manifest "in all the palace;" and many of the brethren had become increasingly bold by his "bonds," and had taken occasion to preach the gospel without fear. (2.) The account given of Epaphroditus imports that, when Paul wrote this epistle, he had been a considerable time at Rome. He was with Paul in Rome, and had been sick there. The Philippians had received an account of his sickness, and he had again been informed how much they had been affected with the intelligence of his illness. Ch. ii. 25, 26. The passing and repassing of this intelligence, Dr. Paley remarks, must have occupied considerable time, and must have all taken place during Paul's residence at Rome. (3.) After a residence at Rome, thus proved to have been of considerable duration, Paul, at the time of writing this epistle, regards the decision of his destiny as at hand. He anticipates that the matter would soon be determined. Ch. ii. 23. "Him therefore (Timothy) I hope to send *presently*, so soon as I see how it will go with me." He had *some* expectation that he might be released, and be permitted to visit them again. Ch. ii. 24. "I trust in the Lord that I also myself shall come shortly." Comp. ch. i. 25. 27. Yet he was not absolutely certain how it would go with him, and though, in one place, he speaks with great confidence that he would be released (ch. i. 25), yet in another he suggests the possibility that he might be put to death. Ch. ii. 17. "Yea, and if I be *offered* upon the sacrifice and service of your faith, I joy and rejoice with you all." These circumstances concur to fix the time of writing the epistle to the period at which the imprisonment in Rome was about to terminate. From Acts xxviii. 30, we learn that Paul was in Rome 'two whole years;' and it was during the latter part of this period that the epistle was written. It is commonly agreed, therefore, that it was written about A. D. 61 or 62. Hug (Intro.) places it at the end of the year 61, or the beginning of the year 62; Lardner, at the close of the year 62. It is evident that it was written before the great conflagration at Rome in the time of Nero (A. D. 64); for it is hardly credible that Paul would have omitted a reference to such an event, if it had occurred. It is certain, from the persecution of the Christians which followed that event, that he would not have been likely to have represented his condition to be so favourable as he has done in this epistle. He could hardly have looked then for a release.

§ 4. *The design and character of the epistle.*

The object of the epistle is apparent. It was sent by Epaphroditus (ch. ii. 25), who appears to have been a resident at Philippi, and a member of the church there, to express the thanks of the apostle for the favours which they had conferred on him, and to comfort them with the hope that he might be soon set at liberty. Epaphroditus had been sent by the Philippians to convey their benefactions to him in the time of his imprisonment. Ch. iv. 18. While at Rome, he had been taken ill. Ch. ii. 26. 27. On his recovery, Paul deemed it proper that he should return at once to Philippi. It was natural that he should give them some information about his condition and prospects. A considerable part of the epistle, therefore, is occupied in giving an account of the effects of his imprisonment in promoting the spread of the gospel, and of his own feelings in the circumstances in which he then was. He was not yet certain what the result of his imprisonment would be (ch. i. 20); but he was prepared either to live or to die, ch. i. 23. He wished to live only that he might be useful to others; and, supposing that he might be made useful, he had some expectation that he might be released from his bonds.

There is, perhaps, no one of the epistles of the apostle Paul which is so tender, and which abounds so much with expressions of kindness, as this. In relation to other churches, he was often under the necessity of using the language of reproof. The prevalence of some error, as in the churches of Galatia; the existence of divisions and strifes, or some aggravated case requiring discipline, or some gross irregularity, as in the church at Corinth; frequently demanded the language of severity. But, in the church at Philippi, there was scarcely anything which required rebuke; there was very much that demanded commendation and gratitude. Their conduct towards him, and their general deportment, had been exemplary, generous, noble. They had evinced for him the tenderest regard in his troubles; providing for his wants, sending a special messenger to supply him when no other opportunity occurred (ch. iv. 10), and sympathizing with him in his trials; and they had, in the order, peace, and harmony of the church, eminently adorned the doctrine of the Saviour. The language of the apostle, therefore, throughout the epistle, is of the most affectionate character—such as a benevolent heart would always choose to employ, and such as must have been exceedingly grateful to them. Paul never hesitated to use the language of commendation where it was deserved, as he never shrank from reproof where it was merited; and he appears to have regarded the one as a matter of duty as much as the other. We are to remember, too, the circumstances of Paul, and to ask what kind of an epistle an affectionate and grateful spiritual father would be *likely* to write to a much-beloved flock, when he felt that he was about to die; and we shall find that *this* is just such an epistle as we should suppose such a man would write. It breathes the spirit of a ripe Christian, whose piety was mellowing for the harvest; of one who felt that he was not far from heaven, and might soon "be with Christ." Though there was some expectation of a release, yet his situation was such as led him to look death in the face. He was lying under heavy accusations; he had no hope of justice from his own countrymen; the character of the sovereign, Nero, was not such as to inspire him with great confidence of having justice done; and it is possible that the fires of persecution had already begun to burn. At the mercy of such a man as Nero; a prisoner; among strangers, and with death staring him in the face, it is natural to suppose that there would be a peculiar solemnity, tenderness, pathos, and ardor of affection, breathing through the entire epistle. Such is the fact; and in none of the writings of Paul are these qualities more apparent than in this letter to the Philippians. He expresses his grateful remembrance of all their kindness; he evinces a tender regard for their welfare; and he pours forth the full-flowing language of gratitude, and utters a father's feelings toward them by tender and kind admonitions. It is important to remember these circumstances in the interpretation of this epistle. It breathes the language of a father, rather than the authority of an apostle; the entreaties of a tender friend, rather than the commands of one in authority. It expresses the affections of a man who felt that he might be near death, and who tenderly loved them; and it will be, to all ages, a model of affectionate counsel and advice.

EPISTLE TO THE PHILIPPIANS.

CHAPTER I.

ANALYSIS OF THE CHAPTER.

This chapter embraces the following points:—

I. The salutation to the church. Vs. 1, 2.

II. In vs. 3—8, the apostle expresses his gratitude for the evidence which they had given of love to God, and for their fidelity in the gospel from the time when it was first proclaimed among them. He says that he was confident that this would continue, and that God, who had so mercifully imparted grace to them to be faithful, would do it to the end.

III. He expresses the earnest hope that they might abound more and more in knowledge, and be without offence to the day of Christ. Vs. 9—11.

IV. In vs. 12—21, he states to them what had been the effect of his imprisonment in Rome—presuming that it would be grateful intelligence to them that even his imprisonment had been overruled for the spread of the gospel. His trials, he says, had been the means of the extension of the knowledge of Christ even in the palace, and many Christians had been emboldened by his sufferings to increased diligence in making known the truth. Some, indeed, he says, preached Christ from unworthy motives, and with a view to increase his affliction, but in the great fact that Christ was preached, he says, he rejoiced. Forgetting himself, and any injury which they might design to do to him, he could sincerely rejoice that the gospel was proclaimed—no matter by whom or with what motives. The whole affair he trusted would be made conducive to his salvation. Christ was the great end and aim of his life; and if he were made known, everything else was of minor importance.

V. The mention of the fact (ver. 21) that his great aim in living was 'Christ,' leads him to advert to the probability that he might soon be with him. Vs. 22—26. So great was his wish to be with him, that he would hardly know which to choose—whether to die at once, or to live and to make him known to others. Believing, however, that his life might be still useful to them, he had an expectation of considerable confidence that his life would be spared, and that he would be released.

VI. The chapter closes, vs. 27—30, with an earnest exhortation that they would live as became the gospel of Christ. Whatever might befall him—whether he should be permitted to see them, or should hear of them, he entreated that he might know that they were living as became the gospel. They were not to be afraid of their adversaries; and if called to suffer, they were to remember that 'it was given' them not only to believe on the Redeemer. but also to suffer in his cause.

1. *Paul and Timotheus.* Paul frequently unites some person with him in his epistles. See Notes on 1 Cor. i. 1. It is clear from this, that Timothy was with Paul at Rome. *Why* he was there is unknown. It is evident that he was not there as a prisoner with Paul, and the proba-

CHAPTER I.

PAUL and Timotheus, the servants of Jesus Christ, to all the saints in Christ Jesus which are at Philippi, [a] with the bishops and deacons;

a Ac. 16. 12. &c.

bility is, that he was one of the friends who had gone to Rome with a view to show his sympathy with him in his sufferings. Comp. Notes on 2 Tim. iv. 9. There was special propriety in the fact that Timothy was joined with the apostle in writing the epistle, for he was with him when the church was founded, and doubtless felt a deep interest in its welfare. Acts xvi. Timothy had remained in Macedonia after Paul went to Athens, and it is not improbable that he had visited them afterwards. ¶ *The servants of Jesus Christ.* Notes, Rom. i. 1. ¶ *To all the saints in Christ Jesus.* The common appellation given to the church, denoting that it was holy. Notes, Rom. i. 7. ¶ *With the bishops.* σὺν ἐπισκόποις. See Notes, Acts xx. 28. The word here used occurs in the New Testament only in the following places. Acts xx. 28, translated *overseers;* and Phil. i. 1. 1 Tim. iii. 2. Tit. i. 7. 1 Pet. ii. 25, in each of which places it is rendered *bishop.* The word properly means *an inspector, overseer,* or *guardian,* and was given to the ministers of the gospel because they exercised this care over the churches, or were appointed to *oversee* their interests. It is a term, therefore, which might be given to any of the officers of the churches, and was originally equivalent to the term *presbyter.* It is evidently used in this sense here. It cannot be used to denote a *diocesan* bishop; or a bishop having the care of the churches in a large district of country, and of a superior rank to other ministers of the gospel, for the word is here used in the plural number, and it is in the highest degree improbable that there were *dioceses* in Philippi. It is clear, moreover, that they were the only officers of the church there except 'deacons;' and the persons referred to, therefore, must have been those who were invested simply with the pastoral office. Thus Jerome, one of the early Fathers, says, respecting the word bishop: "A presbyter is the same as a bishop. And until there arose divisions in religion, churches were governed by a common council of presbyters. But *afterwards,* it was everywhere decreed, that one person, elected from the presbyters, should be placed over the others." "Philippi," says he, "is a single city of Macedonia; and certainly there could not have been several like these who are now called bishops, at one time in the same city. But as, at that time, they called the same bishops, whom they called presbyters also, the apostles spoke indifferently of bishops as of presbyters." Annotations on the Epistle to Titus, as quoted by Dr. Woods on Episcopacy, p. 63. ¶ *And deacons.* On the appointment of deacons, and their duty, see Notes on Acts vi. 1. The word *deacons* does not occur before this place in the common version of the New Testament, though the Greek word here rendered deacon frequently occurs. It is rendered *minister,* and *ministers,* in Matt xx. 26. Mark x. 43. Rom. xiii. 4; xv. 8. 1 Cor. iii. 5. 2 Cor. iii. 6; vi. 4; xi. 15. 23. Gal. ii. 17. Eph. iii. 7; vi. 21. Col. i. 7. 23. 25; iv. 7. 1 Tim. iv. 6; *servant* and *servants,* Matt. xxii. 13; xxiii. 11. Mark ix. 35. John ii. 5. 9; xii. 26. Rom. xvi. 1; and *deacon* or *deacons,* Phil. i. 1. 1 Tim. iii. 8. 12. The word properly means servants, and is then applied to the ministers of the gospel as being the servants of Christ, and of the churches. Hence it came especially to denote those who had charge of the alms of the church, and who were the overseers of the sick and the poor. In this sense the word is probably used in the passage before us, as the officers here referred to were distinct in some way from the bishops. The apostle here mentions but two orders of ministers in the church at Philippi, and this account is of great importance in its bearing on the question about the way in which Christian churches were at first organized, and about the officers which existed in them. In regard to this we may remark, (1.) that but two orders of ministers are mentioned. This is undeniable, whatever rank *they* may have held. (2.) There is no intimation whatever that a minister like a prelatical bishop had ever been appointed there, and that the incumbent of the office was absent, or that the office was now vacant. If the *bishop* was absent, as Bloomfield and others suppose, it is remarkable that no allusion is made to him, and that Paul should have left the impression that there were in fact but two 'orders' there. If there were a prelate there, why did not Paul refer to him with affectionate salutations? Why does he refer to the two other 'orders of clergy' without the slightest allusion to the man who was set over them as "superior in ministerial rank and power?" Was Paul jealous of this prelate? But if they had a prelate, and the see was then vacant, why is there no reference to *this* fact? Why no condolence at their loss? Why no prayer that God would send them a man to enter into the vacant diocese? It is a mere assumption to suppose, as the friends of prelacy often do, that they *had* a prelatical bishop, but that he was then absent. But even granting this, it is an inquiry which has never been answered, why Paul did not make some reference to this fact, and ask their prayers for the absent prelate. (3.) The church was organized by the apostle Paul himself, and there can be no doubt that it was organized on the 'truly primitive and apostolic plan.' (4.) The church at Philippi was in the centre of a large territory; was the capital of Macedonia, and was not likely to be placed in subjection to the diocesan of another region. (5.) It was surrounded by other churches, as we have express mention of the church at Thessalonica, and the preaching of the gospel at Berea. Acts xvii. (6.) There is more than one *bishop* mentioned as connected with the church in Philippi. But these could not have been bishops of the Episcopal or prelatical order. If Episcopalians choose to say that they were *prelates*, then it follows (*a*) that there was a plurality of such persons in the same diocese, the same city, and the same church — which is contrary to the fundamental idea of Episcopacy. It follows also (*b*) that there was entirely wanting in the church at Philippi what the Episcopalians call the "second order" of clergy; that a church was organized by the apostles defective in one of the essential grades, with a body of prelates without presbyters—that is, an order of men of "superior" rank designated to exercise jurisdiction over "priests" who had no existence. If there *were* such presbyters or 'priests' there, why did not Paul name them? If their office was one that was contemplated in the church, and was then vacant, how did this happen? And if *this* were so, why is there no allusion to so remarkable a fact? (7.) It follows, therefore, that in this church there were but two orders of officers; and further that it is right and proper to apply the term *bishop* to the ordinary ministers of the churches.

2 Grace [a] *be* unto you, and peace, from God our Father, and *from* the Lord Jesus Christ.

3 I thank my God upon every [1] remembrance of you,

4 Always in every prayer [b] of mine for you all making request with joy,

5 For your fellowship in the gospel, from the first day until now;

a Ro. 1. 7. [1] or, *mention*.

b Ep. 1. 14, &c. 1 Th. 1. 2.

As no mention is made of a prelate; as there are but two orders of men mentioned to whom the care of the church was intrusted, it follows that there was one church at least organized by the apostles without any prelate. (8.) The same thing may be observed in regard to the distinction between 'teaching' elders and 'ruling' elders. No such distinction is referred to here; and however useful such an office as that of ruling elder may be, and certain as it is, that such an office existed in some of the primitive churches, yet here is one church where no such officer is found, and this fact proves that such an officer is not essential to the Christian church.

2. *Grace be unto you*, &c. See Note, Rom. i. 7.

3. *I thank my God upon every remembrance of you.* Marg., *mention.* The Greek word means *recollection, remembrance.* But this recollection may have been suggested either by his own reflections on what he had seen, or by what he had heard of them by others, or by the favours which they conferred on him reminding him of them. The meaning is, that as often as he thought on them, from whatever cause, he had occasion of thankfulness. He says that he thanked *his* God, intimating that the conduct of the Philippians was a proof of the favour of God to to him; that is, he regarded their piety as one of the tokens of the favour of God to his own soul—for in producing that piety he had been mainly instrumental.

4. *Always*. There is much emphasis in the expressions which are here used. Paul labours to show them that he never forgot them; that he always remembered them in his prayers. ¶ *In every prayer of mine.* This was a proof of particular and special affection, that while there were so many objects demanding his prayers, and so many other churches which he had founded, he never forgot *them.* The person or object that we remember in *every* prayer must be very dear to the heart. ¶ *For you all.* Not for the church in general, but for the individual members. "He industriously repeats the word *all*, that he might show that he loved them all equally well, and that he might the more successfully excite them to the manifestation of the same love and benevolence." *Wetstein.* ¶ *Making request with joy.* With joy at your consistent walk and benevolent lives —mingling thanksgiving with my prayers in view of your holy walk.

5. *For your fellowship in the gospel.* "For your liberality towards me, a preacher of the gospel." *Wetstein.* There has been, however, no little difference of opinion about the meaning of this phrase. Many—as Doddridge, Koppe, and others—suppose it refers to the fact that they participated in the blessings of the gospel from the first day that he preached it until the time when he wrote this epistle. Others suppose that it refers to their constancy in the Christian faith. Others—as Pierce, Michaelis, Wetstein, Bloomfield, and Storr—suppose it refers to their liberality in contributing to the sup-

port of the gospel; to their *participating* with others, or sharing what they had *in common* with others, for the maintenance of the gospel. That this is the true sense seems apparent, (1.) because it accords with the scope of the epistle, and what the apostle elsewhere says of their benefactions. He speaks particularly of their liberality, and indeed this was one of the principal occasions of his writing the epistle. Ch. iv. 10—12, 15—18. (2.) It accords with a frequent meaning of the word rendered *fellowship*—*κοινωνία*. It denotes that which is *in common;* that of which we participate with others, *communion, fellowship.* Acts ii. 42. 1 Cor. i. 9; x. 16. Philem. 6; then it means *communication, distribution, contribution.* Rom. xv. 26. 2 Cor. ix. 13. That it cannot mean 'accession to the gospel' as has been supposed (see Rob. Lex.), is apparent from what he adds—'from the first day until now.' The fellowship must have been something constant, and continually manifest—and the general meaning is, that in relation to the gospel—to its support, and privileges, and spirit, they all shared in common. They felt a common interest in every thing that pertained to it, and they showed this in every suitable way, and especially in ministering to the wants of those who were appointed to preach it. ¶ *From the first day.* The time when it was first preached to them. They had been *constant.* This is honourable testimony. It is much to say of a church, or of an individual Christian, that they have been constant and uniform in the requirements of the gospel. Alas, of how *few* can this be said! On these verses (3—5) we may remark, (1.) That one of the highest joys which a minister of the gospel can have, is that furnished by the holy walk of the people to whom he has ministered. Comp. 3 John 4. It is joy like that of a farmer when he sees his fields whiten for a rich harvest; like that of a teacher in the good conduct and rapid progress of his scholars; like that of a parent in the virtue, success, and piety of his sons. Yet it is superior to all that. The interests are higher and more important; the results are more far-reaching and pure; and the joy is more disinterested. Probably there is nowhere else on earth any happiness so pure, elevated, consoling, and rich, as that of a pastor in the piety, peace, benevolence, and growing zeal of his people. (2.) It is right to commend Christians when they do well. Paul never hesitated to do this, and never supposed that it would do injury. Flattery would injure—but Paul never flattered. Commendation or praise, in order to do good, and not to injure, should be (*a*) the simple statement of the truth; (*b*) it should be without exaggeration; (*c*) it should be connected with an equal readiness to rebuke when wrong; to admonish when in error, and to counsel when one goes astray. Constant fault-finding, scolding, or fretfulness, does no good in a family, a school, or a church. The tendency is to dishearten, irritate, and discourage. To commend a child when he does well, may be as important, and as much a duty, as to rebuke him when he does ill. God is as careful to commend his people when they do well, as he is to rebuke them when they do wrong—and that parent, teacher, or pastor, has much mistaken the path of wisdom, who supposes it to be his duty *always to find fault.* In this world there is nothing that goes so far in promoting happiness as a willingness to be pleased rather than displeased; to be satisfied rather than dissatisfied with the conduct of others. (3.) Our absent friends should be remembered in our prayers. On our knees before God is the best place to remem-

6 Being confident[a] of this very thing, that he[b] which hath begun

a He. 10. 35. b Ps. 138. 8.

ber them. We know not their condition. If they are sick, we cannot minister to their wants; if in danger, we cannot run to their relief; if tempted, we cannot counsel them. But God, who is with them, can do all this; and it is an inestimable privilege thus to be *permitted* to commend them to his holy care and keeping. Besides, it is a *duty* to do it. It is one way—and the best way—to repay their kindness. A child may always be repaying the kindness of absent parents by supplicating the divine blessing on them each morning; and a brother may strengthen and continue his love for a sister, and in part repay her tender love, by seeking, when far away, the divine favour to be bestowed on her.

6. *Being confident.* This is strong language. It means to be fully and firmly persuaded or convinced. Part. Mid. voice from πείθω—to persuade. Comp. Luke xvi. 31. "Neither will they be *persuaded*, though one rose from the dead;" that is, they would not be *convinced.* Acts xvii. 4. Heb. xi. 13. Acts xxviii. 24. It means here that Paul was *entirely convinced* of the truth of what he said. It is the language of a man who had no doubt on the subject. ¶ *That he which hath begun a good work in you.* The 'good work' here referred to, can be no other than religion, or true piety. This is called the work of God; the work of the Lord; or the work of Christ. John vi. 29. Comp. 1 Cor. xv. 58; xvi. 10. Phil. ii. 30. Paul affirms here that that work was *begun* by God. It was not by their own agency or will. Comp. Notes on John i. 13. It was on the fact that it was begun by *God*, that he based his firm conviction that it would be permanent. Had it been the agency of man, he would have had no such conviction, for nothing that man does to-day can lay the foundation of a *certain* conviction that he will do the same thing to-morrow. If the perseverance of the Christian depended wholly on himself, therefore, there could be no sure evidence that he would ever reach heaven. ¶ *Will perform it.* Marg., 'or, *finish.*' The Greek word—ἐπιτελέσει—means that he would carry it forward to *completion;* he would perfect it. It is an *intensive* form of the word, meaning that it would be carried through *to the end.* It occurs in the following places: Luke xiii. 32, "I *do* cures;" Rom. xv. 28, "when *I have performed* this;" 2 Cor. vii. 1, "*perfecting* holiness;" viii. 6, "so he would also *finish* in you;" 11, "*perform* the doing of it;" Gal. iii. 3, "are ye now made *perfect* by the flesh;" Heb. viii. 5, "when he was about to *make* the tabernacle;" ix. 6, "*accomplishing* this service;" and 1 Pet. v. 9, "are *accomplished* in your brethren." The word occurs nowhere else; and here means that God would carry on the work which he had begun to *completion.* He would not leave it unfinished. It would not be commenced and then abandoned. This would or could be 'performed' or 'finished' only (1.) by keeping them from falling from grace, and (2.) by their ultimate entire perfection. ¶ *Until the day of Jesus Christ.* The day when Christ shall so manifest himself as to be the great attractive object, or the day when he shall appear to glorify himself, so that it may be said emphatically to be *his day.* That day is often called "*his* day," or "the day of the Lord," because it will be the day of his triumph and glory. It refers here to the day when the Lord Jesus will appear to receive

a good [a] work in you will [1] perform *it* until the day [b] of Jesus Christ:

a Jno. 6. 29. [1] or, *finish.* b 2 Pe. 3. 10.

7 Even as it is meet for me to think this of you all, because [2] I have you in my heart; inasmuch

[2] or, *ye have me in your.*

his people to himself—the day of judgment. We may remark on this verse, that Paul believed in *the perseverance of saints.* It would be impossible to express a stronger conviction of the truth of that doctrine than he has done here. Language could not be clearer, and nothing can be more unequivocal than the declaration of his opinion that where God has begun a good work in the soul, it will not be finally lost. The *ground* of this belief he has not stated in full, but has merely hinted at it. It is based on the fact that *God* had begun the good work. That ground of belief is something like the following. (1.) It is in God alone. It is not in man in any sense. No reliance is to placed on man in keeping himself. He is too weak; too changeable; too ready to be led astray; too much disposed to yield to temptation. (2.) The reliance, therefore, is on God; and the evidence that the renewed man will be kept is this: (*a*) God *began* the work of grace in the soul. (*b*) He had a *design* in it. It was deliberate, and intentional. It was not by chance or hap-hazard. It was because he had some object that was *worthy* of his interposition. (*c*) There is no reason why he should *begin* such a work and then abandon it. It cannot be because he has no power to complete it, or because there are more enemies to be overcome than he had supposed; or because there are difficulties which he did not foresee; or because it is not desirable that the work should be completed. Why then should he abandon it? (*d*) God abandons nothing that he undertakes. There are no unfinished worlds or systems; no half-made and forsaken works of his hands. There is no evidence in his works of creation of change of plan or of having forsaken what he began from disgust, or disappointment, or want of power to complete them. Why should there be in the salvation of the soul? (*e*) He has *promised* to keep the renewed soul to eternal life. See John x. 27, 28, 29. Heb. vi. 17—20. Comp. Rom. viii. 29, 30.

7. *Even as it is meet for me to think this of you all.* 'There is a reason why I should cherish this hope of you, and this confident expectation that you will be saved. That reason is found in the evidence which you have given that you are sincere Christians. Having evidence of that, it is proper that I should believe that you will finally reach heaven.' ¶ *Because I have you in my heart.* Marg., *Ye have me in your.* The Greek will bear either, though the former translation is the most obvious. The meaning is, that he was warmly attached to them, and had experienced many proofs of their kindness; and that there was, therefore, a propriety in his wishing for their salvation. Their conduct towards him, moreover, in his trials, had convinced him that they were actuated by christian principle; and it was proper that he should believe that they would be kept to eternal life. ¶ *Both in my bonds.* While I have been a prisoner—referring to the care which they had taken to minister to his wants. Ch. iv. 10. 14. 18. ¶ *And in the defence.* Gr., *apology.* Probably he refers to the time when he made his defence before Nero, and vindicated himself from the charges which had been

as both in my bonds, and in the defence [a] and confirmation of the gospel, ye all are partakers [1] of my grace.

8 For God is my record, how greatly I long after you all in the bowels of Jesus Christ.

9 And this I pray, that your love may abound [b] yet more and more in knowledge and *in* all [2] judgment;

a ver. 17. [1] or, *with me of grace.*

b 1 Th. 3. 12. 2 Pe. 3. 18. [2] or, *sense.*

brought against him. See Notes, 2 Tim. iv. 16. Perhaps he means, here, that on that occasion he was abandoned by those who should have stood by him, but that the Philippians showed him all the attention which they could. It is not impossible that they may have sent some of their number to sympathize with him in his trials, and to assure him of the unabated confidence of the church. ¶ *And confirmation of the gospel.* In my efforts to defend the gospel, and to make it known. See ver. 17. The allusion is probably to the fact that, in all his efforts to defend the gospel, he had been sure of their sympathy and co-operation. Perhaps he refers to some assistance which he had derived from them in this cause, which is now to us unknown. ¶ *Ye all are partakers of my grace.* Marg., 'Or, *with me of grace.*' The meaning is, that as they had participated with him in the defence of the gospel; as in all his troubles and persecutions they had made *common cause* with him, so it followed that they would partake of the same tokens of the divine favour. He expected that the divine blessing would follow *his* efforts in the cause of the gospel, and he says that they would share in the blessing. They had shown all the sympathy which they could in his trials; they had nobly stood by him when others forsook him; and he anticipated, as a matter of course, that they would all share in the benefits which would flow to him in his efforts in the cause of the Redeemer.

8. *For God is my record.* My witness; I can solemnly appeal to him. ¶ *How greatly I long after you all.* To see you; and how much I desire your welfare. ¶ *In the bowels of Jesus Christ.* The word 'bowels,' in the Scriptures, denotes the upper viscera—the region of the heart and lungs. See Notes on Isa. xvi. 11. That region was regarded as the seat of affection, sympathy, and compassion, as the *heart* is with us. The allusion here is to the sympathy, tenderness, and love of the Redeemer; and probably the meaning is, that Paul regarded them with something of the affection which the Lord Jesus had for them. This was the tenderest and strongest expression which he could find to denote the ardour of his attachment.

9. *And this I pray.* We pray for those whom we love, and whose welfare we seek. We desire their happiness; and there is no way more appropriate of expressing that desire than of going to God, and seeking it at his hand. Paul proceeds to enumerate the blessings which he sought for them; and it is worthy of observation that he did not ask riches, or worldly prosperity, but that his supplications were confined to spiritual blessings, and he sought these as the most desirable of all favours. ¶ *That your love may abound,* &c. Love to God; love to one another; love to absent Christians; love to the world. This is an appropriate subject of prayer. We cannot wish and pray for a better thing for our christian friends, than that they may abound in *love.* Nothing will promote their welfare like this; and we had better

10 That [a] ye may [1] approve things that are [2] excellent; that ye may be [b] sincere and without offence till the day of Christ;

a Ro. 2. 18. 1 or, *try*. 2 or, *differ*. b Ep. 5. 27.

pray for this, than that they may obtain abundant riches, and share the honours and pleasures of the world. ¶ *In knowledge.* The idea is, that he wished them to have *intelligent* affection. It should not be mere blind affection, but that intelligent love which is based on an enlarged view of divine things—on a just apprehension of the claims of God. ¶ *And in all judgment.* Marg., *sense.* Comp. Notes on Heb. v. 14. The word here means, *the power of discerning;* and the meaning is, that he wished that their love should be exercised with proper *discrimination.* It should be in proportion to the relative value of objects; and the meaning of the whole is, that he wished their religion to be intelligent and discriminating; to be based on knowledge, and a proper sense of the relative value of objects, as well as to be the tender affection of the heart.

10. *That ye may approve things.* Marg., 'Or, *try*.' The word used here denotes the kind of trial to which metals are exposed in order to test their nature; and the sense here is, that the apostle wished them so to try the things that were of real value, as to discern that which was true and genuine. ¶ *That are excellent.* Marg., 'or, *differ*.' The margin here more correctly expresses the sense of the Greek word. The idea is, that he wished them to be able to distinguish between things that *differed* from each other; to have an intelligent apprehension of what was right and wrong—of what was good and evil. He would not have them love and approve all things indiscriminately. They should be esteemed according to their real value. It is remarkable here how anxious the apostle was, not only that they should be *Christians*, but that they should be *intelligent Christians*, and should understand the real worth and value of objects. ¶ *That ye may be sincere.* See Notes on Eph. vi. 24. The word here used—εἰλικρινής—occurs nowhere else in the New Testament, except in 2 Pet. iii. 1, where it is rendered *pure.* The *noun* εἰλικρίνεια, however, occurs in 1 Cor. v. 8; 2 Cor. i. 12; ii. 17; in all which places it is rendered *sincerity.* The word properly means, that which is *judged of in sun-shine* (εἴλη κρίνω); and then that which is clear and manifest. It is that over which there are no clouds; which is not doubtful and dark; which is pure and bright. The word *sincere* means literally *without wax* (*sine cera*); that is, honey which is pure and transparent. Applied to christian character, it means that which is not deceitful, ambiguous, hypocritical; that which is not mingled with error, worldliness, and sin; that which does not proceed from selfish and interested motives, and where there is nothing disguised. There is no more desirable appellation that can be given to a man than to say that he is *sincere*—a sincere friend, benefactor, Christian; and there is nothing more lovely in the character of a Christian than *sincerity.* It implies, (1.) that he is truly converted—that he has not *assumed* Christianity as a mask; (2.) that his motives are disinterested and pure; (3.) that his conduct is free from double-dealing, trick, and cunning; (4.) that his words express the real sentiments of his heart; (5.) that he is true to his word, and faithful to his promises; and (6.) that he is always what he professes to be. A sincere Christian would bear to have the light let in upon him always; to

11 Being filled with the fruits of righteousness, which are by Jesus Christ unto the glory [a] and praise of God.

12 But I would ye should understand, brethren, that the things *which happened* unto me have fallen out rather unto the furtherance of the gospel;

a Jno. 15. 8.

have the emotions of his heart seen; to be scanned everywhere, and at all times, by men, by angels, and by God. ¶ *And without offence.* Inoffensive to others. Not injuring them in property, feelings, or reputation. This is a *negative* virtue, and is often despised by the world. But it is much to say of a man that he *injures* no one; that neither by example, nor opinions, nor conversation, he leads them astray; that he never does injustice to their motives, and never impedes their influence; that he never wounds their feelings, or gives occasion for hard thoughts; and that he so lives that all may see that his is a blameless life. ¶ *Till the day of Christ.* See Notes on ver. 6.

11. *Being filled with the fruits of righteousness.* That which righteousness in the heart produces. The fruits, or results, will be seen in the life; and those fruits are—honesty, truth, charity, kindness, meekness, goodness. The wish of the apostle is, that they might show abundantly by their lives that they were truly righteous. He does not refer to *liberality* merely, but to everything which true piety in the heart is fitted to produce in the life. ¶ *Which are by Jesus Christ.* (1.) Which his religion is fitted to produce. (2.) Which result from endeavouring to follow his example. (3.) Which are produced by his agency on the heart. ¶ *Unto the glory and praise of God.* His honour is never more promoted than by the eminent holiness of his friends. See Notes, John xv. 8. If we wish, therefore, to honour God, it should not be merely with the lips, or by acts of prayer and praise; it should be by a life devoted to him. It is easy to render the service of the lips; it is far more difficult to render that service which consists in a life of patient and consistent piety; and in proportion to the *difficulty* of it, is its value in his sight.

12. *But I would ye should understand.* Paul here turns to himself, and goes into a somewhat extended account of his own feelings in his trials, and of the effects of his imprisonment at Rome. He wished them to understand what his circumstances were, and what had been the effect of his imprisonment, probably, for such reasons as these: (1.) They were tenderly attached to him, and would feel an interest in all that pertained to him. (2.) It was possible that they might hear unfounded rumours about the manner of his treatment, and he wished that they should understand the exact truth. (3.) He had real intelligence to communicate to them that would be joyful to them, about the effect of his imprisonment, and his treatment there; and he wished them to rejoice with him. ¶ *That the things* which happened *unto me.* The accusations against him, and his imprisonment at Rome. He had been falsely accused, and had been constrained to appeal to Cæsar, and had been taken to Rome as a prisoner. Acts xxv.—xxviii. This arrest and imprisonment would *seem* to have been against his success as a preacher; but he now says that the contrary had been the fact. ¶ *Have fallen out.* Have resulted in. Literally, 'have come.' Tindal. 'My business is happened.' ¶ *The furtherance.* The increase, the promotion of the gospel. Instead of

13 So that my bonds [1] in Christ are manifest in all [2] the palace, and [3] in all other *places;*

[1] or, *for.*

[2] or, *Cæsar's court*, c. 4. 22. [3] *to all others.*

being a hindrance, they have been rather an advantage.

13. *So that my bonds in Christ.* Marg., *for.* The meaning is, his bonds *in the cause* of Christ. He was imprisoned *because* he preached Christ (Notes, Eph. vi. 20), and was really suffering because of his attachment to the Redeemer. It was not for crime, but for being a Christian—for had he not been a Christian, he would have escaped all this. The *manner* of Paul's imprisonment was, that he was suffered to occupy a house by himself, though chained to a soldier who was his guard. Acts xxviii. 16. He was not in a dungeon indeed, but he was not at liberty, and this was a severe mode of confinement. Who would wish to be *chained* night and day to a living witness of all that he did; to a spy on all his movements? Who would wish to have such a man always with him, to hear all he said, and to see all that he did? Who could well bear the feeling that he could *never* be alone—and never be at liberty to do any thing without the permission of one too who probably had little disposition to be indulgent? ¶ *Are manifest.* That is, it has become known that I am imprisoned only for the sake of Christ. *Grotius.* The true reason why I am thus accused and imprisoned begins to be understood, and this has awakened sympathy for me as an injured man. They see that it is not for *crime*, but that it is on account of my religious opinions, and the conviction of my innocence has spread abroad, and has produced a favourable impression in regard to Christianity itself. It must have been a matter of much importance for Paul to have this knowledge of the real cause why he was imprisoned go abroad. Such a knowledge would do much to prepare others to listen to what he had to say—for there is no man to whom we listen more readily than to one who is suffering wrongfully. ¶ *In all the palace.* Marg., 'or *Cæsar's court.*' Gr., ἐν ὅλω τῷ πραιτωρίῳ—*in all the prætorium.* This word properly denotes *the general's tent in a camp;* then the house or palace of a governor of a province; then any large hall, house, or palace. It occurs in the New Testament only in the following places: Matt. xxvii. 27, where it is rendered *common hall;* Mark xv. 16, rendered *Prætorium;* John xviii. 28. 33; xix. 9. Acts xxiii. 35, rendered *judgment hall;* and in Phil. i. 13. It is employed to denote (1.) the palace of Herod at Jerusalem, built with great magnificence at the northern part of the upper city, westward of the temple, and overlooking the temple; (2.) the palace of Herod at Cesarea, which was probably occupied by the Roman procurator, and (3.) in the place before us to denote either the palace of the emperor at Rome, or the pretorian camp, the head quarters of the pretorian guards or cohorts. These cohorts were a body of select troops instituted by Augustus to guard his person, and have charge of the city. See *Rob. Lex.* Bloomfield, Rosenmüller, and some others, understand this of the pretorian camp, and suppose that Paul meant to say that the cause of his imprisonment had become known to all the band of the pretorians. Grotius says that the usual word to denote the residence of the emperor at Rome was *palatium—palace*, but that those who resided in the provinces were accustomed to the word *pretorium*, and would use it when speaking of the

14 And many of the brethren in the Lord, waxing confident by

palace of the emperor. Chrysostom says that the palace of the emperor was called *pretorium*, by a Latin word derived from the Greek. See Erasmus *in loc.* Calvin supposes that the palace of Nero is intended. The question about the meaning of the word is important, as it bears on the inquiry to what extent the gospel was made known at Rome in the time of Paul, and perhaps as to the question why he was released from his imprisonment. If the knowledge of his innocence had reached *the palace*, it was a ground of hope that he might be acquitted; and if that palace is here intended, it is an interesting fact, as showing that in some way the gospel had been introduced into the family of the emperor himself. That the palace or residence of the emperor is intended here, may be considered at least probable from the following considerations. (1.) It is the name which would be likely to be used by the Jews who came up from Judea and other provinces, to denote the chief place of judgment, or the principal residence of the highest magistrate. So it was used in Jerusalem, in Cesarea, and in the provinces generally, to denote the residence of the general in the camp, or the procurator in the cities—the highest representative of the Roman power. (2.) If the remark of Chrysostom, above referred to, be well founded, that this was a common name given to the palace in Rome, then this goes far to determine the question. (3.) In ch. iv. 22, Paul, in the salutation of the saints at Rome to those of Philippi, mentions particularly those of "Cæsar's household." From this it would seem that some of the family of the emperor had been made acquainted with the Christian religion, and had been converted. In what way the knowledge of the true cause of Paul's imprisonment had been circulated in the 'palace,' is not now known. There was, however, close intimacy between the military officers and the government, and it was probably by means of some of the soldiers or officers who had the special charge of Paul, that this had been communicated. To Paul, in his bonds, it must have been a subject of great rejoicing, that the government became thus apprized of the true character of the opposition which had been excited against him; and it must have done much to reconcile him to the sorrows and privations of imprisonment, that he was thus the means of introducing religion to the very palace of the emperor. ¶ *And in all other places.* Marg., *to all others.* The Greek will bear either construction. But if, as has been supposed, the reference in the word *pretorium* is to the *palace*, then this should be rendered 'all other *places*.' It then means, that the knowledge of his innocence, and the consequences of that knowledge in its happy influence in spreading religion, were not confined to the palace, but were extended to other places. The subject was *generally* understood, so that it might be said that correct views of the matter pervaded the city, and the fact of his imprisonment was accomplishing extensively the most happy effects on the public mind.

14. *And many of the brethren.* Many Christians. It is evident from this, that there were already '*many*' in Rome who professed Christianity. ¶ *In the Lord.* In the Lord Jesus; that is, united to him and to each other by a professed attachment to him. This is a common phrase to designate Christians. ¶ *Waxing confident by my bonds.* Becoming increasingly bold and zealous in consequence of my being confined.

my bonds, are much more bold to speak the word without fear.

15 Some indeed preach Christ even of envy and strife, and some also of good will.

16 The one preach Christ of

This might have been either (1.) that from the *very fact* that so distinguished a champion of the truth had been imprisoned, they were excited to do all they could in the cause of the gospel. Or (2.) they were aroused by the fact that the cause of his imprisonment had become generally understood, and that there was a strong current of popular favour setting towards Christianity in consequence of it. Or (3.) they had had intercourse with Paul in his own 'hired house,' and had been incited and encouraged by him to put forth great efforts in the cause. Or (4.) it would seem that some had been emboldened to promulgate their views, and set themselves up as preachers, who would have been restrained if Paul had been at liberty. They were disposed to form parties, and to secure followers, and rejoiced in an opportunity to increase their own popularity, and were not unwilling thus to diminish the popularity and lessen the influence of so great a man as Paul. Had *he* been at liberty, they would have had no prospect of success. See ver. 16. To this may be added a suggestion by Theodoret. 'Many of the brethren have increased boldness—θάρσος—on account of my bonds. For seeing me bear such hard things with pleasure, they announce that the gospel [which sustains me] is divine.' The same sentiment occurs in Oecumen. and Theophyl. See *Bloomfield.* In Paul himself they had an illustration of the power of religion, and being convinced of its truth, they went and proclaimed it abroad. ¶ *To speak the word without fear.* That is, they see that I remain safely (comp. Acts xviii. 30), and that there is no danger of persecution, and, stimulated by my sufferings and patience, they go and make the gospel known.

15. *Some indeed preach Christ even of envy and strife.* What was the ground of this 'envy and strife' the apostle does not mention. It would seem, however, that even in Rome there was a party which was jealous of the influence of Paul, and which supposed that this was a good opportunity to diminish his influence, and to strengthen their own cause. He was not now at large so as to be able to meet and confute them. They had access to the mass of the people. It was easy, under plausible pretences, to insinuate hints about the ambitious aims, or improper influence of Paul, or to take strong ground against him and in favour of their own views, and they availed themselves of this opportunity. It would seem most probable, though this is not mentioned, that these persons were *Judaizing teachers,* professing Christianity, and who supposed that Paul's views were derogatory to the honour of Moses and the law. ¶ *And some also of good will.* From pure motives, having no party aims to accomplish, and not intending in any way to give me trouble.

16. *The one preach Christ of contention.* So as to form parties, and to produce strifes among his professed followers. ¶ *Not sincerely.* Not *purely*—ἁγνῶς—not with pure motives or intentions. Their *real* aim is not to preach Christ, but to produce difficulty, and to stir up strife. They are ambitious men, and they have no real regard for the welfare of the church and the honour of religion. ¶ *Supposing to add*

contention, not sincerely, supposing to add affliction to my bonds;

17 But the other of love, knowing that I am set for the defence of the gospel.

18 What then? notwithstand-

---

affliction to my bonds. To make my trial the greater. *How* they did this is unknown. Perhaps they were those who were strongly imbued with Jewish notions, and who felt that his course tended to diminish respect for the law of Moses, and who now took this opportunity to promote their views, knowing that this would be particularly painful to him when he was not at liberty to meet them openly, and to defend his own opinions. It is *possible* also that they may have urged that Paul himself had met with a signal reproof for the course which he had taken, and, as a consequence, was now thrown into chains. Bloomfield suggests that it was the opinion of many of the ancient expositors that they endeavoured to do this by so preaching as to excite the fury of the multitude or the rulers against Paul, and to produce increased severity in his punishment. But the *way* in which they did this is unknown, and conjecture is altogether useless.

17. *But the other of love.* From pure motives, and from sincere affection to me. ¶ *Knowing that I am set for the defence of the gospel.* They believe that I am an ambassador from God. They regard me as unjustly imprisoned, and while I am disabled, they are willing to aid me in the great cause to which my life is devoted. To alleviate his sorrows, and to carry forward the great cause to defend which he was particularly appointed, they engaged in the work which he could not now do, and went forth to vindicate the gospel, and to make its claims better known. Coverdale renders this, "for they know that I lie here for the defence of the gospel." So Piscator, Michaelis, and Endius render it, supposing that the meaning is, that he lay in prison for the defence of the gospel, or as a consequence of his efforts to defend it. But this is not in accordance with the usual meaning of the Greek word (κεῖμαι). It means to lie, and in the perf. pass. to be laid, set, placed. If the apostle had referred to his being in prison, he would have *added* that fact to the statement made. The sense is, that he was appointed to be a defender of the gospel, and that they being well convinced of this, went forth to promulgate and defend the truth. That fact was one of Paul's chief consolations while he was thus in confinement.

18. *What then?* What follows from this? What effect does it have on my mind? Does the fact that some preach from a spirit of envy and contention give me pain? ¶ *Notwithstanding every way.* No matter in what way it is done. We are not to suppose, however, that Paul was indifferent as to the way in which the gospel was preached, or the spirit with which it was done; but the meaning is, that it was a matter of rejoicing that *it was done at all*, whatever the motives might be. ¶ *Whether in pretence or in truth.* Whether as a mere pretext to cover up some other design, or from pure motives. Their pretence was that they preached the gospel because they believed it true and loved it; their real object was to build up a party, and to diminish the influence and authority of Paul. ¶ *Christ is preached.* They made known the name of the Saviour, and announced that the Messiah had come. They could not go forth under *any* pretence as preachers, without making known *some* truth about the Redeemer. So now, it is hardly

ing every way, whether in pretence or in truth, Christ is preached; and I therein do rejoice, yea, and will rejoice.

19 For I know that this [a] shall turn to my salvation through [b] your prayer, and the supply of the Spirit of Jesus Christ,

a Ro. 8. 28. b 2 Co. 1. 11.

possible that any persons should attempt to preach, without stating *some* truth that would not otherwise be known. The *name* of a Saviour will be announced, and that will be something. Some views of his life and work will be presented, which, though they may be far enough from full views, are yet better than none. Though there may be much *error* in what is said, yet there will be also some truth. It would be better to have preachers that were better instructed, or that were more prudent, or that had purer motives, or that held a more perfect system, yet it is much in our world *to have the name of the Redeemer announced in any way*, and even to be told, in the most stammering manner, and from whatever motives, that *man has a Saviour*. The announcement of that fact in any way *may* save a soul; but ignorance of it could save none. ¶ *And I therein do rejoice.* This is an instance of great magnanimity on the part of Paul, and nothing, perhaps, could better show his supreme love for the Saviour. Part preached to increase his afflictions, and the tendency of that preaching was, probably, as it was designed to be, to unsettle confidence in him, and to lessen his influence. Yet this did not move him. The more important matter was secured, and Christ was made known; and if this were secured, he was willing that his own name should be cast into the shade. This may furnish valuable lessons to preachers of the gospel now. When (1.) we are laid aside from preaching by sickness, we should rejoice that others are in health, and are able to make the Saviour known, though we are forgotten. (2.) When we are unpopular and unsuccessful, we should rejoice that others are more popular and successful — for Christ is preached. (3.) When we have rivals, who have better plans than we for doing good, and whose labours are crowned with success, we should not be envious or jealous—for Christ is preached. (4.) When ministers of other denominations preach what we regard as error, and their preaching becomes popular, and is attended with success, we can find occasion to rejoice — for they preach Christ. In the error we should not, we cannot rejoice; but in the fact that the great truth is held up that Christ died for men, we can always find abundant occasion for joy. Mingled as it may be with error, it may be nevertheless the means of saving souls, and though we should rejoice *more* if the truth were preached without any admixture of error, yet still the very fact that Christ is made known lays the foundation for gratitude and rejoicing. Had all Christians, and Christian ministers, the feelings which Paul expresses here, there would be much less envy and uncharitableness than there is now in the churches. May we not hope that the time will yet come when all who preach the gospel will have such supreme regard for the name and work of the Saviour, that they will find sincere joy in the success of a rival denomination, or a rival preacher, or in rival plans for doing good? Then, indeed, contentions would cease, and the hearts of Christians, "like kindred drops," would mingle into one.

19. *For I know that this shall turn to my salvation.* Will be a

20 According to my earnest expectation and *my* hope, that in nothing I shall be ashamed, [a] but *that* with all boldness, [b] as always, *so* now also, Christ shall be mag-

[a] Ro. 5. 5.

[b] Ep 6. 19, 20.

means of my salvation. Whether the effect shall be to turn public favour towards the christian religion, and secure my release; or whether it shall be to instigate my enemies more, so as to lead to my death: I am satisfied that the result, so far as I am concerned, will be well. The word 'salvation,' here, does not refer to his *release* from captivity, as Koppe, Rosenmüller, Clarke, and others, suppose; for he was not absolutely certain of that, and could not expect that to be effected by "the supply of the Spirit of Jesus Christ." But the meaning is, that all these dealings, including his imprisonment, and especially the conduct of those who thought to add affliction to his bonds, would be among the means of his salvation. Trying and painful as all this was, yet trial and pain Paul reckoned *among the means of grace;* and he had no doubt that this would prove so. ¶ *Through your prayer.* See Notes on 2 Cor. i. 11. ¶ *And the supply of the Spirit of Jesus Christ.* To sustain me, and to cause those happy results to come out of these trials. He needed the same spirit which Jesus Christ had, to enable him to bear his trials with patience, and to impart to him the consolations which he required. He had no idea that these trials would produce these effects of their own accord, nor that it could be by any strength of his own.

20. *According to my earnest expectation.* The word here used occurs but in one other place in the New Testament. See it explained in the Notes on Rom. viii. 19. The earnest desire and hope which Paul had was not, primarily, that he might be released; but it was that, in all circumstances, he might be able to honour the gospel, living or dying. To that he looked as a much more important matter than to save his life. Life with him was the secondary consideration; the main thing was, to stand up everywhere as the advocate of the gospel, to maintain its truth, and to exhibit its spirit. ¶ *That in nothing I shall be ashamed.* That I shall do nothing of which I shall have occasion to be ashamed. That in these heavy trials, I may not be left to deny the truth of the christian religion; that, even before the emperor, I may maintain its principles; and that the dread of death may not lead me to do a dishonourable thing, or in any way so to shrink from an avowal of my belief, as to give me or my friends occasion of regret. ¶ *But* that *with all boldness.* By my speaking the truth, and maintaining my principles with all boldness. Notes, 2 Cor. vii. 4. Eph. vi. 19, 20. ¶ *Christ shall be magnified.* Shall be held up to the view of man as the true and only Saviour, whatever becomes of me. ¶ *Whether* it be *by life.* If I am permitted to live. He was not yet certain how the case would terminate with him. He had not been put on his trial, and, whether that trial would result in his acquittal or not, he could not certainly know. But he felt assured that, if he was acquitted, the effect would be to honour Christ. He would ascribe his deliverance to his gracious interposition; he would devote himself with new ardour to his service; and he felt assured, from his past efforts, that he would be able to do something that would '*magnify*' Christ in the estimation of mankind. ¶ *Or by death.* If my trial shall result in my death. Then, he believed, he

nified in my body, whether [a] *it be* by life or by death.

21 For to me to live *is* Christ, and to die [b] *is* gain.

a Ro. 14. 7, 8. *b* Re. 14. 13.

would be able to show such a spirit as to do honour to Christ and his cause. He was not afraid to die, and he was persuaded that he would be enabled to bear the pains of death in such a manner as to show the sustaining power of religion, and the value of Christianity. Christ is 'magnified' in the death of Christians, when his gospel is seen to sustain them; when, supported by its promises, they are enabled to go calmly into the dark valley; and when, in the departing moments, they confidently commit their eternal all into his hands. The effect of this state of feeling on the mind of Paul must have been most happy. In whatever way his trial terminated, he felt assured that the great object for which he lived would be promoted. Christ would be honoured, perhaps, as much by his dying as a martyr, as by his living yet many years to proclaim his gospel. He was, therefore, reconciled to his lot. He had no anxiety. Come what might, the purpose which he had most at heart would be secured, and the name of the Saviour would be honoured.

21. *For to me to live* is *Christ.* My sole aim in living is to glorify Christ. He is the supreme End of my life, and I value it only as being devoted to his honour. *Doddridge.* His aim was not honour, learning, gold, pleasure; it was. to glorify the Lord Jesus. This was the single purpose of his soul—a purpose to which he devoted himself with as much singleness and ardour as ever did a miser to the pursuit of gold, or a devotee of pleasure to amusement, or an aspirant for fame to ambition. This implied the following things: (1.) A purpose to *know* as much of Christ as it was possible to know—to become as fully acquainted as he could with his rank, his character, his plans, with the relations which he sustained to the Father, and with the claims and influences of his religion. See Phil. iii. 10. Eph. iii. 19. Comp. John xvii. 3. (2.) A purpose to *imitate* Christ—to make him the model of his life. It was a design that his Spirit should reign in his heart, that the same temper should actuate him, and that the same great end should be constantly had in view. (3.) A purpose to make his religion known, as far as possible, among mankind. To this Paul seriously gave his life, and devoted his great talents. His aim was to see on how many minds he could impress the sentiments of the christian religion; to see to how many of the human family he could make Christ known, to whom he was unknown before. Never was there a man who gave himself with more ardour to any enterprise, than Paul did to this; and never was one more successful, in any undertaking, than he was in this. (4.) It was a purpose to *enjoy Christ.* He drew his comforts from him. His happiness he found in communion with him. It was not in the works of art; not in the pursuits of elegant literature; not in the gay and fashionable world; but it was in communion with the Saviour, and in endeavouring to please him. Remark, (1.) Paul never had occasion to regret this course. It produced no sadness when he looked over his life. He never felt that he had had an unworthy aim of living; he did not wish that his purpose had been different when he came to die. (2.) If it was Paul's duty thus to live, it is no less that of every Christian. What was there in *his* case that made it his duty to

'live unto Christ,' which does not exist in the case of every sincere Christian on earth? No believer, when he comes to die, will regret that he has lived unto Christ; but how many, alas! regret that this has *not* been the aim and purpose of their souls! ¶ *And to die* is *gain.* Comp. Rev. xiv. 13. A sentiment similar to this occurs frequently in the Greek and Latin classic writers. See Wetstein, *in loc.*, who has collected numerous such passages. With them, the sentiment had its origin in the belief that they would be freed from suffering, and admitted to some happy world beyond the grave. To them, however, all this was conjecture and uncertainty. The word *gain*, here, means *profit, advantage;* and the meaning is, there would be an *advantage* in dying above that of living. Important benefits would result to him *personally*, should he die; and the only reason why he should wish at all to live was, that he might be the means of benefiting others. Vs. 24, 25. But how would it be gain to die? What advantage would there be in Paul's circumstances? What in ours? It may be answered, that it will be gain for a Christian to die in the following respects: (1.) He will be then freed from sin. Here it is the source of perpetual humiliation and sorrow; in heaven he will sin no more. (2.) He will be freed from doubts about his condition. Here the best are liable to doubts about their personal piety, and often experience many an anxious hour in reference to this point; in heaven, doubt will be known no more. (3.) He will be freed from temptation. Here, no one knows when he may be tempted, nor how powerful the temptation may be; in heaven, there will be no allurement to lead him astray; no artful, cunning, and skilful votaries of pleasure to place inducements before him to sin; and no *heart* to yield to them, if there were. (4.) He will be delivered from all his enemies—from the slanderer, the calumniator, the persecutor. Here the Christian is constantly liable to have his motives called in question, or to be met with detraction and slander; there, there will be none to do him injustice; all will rejoice in the belief that he is pure. (5.) He will be delivered from suffering. Here he is constantly liable to it. His health fails, his friends die, his mind is sad. There, there shall be no separation of friends, no sickness, and no tears. (6.) He will be delivered from death. Here, death is ever nigh—dreadful, alarming, terrible to our nature. There, death will be known no more. No face will ever turn pale, and no knees tremble, at his approach; in all heaven there will never be seen a funeral procession, nor will the soil there ever open its bosom to furnish a grave. (7.) To all this may be added the fact, that the Christian will be surrounded by his best friends; that he will be reunited with those whom he loved on earth; that he will be associated with the angels of light; and that he will be admitted to the immediate presence of his Saviour and his God! Why, then, should a Christian be afraid to die? And why should he not hail that hour, when it comes, as the hour of his deliverance, and rejoice that he is going home? Does the prisoner, long confined in a dungeon, dread the hour which is to open his prison, and permit him to return to his family and friends? Does the man in a foreign land, long an exile, dread the hour when he shall embark on the ocean to be conveyed where he may embrace the friends of his youth? Does the sick man dread the hour which restores him to health? the afflicted, the hour of comfort? the wanderer at night, the cheering light of returning day? And why then should the Christian

22 But if I live in the flesh, this *is* the fruit of my labour: yet what I shall choose I wot not.

---

dread the hour which will restore him to immortal vigour; which shall remove all his sorrows; which shall introduce him to everlasting day?

> Death is the crown of life:
> Were death denied, poor man would live in vain;
> Were death denied, to live would not be life;
> Were death denied, even fools would wish to die.
> Death wounds to cure; we fall; we rise; we reign!
> Spring from our fetters; fasten in the skies;
> Where blooming Eden withers in our sight.
> Death gives us more than was in Eden lost.
> The king of terrors is the prince of peace.
>
> *Night Thoughts*, iii.

22. *But if I live in the flesh.* If I continue to live; if I am not condemned and make a martyr at my approaching trial. ¶ *This is the fruit of my labour.* The meaning of this passage, which has given much perplexity to commentators, it seems to me is, 'If I live in the flesh, it will *cost* me labour; it will be attended, as it has been, with much effort and anxious care, and I know not which to prefer—whether to remain on the earth with these cares and the hope of doing good, or to go at once to a world of rest.' A more literal version of the Greek will show that this is the meaning. τοῦτό μοι καρπὸς ἔργου—'this to me is [or would be] the fruit of labour.' Coverdale, however, renders it, "Inasmuch as to live in the flesh is fruitful to me for the work, I wot not what I shall choose." So Luther, 'But since to live in the flesh serves to produce more fruit.' And so Bloomfield, "But if my life in the flesh be of use to the gospel (be it so, I say no more), verily what I shall choose I see and know not." See also Koppe, Rosenmüller, and Calvin, who give the same sense. According to this, the meaning is, that if his life were of value to the gospel, he was willing to live; or that it was a valuable object—*operæ pretium*—worth an effort thus to live. This sense accords well with the connection, and the thought is a valuable one, but it is somewhat doubtful whether it can be made out from the Greek. To do it, it is necessary to suppose that μοι—*my*—is expletive (Koppe), and that καὶ—*and*—is used in an unusual sense. See *Erasmus.* According to the interpretation first suggested, it means, that Paul felt that it would be gain to die, and that he was entirely willing; that he felt that if he continued to live it would involve toil and fatigue, and that, therefore, great as was the natural love of life, and desirous as he was to do good, he did not know which to choose—an immediate departure to the world of rest, or a prolonged life of toil and pain, attended even with the hope that he might do good. There was an intense desire to be with Christ, joined with the belief that his life here must be attended with toil and anxiety; and on the other hand an earnest wish to live in order to do good, and he knew not which to prefer. ¶ *Yet.* The sense has been obscured by this translation. The Greek word (καὶ) means *and*, and should have been so rendered here, in its usual sense. 'To die would be gain; my life here would be one of toil, AND I know not which to choose.' ¶ *What I shall choose I wot not.* I do not know which I should prefer, if it were left to me. On each side there were important considerations, and he knew not which overbalanced the other. Are not Christians often in this state, that if it were left to themselves they would not know which to choose, whether to live or to die?

23 For I am in a strait betwixt two, having a desire [a] to depart, and to be with Christ; which is far better: [b]

a 2 Co. 5. 8. b Ps. 16. 11.

23. *For I am in a strait betwixt two.* Two things, each of which I desire. I earnestly long to be with Christ; and I desire to remain to be useful to the world. The word rendered 'I am in a strait'—συνέχομαι—means to be pressed on or constrained, as in a crowd; to feel one's self pressed or pent up so as not to know what to do; and it here means that he was in perplexity and doubt, and did not know what to choose. 'The words of the original are very emphatic. They appear to be derived from a ship when lying at anchor, and when violent winds blow upon it that would drive it out to sea. The apostle represents himself as in a similar condition. His strong affection for them bound his heart to them—as an anchor holds a ship to its moorings—and yet there was a heavenly influence bearing upon him—like the gale upon the vessel—which would bear him away to heaven.' *Burder*, in Ros. Alt. u. neu. Morgenland, *in loc.* ¶ *Having a desire to depart.* To die—to leave this world for a better. Men, as they are by nature, usually *dread* to die. Few are even made *willing* to die. Almost none *desire* to die—and even then they wish it only as the least of two evils. Pressed down by pain and sorrow; or sick and weary of the world, the mind *may* be wrought up into a *desire* to be away. But this with the world is, in all cases, the result of misanthropy, or morbid feeling, or disappointed ambition, or an accumulation of many sorrows. Wetstein has adduced on this verse several most beautiful passages from the classic writers, in which men expressed a desire to depart—but all of them probably could be traced to disappointed ambition, or to mental or bodily sorrows, or to dissatisfaction with the world. It was from no such wish that Paul desired to die. It was not because he hated man,—for he ardently loved him. It was not because he had been disappointed about wealth and honour—for he had sought neither. It was not because he had not been successful—for no man had been more so. It was not because he had been subjected to pains and imprisonments—for he was willing to bear them. It was not because he was old, and infirm, and a burden to the world—for, from any thing that appears, he was in the vigour of life, and in the fulness of his strength. It was from a purer, higher motive than any of these—the strength of attachment which bound him to the Saviour, and which made him long to be with him. ¶ *And to be with Christ.* We may remark on this expression, (1.) That this was the true reason why he wished to be away. It was his strong love to Christ; his anxious wish to be with him; his firm belief that in his presence was 'fulness of joy.' (2.) Paul believed that the soul of the Christian would be immediately with the Saviour at death. It was evidently his expectation that he would at once pass to his presence, and not that he would remain in an intermediate state to some far distant period. (3.) The soul does not *sleep* at death. Paul expected to be *with* Christ, and to be conscious of the fact—to see him, and to partake of his glory. (4.) The soul of the believer is made happy at death. To be with Christ is synonymous with being in heaven—for Christ is in heaven, and is its glory. We may add, (*a*) that this wish to be with Christ constitutes a marked difference between a Christian and

24 Nevertheless to abide in the flesh *is* more needful for you.

25 And having this confidence, I know that I shall abide and con-

other men. Other men may be willing to die; perhaps be desirous to die, because their sorrows are so great that they feel that they cannot be borne. But the Christian desires to depart from a different motive altogether. It is *to be with Christ*—and this constitutes a broad line of distinction between him and other men. (*b*) A mere *willingness* to die, or even a *desire* to die, is no certain evidence of preparation for death. If this willingness or desire is caused by mere intensity of suffering; if it is produced by disgust at the world or by disappointment; if it arises from some view of fancied Elysian fields beyond the grave, it constitutes no evidence whatever of a preparation for death. I have seen not a few persons who were not professed Christians on a bed of death, and not a few *willing* to die, nay, not a few who *wished* to depart. But in the vast majority of instances it was because they were sick of life, or because their pain made them sigh for relief, or *because they were so wretched that they did not care what happened*—and this they and their friends construed into an evidence that they were prepared to die! In most instances this is a miserable delusion; in *no* case is a mere willingness to die an evidence of preparation for death. ¶ *Which is far better.* Would be attended with more happiness; and would be a higher, holier state than to remain on earth. This proves also that the soul of the Christian at death is made at once happy—for a state of insensibility can in no way be said to be a better condition than to remain in this present world. The Greek phrase here—πολλῷ μᾶλλον κρεῖσσον—is very emphatic, and the apostle seems to labour for language which will fully convey his idea. It means, 'by much more, or rather better,' and the sense is, 'better beyond all expression.' *Doddridge.* See numerous examples illustrating the phrase in Wetstein. Paul did not mean to say that he was merely *willing* to die, or that he *acquiesced* in its necessity, but that the fact of being with Christ was a condition *greatly to be preferred* to remaining on earth. This is the true feeling of Christian piety; and having this feeling, death to us will have no terrors.

24. *Nevertheless to abide in the flesh.* To live. All this is language derived from the belief that the soul will be separate from the body at death, and will occupy a separate state of existence. ¶ Is *more needful for you.* Another object that was dear to the heart of Paul. He never supposed that his life was useless; or that it was a matter of no importance to the cause of religion whether he lived or died. He knew that God works by means; and that the life of a minister of the gospel is of real value to the church and the world. His experience, his influence, his paternal counsels, he felt assured would be of value to the church, and he had, therefore, a desire to live—and it was no part of his religion affectedly to undervalue or despise himself.

25. *And having this confidence.* 'Being persuaded of this, that my continuance on earth is desirable for your welfare, and that the Lord has a work for me to do, I confidently expect that I shall be permitted to live.' The 'confidence' here referred to was, that his life was needful for them, and hence that God would spare him. A literal translation would be, 'And being persuaded as to this, or of this'—τοῦτο πεποιθὼς—'I know,' &c. The foundation of his expectation that he should live

tinue with you all, for your furtherance and joy of faith;

26 That your rejoicing may be more abundant in Jesus Christ for me, by my coming to you again.

27 Only [a] let your conversation be as it becometh the gospel of Christ; that, whether I come and see you, or else be absent, I may

a Ep. 4. 1. c. 3. 20.

---

does not appear to have been any revelation to that effect, as Doddridge supposes; or any intimation which he had from the palace, of the intentions of the government, as some others suppose, but the fact that he believed his life to be necessary for them, and that therefore God would preserve it. ¶ *I know that I shall abide.* The word *know*, however, (οἶδα) is not to be *pressed* as denoting absolute necessity—for it appears from ver. 27, and ch. ii. 17, that there was *some* ground for doubt whether he would live—but is to be taken in a *popular* sense, as denoting good courage, and an earnest hope, that he would be permitted to live and visit them. *Heinrichs.* ¶ *And continue with you all.* That is, that he would be permitted not only to live, but to enjoy their society. ¶ *For your furtherance and joy of faith.* For the increase of your faith, and the promotion of that joy which is the consequence of faith. Wetstein has quoted a beautiful passage from Seneca (Epis. 104) which strikingly resembles this sentiment of Paul. He says that when a man had meditated death, and when on his own account he would be willing to die, yet that he ought to be willing to live—to come back again to life—for the sake of his friends. He then adds, 'It pertains to a great mind to be willing to come back to life for the sake of others; which distinguished men often do.'

26. *That your rejoicing may be more abundant in Christ Jesus.* Through the mercy and grace of Christ. If he was spared, his deliverance would be traced to Christ, and they would rejoice together in one who had so mercifully delivered him. ¶ *For me by my coming to you again.* Their joy would not only be that he was delivered, but that he was permitted to see them again.

27. *Only let your conversation.* The word *conversation* we now apply almost exclusively to oral discourse, or to *talking*. But it was not formerly confined to that, and is never so used in the Scriptures. It means conduct in general—including, of course, our manner of speaking, but not limited to that—and should be so understood in every place where it occurs in the Bible. The original word here used—πολιτεύω—*politeuo*, means properly *to administer the State; to live as a citizen; to conduct oneself according to the laws and customs of a State.* See Acts xxiii. 1. Comp. examples in Wetstein. It would not be improperly rendered, 'let your conduct as a citizen be as becomes the gospel;' and might without impropriety, though not exclusively, be referred to our deportment as members of a community, or citizens of a State. It undoubtedly implies that, *as* citizens, we should act, in all the duties which that relation involves—in maintaining the laws, in submission to authority, in the choice of rulers, &c., as well as in other relations—on the principles of the gospel; for the believer is bound to perform every duty on christian principles. But the direction here should not be confined to that. It doubtless includes our conduct in all relations in life, and refers to our deportment in general; not merely as citizens of the State, but as members of the church, and in all other rela-

hear of your affairs, that ye[a] stand fast in one spirit, with one mind, striving[b] together for the faith of the gospel;

28 And in nothing terrified[a] by your adversaries: which[b] is to them an evident token of perdi-

a c. 4. 1. b Jude 3.

a Is. 51. 7, 12. Mat. 10 28. b 2 Th. 1. 5.

tions. In our manner of speech, our plans of living, our dealings with others, our conduct and walk *in* the church and out of it—all should be done as becomes the gospel. The direction, therefore, in this place, is to be understood of everything pertaining to *conduct.* ¶ *As it becometh the gospel of Christ.* (1.) The rules of the gospel are to be applied to all our conduct—to our conversation, business transactions, modes of dress, style of living, entertainments, &c. There is nothing which we do, or say, or purpose, that is to be excepted from those rules. (2.) There *is* a way of living which is *appropriate to the gospel,* or which is such as the gospel requires. There is something which the gospel would secure as *its proper fruits* in all our conduct, and by which our lives should be regulated. It would distinguish us from the gay, and from those who seek honour and wealth as their supreme object. If all Christians were under the influence of the gospel, there would be *something* in their dress, temper, conversation, and aims, which would distinguish them from others. The gospel is not a thing of naught; nor is it intended that it should exert *no* influence on its friends. (3.) It is very important that Christians should frame their lives by the rules of the gospel, and, to this end, should *study* them and know what they are. This is important, (*a*) because they are the *best* and *wisest* of all rules; (*b*) because it is only in this way that Christians can do good; (*c*) because they have solemnly covenanted with the Lord to take his laws as their guide; (*d*) because it is only in this way that they can enjoy religion; and (*e*) because it is only by this tha they can have peace on a dying bed. If men live as 'becometh the gospel,' they live well. Their lives are honest and honourable; they are men of truth and uprightness; they will have no sources of regret when they die, and they will not give occasion to their friends to hang their heads with shame in the remembrance of them. No man on a dying bed ever yet regretted that he had framed his life by the rules of the gospel, or felt that his conduct had been conformed too much to it. ¶ *That whether I come and see you.* Alluding to the possibility that he might be released, and be permitted to visit them again. ¶ *Or else be absent.* Either at Rome, still confined, or released, and permitted to go abroad. ¶ *I may hear of your affairs,* &c. I may hear always respecting you that you are united, and that you are vigorously striving to promote the interests of the gospel.

28. *And in nothing terrified by your adversaries.* Adversaries, or opponents, they had, like most of the other early Christians. There were Jews there who would be likely to oppose them (comp. Acts xvii. 5), and they were exposed to persecution by the heathen. In that city, Paul had himself suffered much (Acts xvi.); and it would not be strange if the same scenes should be repeated. It is evident from this passage, as well as from some other parts of the epistle, that the Philippians were at this time experiencing some form of severe suffering. But in what way, or why, the opposition to them was excited, is nowhere stated. The meaning here is, 'do not be alarmed at anything which

tion, but [a] to you of salvation, and that of God.

29 For unto you it is given [b] in the behalf of Christ, not only to

a Ro. 8. 17.

b Ac. 5. 41.

they can do. Maintain your christian integrity, notwithstanding all the opposition which they can make. They will, in the end, certainly be destroyed, and you will be saved.' ¶ *Which is to them an evident token of perdition. What*, it may be asked, would be the token of their perdition? What is the evidence to which Paul refers that they will be destroyed? The relative 'which' —ἥτις—is probably used as referring to the *persecution* which had been commenced, and to the *constancy* which the apostle supposed the Philippians would evince. The sentence is elliptical; but it is manifest that the apostle refers either to the circumstance then occurring, that they were persecuted, and that they evinced constancy; or to the constancy which he *wished* them to evince in their persecutions. He says that *this circumstance of persecution, if they evinced such a spirit as he wished*, would be to them an evidence of two things: (1.) Of the destruction of those who were engaged in the persecution. This would be, because they knew that such persecutors could not ultimately prevail. Persecution of the church would be a certain indication that they who did it would be finally destroyed. (2.) It would be a proof of their own salvation, because it would show that they were the friends of the Redeemer; and they had the assurance that all those who were persecuted for his sake would be saved. The gender of the Greek relative here is determined by the following noun (ἔνδειξις), in a manner that is not uncommon in Greek. See Wetstein, *in loc.*, and Koppe. ¶ *And that of God.* That is, their persecution is a proof that God will interpose in due time and save you. The hostility of the wicked to us is one evidence that we are the friends of God, and shall be saved.

29. *For unto you.* Unto you as Christians. This favour is granted unto you in your present circumstances. ¶ *It is given.* God concedes to you this privilege or advantage. ¶ *In the behalf of Christ.* In the cause of Christ, or with a view to honour Christ. Or, these things are brought on you in consequence of your being Christians. ¶ *Not only to believe on him.* It is represented here as a *privilege* to be permitted to believe on Christ. It is so. (1.) It is an honour to a man to believe one who ought to be believed, to trust one who ought to be trusted, to love one who ought to be loved. (2.) It is a privilege to believe on Christ, because it is by such faith that our sins are forgiven; that we become reconciled to God, and have the hope of heaven. (3.) It is a privilege, because it saves the mind from the *tortures* and the deadly influence of unbelief—the agitation, and restlessness, and darkness, and gloom of a skeptic. (4.) It is a privilege, because we have then a friend to whom we may go in trial, and on whom we may roll all our burdens. If there is anything for which a Christian ought to give unfeigned thanks, it is that he has been permitted to believe on the Redeemer. Let a sincere Christian compare his peace, and joy, and hope of heaven, and support in trials, with the restlessness, uneasiness, and dread of death, in the mind of an unbeliever; and he will see abundant occasion for gratitude. ¶ *But also to suffer for his sake.* Here it is represented as a *privilege* to suffer in the cause of the Redeemer—a declaration which may sound strange to the

believe on him, but also to suffer for his sake;

30 Having the same conflict which ye saw [a] in me, *and* now hear *to be* in me.

a Ac. 16. 19. 1 Th. 2. 2.

---

world. Yet this sentiment frequently occurs in the New Testament. Thus it is said of the apostles (Acts v. 41), that "they departed from the presence of the council, rejoicing that they were counted worthy to suffer shame for his name." Col. i. 24. "Who now rejoice in my sufferings for you." 1 Pet. iv. 13. "But rejoice, inasmuch as ye are partakers of Christ's sufferings." Comp. James i. 2. Mark x. 30. See Notes on Acts v. 41. It is a *privilege* thus to suffer in the cause of Christ, because (1.) we then resemble the Lord Jesus, and are united with him in trials; (2.) because we have evidence that we are his, if trials come upon us in his cause; (3.) because we are engaged in a good cause, and the privilege of maintaining such a cause is worth much of suffering; and (4.) because it will be connected with a brighter crown and more exalted honour in heaven.

30. *Having the same conflict.* The same *agony*—ἀγῶνα—the same strife with bitter foes, and the same struggle in the warfare. ¶ *Which ye saw in me.* When I was in Philippi, opposed by the multitude, and thrown into prison. Acts xvi. ¶ *And now hear to be in me.* In Rome. He was a prisoner there, was surrounded by enemies, and was about to be tried for his life. He says that they ought to rejoice if they were called to pass through the same trials.

In this chapter we have a beautiful illustration of the true spirit of a Christian in circumstances exceedingly trying. The apostle was in a situation where religion would show itself, if there were any in the heart; and where, if there was none, the bad passions of our nature would be developed. He was a prisoner. He had been unjustly accused. He was about to be put on trial for his life, and it was wholly uncertain what the result would be. He was surrounded with enemies, and there were not a few false friends and rivals who took advantage of his imprisonment to diminish his influence and to extend their own. He was, perhaps, about to die; and at any rate, was in such circumstances as to be under a necessity of looking death in the face.

In this situation he exhibited some of the tenderest and purest feelings that ever exist in the heart of man—the genuine fruit of pure religion. He remembered them with affectionate and constant interest in his prayers. He gave thanks for all that God had done for them. Looking upon his own condition, he said that the trials which had happened to him, great as they were, had been overruled to the furtherance of the gospel. The gospel had become known even in the imperial palace. And though it had been preached by some with no good will towards him, and with much error, yet he cherished no hard feeling; he sought for no revenge; he rejoiced that in any way, and from any motives, the great truth had been made known that a Saviour died. Looking forward to the possibility that his trial before the emperor might terminate in his death, he calmly anticipated such a result, and looked at it with composure. He says that in reference to the great purpose of his life, it would make no difference whether he lived or died, for he was assured that Christ would be honoured, whatever was the result. To him personally it would be gain to die; and, as an individual, he longed for the hour when he might be with Christ. This feeling is religion, and this is produced only by the hope of eternal life through the Redeemer. An impenitent sinner never expressed such feelings as these; nor does any other form of religion but Christianity enable a man to look upon death in this manner. It is not often that a man is even *willing* to die—and then this state of mind is produced, not by the hope of heaven, but by disgust at the world; by disappointed ambition; by painful sickness, when the sufferer feels that *any* change would be for the better. But Paul had none of these feelings. His desire to depart was not produced by a hatred of life; nor by the greatness of his sufferings; nor by disgust at the world. It was the noble, elevated, and pure wish *to be with Christ*—to see him whom he supremely loved, whom he had so long and so faithfully served, and with whom he was to dwell for ever. To that world where Christ dwelt he would gladly rise; and the only reason why he could be content to remain here was, that he might be a little longer useful to his fellow men. Such is the elevated nature of christian feeling. But, alas! how few attain to it; and even among Christians, how few are they that can habitually *feel* and *realize* that it would be gain for them to die! How few can say with sincerity that they *desire* to depart and to be with Christ! How rarely does even the Christian reach that state of mind, and gain that view of heaven, that, standing amidst his comforts here, and looking on his family, and friends, and property, he can say from the depths of his soul, that he *feels* it would be gain for him to go to heaven! Yet such deadness to the world *may* be produced—as it was in the case of Paul; such deadness to the world *should* exist in the heart of every sincere Christian. Where it *does* exist, death loses its terror, and the heir of life can look calmly on the bed where he will lie down to die; can think calmly of the moment when he will give the parting hand to wife and child, and press them to his bosom for the last time, and imprint on them the last kiss; can look peacefully on the spot where he will moulder back to dust, and in view of all can triumphantly say, "Come, Lord Jesus, come quickly."

CHAPTER II.

ANALYSIS OF THE CHAPTER.

This chapter is made up principally of exhortations to the performance of various christian duties, and the exhibition of christian virtues. The apostle first exhorts the Philippians, in the most tender manner, so to live as to give him joy, by evincing among themselves unity and concord. He entreats them to do nothing by strife and a desire of distinction, but to evince that humility which is manifested when we regard others as more worthy than we are. Vs. 1—4. This exhortation he enforces in a most impressive manner by a reference to the example of Christ—an example of condescension and humiliation fitted to repress in us all the aspirings of ambition, and to make us ready to submit to the most humble offices to benefit others. Vs. 5—11. He then exhorts them to work out their salvation with diligence, assuring them, for their encouragement, that God worked in them to will and to do of his good pleasure. Vs. 12, 13. To this he adds an exhortation that they would avoid everything like murmuring and disputing—that they would be blameless and harmless in their walk, showing the excellency of the religion which they loved to all around them, and exerting such an influence on others that Paul might feel that he had not laboured

CHAPTER II.

IF *there be* therefore any consolation in Christ, if any comfort of love, if any fellowship of the Spirit, if any bowels [a] and mercies,

a Co. 3. 12.

in vain. Vs. 14—16. To excite them to this, he assures them that he was ready himself to be sacrificed for their welfare, and should rejoice if by his laying down his life their happiness would be promoted. He asked the same thing in return from them. Vs. 17, 18. He then tells them, in expressing his interest in them, that he hoped soon to be able to send Timothy to them again—a man who felt a deep interest in their welfare, and whose going to them would be one of the highest proofs of the apostle's love. Vs. 19—24. The same love for them, he says, he had now shown by sending to them Epaphroditus—a man to whom he was tenderly attached, and who had an earnest desire again to return to the church from which he had been sent. Paul sent him, therefore, again to Philippi, that he might be with them and comfort them, and he asked for him a kind reception and affectionate treatment, in view of the sufferings which he had experienced in the cause of the Redeemer. Vs. 25—30.

1. *If* there be *therefore any consolation in Christ.* This, with what is said in the remainder of the verse, is designed as a *motive* for what he exhorts them to in ver. 2—that they would be of the same mind, and would thus fulfil his joy. To urge them to this, he appeals to the tender considerations which religion furnished—and begins by a reference to the consolation which there was in Christ. The meaning here may be this: 'I am now persecuted and afflicted. In my trials it will give me the highest joy to learn that you act as becomes Christians. You also are persecuted and afflicted (ch. i. 28—30); and, in these circumstances, I entreat that the highest consolation may be sought; and by all that is tender and sacred in the christian religion, I conjure you, so to live as not to dishonour the gospel. So live as to bring down the highest consolation which *can* be obtained—the consolation which Christ alone can impart.' We are not to suppose that Paul *doubted* whether there *was* any consolation in Christ, but the form of expression here is one that is designed to urge upon them the duty of seeking the *highest* possible. The *consolation in Christ* is that which *Christ furnishes* or *imparts.* Paul regarded him as the source of all comfort, and earnestly prays that they might so live that he and they might avail themselves in the fullest sense of that unspeakable enjoyment. The idea is, that Christians ought at all times, and especially in affliction, so to act as to secure the highest possible happiness which their Saviour can impart to them. Such an object is worth their highest effort; and if God sees it needful, in order to that, that they should endure much affliction, still it is gain. *Religious consolation is always worth all which it costs to secure it.* ¶ *If any comfort of love.* If there be any comfort in the exercise of tender affection. That there *is*, no one can doubt. Our happiness is almost all centred in love. It is when we love a parent, a wife, a child, a sister, a neighbour, that we have the highest earthly enjoyment. It is in the love of God, of Christ, of Christians, of the souls of men, that the redeemed find their highest happiness. Hatred is a passion full of misery; love an emotion full of joy.

2 Fulfil [a] ye my joy, that ye be [b] like-minded, having the same love, *being* of one accord, of one mind.

a Jno. 3. 29. *b* 2 Co. 13. 11. 1 Pe. 3. 8.

3 *Let* nothing [c] *be done* through strife or vain glory; but in lowliness of mind let each [d] esteem other better than themselves.

c Ga. 5. 26. Ja. 3. 14. *d* 1 Pe. 5. 5.

By this consideration, Paul appeals to them, and the motive here is drawn from all the joy which mutual love and sympathy are fitted to produce in the soul. Paul would have that love exercised in the highest degree, and would have them enjoy all the happiness which its mutual exercise could furnish. ¶ *If any fellowship of the Spirit.* The word 'fellowship'—κοινωνία—means that which is *common* to two or more; that of which they partake together. Notes, Eph. iii. 9. Phil. i. 5. The idea here is, that among Christians there was a *participation* in the influences of the Holy Ghost; that they shared in some degree the feelings, views, and joys of the sacred Spirit himself; and that this was a privilege of the highest order. By this fact, Paul now exhorts them to unity, love, and zeal—so to live that they might partake in the highest degree of the consolations of this Spirit. ¶ *If any bowels and mercies.* If there is any affectionate bond by which you are united to me, and any regard for my sorrows, and any desire to fill up my joys, so live as to impart to me, your spiritual father and friend, the consolation which I seek.

2. *Fulfil ye my joy.* Fill up my joy so that nothing shall be wanting to complete it. This, he says, would be done by their union, zeal, and humility. Comp. John iii. 29. ¶ *That ye be like minded.* Gr. That ye think the same thing. See Notes on 2 Cor. xiii. 11. Perfect unity of sentiment, opinion, and plan would be desirable if it could be attained. It may be, so far as to prevent discord, schism, contention and strife in the church, and so that Christians may be harmonious in promoting the same great work—the salvation of souls. ¶ *Having the same love.* Love to the same objects, and the same love one for another. Though their opinions might differ on some points, yet they might be united in love. See Notes on 1 Cor. i. 10. ¶ Being *of one accord.* σύμψυχοι—*of one soul; having your souls joined together.* The word used here does not occur elsewhere in the New Testament. It means a union of soul; or an acting together *as if* but one soul actuated them. ¶ *Of one mind.* Gr. *Thinking the same thing.* The apostle here uses a great variety of expressions to denote the same thing. The object which he aimed at was union of heart, of feeling, of plan, of purpose. He wished them to avoid all divisions and strifes; and to show the power of religion by being united in the common cause. Probably there is no single thing so much insisted on in the New Testament as the importance of harmony among Christians. Now, there is almost nothing so little known; but *if* it prevailed, the world would soon be converted to God. Comp. Notes on John xvii. 21—or see the text itself without the Notes.

3. Let *nothing* be done *through strife.* With a spirit of contention. This command forbids us to do any thing, or attempt any thing as *the mere result of strife.* This is not the principle from which we are to act, or by which we are to be governed. We are to form *no* plan, and aim at no object which is to be secured in this way. The command prohibits all attempts to secure any thing over others by mere physical

strength, or by superiority of intellect or numbers, or as the result of dark schemes and plans formed by rivalry, or by the indulgence of angry passions, or with the spirit of ambition. We are not to attempt to do any thing *merely* by outstripping others, or by showing that we have more talent, courage, or zeal. What we do is to be by principle, and with a desire to maintain the truth, and to glorify God. And yet how often is this rule violated! How often do christian denominations attempt to outstrip each other, and to see which shall be the greatest! How often do ministers preach with no better aim! How often do we attempt to outdo others in dress, and in the splendour of furniture and equipage! How often, even in plans of benevolence, and in the cause of virtue and religion, is the secret aim to *outdo others*. This is all wrong. There is no holiness in such efforts. Never once did the Redeemer act from such a motive, and never once should this motive be allowed to influence us. The conduct of others may be allowed to show us what we *can* do, and *ought* to do; but it should not be our sole aim to outstrip them. Comp. 2 Cor. ix. 2—4. ¶ *Or vain glory.* The word here used—κενοδοξία—*kenodoxia*, occurs nowhere else in the New Testament, though the adjective—κενόδοξος—*kenodoxos*, occurs once in Gal. v. 26. See Notes on that place. It means properly *empty pride*, or *glory*, and is descriptive of vain and hollow parade and show. Suidas renders it, 'any vain opinion about one's self'—ματαία τις περὶ ἑαυτοῦ οἴησις. The idea seems to be that of mere self-esteem; a mere desire to honour ourselves, to attract attention, to win praise, to make ourselves uppermost, or foremost, or the main object. The command here solemnly forbids our doing *any thing* with such an aim—no matter whether it be in intellectual attainments, in physical strength, in skill in music, in eloquence or song, in dress, furniture, or religion. *Self* is not to be foremost; selfishness is not to be the motive. Probably there is no command of the Bible which would have a wider sweep than this, or would touch on more points of human conduct, if fairly applied. Who is there who passes a single day without, in some respect, desiring to display himself? What minister of the gospel preaches, who never has any wish to exhibit his talents, eloquence, or learning? How few make a gesture, but with some wish to display the grace or power with which it is done! Who, in conversation, is always free from a desire to show his wit, or his power in argumentation, or his skill in repartee? Who plays at the piano without the desire of commendation? Who thunders in the senate, or goes to the field of battle; who builds a house, or purchases an article of apparel; who writes a book, or performs a deed of benevolence, altogether uninfluenced by this desire? If all could be taken out of human conduct which is performed merely from "strife," or from "vain-glory," how small a portion would be left! ¶ *But in lowliness of mind.* Modesty, or humility. The word here used is the same which is rendered *humility* in Acts xx. 19. Col. ii. 18. 23. 1 Pet. v. 5; *humbleness*, in Col. iii. 12; and *lowliness*, in Eph. iv. 2. Phil. ii. 3. It does not elsewhere occur in the New Testament. It here means *humility*, and it stands opposed to that pride or self-valuation which would lead us to strive for the ascendancy, or which acts from a wish for flattery, or praise. The best and the only true correction of these faults is humility. This virtue consists in estimating ourselves *according to truth*. It is a willingness to take

4 Look not every man on his[a] own things, but every man also on the things of others.

a 1 Co. 13.5.

the place which we *ought* to take in the sight of God and man; and, having the low estimate of our own importance and character which the *truth* about our insignificance as creatures and vileness as sinners would produce, it will lead us to a willingness to perform lowly and humble offices that we may benefit others. ¶ *Let each esteem other better than themselves.* Comp. 1 Pet. v. 5. This is one of the effects produced by true humility, and it naturally exists in every truly modest mind. The reasons are these. (1.) We are sensible of our own defects, but we have not the same clear view of the defects of others. We see our own hearts; we are conscious of the great corruption there; we have painful evidence of the impurity of the motives which often actuate us—of the evil thoughts and corrupt desires in our own souls; but we have not the same view of the errors, defects, and follies of others. We can see only their *outward* conduct; but, in our own case, we can look *within*. It is natural for those who have any just sense of the depravity of their own souls, charitably to hope that it is not so with others, and to believe that they have purer hearts. This will lead us to feel that they are worthy of more respect than we are. Hence this is always the characteristic of modesty and humility—graces which the gospel is fitted eminently to produce. A truly pious man will be always, therefore, an humble man, and will wish that others should be preferred in office and honour to himself. Of course, this will not make him blind to the defects of others when they are manifested; but he will be himself retiring, modest, unambitious, unobtrusive. *This* rule of Christianity would strike a blow at all the ambition of the world. It would rebuke the love of office, and would produce universal contentment in any low condition of life where the providence of God may have cast our lot. Comp. Notes on 1 Cor. vii. 21.

4. *Look not every man on his own things.* That is, be not selfish. Do not let your care and attention be wholly absorbed by your own concerns, or by the concerns of your own family. Evince a tender interest for the happiness of the whole, and let the welfare of others lie near your hearts. This, of course, does not mean that there is to be any improper interference in the business of others, or that we are to have the character of "busy-bodies in other men's matters" (comp. Notes, 2 Thess. iii. 11. 1 Tim. v. 13. 1 Pet. iv. 15); but that we are to regard with appropriate solicitude the welfare of others, and to strive to do them good. ¶ *But every man also on the things of others.* It is the duty of *every man* to do this. No one is at liberty to live for himself, or to disregard the wants of others. The *object* of this rule is to break up the narrow spirit of selfishness, and to produce a benevolent regard for the happiness of others. In respect to the rule we may observe, (1.) We are *not* to be "busy-bodies" in the concerns of others. See the references above. We are *not* to attempt to pry into their secret purposes. Every man has his own plans, and thoughts, and intentions, which no other one has a right to look into. Nothing is more odious than an intermeddler in the concerns of others. (2.) We are not to obtrude our advice where it is not sought, or at unseasonable times and places, even if the advice is in itself good. No man likes to be interrupted to hear *advice;* and I have no right to require

that he should suspend his business in order that *I* may give him counsel. (3.) We are not to find fault with what pertains exclusively to him. We are to remember that there are some things which are *his* business, not *ours;* and we are to learn to 'possess our souls in patience,' if he does not give just as much as we think he ought to benevolent objects, or if he dresses in a manner not to please our taste, or if he indulges in things which do not accord exactly with our views. He may see reasons for his conduct which we do not; and it is *possible* that he may be right, and that, if we understood the whole case, we should think and act as he does. We often complain of a man because he does not give as much as we think he ought, to objects of charity; and it is *possible* that he may be miserably niggardly and narrow. But it is also *possible* that he may be more embarrassed than we know of; or that he may just then have demands against him of which we are ignorant; or that he may have numerous poor relatives dependant on him; or that he gives much with 'the left hand' which is not known by 'the right hand.' At any rate, it is *his* business, not ours; and we are not qualified to judge until we understand *the whole case.* (4.) We are not to be *gossips* about the concerns of others. We are not to hunt up small stories, and petty scandals respecting their families; we are not to pry into domestic affairs, and divulge them abroad, and find pleasure in circulating such things from house to house. There are domestic secrets, which are not to be betrayed; and there is scarcely an offence of a meaner or more injurious character than to divulge to the public what we have seen in a family whose hospitality we have enjoyed. (5.) Where christian duty and kindness require us to look into the concerns of others, there should be the utmost delicacy. Even children have their own secrets, and their own plans and amusements, on a small scale, quite as important to them as the greater games which we are playing in life; and they will feel the meddlesomeness of a busy-body to be as odious to them as we should in our plans. A delicate parent, therefore, who has undoubtedly a *right* to know all about his children, will not rudely intrude into their privacies, or meddle with their concerns. So, when we visit the sick, while we show a tender sympathy for them, we should not be too particular in inquiring into their maladies or their feelings. So, when those with whom we sympathize have brought their calamities on themselves by their own fault, we should not ask too many questions about it. We should not too closely examine one who is made poor by intemperance, or who is in prison for crime. And so, when we go to sympathize with those who have been, by a reverse of circumstances, reduced from affluence to penury, we should not ask too many questions. We should let them tell their own story. If they voluntarily make us their confidants, and tell us all about their circumstances, it is well; but let us not drag out the circumstances, or wound their feelings by our impertinent inquiries, or our indiscreet sympathy in their affairs. *There are always secrets which the sons and daughters of misfortune would wish to keep to themselves.* But, while these things are true, it is also true that the rule before us positively requires us to show an interest in the concerns of others; and it may be regarded as implying the following things: (1.) We are to feel that the spiritual interests of every one in the church is, in a certain sense, our own interest. The church is one. It is confederated together for a common object.

5 Let this [a] mind be in you, which was also in Christ Jesus:

a Jno. 13. 14. 1 Pe. 2. 21.

Each one is intrusted with a portion of the honour of the whole, and the conduct of one member affects the character of all. We are, therefore, to promote, in every way possible, the welfare of every other member of the church. If they go astray, we are to admonish and entreat them; if they are in error, we are to instruct them; if they are in trouble, we are to aid them. Every member of the church has a claim on the sympathy of his brethren, and should be certain of always finding it when his circumstances are such as to demand it. (2.) There are circumstances where it is proper to look with special interest on the temporal concerns of others. It is when the poor, the fatherless, and the afflicted must be *sought out* in order to be aided and relieved. They are too retiring and modest to press their situation on the attention of others, and they need that others should manifest a generous care in their welfare in order to relieve them. This is not improper interference in their concerns, nor will it be so regarded. (3.) For a similar reason, we should seek the welfare of all others in a spiritual sense. We should seek to arouse the sinner, and lead him to the Saviour. He is blind, and will not come himself; unconcerned, and will not seek salvation; filled with the love of this world, and will not seek a better; devoted to pursuits that will lead him to ruin, and he ought to be apprized of it. It is no more an improper interference in his concerns to apprize him of his condition, and to attempt to lead him to the Saviour, than it is to warn a man in a dark night, who walks on the verge of a precipice, of his peril; or to arouse one from sleep whose house is in flames. In like manner, it is no more intermeddling with the concerns of another to tell him that there is a glorious heaven which may be his, than it is to apprize a man that there is a mine of golden ore on his farm. It is for the man's own interest, and it is the office of a friend to remind him of these things. He does a man a favour who tells him that he has a Redeemer, and that there is a heaven to which he may rise; he does his neighbour the greatest possible kindness who apprizes him that there is a world of infinite woe, and tells him of an easy way by which he may escape it. The world around is dependant on the church of Christ to be apprized of these truths. The gay will not warn the gay of their danger; the crowd that presses to the theatre or the ball-room will not apprize those who are there that they are in the broad way to hell; and every one who loves his neighbour, should feel sufficient interest in him to tell him that he *may be* eternally happy in heaven.

5. *Let this mind be in you, which was also in Christ Jesus.* The object of this reference to the example of the Saviour is particularly to enforce the duty of humility. This was the highest example which could be furnished, and it would illustrate and confirm all the apostle had said of this virtue. The *principle* in the case is, that we are to make the Lord Jesus our model, and are in all respects to frame our lives, as far as possible, in accordance with this great example. The point here is, that he left a state of inexpressible glory, and took upon him the most humble form of humanity, and performed the most lowly offices, that he might benefit us.

6 Who, being [a] in the form of God, thought it not robbery to be equal [b] with God;

a Jno. 1. 1, 2. Co. 1. 15.

b Jno. 5. 18.

6. *Who being in the form of God.* There is scarcely any passage in the New Testament which has given rise to more discussion than this. The importance of the passage on the question of the Divinity of the Saviour will be perceived at once, and no small part of the point of the appeal by the apostle depends, as will be seen, in the fact that Paul regarded the Redeemer as equal with God. If he was truly divine, then his consenting to become a man was the most remarkable of all possible acts of humiliation. The word rendered *form*—μορφή—*morphē*, occurs only in three places in the New Testament, and in each place is rendered *form.* Mark xvi. 12. Phil. ii. 6, 7. In Mark it is applied to the *form* which Jesus assumed after his resurrection, and in which he appeared to two of his disciples on his way to Emmaus. "After that he appeared in another *form* unto two of them." This 'form' was so unlike his usual appearance, that they did not know him. The word properly means, *form, shape, bodily shape*, especially a beautiful form, a beautiful bodily appearance. *Passow.* In ver. 7, it is applied to the appearance of a servant—'and took upon him *the form* of a servant;' that is, he was in the condition of a servant—or of the lowest condition. The word *form* is often applied to the gods by the classic writers, denoting their aspect or appearance when they became visible to men. See Cic. de Nat. Deor. ii. 2; Ovid, Meta. i. 73; Silius xiii. 643; Xeno. Memora. iv; Æniad, iv. 556, and other places cited by Wetstein, *in loc.* Hesychius explains it by ἰδέα, εἶδος. The word occurs often in the Septuagint, (1.) as the translation of the word זִיו—*Ziv—splendour*, Dan. iv. 33; v. 6. 9, 10; vii. 28; (2.) as the translation of the word תַּבְנִית—*Tabnith*, structure, model, pattern—as in building Isa. xliv. 13; (3.) as the translation of תְּמוּנָה—*temuna*—appearance, form, shape, image, likeness, Job, iv. 16. See also the Book of Wisdom xviii. 1. The word can have here only one of two meanings, either (1.) splendour, majesty, glory—referring to the honour which the Redeemer had, his power to work miracles, &c.—or (2.) nature, or essence—meaning the same as φύσις, *nature*, or οὐσία, *being*. The first is the opinion adopted by Crellius, Grotius, and others, and substantially by Calvin. Calvin says, "The form of God here denotes majesty. For as a man is known from the appearance of his form, so the majesty which shines in God, is his figure. Or to use a more appropriate similitude, the form of a king consists of the external marks which indicate a king—as his sceptre, diadem, coat of mail, attendants, throne, and other insignia of royalty; the form of a consul is the toga, ivory chair, attending lictors, &c. Therefore Christ before the foundation of the world was in the form of God, because he had glory with the Father before the world was. John xvii. 5. For in the wisdom of God, before he put on our nature, there was nothing humble or abject, but there was magnificence worthy of God." *Comm. in loc.* The second opinion is, that the word is equivalent to *nature*, or *being;* that is, that he was in the nature of God, or his mode of existence was that of God, or was divine. This is the opinion adopted by Schleusner (Lex.); Prof. Stuart (Letters to Dr. Channing, p. 40); Doddridge, and by orthodox expositors in general, and

seems to me to be the correct interpretation. In support of this interpretation, and in opposition to that which refers it to his power of working miracles, or his divine appearance when on earth, we may adduce the following considerations. (1.) The 'form' here referred to must have been something *before* he became a man, or before he took upon him the form of a servant. It was something *from* which he humbled himself by making 'himself of no reputation;' by taking upon himself 'the form of a servant;' and *by being made* '*in the likeness of men.*' Of course, it must have been something which existed when he had *not* the likeness of men; that is, *before* he became incarnate. He must therefore have had an existence before he appeared on earth as a man, and *in* that previous state of existence there must have been something which rendered it proper to say that he was '*in the form of God.*' (2.) That it does not refer to any moral qualities, or to his power of working miracles on earth, is apparent from the fact that these were not laid aside. When did he divest himself of these in order that he might humble himself? There was something which he possessed which made it proper to say of him that he was 'in the form of God,' which he laid aside when he appeared in the form of a servant, and in the likeness of men. But assuredly that could not have been his moral qualities, nor is there any conceivable sense in which it can be said that he divested himself of the power of working miracles in order that he might take upon himself the 'form of a servant.' All the miracles which he ever wrought were performed when he sustained the form of a servant, in his lowly and humble condition. These considerations make it certain that the apostle refers to a period before the incarnation. It may be added (3.) that the phrase 'form of God' is one that naturally conveys the idea that he was God. When it is said that he was 'in the form of a servant,' the idea is, that he was *actually* in a humble and depressed condition, and not merely that he *appeared* to be. Still it may be asked, what *was* the 'form' which he had before his incarnation? What is meant by his having been *then* 'in the form of God?' To these questions perhaps no satisfactory answer can be given. He himself speaks (John xvii. 5) of "the glory which he had with the Father before the world was;" and the language naturally conveys the idea that there was then a manifestation of the divine nature through him, which in some measure ceased when he became incarnate; that there was some visible splendour and majesty which was then laid aside. What manifestation of his glory God may make in the heavenly world, of course, we cannot now fully understand. Nothing forbids us, however, to suppose that there *is* some such visible manifestation; some splendour and magnificence of God in the view of the angelic beings such as *becomes* the Great Sovereign of the universe—for he 'dwells in light which no man can approach unto.' 1 Tim. vi. 16. *That* glory, visible manifestation, or splendour, indicating the nature of God, it is here said that the Lord Jesus possessed before his incarnation. ¶ *Thought it not robbery to be equal with God.* This passage, also, has given occasion to much discussion. Prof. Stuart renders it, "did not regard his equality with God as an object of solicitous desire;" that is, that though he was of a divine nature or condition, he did not eagerly seek to retain his equality with God, but took on him an humble condition—even that of a servant. Letters to Channing, pp. 88—92. That this is the correct rendering of the passage is apparent from the following considerations;—(1.) It accords with the scope and design of the apostle's reasoning. His object is not to show, as our common translation would seem to imply, that he *aspired* to be equal with God, or that he did not regard it as an improper invasion of the prerogatives of God *to be* equal with him, but that he did not regard it, in the circumstances of the case, as an object to be greatly desired, or eagerly sought *to retain* his equality with God. Instead of retaining this by an earnest effort, or by a grasp which he was unwilling to relinquish, he chose to forego the dignity, and to assume the humble condition of a man. (2.) It accords better with the Greek than the common version. The word rendered *robbery*—ἁρπαγμος—is found nowhere else in the New Testament, though the verb from which it is derived frequently occurs. Matt. xi. 12; xiii. 19. John vi. 15; x. 12. 28, 29. Acts viii. 29; xxxiii. 10. 2 Cor. xii. 2. 4. 1 Thess. iv. 17. Jude 23. Rev. xii. 5. The notion of *violence*, or *seizing*, or *carrying away*, enters into the meaning of the word in all these places. The word here used does not properly mean *an act of robbery*, but *the thing robbed—the plunder—das Rauben* (*Passow*), and hence something to be eagerly seized and appropriated. *Schleusner*. Comp. Storr, Opuscul. Acade. i. 322, 323. According to this, the meaning of the word here is, something to be seized and eagerly sought, and the sense is, *that his being equal with God was not a thing to be anxiously retained*. The phrase "thought it not," means 'did not consider;' it was not judged to be a matter of such importance that it could not be dispensed with. The sense is, 'he did not eagerly seize and tenaciously hold' as one does who seizes prey or spoil. So Rosenmüller, Schleusner, Bloomfield, Stuart, and others understand it. ¶ *To be equal with God.* τὸ ἑιναι ἴσα θεῷ. That is, the being equal with God he did not consider a thing to be tenaciously retained. The plural neuter form of the word *equal* in Greek—ἴσα—is used in accordance with a known rule of the language, thus stated by Buttman. "When an adjective as *predicate* is separated from its substantive, it often stands in the neuter where the substantive is a masculine or feminine, and in the singular where the substantive is in the plural. That which the predicate expresses is, in this case, considered in general as a *thing*." Gr. Gram., § 129. 6. The phrase 'equal with God,' or 'equal with the gods,' is of frequent occurrence in the Greek Classics. See Wetstein *in loc.* The very phrase here used occurs in the Odyssey, O.

Τὸν νῦν ἶσα Θεῷ 'Ιθακήσιοι εἰσορόωσι.

Comp. John v. 18. "Made himself equal with God." The phrase means one who sustains the same rank, dignity, nature. Now it could not be said of an angel that he was in any sense equal with God; much less could this be said of a mere man. The natural and obvious meaning of the language is, that there was an equality of nature and of rank with God, from which he humbled himself when he *became* a man. The meaning of the whole verse, according to the interpretation suggested above, is, that Christ, before he became a man, was invested with honour, majesty, and glory, such as was appropriate to God himself; that there was some manifestation, or splendour in his existence and mode of being then, which showed that he was equal with God; that he did not consider that that honour, indicating equality with God, was to be retained at all events, and so as to do violence, as it were, to other interests,

7 But [a] made himself of no reputation, and took upon him the

a Ps. 22. 6.

and to rob the universe of the glory of redemption; and that he was willing, therefore, to forget that, or lay it by for a time, in order that he might redeem the world. There were a glory and majesty which were *appropriate* to God, and which indicated *equality* with God—such as none but God could assume. For how could an angel have such glory, or such external splendour in heaven, as to make it proper to say that he was 'equal with God?' With what glory could he be invested which would be such as became *God only?* The fair interpretation of this passage, therefore, is, that Christ before his incarnation was equal with God.

7. *But made himself of no reputation.* This translation by no means conveys the sense of the original. According to this it would seem that he consented to be without distinction or honour among men; or that he was willing to be despised or disregarded. The Greek is ἑαυτὸν ἐκένωσε. The word κενόω means literally, *to empty, to make empty, to make vain, or void.* It is rendered *made void* in Rom. iv. 14; *made of none effect,* 1 Cor. i. 17; *make void,* 1 Cor. ix. 15; *should be vain,* 2 Cor. ix. 3. The word does not occur elsewhere in the New Testament, except in the passage before us. The essential idea is that of bringing to emptiness, vanity, or nothingness; and hence it is applied to a case where one lays aside his rank and dignity, and becomes in respect to that as *nothing;* that is, he assumes a more humble rank and station. In regard to its meaning here, we may remark (1.) that it cannot mean that he *literally* divested himself of his divine nature and perfections, for that was impossible. He could not cease to be omnipotent, and omnipresent, and most holy, and true, and good. (2.) It is conceivable that he might have laid aside, for a time, the symbols or the manifestation of his glory, or that the outward expressions of his majesty in heaven might have been withdrawn. It is conceivable for a divine being to intermit the exercise of his almighty power, since it cannot be supposed that God is *always* exerting his power to the utmost. And in like manner there might be for a time a laying aside or intermitting of these manifestations or symbols, which were expressive of the divine glory and perfections. Yet (3.) this supposes no change in the divine nature, or in the essential glory of the divine perfections. When the sun is obscured by a cloud, or in an eclipse, there is no real change of its glory, nor are his beams extinguished, nor is the sun himself in any measure changed. His lustre is only for a time obscured. So it might have been in regard to the manifestation of the glory of the Son of God. Of course, there is much in regard to this which is obscure, but the language of the apostle undoubtedly implies more than that he took an humble place, or that he demeaned himself in an humble manner. In regard to the actual change respecting his manifestations in heaven, or the withdrawing of the symbols of his glory there, the Scriptures are nearly silent, and conjecture is useless—perhaps improper. The language before us fairly implies that he laid aside that which was expressive of his being divine—that glory which is involved in the phrase 'being in the form of God'—and took upon himself another form and manifestation in the condition of a servant. ¶ *And took upon him the form of a servant.* The phrase

form of a servant, [a] and was made in the [1] likeness of men:

8 And being found in fashion as a man, he humbled himself

a Lu. 22. 27. [1] or, *habit*.

'form of a servant,' should be allowed to explain the phrase 'form of God,' in ver. 6. The 'form of a servant' is that which indicates the condition of a servant, in contradistinction from one of higher rank. It means to appear as a servant, to perform the offices of a servant, and to be regarded as such. He was made like a servant in the lowly condition which he assumed. The whole connection and force of the argument here demands this interpretation. Storr and Rosenmüller interpret this as meaning that he became *the servant or minister of God*, and that in doing it, it was necessary that he should become a man. But the objection to this is obvious. It greatly weakens the force of the apostle's argument. His object is to state the depth of humiliation to which he descended, and this was best done by saying that he descended to the lowest condition of humanity, and appeared in the most humble garb. The idea of being a 'servant or minister of God' would not express that, for this is a term which might be applied to the highest angel in heaven. Though the Lord Jesus was not *literally* a servant or slave, yet what is here affirmed was true of him in the following respects:—(1.) he occupied a most lowly condition in life; and (2.) he condescended to perform such acts as are appropriate only to those who are servants. "I am among you as he that serveth." Luke xxii. 27. Comp. John xiii. 4—15. ¶ *And was made in the likeness of men.* Marg., *habit.* The Greek word means *likeness, resemblance.* The meaning is, he was made like unto men by assuming such a body as theirs. See Notes, ch. viii. 3.

8. *And being found.* That is, being such, or existing as a man, he humbled himself. ¶ *In fashion as a man.* The word rendered *fashion*—σχῆμα—means figure, mien, deportment. Here it is the same as *state*, or *condition.* The sense is, that when he was reduced to this condition he humbled himself, and obeyed even unto death. He took upon himself all the attributes of a man. He assumed all the innocent infirmities of our nature. He appeared as other men do, was subjected to the necessity of food and raiment, like others, and was made liable to suffering, as other men are. It was still he who had been in the 'form of God' who thus appeared; and, though his divine glory had been for a time laid aside, yet it was not extinguished or lost. It is important to remember, in all our meditations on the Saviour, that it was *the same Being* who had been invested with so much glory in heaven, that appeared on earth in the form of a man. ¶ *He humbled himself.* Even then, when he appeared as a man. He had not only laid aside the symbols of his glory (ver. 7), and become a man; but, when *he was a man*, he humbled himself. Humiliation was a constant characteristic of him as a man. He did not aspire to high honours; he did not affect pomp and parade; he did not demand the service of a train of menials; but he condescended to the lowest conditions of life. Luke xxii. 27. The words here are very carefully chosen. In the former case (ver. 7), when he *became* a man, he 'emptied himself,' or laid aside the symbols of his glory; now, *when* a man, he *humbled* himself. That is, though he was God appearing in the form of man—a divine person on earth—yet he did not assume and assert the dignity and

and became [a] obedient unto death, even the death of the cross.

9 Wherefore [b] God also hath highly exalted him, and given him

a He. 12. 2.

b He. 2. 9. Re. 3. 21.

prerogatives appropriate to a divine being, but put himself in a condition of obedience. For *such* a being to obey law, implied voluntary humiliation; and the greatness of his humiliation was shown by his becoming entirely obedient, even till he died on the cross. ¶ *And became obedient.* He subjected himself to the law of God, and wholly obeyed it. Heb. x. 7. 9. It was a characteristic of the Redeemer that he yielded perfect obedience to the will of God. Should it be said that, if he was God himself, he must have been himself the lawgiver, we may reply that this rendered his obedience the more wonderful and the more meritorious. If a monarch should for an important purpose place himself in a position to obey his own laws, nothing could show in a more striking manner their importance in his view. The highest honour that has been shown to the law of God on earth was, that it was perfectly observed by him who made the law—the great Mediator. ¶ *Unto death.* He obeyed even when obedience terminated in death. The point of this expression is this: One may readily and cheerfully obey another where there is no particular peril. But the case is different where obedience is attended with danger. The child shows a spirit of true obedience when he yields to the commands of a father, though it should expose him to hazard; the servant who obeys his master, when obedience is attended with risk of life; the soldier, when he is morally certain that to obey will be followed by death. Thus many a company or platoon has been ordered into the 'deadly breach,' or directed to storm a redoubt, or to scale a wall, or to face a cannon, when it was morally certain that death would be the consequence. No profounder spirit of obedience can be evinced than this. It should be said, however, that the obedience of the soldier is in many cases scarcely voluntary, since, if he did *not* obey, death would be the penalty. But, in the case of the Redeemer, it was wholly voluntary. He placed himself in the condition of a servant to do the will of God, and then never shrank from what that condition involved. ¶ *Even the death of the cross.* It was not such a death as a servant might incur by crossing a stream, or by falling among robbers, or by being worn out by toil; it was not such as the soldier meets when he is suddenly cut down, covered with glory as he falls; it was the long, lingering, painful, humiliating death of the cross. Many a one might be willing to obey if the death that was suffered was regarded as glorious; but when it is ignominious, and of the most degrading character, and the most torturing that human ingenuity can invent, then the whole character of the obedience is changed. Yet this was the obedience the Lord Jesus evinced; and it was in this way that his remarkable readiness to suffer was shown.

9. *Wherefore.* As a reward of this humiliation and these sufferings. The idea is, that there was an appropriate reward for it, and that that was bestowed upon him by his exaltation as Mediator to the right hand of God. Comp. Notes on Heb. ii. 9. ¶ *God also hath highly exalted him.* As Mediator. Though he was thus humbled, and appeared in the form of a servant, he is now raised up to the throne of glory, and to universal dominion. This exaltation is spoken of the Redeemer *as he was,* sustaining a divine and a human nature

a name which is above every name.

10 That at the name of Jesus every [a] knee should bow, of *things*

a Is. 45. 23. Re. 5. 13.

If there was, as has been supposed, some obscuration or withdrawing of the symbols of his glory (ver. 7), when he became a man, then this refers to the restoration of that glory, and would seem to imply, also, that there was additional honour conferred on him. There was all the augmented glory resulting from the work which he had performed in redeeming man. ¶ *And given him a name which is above every name.* No other name can be compared with his. It stands alone. He only is Redeemer, Saviour. He only is Christ, the Anointed of God. See Notes on Heb. i. 4. He only is the Son of God. His rank, his titles, his dignity, are above all others. See this illustrated in the Notes on Eph. i. 20, 21.

10. *That at the name of Jesus every knee should bow.* The *knee* should bow, or bend, in token of honour, or worship; that is, all men should adore him. This cannot mean merely that at the mention of the name of *Jesus* we should bow; nor is there any evidence that God requires this. Why should we bow at the mention of *that* name, rather than at any of the other titles of the Redeemer? Is there any *special* sacredness or honour in it above the other names which he bears? And why should we bow at *his* name, rather than at the name of the Father? Besides, if any *special* homage is to be paid to the name of the Saviour under the authority of *this* passage—and this is the only one on which the authority of this custom is based—it should be by bowing the *knee*, not the '*head*.' But the truth is, this authorizes and requires neither; and the custom of bowing at the name of Jesus, in some churches, has arisen entirely from a misinterpretation of this passage. There is no other place in the Bible to which an appeal is made to authorize the custom. Comp. Neal's History of the Puritans, ch. 5. Ninth. 5. The meaning here is, not that a *special* act of respect or adoration should be shown wherever the *name* 'Jesus' occurs in reading the Scriptures, or whenever it is mentioned, but that he was so exalted that it would be proper that all in heaven and on earth should worship him, and that the time would come when he would be thus everywhere acknowledged as Lord. The bowing of the knee properly expresses homage, respect, adoration (comp. Notes, Rom. xi. 4); and it cannot be done to the Saviour by those who are in heaven, unless he be divine. ¶ *Of* things *in heaven.* ἐπουρανίων—rather, of *beings* in heaven, the word 'things' being improperly supplied by our translators. The word *may* be in the neuter plural; but it may be also in the masculine plural, and denote *beings* rather than *things*. *Things* do not bow the knee; and the reference here is undoubtedly to angels, and to the 'spirits of the just made perfect' in heaven. If Jesus is worshipped there, he is divine; for there is no idolatry of a creature in heaven. In this whole passage there is probably an allusion to Isa. xlv. 23. See it illustrated in the Notes on Rom. xiv. 11. In the great divisions here specified—of those in heaven, on the earth, and under the earth—the apostle intends, doubtless, to denote the universe. The same mode of designating the universe occurs in Rev. v. 13. Ex. xx. 4. Comp. Ps. xcvi. 11, 12. This mode of expression is equivalent to saying, 'all that is above, around, and beneath us,' and arises from what *appears* to us.

in heaven, and *things* in earth, and *things* under the earth.

11 And *that* every tongue should confess that Jesus Christ *is* Lord,[a] to the glory of God the Father.

12 Wherefore, my beloved, as ye have always obeyed, not as in

a Jno. 13. 13. Ro. 14. 9.

The division is natural and obvious—that which is above us in the heavens, that which is on the earth where we dwell, and all that is beneath us. ¶ *And* things *in earth.* Rather, 'beings on earth,' to wit, *men;* for they only are capable of rendering homage. ¶ *And* things *under the earth.* Beings under the earth. The whole universe shall confess that he is Lord. This embraces, doubtless, those who have departed from this life, and perhaps includes also fallen angels. The meaning is, that they shall all acknowledge him as universal Lord; all bow to his sovereign will; all be subject to his control; all recognise him as divine. The fallen and the lost will do this; for they will be constrained to yield an unwilling homage to him by submitting to the sentence from his lips that shall consign them to woe; and thus the whole universe shall acknowledge the exalted dignity of the Son of God. But this does not mean that they will all be *saved,* for the guilty and the lost may be compelled to acknowledge his power, and submit to his decree as the sovereign of the universe. There is the free and cheerful homage of the heart which they who worship him in heaven will render; and there is the constrained homage which they must yield who are compelled to acknowledge his authority.

11. *And* that *every tongue should confess.* Every one should acknowledge him. On the duty and importance of *confessing Christ,* see Notes on Rom. x. 9, 10. ¶ *That Jesus Christ* is *Lord.* The word *Lord,* here, is used in its primitive and proper sense, as denoting owner, ruler, sovereign. Comp. Notes, Rom. xiv. 9. The meaning is, that all should acknowledge him as the universal sovereign. ¶ *To the glory of God the Father.* Such a universal confession would honour God. See Notes on John v. 23, where this sentiment is explained.

12. *Wherefore, my beloved, as ye have always obeyed.* The Philippians had from the beginning manifested a remarkable readiness to show respect to the apostle, and to listen to his teaching. This readiness he more than once refers to and commends. He still appeals to them, and urges them to follow his counsels, that they might secure their salvation. ¶ *Now much more in my absence.* Though they had been obedient when he was with them, yet circumstances had occurred in his absence which made their obedience more remarkable, and more worthy of special commendation. ¶ *Work out your own salvation.* This important command was first addressed to Christians, but there is no reason why the same command should not be regarded as addressed to all—for it is equally applicable to all. The *duty* of doing this is enjoined here; the *reason* for making the effort, or the *encouragement* for the effort, is stated in the next verse. In regard to the command here, it is natural to inquire why it is a duty; and what is necessary to be done in order to comply with it? On the first of these inquiries, it may be observed that it is a *duty* to make a personal effort to secure salvation, or to work out our salvation: (1.) Because God *commands* it. There is no command more frequently repeated in the Scriptures, than the

my presence only, but now much more in my absence, work[a] out your own salvation with fear[b] and trembling:

a Pr. 10. 16. Jno. 6. 27-29. He. 4. 11. 2 Pe. 1. 5-10.

b Ep. 6. 5.

command to make to ourselves a new heart; to strive to enter in at the strait gate; to break off from sin, and to repent. (2.) It is a duty because it is our own personal interest that is at stake. No other one has, or can have, as much interest in our salvation as we have. It is every man's *duty* to be as happy as possible here, and to be prepared for eternal happiness in the future world. No man has a *right* either to throw away his life or his soul. He has no more right to do the one than the other; and if it is a man's duty to endeavour to save his life when in danger of drowning, it is no less his duty to endeavour to save his soul when in danger of hell. (3.) Our earthly friends cannot save us. No effort of theirs can deliver us from eternal death without our own exertion. Great as may be their solicitude for us, and much as they may do, there *is* a point where their efforts must stop—and that point is *always* short of our salvation, unless *we* are roused to seek salvation. They may pray, and weep, and plead, but they cannot save us. There is a work to be done on our own hearts which *they* cannot do. (4.) It is a duty, because the salvation of the soul will not take care of itself without an effort on our part. There is no more reason to suppose this than that health and life will take care of themselves without our own exertion. And yet many live as if they supposed that *somehow* all would yet be well; that the matter of salvation need not give them any concern, for that things *will so arrange themselves* that they will be saved. Why should they suppose this any more in regard to religion than in regard to anything else? (5.) It is a duty, because there is no reason to expect the divine interposition without our own effort. No such interposition is *promised* to any man, and why should he expect it? In the case of all who *have* been saved, they have made an effort—and why should we expect that God will favour us more than he did them? 'God helps them who help themselves;' and what reason has any man to suppose that he will interfere in his case and save him, if he will put forth no effort to 'work out his own salvation?' In regard to the other inquiry—What does the command imply; or what is necessary to be done in order to comply with it? we may observe, that it does *not* mean (1.) that we are to attempt to *deserve* salvation on the ground of merit. That is out of the question; for what *can* man do that shall be an *equivalent* for eternal happiness in heaven? Nor (2.) does it mean that we are to endeavour to make atonement for past sins. That would be equally impossible, and it is, besides, unnecessary. *That* work has been done by the great Redeemer But it means, (1.) that we are to make an honest *effort* to be saved in the way which God has appointed; (2.) that we are to break off from our sins by true repentance; (3.) that we are to believe in the Saviour, and honestly to put our trust in him; (4.) that we are to give up all that we have to God; (5.) that we are to break away from all evil companions and evil plans of life; and (6.) that we are to resist all the allurements of the world, and all the temptations which may assail us that would lead us back from God, and *are to persevere unto the end.* The great difficulty in working out

13 For it is God [a] which worketh in you both to will and to do of *his* good pleasure.

a He. 13. 21.

salvation is in forming a purpose *to begin at once.* When *that* purpose is formed, salvation is easy. ¶ *With fear and trembling.* That is, with that kind of anxiety which one has who feels that he has an important interest at stake, and that he is in danger of losing it. The reason or the ground for 'fear' in this case is in general this: *there is danger of losing the soul.* (1.) So many persons make shipwreck of all hope and perish, that there is danger that we may also. (2.) There are so many temptations and allurements in the world, and so many things that lead us to defer attention to religion, that there is danger that we may be lost. (3.) There is danger that if the present opportunity passes, another may not occur. Death may soon overtake us. No one has a moment to lose. No one can designate *one single moment* of his life, and say, 'I may *safely* lose that moment. I may *safely* spend it in the neglect of my soul.' (4.) It should be done with the most earnest concern, from the immensity of the interest at stake. If the soul is lost, all is lost. And who is there that can estimate the value of that soul which is thus in danger of being lost for ever?

13. *For it is God that worketh in you.* This is given as a *reason* for making an effort to be saved, or for working out our salvation. It is often thought to be the very reverse, and men often feel that if *God* works 'in us to will and to do,' there can be no need of our making an effort, and that there would be no use in it. If God does all the work, say they, why should we not patiently sit still, and wait until he puts forth his power and accomplishes in us what he wills? It is of importance, therefore, to understand what this declaration of the apostle *means,* in order to see whether this objection is valid, or whether the fact that God 'works in us' is to be regarded as a reason why *we* should make no effort. The word rendered *worketh* —ἐνεργῶν—*working*—is from a verb meaning to work, to be active, to produce effect—and is that from which we have derived the word *energetic.* The meaning is, that God *produces a certain effect in us;* he exerts such an influence over us as to lead to a certain result in our minds—to wit, 'to will and to do.' Nothing is said of the *mode* in which this is done, and probably this cannot be understood by us here. Comp. John iii. 8. In regard to the divine agency here referred to, however, certain things, though of a *negative* character, are clear. (1.) It is not God who *acts for us.* He leads *us* to 'will and to do.' It is not said that *he wills and does for us,* and it cannot be. It is *man* that 'wills and does'—though God so influences him that he does it. (2.) He does not *compel* or *force* us against our will. He leads us to '*will*' as well as to 'do.' The *will* cannot be forced; and the meaning here must be that God exerts such an influence as to make us *willing* to obey him. Comp. Ps. cx. 3. (3.) It is not a *physical* force, but it must be a *moral* influence. A physical power cannot act on the *will.* You may chain a man, incarcerate him in the deepest dungeon, starve him, scourge him, apply red-hot pincers to his flesh, or place on him the thumb-screw, but the *will* is still free. You cannot bend that or control it, or make him believe otherwise than as he *chooses* to believe. The declaration here, therefore, cannot mean that God compels us, or that we are any thing else but free agents still, though he 'works in us to will and

to do.' It must mean merely that he exerts such an influence as to secure this result. ¶ *To will and to do of* his *good pleasure.* Not to will and to do *every thing*, but his 'good pleasure.' The extent of the divine agency *here* referred to, is limited to that, and no man should adduce this passage to prove that God 'works' in him to lead him to commit sin. This passage teaches no such doctrine. It refers here to Christians, and means that he works in *their* hearts that which is agreeable to him, or leads them to 'will and to do' that which is in accordance with his own will. The word rendered 'good pleasure'—εὐδοκία—means *delight*, *good-will*, *favour*; then *good pleasure*, *purpose*, *will*. See Eph. i. 5. 2 Thess. i. 11. Here it means that which would be agreeable to him; and the idea is, that he exerts such an influence as to lead men to *will* and to *do* that which is in accordance with *his* will. Paul regarded this fact as a *reason* why we should work out our salvation with fear and trembling. It is with that view that he urges it, and not with any idea that it will embarrass our efforts, or be a hindrance to us in seeking salvation. The question then is, how this fact can be a motive to us to make an effort? In regard to this we may observe, (1.) That the work of our salvation is such that we need *help*, and such help as God only can impart. We need it to enable us to overcome our sins; to give us such a view of them as to produce true penitence; to break away from our evil companions; to give up our plans of evil, and to resolve to lead different lives. We need help that our minds may be enlightened; that we may be led in the way of truth; that we may be saved from the danger of error, and that we may not be suffered to fall back into the ways of transgression. *Such* help we should welcome from any quarter; and any assistance furnished on these points will not interfere with our freedom. (2.) The influence which God exerts on the mind is in the way of *help* or aid. What *he* does will not embarrass or hinder us. It will prevent no effort which we make to be saved, it will throw no hindrance or obstacle in the way. When we speak of God's working 'in us to will and to do,' men often seem to suppose that his agency will *hinder* us, or throw some obstacle in our way, or exert some *evil* influence on our minds, or make it more difficult for us to work out our salvation than it would be without his agency. But this cannot be. We may be sure that *all* the influence which God exerts over our minds, will be to aid us in the work of salvation, not to embarrass us; will be to enable us to overcome our spiritual enemies and our sins, and not to put additional weapons into their hands or to confer on them new power. Why should men ever dread the influence of God on their hearts, *as if* he would hinder their efforts for their own good? (3.) The fact that *God works* is an encouragement for us to work. When a man is about to set out a peach or an apple tree, it is an *encouragement* for him to reflect that the agency of God is around him, and that *he* can cause the tree to produce blossoms, and leaves, and fruit. When he is about to plough and sow his farm, it is an encouragement, not a hindrance, to reflect that *God works*, and that he can quicken the grain that is sown, and produce an abundant harvest. What encouragement of a higher order can man ask? And what farmer *is afraid of the agency of God* in the case, or supposes that the fact that God exerts an agency is a reason why he should not plough and plant his field, or set out his orchard? Poor encouragement would a man

14 Do all things without murmurings[a] and disputings;[b]

15 That ye may be blameless and [1] harmless, the sons[c] of God, without rebuke, in the midst of a crooked[d] and perverse nation, among whom[2] ye shine as lights[e] in the world;

a 1 Co. 10. 10. b Ro. 14. 1. 1 or, *sincere*. c Mat. 5. 45. Ep. 5. 1. d De. 32. 5. 2 or, *shine ye*. e Mat. 5. 14, 16.

have in these things if God did not exert any agency in the world, and could not be expected to make the tree grow or to cause the grain to spring up; and *equally* poor would be all the encouragement in religion without his aid.

14. *Do all things without murmurings and disputings.* In a quiet, peaceful, inoffensive manner. Let there be no brawls, strifes, or contentions. The object of the apostle here is, probably, to illustrate the sentiment which he had expressed in vs. 3—5, where he had inculcated the general duties of humbleness of mind, and of esteeming others better than themselves. In order that that spirit might be fully manifested, he now enjoins the duty of doing every thing in a quiet and gentle manner, and of avoiding any species of strife. See Notes on Eph. iv. 31, 32.

15. *That ye may be blameless.* That you may give no occasion for others to accuse you of having done wrong. ¶ *And harmless.* Marg., *sincere.* The Greek word (ἀκέραιος) means properly that which is *unmixed;* and then *pure, sincere.* The idea here is, that they should be artless, simple, without guile. Then they would injure no one. The word occurs only in Matt. x. 16. Phil. ii. 15, where it is rendered *harmless,* and Rom. xvi. 19, where it is rendered *sincere.* See Notes on Matt. x. 16, and Rom. xvi. 19. ¶ *The sons of God.* The children of God; a phrase by which true Christians were denoted. See Notes, Matt. v. 45. Eph. v. 1. ¶ *Without rebuke.* Without blame; without giving occasion for any one to complain of you. ¶ *In the midst of a crooked and perverse nation.* Among those of perverted sentiments and habits; those who are disposed to complain and find fault; those who will take every occasion to pervert what you do and say, and who seek every opportunity to retard the cause of truth and righteousness. It is not certainly known to whom the apostle refers here, but it seems not improbable that he had particular reference to the Jews who were in Philippi. The language here used was employed by Moses (Deut. xxxii. 5), as applicable to the Jewish people, and it is accurately descriptive of the character of the nation in the time of Paul. The Jews were among the most bitter foes of the gospel, and did perhaps more than any other people to embarrass the cause of truth and prevent the spread of the true religion. ¶ *Among whom ye shine.* Marg., 'or, *shine ye.*' The Greek will admit of either construction, and expositors have differed as to the correct interpretation. Rosenmüller, Doddridge, and others regard it as *imperative,* and as designed to enforce on them the *duty* of letting their light shine. Erasmus says it is doubtful whether it is to be understood in the *indicative* or *imperative.* Grotius, Koppe, Bloomfield, and others regard it as in the *indicative,* and as teaching that they did *in fact* shine as lights in the world. The sense can be determined only by the connection; and in regard to it different readers will form different opinions. It seems to me that the connection seems rather to require the sense of *duty* or *obligation* to be understood. The apostle is

16 Holding forth the word of life; that I may rejoice in the day

enforcing on them the duty of being blameless and harmless; of holding forth the word of life; and it is in accordance with his design to remind them that they *ought* to be lights to those around them. ¶ *As lights in the world.* The comparison of Christians with *light*, often occurs in the Scriptures. See Notes on Matt. v. 14. 16. The image here is not improbably taken from *light-houses* on a sea-coast. The image then is, that as those light-houses are placed on a dangerous coast to apprize vessels of their peril, and to save them from shipwreck, so the light of christian piety shines on a dark world, and in the dangers of the voyage which we are making. See the Note of Burder, in Ros. Alt. u. neu. Morgenland, *in loc.*

16. *Holding forth the word of life.* That is, you are under obligation to hold forth the word of life. It is a duty incumbent on you as Christians to do it. The 'word of life' means the gospel, called the 'word of life' because it is the message that promises life; or perhaps this is a Hebraism, denoting *the living*, or *life-giving word.* The gospel stands thus in contrast with all human systems of religion—for they have no efficacy to save—and to the law which 'killeth.' See Notes on John vi. 63, and 2 Cor. iii. 6. The *duty* here enjoined is that of making the gospel known to others, and of thus keeping up the knowledge of it in the world. This duty rests on Christians (comp. Matt. v. 14. 16), and they cannot escape from the obligation. They are bound to do this, not only because God commands it, but (1.) because they are called into the church that they may be witnesses for God. Isa. xliii. 10. (2.) Because they are kept on the earth for that purpose. If it were not for some such design, they would be removed to heaven at once on their conversion. (3.) Because there are no others to do it. The gay will not warn the gay, nor the proud the proud, nor the scoffer the scoffer. The thoughtless and the vain will not go and tell others that there is a God and a Saviour; nor will the wicked warn the wicked, and tell them that they are in the way to hell. There are none who *will* do this but Christians; and, if *they* neglect it, sinners will go unwarned and unalarmed down to death. This duty rests on *every Christian.* The exhortation here is not made to the pastor, or to any officer of the church particularly; but *to the mass of communicants. They* are to shine as lights in the world; *they* are to hold forth the word of life. There is not one member of a church who is so obscure as to be exempt from the obligation; and there is not one who may not do something in this work. If we are asked *how* this may be done, we may reply, (1.) They are to do it by *example.* Every one is to hold forth the living word in that way. (2.) By efforts to send the gospel to those who have it not. There is almost no one who cannot contribute *something*, though it may be but two mites, to accomplish this. (3.) By conversation. There is no Christian who has not some influence over the minds and hearts of others; and he is bound to use that influence in holding forth the word of life. (4.) By defending the divine origin of religion when attacked. (5.) By rebuking sin, and thus testifying to the value of holiness. The defence of the truth, under God, and the diffusion of a knowledge of the way of salvation, rests on those who are Christians. Paganism never originates a system which it would not be an advantage to the world to have destroyed as soon as it is conceived

of Christ, that I have not run in vain, [a] neither laboured in vain.

17 Yea, and if I be [1] offered upon the sacrifice and service of

a 1 Co. 9. 26.

1 poured forth. b 2 Ti. 4. 6.

Philosophy has never yet told of a way by which a sinner may be saved. The world at large devises no plan for the salvation of the soul. The most crude, ill-digested, and perverse systems of belief conceivable, prevail in the community called '*the world*.' Every form of opinion has an advocate there; every monstrous vagary that the human mind ever conceived, finds friends and defenders there. The human mind has of itself no elastic energy to bring it from the ways of sin; it has no recuperative power to lead it back to God. *The world at large is dependant on the church for any just views of God, and of the way of salvation;* and every Christian is to do *his* part in making that salvation known. ¶ *That I may rejoice.* This was *one* reason which the apostle urged, and which it was proper to urge, why they should let their light shine. He had been the instrument of their conversion, he had founded their church, he was their spiritual father, and had shown the deepest interest in their welfare; and he now entreats them, as a means of promoting his highest joy, to be faithful and holy. The exemplary piety and holy lives of the members of a church will be one of the sources of highest joy to a pastor in the day of judgment. Comp. 3 John 4. ¶ *In the day of Christ.* The day when Christ shall appear—the day of judgment. It is called *the day of Christ*, because he will be the glorious object which will be prominent on that day; it will be the day in which he will be honoured as the judge of all the world. ¶ *That I have not run in vain.* That is, that I have not lived in vain—life being compared with a race. See Notes on 1 Cor. ix. 26. ¶ *Neither laboured in vain.* In preaching the gospel. Their holy lives would be the fullest proof that he was a faithful preacher.

17. *Yea, and if I be offered.* Marg., *poured forth.* The mention of his labours in their behalf, in the previous verse, seems to have suggested to him the sufferings which he was likely yet to endure on their account. He had laboured for their salvation. He had exposed himself to peril that they and others might have the gospel. On their account he had suffered much; he had been made a prisoner at Rome; and there was a possibility, if not a probability, that his life might be a forfeit for his labours in their behalf. Yet he says that, even if this should happen, he would not regret it, but it would be a source of joy. The word which is here used — σπένδομαι — properly means, to pour out, to make a libation; and is commonly used, in the classic writers, in connection with sacrifices. It refers to a drink-offering, where one who was about to offer a sacrifice, or to present a drink-offering to the gods, before he tasted of it himself, poured out a part of it on the altar. *Passow.* It is used also to denote the fact that, when an animal was about to be slain in sacrifice, wine was poured on it as a solemn act of devoting it to God. Comp. Num. xv. 5; xxviii. 7. 14. In like manner, Paul may have regarded himself as a victim prepared for the sacrifice. In the New Testament it is found only in this place, and in 2 Tim. iv. 6, where it is rendered, 'I am ready to be offered.' Comp. Notes on that place. It does not here mean that Paul really expected to be *a sacrifice*, or to make an expiation for sin by his death, but that he might be called to *pour out* his blood, or to offer up his life

your faith, I joy, and rejoice with you all.

18 For the same cause also do ye joy, and rejoice with me.

as if he were a sacrifice, or an offering to God. We have a similar use of language, when we say that a man *sacrifices himself* for his friends or his country. ¶ *Upon the sacrifice.* επὶ τῇ θυσίᾳ. The word here rendered *sacrifice*, means (1.) the *act* of sacrificing; (2.) the *victim* that is offered; and (3.) any oblation or offering. *Robinson, Lex.* Here it must be used in the latter sense, and is connected with '*faith*'—'the sacrifice of your faith.' The reference is probably to the faith, *i. e.*, the religion of the Philippians, regarded as a sacrifice or an *offering* to God; the worship which they rendered to him. The idea of Paul is, that if, *in order* to render that offering what it should be—to make it as complete and acceptable to God as possible—it were necessary for him to die, pouring out his blood, and strength, and life, as wine was poured out to prepare a sacrifice for the altar and make it complete, he would not refuse to do it, but would rejoice in the opportunity. He seems to have regarded them as engaged in making an offering of faith, and as endeavouring to make the offering complete and acceptable; and says that if *his* death were necessary to make their piety of the highest and most acceptable kind, he was ready to die. ¶ *And service.* λειτουργία—a word taken from an act of worship, or public service, and especially the *ministry* of those engaged in offering sacrifices. Luke i. 23. Heb. viii. 6. Here it means, the *ministering* or service which the Philippians rendered to God; the worship which they offered, the essential element of which was *faith.* Paul was willing to endure anything, even to suffer death in their cause, if it would tend to make their 'service' more pure, spiritual, and acceptable to God. The meaning of the whole is, (1.) that the sufferings and dangers which he now experienced were in their cause, and on their behalf; and (2.) that he was willing to lay down his life, if their piety would be promoted, and their worship be rendered more pure and acceptable to God. ¶ *I joy.* That is, I am not afraid of death; and if my dying can be the means of promoting your piety, it will be a source of rejoicing. Comp. Notes on ch. i. 23. ¶ *And rejoice with you all.* My joy will be increased in anything that promotes yours. The fruits of my death will reach and benefit you, and it will be a source of mutual congratulation.

18. *For the same cause.* Because we are united, and what affects one of us should affect both. ¶ *Do ye joy and rejoice with me.* That is, 'do not grieve at my death. Be not overwhelmed with sorrow, but let your hearts be filled with congratulation. It will be a privilege and a pleasure thus to die.' This is a noble sentiment, and one that could have been uttered only by a heroic and generous mind—by a man who did not dread death, and who felt that it was honourable thus to die. Doddridge has illustrated the sentiment by an appropriate reference to a fact stated by Plutarch. A brave Athenian returned from the battle of Marathon, bleeding with wounds and exhausted, and rushed into the presence of the magistrates, and uttered only these two words—χαιρετε, χαιρομεν—'*rejoice, we rejoice*,' and immediately expired. So Paul felt that there was occasion for him, and for all whom he loved, to rejoice, if he was permitted to die in the cause of others, and in such a manner that his death would benefit the world.

19 [1] But I trust in the Lord Jesus to send Timotheus [a] shortly unto you, that I also may be of good comfort, when I know your state.

20 For I have no man [1] like-minded, who will naturally care for your state.

[1] *moreover.* *a* 1 Th. 3. 2.

[1] or, *so dear unto me.*

---

19. *But I trust in the Lord Jesus.* His hope was that the Lord Jesus would so order affairs as to permit this—an expression that no man could use who did not regard the Lord Jesus as on the throne, and as more than human. ¶ *To send Timotheus shortly unto you.* There was a special reason why Paul desired to send Timothy to them rather than another person, which he himself states, ver. 22. "*Ye know the proof of him*, that as a son with the father, he hath served with me in the gospel." From this passage, as well as from ch. i. 1, where Timothy is joined with Paul in the salutation, it is evident that he had been with the apostle at Philippi. But this fact is nowhere mentioned in the sixteenth chapter of the Acts of the Apostles, which contains an account of the visit of Paul to that place. The narrative in the Acts, however, as Dr. Paley has remarked (*Horæ Paulinæ, in loc.*), is such as to render this altogether probable, and the manner in which the fact is adverted to here is such as would have occurred to no one forging an epistle like this, and shows that the Acts of the Apostles and the epistle are independent books, and are not the work of imposture. In the Acts of the Apostles it is said that when Paul came to Derbe and Lystra he found a certain disciple named Timothy, whom he would have go forth with him. Ch. xvi. 1—3. The narrative then proceeds with an account of the progress of Paul through various provinces of Asia Minor, till it brings him to Troas. There he was warned in a vision to go over into Macedonia. In pursuance of this call, he passed over the Ægean sea, came to Samothracia, and thence to Neapolis, and thence to Philippi. No mention is made, indeed, of Timothy as being with Paul at Philippi, but after he had left that city, and had gone to Berea, where the 'brethren sent away Paul,' it is added, "but Silas and *Timotheus* abode there still." From this it is evident that he had accompanied them in their journey, and had no doubt been with them at Philippi. For the argument which Dr. Paley has derived from the manner in which this subject is mentioned in the Acts, and in this epistle, in favour of the genuineness of the Scripture account, see Horæ Paul. on the epistle to the Philippians, No. iv. ¶ *When I know your state.* It was a considerable time since Epaphroditus had left the Philippians, and since, therefore, Paul had been informed of their condition.

20. *For I have no man like-minded.* Marg. *so dear unto me.* The Greek is, ἰσόψυχον—*similar in mind*, or like-minded. The meaning is, that there was no one with him who would feel so deep an interest in their welfare. ¶ *Who will naturally care.* The word rendered *naturally*—γνησίως—means *sincerely*, and the idea is, that he would regard their interests with a sincere tenderness and concern. He might be depended on to enter heartily into their concerns. This arose doubtless from the fact that he had been with them when the church was founded there, and that he felt a deeper interest in what related to the apostle Paul than any other man. Paul regarded Timothy *as a son*, and his sending him on such an occasion would evince the feelings of a father who should

21 For all seek their own, [a] not the things which are Jesus Christ's.

22 But ye know the proof of him, that, as a son with the father, he hath served with me in the gospel.

23 Him therefore I hope to

a 2 Ti. 3. 2.

send a beloved son on an important message.

21. *For all seek their own.* That is, all who are with me. Who Paul had with him at this time is not fully known, but he doubtless means that this remark should apply to the mass of Christians and christian ministers then in Rome. Perhaps he had proposed to some of them to go and visit the church at Philippi, and they had declined it because of the distance and the dangers of the way. When the trial of Paul came on before the emperor, all who were with him in Rome fled from him (2 Tim. iv. 16), and it is possible that the same disregard of his wishes and his welfare had already begun to manifest itself among the Christians who were at Rome, so that he was constrained to say that, as a general thing, they sought their own ease and comfort, and were unwilling to deny themselves in order to promote the happiness of those who lived in the remote parts of the world. Let us not be harsh in judging them. How many professing Christians in *our* cities and towns are there now who would be willing to leave their business and their comfortable homes and go on embassy like this to Philippi? How many are there who would not seek some excuse, and show that it was a characteristic that they 'sought their own' rather than the things which pertained to the kingdom of Jesus Christ? ¶ *Not the things which are Jesus Christ's.* Which pertain to his cause and kingdom. They are not willing to practise self-denial in order to promote that cause. It is implied here (1.) that it is the *duty* of those who profess religion to seek the things which pertain to the kingdom of the Redeemer, or to make that the great and leading object of their lives. They are bound to be willing to sacrifice 'their own' things—to deny themselves of ease, and to be always ready to expose themselves to peril and want if they may be the means of advancing his cause. (2.) That frequently this is *not* done by those who profess religion. It was the case with the professed Christians at Rome, and it is often the case in the churches now. There are few Christians who deny themselves much to promote the kingdom of the Redeemer; few who are willing to lay aside what they regard as '*their own*' in order to advance *his* cause. Men live for their own ease; for their families; for the prosecution of their own business—as if a Christian *could* have anything which he has a right to pursue independently of the kingdom of the Redeemer, and without regard to his will and glory.

22. *But ye know the proof of him.* You have had evidence among yourselves how faithfully Timothy devoted himself to the promotion of the gospel, and how constantly he served with me. This proves that Timothy was with Paul when he was at Philippi. ¶ *As a son with the father.* Manifesting the same spirit towards me which a son does towards a father, and evincing the same interest in my work. He did all he could do to aid me, and lighten my labours and sufferings.

23. *So soon as I shall see how it will go with me.* Paul was a prisoner at Rome, and there was not a little uncertainty whether he would be condemned or acquitted. He was,

send presently, so soon as I shall see how it will go with me.

24 But [a] I trust in the Lord that I also myself shall come shortly.

25 Yet I supposed it necessary to send to you Epaphroditus, [b] my brother, and companion in labour, and fellow-soldier, [c] but your messenger, and he that ministered to my wants.

a c. 1. 25. b c. 4. 18. c Phi. 2.

---

it is commonly supposed, in fact released on the first trial. 2 Tim. iv. 16. He now felt that he would soon be able to send Timothy to them at any rate. If he was condemned and put to death, he would, of course, have no further occasion for his services, and if he was released from his present troubles and dangers, he could spare him for a season to go and visit the churches.

24. *But I trust in the Lord*, &c. Note, ch. i. 25.

25. *Yet I supposed it necessary to send to you Epaphroditus.* Epaphroditus is nowhere else mentioned but in this epistle. See ch. iv. 18. All that is known of him, therefore, is what is mentioned here. He was from Philippi, and was a member of the church there. He had been employed by the Philippians to carry relief to Paul when he was in Rome (ch. iv. 18), and while in Rome he was taken dangerously sick. News of this had been conveyed to Philippi, and again intelligence had been brought to him that they had heard of his sickness and that they were much affected by it. On his recovery, Paul thought it best that he should return at once to Philippi, and doubtless sent this epistle by him. He is much commended by Paul for his faithfulness and zeal. ¶ *My brother.* In the gospel; or brother Christian. These expressions of affectionate regard must have been highly gratifying to the Philippians. ¶ *And companion in labour.* It is not impossible that he may have laboured with Paul in the gospel, at Philippi; but more probably the sense is, that he regarded him as engaged in the same great work that he was. It is not probable that he assisted Paul much in Rome, as he appears to have been sick during a considerable part of the time he was there. ¶ *And fellow-soldier.* Christians and christian ministers are compared with soldiers (Philem. 2. 2 Tim. ii. 3, 4), because of the nature of the service in which they are engaged. The christian life is a warfare; there are many foes to be overcome; the period which they are to serve is fixed by the Great Captain of salvation, and they will soon be permitted to enjoy the triumphs of victory. Paul regarded himself as enlisted to make war on all the spiritual enemies of the Redeemer, and he esteemed Epaphroditus as one who had shown that he was worthy to be engaged in so good a cause. ¶ *But your messenger.* Sent to convey supplies to Paul. Ch. iv. 18. The original is, 'your apostle'—ὑμῶν δὲ ἀπόστολον—and some have proposed to take this *literally*, meaning that he was the *apostle* of the church at Philippi, or that he was their *bishop.* The advocates for Episcopacy have been the rather inclined to this, because in ch. i. 1, there are but two orders of ministers mentioned—'bishops and deacons'—from which they have supposed that '*the* bishop' might have been absent, and that 'the bishop' was probably this Epaphroditus. But against this supposition the objections are obvious. (1.) The word ἀπόστολος means properly *one sent forth*, a messenger, and it is uniformly used in this sense unless there is something in the connection

26 For he longed after you all, and was full of heaviness, because that ye had heard that he had been sick.

27 For indeed he was sick nigh unto death: but God had mercy on him; and not on him only, but on me also, lest I should have sorrow upon sorrow.

28 I send him therefore the more carefully, that, when ye see him again, ye may rejoice, and that I may be the less sorrowful.

29 Receive him therefore in

---

to limit it to *an apostle*, technically so called. (2.) The supposition that it here means *a messenger* meets all the circumstances of the case, and describes exactly what Epaphroditus did. He was in fact sent as *a messenger* to Paul. Ch. iv. 18. (3.) He was *not* an apostle in the proper sense of the term—the apostles having been chosen to be witnesses of the life, the teachings, the death, and the resurrection of the Saviour. See Acts i. 22. Comp. Notes, 1 Cor. ix. 1. (4.) If he *had been* an apostle, it is altogether improbable that he would have been sent on an errand comparatively so humble as that of carrying supplies to Paul. Was there no one else who could do this without sending their *bishop?* Would a diocese be likely to employ a 'bishop' for such a purpose now? ¶ *And he that ministered to my wants.* Ch. iv. 18.

26. *For he longed after you all.* He was desirous to see you all, and to relieve your anxiety in regard to his safety.

27. *For indeed he was sick nigh unto death.* Dr. Paley has remarked (*Hor. Paul.* on Phil. No. ii.) that the account of the sickness and recovery of Epaphroditus is such as to lead us to suppose that he was not restored by miracle; and he infers that the power of healing the sick was conferred on the apostles only occasionally, and did not depend at all on their will, since, if it had, there is every reason to suppose that Paul would at once have restored him to health. This account, he adds, shows also that this epistle is not the work of an impostor. Had it been, a miracle would not have been spared. Paul would not have been introduced as showing such anxiety about a friend lying at the point of death, and as being unable to restore him. It would have been said that he interposed at once, and raised him up to health. ¶ *But God had mercy on him.* By restoring him to health, evidently not by miracle, but by the use of ordinary means. ¶ *On me also, lest I should have sorrow upon sorrow.* In addition to all the sorrows of imprisonment, and the prospect of a trial, and the want of friends. The sources of his sorrow, had Epaphroditus died, would have been such as these: (1.) He would have lost a valued friend, and one whom he esteemed as a brother and worthy fellow-labourer. (2.) He would have felt that the church at Philippi had lost a valuable member. (3.) His grief might have been aggravated from the consideration that his life had been lost in endeavouring to do *him* good. He would have felt that he was the occasion, though innocent, of his exposure to danger.

28. *I send him therefore the more carefully.* With more diligence, or speed; I was the more ready to send him. ¶ *That I may be the less sorrowful.* That is, on account of my solicitude for you; that I may know that your minds are at ease, and that you rejoice in his being among you.

29. *Receive him therefore in the Lord.* As the servant of the Lord, or as now restored to you by the Lord, and therefore to be regarded as a fresh gift from God. Our friends

the Lord with all gladness; and [1] hold such in reputation:

30 Because for the work of Christ he was nigh unto death, not regarding his life [a] to supply your lack of service toward me.

[1] or, *honour such.* 1 Co. 16. 18.

[a] 1 Co. 16. 17.

restored to us after a long absence, we should receive as the gift of God, and as a proof of his mercy. ¶ *And hold such in reputation.* Marg., *honour such.* This is a high commendation of Epaphroditus, and, at the same time, it enjoins an important duty in regard to the proper treatment of those who sustain such a character. It is a christian duty to honour those who ought to be honoured, to respect the virtuous and the pious, and especially to honour those who evince fidelity in the work of the Lord.

30. *Because for the work of Christ.* That is, either by exposing himself in his journey to see the apostle in Rome, or by his labours there. ¶ *Not regarding his life.* There is a difference in the MSS. here, so great that it is impossible now to determine which is the true reading, though the sense is not materially affected. The common reading of the Greek text is, παραβουλευσάμενος; literally, *misconsulting*, *not consulting carefully, not taking pains.* The other reading is, παραβολευσάμενος; *exposing oneself to danger*, regardless of life. See the authorities for this reading in Wetstein. Comp. Bloomfield, *in loc.* This reading suits the connection, and is generally regarded as the correct one. ¶ *To supply your lack of service toward me.* Not that they had been indifferent to him, or inattentive to his wants, for he does not mean to blame them; but they had not had an opportunity to send to his relief (see ch. iv. 10), and Epaphroditus therefore made a special journey to Rome on his account. He came and rendered to him the service which they could not do *in person;* and what the church *would* have done if Paul had been among them, he performed in their name and on their behalf.

REMARKS.

1. Let us learn to esteem others as they ought to be. Ver. 3. *Every* person who is virtuous and pious has *some* claim to esteem. He has a reputation which is valuable to him and to the church, and we should not withhold respect from him. It is one evidence, also, of true humility and of right feeling, when we esteem them as better than ourselves, and when we are willing to see them honoured, and are willing to sacrifice our own ease to promote their welfare. It is one of the instinctive promptings of true humility to feel that other persons are better than we are.

2. We should not be disappointed or mortified if others think little of us—if we are not brought into prominent notice among men. Ver. 3. We *profess* to have a low opinion of ourselves, if we are Christians, and we *ought* to have; and why should we be chagrined and mortified if others have the same opinion of us? Why should we not be willing that they should accord in judgment with us in regard to ourselves?

3. We should be willing to occupy our appropriate place in the church. Ver. 3. That is true humility; and why should any one be unwilling to be esteemed just as he *ought* to be? Pride makes us miserable, and is the grand thing that stands in the way of the influence of the gospel on our hearts. No one can become a Christian who is not willing to occupy just the place which he *ought* to occupy; to take the lowly position as a penitent which he *ought* to take; and to

have God regard and treat him just as he *ought* to be treated. The first, second, and third thing in religion is humility; and no one ever becomes a Christian who is not willing to take the lowly condition of a child.

4. We should feel a deep interest in the welfare of others. Ver. 4. Men are by nature selfish, and it is the design of religion to make them benevolent. They seek their own interests by nature, and the gospel would teach them to regard the welfare of others. If we are truly under the influence of religion, there is not a member of the church in whom we should not feel an interest, and whose welfare we should not strive to promote as far as we have opportunity. And we *may* have opportunity every day. It is an easy matter to do good to others. A kind word, or even a kind *look*, does good; and who so poor that he cannot render this? Every day that we live, we come in contact with *some* who may be benefited by our example, our advice, or our alms; and every day, therefore, *may* be closed with the feeling that we have not lived in vain.

5. Let us in all things look to the example of Christ. Ver. 5. He came that he might be an example; and he *was* exactly such an example as we need. We may be *always* sure that we are right when we follow his example and possess his spirit. We cannot be *so* sure that we are right in any other way. He came to be our model in all things, and in all the relations of life. (1.) He showed us what the law of God requires of us. (2.) He showed us what we should aim to be, and what human nature would be if it were wholly under the influence of religion. (3.) He showed us what true religion is, for it is just such as was seen in his life. (4.) He showed us how to act in our treatment of mankind. (5.) He showed us how to bear the ills of poverty, and want, and pain, and temptation, and reproach from the world. We should learn to manifest the same spirit in suffering which he did, for then we are sure we are right. (6.) And he has showed us how to die. He has exhibited in death just the spirit which *we* should when we die; for it is not less desirable *to die well* than *to live well.*

6. It is right and proper to worship Christ. Ver. 6. He was in the form of God, and equal with God; and, being such, we should adore him. No one need be afraid to render too high honour to the Saviour; and all piety may be measured by the respect which is shown to him. Religion advances in the world just in proportion as men are disposed to render honour to the Redeemer; it becomes dim and dies away just in proportion as that honour is withheld.

7. Like the Redeemer, we should be willing to deny ourselves in order that we may promote the welfare of others. Vs. 6—8. We can never, indeed, equal his condescension. We can never stoop from such a state of dignity and honour as he did; but, in our measure, we should aim to imitate him. If we have comforts, we should be willing to deny ourselves of them to promote the happiness of others. If we occupy an elevated rank in life, we should be willing to stoop to one more humble. If we live in a palace, we should be willing to enter the most lowly cottage, if we can render its inmates happy.

8. Christ was obedient unto death. Ver. 8. Let *us* be obedient also, doing the will of God in all things. If in his service we are called to pass through trials, even those which will terminate in death, let us obey. He has a right to command us, and we have the example of the Saviour to sustain us. If he requires us, by his providence, and by the leadings

of his Spirit, to forsake our country and home; to visit climes of pestilential air, or to traverse wastes of burning sand, to make his name known; if he demands that, in that service, we shall die far away from kindred and home, and that our bones shall be laid on the banks of the Senegal or the Ganges,—still, let us remember that these sufferings are not equal to those of the Master. He was an exile from heaven, in a world of suffering. *Our* exile from our own land is not like that from heaven; nor will our sufferings, though in regions of pestilence and death, be like *his* sufferings in the garden and on the cross.

9. Let us rejoice that we have a Saviour who has ascended to heaven, and who is to be forever honoured there. Vs. 9—11. He is to suffer no more. He has endured the last pang; has passed through a state of humiliation and woe which he will never repeat; and has submitted to insults and mockeries to which it will not be necessary for him to submit again. When we now think of the Redeemer, we can think of him as always happy and honoured. There is no moment by day or by night in which he is not the object of adoration, love, and praise—nor will there *ever* be such a moment to all eternity. Our best friend is thus to be eternally reverenced, and in heaven he will receive a full reward for all his unparalleled woes.

10. Let us diligently endeavour to work out our salvation. Vs. 12, 13. Nothing else so much demands our unceasing solicitude as this, and in nothing else have we so much encouragement. We are assured that God aids us in this work. He throws no obstructions in our path, but all that God *does* in the matter of salvation is in the way of *help*. He does not work in us evil passions, or impure desires, or unbelief;—his agency is to enable us to perform 'his good pleasure,' or that which will *please* him—that is, that which is holy. The farmer is encouraged to plough and plant his fields when *God works* around him by sending the warm breezes of the spring, and by refreshing the earth with gentle dews and rains. And so *we* may be encouraged to seek our salvation when God works in our hearts, producing serious thoughts, and a feeling that we need the blessings of salvation.

11. Christians should let their light shine. Vs. 14—16. God has called them into his kingdom that they may show what is the nature and power of true religion. They are to illustrate in their lives the nature of that gospel which he has revealed, and to show its value in purifying the soul and in sustaining it in the time of trial. The world is dependent on Christians for just views of religion, and every day that a Christian lives he is doing *something* to honour or dishonour the gospel. Every word that he speaks, every expression of the eye, every cloud or beam of sunshine on his brow, will have *some* effect in doing this. He *cannot* live without making *some* impression upon the world around him, either favourable or unfavourable to the cause of his Redeemer.

12. We should be ready *to die*, if called to such a sacrifice in behalf of the church of Christ. Ver. 17. We should *rejoice* in being permitted to suffer, that we may promote the welfare of others, and be the means of saving those for whom Christ died. It has been an honour to be a martyr in the cause of religion, and so it ever will be when God calls to such a sacrifice of life. If he calls *us* to it, therefore, we should not shrink from it, nor should we shrink from any sufferings by which we may honour the Saviour, and rescue souls from death.

13. Let us learn, from the interesting narrative respecting Epaphroditus at the close of this chapter, to live and act as becomes Christians in every situation in life. Vs. 25—30. It was much to have the praise of an apostle, and to be commended for his christian conduct, as this stranger in Rome was. He went there, not to view the wonders of the imperial city, and not to run the rounds of giddy pleasure there, but to perform an important duty of religion. While there be became sick—not by indulgence in pleasures; not as the result of feasting and revelry, but in the work of Christ. In a strange city, far from home, amidst the rich, the great, the gay; in a place where theatres opened their doors, and where places of amusement abounded, he led a life which an apostle could commend as pure. There is nothing more difficult for a Christian than to maintain an irreproachable walk when away from the usual restraints and influences that serve to keep him in the paths of piety, and when surrounded with the fascinations and allurements of a great and wicked city. There strangers, extending the rites of hospitality, often invite the guest to places of amusement which the Christian would not visit were he at home. There the desire to see all that is to be seen, and to hear all that is to be heard, attracts him to the theatre, the opera, and the gallery of obscene and licentious statuary and painting. There the plea readily presents itself that an opportunity of witnessing these things may never occur again; that he is unknown, and that his example, therefore, can do no harm; that it is desirable, from personal observation, to know what is the condition of the world; or that perhaps his former views in these matters may have been precise and puritanical. To such considerations he yields; but yields only to regret it in future life. Rarely is such a thing done without its being in some way soon known; and rarely, very rarely does a Christian minister or other member of the church travel much without injury to his piety, and to the cause of religion. A christian man who is under a *necessity* of visiting Europe from this country, should feel that he has special need of the prayers of his friends, that he may not dishonour his religion abroad; he who is permitted to remain at home, and to cultivate the graces of piety in his own family, and in the quiet scenes where he has been accustomed to move, should regard it as a cause of special thankfulness to God.

CHAPTER III.

ANALYSIS OF THE CHAPTER.

This chapter consists in the main, of exhortations to holy living, and to an effort to make great attainments in the divine life. It is full of tenderness and affection, and is one of the most beautiful appeals which can anywhere be found to induce Christians to devote themselves to the service of the Redeemer. The appeal is drawn in a great measure from the apostle's statement of his own feelings, and is one which the Philippians could not but feel, for they knew him well. In the course of the chapter, he adverts to the following points.

He exhorts them to rejoice in the Lord. Ver. 1.

He warns them against the Jewish teachers who urged the necessity of complying with the Mosaic laws, and who appear to have boasted of their being Jews, and to have regarded themselves as the favourites of God on that account. Vs. 2, 3.

To meet what they had said, and to show how little all that on which they relied was to be valued, Paul

CHAPTER III.

FINALLY, my brethren, rejoice [a] in the Lord. To write the same [b] things to you, to me indeed *is* not grievous, but for you *it is* safe.

a 1 Th. 5. 16.

b 2 Pe. 1. 12-15.

says that *he* had had advantages of birth and education which surpassed them all, and that all the claim to the favour of God, and all the hope of salvation which could be derived from birth, education, and a life of zeal and conformity to the law, had been his. Vs. 4—5.

Yet he says, he had renounced all this, and now regarded it as utterly worthless in the matter of salvation. He had cheerfully suffered the loss of all things, and was willing still to do it, if he might obtain salvation through the Redeemer. Christ was more to him than all the advantages of birth, and rank, and blood; and all other grounds of dependence for salvation, compared with reliance on him, were worthless. Vs. 7—11.

The object which he had sought in doing this, he says, he had not yet fully attained. He had seen enough to know its inestimable value, and he now pressed onward that he might secure all that he desired. The mark was before him, and he pressed on to secure the prize. Vs. 12—14.

He exhorts them to aim at the same thing, and to endeavour to secure the same object, assuring them that God was ready to disclose to them all that they desired to know, and to grant all that they wished to obtain. Vs. 15, 16.

This whole exhortation he enforces in the end of the chapter (vs. 17—21) by two considerations. One was, that there were not a few who had been deceived and who had no true religion—whom he had often warned with tears, vs. 18, 19; the other was, that the home, the citizenship of the true Christian, was in heaven, and they who were Christians ought to live as those who expected soon to be there. The Saviour would soon return to take them to glory. He would change their vile body, and make them like himself, and they should therefore live as became those who had a hope so blessed and transforming.

1. *Finally, my brethren, rejoice in the Lord.* That is, in the Lord Jesus. See ver. 3. Comp. Notes on Acts i. 24, and 1 Thess. v. 16. The idea here is, that it is the duty of Christians to rejoice in the Lord Jesus Christ. This duty implies the following things. (1.) They should rejoice that they *have* such a Saviour. Men everywhere have felt the need of a Saviour, and to us it should be a subject of unfeigned joy that one has been provided for us. When we think of our sins, we may now rejoice that there is one who can deliver us from them; when we think of the worth of the soul, we may rejoice that there is one who can save it from death; when we think of our danger, we can rejoice that there is one who can rescue us from all peril, and bring us to a world where we shall be forever safe. (2.) We may rejoice that we have *such* a Saviour. He is just such as we need. He accomplishes just what we want a Saviour to do. We need one to make known to us a way of pardon, and he does it. We need one to make an atonement for sin, and he does it. We need one to give us peace from a troubled conscience, and he does it. We need one to support us in trials and bereavements, and he does it. We need one who can comfort us on the bed of death, and guide us through

2 Beware of dogs, [a] beware of [b] evil workers, beware of the [c] concision.

a Is. 56. 10-11. Re. 22. 15. b Ps. 119. 115. c Ga. 5. 1-3.

the dark valley, and the Lord Jesus is just what we want. When we look at his character, it is just such as it should be to win our hearts, and to make us love him; and when we look at what he has done, we see that he has accomplished all that we can desire, and why should we not rejoice? (3.) We may and should rejoice *in* him. The principal joy of the true Christian should be *in* the Lord. He should find his happiness not in riches, or gayety, or vanity, or ambition, or books, or in the world in any form, but in communion with the Lord Jesus, and in the hope of eternal life through him. In his friendship, and in his service, should be the highest of our joys, and in these we may always be happy. It is the *privilege*, therefore, of a Christian to rejoice. He has more sources of joy than any other man—sources which do not fail when all others fail. Religion is not sadness or melancholy, it is joy; and the Christian should never leave the impression on others that his religion makes him either gloomy or morose. A cheerful countenance, an eye of benignity, a conversation pleasant and kind, should always evince the joy of his heart, and in all his intercourse with the world around him he should show that his heart is full of joy. ¶ *To write the same things.* That is, to repeat the same truths and admonitions. Perhaps he refers in this to the exhortations which he had given them when he was with them, on the same topics on which he is now writing to them. He says, that for him to *record* these exhortations, and transmit them by a letter, might be the means of permanent welfare to them, and would not be burdensome or oppressive to him. It was not absolutely *necessary* for them, but still it would be conducive to their order and comfort as a church. We may suppose that this chapter is a summary of what he had often inculcated when he was with them. ¶ *To me indeed* is *not grievous.* It is not burdensome or oppressive to me to repeat these exhortations in this manner. They might suppose that in the multitude of cares which he had, and in his trials in Rome, it might be too great a burden for him to bestow so much attention on their interests. ¶ *But for you* it is *safe.* It will contribute to your security as Christians, to have these sentiments and admonitions on record. They were exposed to dangers which made them proper. What those dangers were, the apostle specifies in the following verses.

2. *Beware of dogs.* Dogs in the east are mostly without masters; they wander at large in the streets and fields, and feed upon offals, and even upon corpses. Comp. 1 Kings xiv. 11; xvi. 4; xxi. 19. They are held as unclean, and to call one *a dog* is a much stronger expression of contempt there than with us. 1 Sam. xvii. 43. 2 Kings viii. 13. The Jews called the heathen *dogs*, and the Mohammedans call Jews and Christians by the same name. The term *dog* also is used to denote a person that is shameless, impudent, malignant, snarling, dissatisfied, and contentious, and is evidently so employed here. It is possible that the *language* used here may have been derived from some custom of affixing a caution, on a house that was guarded by a dog, to persons approaching it. Lenfant remarks that at Rome it was common for a dog to lie chained before the door of a house, and that a notice was placed

3 For we [a] are the circumcision, which worship God in the spirit, and rejoice in Christ Jesus,

a Ro. 2. 28, 29.

in sight, 'Beware of the dog.' The same notice I have seen in this city affixed to the kennel of dogs in front of a bank, that were appointed to guard it. The reference here is, doubtless, to Judaizing teachers, and the idea is, that they were contentious, troublesome, dissatisfied, and would produce disturbance. The strong language which the apostle uses here, shows the sense which he had of the danger arising from their influence. It may be observed, however, that the term *dogs* is used in ancient writings with great frequency, and even by the most grave speakers. It is employed by the most dignified characters in the Iliad (*Bloomfield*), and the name was given to a whole class of Greek philosophers — the *Cynics*. It is used in one instance by the Saviour. Matt. vii. 6. By the use of the term here, there can be no doubt that the apostle meant to express strong disapprobation of the character and course of the persons referred to, and to warn the Philippians in the most solemn manner against them. ¶ *Beware of evil workers.* Referring, doubtless, to the same persons that he had characterized as *dogs*. The reference is to Jewish teachers, whose doctrines and influence he regarded only as evil. We do not know what was the nature of their teaching, but we may presume that it consisted much in urging the obligations of the Jewish rites and ceremonies; in speaking of the advantage of having been born Jews; and in urging a compliance with the law in order to justification before God. In this way their teachings tended to set aside the great doctrine of salvation by the merits of the Redeemer. ¶ *Beware of the concision.* Referring, doubtless, also to the Jewish teachers. The word rendered *concision* — κατατομή — means properly *a cutting off, a mutilation.* It is used here contemptuously for the Jewish circumcision in contrast with the true circumcision. *Robinson, Lex.* It is not to be understood that Paul meant to throw contempt on circumcision as enjoined by God, and as practised by the pious Jews of other times (comp. Acts xvi. 3), but only as it was held by the false Judaizing teachers. As they held it, it was not the true circumcision. They made salvation to depend on it, instead of its being only a sign of the covenant with God. Such a doctrine, as they held it, was a mere *cutting off of the flesh*, without understanding anything of the true nature of the rite, and hence the unusual term by which he designates it. Perhaps, also, there may be included the idea that a doctrine so held would be in fact a cutting off of the soul; that is, that it tended to destruction. Their cutting and mangling the flesh might be regarded as an emblem of the manner in which their doctrine would cut and mangle the church. *Doddridge.* The meaning of the whole is, that they did not understand the true nature of the doctrine of circumcision, but that with them it was a mere cutting of the flesh, and tended to destroy the church.

3. *For we are the circumcision.* We who are Christians. We have and hold the true doctrine of circumcision. We have that which was intended to be secured by this rite — for we are led to renounce the flesh, and to worship God in the spirit. The apostle in this verse teaches that the ordinance of circumcision was not designed to be a mere *outward* ceremony, but was intended to be emblematic of the renunciation of the flesh with its corrupt propen-

and have no confidence in the flesh:

4 Though I might also have confidence in the flesh. If any other man thinketh that he hath whereof he might trust in the flesh, I more:

5 Circumcised the eighth day,

---

sities, and to lead to the pure and spiritual worship of God. In this, he has undoubtedly stated its true design. They who now urged it as necessary to salvation, and who made salvation depend on its mere outward observance, had lost sight of this object of the rite. But this, the real design of circumcision, was attained by those who had been led to renounce the flesh, and who had devoted themselves to the worship of God. See Notes on Rom. ii. 28, 29. ¶ *Which worship God in the spirit.* See Notes on John iv. 24. Comp. Gen. xvii. 10—14. ¶ *And rejoice in Christ Jesus.* See ver. 1. That is, we have, through him, renounced the flesh; we have become the true worshippers of God, and have thus attained what was originally contemplated by circumcision, and by all the other rites of religion. ¶ *And have no confidence in the flesh.* In our own corrupt nature; or in any ordinances that relate merely to the flesh. We do not depend on circumcision for salvation, or on any external rites and forms whatever — on any advantage of rank, or blood. The word '*flesh*' here seems to refer to every advantage which any may have of birth; to any external conformity to the law, and to everything which unaided human nature can do to effect salvation. On none of these things can we put reliance for salvation; none of them will constitute a ground of hope.

4. *Though I might also have confidence in the flesh.* That is, though I had uncommon advantages of this kind; and if any one could have trusted in them, I could have done it. The object of the apostle is to show that he did not despise those things because he did not possess them, but because he now saw that they were of no value in the great matter of salvation. Once he had confided in them, and if any one could find any ground of reliance on them, he could have found more than any of them. But he had seen that all these things were valueless in regard to the salvation of the soul. We may remark here, that Christians do not despise or disregard advantages of birth, or amiableness of manners, or external morality, because they do not possess them—but because they regard them as insufficient to secure their salvation. They who have been most amiable and moral before their conversion will speak in the most decided manner of the insufficiency of these things for salvation, and of the danger of relying on them. They have once tried it, and they now see that their feet were standing on a slippery rock. The Greek here is, literally, 'although I [was] having confidence in the flesh.' The meaning is, that he had every ground of confidence in the flesh which any one could have, and that if there was any advantage for salvation to be derived from birth, and blood, and external conformity to the law, he possessed it. He had *more* to rely on than most other men had; nay, he could have boasted of advantages of this sort which could not be found united in any other individual. What those advantages were, he proceeds to specify.

5. *Circumcised the eighth day.* That is, he was circumcised in exact compliance with the law. If there was any ground of confidence from such compliance with the law, he had it. The law required that circumcision should be performed on

of the stock of Israel, *of* the tribe of Benjamin, an Hebrew of the Hebrews; as touching the law, a Pharisee; [a]

[a] Ac. 23. 6.

the eighth day (Gen. xvii. 12. Lev. xii. 3. Luke i. 59); but it is probable that, in some cases, this was delayed on account of sickness, or from some other cause; and, in the case of proselytes, it was not performed until adult age. See Acts xvi. 3. But Paul says that, in his case, the law had been literally complied with; and, consequently, all the advantage which could be derived from such a compliance, was his. ¶ *Of the stock of Israel.* Descended from the patriarch Israel, or Jacob; and, therefore, able to trace his genealogy back as far as any Jew could. He was not a proselyte himself from among the heathen, nor were any of his ancestors proselytes. He had all the advantages which could be derived from a regular descent from the venerable founders of the Jewish nation. He was thus distinguished from the Edomites and others who practised circumcision; from the Samaritans, who were made up of a mixture of people; and from many, even among the Jews, whose ancestors had been once heathen, and who had become proselytes. ¶ *Of the tribe of Benjamin.* Benjamin was one of the two tribes which remained when the ten tribes revolted under Jeroboam, and, with the tribe of Judah, it ever afterwards maintained its allegiance to God. The idea of Paul is, that he was not one of the revolted tribes, but that he had as high a claim to the honour of being a Jew as any one could boast. The tribe of Benjamin, also, was located near the temple, and indeed it has been said that the temple was on the dividing line between that tribe and the tribe of Judah; and it might have been supposed that there was some advantage in securing salvation from having been born and reared so near where the holy rites of religion were celebrated. If there were any such derived from the proximity of the tribe to the temple, he could claim it; for, though his birth was in another place, yet he was a member of the tribe. ¶ *An Hebrew of the Hebrews.* This is the Hebrew mode of expressing the superlative degree; and the idea is, that Paul enjoyed every advantage which could possibly be derived from the fact of being a Hebrew. He had a lineal descent from the very ancestor of the nation; he belonged to a tribe that was as honourable as any other, and that had its location near the very centre of religious influence; and he was an Hebrew by both his parents, with no admixture of Gentile blood. On this fact—that no one of his ancestors had been a proselyte, or of Gentile extraction—a Jew would pride himself much; and Paul says that he was entitled to all the advantage which could be derived from it. ¶ *As touching the law, a Pharisee.* In my views of the law, and in my manner of observing it, I was of the straitest sect—a Pharisee. See Notes on Acts xxvi. 5. The Pharisees were distinguished among the Jewish sects for their rigid adherence to the letter of the law, and had endeavoured to guard it from the possibility of violation by throwing around it a vast body of traditions, which they considered to be equally binding with the written law. See Notes on Matt. iii. 7. The Sadducees were much less strict; and Paul here says that whatever advantage could be derived from the most rigid adherence to the letter of the law, was his.

6. *Concerning zeal, persecuting the church.* Showing the greatness of my zeal for the religion which I

6 Concerning zeal,[a] persecuting the church; touching the righteousness which is in the law, blameless.[b]

a Ac. 22. 3, 4. Ga. 1. 13, 14. *b* Lu. 1. 6.

7 But what things were gain to me, those I counted loss[c] for Christ.

c Mat. 13. 44.

believed to be true, by persecuting those whom I considered to be in dangerous error. Zeal was supposed to be, as it is, an important part of religion. See 2 Kings x. 16. Ps. lxix. 9; cxix. 139. Isa. lix. 17. Rom. x. 2. Paul says that *he* had shown the highest degree of zeal that was possible. He had gone so far in his attachment for the religion of his fathers, as to pursue with purposes of death those who had departed from it, and who had embraced a different form of belief. If any, therefore, could hope for salvation on the ground of extraordinary devotedness to religion, he said that he could. ¶ *Touching the righteousness which is in the law, blameless.* So far as the righteousness which can be obtained by obeying the law is concerned. It is not needful to suppose here that he refers merely to the ceremonial law; but the meaning is, that he did all that could be done to obtain salvation by the mere observance of law. It was supposed by the Jews, and especially by the Pharisees, to which sect he belonged, that it was possible to be saved in that way; and Paul says that he had done all that was supposed to be necessary for that. We are not to imagine that, when he penned this declaration, he meant to be understood as saying that he had wholly complied with the law of God; but that, before his conversion, he supposed that he had done all that was necessary to be done in order to be saved by the observance of law. He neglected no duty that he understood it to enjoin. He was not guilty of deliberately violating it. He led a moral and strictly upright life, and no one had occasion to 'blame' or to accuse him as a violator of the law of God. There is every reason to believe that Paul, before his conversion, was a young man of correct deportment, of upright life, of entire integrity; and that he was free from the indulgences of vice and passion, into which young men often fall. In all that he ever says of himself as being 'the chief of sinners,' and as being 'unworthy to be called an apostle,' he never gives the least intimation that his early life was stained by vice, or corrupted by licentious passions. On the contrary, we are left to the fair presumption that, if *any* man could be saved by his own works, he was that man. This fact should be allowed to make its proper impression on those who are seeking salvation in the same way; and they should be willing to inquire whether they may not be deceived in the matter, as he was, and whether they are not in as much real danger in depending on their own righteousness, as was this most upright and zealous young man.

7. *But what things were gain to me.* The advantages of birth, of education, and of external conformity to the law. 'I thought these to be gain—that is, to be of vast advantage in the matter of salvation. I valued myself on these things, and supposed that I was *rich* in all that pertained to moral character and to religion.' Perhaps, also, he refers to these things as laying the foundation of a hope of future advancement in honour and in wealth in this world. They commended him to the rulers of the nation; they opened before him a brilliant prospect of distinction; they made it certain that

8 Yea, doubtless, and I count all things *but* loss for [a] the excellency of the knowledge of Christ Jesus my Lord: for whom I have [b] suffered the loss of all things, and do count them *but* dung, that I may win Christ,

a Is. 53. 11. Je. 9. 23, 24. Jno. 17. 3. 1 Co. 2. 2.

b 2 Co. 11. 23, 27

he could rise to posts of honour and of office, and could easily gratify all the aspirings of his ambition.—¶ *Those I counted loss.* 'I now regard them all as so much loss. They were really a disadvantage—a hindrance—an injury. I look upon them, not as gain or an advantage, but as an obstacle to my salvation.' He had relied on them. He had been led by these things to an improper estimate of his own character, and he had been thus hindered from embracing the true religion. He says, therefore, that he now renounced all dependence on them; that he esteemed them not as contributing to his salvation, but, so far as *any* reliance should be placed on them, as in fact so much loss. ¶ *For Christ.* Gr., 'On account of Christ.' That is, so far as Christ and his religion were concerned, they were to be regarded as worthless. In order to obtain salvation by him, it was necessary to renounce all dependence on these things.

8. *Yea, doubtless, and I count all things* but *loss.* Not only those things which he had just specified, and which he had himself possessed, he says he would be willing to renounce in order to obtain an interest in the Saviour, but *every thing* which could be imagined. Were all the wealth and honour which could be conceived of his, he would be willing to renounce them in order that he might obtain the knowledge of the Redeemer. He would be a gainer who should sacrifice every thing in order to win Christ. Paul had not only acted on this principle when he became a Christian, but had ever afterwards continued to be ready to give up every thing in order that he might obtain an interest in the Saviour. He uses here the same word —ζημίαν—which he does in the Acts of the Apostles, ch. xxvii. 21, when speaking of the *loss* which had been sustained by loosing from Crete, contrary to his advice, on the voyage to Rome. The idea here seems to be, 'What I might obtain, or did possess, I regard as loss in comparison with the knowledge of Christ, even as seamen do the goods on which they set a high value, in comparison with their lives. Valuable as they may be, they are willing to throw them all overboard in order to save themselves.' *Burder*, in Ros. Alt. u. neu. Morgenland, *in loc.* ¶ *For the excellency of the knowledge.* A Hebrew expression to denote *excellent knowledge.* The idea is, that he held everything else to be worthless in comparison with that knowledge, and he was willing to sacrifice everything else in order to obtain it. On the value of this knowledge of the Saviour, see Notes on Eph. iii. 19. ¶ *For whom I have suffered the loss of all things.* Paul, when he became a Christian, gave up his brilliant prospects in regard to this life, and everything indeed on which his heart had been placed. He abandoned the hope of honour and distinction; he sacrificed every prospect of gain or ease; and he gave up his dearest friends and separated himself from those whom he tenderly loved. He might have risen to the highest posts of honour in his native land, and the path which an ambitious young man desires was fully open before him. But all this had been cheerfully sacrificed in order that he might obtain an interest in the Saviour, and partake of the

9 And be found in him, not having mine own [a] righteousness, which is of the law, but that which is through the faith of Christ, the righteousness [b] which is of God by faith:

a Ro. 10. 3, 5.

b Ro. 1. 17. 3. 21, 22.

blessings of his religion. He has not, indeed, informed us of the exact extent of his loss in becoming a Christian. It is by no means improbable that he had been excommunicated by the Jews; and that he had been disowned by his own family. ¶ *And do count them* but *dung.* The word here used—σκύβαλον—occurs nowhere else in the New Testament. It means, properly, *dregs; refuse;* what is thrown away as worthless; chaff; offal, or the refuse of a table or of slaughtered animals, and then filth of any kind. No language could express a more deep sense of the utter worthlessness of all that external advantages can confer in the matter of salvation. In the question of justification before God, all reliance on birth, and blood, and external morality, and forms of religion, and prayers, and alms, is to be renounced, and, in comparison with the merits of the great Redeemer, to be esteemed as vile. Such were Paul's views, and we may remark that if this was so in his case, it should be in ours. Such things can no more avail for our salvation than they could for his. We can no more be justified by them than he could. Nor will they do anything more in our case to commend us to God than they did in his.

9. *And be found in him.* That is, united to him by a living faith. The idea is, that when the investigations of the great day should take place in regard to the ground of salvation, it might be found that he was united to the Redeemer and depended solely on his merits for salvation. Comp. Notes on John vi. 56. ¶ *Not having mine own righteousness.* That is, not relying on that for salvation. This was now the great aim of Paul, that it might be found at last that he was not trusting to his own merits, but to those of the Lord Jesus. ¶ *Which is of the law.* See Notes on Rom. x. 3. The 'righteousness which is of the law' is that which could be obtained by conformity to the precepts of the Jewish religion, such as Paul had endeavoured to obtain before he became a Christian. He now saw that no one complied perfectly with the holy law of God, and that all dependence on such a righteousness was vain. All men by nature seek salvation by the law. They set up some standard which they mean to comply with, and expect to be saved by conformity to that. With some it is the law of honour, with others the laws of honesty, with others the law of kindness and courtesy, and with others the law of God. If they comply with the requirements of these laws, they suppose that they will be safe, and it is only the grace of God showing them how defective their standard is, or how far they come from complying with its demands, that can ever bring them from this dangerous dependence. Paul in early life depended on his compliance with the laws of God as he understood them, and supposed that he was safe. When he was brought to realize his true condition, he saw how far short he had come of what the law of God required, and that all dependence on his own works was vain. ¶ *But that which is through the faith of Christ.* That justification which is obtained by believing on the Lord Jesus Christ. See Notes on Rom. i. 17; iii. 24; iv. 5. ¶ *Righteousness which is of God by faith.* Which proceeds from God, or of which he is the great source and fountain

10 That I may know him, and the power of his resurrection, and

This may include the following things. (1.) God is the author of pardon—and this is a part of the righteousness which the man who is justified has. (2.) God purposes to treat the justified sinner *as if* he had not sinned—and thus his righteousness is of God. (3.) God is the source of all the grace that will be imparted to the soul, making it really holy. In this way, all the righteousness which the Christian has is "of God." The idea of Paul is, that he now saw that it was far more desirable to be saved by righteousness obtained from God than by his own. That obtained from God was perfect, and glorious, and sufficient; that which he had attempted to work out was defective, impure, and wholly insufficient to save the soul. It is far more honourable to be saved by God than to save ourselves; it is more glorious to depend on him than to depend on anything that we can do.

10. *That I may know him.* That I may be fully acquainted with his nature, his character, his work, and with the salvation which he has wrought out. It is one of the highest objects of desire in the mind of the Christian to *know* Christ. See Notes on Eph. iii. 19. ¶ *And the power of his resurrection.* That is, that I may understand and experience the proper influence which the fact of his resurrection should have on the mind. That influence would be felt in imparting the hope of immortality; in sustaining the soul in the prospect of death, by the expectation of being raised from the grave in like manner; and in raising the mind above the world. Rom. vi. 11. There is no one truth that will have greater *power* over us, when properly believed, than the truth that Christ has risen from the dead. His resurrection confirms the truth of the christian religion (Notes, 1 Cor. xv.); makes it certain that there is a future state, and that the dead will also rise; dispels the darkness that was around the grave, and shows us that our great interests are in the future world. The fact that Christ has risen from the dead, when fully believed, will produce a sure hope that we also shall be raised, and will animate us to bear trials for his sake, with the assurance that we shall be raised up as he was. One of the things which a Christian ought most earnestly to desire is, to feel the power of this truth on his soul—that his great Redeemer has burst the bands of death; has brought life and immortality to light, and has given us the pledge that our bodies shall rise. What trials may we not bear with this assurance? What is to be dreaded in death, if this is so? What glories rise to the view when we think of the resurrection! And what trifles are all the things which men seek here, when compared with the glory that shall be ours when we shall be raised from the dead! ¶ *And the fellowship of his sufferings.* That I may participate in the same kind of sufferings that he endured; that is, that I may in all things be identified with him. Paul wished to be just like his Saviour. He felt that it was an honour to live as he did; to evince the spirit that he did, and to suffer in the same manner. All that Christ did and suffered was glorious in his view, and he wished in all things to resemble him. He did not desire merely to share his honours and triumphs in heaven, but, regarding his *whole* work as glorious, he wished to be wholly conformed to that, and, as far as possible, to be *just like Christ.* Many are willing to reign with Christ, but they would not be willing to suffer with him; many would be willing to

the [a] fellowship of his sufferings, being made conformable unto his death;

a 1 Pe. 4. 13.

wear a crown of glory like him, but not the crown of thorns; many would be willing to put on the robes of splendour which will be worn in heaven, but not the scarlet robe of contempt and mockery. They would desire to share the glories and triumphs of redemption, but not its poverty, contempt, and persecution. This was not the feeling of Paul. He wished in all things to be *just like Christ*, and hence he counted it an honour to be permitted to suffer as he did. So Peter says, "Rejoice, inasmuch as ye are partakers of Christ's sufferings." 1 Pet. iv. 13. So Paul says (Col. i. 24) that he rejoiced in his sufferings in behalf of his brethren, and desired "to fill up that which was behind, of the afflictions of Christ," or that in which he had hitherto come short of the afflictions which Christ endured. The idea is, that it is an honour to suffer as Christ suffered; and that the true Christian will esteem it a privilege *to be made just like him*, not only in glory, but in trial. To do this, is one evidence of piety; and we may ask ourselves, therefore, whether these are the feelings of our hearts. Are we seeking merely the honours of heaven, or should we esteem it a privilege to be reproached and reviled as Christ was—to have our names cast out as his was—to be made the object of sport and derision as he was—and to be held up to the contempt of a world as he was? If so, it is an evidence that we love him; if not so, and we are merely seeking the crown of glory, we should doubt whether we have ever known anything of the nature of true religion. ¶ *Being made conformable to his death.* In all things, being just like Christ—to live as he did, and to die as he did. There can be no doubt that Paul means to say that he esteemed it so desirable to be *just like Christ*, that he would regard it as an honour to die in the same manner. He would rejoice to go with him to the cross, and to pass through the circumstances of scorn and pain which attended such a death. Yet how few there are who would be willing to die as Christ died, and how little would the mass of men regard it as a privilege and honour! Indeed, it requires an elevated state of pious feeling to be able to say that it would be regarded as a privilege and honour to die like Christ; to have such a sense of the loveliness of his character in all things, and such ardent attachment to him, as to rejoice in the opportunity of dying as he did! When we think of dying, we wish to have our departure made as comfortable as possible. We would have our sun go down without a cloud. We would wish to lie on a bed of down; we would have our head sustained by the kind arm of a friend, and not left to fall, in the intensity of suffering, on the breast; we would wish to have the place where we die surrounded by sympathizing kindred, and not by those who would mock our dying agonies. And, if such is the will of God, it is not improper to desire that our end may be peaceful and happy; but we should also feel, if God should order it otherwise, that it would be an honour, in the cause of the Redeemer, to die amidst reproaches—to be led to the stake, as the martyrs have been—or to die, as our Master did, on a cross. They who are most like him in the scenes of humiliation here, will be most like him in the realms of glory.

11. *If by any means.* Implying, that he meant to make use of the most strenuous exertions to obtain the object. ¶ *I might attain unto*

11 If by any means I might [a] attain unto the resurrection of the dead.

a Ac. 26. 7.

12 Not as though I had already attained, either were already perfect: [b] but I follow after, if that I

b He. 12. 23.

I may come to, or may secure this object. ¶ *The resurrection of the dead.* Paul believed that *all* the dead would be raised (Acts xxiv. 15; xxvi. 6—8); and in this respect he would certainly attain to the resurrection of the dead, in common with all mankind. But the phrase, 'the resurrection of the dead,' also might be used, in a more limited sense, to denote the resurrection of the righteous as a most desirable object; and this might be secured by effort. It was this which Paul sought—this for which he strove—this that was so bright an object in his eye that it was to be secured at any sacrifice. To rise with the saints; to enter with them into the blessedness of the heavenly inheritance, was an object that the apostle thought was worth every effort which could be made. The doctrine of the resurrection was, in his view, that which distinguished the true religion, and which made it of such inestimable value (Acts xxvi. 6, 7; xxiii. 6. 1 Cor. xv.); and he sought to participate in the full honour and glory of such a resurrection.

12. *Not as though I had already attained.* This verse and the two following are full of allusions to the Grecian races, and it will illustrate the whole passage to insert a cut representing a Grecian foot-race. We shall thus have the image before us which probably the apostle had in his eye when he penned the passage. (See opposite page.) "The word rendered 'attained' signifies, to have arrived at the goal and won the prize, but without having as yet received it." *Pict. Bib.* The meaning here is, I do not pretend to have attained to what I wish or hope to be. He had indeed been converted; he had been raised up from the death of sin; he had been imbued with spiritual life and peace; but there was a glorious object before him which he had not yet received. There was to be a kind of resurrection which he had not arrived at. It is possible that Paul here may have had his eye on an error which prevailed to some extent in the early church, that 'the resurrection was already past' (2 Tim. ii. 18), by which the faith of some had been perverted. How far this error had spread, or on what it was founded, is not now known; but it is possible that it might have found advocates extensively in the churches. Paul says, however, that he entertained no such opinion. He looked forward to a resurrection which had not yet occurred. He anticipated it as a glorious event yet to come, and he purposed to secure it by every effort which he could make. ¶ *Either were already perfect.* This is a distinct assertion of the apostle Paul that he did not regard himself as a perfect man. He had not reached that state where he was free from sin. It is not indeed a declaration that no one was perfect, or that no one could be in this life; but it is a declaration that he did not regard himself as having attained to it. Yet who can urge better claims to having attained perfection than Paul could have done? Who has surpassed him in love, and zeal, and self-denial, and true devotedness to the service of the Redeemer? Who has more elevated views of God, and of the plan of salvation? Who prays more, or lives nearer to God than he did? That must be extraordinary

Grecian Foot-race. (Olympic Games

may apprehend that for which also I am apprehended of Christ Jesus.

piety which surpasses that of the apostle Paul; and he who lays claim to a degree of holiness which even Paul did not pretend to, gives little evidence that he has any true knowledge of himself, or has ever been imbued with the true humility which the gospel produces. It should be observed, however, that many critics, as Bloomfield, Koppe, Rosenmüller, Robinson (*Lex.*), Clarke, the editor of the Pictorial Bible, and others, suppose the word here used—τελειόω—not to refer to *moral* or *christian* perfection, but to be an allusion to the *games* that were celebrated in Greece, and to mean that he had not completed his course and arrived at the goal, so as to receive the prize. According to this, the sense would be, that he had not yet received the crown which he aspired after as the result of his efforts in this life. It is of importance to understand precisely what he meant by the declaration here; and, in order to this, it will be proper to look at the meaning of the word elsewhere in the New Testament. The word properly means, to *complete*, to *make perfect*, so as to be full, or so that nothing shall be wanting. In the New Testament it is used in the following places, and is translated in the following manner: It is rendered *fulfilled* in Luke ii. 23. John xix. 28: *perfect*, and *perfected*, in Luke xiii. 32. John xvii. 23. 2 Cor. xii. 9. Phil. iii. 12. Heb. ii. 10; v. 9; vii. 19; ix. 9; x. 1. 14; xi. 40; xii. 23. James ii. 22. 1 John ii. 5; iv. 12. 17, 18: *finish*, and *finished*, John v. 36. Acts xx. 24: and *consecrated*, Heb. vii. 28. In one case (Acts xx. 24), it is applied to a *race* or *course* that is run—'That I might finish my course with joy;' but this is the only instance, unless it be in the case before us. The proper sense of the word is that of *bringing to an end*, or rendering complete, so that nothing shall be wanting. The idea of Paul evidently is, that he had not yet attained that which would be the *completion* of his hopes. There was something which he was striving after, which he had not obtained, and which was needful to render him perfect, or complete. He *lacked* now what he hoped yet to attain to; and that which he lacked may refer to all those things which were wanting in his character and condition then, which he expected to secure in the resurrection. What he would then obtain, would be—perfect freedom from sin, deliverance from trials and temptations, victory over the grave, and the possession of immortal life. As those things were needful in order to the completion of his happiness, we may suppose that he referred to them now, when he says that he was not yet 'perfect.' This word, therefore, while it will embrace an allusion to moral character, need not be understood of that only, but may include all those things which were necessary to be observed in order to his complete felicity. Though there may be, therefore, an allusion in the passage to the Grecian foot-races (comp. the cut above,) yet still it would teach that he did not regard himself as in any sense perfect. In all respects, there were things wanting to render his character and condition complete, or what he desired they might ultimately be. The same is true of all Christians now. We are imperfect in our moral and religious character, in our joys, in our condition. Our state here is far different from that which will exist in heaven; and no Christian can say, any more than Paul could, that he has obtained that which is requisite to the *completion*

13 Brethren, I count not myself to have apprehended: but

---

or *perfection* of his character and condition. He looks for something brighter and purer in the world beyond the grave. Though, therefore, there may be—as I think the connection and phraseology seem to demand—a reference to the Grecian games, yet the sense of the passage is not materially varied. It was still a struggle for the crown of perfection—a crown which the apostle says he had not yet obtained. ¶ *But I follow after.* I pursue the object, striving to obtain it. The prize was seen in the distance, and he diligently sought to obtain it. There is a reference here to the Grecian races, and the meaning is, 'I steadily pursue my course.' Comp. Notes on 1 Cor. ix. 24. ¶ *If that I may apprehend.* If I may obtain, or reach, the heavenly prize. There was a glorious object in view, and he made most strenuous exertions to obtain it. The idea in the word 'apprehend' is that of taking hold of, or of seizing suddenly and with eagerness; and, since there is no doubt of its being used in an allusion to the Grecian foot-races, it is not improbable that there is a reference to the laying hold of the pole or post which marked the goal, by the racer who had outstripped the other competitors, and who, by that act, might claim the victory and the reward. See the cut above. ¶ *That for which also I am apprehended of Christ Jesus. By* Christ Jesus. The idea is, that he had been called into the service of the Lord Jesus, *with a view* to the obtaining of an important object. He recognised (1.) *the fact* that the Lord Jesus had, as it were, *laid hold* on him, or seized him with eagerness or suddenness, for so the word used here—κατελήφθην—means (comp. Mark ix. 18. John viii. 3, 4; xii. 35. 1 Thess. v. 4); and (2.) the fact that the Lord Jesus had laid hold on him, *with a view* to his obtaining the prize. He had done it in order that he might obtain the crown of life, that he might serve him faithfully here, and then be rewarded in heaven. We may learn, from this, (1.) That Christians are seized, or laid hold on, when they are converted, by the power of Christ, to be employed in his service. (2.) That there is an object or purpose which he has in view. He designs that they shall obtain a glorious prize, and he 'apprehends' them with reference to its attainment. (3.) That the fact that Christ has called us into his service with reference to such an object, and designs to bestow the crown upon us, need not and should not dampen our exertions, or diminish our zeal. It should rather, as in the case of Paul, excite our ardour, and urge us forward. We should seek diligently to gain that, for the securing of which, Christ has called us into his service. The fact that he has thus arrested us in our mad career of sin; that he has by his grace constrained us to enter into his service, and that he contemplates the bestowment upon us of the immortal crown, should be the highest motive for effort. The true Christian, then, who feels that heaven is to be his home, and who believes that Christ means to bestow it upon him, will make the most strenuous efforts to obtain it. The prize is so beautiful and glorious, that he will exert every power of body and soul that it may be his. The belief, therefore, that God *means* to save us, is one of the highest incentives to effort in the cause of religion.

13. *Brethren, I count not myself to have apprehended.* That is, to have obtained that for which I have been called into the service of the Redeemer. There is something which I strive after which I have not

this one thing *I do*, forgetting [a] those things which are behind, and reaching forth unto those things which are before,

a Ps. 45. 10. He. 6. 1.

yet gained. This statement is a confirmation of the opinion that in the previous verse, where he says that he was not 'already perfect,' he includes a moral perfection, and not merely the obtainment of the prize or reward; for no one could suppose that he meant to be understood as saying that he had obtained the crown of glory. ¶ This *one thing* I do. Paul had one great aim and purpose of life. He did not attempt to mingle the world and religion, and to gain both. He did not seek to obtain wealth and salvation too; or honour here and the crown of glory hereafter, but he had one object, one aim, one great purpose of soul. To this singleness of purpose he owed his extraordinary attainments in piety, and his uncommon success as a minister. A man will accomplish little who allows his mind to be distracted by a multiplicity of objects. A Christian will accomplish nothing who has not a single great aim and purpose of soul. That purpose should be to secure the prize, and to renounce everything that would be in the way to its attainment. Let us then so live that we may be able to say, that there is one great object which we always have in view, and that we mean to avoid everything which would interfere with that. ¶ *Forgetting those things which are behind.* There is an allusion here undoubtedly to the Grecian races. One running to secure the prize would not stop to look behind him to see how much ground he had run over, or who of his competitors had fallen or lingered in the way. He would keep his eye steadily on the prize, and strain every nerve that he might obtain it. If his attention was diverted for a moment from that, it would hinder his flight, and might be the means of his losing the crown. See cut on page 229. So the apostle says it was with him. He looked *onward* to the prize. He fixed the eye intently on that. It was the single object in his view, and he did not allow his mind to be diverted from that *by anything*—not even by the contemplation of the past. He did not stop to think of the difficulties which he had overcome, or the troubles which he had met, but he thought of what was yet to be accomplished. This does not mean that he would not have regarded a proper contemplation of the past life as useful and profitable for a Christian (comp. Notes on Eph. ii. 11), but that he would not allow any reference to the past to interfere with the one great effort to win the prize. It may be, and is, profitable for a Christian to look over the past mercies of God to his soul, in order to awaken emotions of gratitude in the heart, and to think of his shortcomings and errors, to produce penitence and humility. But none of these things should be allowed for one moment to divert the mind from the purpose to win the incorruptible crown. And it may be remarked in general, that a Christian will make more rapid advances in piety by looking *forward* than by looking *backward.* Forward we see everything to cheer and animate us—the crown of victory, the joys of heaven, the society of the blessed—the Saviour beckoning to us and encouraging us. Backward, we see everything to dishearten and to humble. Our own unfaithfulness; our coldness, deadness, and dulness; the little zeal and ardour which we have, all are fitted to humble and discourage. He is the most cheerful Chris-

14 I press [a] toward the mark for the prize of the high [b] calling of God in Christ Jesus.

15 Let us therefore, as many as be perfect, [c] be thus [d] minded: and if in any thing ye be other-

a 1 Co. 9. 24. He. 12. 1. b He. 3. 1. c 1 Co. 2. 6. d Ga. 5. 10.

---

tian who looks *onward*, and who keeps heaven always in view; he who is accustomed much to dwell on the past, though he may be a true Christian, will be likely to be melancholy and dispirited, to be a recluse rather than a warm-hearted and active friend of the Saviour. Or if he looks backward to contemplate what he has done—the space that he has run over—the difficulties which he has surmounted—and his own rapidity in the race, he will be likely to become self-complacent and self-satisfied. He will trust in his past endeavours, and feel that the prize is now secure, and will relax his future efforts. Let us then look onward. Let us not spend our time either in pondering the gloomy past, and our own unfaithfulness, or in thinking of what we have done, and thus becoming puffed up with self-complacency; but let us keep the eye steadily on the prize, and run the race as though we had just commenced it. ¶ *And reaching forth.* As one does in a race. ¶ *Unto those things which are before.* Before the racer there was a crown or garland to be bestowed by the judges of the games. Before the Christian there is the crown of glory, the eternal reward of heaven. There is the favour of God, victory over sin and death, the society of the redeemed and of angelic beings, and the assurance of perfect and eternal freedom from all evil. These are enough to animate the soul, and to urge it on with ever-increasing vigour in the christian race.

14. *I press toward the mark.* As he who was running a race did. The '*mark*' means properly the object set up at a distance at which one looks or aims, and hence the *goal*, or *post* which was set up at the end of a race-course, and which was to be reached in order that the prize might be won. Here it means that which is at the end of the Christian race—in heaven. ¶ *For the prize.* The prize of the racer was a crown or garland of olive, laurel, pine, or apple. See Notes on 1 Cor. ix. 24. The prize of the Christian is the crown that is incorruptible in heaven. ¶ *Of the high calling of God.* Which is the end or result of that calling. God has called us to great and noble efforts; to a career of true honour and glory; to the obtainment of a bright and imperishable crown. It is a calling which is '*high*,' or *upward*—(ἄνω)—that is, which tends to the skies. The calling of the Christian is *from* heaven, and *to* heaven. Comp. Prov. xv. 24. He has been summoned by God through the gospel of the Lord Jesus to secure the crown. It is placed before and above him in heaven. It may be his, if he will not faint or tire or look backward. It demands his highest efforts, and it is *worth* all the exertions which a mortal can make even in the longest life.

15. *Let us, therefore, as many as be perfect.* See Notes on ver. 12. Or, rather, those who *would be* perfect; or who are *aiming at* perfection. It can hardly be supposed that the apostle would address them as already perfect, when he had just said of himself that he had not attained to that state. But those whom he addressed might be supposed to be aiming at perfection, and he exhorts them, therefore, to have the same spirit that he himself had,

wise minded, God shall reveal even this unto you.

16 Nevertheless, whereto we have already attained, let us walk by the same rule, [a] let us mind the same thing.

a Ga. 6. 16.

and to make the same efforts which he himself put forth. ¶ *Be thus minded.* That is, be united in the effort to obtain the prize, and to become entirely perfect. 'Let them put forth the same effort which I do, forgetting what is behind, and pressing forward to the mark.' ¶ *And if in anything ye be otherwise minded.* That is, if there were any among them who had not these elevated views and aims, and who had not been brought to see the necessity of such efforts, or who had not learned that such high attainments were possible. There might be those among them who had been very imperfectly instructed in the nature of religion; those who entertained views which impeded their progress, and prevented the simple and earnest striving for salvation which Paul was enabled to put forth. He had laid aside every obstacle; renounced all the Jewish opinions which had impeded his salvation, and had now one single aim—that of securing the prize. But there might be those who had not attained to these views, and who were still impeded and embarrassed by erroneous opinions. ¶ *God shall reveal even this unto you.* He will correct your erroneous opinions, and disclose to you the importance of making this effort for the prize. This is the expression of an opinion, that to those who were sincere and true Christians, God would yet make a full revelation of the nature of religion, or would lead them on so that they would fully understand it. They who are acquainted with religion at all, or who have been truly converted, God will teach and guide until they shall have a full understanding of divine things.

16. *Nevertheless, whereto we have already attained, let us walk by the same rule.* This is a most wise and valuable rule, and a rule that would save much difficulty and contention in the church, if it were honestly applied. The meaning is this, that though there might be different degrees of attainment among Christians, and different views on many subjects, yet there were points in which all could agree; there were attainments which they all had made, and in reference to them they should walk in harmony and love. It might be that some had made much greater advances than others. They had more elevated views of religion; they had higher knowledge; they were nearer perfection. Others had had less advantages of education and instruction, had had fewer opportunities of making progress in the divine life, and would less understand the higher mysteries of the christian life. They might not see the truth or propriety of many things which those in advance of them would see clearly. But it was not worth while to quarrel about these things. There should be no angry feeling, and no fault-finding on either side. There *were* many things in which they could see alike, and where there were no jarring sentiments. In those things they could walk harmoniously; and they who were in advance of others should not complain of their less informed brethren as lacking all evidence of piety; nor should those who had not made such advances complain of those before them as fanatical, or as disposed to push things to extremes. They who had the higher views should, as Paul did, believe that God will yet

17 Brethren, be followers [a] together of me, and mark them which walk so, as ye have us [b] for an ensample.

a 1 Th. 1. 6. b 1 Pe. 5. 3.

communicate them to the church at large, and in the mean time should not denounce others; and those who had less elevated attainments should not censure their brethren as wild and visionary. There were *common grounds* on which they might unite, and thus the harmony of the church would be secured. No better rule than this could be applied to the subjects of inquiry which spring up among Christians respecting temperance, slavery, moral reform, and the various doctrines of religion; and, if this rule had been always observed, the church would have been *always* saved from harsh contention and from schism. If a man does not see things just as I do, let me try with mildness to 'teach' him, and let me believe that, if he is a Christian, God will make this known to him yet; but let me not quarrel with him, for neither of us would be benefited by that, nor would the object be likely to be attained. In the mean time, there are many things in which we can agree. In them let us work together, and strive, as far as we can, to promote the common object. Thus we shall save our temper, give no occasion to the world to reproach us, *and be much more likely to come together in all our views.* The best way to make true Christians harmonious is, to labour together in the common cause of saving souls. As far as we *can* agree, let us go and labour together; and where we cannot *yet*, let us 'agree to differ.' We shall all think alike by-and-by.

17. *Brethren, be followers together of me.* That is, live as I do. A minister of the gospel, a parent, or a Christian of any age or condition, *ought* so to live that he can refer to his own example, and exhort others to imitate the course of life which he had led. Paul could do this without ostentation or impropriety. *They* knew that he lived so as to be a proper example for others; and *he* knew that they would feel that his life had been such that there would be no impropriety in his referring to it in this manner. But, alas! how few are there who can safely imitate Paul in this! ¶ *And mark them which walk so, as ye have us for an ensample.* There were those in the church who endeavoured to live as he had done, renouncing all confidence in the flesh, and aiming to win the prize. There were others, it would seem, who were actuated by different views. See ver. 18. There are *usually* two kinds of professing Christians in every church—those who imitate the Saviour, and those who are worldly and vain. The exhortation here is, to 'mark'—that is, to observe with a view to imitate—those who lived as the apostles did. We should set before our minds the best examples, and endeavour to imitate the most holy men. A worldly and fashionable professor of religion is a very bad example to follow; and, especially, *young* Christians should set before their minds for imitation, and associate with, the purest and most spiritual members of the church. Our religion takes its form and complexion much from those with whom we associate; and he will usually be the most holy man who associates with the most holy companions.

18. *For many walk.* Many *live*, the christian life being often in the Scriptures compared with a journey. In order to induce them to imitate those who were the most holy, the apostle says that there were many, even in the church, whom it would not be safe for them to imitate. He

18 (For many walk, of whom I have told you often, and now tell you even weeping, *that they are* the enemies [a] of the cross of Christ;

[a] Ga. 1. 7. 6. 12.

evidently here refers mainly to the church at Philippi, though it may be that he meant to make the declaration general, and to say that the same thing existed in other churches. There has not probably been any time yet in the christian church when the same thing might not be said. ¶ *Of whom I have told you often.* When he preached in Philippi. Paul was not afraid to speak of church-members when they did wrong, and to warn others not to imitate their example. He did not attempt to cover up or excuse guilt because it was in the church, or to apologize for the defects and errors of those who professed to be Christians. The true way is, to admit that there *are* those in the church who do not honour their religion, and to warn others against following their example. But this fact does not make religion any the less true or valuable, any more than the fact that there is counterfeit money makes all money bad, or makes genuine coin of no value. ¶ *And now tell you even weeping.* This is the true spirit with which to speak of the errors and faults of Christians. It is not to go and blazon their inconsistencies abroad. It is not to find pleasure in the fact that they *are* inconsistent. It is not to reproach religion on that account, and to say that all religion is false and hollow, and that all professors are hypocrites. We should rather speak of the fact with tears; for, if there is *any* thing that should make us weep, it is, that there are those in the church who are hypocrites, or who dishonour their profession. We should weep, (1.) because they are in danger of destroying their own souls; (2.) because they are destined to certain disappointment when they come to appear before God; and (3.) because they injure the cause of religion, and give occasion to the 'enemies of the Lord to speak reproachfully.' He who loves religion, will *weep* over the inconsistencies of its friends; he who does not, will exult and triumph. ¶ That they are *the enemies of the cross of Christ.* The 'cross' was the instrument of death on which the Redeemer died to make atonement for sin. As the atonement made by Christ for sin is that which peculiarly distinguishes his religion from all others, the 'cross' comes to be used to denote his religion; and the phrase here means, that they were the enemies of his religion, or were strangers to the gospel. It is not to be supposed that they were open and avowed enemies of the cross, or that they denied that the Lord Jesus died on the cross to make an atonement. The characteristic of those persons mentioned in the following verse is, rather, that they were *living* in a manner which showed that they were strangers to his pure gospel. An immoral life is enmity to the cross of Christ; for he died to make us holy. A life where there is no evidence that the heart is renewed, is enmity to the cross; for he died that we might be renewed. They are the enemies of the cross, in the church, (1.) who have never been born again; (2.) who are living in the indulgence of known sin; (3.) who manifest none of the peculiarities of those who truly love him; (4.) who have a deeper interest in worldly affairs than they have in the cause of the Redeemer; (5.) whom nothing can induce to give up their worldly concerns when God demands it; (6.) who are opposed to all the peculiar *doctrines* of Christtianity; and (7.) who are opposed

19 Whose end [a] *is* destruction, whose God [b] *is their* belly, and *whose* glory [c] *is* in their shame, who mind earthly things.)

a 2 Co. 11. 15. 2 Pe. 2 1.
b 1 Ti. 6. 5. c Hos. 4. 7.

20 For our conversation [d] is in heaven; from whence also we look [e] for the Saviour, the Lord Jesus Christ;

d Ep. 2. 6, 19. e He. 9. 28.

to all the peculiar *duties* of religion, or who live in the habitual neglect of them. It is to be feared that at all times there are such enemies of the cross in the church, and the language of the apostle implies that it is a proper subject of grief and tears. He wept over it, and so should we. It is from this cause that so much injury is done to the true religion in the world. One secret enemy in a camp may do more harm than fifty men who are open foes; and a single unholy or inconstant member in a church may do much more injury than many men who are avowedly opposed to religion. It is not by infidels, and scoffers, and blasphemers, so much, that injury is done to the cause of religion; it is by the unholy lives of its professed friends—the worldliness, inconsistency, and want of the proper spirit of religion, among those who are in the church. Nearly all the objections that are made to religion are from this quarter; and, if this objection were taken away, the religion of Christ would soon spread its triumphs around the globe.

19. *Whose end* is *destruction.* That is, as they have no true religion, they must perish in the same manner as all sinners. A mere profession will not save them. Unless they are converted, and become the true friends of the cross, they cannot enter heaven. ¶ *Whose God is* their *belly.* Who worship their own appetites; or who live not to adore and honour God, but for self-indulgence and sensual gratifications. See Rom. xvi. 18. ¶ *And* whose *glory* is *in their shame.* That is, they glory in things of which they ought to be ashamed. They indulge in modes of living which ought to cover them with confusion. ¶ *Who mind earthly things.* That is, whose hearts are set on earthly things, or who live to obtain them. Their attention is directed to honour, gain, or pleasure, and their chief anxiety is that they may secure these objects. This is mentioned as one of the characteristics of enmity to the cross of Christ; and if this be so, how many are there in the church now who are the real enemies of the cross! How many professing Christians are there who regard little else than worldly things! How many who live only to acquire wealth, to gain honour, or to enjoy the pleasures of the world! How many are there who have no interest in a prayer-meeting, in a Sabbath-school, in religious conversation, and in the advancement of true religion on the earth! These are the real enemies of the cross. It is not so much those who deny the doctrines of the cross, as it is those who oppose its influence on their hearts; not so much those who live to scoff and deride religion, as it is those who 'mind earthly things,' that injure this holy cause in the world.

20. *For our conversation is in heaven.* That is, this is true of all who are sincere Christians. It is a characteristic of Christians, in contradistinction from those who are the 'enemies of the cross,' that their conversation is in heaven. The word 'conversation' we now apply almost entirely to oral discourse. It formerly, however, meant *conduct in general*, and it is usually employed in this sense in the Scriptures. See Notes on ch. i. 27, where the *verb* occurs, from which the noun here is

derived. The word here used—πολίτευμα—is found nowhere else in the New Testament. It properly means, *any public measure*, *administration of the state*, the manner in which the affairs of a state are administered; and then *the state itself*, *the community*, *commonwealth*, those who are bound under the same laws, and associated in the same society. Here it cannot mean that their 'conversation,' in the sense of *discourse* or *talking*, was in heaven; nor that their '*conduct*' was in heaven—for this would convey no idea, and the original word does not demand it; but the idea is, that they were *heavenly citizens*, or citizens of the *heavenly* world, in contradistinction from a *worldly* community. They were governed by the laws of heaven; they were a community associated as citizens of that world, and expecting there to dwell. The idea is, that there are two great communities in the universe—that of the world, and that of heaven; that governed by worldly laws and institutions, and that by the laws of heaven; that associated for worldly purposes, and that associated for heavenly or religious purposes; and that the Christian belonged to the latter,—the enemy of the cross, though in the church, belonged to the former. Between true Christians, therefore, and others, there is all the difference which arises from belonging to different communities; being bound together for different purposes; subject to different laws; and altogether under a different administration. There is *more* difference between them than there is between the subjects of two earthly governments. Comp. Notes on Eph. ii. 6.

19. ¶ *From whence also we look for the Saviour*. From heaven. That is, it is one of the characteristics of the Christian that he believes that the Lord Jesus will return from heaven, and that he looks and waits for it. Other men do not believe this (2 Pet. iii. 4), but the Christian confidently expects it. His Saviour has been taken away from the earth, and is now in heaven, but it is a great and standing article of his faith that that same Saviour will again come, and take the believer to himself. See Notes on John xiv. 2, 3. 1 Thess. iv 14. This was the firm belief of the early Christians, and this expectation with them was allowed to exert a constant influence on their hearts and lives. It led them (1.) to desire to be prepared for his coming; (2.) to feel that earthly affairs were of little importance, as the scene here was soon to close; (3.) to live above the world, and in the desire of the appearing of the Lord Jesus. This was one of the elementary doctrines of their faith, and one of the means of producing deadness to the world among them; and among the early Christians there was, perhaps, no doctrine that was more the object of firm belief, and the ground of more delightful contemplation, than that their ascended Master would return. In regard to the certainty of their belief on this point, and the effect which it had on their minds, see the following texts of the New Testament. Matt. xxiv. 42. 44. Luke xii. 37. John xiv. 3. Acts i. 11. 1 Cor. iv. 5. Col. iii. 4. 1 Thess. ii. 19. 2 Thess. ii. 1. Heb. x. 37. James v. 7, 8. 1 John iii. 2. Rev. xxii. 7. 12. 20. It may be asked, with great force, whether Christians in general have now any such expectation of the second appearing of the Lord Jesus, or whether they have not fallen into the dangerous error of prevailing unbelief, so that the expectation of his coming is allowed to exert almost no influence on the soul. In the passage before us, Paul says that it was one of the distinct characteristics of Christians that they *looked for* the coming of the Saviour from heaven.

21 Who shall change [a] our vile body, that it may be fashioned like unto his glorious body, according to the working [b] whereby he is able even [c] to subdue all things unto himself.

a 1 Co. 15. 43, &c. 1 Jno. 3. 2. b Ep. 1. 19. c 1 Co. 15. 26, 27.

They believed that he would return. They anticipated that important effects would follow to them from his second coming. So *we* should look. There may be, indeed, a difference of opinion about the time when he will come, and about the question whether he will come to reign 'literally, on the earth—but *the fact that Christ will return to our world* is common ground on which *all* Christians may meet, and is a fact which should be allowed to exert its full influence on the heart. It is a glorious truth—for what a sad world would this be, and what a sad prospect would be before the Christian, if the Saviour were never to come to raise his people from their graves, and to gather his redeemed to himself! The *fact* that he will come is identified with all our hopes. It is fitted to cheer us in trial; to guard us in temptation; to make us dead to the world; to lead us to keep the eye turned toward heaven.

21. *Who shall change our vile body.* Comp. Notes on 1 Cor. xv. The original words, which are here rendered 'vile body,' properly mean 'the body of humiliation;' that is, our *humble body.* It refers to the body as it is in its present state, as subject to infirmities, disease, and death. It is different far from what it was when man was created, and from what it will be in the future world. Paul says that it is one of the objects of the christian hope and expectation, that this body, so subject to infirmities and sicknesses, will be changed. ¶ *That it may be fashioned like unto his glorious body.* Gr., 'The body of his glory;' that is, the body which he has in his glorified state. What change the body of the Redeemer underwent when he ascended to heaven, we are not informed,—nor do we know what is the nature, size, appearance, or form of the body which he now has. It is certain that it is adapted to the glorious world where he dwells; that it has none of the infirmities to which it was liable when here; that it is not subject, as here, to pain or death; that it is not sustained in the same manner. The body of Christ in heaven is of the same nature as the bodies of the saints will be in the resurrection, and which the apostle calls 'spiritual bodies,' (Notes, 1 Cor. xv. 44); and it is doubtless accompanied with all the circumstances of splendour and glory which are appropriate to the Son of God. The idea here is, that it is the object of the desire and anticipation of the Christian, to be made *just like Christ* in all things. He desires to resemble him in moral character here, and to be like him in heaven. Nothing else will satisfy him but such conformity to the Son of God; and when he shall resemble him in all things, the wishes of his soul will all be met and fulfilled. ¶ *According to the working,* &c. That is, such a change demands the exertion of vast power. No creature can do it. But there is One who has power intrusted to him over all things, and he can effect this great transformation in the bodies of men. Comp. 1 Cor. xv. 26, 27. He can mould the mind and the heart to conformity to his own image, and thus also he can transform the body so that it shall resemble his. Every thing he can make subject to his will. (Notes on Matt. xxviii. 18. John xvii. 2.) And he that has this power *can* change our humbled and debased bodies, so that they shall put on the glorious appear

ance and form of that of the Son of God himself. What a contrast between our bodies here—frail, feeble, subject to sickness, decay, and corruption—and the body as it will be in heaven! And what a glorious prospect awaits the weak and dying believer, in the future world!

REMARKS.

1. It is a privilege of the Christian to rejoice. Ver. 1. He has more sources of real joy than any other persons. See 1 Thess. v. 16. He has a Saviour in whom he may always find peace; a God whose character he can always contemplate with pleasure; a heaven to look forward to where there is nothing but happiness; a Bible that is full of precious promises, and at all times the opportunity of prayer, in which he may roll all his sorrows on the arms of an unchanging friend. If there is any one on earth who *ought* to be happy, it is the Christian.

2. The Christian should so live as to leave on others the impression that religion *produces* happiness. In our intercourse with our friends, we should show them that religion does not cause sadness or gloom, sourness or misanthropy, but that it produces cheerfulness, contentment, and peace. This may be shown by the countenance, and by the whole demeanour—by a calm brow, and a benignant eye, and by a cheerful aspect. The internal peace of the soul should be evinced by every proper external expression. A Christian may thus be *always* doing good—for he is always doing good who leaves the impression on others that religion makes its possessors happy.

3. The nature of religion is almost always mistaken by the world. They suppose that it makes its possessors melancholy and sad. The reason is, not that they are told so by those who are religious, and not that even *they* can see anything in religion to produce misery, but because they have fixed their affections on certain things which they suppose to be *essential* to happiness, and which they suppose religion would require them to give up without substituting anything in their place. But never was there a greater mistake. Let them go and ask Christians, and they will obtain but one answer from them. It is, that they never knew what true happiness was till they found it in the Saviour. This question may be proposed to a Christian of any denomination, or in any land, and the answer will be uniformily the same. Why is it, then, that the mass of persons regard religion as adapted only to make them unhappy? Why will they not take the testimony of their friends in the case, and believe those whom they would believe on any other subject, when they declare that it is only true religion that ever gives them solid peace?

4. We cannot depend on any external advantages of birth or blood for salvation. Vs. 4, 5, 6. Few or no persons have as much in this respect to rely on as Paul had. Indeed, if salvation were to be obtained at all by such external advantages, it is impossible to conceive that more could have been united in one case than there was in his. He had not only the advantage of having been born a Hebrew; of having been early trained in the Jewish religion; of being instructed in the ablest manner, but also the advantage of entire blamelessness in his moral deportment. He had showed in every way possible that he was heartily attached to the religion of his fathers, and he began life with a zeal in the cause which seemed to justify the warmest expectations of his friends. But all this was renounced, when he came to see the true method of salvation, and saw the better way by which eternal life

is to be obtained. And if Paul could not depend on this, we cannot safely do it. It will not save us that we have been born in the church; that we have had pious parents; that we were early baptized and consecrated to God; that we were trained in the Sabbath-school. Nor will it save us that we attend regularly on the place of worship, or that we are amiable, correct, honest, and upright in our lives. We can no more depend on these things than Saul of Tarsus could, and if all his eminent advantages failed to give him a solid ground of hope, our advantages will be equally vain in regard to our salvation. It almost seems as if God *designed* in the case of Saul of Tarsus, that there should be *one* instance where *every possible* external advantage for salvation should be found, and there should be everything that men ever could rely on in moral character, in order to show that no such things could be sufficient to save the soul. All these may exist, and yet there may not be a particle of love to God, and the heart may be full of selfishness, pride, and ambition, as it was in his case.

5. Religion demands humility. Vs. 7, 8. It requires us to renounce all dependence on our own merits, and to rely simply on the merits of another—the Lord Jesus Christ. If we are ever saved, we must be brought to esteem all the advantages which birth and blood and our own righteousness can bestow as worthless, and even vile, in the matter of justification. We shall not despise these things in themselves, nor shall we consider that vice is as desirable as virtue, nor that a bad temper is to be sought rather than an amiable disposition, nor that dishonesty is as commendable as honesty; but we shall feel that in comparison with the merits of the Redeemer all these are worthless. But the mind is not brought to this condition without great humiliation. Nothing but the power of God can bring a proud and haughty and self-righteous sinner to this state, where he is willing to renounce all dependence on his own merits, and to be saved in the same way as the vilest of the species.

6. Let us seek to obtain an interest in the righteousness of the Redeemer. Ver. 9. Our own righteousness cannot save us. But in him there is enough. There is all that we want, and if we have that righteousness which is by faith, we have all that is needful to render us accepted with God, and to prepare us for heaven. When there is *such* a way of salvation—so easy, so free, so glorious, so ample for all, how unwise is any one to rest on his own works, and to expect to be saved by what he has done! The highest honour of man is to be saved by the merits of the Son of God, and he has reached the most elevated rank in the human condition who has the most certain hope of salvation through him.

7. There is enough to be gained to excite us to the utmost diligence and effort in the christian life. Vs. 10—14. If men can be excited to effort by the prospect of an earthly crown in a race or a game, how much more should we be urged forward by the prospect of the eternal prize! To seek to know the Redeemer; to be raised up from the degradation of sin; to have part in the resurrection of the just; to obtain the prize of the high calling in heaven—to be made everlastingly happy and glorious there—what object was ever placed before the mind like this? What ardour should it excite that we may gain it! Surely, the hope of obtaining such a prize as is before the Christian, should call forth all our powers. The struggle will not be long. The race will soon be won. The victory will be glorious; the defeat would be overwhelm-

ing and awful. No one need fear that he can put forth *too much* effort to obtain the prize. It is worth every exertion, and we should never relax our efforts, or give over in despair.

8. Let us, like Paul, ever cherish an humble sense of our attainments in religion. Vs. 12, 13. If Paul had not reached the point of perfection, it is not to be presumed that we have; if he could not say that he had 'attained,' it is presumption in us to suppose that we have; if he had occasion for humiliation, we have more; if he felt that he was far short of the object which he sought, and was pressed down with the consciousness of imperfection, such a feeling becomes us also. Yet let us not sink down in despondency and inaction. Like him, let us strain every nerve that we may overcome our imperfections and win the prize. That prize is before us. It is glorious. We may be sensible that we, as yet, have not reached it, but if we will strive to obtain it, it will soon be certainly ours. We may feel that we are far distant from it now in the degree of our attainments, but we are not far from it in fact. It will be but a short period before the Christian will lay hold on that immortal crown, and before his brow will be encircled with the diadem of glory. For the race of life, whether we win or lose, is soon run; and when a Christian begins a day, he knows not but he may end it in heaven; when he lies down on his bed at night, he knows not but he may awake with the 'prize' in his hand, and with the diadem of glory sparkling on his brow.

9. Our thoughts should be much in heaven. Ver. 20. Our home is there; our citizenship is there. Here we are strangers and pilgrims. We are away from home, in a cold and unfriendly world. Our great interests are in the skies; our eternal dwelling is to be there; our best friends are already there. There is our glorious Saviour, with a body adapted to those pure abodes, and there are many whom we have loved on earth already with him. They are happy now, and we should not love them less because they are in heaven. Since, therefore, our great interests are there, and our best friends there; and since we ourselves are citizens of that heavenly world, our best affections should be there.

10. We look for the Saviour. Vs. 20, 21. He will return to our world He will change our vile bodies, and make them like his own glorious body. And since this is so, let us (1.) bear with patience the trials and infirmities to which our bodies here are subject. These trials will be short, and we may well bear them for a few days, knowing that soon all pain will cease, and that all that is humiliating in the body will be exchanged for glory. (2.) Let us not think too highly or too much of our bodies here. They may be now beautiful and comely, but they are 'vile' and degraded, compared with what they will soon be. They are subject to infirmity and to numerous pains and sicknesses. Soon the most beautiful body may become loathsome to our best friends. Soon, too offensive to be looked upon, it will be hidden in the grave. Why then should we seek to pamper and adorn these mortal frames? Why live only to decorate them? Why should we idolize a mass of moulded and animated clay? Yet (3.) let us learn to honour the body in a true sense. It is soon to be changed. It will be made like the glorified body of Christ. Yes, this frail, diseased, corruptible, and humbled body; this body, that is soon to be laid in the grave, and to return to the dust, is soon to put on a new form, and to be clothed with immortality. It will be what the body of Christ now is—glorious and immortal. What a

change! Christian, go and look on the creeping caterpillar, and see it changed to the gay and gilded butterfly — yesterday, a crawling and offensive insect; to-day, with gaudy colours, an inhabitant of the air, and a dweller amidst flowers; and see an *image* of what thy body shall be, and of the mighty transformation which thou wilt soon undergo. See the change from the cold death of winter to the fragrance and life of spring, and behold an image of the change which thou thyself wilt ere long experience, and a *proof* that some such change awaits thee.

"Shall spring the faded world revive?
Shall waning moons their light renew?
Again shall setting suns ascend
And chase the darkness from our view?

Shall life revisit dying worms,
And spread the joyful insect's wing?
And, oh, shall man awake no more,
To see thy face, thy name to sing?

Faith sees the bright, eternal doors
Unfold to make her children way;
They shall be clothed with endless life,
And shine in everlasting day."

DWIGHT.

11. Let us look for the coming of the Lord. Ver. 21. All that we hope for depends on his reappearing. Our day of triumph and of the fulness of our joy, is to be when he shall return. Then we shall be raised from the grave; then our vile bodies shall be changed; then we shall be acknowledged as his friends; then we shall go to be forever with him. The earth is not our home; nor is the grave to be our everlasting bed of rest. Our home is heaven—and the Saviour will come, that he may raise us up to that blessed abode. And who knows when he may appear? He himself commanded us to be ready, for he said he would come at an hour when we think not. We should so desire his coming, that the hours of his delay would seem to be heavy and long, and should so live that we can breathe forth with sincerity, at all times, the fervent prayer of the beloved disciple, "Come, Lord Jesus, COME QUICKLY." Rev. xxii. 20.

"My faith shall triumph o'er the grave,
And trample on the tombs;
My Jesus, my Redeemer, lives,
My God, my Saviour, comes;
Ere long I know he shall appear,
In power and glory great;
And death, the last of all his foes,
Lie vanquish'd at his feet.

Then, though the worms my flesh devour,
And make my form their prey,
I know I shall arise with power,
On the last judgment-day;—
When God shall stand upon the earth,
Him then mine eyes shall see;
My flesh shall feel a sacred birth;
And ever with him be.

Then his own hand shall wipe the tears
From every weeping eye;
And pains, and groans, and griefs, and fears,
Shall cease eternally.
How long, dear Saviour! Oh, how long
Shall this bright hour delay?
Fly swift around, ye wheels of time,
And bring the welcome day."

WATTS.

CHAPTER IV.

ANALYSIS OF THE CHAPTER.

This chapter comprises the following points:

I. Exhortations.

II. Solemn commands to live as became Christians.

III. The expression of a grateful acknowledgment of the favours which he had received from them; and,

IV. The customary salutations.

I. *Exhortations.* Vs. 1—3. (1.) He exhorts them to stand fast in the Lord. Ver. 1. (2.) He entreats Euodias and Syntyche, who appear to have been alienated from each other, to be reconciled. Ver. 2. (3.) He entreats one whom he calls a 'true yoke-fellow' to render assistance to those women who had laboured with him in the gospel. Ver. 3.

II. *Commands.* Vs. 4—9. He commands them to rejoice in the Lord always, ver. 4; to let their moderation be known to all, ver. 5; to have no anxiety about worldly

CHAPTER IV.

THEREFORE, my brethren dearly beloved and longed for, my joy and crown, so stand fast in the Lord, *my* dearly beloved.

2 I beseech Euodias, and be

---

matters, but in all their necessities to go to God, vs. 6, 7; and to do whatever was honest, just, pure, lovely, and of good report. Vs. 8, 9.

III. *A grateful acknowledgment of their kindness.* Vs. 10—19. He says that their care of him had been manifested again, in such a way as to be highly grateful to his feelings. Ver. 10. He did not indeed say that he had suffered, for he had learned, in whatever state he was, to be content (vs. 11—13); but they had shown a proper spirit in endeavouring to relieve his necessities, ver. 14. He remarks that their church was the only one that had aided him when he was in Macedonia, and that they had sent to him more than once when he was in Thessalonica, and says that their favour now was an offering acceptable to God, who would abundantly reward them. Vs. 15—20.

IV. *Salutations.* Vs. 21—23.

1. *Therefore, my brethren dearly beloved and longed for.* Doddridge unites this verse with the previous chapter, and supposes that it is the proper close of the solemn statement which the apostle makes there. The word *therefore*—ὥστε—has undoubted reference to the remarks made there; and the meaning is, that in view of the fact that there were many professed Christians who were not sincere—that the 'citizenship' of all true Christians was in heaven, and that Christians looked for the coming of the Lord Jesus, who would make them like to himself, the apostle exhorts them to stand fast in the Lord. The accumulation of epithets of endearment in this verse shows his tender regard for them, and is expressive of his earnest solicitude for their welfare, and his deep conviction of their danger. The term '*longed for*' is expressive of strong affection. See ch. i. 8, and ii. 26. ¶ *My joy.* The source of my joy. He rejoiced in the fact that they had been converted under him; and in their holy walk and their friendship. Our chief joy is in our friends; and the chief happiness of a minister of the gospel is in the pure lives of those to whom he ministers. See 3 John 4. ¶ *And crown.* Comp. 1 Thess. ii. 19. The word *crown* means a circlet, chaplet, or diadem, (1) as the emblem of royal dignity—the symbol of office; (2) as the prize conferred on victors in the public games, 1 Cor. ix. 25, and hence as an emblem of the rewards of a future life, 2 Tim. iv. 8. James i. 12. 1 Pet. v. 4; (3) anything that is an ornament or honour, as one *glories* in a crown. Comp. Prov. xii. 4, "A virtuous woman is a crown to her husband;" xiv. 24, "The crown of the wise is their riches;" xvi. 31, "The hoary head is a crown of glory;" xvii. 6, "Children's children are the crown of old men." The idea here is, that the church at Philippi was that in which the apostle gloried. He regarded it as a high honour to have been the means of founding such a church, and he looked upon it with the same interest with which a monarch looks upon the diadem which he wears. ¶ *So stand fast in the Lord.* In the service of the Lord, and in the strength which he imparts. See Notes on Eph. vi. 13, 14.

2. *I beseech Euodias, and beseech Syntyche.* These are doubtless the names of females. The name Syn

seech Syntyche, that they be of the same mind in the Lord.

3 And I entreat thee also, true yoke-fellow, help those women which laboured with me in the gospel, with Clement also, and

---

tyche is sometimes the name of a man; but, if these persons are referred to in ver. 3, there can be no doubt that they were females. Nothing more is known of them than is here mentioned. It has been commonly supposed that they were deaconesses, who preached the gospel to those of their own sex; but there is no certain evidence of this. All that is known is, that there was some disagreement between them, and the apostle entreats them to be reconciled to each other. ¶ *That they be of the same mind.* That they be united, or reconciled. Whether the difference related to doctrine, or to something else, we cannot determine from this phrase. The language is such as would properly relate to *any* difference. ¶ *In the Lord.* In their christian walk and plans. They were doubtless professing Christians, and the apostle exhorts them to make *the Lord* the great object of their affections, and, in their regard for him, to bury all their petty differences and animosities.

3. *And I entreat thee also, true yoke-fellow.* It is not known to whom the apostle refers here. No name is mentioned, and conjecture is useless. All that is known is, that it was some one whom Paul regarded as associated with himself in labour, and one who was so prominent at Philippi that it would be understood who was referred to, without more particularly mentioning him. The presumption, therefore, is, that it was one of the ministers, or 'bishops' (see Notes, ch. i. 1) of Philippi, who had been particularly associated with Paul when he was there. The epistle was addressed to the 'church with the bishops and deacons' (ch. i. 1); and the fact that this one had been particularly associated with Paul, would serve to designate him with sufficient particularity. Whether he was related to the women referred to, is wholly unknown. Doddridge supposes that he might be the husband of one of these women; but of that there is no evidence. The term 'yoke-fellow'—σύζυγος—some have understood as a proper name (*Syzygus*); but the proper import of the word is *yoke-fellow*, and there is no reason to believe that it is used here to denote a proper name. If it had been, it is probable that some other word than that here used and rendered *true*—γνήσιος—would have been employed. The word *true*—γνήσιος—means that he was sincere, faithful, worthy of confidence. Paul had had evidence of his sincerity and fidelity; and he was a proper person, therefore, to whom to intrust a delicate and important business. ¶ *Help those women.* The common opinion is, that the women here referred to were Euodias and Syntyche, and that the office which the friend of Paul was asked to perform was, to secure a reconciliation between them. There is, however, no certain evidence of this. The reference seems rather to be to influential females who had rendered important assistance to Paul when he was there. The kind of 'help' which was to be imparted was probably by counsel, and friendly cooperation in the duties which they were called to perform. There is no evidence that it refers to pecuniary aid; and, had it referred to a reconciliation of those who were at variance, it is probable that some other word would have been used than that here rendered *help*—συλλαμβάνου. ¶ *Which laboured with me in the gospel.* As Paul did not per-

with other my fellow-labourers, whose names *are* in the book of life.

4 Rejoice [a] in the Lord alway: *and* again I say, Rejoice.

5 Let your moderation [b] be

a c. 3. 1. b 1 Co. 9. 25.

mit women to preach (see 1 Tim. ii. 12; comp. Notes on 1 Cor. x. 5), he must have referred here to some other services which they had rendered. There were deaconesses in the primitive churches (Notes, Rom. xvi. 1. 1 Tim. v. 9, seq.), to whom was probably intrusted particularly the care of the female members of a church. In the custom which prevailed in the oriental world, of excluding females from the public gaze, and of confining them to their houses, it would not be practicable for the apostles to have access to them. The duties of instructing and exhorting them were then probably intrusted chiefly to pious females; and in this way important aid would be rendered in the gospel. Paul could regard such as 'labouring with him,' though they were not engaged in preaching. ¶ *With Clement also.* That is, they were associated with Clement, and with the other fellow-labourers of Paul, in aiding him in the gospel. Clement was doubtless some one who was well known among them; and the apostle felt that, by associating them with him, as having been real helpers in the gospel, their claim to respectful attention would be better appreciated. Who Clement was, is unknown. Most of the ancients say it was Clement of Rome, one of the primitive fathers. But there is no evidence of this. The name Clement was common, and there is no improbability in supposing that there might have been a preacher of this name in the church at Philippi. ¶ *Whose names* are *in the book of life.* See Notes on Isa. iv. 3. The phrase, 'the book of life,' which occurs here, and in Rev. iii. 5; xiii. 8; xx. 12. 15: xxi. 27; xxii. 19, is a Jewish phrase, and refers originally to a record or catalogue of names, as the roll of an army. It then means to be among the living, as the name of an individual would be erased from a catalogue when he was deceased. The word *life* here refers to eternal life; and the whole phrase refers to those who were enrolled among the true friends of God, or who would certainly be saved. The use of this phrase here implies the belief of Paul that these persons were true Christians. Names that are written in the book of life will not be blotted out. If the hand of God records them there, who can obliterate them?

4. *Rejoice in the Lord alway.* See Notes, ch. iii. 1. It is the privilege of Christians to do this, not at certain periods and at distant intervals, but at all times they may rejoice that there is a God and Saviour; they may rejoice in the character, law, and government of God—in his promises, and in communion with him. The Christian, therefore, may be, and should be, always a happy man. If everything else changes, yet the Lord does not change; if the sources of all other joy are dried up, yet this is not; and there is not a moment of a Christian's life in which he may not find joy in the character, law, and promises of God.

5. *Let your moderation be known unto all men.* That is, let it be such that others may see it. This does not mean that they were to make an ostentatious display of it, but that it should be such a characteristic of their lives that it would be constantly visible to others. The word *moderation*—ἐπιεικὲς—refers to restraint on the passions, general so-

known unto all men: The Lord[a] *is* at hand.

6 Be careful[b] for nothing; but in every thing by prayer and sup-

a Re. 22. 7, 20.

b Mat. 6. 25. 1 Pe. 5. 7.

berness of living, being free from all excesses. The word properly means that which is *fit* or *suitable*, and then propriety, gentleness, mildness.—They were to indulge in no excess of passion, or dress, or eating, or drinking. They were to govern their appetites, restrain their temper, and to be examples of what was proper for men in view of the expectation that the Lord would soon appear. ¶ *The Lord is at hand.* Is near. See Notes, ch. iii. 20. 1 Cor. xvi. 22. This has the appearance of being a phrase in common use among the early Christians, and as being designed to keep before their minds a lively impression of an event which ought, by its anticipation, to produce an important effect. Whether, by this phrase, they commonly understood the coming of the Lord to destroy Jerusalem, or to remove them by death, or to judge the world, or to reign personally on the earth, it is impossible now to determine, and is not very material to a proper understanding of its use here. The idea is, that the expectation that the Lord Jesus will 'come,' *ought* to be allowed to produce moderation of our passions, in our manner of living, in our expectations of what this world can furnish, and in our desires of earthly good. On him who feels that he is soon to die, and to stand at the bar of God—on him who expects soon to see the Lord Jesus coming in the clouds of heaven, it cannot fail to have this effect. Men indulge their passions—are extravagant in their plans of life, and in their expectations of earthly good for themselves and for their families, because they have no realizing sense of the truth that there is before them a vast eternity. He that has a lively expectation that heaven will soon be his, will form very moderate expectations of what this world can furnish.

6. *Be careful for nothing.* That is, be not *anxious* or *solicitous* about the things of the present life. The word here used—μεριμνᾶτε—does not mean that we are to exercise no *care* about worldly matters—no care to preserve our property, or to provide for our families (comp. 1 Tim. v. 8); but that there is to be such confidence in God as to free the mind from anxiety, and such a sense of dependence on him as to keep it calm. See the subject explained in the Notes on Matt. vi. 25. ¶ *But in everything.* Everything in reference to the supply of your wants, and the wants of your families; everything in respect to afflictions, embarrassments, and trials; and everything relating to your spiritual condition. There is nothing which pertains to body, mind, estate, friends, conflicts, losses, trials, hopes, fears, in reference to which we may not go and spread it all out before the Lord. ¶ *By prayer and supplication.* The word rendered *supplication* is a stronger term than the former. It is the mode of prayer peculiarly which arises from the sense of *need*, or *want*—from δέομαι, *to want, to need.* ¶ *With thanksgiving.* Thanksgiving connected with prayer. We can always find *something* to be thankful for, no matter what may be the burden of our wants, or the special subject of our petitions. When we pray for the supply of our wants, we may be thankful for that kind providence which has hitherto befriended us; when we pray for restoration from sickness, we may be thankful for the health we have hitherto enjoyed, and for God's merciful interposition in the former days of trial, and for his goodness in now

plication, with thanksgiving, let your request be made known unto God:

7 And the peace [a] of God, which passeth all understanding, shall keep your hearts and minds through Christ Jesus.

8 Finally, brethren, whatsoever

a Is. 26. 3. Jno. 14. 27.

sparing our lives; when we pray that our children and friends may be preserved from danger and death, we may remember how often God has interposed to save them; when, oppressed with a sense of sin, we pray for pardon, we have abundant cause of thanksgiving that there *is* a glorious way by which we may be saved. The greatest sufferer that lives in this world of redeeming love, and who has the offer of heaven before him, has cause of gratitude. ¶ *Let your request be made known unto God.* Not as if you were to give him *information*, but to *express* to him to your wants. God needs not to be informed of our necessities, but he requires that we come and express them to him. Comp. Ezek. xxxvi. 37. "Thus saith the Lord God, I will yet for this be inquired of by the house of Israel to do it for them."

7. *And the peace of God.* The peace which God gives. The peace here particularly referred to is that which is felt when we have no anxious care about the supply of our wants, and when we go confidently and commit everything into the hands of God. "Thou wilt keep him in perfect peace whose mind is stayed on thee." Isa. xxvi. 3. See Notes on John xiv. 27. ¶ *Which passeth all understanding.* That is, which surpasses all that men had conceived or imagined. The expression is one that denotes that the peace imparted is of the highest possible kind. The apostle Paul frequently used terms which had somewhat of a hyperbolical cast (see Notes on Eph. iii. 19. Comp. John xxi. 25), and the language here is that which one would use who designed to speak of that which was of the highest order. The Christian, committing his way to God, and feeling that he will order all things aright, *has* a peace which is nowhere else known. Nothing else will furnish it but religion. No confidence that a man can have in his own powers; no reliance which he can repose on his own plans or on the promises or fidelity of his fellow-men, and no calculations which he can make on the course of events, can impart such peace to the soul as simple confidence in God. ¶ *Shall keep your hearts and minds.* That is, shall keep them from anxiety and agitation. The idea is, that by thus making our requests known to God, and going to him in view of all our trials and wants, the mind would be preserved from distressing anxiety. The way to find peace, and to have the heart kept from trouble, is thus to go and spread out all before the Lord. Comp. Isa. xxvi. 3, 4. 20; xxxvii. 1—7. The word here rendered *shall keep*, is a military term, and means that the mind would be guarded as a camp or castle is. It would be preserved from the intrusion of anxious fears and alarms. ¶ *Through Christ Jesus.* By his agency, or intervention. It is only in him that the mind can be preserved in peace. It is not by mere confidence in God, or by mere prayer, but it is by confidence in God as he is revealed through the Redeemer, and by faith in him. Paul never lost sight of the truth that all the security and happiness of a believer were to be traced to the Saviour.

8. *Finally, brethren.* As for what remains — τὸ λοιπὸν — or as a final counsel or exhortation. ¶ *What-*

things are true, [a] whatsoever things are [1] honest, [b] whatsoever things

a Ep. 4. 25. [1] or, *venerable*. b 2 Co. 8. 21.

soever things are true. In this exhortation the apostle assumes that there were certain things admitted to be true, and pure, and good, in the world, which had not been directly revealed, or which were commonly regarded as such by the men of the world, and his object is to show them that such things ought to be exhibited by the Christian. Everything that was honest and just towards God and towards men was to be practised by them, and they were in all things to be examples of the highest kind of morality. They were not to exhibit partial virtues; not to perform one set of duties to the neglect or exclusion of others; not to be faithful in their duties to God, and to neglect their duty to men; not to be punctual in their religious rites, and neglectful of the common laws of morality; but they were to do *everything* that could be regarded as the fair subject of commendation, and that was implied in the highest moral character. The word *true* refers here to everything that was the reverse of falsehood. They were to be true to their engagements; true to their promises; true in their statements; and true in their friendships. They were to maintain the truth about God; about eternity; about the judgment; and about every man's character. Truth is a representation of things as they are; and they were constantly to live under the correct impression of objects. A man who is false to his engagements, or false in his statements and promises, is one who will always disgrace religion. ¶ *Whatsoever things are honest.* σεμνά. Properly, *venerable, reverend*; then *honourable, reputable.* The word was originally used in relation to the gods, and to the things that pertained to them, as being worthy of honour or veneration. *Passow.* As applied to men, it commonly means grave, dignified, worthy of veneration or regard. In the New Testament it is rendered *grave* in 1 Tim. iii. 8. 11, and Titus ii. 2, the only places where the word occurs except this; and the *noun* (σεμνότης) is rendered *honesty* in 1 Tim. ii. 2, and *gravity* in 1 Tim. iii. 4, and Tit. ii. 7. It occurs nowhere else in the New Testament. The word, therefore, does not express precisely what the word *honest* does with us, as confined to *dealings* or *business transactions*, but rather has reference to what was regarded as worthy of reputation or honour; what there was in the customs of society, in the respect due to age and rank, and in the intercourse of the world, that deserved respect or esteem. It *includes* indeed what is right in the transaction of business, but it embraces also much more, and means that the Christian is to show respect to all the venerable and proper customs of society, when they did not violate conscience or interfere with the law of God. Comp. 1 Tim. iii. 7. ¶ *Whatsoever things are just.* The things which are right between man and man. A Christian should be *just* in all his dealings. His religion does not exempt him from the strict laws which bind men to the exercise of this virtue, and there is no way by which a professor of religion can do more injury perhaps than by injustice and dishonesty in his dealings. It is to be remembered that the men of the world, in estimating a man's character, affix much more importance to the virtues of justice and honesty than they do to regularity in observing the ordinances of religion; and therefore if a Christian would make an impression on his fellow-men favourable to religion, it is indispensa-

are just, [a] whatsoever things *are* pure, [b] whatsoever things *are* lovely, [c] whatsoever things *are* of good report; [d] if *there be* any virtue, [e] and if *there be* any praise, [f] think on these things.

9 Those things which ye have both learned, and received, and heard, and seen in me, do: and the God [g] of peace shall be with you.

a De. 16. 20. Is. 26. 7. b Ja. 3. 17. 1 Jno. 3. 3. c 1 Co. c. 13. d Col. 4. 5. He. 11. 2. e 2 Pe. 1. 3, 4. f Ro. 13. 3. g He. 13. 20.

ble that he manifest uncorrupted integrity in his dealings. ¶ *Whatsoever things* are *pure.* Chaste—in thought, and feeling, and in the intercourse between the sexes. Comp. Notes, 1 Tim. v. 2. ¶ *Whatsoever things* are *lovely.* The word here used means properly what is *dear* to any one; then what is pleasing. Here it means what is *amiable*—such a temper of mind that one can love it; or such as to be agreeable to others. A Christian should not be sour, crabbed, and irritable in his temper—for nothing almost tends so much to injure the cause of religion as a temper always chafed; a brow morose and stern; an eye that is severe and unkind, and a disposition to find fault with everything. And yet it is to be regretted that there are many persons, who make no pretensions to piety, who far surpass many professors of religion in the virtue here commended. A sour and crabbed temper in a professor of religion will undo all the good that he attempts to do. ¶ *Whatsoever things* are *of good report.* That is, whatsoever is truly *reputable* in the world at large. There are actions which all men agree in commending, and which in all ages and countries are regarded as virtues. Courtesy, urbanity, kindness, respect for parents, purity between brothers and sisters, are among those virtues, and the Christian should be a pattern and an example in them all. His usefulness depends much more on the cultivation of these virtues than is commonly supposed. ¶ *If* there be *any virtue.* If there is anything truly virtuous. Paul did not suppose that he had given a full catalogue of the virtues which he would have cultivated. He, therefore, adds, that if there was anything else that had the nature of true virtue in it, they should be careful to cultivate that also. The Christian should be a pattern and example of every virtue. ¶ *And if* there be *any praise.* Anything worthy of praise, or that ought to be praised. ¶ *Think on these things.* Let them be the object of your careful attention and study, so as to practise them. Think what they are; think on the obligation to observe them; think on the influence which they would have on the world around you.

9. *Those things which ye have both learned, and received, and heard, and seen in me, do.* That is, what you have witnessed in me, and what you have learned of me, and what you have heard about me, practise yourselves. Paul refers them to his uniform conduct—to all that they had seen, and known, and heard of him, as that which it was proper for them to imitate. The same thing, substantially, he urges in ch. iii. 17. See Notes on that verse. It could have been only the consciousness of a pure and upright life which would make such counsel proper. How few are the men at this day who can urge others to imitate all that they have seen in them, and learned from them, and *heard* of them. ¶ *And the God of peace shall be with you.* The God who gives peace. Comp. Heb. xiii. 20. 1 Thess. v. 23. See also Notes on ver. 7. The meaning here is, that Paul, by pursuing the course of life

10 But I rejoiced in the Lord greatly, that now at the last your care of me [1] hath flourished again; wherein ye were also careful, but ye lacked opportunity. [a]

11 Not that I speak in respect of want: for I have learned, in whatsoever state I am, *therewith* to be content. [b]

[1] or, *is revived.* [a] 2 Cor. 6. 7.

[b] He. 13. 5.

which he had led, and which he here counsels them to follow, had found that it had been attended with the blessing of the God of peace, and he felt the fullest assurance that the same blessing would rest on them if they imitated his example. The way to obtain the blessing of the God of peace, is to lead a holy life, and to perform with faithfulness all the duties which we owe to God and to our fellow-men.

10. *But I rejoiced in the Lord greatly.* The favour which Paul had received, and for which he felt so much gratitude, had been received of the Philippians; but he regarded 'the Lord' as the source of it, and rejoiced in it as the expression of his kindness. The effect was to lead his heart with cheerfulness and joy up to God. ¶ *That now at the last.* After so long a time. The reason why he had not before received the favour, was not neglect or inattention on their part, but the difficulty of having communication with him. ¶ *Your care of me hath flourished again.* In the margin this is rendered '*is revived*,' and this is the proper meaning of the Greek word. It is a word properly applicable to plants or flowers, meaning to grow green again; to flourish again; to spring up again. Here the meaning is, that they had been again *prospered* in their care of him, and to Paul it seemed *as if* their care had sprung up anew. ¶ *Wherein ye were also careful.* That is, they were desirous to render him assistance, and to minister to his wants. Paul adds this, lest they should think he was disposed to blame them for inattention. ¶ *But ye lacked opportunity.* Because there were no persons going to Rome from Philippi by whom they could send to him. The distance was considerable, and it is not probable that the intercourse between the two places was very constant.

11. *Not that I speak in respect of want.* Though Paul was doubtless often in circumstances of necessity, yet he did not make these remarks on that account. In his journeys, in his imprisonments, he could not but be at times in want; but he had learned to bear all this; and that which most impressed itself on his mind was the interest which the church *ought* to show in the cause of religion, and the evidence which it would thus furnish of attachment to the cause. As to his own personal trials, he had learned to bear them, so that they did not give him great uneasiness. ¶ *For I have learned, in whatsoever state I am,* therewith *to be content.* That is, to have a contented mind. Paul says that he had '*learned*' this. Probably by nature he had a mind as prone to impatience as others, but he had been in circumstances fitted to produce a different state of feeling. He had had ample experience (2 Cor. xi. 26), and, in his life of trials, he had acquired invaluable lessons on the subject. He had had abundant time for reflection, and he had found that there was grace enough in the gospel to enable him to bear trials with resignation. The *considerations* by which he had been taught this, he does not state; but they were probably such as the follow-

12 I know both how to be abased, and I know how to abound: every where, and in all things, I am instructed, both to be full and

ing: that it is wrong to murmur at the allotments of Providence; that a spirit of impatience does no good, remedies no evil, and supplies no want; that God could provide for him in a way which he could not foresee, and that the Saviour was able abundantly to sustain him. A contented mind is an invaluable blessing, and is one of the fruits of religion in the soul. It arises from the belief that God is right in all his ways. Why should we be impatient, restless, discontented? What evil will be remedied by it? what want supplied? what calamity removed? "He that is of a merry heart hath a continual feast" (Prov. xv. 15); and one of the secrets of happiness is to have a mind satisfied with all the allotments of Providence. The members of the Episcopal church beautifully pray, every day, 'Give us minds always contented with our present condition.' No prayer can be offered which will enter more deeply into all our happiness on earth.

12. *I know both how to be abased.* To be in circumstances of want. ¶ *And I know how to abound.* To have an abundance. He had been in circumstances where he had an ample supply for all his wants, and knew what it was to have enough. It requires as much grace to keep the heart right in prosperity, as it does in adversity, and perhaps more. Adversity, *of itself*, does something to keep the mind in a right state; prosperity does nothing. ¶ *Everywhere and in all things.* In all my travels and imprisonments, and in reference to everything that occurs, I learn important lessons on these points. ¶ *I am instructed.* The word here used—μεμύημαι—is one that is commonly used in relation to *mysteries*, and denoted being instructed in the secret doctrines that were taught in the ancient 'mysteries.' *Passow.* In those mysteries, it was only the 'initiated' who were made acquainted with the lessons that were taught there. Paul says that *he* had been initiated into the lessons taught by trials and by prosperity. The secret and important lessons which these schools of adversity are fitted to teach, he had had an ample opportunity of learning; and he had faithfully embraced the doctrines thus taught. ¶ *Both to be full.* That is, he had learned to have an ample supply of his wants, and yet to observe the laws of temperance and soberness, and to cherish gratitude for the mercies which he had enjoyed. ¶ *And to be hungry.* That is, to be in circumstances of want, and yet not to murmur or complain. He had learned to bear all this without discontent. This was then, as it is now, no easy lesson to learn; and it is not improper to suppose that, when Paul says that he had 'been instructed' in this, even he means to say that it was only *by degrees* that he had acquired it. It is a lesson which we slowly learn, not to murmur at the allotments of Providence; not to be envious at the prosperity of others; not to repine when our comforts are removed. There may be another idea suggested here. The condition of Paul was not always the same. He passed through great reverses. At one time he had abundance; then he was reduced to want;—now he was in a state which might be regarded as affluent; then he was brought down to extreme poverty. Yesterday, he was poor and hungry; today, all his necessities are supplied. Now, it is in these sudden reverses that grace is most needed, and in these rapid changes of life that it is

to be hungry, both to abound and to suffer need.

13 I can do all things through [a] Christ which strengtheneth me.

a Jno. 15. 5. 2 Co. 12. 9.

most difficult to learn the lessons of calm contentment. Men get accustomed to an even tenor of life, no matter what it is, and learn to shape their temper and their calculations according to it. But these lessons of philosophy vanish when they pass suddenly from one extreme to another, and find their condition in life suddenly changed. The garment that was adapted to weather of an uniform temperature, whether of heat or cold, fails to be fitted to our wants when these transitions rapidly succeed each other. Such *changes* are constantly occurring in life. God tries his people, not by a steady course of prosperity, or by long-continued and uniform adversity, but by *transition* from the one to the other; and it often happens that the grace which would have been sufficient for either continued prosperity or adversity, would fail in the transition from the one to the other. Hence, new grace is imparted for this new form of trial, and new traits of christian character are developed in these rapid transitions in life, as some of the most beautiful exhibitions of the laws of matter are brought out in the transitions produced in chemistry. The rapid changes from heat to cold, or from a solid to a gaseous state, develope properties before unknown, and acquaint us much more intimately with the wonderful works of God. The gold or the diamond, unsubjected to the action of intense heat, and to the changes produced by the powerful agents brought to bear on them, might have continued to shine with steady beauty and brilliancy; but we should never have witnessed *the peculiar* beauty and brilliancy which may be produced in rapid chemical changes. And so there is many a beautiful trait of character which would never have been known by either continued prosperity or adversity. There might have been *always* a beautiful exhibition of virtue and piety, but not that peculiar manifestation which is produced in the transitions from the one to the other.

13. *I can do all things.* From the experience which Paul had in these various circumstances of life, he comes here to the general conclusion that he could 'do all things.' He could bear any trial, perform any duty, subdue any evil propensity of his nature, and meet all the temptations incident to any condition of prosperity or adversity. His own experience in the various changes of life had warranted him in arriving at this conclusion; and he now expresses the firm confidence that nothing would be required of him which he would not be able to perform. In Paul, this declaration was not a vain self-reliance, nor was it the mere result of his former experience. He knew well where the strength was to be obtained by which to do all things, and on that arm that was able to uphold him he confidently relied. ¶ *Through Christ which strengtheneth me.* See Notes on John xv. 5. Of the strength which Christ can impart, Paul had had abundant experience; and now his whole reliance was there. It was not in any native ability which he had; not in any vigour of body or of mind; not in any power which there was in his own resolutions; it was in the strength that he derived from the Redeemer. By that he was enabled to bear cold, fatigue, and hunger; by that, he met temptations and persecutions; and by that, he engaged in the performance of his arduous duties. Let us learn,

14 Notwithstanding, ye have well done that ye did communicate with my affliction.

15 Now, ye Philippians, know also, that in the beginning of the gospel, when I departed from Macedonia, no [a] church communicated with me as concerning giving and receiving, but ye only.

a 2 Co. 11. 8, 9.

hence, (1.) That we need not sink under any trial, for there is one who can strengthen us. (2.) That we need not yield to temptation. There is one who is able to make a way for our escape. (3.) That we need not be harassed, and vexed, and tortured with improper thoughts and unholy desires. There is one who can enable us to banish such thoughts from the mind, and restore the right balance to the affections of the soul. (4.) That we need not dread what is to come. Trials, temptations, poverty, want, persecution, may await us; but we need not sink into despondency. At every step of life, Christ is able to strengthen us, and can bring us triumphantly through. What a privilege it is, therefore, to be a Christian—to feel, in the trials of life, that we have one friend, unchanging and most mighty, who can always help us! How cheerfully should we engage in our duties, and meet the trials that are before us, leaning on the arm of our Almighty Redeemer! Let us not shrink from duty; let us not dread persecution; let us not fear the bed of death. In all circumstances, Christ, our unchanging Friend, can uphold us. Let the eye and the affections of the heart be fixed on him; let the simple, fervent, believing prayer be directed always to him when trials come, when temptations assail, when duty presses hard upon us, and when a crowd of unholy and forbidden thoughts rush into the soul; and we shall be safe.

14. *Notwithstanding, ye have well done.* Though he had learned the grace of contentment, and though he knew that Christ could enable him to do all things, it was well for them to show sympathy for his sufferings; for it evinced a proper regard for a benefactor and an apostle. ¶ *Ye did communicate.* You took part with my affliction. That is, you sympathized with me, and assisted me in bearing it. The relief which they had sent, not only supplied his wants, but it sustained him by the certainty that he was not forgotten.

15. *In the beginning of the gospel.* 'At the time when I first preached the gospel to you; or when the gospel began its benign influence on your hearts.' ¶ *When I departed from Macedonia.* See Acts xvii. 14. The last place that Paul visited in Macedonia, at that time, was Berea. There a tumult was excited by the Jews, and it was necessary for him to go away. He left Macedonia to go to Athens; and left it in haste, amidst scenes of persecution, and when he needed sympathizing aid. At that time, as well as when he was in Thessalonica (Acts xvii. 1—10), he needed the assistance of others to supply his wants; and he says that aid was not withheld. The meaning here is, that this aid was sent to him 'as he was departing from Macedonia;' that is, alike in Thessalonica and afterwards. This was about twelve years before this epistle was written. *Doddridge.* ¶ *No church communicated with me.* No church so participated with me in my sufferings and necessities, as to send to my relief. Comp. 2 Cor. xi. 8, 9. *Why* they did not, Paul does not intimate. It is not necessary to suppose that he meant to blame them. They might not have been acquainted with his necessities. All that is

16 For even in Thessalonica ye sent once and again unto my necessity.

17 Not because I desire a gift; but I desire fruit that may abound to your account.

18 But I [1] have all, and abound: I am full, having received of Epaphroditus the things *which were sent* from you, an odour of a sweet smell, a sacrifice [a] acceptable, well-pleasing to God.

[1] or, *have received.* [a] He. 13. 16.

---

implied here is, that he specially commends the Philippians for their attention to him.

16. *For even in Thessalonica.* Notes, Acts xvii. 1. Paul remained there long enough to establish a flourishing church. He met, indeed, with much opposition and persecution there; and hence it was necessary that his wants should be supplied by others.

17. *Not because I desire a gift.* 'The reason why I rejoice in the reception of what you have sent to me, is not that I am covetous.' From the interest with which he had spoken of their attention to him, some might, perhaps, be disposed to say, that it arose from this cause. He says, therefore, that, grateful as he was for the favour which he had received, his chief interest in it arose from the fact that it would contribute ultimately to their own good. It showed that they were governed by christian principle, and this would not fail to be rewarded. What Paul states here is by no means impossible; though it may not be very common. In the reception of favours from others, it is practicable to rejoice in them mainly, because their bestowment will be a means of good to the benefactor himself. All our selfish feelings and gratifications may be absorbed and lost in the superior joy which we have in seeing others actuated by a right spirit, and in the belief that they will be rewarded. This feeling is one of the fruits of christian kindness. It is that which leads us to look away from self, and to rejoice in every evidence that others will be made happy. ¶ *I desire fruit.* The word 'fruit' is often used in the Scriptures, as elsewhere, to denote *results*, or that which is *produced.* Thus we speak of punishment as the fruit of sin, poverty as the fruit of idleness, and happiness as the fruit of a virtuous life. The language is taken from the fact, that a man reaps or gathers the fruit or result of that which he plants. ¶ *To your account.* A phrase taken from commercial dealings. The apostle wished that it might be set down *to their credit.* He desired that when they came to appear before God, they might reap the benefit of all the acts of kindness which they had shown him.

18. *But I have all.* Marg., 'or, *have received.*' The phrase here is equivalent to, 'I have received every thing. I have all I want, and desire no more.' He was entirely satisfied. What they had sent to him is, of course, now unknown. It is sufficient to know, that it was of such a nature as to make his situation comfortable. ¶ *I am full.* I have enough. This is a strong expression, denoting that nothing was lacking. ¶ *Having received of Epaphroditus.* See Notes, ch. ii. 25. ¶ *An odour of a sweet smell.* This does not mean that it was such an odour to Paul, but to God. He regarded it as an offering which they had made to God himself; and he was persuaded that he would regard it as acceptable to him. They had doubtless made the offering, not merely from personal friendship for Paul, but because he was a minister of Christ,

19 But my God shall supply [a] all your need, according to his riches [b] in glory by Christ Jesus.
20 Now [c] unto God and our

a Ps. 23. 1. b Ep. 3. 16. c Ro. 16. 27.

and from love to his cause; and Paul felt assured that this offering would be acceptable to him. Comp. Matt. x. 41, 42. The word '*odour*' refers properly to the pleasant fragrance produced in the temple by the burning of incense. Notes on Luke i. 9. On the meaning of the word rendered 'a sweet smell,'—εὐωδιά—see Notes on 2 Cor. ii. 15. The whole language here is taken from an act of worship; and the apostle regarded what he had received from the Philippians as, in fact, a thank-offering to God, and as presented with the spirit of true devotion to him. It was not, indeed, a formal act of worship; but it was acceptable to God as an expression of their regard for his cause. ¶ *A sacrifice acceptable.* Acceptable to God. Comp. Heb. xiii. 16. Notes, Rom. xii. 1. ¶ *Well-pleasing to God.* Because it evinced a regard for true religion. Learn hence, (1.) that kindness done to the ministers of the gospel, is regarded as an acceptable offering to God. (2.) That kindness to the servants of God *in distress and want*, is as well-pleasing to God as direct acts of worship. (3.) That such acts of benevolence are evidences of attachment to the cause of religion, and are proofs of genuine piety. Notes, Matt. x. 42.

19. *But my God shall supply all your need.* That is, 'You have shown your regard for me as a friend of God, by sending to me in my distress, and I have confidence that, in return for all this, God will supply all your wants, when you are in circumstances of necessity.' Paul's confidence in this seems not to have been founded on any express revelation; but on the general principle that God would regard their offering with favour. Nothing is lost, even in the present life, by doing good. In thousands of instances it is abundantly repaid. The benevolent are not usually poor; and if they are, God often raises up for them benefactions, and sends supplies in a manner as unexpected, and bearing proofs of divine interposition as decided, as when supplies were sent by the ravens to the prophet. ¶ *According to his riches in glory.* Notes, Eph. iii. 16. The word *riches* here means, his abundant fulness; his possessing all things; his inexhaustible ability to supply their wants. The phrase '*in glory*,' is probably to be connected with the following phrase, 'in Christ Jesus;' and means that the method of imparting supplies to men was through Jesus Christ, and was a glorious method; or, that it was done in a glorious manner. It is such an expression as Paul is accustomed to use, when speaking of what God does. He is not satisfied with saying simply that *it is so;* but connects with it the idea that whatever God does is done in a way worthy of himself, and so as to illustrate his own perfections. ¶ *In Christ Jesus.* By the medium of Christ; or through him. All the favours that Paul expected for himself, or his fellow-men, he believed would be conferred through the Redeemer. Even the supply of our temporal wants comes to us through the Saviour. Were it not for the atonement, there is no more reason to suppose that blessings would be conferred on *men* than that they would be on fallen angels. For them no atonement has been made; and at the hand of justice they have received only wretchedness and wo.

20. *Now unto God and our Father,* &c. See Notes on Rom. xvi.

Father *be* glory for ever and ever. Amen.

21 Salute every saint in Christ Jesus. The brethren which are with me greet you.

22 All the saints salute you, chiefly they that are of Cæsar's household.

23 The grace of our Lord Jesus Christ *be* with you all. Amen.

It was written to the Philippians from Rome, by Epaphroditus.

---

27. It was common for Paul to address such an ascription of praise to God, at the close of his epistles.

21. *Salute every saint in Christ Jesus.* It was usual for him also to close his epistles with affectionate salutations to various members of the churches to which he wrote. These salutations are generally specific, and mention the names, particularly if prominent members of the churches. See the close of the epistles to the Romans; 1 Corinthians; Colossians, and 2 Timothy. In this epistle, however, as in some others, the salutation is general. Why none are specified in particular is not certainly known. ¶ *The brethren which are with me*, &c. The word 'brethren' here probably refers to ministers that were with Paul, as the '*saints*' in general are mentioned in the next verse. It is possible that at Rome the ministers were known by the general name of *the brethren. Pierce.*

22. *All the saints salute you.* All in Rome, where this epistle was written. No individuals are specified, perhaps because none of the Christians at Rome were personally known to the church at Philippi. They would, however, feel a deep interest in a church which had thus the confidence and affection of Paul. There is reason to believe that the bonds of affection among the churches then were much stronger than they are now. There was a generous warmth in the newness of the christian affection—the first ardour of love; and the common trials to which they were exposed would serve to bind them closely together. ¶ *Chiefly they that are of Cæsar's household.* That is, of Nero, who was at that time the reigning emperor. The name *Cæsar* was given to all the emperors after the time of Julius Cæsar, as the name *Pharaoh* was the common name of the kings of Egypt. The *phrase* here used—'the household of Cæsar'—*may* refer to the *relatives* of the emperor; and it is certainly possible that some of them may have been converted to Christianity. But it does not of necessity refer to those related to him, but may be applied to his domestics, or to some of the officers of the court that were more particularly employed around his person; and as it is more probable that some of them would be converted than his own relatives, it is more safe to suppose that they were intended. See Notes on ch. i. 13.

23. *The grace of our Lord Jesus Christ*, &c. Notes, Rom. xvi. 20.

In regard to the subscription at the end of this epistle, it may be remarked, as has been done of the other subscriptions at the end of the epistles, that it is of no authority whatever. There is no reason, however, to doubt that in this case it is correct. The epistle bears internal evidence of having been written from Rome, and was doubtless sent by Epaphroditus. See the Intro., § 3 There is considerable variety in the subscription. The Greek is, "It was written to the Philippians from Rome by Epaphroditus." The Syriac, "The epistle to the Philippians was written from Rome, and sent by Epaphroditus." The Æthiopic, "To the Philippians, by Timothy."

REMARKS.

The principal lessons taught in this closing chapter are the following:—

1. It is our duty to be firm in the Lord, in all the trials, temptations, and persecutions to which we may be exposed. Ver. 1. This duty should be pressed on Christians by their teachers, and by each other, by all that is tender and sacred in the christian profession, and all that is endearing in christian friendship. Like Paul, we should appeal to others as 'brethren dearly beloved and longed for,' and by all their affection for us we should entreat them to be steadfast in the christian profession. As their "joy and crown," also, ministers should desire that their people should be holy. Their own happiness and reward is to be closely connected with the firmness with which their people maintain the principles of the christian faith. If Christians, therefore, wish to impart the highest joy to their religious teachers, and to exalt them as high as possible in future happiness and glory, they should strive to be faithful to their great Master, and to be steadfast in attachment to his cause.

2. It is the duty of those who have from any cause been alienated, to seek to be reconciled. Ver. 2. They should be of the same mind. Almost nothing does more to hinder the cause of religion than alienations and bickerings among its professed friends. It is *possible* for them to live in harmony, and to be of the same mind in the Lord; and such is the importance of this, that it well deserves to be enforced by apostolic authority and persuasion. It may be observed, also, that in the case referred to in this chapter—that of Euodias and Syntyche—the exhortation to reconciliation is addressed to *both*. Which was in the wrong, or whether both were, is not intimated, and is not needful for us to know. It is enough to know that there was alienation, and *both* of them were exhorted to see that the quarrel was made up. So, in all cases where members of the church are at variance, it is the business of both parties to seek to be reconciled, and neither party is right if he waits for the other before he moves in the matter. If you feel that you have been injured, go and tell your brother kindly wherein you think he has done you wrong. He may at once explain the matter, and show that you have misunderstood it, or he may make proper confession or restitution. Or, if he will do neither, you will have done your duty. Matt. xviii. 15. If you are conscious that you have injured him, then nothing is more proper than that you should go and make confession. The blame of the quarrel rests wholly on you. And if some meddling third person has got up the quarrel between you, then go and see your brother, and disappoint the devices of the enemy of religion.

3. It is our duty and our privilege to rejoice in the Lord always. Ver. 4. As God is unchanging, we may always find joy in him. The character of God which we loved yesterday, and in the contemplation of which we found happiness then, is the same to-day, and its contemplation will furnish the same joy to us now. His promises are the same; his government is the same; his readiness to impart consolation is the same; the support which he can give in trial and temptation is the same. Though in our own hearts we may find much over which to mourn, yet when we look away from ourselves we may find abundant sources of consolation and peace. The Christian, therefore, *may* be always happy. If he will look to God and not to himself; to heaven and not to earth, he will find perma-

nent and substantial sources of enjoyment. But in nothing else than God can we rejoice *always.* Our friends, in whom we find comfort, are taken away; the property that we thought would make us happy, fails to do so; and pleasures that we thought would satisfy, pall upon the sense and make us wretched. No man can be permanently happy who does not make THE LORD the source of joy, and who does not expect to find his chief pleasure in him.

4. It is a privilege to be permitted to go and commit everything to God. Vs. 6, 7. The mind *may be* in such a state that it shall feel no *anxiety* about anything. We may feel so certain that God will supply all our wants; that he will bestow upon us all that is really necessary for us in this life and the next, and that he will withhold from us nothing which it is not for our real good to have withheld, that the mind may be constantly in a state of peace. With a thankful heart for all the mercies which we *have* enjoyed—and in all cases they are many — we may go and commit ourselves to God for all that we need hereafter. Such is the privilege of religion; such an advantage is it to be a Christian. Such a state of mind will be followed by peace. And it is only in such a way that true peace can be found. In every other method there will be agitation of mind and deep anxiety. If we have not this confidence in God, and this readiness to go and commit all to him, we shall be perplexed with the cares of this life; losses and disappointments will harass us; the changes which occur will weary and wear out our spirits, and through life we shall be tossed as on a restless ocean.

5. It is the duty of Christians to be upright in every respect. Ver. 8. Every friend of the Redeemer should be a man of incorruptible and unsuspected integrity. He should be one who can always be depended on to do what is right, and pure, and true, and lovely. I know not that there is a more important verse in the New Testament than the *eighth* verse of this chapter. It deserves to be recorded in letters of gold in the dwelling of every Christian, and it would be well if it could be made to shine on his way as if written in characters of living light. There should be no virtue, no truth, no noble plan of benevolence, no pure and holy undertaking in society, of which the Christian should not be, according to his ability, the patron and the friend. The reasons are obvious. It is not only because this is in accordance with the law of God, but it is from its effect on the community. The people of the world judge of religion by the character of its professed friends. It is not from what they hear in the pulpit, or learn from the Bible, or from treatises on divinity; it is from what they see in the lives of those who profess to follow Christ. They mark the expression of the eye; the curl of the lip; the words that we speak—and if they perceive peevishness and irritability, they set it down to the credit of religion. They watch the conduct, the temper and disposition, the manner of doing business, the respect which a man has for truth, the way in which he keeps his promises, and set it all down to the credit of religion. If a professed Christian fails in *any one* of these things, he dishonours religion and neutralizes all the good which he might otherwise do. It is not only the man in the church who is untrue, *and* dishonest, *and* unjust, *and* unlovely in his temper, that does evil; it is he who is *either* false, *or* dishonest, *or* unjust, *or* unlovely in his temper. One evil propensity will neutralize all that is good; and one member of the church who fails to lead a moral and upright life will do much to neutralize all the good

that can be done by all the rest of the church. Comp. Eccl. x. 1.

6. It is the duty of Christians to show kindness to the ministers of the gospel, especially in times and circumstances of want. Vs. 10. 14—17. Paul commended much what the Philippians had done for him. Yet they had done no more than they ought to do. See 1 Cor. ix. 11. He had established the gospel among them, carrying it to them by great personal sacrifice and self-denial. What he had done for *them* had cost him much more than what they had done for *him* — and was of much more value. He had been in want. He was a prisoner; among strangers; incapable of exerting himself for his own support; not in a situation to minister to his own wants, as he had often done by tent-making, and in these circumstances he *needed* the sympathizing aid of friends. He was not a man to be voluntarily dependent on others, or to be at any time a burden to them. But circumstances beyond his control had made it necessary for others to supply his wants. The Philippians nobly responded to his claims on them, and did all that he could ask. Their conduct is a good example for other Christians to imitate in their treatment of the ministers of the gospel. Ministers now are often in want. They become old, and are unable to labour; they are sick, and cannot render the service which they have been accustomed to; their families are afflicted, and they have not the means of providing for them comfortably in sickness. It is to be remembered also that such cases often happen where a minister has spent the best part of his life in the service of a people; where he has devoted his most vigorous days to their welfare; where he has been unable to lay up anything for sickness or old age; where he may have abandoned what would have been a lucrative calling in life, for the purpose of preaching the gospel. If there ever is a claim on the generosity of a people, his case is one, and there is no debt of gratitude which a people ought more cheerfully to pay than that of providing for the wants of an aged or an afflicted and disabled servant of Christ, who has spent his best years in endeavouring to train them and their children up for heaven. Yet, it cannot be denied, that great injustice is often done in such cases. The poor beast that has served a man and his family in the days of his vigour, is often turned out in old age to die; and something like this sometimes occurs in the treatment of ministers of the gospel. The conduct of a people, generous in many other respects, is often unaccountable in their treatment of their pastors; and one of the lessons which ministers often have to learn, like their Master, by bitter experience, is the ingratitude of those for whose welfare they have toiled, and prayed, and wept.

7. Let us learn to be contented with our present condition. Vs. 11, 12. Paul *learned* this lesson. It is not a *native* state of mind. It is a lesson to be acquired by experience. By nature we are all restless and impatient; we are reaching after things that we have not, and often after things that we cannot and ought not to have. We are envious of the condition of others, and suppose that if we had what they have we should be happy. Yet, if we have right feelings, we shall always find enough in our present condition to make us *contented.* We shall have such confidence in the arrangements of Providence as to feel that things are ordered for the best. If we are poor, and persecuted, and in want, or are prostrated by sickness, we shall feel that there is some good reason why this is so arranged — though the reason may not be known

to us. If we are benevolent, as we ought to be, we shall be willing that others shall be made happy by what they possess, instead of coveting it for ourselves, and desiring to wrest it from them. If we are disposed to estimate our mercies, and not to give up our minds to a spirit of complaining, we shall see enough around us to make us contented. Paul was a prisoner; he was poor; he was among strangers; he had neither wife nor children; he was about to be tried for his life, and probably put to death—yet he learned to be content. He had a good conscience; the hope of heaven; a sound intellect; a heart disposed to do good, and confidence in God, and why should a man in such circumstances murmur? Says Jeremy Taylor, "Am I fallen into the hands of publicans and sequestrators, who have taken all from me? What now? Let me look about me. They have left me the sun and moon, fire and water, a loving wife, and many friends to pity me, and some to relieve me, and I can still discourse; and unless I list, they have not taken away my merry countenance, and a cheerful spirit, and a good conscience; they still have left me the providence of God, and all the promises of the gospel, and my religion, and my hopes of heaven, and my charity to them too; and still I sleep and digest; I eat and drink; I read and meditate; I can walk in my neighbour's pleasant fields, and see the varieties of natural beauties, and delight in all in which God delights, that is, in virtue and wisdom, in the whole creation, and in God himself. And he who hath so many causes of joy, and so great, is very much in love with sorrow and peevishness, who loses all these pleasures, and chooses to sit down upon his little handful of thorns." Holy living, ch. ii. sect. vi. Let the whole of this section "on Contentedness" be read. It is one of the most beautiful arguments for *contentment* that ever proceeded from uninspired lips.

8. In all these things; in all the duties and the trials of life; in all our efforts to meet temptation, and to cultivate contentment with our present condition, let us put our trust in the Saviour. Ver. 13. Paul said that he could "do all things through Christ who strengthened him." His strength was there; ours is there also. If we attempt these things, relying on our own strength, we shall certainly fail. The bad passions of our nature will get the ascendency, and we shall be left to discontent and murmuring. The arm that is to uphold us is that of the Redeemer; and relying on that, we shall find no duty so arduous that we may not be able to perform it; no temptation so formidable that we may not be able to meet it; no trial so great that we may not be able to bear it; no situation in life through which we may be called to pass, where we may not find contentment and peace. And may God of his rich mercy give to each one who shall read these Notes on this beautiful epistle to the Philippians, abundant grace thus to confide in the Saviour, and to practise all the duties so tenderly enjoined on the Philippian Christians and on us by this illustrious prisoner in the cause of Christ.

THE

EPISTLE TO THE COLOSSIANS

INTRODUCTION.

§ 1. *The situation of Colosse.*

Colosse, or, as it is written in many manuscripts, *Colasse*, was a celebrated city of Phrygia, in Asia Minor. See the map prefixed to the Notes on the Acts of the Apostles. It was in the southern part of that province, was nearly directly east of Ephesus, north of Laodicea, and nearly west of Antioch in Pisidia. It is mentioned by Herodotus (Polyhymn. Lib. viii. c. 30) as 'a great city of Phrygia, in that part where the river Lycus descends into a chasm of the earth and disappears, but which, after a distance of five stadia, rises again and flows into the Meander'—ες τον Μαιανδρον. Xenophon also mentions the city of Colosse as being Πολις οικουμενη ευδαιμων και μεγαλη—'a city well inhabited, pleasant, and large.' Expedi. Cyr. Lib. i. In the time of Strabo, however, it seems to have been much diminished in size, as it is mentioned by him among the 'smaller towns'—πολισματα. Lib. xii. p. 864. In the latter part of the reign of Nero, and not long after this epistle was written, Colosse, Laodicea, and Hierapolis were at the same time overwhelmed by an earthquake. Pliny, Hist. Nat. Lib. v. c. 41. Colosse recovered, however, from this shock, and is mentioned by the Byzantine writers as among the most opulent cities. See Koppe, *Proleg*. The ancient town is now extinct, but its site is occupied by a village called *Chonos*, or *Khonas*. This village is described by Mr. Arundell as being situated most picturesquely under the immense range of Mount Cadmus, which rises to a very lofty and perpendicular height behind the village, in some parts clothed with pines, in others bare of soil, with vast chasms and caverns. The immense perpendicular chasm, seen in the view, affords an outlet to a wide mountain torrent, the bed of which is dry in summer. The approach to the village is as wild as the village itself is beautiful, abounding in tall trees, from which vines of most luxuriant growth are suspended. In the immediate neighbourhood are several vestiges of an ancient city, consisting of arches, vaults, squared stones, while the ground is strewed with broken pottery, which so generally and so remarkably indicates the site of ancient towns in the East. That these ruins are all that now remain of Colosse, there seems no reason to doubt. The opposite cut will furnish an idea of their appearance.

Colosse, as has been remarked, was situated in Phrygia. On the name Phrygia, and the origin of the Phrygians, very different opinions have been entertained, which it is necessary to specify in order to an understanding of this epistle. They claimed to be the most ancient people of the world; and it is said that this claim was admitted by the Egyptians, who, though boastful of their own antiquity, were content to regard themselves as second to the Phrygians. *Pict. Bib.* Like other parts of Asia Minor which were distinguished as provinces under the Roman empire, Phrygia is first historically known as a kingdom, and continued such until it was made a province of the Lydian monarchy. It remained a province of that monarchy until Crœsus, king of Lydia, was conquered by Cyrus of Persia, who added the Lydian kingdom to his empire. After that, Phrygia, like the rest of Asia Minor, became successively subject to the Greeks, the Romans, and the Turks. In the time when the gospel was preached there, it was subject to the Romans; it is now under the dominion of the Turks. Phrygia was anciently celebrated for its fertility; but under the Moslem yoke, a great part of the country lies uncultivated.

§ 2. *The establishment of the church in Colosse.*

The gospel was first preached in Phrygia by Paul and Silas, accompanied also by Timothy. Acts xv. 40, 41; xvi. 1—3. 6. It is said that they "went throughout Phrygia," which means, doubtless, that they went to the principal cities and towns. In Acts xviii. 23, it is said that Paul visited Phrygia again, after he had been to Philippi, Athens, Jerusalem, and Antioch. He "went over all the country of Galatia and Phrygia in order, strengthening all the disciples." It is not, indeed, expressly said of Paul and Silas that they went to Colosse; but, as this was one of the principal cities of Phrygia, there is every reason to suppose that they preached the gospel there.

It has been doubted, however, whether Paul was ever at Colosse. It is expressly affirmed by Hug (*Intro.*), and by Koppe (*Proleg.*), that Paul had not taught at Colosse himself, and that he had no personal acquaintance with the Christians there. It has been maintained that the gospel was, probably, first preached there by Epaphras, who heard the apostle at Ephesus, and who returned and preached the gospel to his own countrymen. The opinion that Paul had not been there, and was personally unacquainted with the church, is founded on his declaration in ch. ii. 1—"For I would that ye knew what great conflict I have for you, and for them at Laodicea, *and for as many as have not seen my face in the flesh.*" From this it is inferred that he was neither at Colosse nor at Laodicea. Yet it may be justly doubted whether this passage will authorize this conclusion. Theodoret long since suggested that the meaning of this was—'I have not only a concern for you, but I have also great concern for those who have not seen me.' Dr. Lardner, however, maintains that the gospel was preached in Colosse by Paul. The reasons which he gives for the opinion are briefly these:

(1.) The declarations of Luke, already quoted, that Paul more than once passed through Phrygia. The presumption is, that he would visit the chief cities of that province in passing and repassing through it. It is

Colosse, present state.

to be remembered that, according to ch. ii. 1, Colosse and *Laodicea* are placed on the same footing; and hence the difficulty of the supposition that he did not visit the former is increased. Can it be supposed that Paul would go again and again through that region, preaching the gospel in the points where it would be likely to exert the widest influence, and yet never visit either of these principal cities of the province, especially when it is remembered that Laodicea was the capital? (2.) Dr. Lardner appeals to what Paul says in ch. i. 6, and ii. 6, 7, in proof that he knew that they had been rightly taught the gospel. From this he infers that Paul had himself communicated it to them. This conclusion is not perfectly clear, since it is certain that Paul might have known their first teachers, and been satisfied that they taught the truth; but it is such language as he would have used on the supposition that he was the spiritual father of the church. (3.) Epaphras, says Dr. Lardner, was not their first instructor in the gospel. This he infers from what is said of him in ch. i. 7, and in ch. iv. 12, 13. He is commended as "one of them," as a "fellow-servant," as "a faithful minister of Christ," as one "beloved." But he is not spoken of as sustaining any nearer relation to them. If he had been the founder of their church, he thinks it is incredible that there is no allusion to this fact in writing to them; that the apostle should have spoken more than once of him, and never referred to his agency in establishing the church there. (4.) Paul does, in effect, say that he had himself dispensed the gospel to these Colossians. Ch. i. 21—25. The salutations at the end of the epistle, to various persons at Laodicea and Colosse, show that he was personally acquainted there. See these and other reasons drawn out in Lardner's Works, vol. vi., pp. 151 seq., Ed. Lond. 1829. The considerations suggested by Dr. Lardner seem to me to be sufficient to render it in the highest degree probable that the church at Colosse was founded by Paul.

§ 3. *When and where the epistle was written.*

This epistle is believed to have been written at Rome, when Paul was a prisoner there, and at about the same time that the epistle to the Ephesians, and the epistle to Philemon, were written; and that they were all sent by the same persons. It is said in the epistle itself (ch. iv. 7. 9), that it was sent by Tychicus and Onesimus, both of whom are commended as 'faithful and beloved' brethren. But the epistle to the Ephesians was written at Rome (see the Intro.), and was sent by Tychicus (Eph. vi. 21); and the epistle to Philemon was sent by Onesimus. It is probable, therefore, that these persons visited Ephesus, Colosse, and the place where Philemon resided; or, rather, that Tychicus and Onesimus visited Colosse together, and that then Tychicus went to Ephesus, and Onesimus went to his former master Philemon. That this epistle and the one to Philemon were written at about the same time, is further apparent from the fact that Epaphras is mentioned in both as with the apostle, and as joining in the salutation. Col. iv. 12. Phil. 23. The epistle to the Colossians bears *internal* marks of having been written at Rome, when the apostle was a prisoner. Thus, in ch. i. 24, he says, "who now rejoice in my sufferings for you." Ch. iv. 18, "Remember my bonds." If this be so, then it is not difficult to fix the date of the epistle with some degree of accuracy. This would be about the year 62.

§ 4. *The occasion and design of the epistle.*

The general drift of this epistle has a strong resemblance to that addressed to the Ephesians, and it bears internal marks of being from the same hand. It was evidently written in view of errors which extensively prevailed among the churches of that part of Asia Minor, and was designed to inculcate the same general duties. It is of importance, therefore, to possess a general understanding of the nature of these errors, in order to a correct interpretation of the epistle.

The church at Colosse was one of a circle or group of churches, lying near each other, in Asia Minor; and it is probable that the same general views of philosophy, and the same errors, prevailed throughout the entire region where they were situated. That group of churches embraced those at Ephesus, Laodicea, Thyatira, and, in general, those addressed in the Apocalypse as 'the seven churches of Asia.' From some of the notices of those churches in the New Testament, as well as from the epistle before us, we may learn what errors prevailed there in general, and against what form of error particularly the epistle to the Colossians was designed to guard.

(1.) Several classes of errorists are mentioned as existing within the limits of the 'seven churches of Asia.' Thus, in the church at Ephesus, "those which say they are apostles, and are not, and hast found them liars" (Rev. ii. 2); in Smyrna, those "which say they are Jews, and are not, but are of the synagogue of Satan" (Rev. ii. 9); in Thyatira, "that woman Jezebel, which calleth herself a prophetess" (Rev. ii. 20); in Pergamos, "them that hold the doctrine of the Nicolaitanes;" those "who hold the doctrine of Balaam, who taught Balak to cast a stumbling-block before the children of Israel." Rev. ii. 14, 15. The near proximity of these churches to Colosse would render it probable that the infection of these errors might have reached that church also.

(2.) The apostle Paul, in his parting speech to the elders of the church at Ephesus, alludes to dangerous teachers to which the church there might be exposed, in such a manner as to show that there was some peculiar danger from such teachers in that community. "For I know that after my departure shall grievous wolves enter in among you, not sparing the flock. Also of your ownselves shall men arise, speaking perverse things, to draw away disciples after them." Acts xx. 29, 30. He does not specify, indeed, the kind of danger to which they would be exposed; but it is evident that the danger arose from plausible teachers of error. These were of two classes—those who would come in from abroad, implying probably that there were such teachers in the neighbouring churches; and such as would spring up among themselves.

(3.) In that vicinity there appear to have been numerous disciples of John the Baptist, retaining many Jewish prejudices and prepossessions, who would be tenacious of the observances of the Mosaic law. What were their views, is not precisely known. But it is clear that they regarded the Jewish law as still binding; that they would be rigid in its observance, and in insisting on its observance by others; that they had at best, if any, a very imperfect acquaintance with Christianity; and that they were ignorant of the miraculous power of the Holy Spirit, and of the fact that that had been poured out in a remarkable manner under the preaching of the apostles Paul found a number of these disciples of John at Ephesus, who professed not to have received the Holy Ghost, and who said that they had been baptized unto John's baptism. Acts xix. 1—3. Among the most distinguished and influential of the disciples of John in that region was Apollos (Acts xviii. 24, 25), who is represented as an eloquent man, and mighty in the Scriptures. He taught at Ephesus, but how long before he was made more fully acquainted with the gospel, is unknown. He is represented as having been zealously engaged in that work, and as being eminently successful. Acts xviii. 25. There is no reason to doubt that he contributed not a little in diffusing, in that region, the peculiar views held by those who were known as the disciples of John. What was precisely the doctrine which Apollos taught, before 'the way of God was expounded more perfectly to him' (Acts xviii. 26), is not now known. There is every reason, however, to suppose that he would insist on the observance of the Jewish laws, and the customs of their nation. The opinions which would be *likely* to be defended by one in his circumstances, would be those which prevailed when John preached—when the law of Moses was considered to be in full force, and when it was necessary to observe all his institutions. The advocates for the Jewish law among the churches would be likely to appeal with great force to the sentiments of so good and so eloquent a man as Apollos. So extensive was his influence, that Koppe supposes that the principal errors prevailing in the churches in Phrygia, which it was the design of the apostle in this epistle to correct, could be traced to the influence of the disciples of John, and especially to the teachings of this eloquent man. Proleg., p. 160.

(4.) If we look into the epistle itself, we shall be able to determine with some degree of certainty the errors which prevailed, and which it was the design of this epistle to correct, and we shall find that they correspond remarkably with what we might anticipate, from what we have seen to be the errors abounding in that region. (*a*) Their first danger arose from the influence of philosophy. Ch. ii. 4—8. The apostle warns them to beware lest any one should "beguile them with enticing words;" he cautions them against "philosophy and vain deceit"—a philosophy that was based on the "tradition of men," "after the rudiments of the world, and not after Christ." Such philosophy might be expected to prevail in those cities so near to Greece, and so much imbued with the Grecian spirit, and one of the chief dangers which would beset them would arise from its prevalence. (*b*) A second source of danger referred to, was that arising from the influence of those who insisted on the observance of the rites and customs of the Jewish religion. This the apostle refers to in ch. ii. 16. "Let no man, therefore, judge you in meat or in drink, or in respect of an holy day, or of the new moon, or of the Sabbath days." These are subjects on which the Jews would insist much, and in this respect the disciples of John would be likely to sympathize entirely with them. It is evident that there were those among them who were endeavouring to enforce the observance of these things. (*c*) There is some evidence of the prevalence there of a philosophy more Oriental than Grecian—a philosophy that savoured of Gnosticism. This philosophy was subsequently the foundation of a large part of the errors that crept into the church. Indications of its prevalence in Colosse, occur in places like the following. Ch. ii. 9. "For in him [Christ] dwelleth all the fulness of the Godhead *bodily;*" from which it would seem probable that there were those who denied that the fulness of the Godhead dwelt *bodily* in the Lord Jesus — a favourite doctrine of the Gnostics, who maintained that the assumption of human nature, by the Son of God, was *in appearance* only, and that he died on the cross only *in appearance*, and not in reality. So in ch. ii. 18, there is a reference to 'a voluntary humility and worshipping of angels, intruding into those things which are not seen, and which tend vainly to puff up a fleshly mind'—a description that will apply with remarkable accuracy to the homage paid by the Gnostics to the Æons, and to the general efforts of those who held the doctrines of that philosophy to intrude into those things which are not seen, and to offer an explanation of the mode of the divine existence, and the nature of the divine agency. See Notes on the verses here referred to. It will contribute not a little to a proper understanding of this epistle, to keep these things in remembrance respecting the kind of philosophy which prevailed in the region in which Colosse was situated, and the nature of the dangers to which they were exposed.

(5.) It will be seen from these remarks, and from the epistle itself, that the difficulties in the church at Colosse did not relate to the moral and religious character of its members. There is no mention of any improper conduct, either in individuals or in the church at large, as there was in the church at Corinth; there is no intimation that they had been guilty of any sins but such as were common to all heathens before conversion. There are, indeed, intimations that they were exposed to sin, and there are solemn charges against indulgence in it. But the sins to which they were exposed were such as prevailed in all the ancient heathen world, and doubtless such as the Gentile part of the church, particularly, had been guilty of before their conversion. The following sins particularly are mentioned: "Fornication, uncleanness, inordinate affection, covetousness, anger, wrath, malice, blasphemy, filthy communications, and lying." Ch. iii. 5—9. These were common sins among the heathen (comp. Notes on Rom. i.), and to a relapse into these they were particularly exposed; but it does not appear that any of the members of the church had given occasion for public reproach, or for apostolic reproof, by falling into them. As they were sins, however, in which they had formerly indulged (ch. iii. 7), and as they were, therefore, the more liable to fall into them again, there was abundant occasion for all the solicitude which the apostle manifests on the subject.

From the remarks now made, it is easy to see what was the *design* of the epistle to the Colossians. It was primarily to guard the church against the errors to which it was exposed from the prevalence of false philosophy, and from the influence of false teachers in religion; to assert the superior claims of Christianity over all philosophy, and its independence of the *peculiar* rites and customs of the Jewish religion.

It has been asked *why* the apostle wrote an epistle to the church at Colosse, rather than to the church in Laodicea, especially as Laodicea was the capital of Phrygia? And it has been asked also, why an epistle was addressed to that church so strikingly resembling the Epistle to the Ephesians (see § 5), especially as it has been supposed that the Epistle to the Ephesians was designed to be a *circular* letter, to be read by the churches in the vicinity? The reasons why an epistle was addressed particularly to the church at Colosse, seem to have been such as the following:—

(1.) Onesimus was at that time with Paul at Rome, and was about to return to his master Philemon, at Colosse. See the Introduction to the Epistle to Philemon. It was perfectly natural that Paul should avail him self of the opportunity thus afforded him, to address a letter to the church at Colosse also.

(2.) Epaphras, a principal teacher of the church at Colosse, was also with Paul at Rome. Ch. i. 7; iv. 12. He was at that time a fellow-prisoner with him (Philem. 23), and it is not improbable that it was at his solicitation particularly that this epistle was written. Paul had learned from him the state of the church at Colosse (ch. i. 6, 7), and it is not impossible, as Koppe conjectures, that he had been sent to Rome by the church to seek the counsel of the apostle in the state of things which then existed in Colosse. Epaphras was, at any rate, greatly interested in the state of things in the church, as well as in the condition of the churches at Laodicea and Hierapolis (ch. iv. 13), and nothing was more natural than that he should endeavour to induce the apostle to direct a letter that might be of benefit to them all.

(3.) A particular reason for sending this epistle appears to have been, to confirm the authority of Epaphras, and to give the sanction of the apostle to the truths which he had taught. In their difficulties and dangers, Epaphras had taken an important part in giving them counsel. His views might have been opposed; or his authority might have been disputed by the teachers of error there, and it was important that the apostolic sanction should be given to what he had taught. Hence the apostle speaks with so much affection of Epaphras, and so warmly of him as a faithful servant of Christ. Ch. i. 7; iv. 12, 13.

(4.) It may be added, that although there is a strong resemblance between this epistle and that to the Ephesians, and although it may be regarded as probable that the epistle to the Ephesians was intended in part as a circular, yet this epistle would not have been needless. It contains many things which are not in that epistle; is especially adapted to the state of things in the church at Colosse, and would have the greater weight with Christians there from being specifically addressed to them. See Michaelis' Intro. to the New Testament, vol. iv. 122, and Koppe, Proleg. pp. 163, 164.

§ 5. *The resemblance between this epistle and that to the Ephesians.*

Every person who has given any considerable degree of attention to this epistle, must have been struck with its remarkable similarity to the epistle to the Ephesians. That resemblance is greater by far than exists between any other two of the epistles of Paul—a resemblance not only in the general style and manner which may be expected to characterize the different productions of the same author, but extending to the course of thought; the structure of the argument; the particular instructions, and to some phrases which do not occur elsewhere. This similarity relates particularly to the following points:—

(1.) In the representation of the reason for which the apostle was imprisoned at Rome. This resemblance, Dr. Paley (*Horæ Paul.*) remarks, is "too close to be accounted for from accident, and yet too indirect and latent to be imputed to design, and is one which cannot easily be resolved into any other source than truth." It is not found in any other of his epistles. It consists in this, that Paul in these two epistles attributes his imprisonment not to his preaching Christianity in general, but to his asserting the right of the Gentiles to be admitted into the church on an equal footing with the Jews, and without being obliged to conform themselves to the Jewish law. This was the doctrine to which he considered himself a martyr. Thus in ch. i. 24, he says, 'Who now rejoice in my sufferings *for you*;" and in ch. ii. 1, "for I would that ye knew what great conflict I have *for you*, and for them at Laodicea." That is, his conflicts and trials, his imprisonment and danger of death, had somehow come upon him in consequence of his endeavouring to spread the gospel in such places as Colosse and Laodicea. These were Gentile communities; and the meaning is, that his trials were the result of his efforts to preach among *the Gentiles*. The same representation is made in the epistle to the Ephesians—likewise written from Rome during his imprisonment. "For this cause I, Paul, the prisoner of Jesus Christ *for you Gentiles*." Ch. iii. 1. And this coincidence is also apparent by comparing two other places in the epistles. Thus Col. iv. 3. "Praying for us, that God would open unto us a door of utterance to speak the *mysteries of Christ, for which I am in bonds*." An allusion to the same '*mystery*' occurs also in the Epistle to the Ephesians. "Whereby when ye read, ye may understand my knowledge in the *mystery of Christ—that the Gentiles should be fellow-heirs of the same body, and partakers of his promise in Christ by the gospel.*" Ch. iii. 4—6. In the Acts of the Apostles the same statement occurs in regard to the cause for which the apostle was persecuted and imprisoned—and it is on this coincidence, which is so evidently undesigned, that Paley has founded the argument for the genuineness of the epistles to the Ephesians and Colossians. *Horæ Paulinæ.* The statement in the Acts of the Apostles is, that the persecutions of Paul which led to his appeal to the Roman emperor and to his imprisonment at Rome, were in consequence of his maintaining that the Gentiles were, in the Christian administration, to be admitted to the same privileges as the Jews, or that there was no distinction between them in the matter of salvation; and his sufferings, therefore, were, as he says, 'in behalf of the Gentiles.' See, particularly, Acts xxi. 28; xxii. 21, 22. From these passages it appears that the offence which drew down on Paul the vengeance of his countrymen was, his mission *to the Gentiles*, and his maintaining that they were to be admitted to the privileges of salvation on the same terms as the Jews.

(2.) There is a strong resemblance between the course of thought and the general structure of the Epistles to the Ephesians and the Colossians. To an extent that does not occur in any other of Paul's epistles, the same topics are introduced, and in the same order and connection. Indeed, in some portions, they are almost identical. Particularly the *order* in which the various topics are introduced is nearly the same. The following portions of the two epistles will be seen to correspond with each other.

Ephesians.		*Colossians.*
i. 15—19	with	i. 9—11.
i. 20—23	"	i. 15—19.
i. 10	"	i. 20.
ii. 1—10	"	i. 21—23.
iii. 7	"	i. 25.
iii. 9, 10	"	i. 26, 27.
iii. 17	"	ii. 7.
ii. 11—22	"	ii. 11—15.

Ephesians.		Colossians.
iv. 14	with	ii. 8.
iv. 15, 16	"	ii. 19.
iv. 25	"	iii. 9.
iv. 22—24	"	iii. 9, 10.
iv. 32	"	iii. 12.
v. 19, 20	"	iii. 16, 17.
v. 21; vi. 6—9	"	iii. 18—22; iv. 1.
vi. 19	"	iv. 3.
v. 16	"	iv. 5.
vi. 21	"	iv. 7.

This resemblance, thus carried almost through the epistle, shows that there was a similarity of condition in the two churches in reference to the dangers to which they were exposed, the kind of philosophy which prevailed, the false teachers who might have an influence over them, and the particular duties to which it was desirable their attention should be turned. There is, indeed, some considerable variety of phraseology in the discussion of these topics, but still the resemblance is remarkable, and would indicate that the epistles were written not far from the same time, and clearly by the same person. It is remarkable, among other things, as Michaelis has observed, that it is only in these two epistles that the apostle warns his readers against *lying*. Eph. iv. 25. Col. iii. 9. Hence we may conclude that this vice was one that particularly prevailed in the region where these churches were situated, and that the members of these churches had been particularly addicted to this vice before their conversion.

§ 6. *The epistle from Laodicea.*

In ch. iv. 16 of this epistle, the apostle gives this direction: "And when this epistle is read among you, cause that it be read also in the church of the Laodiceans, and that ye likewise read the epistle from Laodicea." The former part of this verse is clear, and the direction was given, doubtless, because the churches of Colosse and Laodicea were in the vicinity of each other, and the instructions were adapted to both churches. Doubtless the same form of philosophy prevailed, and the churches were exposed to the same errors. But it is not so clear what is meant by the "epistle from Laodicea." The most natural and obvious interpretation would be, that Paul had sent a letter also to that church, and that he wished them to procure it and read it. But no such epistle is now extant, and, consequently, much difficulty has been felt in determining what the apostle referred to. A brief examination of the opinions entertained on the subject, seems necessary in this place. They are the following:

1. It has been supposed that the reference is to a letter sent *from* the Laodiceans *to* Paul, proposing to him some questions which they desired him to answer, and that he now wishes the Colossians to procure that letter, in order that they might more fully understand the drift of the epistle which he now sent to them. This opinion was held by Theodoret, and has been defended by Storr, Rosenmüller, and others. But the objections to it are obvious and conclusive. (1.) It is not the fair meaning of the language used by Paul. If he had referred to a letter *to him*, he

would have said so; whereas the obvious meaning of the language used is, that the Colossians were to procure a letter in the possession of the Laodiceans, in exchange for the one which they now received from Paul. The churches were to make an exchange of letters, and one church was to read that which had been addressed to the other. (2.) If the letter had been addressed *to* Paul, it was doubtless in his possession; and if he wished the church at Colosse to read it, nothing would be more natural or obvious than to send it, by Tychicus, along with the letter which he now sent. Why should he give directions to send to Laodicea to procure a copy of it? (3.) If a letter had been sent *to* him by the Laodiceans, proposing certain questions, why did he send the answer to the church at Colosse, and not to the church at Laodicea? The church at Laodicea would certainly have been the one that was entitled to the reply. There would have been a manifest impropriety in sending an epistle to one church, made up of answers to questions proposed by another, and then at the end requesting them to procure those questions, that they might understand the epistle. (4.) It may be added, that it is not necessary to suppose that there was any such epistle, in order to understand this epistle to the Colossians. This is not more difficult of interpretation than the other epistles of Paul, and does not furnish in its structure any particular evidence that it was sent in answer to inquiries which had been proposed to the author.

2. It has been supposed by some that the epistle referred to was one written to Timothy, by the apostle himself, *at* Laodicea. This opinion was defended by Theophylact. The only show of authority for it is the subscription at the end of the First Epistle to Timothy—"The first to Timothy was written from Laodicea, which is the chiefest city of Phrygia Pacatiana." But that this is erroneous, can be easily shown. (1.) The subscription to the epistle to Timothy is of no authority. (2.) If this epistle had been referred to, Paul would not have designated it in this manner. It would have been rather by mentioning the *person* to whom it was addressed, than the *place* where it was written. (3.) There is nothing in the epistle to Timothy which would throw any important light on this to the Colossians, or which would be particularly important to them as a church. It was addressed to one individual, and it contains counsels adapted to a minister of the gospel, rather than to a church.

3. Many have supposed that the 'epistle from Laodicea,' referred to, was one which Paul had written to the Laodiceans, partly for their use, but which was of the nature of a *circular* epistle, and that we still have it under another name. Those who hold this opinion suppose that the epistle to the Ephesians is the one referred to, and that it was, in fact, sent also to the church at Laodicea. See this question treated at length in the Introduction to the Epistle to the Ephesians, § 5. The reasons for supposing that the epistle now known as the 'Epistle to the Ephesians' was neither a *circular* letter, nor addressed to the church at Laodicea, are there given. But if the common reading of the text in Eph. i. 1, 'the saints which are *at Ephesus*,' be correct, then it is clear that *that* epistle was really sent to the church in that place. The only question, then, is, whether it is of so general a character that it might as well be sent to other churches as to that, and whether Paul actually sent it as a circular, with a direction to different churches? Against this supposition, there are strong improbabilities. (1.) It is contrary to the usual practice of Paul. He addressed letters to particular churches and individuals; and

unless this case be one, there is no evidence that he ever adopted the practice of sending the same letter to different individuals or churches. (2.) There would have been some impropriety in it, if not dishonesty. An avowed circular letter, addressed to churches in general, or to any number whose names are enumerated, would be perfectly honest. But how would this be, if the same letter was addressed to one church, and then, with a new direction, addressed to another, with no intimation of its circular character? Would there not be a species of concealment in this which we should not expect of Paul? (3.) How happens it, if this had occurred, that all remembrance of it was forgotten? When those epistles were collected, would not the attention be called to the fact, and some record of it be found in some ancient writer? Would it fail to be adverted to that the same epistle had been found to have been addressed to different churches, with a mere change in the name?

4. There is but one other opinion which can exist on this question; and that is, that the apostle refers to some letter which had been sent to the Laodiceans, which we have not now in the New Testament. If this be so, then the reference could only be to some epistle which may be extant elsewhere, or which is now lost. There is an epistle extant which is known by the name of "St. Paul's Epistle to the Laodiceans;" but it has no well-founded claims to being a genuine epistle of Paul, and is universally regarded as a forgery. "It is," says Michaelis, "a mere rhapsody, collected from St. Paul's other epistles, and which no critic can receive as a genuine work of the apostle. It contains nothing which it was necessary for the Colossians to know, nothing which is not ten times better and more fully explained in the epistle which St. Paul sent to the Colossians; in short, nothing which could be suitable to St. Paul's design." Intro. to the New Tes. iv. 127. The Greek of this epistle may be found at length in Michaelis; and, as it may be a matter of curiosity, and will show that this cannot be the epistle referred to by Paul in Col. iv. 16, I will subjoin here a translation. It is as follows: "Paul, an apostle, not of men, neither by men, but by Jesus Christ, to the brethren in Laodicea. Grace be to you, and peace, from God the Father, and our Lord Jesus Christ. I give thanks to my God in Christ always in my prayers, that you are mindful of and are persevering in good works, waiting for the promise in the day of judgment. And let not the vain speeches of some who would conceal the truth disturb you, to turn you away from the truth of the gospel which has been preached unto you. Now God grant that all they who are of me may be borne forward to the perfection of the truth of the gospel, to perform those excellent good works which become the salvation of eternal life. And now are my bonds manifest, in which bonds I am in Christ, and at the present time; but I rejoice, for I know that this shall be for the furtherance of my salvation, which is through your prayer and the supply of the Holy Ghost, whether by life or by death. For to me to live is Christ, and to die is joy. But our Lord himself shall grant you his mercy with us, that possessing love you may be of the same mind, and think the same thing. On this account, brethren, as ye have heard of the appearing of the Lord, so think and do in the fear of God, and it shall be eternal life to you, for it is God who worketh in you. Do all things without murmurings and disputings. And for the remainder, brethren, rejoice in the Lord Jesus Christ, and see that ye keep yourselves from all base gain of covetousness. Let all your requests be made known with boldness unto God, and

be firm in the mind of Christ. And finally, brethren, whatsoever things are true, whatsoever things are honest, whatsoever things are holy, whatsoever things are just, whatsoever things are lovely, these things do. And what you have heard and received, keep in your hearts, and it shall give you peace. Salute all the brethren with an holy kiss. All the saints salute you. The grace of our Lord Jesus Christ be with your spirit. Amen. Cause that this epistle be read in the church of the Colossians, and do you also read the epistle from Colosse." Nothing can be plainer than that this is not such an epistle as the apostle Paul would have written; it is therefore a mere forgery. The conclusion to which we are conducted is, that the reference in Col. iv. 16 is to some epistle of Paul to the church at Laodicea which is not now extant, and that the probability is, that, having accomplished the object for which it was sent, it has been suffered to be lost. Thus, it is to be numbered with the writings of Gad, and Iddo the Seer, and Nathan, and the prophecy of Ahijah the Shilonite, and the book of Jehu (1 Chron. xix. 29. 2 Chron. ix. 29; xx. 34. 1 Kings xvi. 1); works which, having accomplished the object for which they were composed, have been suffered to become extinct. Nor is there anything improbable or absurd in the supposition that an inspired book may have been lost. There is no special sacredness in a mere *writing*, or in the fact that inspired truth was *recorded*, that makes it indispensable that it should be preserved. The *oral discourses* of the Saviour were as certainly inspired as the *writings* of Paul; and yet but a small part of what he said has been preserved. John xxi. 25. Why should there be any improbability in supposing that an inspired *book* may also have been lost? And, if it has, how does that fact weaken the evidence of the importance or the value of what we now possess? How does the fact that a large part of the sermons of the Saviour have perished, by not being recorded, diminish the value, or lessen the evidence of the divine authority, of the Sermon on the Mount?

THE

EPISTLE TO THE COLOSSIANS.

CHAPTER I.

PAUL, [a] an apostle of Jesus Christ, by the will of God, and Timotheus *our* brother.

a Ep. 1. 1.

CHAPTER I.

ANALYSIS OF THE CHAPTER.

This chapter embraces the following topics:—

(1.) The usual salutation to the church. Vs. 1, 2.

(2.) Thanks to God for what he had done for the Colossians, and for the fruits of the gospel among them. Vs. 3—8.

(3.) Prayer that they might persevere in the same course, and might walk worthy of their calling. Vs. 9—11.

(4.) An exhortation to render thanks to God for what he had done for them in redemption. Vs. 12—14.

(5.) A statement of the exalted dignity of the Redeemer. Vs. 15—18.

(6.) A statement of what he had done in the work of redemption, in making peace by the blood of his cross and reconciling the world to God. Vs. 19, 20.

(7.) Through this gospel, Paul says, they had been reconciled to God, and were now brought into a state in which they might be presented as holy and unblameable in his sight. Vs. 21—23.

(8.) Of this gospel, Paul says he was a minister; in preaching it he had been called to endure trials, but those trials he endured with joy; and in preaching this gospel he used the utmost diligence, warning every man, and teaching every man in all wisdom, that he might present every one perfect in Christ Jesus. Vs. 24—29.

1. *Paul, an apostle of Jesus Christ.* See Notes, Rom. i. 1. ¶ *By the will of God.* Notes, 1 Cor. i. 1. ¶ *And Timotheus* our *brother.* On the question why Paul associated others with him in his epistles, see Notes on 1 Cor. i. 1. There was a particular reason why Timothy should be associated with him in writing this epistle. He was a native of the region where the church was situated (Acts xvi. 1—3), and had been with Paul when he preached there, and was doubtless well known to the church there. Acts xvi. 6. It is evident, however, from the manner in which Paul mentions him here, that he did not regard him as 'an apostle,' and did not wish the church at Colosse to consider him as such. It is not 'Paul *and* Timothy, apostles of Jesus Christ,' but 'Paul, an apostle of Jesus Christ, and Timothy *our brother*.' Paul is careful never to apply the term apostle to Timothy. Phil. i. 1. "Paul and Timotheus, *the servants* of Jesus Christ." Comp. 1 Thess. i. 1. 2 Thess. i. 1. If he had regarded Timothy as an apostle, or as having apostolic authority, it is not easy to conceive why he should not have referred to him as such in these letters to the churches. Could he have fail-

2 To the saints [a] and faithful brethren in Christ which are at Colosse: [b] Grace *be* unto you, and peace, from God our Father, and the Lord Jesus Christ.

3 We [c] give thanks to God and the Father of our Lord Jesus Christ, praying always for you,

4 Since we heard of your faith in Christ Jesus, and of the love *which ye have* to all the saints;

5 For the hope which is laid up [d] for you in heaven, whereof ye heard before in the word of the truth of the gospel,

6 Which is come unto you, as *it is* in all [e] the world; and bringeth [f] forth fruit as *it doth* also in

a Ps. 16. 3. b Ga. 1. 3. c Ep. 1. 15, 16. d 2 Ti. 4. 8. 1 Pe. 1. 4. e ver. 23. f Jno. 15. 16.

---

ed to see that the manner in which he referred to him was adapted to produce a very important difference in the estimate in which he and Timothy would be held by the Colossians?

2. *Grace* be *unto you.* See Notes, Rom. i. 7.

3. *We give thanks to God.* See Notes on the parallel place in Eph. i. 15, 16. ¶ *Praying always for you.* See Notes on Rom. i. 9. Eph. i. 16. Comp. 1 Thess. i. 2.

4. *Since we heard of your faith in Christ Jesus.* To wit, by Epaphras, who had informed Paul of the steadfastness of their faith and love. Vs. 7, 8. This does not prove that Paul had never been at Colosse, or that he did not establish the church there, for he uses a similar expression respecting the church at Ephesus (Eph. i. 15), of which he was undoubtedly the founder. The meaning is, that he had heard of their faith *at that time*, or of their *perseverance* in faith and love. ¶ Which ye have *to all the saints.* In what way they had manifested this is not known. It would seem that Paul had been informed that this was a character of their piety, that they had remarkable love for all who bore the christian name. Nothing could be more acceptable information respecting them to one who himself so ardently loved the church; and nothing could have furnished better evidence that they were influenced by the true spirit of religion. Comp. 1 John iii. 14.

5. *For the hope which is laid up for you in heaven.* That is, 'I give thanks that there *is* such a hope laid up for you.' The *evidence* which he had that this hope was theirs, was founded on the faith and love to the saints which he heard they had evinced. He fully believed that where there was such faith and love, there was a well-founded hope of heaven. The word 'hope' here is used, as it often is, for *the thing hoped for.* The *object* of hope—to wit, eternal happiness, was reserved for them in heaven. ¶ *Whereof ye heard before.* When the gospel was first preached to you. You were told of the blessed rewards of a life of faith, in heaven. ¶ *In the word of the truth of the gospel.* In the true word of the gospel.

6. *Which is come unto you.* It has not been confined to the Jews, or limited to the narrow country where it was first preached, but has been sent abroad to the Gentile world. The object of the apostle here seems to be, to excite in them a sense of gratitude that the gospel had been sent to *them.* It was owing entirely to the goodness of God in sending them the gospel, that they had this hope of eternal life. ¶ *As it is in all the world.* It is confined to no place or people, but is designed to be a universal religion. It offers the same blessedness in heaven to all.

you, since the day ye heard [a] *of it*, and knew the [b] grace of God in truth. [c]

7 As ye also learned of [d] Epaphras our dear fellow-servant, who is for you a faithful minister of Christ;

8 Who also declared unto us your love [e] in the Spirit.

9 For this cause we also, since the day we heard *it*, do not cease to pray for you, and to desire that ye might be filled with the knowledge of his will, [f] in all

a Ro. 10. 17. b Tit. 2. 11, 12. c Jno. 4. 23. d Phi. 23. e Ro. 15. 30. f Ro. 12. 2. Ep. 5. 10, 17.

Comp. Notes on ver. 23. ¶ *And bringing forth fruit.* The fruits of righteousness or good living. See Notes on 2 Cor. ix. 10. The meaning is, that the gospel was not without effect wherever it was preached. The same results were observable everywhere else as in Colosse, that it produced most salutary influences on the hearts and lives of those who received it. On the nature of the 'fruits' of religion, see Notes on Gal. v. 22, 23. ¶ *Since the day ye heard* of it. It has constantly been producing these fruits since you first heard it preached. ¶ *And knew the grace of God in truth.* Since the time ye knew the *true* grace of God; since you became acquainted with the *real* benevolence which God has manifested in the gospel. The meaning is, that ever since they had heard the gospel it had been producing among them abundantly its appropriate fruit, and that the same thing had also characterized it wherever it had been dispensed.

7. *As ye also learned of Epaphras.* Epaphras was then with Paul. Philem. 23. He had probably been sent to him by the church at Colosse to consult him in reference to some matters pertaining to the church there. It is evident from this, that Epaphras was a minister of the church at Colosse, though there is no evidence, as has been often supposed, that he was the founder of the church. The apostle here says, that they had learned from Epaphras *the true nature of the gospel*, and he designs undoubtedly to confirm what he had taught them, in opposition to the teachings of errorists. See the Introduction, § 4. He had doubtless conferred with Epaphras respecting the doctrines which he had taught there. ¶ *Our dear fellow-servant.* This shows that Paul had contracted a strong friendship for Epaphras. There is no reason to believe that he had known him before, but his acquaintance with him now had served to attach him strongly to him. It is possible, as has been conjectured (see the Introduction), that there was a party in the church at Colosse opposed to Epaphras and to the doctrines which he preached, and if this were so, Paul's strong expression of attachment for him would do much to silence the opposition. ¶ *Who is for you a faithful minister of Christ.* 'For you,' when he is with you, and in managing your interests here.

8. *Who also declared unto us your love in the Spirit.* The love wrought in you by the Holy Spirit. It was not mere natural affection, but love wrought in their hearts by the agency of the Holy Ghost.

9. *Do not cease to pray for you.* Ver. 3. The progress which they had already made, and the love which they had shown, constituted an encouragement for prayer, and a reason why higher blessings still should be sought. We always feel stimulated and encouraged to pray for those who are doing well. ¶ *That ye might be filled with the knowledge of his will.* They had shown by their faith and love that they were disposed to do his will, and the

wisdom [a] and spiritual understanding; [b]

10 That ye might walk worthy [c] of the Lord unto all pleasing, [d] being fruitful in every good work, and increasing [f] in the knowledge of God;

11 Strengthened [g] with all might, according to his glorious power, unto all patience [h] and long-suffering, with joyfulness; [i]

a Ps. 119. 99. b 1 Jno. 5. 20. c Ph. 1. 27. d 1 Th. 4. 1. e Jno. 15. 8, 16.

f 2 Pe. 3. 18. g Is. 45. 24. h Ja. 1. 4. i Ro. 5. 3.

apostle now prays that they might be fully acquainted with what he would have them do. He offered a similar prayer in behalf of the Ephesians. See the parallel place in Eph. i. 17—19, and the Notes on those verses. ¶ *In all wisdom.* That you may be truly wise in all things. Eph. i. 17. ¶ *And spiritual understanding.* In understanding those things that pertain to the 'Spirit;' that is, those things taught by the Holy Spirit, and those which he produces in the work of salvation. See Notes on 1 Cor. ii. 12, 13. Comp. 1 John ii. 20; v. 20.

10. *That ye might walk worthy of the Lord.* That you may live as becomes the followers of the Lord. How this was to be done he states in this and the following verses. ¶ *Unto all pleasing.* So as to please him in all things. Comp. Heb. xi. 5. ¶ *Being fruitful in every good work.* This is one way in which we are to walk worthy of the Lord, and so as to please him. See Notes on John xv. 8. ¶ *And increasing in the knowledge of God.* This is another way in which we may walk worthy of the Lord, and so as to please him. It is by endeavouring to become better acquainted with his true character. God is *pleased* with those who desire to understand what he is; what he does; what he purposes; what he commands. Hence he not only *commands* us to study his works (comp. Ps. cxi. 2), but he has made a world so beautiful as to *invite* us to contemplate his perfections as reflected in that world. All good beings desire that others should understand their character, and God delights in those who are sincerely desirous of knowing what he is, and who inquire with humility and reverence into his counsels and his will. Men are often displeased when others attempt to look into their plans, for they are sensible they will not bear the light of investigation. God has no plans which would not be seen to be, in the highest degree, glorious to him.

11. *Strengthened with all might.* This was also an object of Paul's earnest prayer. He desired that they might be strengthened for the performance of duty; to meet temptations; and to bear up under the various trials of life. ¶ *According to his glorious power.* Not by any human means, but by the power of God. There is a manifestation of *power* in the spirit with which Christians are enabled to bear up under trials, which shows that it is not of human origin. It is the power which God gives them in the day of trial. This power is 'glorious,' or, as it is in the Greek, it is the 'power of his glory.' It is manifestly the power of the great and glorious God, and it tends to promote his glory, and to show forth his praise. ¶ *Unto all patience.* So that you may be enabled to bear all your trials without murmuring. It is only the power of God that can enable us to do that. ¶ *And long-suffering.* Notes, 1 Cor. xiii. 4. ¶ *With joyfulness.* Notes, Rom. v. 3. 2 Cor. vii. 4. The Syriac version, Chrysostom, and a few MSS. attach this to the following verse, and read it, 'With joyfulness giving thanks to the Father,' &c. The only difference is in the pointing, and either reading makes good sense.

12 Giving thanks unto the Father, which hath made us meet[a]

a Re. 22. 14.

12. *Giving thanks to the Father.* This is another mode by which we may 'walk worthy of the Lord unto all pleasing' (ver. 10); to wit, by rendering appropriate thanks to God for his mercy. The particular point which the apostle here says demanded thanksgiving was, that they had been called from the kingdom of darkness to the kingdom of light. This had been done by the special mercy of the Father, who had provided the plan of salvation, and had sent his Son to redeem them. The connection shows that the word 'Father' refers, in this place, not to God as the Father of his creatures, but to the Father as distinguished from the Son. It is the "Father" who has translated us into the kingdom of the "Son." Our especial thanks are due to the "Father" in this, as he is represented as the great Author of the whole plan of salvation—as he who sent his Son to redeem us. ¶ *Who hath made us meet.* The word here used—ἱκανόω—means properly *to make sufficient*, from ἱκανός—*sufficient*, *abundant*, *much.* The word conveys the idea of having *sufficient* or *enough* to accomplish anything. See it explained in the Notes on 2 Cor. iii. 6. The verb is not elsewhere used in the New Testament. In its use here, there seems to be implied the idea of conferring the privilege or the ability to be thus made the partakers of the kingdom, and the idea also of rendering us *fit* for it. The sense is, he has conferred on us grace *sufficient* to make it proper that we should partake of the blessings of his kingdom. In regard to this 'fitness' or 'meetness' for that kingdom, we may remark, (1.) that it does not mean that we are rendered fit by our own merits, or by anything which we have done; for it is expressly said that it is God who has thus rendered us 'meet' for it. No one, by his own merits, ever made himself *fit* for heaven. His good works cannot be an equivalent for the eternal rewards of heaven; nor is the heart, when unrenewed, even in the best state, *fit* for the society and the employments of heaven. There is no *adaptedness* of such a heart, however amiable and however refined, to the pure spiritual joys of the upper world. Those joys are the joys of religion, of the love of God, of pleasure in holiness; and the unrenewed heart can never be *wrought up* to a fitness to enter into those joys. Yet (2.) there *is* a fitness or meetness which Christians possess for heaven. It consists in two things. *First*, in their having complied with the conditions on which God promises heaven, so that, although they have no merit in themselves, and no fitness by their own works, they have that meetness which results from having complied with the terms of favour. They have truly repented of their sins, and believed in the Redeemer; and they are thus in the proper state of mind to receive the mercy of God; for, according to the terms of mercy, there is a propriety that pardon should be bestowed on the penitent, and peace on the believing. A child that is truly broken-hearted for a fault, is in a fit state of mind to be forgiven; a proud, and obstinate, and rebellious child, is not. *Secondly*, there is, *in fact*, a fitness in the Christian for the participation of the inheritance of the saints in light. He has a state of feeling that is *adapted* to that. There is a congruity between his feelings and heaven—a state of mind that can be satisfied with nothing but heaven. He has in his heart substantially the same principles which reign in hea-

to be partakers of the inheritance [a] of the saints in light:

13 Who hath delivered us from the power of darkness, [b] and hath

a Ac. 20. 32.

b 1 Pe. 2. 9.

ven; and he is fitted to find happiness only in the same objects in which the inhabitants of heaven do. He loves the same God and Saviour; has pleasure in the same truths; prefers, as they do, holiness to sin; and, like the inhabitants of heaven, he would choose to seek his pleasure in holy living, rather than in the ways of vanity. His preferences are all on the side of holiness and virtue; and, with such preferences, he is fitted for the enjoyments of heaven. In character, views, feelings, and preferences, therefore, the Christian is made 'fit' to participate in the employments and joys of the saints in light. ¶ *To be partakers of the inheritance.* The privileges of religion are often represented as an *heirship*, or an *inheritance.* See Notes on Rom. viii. 17. ¶ *Of the saints in light.* Called, in ver. 13, 'the kingdom of his dear Son.' This is a kingdom of *light*, as opposed to the kingdom of darkness in which they formerly were. In the East, and particularly in Persia, there prevailed early the belief that there were two great kingdoms in the universe—that of light, and that of darkness. We find traces of this opinion in the Scriptures, where the kingdom of God is called 'light,' and that of Satan is called 'darkness.' These are, of course, figurative expressions; but they convey important truth. Light, in the Scriptures, is the emblem of holiness, knowledge, happiness; and all these are found in the kingdom over which God presides, and of which Christians are the heirs. Accordingly, we find the word *light* often used to describe this kingdom. Thus it is said of God, who presides over it, that he "is *light*, and in him is no darkness at all," 1 John i. 5; of Christ, that he is "the light of man," John i. 4; that he is "the true light," John i. 9; that he is "the light of the world," John viii. 12 Comp. xii. 35. Luke ii. 32. The angels of that kingdom are 'angels of light,' 2 Cor. xi. 14. Those who compose that kingdom on earth are 'the children of light,' Luke xvi. 8. 1 Thess. v. 5. And all the descriptions of that kingdom in heaven represent it as filled with light and glory. Isa. lx. 19. Rev. xx. 23; xxii. 5.

13. *Who hath delivered us from the power of darkness.* The power exerted over us in that dark kingdom to which we formerly belonged—the kingdom of Satan. The characteristic of this empire is *darkness*—the emblem of (1.) sin; (2.) error; (3.) misery and death. Over us, by nature, these things had uncontrollable power; but now we are delivered from them, and brought to the enjoyment of the privileges of those who are connected with the kingdom of light. Darkness is often used to represent the state in which men are by nature. Comp. Luke i. 79. Acts xxvi. 18. Rom. xiii. 12. 1 Pet. ii. 9. 1 John ii. 8. ¶ *And hath translated* us. The word here rendered 'translated' is often used in the sense of removing *a people* from one country to another. See Josephus, Ant. ix. 11. 1. It means, here, that they who are Christians have been transferred from one kingdom to another, *as if* a people were thus removed. They become subjects of a new kingdom, are under different laws, and belong to a different community. This change is made in regeneration, by which we pass from the kingdom of darkness to the kingdom of light; from the empire of sin, ignorance, and misery, to one of

translated *us* into the kingdom of [1] his dear Son;

14 In [a] whom we have redemption through his blood, *even* the forgiveness of sins:

15 Who is the image [b] of the

[1] *the Son of his love.* a Ep. 1. 7. b He. 1. 3.

holiness, knowledge, and happiness. No change, therefore, in a man's life is so important as this; and no words can suitably express the gratitude which they should feel who are thus transferred from the empire of darkness to that of light.

14. *In whom we have redemption.* See this explained in the Notes on Eph. i. 7. The passage here proves that we obtain forgiveness of sins through the blood of Christ; but it does not prove that this is *all* that we obtain through that blood.

15. *Who is the image of the invisible God.* εἰκὼν τοῦ θεοῦ τοῦ ἀοράτου. The object here, as it is in the parallel place in Eph. i. 20—23, is to give a just view of the exaltation of the Redeemer. It is probable that, in both cases, the design is to meet some erroneous opinion on this subject that prevailed in those churches, or among those that claimed to be teachers there. See the Introduction to this epistle, and comp. the Notes on Eph. i. 20—23. For the meaning of the phrase occurring here, '*the image of the invisible God*,' see the Notes on Heb. i. 3, and 2 Cor. iv. 4. The meaning is, that he represents to mankind the perfections of God, as an image, figure, or drawing does the object which it is made to resemble. See the word *image*—εἰκὼν—explained in the Notes on Heb. x. 1. It properly denotes that which is a copy or delineation of a thing; which accurately and fully represents it, in contradistinction from a rough sketch, or outline. Comp. Rom. viii. 29. 1 Cor. xi. 7; xv. 49. The meaning here is, that the being and perfections of God are accurately and fully represented by Christ. In what respects particularly he was thus a representative of God, the apostle proceeds to state in the following verses, to wit, in his creative power, in his eternal existence, in his heirship over the universe, in the fulness that dwelt in him. This cannot refer to him merely as incarnate, for some of the things affirmed of him pertained to him *before* his incarnation; and the idea is, that *in all things* Christ fairly represents to us the divine nature and perfections. God is manifest to us through him. 1 Tim. iii. 16. We see God in him as we see an object in that which is in all respects an exact copy of it. God is invisible. No eye has seen him, or can see him; but in what Christ is, and has done in the works of creation and redemption, we have a fair and full representation of what God is. See Notes on John i. 18; xiv. 9. ¶ *The first-born of every creature.* Among all the creatures of God, or over all his creation, occupying the rank and pre-eminence of the first-born. The first-born, or the eldest son, among the Hebrews as elsewhere, had peculiar privileges. He was entitled to a double portion of the inheritance. It has been, also, and especially in oriental countries, a common thing for the eldest son to succeed to the estate and the title of his father. In early times, the first-born son was the officiating priest in the family, in the absence or on the death of the father. There can be no doubt that the apostle here has reference to the *usual* distinctions and honours conferred on the first-born, and means to say that, among all the creatures of God, Christ occupied a pre-eminence *similar* to that. He does not say that, *in all respects*, he resembled the first-born in a family; nor does he say that he

invisible God, the first-born of every creature:

16 For by him [a] were all things created, that are in heaven, and

a Jno. 1. 3.

himself was a creature, for the point of his comparison does not turn on these things, and what he proceeds to affirm respecting him is inconsistent with the idea of his being a created being himself. He that 'created all things that are in heaven and that are in earth,' was not himself *created.* That the apostle did not mean to represent him as a creature, is also manifest *from the reason which he assigns* why he is called the first-born. 'He is the image of God, and the first-born of every creature, *for*—ὅτι—by him were all things created.' That is, he sustains the elevated rank of the first-born, or a high eminence over the creation, *because* by him 'all things were created in heaven and in earth.' The *language* here used, also, does not fairly imply that he was a creature, or that he was in nature and rank one of those in relation to whom it is said he was the first-born. It is true that the word first-born — πρωτότοκος — properly means the first-born child of a father or mother, Matt. i. 25. Luke ii. 7; or the first-born of animals. But two things are also to be remarked in regard to the use of the word: (1.) It does not necessarily imply that any one is born *afterwards* in the family, for it would be used of the first-born, though an only child; and (2.) it is used to denote one who is chief, or who is highly distinguished and pre-eminent. Thus it is employed in Rom. viii. 29, "That he might be the first-born among many brethren." So, in ver. 18 of this chapter, it is said that he was "the first-born from the dead;" not that he was literally the first that was raised from the dead, which was not the fact, but that he might be pre-eminent among those that are raised. Comp. Ex. iv. 22. The meaning, then, is, that Christ sustains the most exalted rank in the universe; he is pre-eminent above all others; he is at the head of all things. The expression does not mean that he was 'begotten before all creatures,' as it is often explained, but refers to the simple fact that he sustains the highest rank over the creation. He is the Son of God. He is the heir of all things. All other creatures are also the 'offspring of God;' but he is exalted as the Son of God above all.

16. *For by him were all things created.* This is one of the *reasons* why he is called 'the image of God, and the 'first-born.' He makes God known to us by his creative power, and by the same power in creation shows that he is exalted over all things as the Son of God. The phrase which is here used by the apostle is universal. He does not declare that he created all things in the spiritual kingdom of God, or that he arranged the events of the gospel dispensation, as Socinians suppose (see Crellius); but that *everything* was created by him. A similar form of expression occurs in John i. 3. See Notes on that verse. There could not possibly be a more explicit declaration that the universe was created by Christ, than this. As if the simple declaration in the most comprehensive terms were not enough, the apostle goes into a specification of things existing in heaven and earth, and so varies the statement as if to prevent the possibility of mistake. ¶ *That are in heaven.* The division of the universe into 'heaven and earth' is natural and obvious, for it is the one that is *apparent.* See Gen. i. 1. *Heaven,* then, according to this division, will

that are in earth, visible and invisible, whether *they be* thrones, or dominions, or principalities, or powers: all things were created by [a] him, and for him:

a Ro. 11. 36.

embrace all the universe, *except* the earth; and will include the heavenly bodies and their inhabitants, the distant worlds as well as *heaven*, more strictly so called, where God resides. The declaration, then, is, that all things that were in the worlds above us were the work of his creative power. ¶ *And that are in earth.* All the animals, plants, minerals, waters, hidden fires, &c. Everything which the earth contains. ¶ *Visible and invisible.* We see but a small part of the universe. The angels we cannot see. The inhabitants of distant worlds we cannot see. Nay, there are multitudes of worlds which, even with the best instruments, we cannot see. Yet all these things are said to have been created by Christ. ¶ *Whether* they be *thrones.* Whether those invisible things be thrones. The reference is to the ranks of angels, called here *thrones, dominions,* &c. See Notes on Eph. i. 21. The word '*thrones*' does not occur in the parallel place in Ephesians; but there can be no doubt that the reference is to an order of angelic beings, as those to whom dominion and power were intrusted. The other orders enumerated here are also mentioned in Eph. i. 21. ¶ *All things were created by him.* The repetition, and the varied statement here, are designed to express the truth with emphasis, and so that there could not be the possibility of mistake or misapprehension. Comp. Notes on John i. 1—3. The importance of the doctrine, and the fact that it was probably denied by false teachers, or that they held philosophical opinions that tended to its practical denial, are the reasons why the apostle dwells so particularly on this point. ¶ *And for him.* For his glory; for such purposes as *he* designed. There was a reference to himself in the work of creation, just as, when a man builds a house, it is with reference to some important purposes which he contemplates, pertaining to himself. The universe was built by the Creator to be his own property; to be the theatre on which he would accomplish his purposes, and display his perfections. Particularly the earth was made by the Son of God to be the place where he would become incarnate, and exhibit the wonders of redeeming love. There could not be a more positive declaration than this, that the universe was created by Christ; and, if so, he is divine. The work of creation is the exertion of the highest power of which we can form a conception, and is often appealed to in the Scriptures by God to prove that he is divine, in contradistinction from idols. If, therefore, this passage be understood literally, it settles the question about the divinity of Christ. Accordingly, Unitarians have endeavoured to show that the creation here referred to is a *moral* creation; that it refers to the arrangement of affairs in the christian church, or to the kingdom of God on earth, and not to the creation of the material universe. This interpretation has been adopted even by Grotius, who supposes that it refers to the arrangement by which all things are fitted up in the new creation, and by which angels and men are reconciled. By the 'things in heaven and in earth, some Unitarian expositors have understood the Jews and the Gentiles, who are reconciled by the gospel; others, by the things in heaven, understand the angels, and, by the things on earth, men, who are brought into harmony by the gospel plan of salvation. But the objections to this

17 And he is before [a] all things, and by him all things consist:

a Jno. 1. 1.

interpretation are insuperable: (1.) The word *created* is not used in this sense properly, and cannot be. That it *may* mean *to arrange, to order*, is true; but it is not used in the sense of *reconciling*, or of bringing discordant things into harmony. To the great mass of men, who have no theory to support, it would be understood in its natural and obvious sense, as denoting the literal creation. (2.) The assertion is, that the 'creative' power of Christ was exerted on 'all *things*.' It is not in reference to angels only, or to men, or to Jews, or to Gentiles; it is in relation to '*everything* in heaven and in earth;' that is, to the whole universe. Why should so universal a declaration be supposed to denote merely the intelligent creation? (3.) With what propriety, or in what tolerable sense, can the expression 'things in heaven and things in earth' be applied to the Jews and Gentiles? In what sense can it be said that they are 'visible and invisible?' And, if the language could be thus used, how can the fact that Christ is the means of reconciling them be a reason why he should be called 'the image of the invisible God?' (4.) If it be understood of *a moral creation*, of a renovation of things, of a change of nature, how can this be applied to *the angels?* Has Christ *created* them anew? Has he changed their nature and character? Good angels cannot need a spiritual renovation; and Christ did not come to convert fallen angels, and to bring them into harmony with the rest of the universe. (5.) The phrase here employed, of 'creating all things in heaven and on earth,' is *never* used elsewhere to denote a moral or spiritual creation. It appropriately expresses the creation of the universe. It is language strikingly similar to that used by Moses, Gen. i. 1; and it would be so understood by the great mass of mankind. If this be so, then Christ is divine, and we can see in this great work a good reason why he is called 'the *image* of the invisible God,' and why he is at the head of the universe—the first-born of the creation. It is because, through him, God is made known to us in the work of creation; and because, being the great agent in that work, there is a propriety that he should occupy this position at the head of all things.

17. *And he is before all things.* As he must be, if he *created* all things. Those who regard this as referring to a moral creation, interpret it as meaning that he has the *pre-eminence over* all things; not as referring to his *pre-existence.* But the fair and proper meaning of the word *before* (πρὸ) is, that he was *before* all things in the order of existence. Comp. Matt. viii. 29. John xi. 55; xiii. 1. Acts v. 36; xxi. 38. 2 Cor. xii. 2. It is equivalent to saying that he was eternal—for he that had an existence before *anything* was created, must be eternal. Thus it is equivalent to the phrase 'In the beginning.' Gen. i. 1. Comp. Notes, John i. 1. ¶ *And by him all things subsist.* Or are sustained. See Notes on Heb. i. 3. The meaning is, that they are kept in the present state; their existence, order, and arrangement are continued by his power. If unsupported by him, they would fall into disorder, or sink back to nothing. If this be the proper interpretation, then it is the ascription to Christ of infinite *power*—for nothing less could be sufficient to uphold the universe; and of infinite *wisdom*—for this is needed to preserve the harmonious action of the suns and systems of which it is composed. None could do this but one

18 And he is the head [a] of the body, the church; who is the beginning, [b] the first-born from the dead; that [1] in all *things* he might have the pre-eminence.

19 For it pleased *the Father*

a Ep. 5. 23. *b* 1 Co. 15. 20.

[1] *among all.*

who is divine; and hence we see the reason why he is represented as the image of the invisible God. He is the great and glorious and ever-active agent by whom the perfections of God are made known.

18. *And he is the head of the body, the church.* Notes, Eph. i. 22; v. 23. ¶ *Who is the beginning.* In all things—alike in the work of creation and in the church. He is the fountain of authority and power, and commences everything that is designed to uphold the order of the universe, and to save the world. ¶ *The first-born from the dead.* At the head of those who rise from their graves. This does not mean literally that he was the first who rose from the dead, for he himself raised up Lazarus and others, and the bodies of saints arose at his crucifixion; but it means that he had the pre-eminence among them all; he was the most illustrious of those who will be raised from the dead, and is the head over them all. Especially, he had this pre-eminence in the resurrection in this respect, that he was the first who rose from death to immortality. Others who were raised undoubtedly died again. Christ rose to die no more. See Notes on 1 Cor. xv. 20. ¶ *That in all* things. Marg., *among all.* The Greek will bear either construction, and either will accord with the scope of the apostle's remarks. If the former, it means that he is at the head of all *things*—the universe; if the latter, that he is chief among those who rose from the dead. Each of these is true, but the scope of the passage seems rather to require us to understand this of *everything*, and to mean that all the arrangements respecting him were such as to give him supremacy over the universe. ¶ *He might have the pre-eminence.* Gr., *might be first*—πρωτεύων. That is, might be first in rank, dignity, honour, power. He has the pre-eminence (1.) as over the universe which he has formed—as its Creator and Proprietor; (2.) as chief among those who shall rise from the dead—since he first rose to die no more, and their resurrection depends on him; (3.) as head of the church — all synods, councils, and governments being subject to him, and he alone having a right to give law to his people; and (4.) in the affections of his friends—being in their affections and confidence superior to all others.

19. *For it pleased* the Father. The words 'the Father' are not in the original, but they are not improperly supplied. Some word must be understood, and as the apostle in ver. 12 referred to 'the Father' as having a claim to the thanks of his people for what he had done, and as the great favour for which they ought to be thankful is that which he immediately specifies—the exaltation of Christ, it is not improper to suppose that this is the word to be understood here. The meaning is, that he chose to confer on his Son such a rank, that in all things he might have the pre-eminence, and that there might be in him 'all fulness.' Hence, by his appointment, he was the agent in creation, and hence he is placed over all things as the head of the church. ¶ *That in him should all fulness dwell.* That in him there should be such dignity, authority, power, and moral excellence as to be fitted to the work of creating the world, redeeming his people, and supplying everything needful for their salvation. On the

that in him [a] should all fulness dwell;

20 And, [1] having made [b] peace through the blood of his cross, by him to reconcile all things unto himself; by him, *I say*, whether

a Jno. 1. 16. 1 or, *making*. b Ep. 2. 14-16.

word *fulness*, see Notes on John i. 14. 16. Comp. Rom. xi. 12. 25. Gal. iv. 4. Eph. i. 23; iii. 19. Col. ii. 9. This is to us a most precious truth. We have a Saviour who is in no respect deficient in wisdom, power, and grace to redeem and save us. There is nothing necessary to be done in our salvation which he is not qualified to do; there is nothing which we need to enable us to perform our duties, to meet temptation, and to bear trial, which he is not able to impart. In no situation of trouble and danger will the church find that there is a deficiency in him; in no enterprise to which she can put her hands will there be a lack of power in her great Head to enable her to accomplish what he calls her to. We may go to him in all our troubles, weaknesses, temptations, and wants, and may be supplied from his fulness—just as, if we were thirsty, we might go to *an ocean* of pure water and drink.

20. *And having made peace.* Marg., *making*. The Greek will bear either. The meaning is, that by his atonement he produces reconciliation between those who were alienated from each other. See Notes on Eph. ii. 14. It does not mean here that he had actually effected peace by his death, but that he had laid the foundation for it; he had done that which would secure it. ¶ *By the blood of his cross.* By his blood shed on the cross. That blood, making atonement for sin, was the means of making reconciliation between God and man. On the meaning of the word *blood*, as used in this connection, see Notes on Rom. iii. 25. ¶ *By him to reconcile all things to himself.* On the meaning of the word *reconcile*, see Notes on Matt. v. 24. Rom. v. 10, and 2 Cor. v. 18. When it is said that 'it pleased the Father by Christ to reconcile *all things* to himself,' the declaration must be understood with some limitation. (1.) It relates only to those things which are *in heaven and earth*—for those only are specified. Nothing is said of the inhabitants of hell, whether fallen angels, or the spirits of wicked men who are there. (2.) It cannot mean that all things *are* actually reconciled—for that never has been true. Multitudes on earth have remained alienated from God, and have lived and died his enemies. (3.) It can mean then, only, that he had executed a plan that was adapted to this; that if fairly and properly applied, the blood of the cross was fitted to secure entire reconciliation between heaven and earth. There was no enemy which it was not fitted to reconcile to God; there was no guilt, now producing alienation, which it could not wash away. ¶ *Whether* they be *things in earth, or things in heaven.* That is, to produce *harmony* between the things in heaven and in earth; so that all things shall be reconciled to him, or so that there shall be harmony between heaven and earth. The meaning is not, that 'the things *in heaven*' were alienated from God, but that there was alienation in the universe which *affected* heaven, and the object was to produce again universal concord and love. Substantially the same sentiment is found in Eph. i. 10. See Notes on that verse. Much has been written on the meaning of this expression, and a great variety of opinions have been entertained of it. It is best, always, unless necessity require a different interpretation, to take

they be things in earth, or things in heaven.

21 And you, that were sometime alienated, and enemies [1] in *your* mind [2] by wicked works, yet now hath he reconciled,

22 In the body of his flesh through death, to present [a] you

[1] or, *by*.

[2] or, *in*.

[a] Jude 24.

words in their usual signification. If that rule be adopted here, 'things in heaven' will refer to God and the angels, and perhaps may include the principles of the divine government. 'Things on earth,' will embrace *men*, and the various things on earth which are now at variance with God and with heaven. Between these, it is designed to produce harmony by the blood of the cross, or by the atonement. As in heaven nothing is *wrong;* as it is not desirable that anything should be changed there, all the *change* that is to take place in order to produce reconciliation, is to be on the part of men and the things of this world. The only effect of the blood of the atonement on the 'things' of heaven in effecting the reconciliation is, to render it consistent for God *to be* at peace with sinners. The effect on earth is, to dispose the sinner to a willingness to be reconciled; to lead him to lay aside his enmity; to change his heart, and to effect a change in the views and principles prevailing on earth which are now at variance with God and his government. When this shall be done there will be *harmony* between heaven and earth, and an alienated world will be brought into conformity with the laws and government of the Creator.

21. *And you, that were sometime alienated.* In this work of reconciling heaven and earth, you at Colosse, who were once enemies of God, have been reached. The benefit of that great plan has been extended to you, and it has accomplished in you what it is designed to effect everywhere—to reconcile enemies to God. The word *sometime* here—ποτε—means *formerly.* In common with all other men they were, by nature, in a state of enmity against God. Comp. Notes on Eph. ii. 1—3. ¶ *In your mind.* It was not merely by wicked works, or by an evil life; it was alienation seated *in the mind*, and leading to wicked works. It was deliberate and purposed enmity. It was not the result of passion and excitement; it had a deeper seat, and took hold of the intellectual powers. The understanding was perverse and alienated from God, and all the powers of the soul were enlisted against him. It is this fact which renders reconciliation with God so difficult. Sin has corrupted and perverted alike the moral and the intellectual powers, and thus the whole man is arrayed against his Creator. Comp. Notes on Eph. iv. 18. ¶ *By wicked works.* The alienation of the mind showed itself by wicked works, and those works were the public evidence of the alienation. Comp. Eph. ii. 1, 2. ¶ *Yet now hath he reconciled.* Harmony has been secured between you and God, and you are brought to friendship and love. Such a change has been produced in you as to bring your minds into friendship with that of God. All the *change* in producing this is on the part of man, for God *cannot* change, and there is no reason why he *should*, if he could. In the work of reconciliation man lays aside his hostility to his Maker, and thus becomes his friend. See Notes, 2 Cor. v. 18.

22. *In the body of his flesh through death.* The death of his body, or his death in making an atonement, has been the means of producing

holy and unblameable and unreproveable in his sight;

23 If ye continue [a] in the faith grounded and settled, and *be* not

a He. 10. 38.

this reconciliation. It (1.) removed the obstacles to reconciliation on the part of God — vindicating his truth and justice, and maintaining the principles of his government as much as if the sinner had himself suffered the penalty of the law—thus rendering it *consistent* for God to indulge the benevolence of his nature in pardoning sinners; and (2.) it was the means of bringing the sinner himself to a willingness to be reconciled—furnishing the strongest possible appeal to him; leading him to reflect on the love of his Creator, and showing him his own guilt and danger. No means ever used to produce reconciliation between two alienated parties has had so much tenderness and power as those which God has adopted in the plan of salvation; and if the dying love of the Son of God fails to lead the sinner back to God, everything else will fail. The phrase 'the body of his flesh' means, the *body of flesh* which he assumed in order to suffer in making an atonement. The reconciliation could not have been effected but by his assuming such a body, for his divine nature could not so suffer as to make atonement for sins. ¶ *To present you.* That is, before God. The object of the atonement was to enable him to present the redeemed to God freed from sin, and made holy in his sight. The whole work had reference to the glories of that day when the Redeemer and the redeemed will stand before God, and he shall present them to his Father as completely recovered from the ruins of the fall. ¶ *Holy.* Made holy, or made free from sin. Comp. Luke xx. 36. ¶ *And unblameable.* Not that in themselves they will not be deserving of *blame*, or will not be unworthy, but that they will be purified from their sins. The word here used—ἄμωμος—means, properly, *spotless, without blemish.* See the Notes on Eph. i. 4; v. 27. Heb. ix. 4. It is applied to a lamb, 1 Pet. i. 19; to the Saviour, Heb. ix. 14, and to the church, Eph. i. 4; v. 27. Jude 24. Rev. xiv. 5. It does not elsewhere occur. When the redeemed enter heaven, all their sins will have been taken away; not a *spot* of the deep dye of iniquity will remain on their souls. Rev. i. 5; vii. 14. ¶ *And unreproveable in his sight.* There will be none to *accuse* them before God; or they will be free from all *accusation.* The *law* will not accuse them — for the death of their Redeemer has done as much to honour it as their own punishment would have done; God will not accuse them—for he has freely forgiven them; their consciences will not accuse them — for their sins will all have been taken away, and they will enjoy the favour of God *as if* they had not sinned; holy angels will not accuse them—for they will welcome them to their society; and even Satan will not accuse them, for he will have seen that their piety is sincere, and that they are truly what they profess to be. Comp. Notes on Rom. viii. 33, 34.

23. *If ye continue in the faith.* In the belief of the gospel, and in holy living. If this were done, they would be presented unblameable before God; if not, they would not be. The meaning is, that it will be impossible to be saved unless we continue to lead lives becoming the gospel. ¶ *Grounded.* On a firm foundation. See Notes on Eph. iii. 17, where the same word occurs. ¶ *And settled.* Gr., *firm;* as a building is that is founded on a rock. Comp. Matt. vii. 25. ¶ *And be not moved*

moved away from the hope of the gospel, which ye have heard, *and* which was preached to every[a] creature which is under heaven; whereof I Paul am made a minister;

24 Who now rejoice in my sufferings for you, and fill up that

a Mat. 24. 14. Mar. 16 15.

---

away from the hope of the gospel. By the arts of philosophy, and the allurements of sin. ¶ *Which was preached to every creature which is under heaven.* It cannot be supposed that it was literally true that every creature under heaven had actually *heard* the gospel. But this may mean, (1.) that it was *designed* to be preached to every creature, or that the commission to make it known embraced every one, and that, so far as the provisions of the gospel are concerned, it may be said that it was a system proclaimed to all mankind. See Mark xvi. 15. If a vast army, or the inhabitants of a distant province, were in rebellion against a government, and a proclamation of pardon were issued, it would not be improper to say that *it was made to every one of them*, though, as a matter of fact, it might not be true that every one in the remote parts of the army or province had actually heard of it. (2.) The gospel in the time of Paul seems to have been so extensively preached, that it might be said that it was proclaimed to everybody. All known countries appear to have been visited; and so zealous and laborious had been the heralds of salvation, that it might be said that the message had been proclaimed to all the world. See ver. 6. Comp. Notes on Matt. xxiv. 14. ¶ *Whereof I Paul am made a minister.* See Notes, Eph. iii. 1—7. Paul here pursues the same train of thought which he does in the epistle to the Ephesians, where, having shown the exalted nature of the Redeemer, and the design of the gospel, he adverts to his own labours and sufferings in making it known. The object seems to be to show that he regarded it as the highest honour to be thus intrusted with the message of mercy to mankind, and considered it as a privilege to suffer in that cause.

24. *Who now rejoice in my sufferings for you.* For you as a part of the Gentile world. It was not for the Colossians alone, but he regarded himself as suffering on account of his labours in preaching to the heathen at large. His trials at Rome had come upon him because he had maintained that the wall of partition between Jews and Gentiles was broken down, and that the gospel was to be preached indiscriminately to all mankind. See this illustrated in the Introduction, § 5. ¶ *And fill up that which is behind of the afflictions of Christ.* That which I lack of coming up to the sufferings which Christ endured in the cause of the church. The apostle seems to mean, (1.) that he suffered in the same cause as that for which Christ suffered; (2.) that he endured the same kind of sufferings, to some extent, in reproaches, persecutions, and opposition from the world; (3.) that he had not yet suffered *as much* as Christ did in this cause, and, though he had suffered greatly, yet there was much that was lacking to make him equal in this respect to the Saviour; and (4.) that he felt that it was an object to be earnestly desired to be made in all respects *just like Christ*, and that in his present circumstances he was fast filling up that which was lacking, so that he would have a more complete resemblance to him. What he says here is based on the leading desire

which is behind of the afflictions [a] of Christ in my flesh for his body's sake, which is the church;

25 Whereof I am made a minister, according to the dispensation of God which is given to me for you, [1] to fulfil the word of God;

26 *Even* the mystery [b] which hath been hid from ages and from generations, but now [c] is made manifest to his saints:

27 To whom God would make known what *is* the riches of the glory of this mystery among the

a Ph. 3. 10. [1] or, *fully to preach.* b Ep. 3. 9. c 2 Ti. 1. 10.

of his soul—the great principle of his life—TO BE JUST LIKE CHRIST; alike in moral character, in suffering, and in destiny. See Notes on Phil. iii. 10. Having this strong wish, he had been led to pursue a course of life which conducted him through trials strongly resembling those which Christ himself endured; and, as fast as possible, he was filling up that in which he now fell short. He does not mean that there was anything lacking or deficient in the sufferings which Christ endured in making an atonement which was to be supplied by his followers, so that *their* merits might be added to *his* in order to secure the salvation of men, as the Romanists seem to suppose; but that there was still much lacking on *his* part before he should be entirely conformed to the Saviour in his sufferings, and that his present condition was such as rapidly to fill that up. This seems to me to be the fair meaning of this expression, though not the one commonly given. The usual interpretation is, 'that which remains to me of affliction to be endured in the cause of Christ.' But this seems to me to be cold and tame, and not to suit the genius of Paul. ¶ *In my flesh.* In bodily sufferings. ¶ *For his body's sake, which is the church.* See Notes on Eph. i. 23.

25. *According to the dispensation of God.* The arrangement which God has made. That is, he designed that the gospel should be preached to the Gentiles, and, in accordance with that arrangement, he has called me to be a minister. Notes, Eph. iii. 2. ¶ *To fulfil the word of God.* Marg., '*fully to preach.*' The Greek is, 'to fill up the word of God;' the meaning is, 'fully to teach and promulgate the gospel.' Comp. Notes, Rom. xv. 19.

26. Even *the mystery.* To make that mystery fully known. See this explained in the Notes on Eph. iii. 2—9. The great doctrine that salvation was to be proclaimed to all mankind, Paul says, had been *concealed* for many generations. Hence it was called a *mystery*, or a hidden truth. ¶ *But now is made manifest to his saints.* It was communicated especially to the apostles who were appointed to proclaim it, and through them to all the saints. Paul says that he regarded himself as specially called to make this truth known, as far as possible, to mankind.

27. *To whom.* To the saints. ¶ *God would make known.* '*Willed* (Gr.) to make known;' that is, he was pleased to make this known. It was concealed in his bosom until he chose to reveal it to his apostles. It was a doctrine which the Jewish people did not understand. Eph. iii. 5, 6. ¶ *What* is *the riches of the glory of this mystery.* The rich glory of this great, long-concealed truth. On the use of the word *riches*, see Notes on Rom. ii. 4. It is a favourite word with the apostle Paul to denote that which is valuable, or that which *abounds.* The meaning here is, that the truth that the gospel was to be preached to all mankind, was a truth *abounding in*

Gentiles; which is Christ [1] in you, the [a] hope of glory:

28 Whom we preach, warning [b] every man, and teaching [c] every man in all wisdom; that [d] we may present every man perfect in Christ Jesus:

29 Whereunto [e] I also labour,

[1] or, *among*. a 1 Ti. 1. 1. b Ac. 20. 28, 31. c 2 Ti. 2. 25. d 2 Co. 11. 2. e 1 Co. 15. 10.

---

glory. ¶ *Among the Gentiles.* That is, the glory of this truth is manifested by the effects which it has produced among the Gentiles.—¶ *Which is Christ in you, the hope of glory.* Or, Christ *among* you. *Margin.* The meaning is, that the whole of that truth, so full of glory, and so rich and elevated in its effect, is summed up in this—that Christ is revealed among you as the source of the hope of glory in a better world. This was the great truth which so animated the heart and fired the zeal of the apostle Paul. The wonderful announcement had burst on his mind like a flood of day, that the offer of salvation was not to be confined, as he had once supposed, to the Jewish people, but that all men were now placed on a level; that they had a common Saviour; that the same heaven was now opened for all, and that there were none so degraded and vile that they might not have the offer of life as well as others. This great truth Paul burned to communicate to the whole world; and for holding it, and in making it known, he had involved himself in all the difficulties which he had with his own countrymen; had suffered from want, and peril, and toil; and had finally been made a captive, and was expecting to be put to death. It was just such a truth as was fitted to fire such a mind as that of Paul, and to make it known was *worth* all the sacrifices and toils which he endured. Life is well sacrificed in making known such a doctrine to the world.

28. *Whom we preach, warning every man.* This does not mean *warning* of danger, but '*admonishing* all of the claims of the gospel to attention.' Our word *warn* is commonly used in the sense of *cautioning against danger*. The Greek word here means *to put in mind; to admonish; to exhort.* The idea of the apostle is, that he made it his great business to bring the offers of the gospel fairly before the mind of every man. As it had the same claims on all; as it might be freely offered to all, and as it furnished the only hope of glory, he made it the object of his life to apprize *every man* of it, as far as he could. ¶ *And teaching every man.* Paul made it his business to *instruct* men, as well as to exhort them. Exhortation and warning are of little use where there is not sound instruction and a careful inculcation of the truth. It is one of the duties of the ministry to *instruct* men in those truths of which they were before ignorant. See Matt. xxviii. 19. 2 Tim. ii. 25. ¶ *In all wisdom.* Comp. Notes on Matt. x. 16. Col. i. 9. The meaning is, that he and his fellow-labourers endeavoured to *manifest* true wisdom in the method in which they instructed others. ¶ *That we may present every man.* When we come to appear before God. Notes, 2 Cor. xi. 2. Paul was anxious that no one to whom this gospel was preached should be lost. He believed it to be adapted to save every man; and as he expected to meet all his hearers at the bar of God, his aim was to present them made perfect by means of that gospel which he preached.

29. *Whereunto I also labour.* See Notes, 1 Cor. xv. 10. ¶ *Striving.* Gr. *agonizing.* He taxed all his energies to accomplish this, as the

striving according to his working, which worketh in me mightily.

wrestlers strove for the mastery in the Grecian games. ¶ *According to his working.* Not by my own strength, but by the power which God alone can give. See Notes on 1 Cor. xv. 10.

REMARKS.

Among the truths of practical importance taught by this chapter, are the following:—

1. We should rejoice in the piety of others. Vs. 2—8. It should be to us a subject of unfeigned gratitude to God, when others are faithful to their high calling, and when they so live as to adorn the blessed gospel. In all their faith, and love, and joy, we should find occasion for thankfulness to God. We should not envy it, or be disposed to charge it to wrong motives, or suspect it of insincerity or hypocrisy; but should welcome every account of the zeal and faithfulness of those who bear the christian name—no matter who the persons are, or with what denomination of Christians they may be connected. Especially is this true in relation to our friends, or to those for whose salvation we have laboured. The source of highest gratitude to a Christian, in relation to his friends, should be, that they act as becomes the friends of God; the purest joy that can swell the bosom of a minister of Christ, is produced by the evidence that they to whom he has ministered are advancing in knowledge and love.

2. We should earnestly pray that they who have been much favoured should be prospered more and more. Vs. 9—11.

3. It is a good time to pray for Christians when they are already prosperous, and are distinguished for zeal and love. Vs. 9—11. We have then *encouragement* to do it. We feel that our prayers will not be in vain. For a man that is doing well, we feel encouraged to pray that he may do still better. For a Christian who has true spiritual joy, we are encouraged to pray that he may have more joy. For one who is aiming to make advances in the knowledge of God, we are encouraged to pray that he may make still higher advances; and if, therefore, we *wish* others to pray for us, we should show them by our efforts that there is some encouragement for them to do it.

4. Let us cherish with suitable gratitude the remembrance of the goodness of God, who has translated us from the kingdom of darkness into the kingdom of his dear Son. Vs. 12, 13. By nature we, like others, were under the power of darkness. In that kingdom of sin, and error, and misery, we were born and reared, until God, in great compassion brought us out from it, and made us heirs of light. Now, if we are true Christians, we belong to a kingdom of holiness, and knowledge, and happiness. No words can express appropriately the goodness of God in thus making us heirs of light; and not an hour of our lives should pass without a thoughtful remembrance of his mercy.

5. In the affections of our hearts let the Saviour in all things have the pre-eminence. Vs. 15—18. He is the image of God; and when we think of him, we see what God is—how holy, pure, benevolent. He is the first-born of all things; the Son of God; exalted to the highest seat in the universe. When we look on the sun, moon, and stars, let us remember that he created them all. When we think of the angels, let us remember that they are the workmanship of his hands. When we look on the earth—the floods, the rivers, the hills, let us remember that all these were made by his power. The

vast universe is still sustained by him. Its beautiful order and harmony are preserved by him; and all its movements are under his control. So the church is under him. It is subject to his command; receives its laws from his lips, and is bound to do his will. Over all councils and synods; over all rule and authority in the church, Christ is the Head; and whatever may be ordained by man, his will is to be obeyed. So, when we think of the resurrection, Christ is *chief*. He first rose to return to death no more; he rose as the pledge that his people should also rise. As Christ is thus head over all things, so let him be first in the affections of our hearts; as it is designed that in every thing he shall have the pre-eminence, so let him have the pre-eminence in the affections of our souls. None should be loved by us as Christ is loved; and no friend, however dear, should be allowed to displace him from the supremacy in our affections.

6. In all our wants let us go to Christ. Ver. 19. 'It pleased the Father that in him should all fulness dwell.' We have not a want which he cannot supply; there is not a sorrow of our lives in which he cannot comfort us; not a temptation from which he cannot deliver us; not a pain which he cannot relieve, or enable us to bear. Every necessity of body or mind he can supply; and we *never* can go to him, in any circumstance of life in which we can possibly be placed, where we shall fail of consolation and support *because* Christ is not able to help us. True piety learns day by day to live more by simple dependence on the Saviour. As we advance in holiness, we become more and more sensible of our weakness and insufficiency, and more and more disposed to live by the faith of the Son of God.'

7. By religion we become united with the angels. Ver. 20. Harmony is produced between heaven and earth. Alienated worlds are reconciled again, and from jarring elements there is rearing one great and harmonious empire. The work of the atonement is designed to remove what separated earth from heaven; men from angels; man from God. The redeemed have substantially the same feelings now, which they have who are around the throne of God; and though we are far inferior to them in rank, yet we shall be united with them in affection and purpose, forever and ever. What a glorious work is that of the gospel! It reconciles and harmonizes distant worlds, and produces concord and love in millions of hearts which *but* for that would have been alienated forever!

8. By religion we become fitted for heaven. Vs. 12. 22. We are made 'meet' to enter there; we shall be presented there unblamable and unreprovable. No one will accuse us before the throne of God. Nor Satan, nor our own consciences, nor our fellow-men will then urge that we *ought not* to be admitted to heaven. Redeemed and pardoned, renewed and sanctified, the universe will be satisfied that we *ought* to be saved, and will rejoice. Satan will no longer charge the friends of Jesus with insincerity and hypocrisy; our own minds will be no longer troubled with doubts and fears; and holy angels will welcome us to their presence. Not a voice will be lifted up in reproach or condemnation, and the Universal Father will stretch out his arms and press to his bosom the returning prodigals. Clothed in the white robes of salvation, we shall be welcome even in heaven, and the universe will rejoice that we are there.

9. It is a privilege to suffer for the welfare of the church. Ver. 24. Paul regarded it as such, and *re-*

joiced in the trials which came upon him in the cause of religion. The Saviour so regarded it, and shrank not from the great sorrows involved in the work of saving his people. We may suffer much in promoting the same object. We may be exposed to persecution and death. We may be called to part with all we have—to leave country and friends and home, to go and preach the gospel to benighted men. On a foreign shore, far from all that we hold dear on earth, we may lie down and die, and our grave, unmarked by sculptured marble, may be soon forgotten. But to do good; to defend truth; to promote virtue; to save the souls of the perishing, is *worth all which it costs*, and he who accomplishes these things by exchanging for them earthly comforts, and even life, has made a wise exchange. The universe *gains* by it in happiness; and the benevolent heart should rejoice that there *is such a gain*, though attended with our individual and personal suffering.

10. Ministers have a noble office. Vs. 24—29. It is their privilege to make known to men the most glorious truths that can come before the human mind; truths which were hid from ages and generations, but which are now revealed by the gospel. These great truths are intrusted to the ministry to explain and defend, and are by them to be carried around the world. The ministers of religion strive not for gold and honour and worldly pleasures; they strive in the noble effort to show to every man that he has a Saviour; that there is a heaven to which he may come; and to present every one perfect before God. With all its sacrifices and self-denials, therefore, it is an inestimable privilege to be a minister of the gospel —for there is no man who diffuses through a community so much solid happiness; there is no one, the result of whose labours reaches so far into future ages. To a benevolent heart there is no higher privilege than to be permitted to go to *every man*—to the poor, the tempted, the oppressed, the slave, the penitent, and the dying sinner, and to say to him that *he* has a Saviour, that Christ died for *him*, and that, if he will have it so, *he* may have a home in heaven. No matter whom he meets; no matter how debased and degraded he may be to whom he ministers, no matter though it be the poor slave, or the lonely wanderer on pathless sands, or the orphan, or the outcast, the herald of salvation may tell him that there is a heaven for *him* —a Saviour who died for *him*—a God who is ready to pardon and save *his* soul. In such a work, it is a privilege to exhaust our strength; in the performance of the duties of such an office, it is an honour to be permitted to wear out life itself. Doing this, a man when he comes to die will feel that he has not lived in vain; and whatever self-denial he may practise in it; however much comfort, or however many friends he may forsake, all these things will give him no pang of regret when from a bed of death he looks out on the eternal world.

CHAPTER II.

ANALYSIS OF THE CHAPTER.

This entire chapter may be regarded as designed to guard the Colossians against the seductive influence of the false philosophy which tended to draw them away from the gospel. It is evident from the chapter that there were at Colosse, or in the vicinity, professed instructors in religion, who taught an artful and plausible philosophy, adapting themselves to the prejudices of the people, and inculcating opinions that tended to lead them away from the truths which they had embraced. These teachers were probably of Jewish

CHAPTER II.

FOR I would that ye knew what great [1] conflict I have for you, and *for* them at Laodicea, [a] and *for* as many as have not seen my face in the flesh;

[1] or, *fear*; or, *care*.

a Re. 3. 14, &c.

origin, and had adopted many of the arts of a plausible rhetoric, from the prevailing philosophy in that region. See the Intro. § 4. Against the seductive influences of this philosophy, it is the design of this chapter to guard them, and though the apostle does not seem to have intended to pursue an exact logical order, yet the argument in the chapter can be conveniently regarded as consisting of two parts:—A statement of the reasons why they should be on their guard against the arts of that philosophy; and a specification of the particular errors to which they were exposed.

I. A statement of the reasons why they should not allow themselves to be drawn away by the influence of the prevalent philosophy. Vs. 1—15. This also consists of two parts.

A. The importance of the subject. Vs. 1—7.

(1.) The apostle felt great solicitude for them, and for all whom he had not seen, that they might hold the truth in reference to the divine existence and perfections. Vs. 1, 2.

(2.) All the treasures of wisdom and knowledge were in Christ, and it was, therefore, of the greatest importance to hold to the truth respecting him. Ver. 3.

(3.) They were in danger of being led astray by enticing words. Ver. 4.

(4.) Paul says that he was with them in spirit, and he exhorted them, therefore, to remain rooted and grounded in the doctrines which they had received respecting the Saviour. Vs. 5—7.

B. Reasons why they should be steadfast and not drawn away by the influence of false philosophy. Vs. 8—15.

(1.) The danger of depending on traditions and worldly principles in religion; of being 'spoiled' or robbed by philosophy. Ver. 8.

(2.) All that we need to desire is to be found in Christ. Vs. 9, 10.

(3.) We have received through him the true circumcision—the putting away our sins. Ver 11.

(4.) We have been buried with him in baptism, and have solemnly devoted ourselves to him. Ver. 12.

(5.) We have been quickened by him; our sins have been forgiven; and everything that hindered our salvation has been taken out of the way by him, and he has triumphed over our foes. Vs. 13—15.

II. Specification of particular errors to which they were exposed, or of particular things to be avoided. Vs. 16—23.

The chapter closes (vs. 20—23) with an earnest exhortation wholly to avoid these things; not to touch or taste or handle them. However plausible the pretences might be on which they were urged; whatever appearance of wisdom or humility there might be, the apostle assures them that there was no real honour in them, and that they were wholly to be avoided.

1. *For I would that ye knew.* I wish you knew or fully understood. He supposes that this would deeply affect them if they understood the solicitude which he had had on their account. ¶ *What great conflict.*

2 That their hearts might be comforted, being knit together in love, [a] and unto all riches of the full [b] assurance of understanding,

a c. 3. 14. b Is. 32. 17. He. 6. 11.

Marg., *fear*, or *care*. The Greek word is *agony*—ἀγῶνα. It is not, however, the word rendered *agony* in Luke xxii. 44 — ἀγωνία — though that is derived from this. The word is rendered *conflict* in Phil. i. 30; *contention*, 1 Thess. ii. 2; *fight*, 1 Tim. vi. 12. 2 Tim. iv. 7; and *race*, Heb. xii. 1. It properly refers to the combats, contests, struggles, efforts at the public games; the toil and conflict to obtain a victory. It refers here to the anxious care, the mental conflict, the earnest solicitude which he had in their behalf, in view of the dangers to which they were exposed from Judaizing Christians and Pagan philosophy. This mental struggle resembled that which the combatants had at the public games. Comp. Notes on 1 Cor. ix. 25. 27. ¶ *And for them at Laodicea.* For Christians there, who were exposed to similar danger. Laodicea was the capital of Phrygia, in Asia Minor, and a little south of Colosse. See Intro. § 1. 6. Notes on ch. iv. 16. There was a church early planted there—the 'lukewarm' church mentioned in Rev. iii. 14. Being in the vicinity of Colosse, the church there would be exposed to the same perils, and the rebuke in Rev. iii. 14, showed that the fears of Paul were well founded, and that the arts of the false teachers were too successful. ¶ *And for as many as have not seen my face in the flesh.* That is, evidently, in that region. He had, doubtless, a general solicitude for all Christians, but his remark here has reference to those in the neighbourhood of the church at Colosse, or in that church. On the question which has been raised, whether this proves that the apostle Paul had never been at Colosse or Laodicea, see Intro. § 2. 4. This passage does not seem to me to prove that he had not been there. It may mean that he had great solicitude for those Christians there whom he knew, and for all others there, or in the vicinity, even though he was not personally acquainted with them. He may refer (1.) to some churches in the neighbourhood formed since he was there; or (2.) to strangers who had come in there since he was with them; or (3.) to those who had been converted since he was there, and with whom he had no personal acquaintance. For all these he would feel the same solicitude, for they were all exposed to the same danger. To 'see one's face in the flesh,' is a Hebraism meaning to become personally acquainted with him.

2. *That their hearts might be comforted.* Like all other Christians in the times of the apostles, they were doubtless exposed to trials and persecutions. ¶ *Being knit together in love.* The same word which is here used (συμβιβάζω) occurs in Eph. iv. 16, and is rendered *compacted.* See Notes on that place. In Acts ix. 22, it is rendered *proving;* Acts xvi. 10, *assuredly gathering;* 1 Cor. ii. 16, *instruct;* and here, and in ver. 19, *knit together.* It means, properly, *to make to come together*, and hence refers to *a firm union*, as where the hearts of Christians are one. Here it means that the way of comforting each other was by solid christian friendship, and that the means of cementing that was *love.* It was not by a mere outward profession, or by mere speculative faith; it was by a union of affection. ¶ *And unto all riches.* On the meaning of the word *riches*, as used by the apostle Paul, see Notes on Rom. ii. 4. There is a great energy of expression here. The meaning

to the acknowledgment of the mystery [a] of God, and of the Father, and of Christ;

a 1 Jno. 5. 7.

3 In [1] whom are hid all the treasures of wisdom and knowledge.

1 or, *wherein*.

is, that the thing referred to—'the full understanding' of the 'mystery' of religion—was an invaluable possession, like abundant wealth. This passage also shows the object for which they should be united. It should be in order that they might obtain this inestimable wealth. If they were divided in affections, and split up into factions, they could not hope to secure it. ¶ *Of the full assurance of understanding.* This word (πληροφορία) means *firm persuasion, settled conviction.* It occurs only here and in 1 Thess. i. 5. Heb. vi. 11; x. 22, and is rendered by *assurance*, or *full assurance*, in every instance. See the *verb*, however, in Luke i. 1. Rom. iv. 21; xiv. 5. 2 Tim. iv. 5. 17. It was the desire of the apostle that they might have *entire conviction* of the truth of the christian doctrines. ¶ *To the acknowledgment.* So as fully and openly to acknowledge or confess this mystery. ¶ *The mystery.* On the meaning of this word, see Notes on Rom. xi. 25. Eph. i. 9. The meaning is, the doctrine respecting God, which had before been concealed or hidden, but which was now revealed in the gospel. It does not mean that there was anything unintelligible or incomprehensible respecting this doctrine when it was made known. That might be as clear as any other truth. ¶ *Of God.* Of God as he *actually* subsists. This does not mean that the mere fact of the *existence* of God was a 'mystery,' or a truth which had been concealed, for that was not true. But the sense plainly is, that there were truths now made known in the gospel to mankind, about the mode of the divine existence, which had not before been disclosed; and *this* 'mystery' he wished them to retain, or fully acknowledge. The 'mystery,' or the hitherto unrevealed truth, related to the fact that God subsisted in more persons than one, as 'Father,' and as 'Christ.' ¶ *And of the Father.* Or, rather, '*even* of the Father;' for so the word καὶ (*and*) is often used. The apostle does not mean that he wished them to acknowledge the hitherto unrevealed truth respecting 'God' *and* another being called 'the Father;' but respecting 'God' *as* the 'Father,' or of God *as* 'Father' and *as* 'Christ.' ¶ *And of Christ.* As a person of the Godhead. What the apostle wished them to acknowledge was, the full revelation now made known respecting the essential nature of God, as the 'Father,' and as 'Christ.' In relation to this, they were in special danger of being corrupted by the prevalent philosophy, as it is in relation to this that error of christian doctrine usually commences. It should be said, however, that there is great variety of reading in the MSS. on this whole clause, and that many critics (see Rosenmüller) regard it as spurious. I do not see evidence that it is not genuine; and the strain of exhortation of the apostle seems to me to demand it.

3. *In whom.* Marg., *wherein.* The more correct translation is 'in whom.' The reference is doubtless to Christ, as his name is the immediate antecedent, and as what is affirmed here properly appertains to him. ¶ *Are hid.* Like treasures that are concealed or garnered up. It does not mean that none of those 'treasures' had been developed; but that, so to speak, Christ, as Mediator, was the great treasure-house where were to be found all the wis-

4 And this I say, lest any man should beguile [a] you with enticing words.

5 For though I be absent in the flesh, yet am I with you in the Spirit, joying and beholding your order, and the stedfastness of your faith in Christ.

6 As ye have therefore received Christ Jesus the Lord, *so* walk [b] ye in him;

a Mar. 13. 22.

b 1 Jno. 2. 6.

dom and knowledge needful for men. ¶ *All the treasures.* It is common to compare any thing valuable with 'treasures' of silver or gold. The idea here is, that in reference to the wisdom and knowledge needful for us, Christ is what abundant treasures are in reference to the supply of our wants. ¶ *Wisdom.* The wisdom needful for our salvation. Notes, 1 Cor. i. 24. ¶ *And knowledge.* The knowledge which is requisite to guide us in the way to life. Christ is able to instruct us in all that it is desirable for us to know, so that it is not necessary for us to apply to philosophy, or to the teachings of men.

4. *And this I say.* Respecting the character and sufficiency of the truth revealed in Christ. ¶ *Lest any man should beguile you.* Deceive you, lead you away from the truth. ¶ *With enticing words.* Artful words, smooth and plausible arguments, such as were employed by the Greek sophists and rhetoricians.

5. *For though I be absent in the flesh, yet am I with you in the spirit.* That is, I *seem* to see you; I feel as if I were there, and were looking upon you; and I have the same solicitude as if I were there, and saw all the danger which exists that your beautiful order and harmony should be disturbed by the influence of false philosophy. See Notes on 1 Cor. v. 3. The word 'spirit,' here, does not refer to the Holy Spirit, or to any *inspiration* by which the apostle was enabled to see them; but it is equivalent to what we mean when we say, 'My *heart* is with you.' He *seemed* to be beholding them. ¶ *Joying and beholding your order.* That is, I rejoice *as if* I *saw* your order. He had such confidence that everything would be done among them as became Christians, that he could rejoice as if he actually saw it.

6. *As ye have therefore received Christ Jesus the Lord.* Have received him by faith as your Saviour, or as you were instructed respecting his rank, character, and work. The *object* here is to induce them not to swerve from the views which they had of Christ when he was made known to them. They had at first probably received their ideas of the Saviour from the apostle himself (see the Intro.); and, at any rate, the apostle designs to assure them that the views which they had when they 'received him,' were founded in truth. ¶ *So walk in him.* Continue in those views of Christ; live in the maintenance of them; let them regulate your whole conduct. The word *walk*, in the Scriptures, is used to denote the manner of life; and the sense here is, that they should live and act wholly under the influence of the conceptions which they had of the Saviour when they first embraced him. The particle '*so*' is supplied by our translators, and rather weakens the sense. No stress should be laid on it, as is often done. The meaning is, simply, 'Since you have received Christ as your Lord as he was preached to you, hold fast the doctrine which you have received, and do not permit yourselves to be turned aside by any Jew-

7 Rooted [a] and built up in him, [b] and stablished in the faith, as ye have been taught, abounding therein with thanksgiving.

8 Beware [c] lest any man spoil you through philosophy and vain deceit, after the tradition of men, after the [1] rudiments of the world, and not after Christ:

9 For in him [d] dwelleth all the fulness of the Godhead bodily.

a Ep. 3. 17. b Jno. 15. 4, 5. c Ro. 16. 17. Ep. 5. 6. He. 13. 9. [1] or, *elements*. d c. 1. 19.

---

ish teachers, or teachers of philosophy.'

7. *Rooted—in him.* As a tree strikes its roots deep in the earth, so our faith should strike deep into the doctrine respecting the Saviour. See the phrase here used explained in the parallel place in Eph. iii. 17. ¶ *And established in the faith, as ye have been taught.* To wit, by the founders of the church, and by those faithful ministers who had succeeded them. Notes, ch. i. 7. ¶ *Abounding therein with thanksgiving.* Expressing overflowing thanks to God that you have been made acquainted with truths so precious and glorious. If there is anything for which we ought to be thankful, it is for the knowledge of the great truths respecting our Lord and Saviour.

8. *Beware lest any man spoil you.* The word *spoil* now commonly means, *to corrupt, to cause to decay and perish*, as fruit is *spoiled* by keeping too long, or paper by wetting, or hay by a long rain, or crops by mildew. But the Greek word here used means to spoil in the sense of *plunder, rob*, as when plunder is taken in war. The meaning is, 'Take heed lest any one plunder or rob you of your faith and hope by philosophy.' These false teachers would strip them of their faith and hope, as an invading army would rob a country of all that was valuable. ¶ *Through philosophy.* The Greek philosophy prevailed much in the regions around Colosse, and perhaps also the oriental or Gnostic philosophy. See the Intro. They were exposed to the influences of these plausible systems. They consisted much of speculations respecting the nature of the divine existence; and the danger of the Colossians was, that they would rely rather on the deductions of that specious *reasoning*, than on what they had been *taught* by their christian teachers. ¶ *And vain deceit.* Mere fallacy. The idea is, that the doctrines which were advanced in those systems were maintained by plausible, not by solid arguments; by considerations not fitted to lead to the truth, but to lead astray. ¶ *After the tradition of men.* There appear to have been two sources of danger to which the Christians at Colosse were exposed, and to which the apostle in these cautions alludes, though he is not careful to distinguish them. The one was that arising from the Grecian philosophy the other, from Jewish opinions The latter is that to which he refers here. The Jews depended much on tradition (see Notes on Matt. xv. 2), and many of those traditions would have tended much to corrupt the gospel of Christ. ¶ *After the rudiments of the world.* Marg., *elements.* See this explained in the Notes on Gal. iv. 3. ¶ *And not after Christ.* Not such as Christ taught.

9. *For in him dwelleth.* That is, this was the great and central doctrine that was to be maintained about Christ, that all the fulness of the Godhead dwelt in him. Every system which denied this was a denial of the doctrine which they had been taught; and against everything

10 And ye are complete [a] in him, which is the head [b] of all principality and power;

a He. 5. 9.

b 1 Pe. 3. 22.

that would go to undermine this, they were especially to be on their guard. Almost all heresy has been begun by some form of the denial of the great central truth of the incarnation of the Son of God. ¶ *All the fulness.* Notes, ch. i. 19. ¶ *Of the Godhead.* Of the Divinity, the divine nature — θεότης. The word is one that properly denotes the divine nature and perfections. *Robinson, Lex.* It occurs nowhere else in the New Testament. ¶ *Bodily.* σωματικῶς. This word also is found nowhere else in the New Testament, though the adjective *bodily*—σωματικός—occurs twice: Luke iii. 22, 'in a *bodily* shape;' and 1 Tim. iv. 8, 'for *bodily* exercise profiteth little.' The word means, 'having a bodily appearance, instead of existing or appearing in a spiritual form;' and the fair sense of the phrase is, that the fulness of the divine nature became incarnate, and was indwelling in the body of the Redeemer. It does not meet the case to say, as Crellius does, that the 'whole divine will was in him,' for the word θεότης—*godhead*—does not mean the *will* of God; and it is as certainly true that the inspired prophets were under the control of the divine will, as that the Saviour was. Nor can it mean, as Socinus supposes, that the fulness of divine *knowledge* dwelt in him, for this is not the proper meaning of the word (θεότης) *godhead;* nor can it mean, for the same reason, that a fulness of *divine gifts* was intrusted to him. The language is such as would be obviously employed on the supposition that God became incarnate, and appeared in human form; and there is no other idea which it so naturally expresses, nor is there any other which it can be *made* to express without a forced construction. The meaning is, that it was not any *one* attribute of the Deity that became incarnate in the Saviour; that he was not merely endowed with the knowledge, *or* the power, *or* the wisdom of God; but that the whole Deity thus became incarnate, and appeared in human form. Comp. John xiv. 9; i. 18. No language could, therefore, more clearly demonstrate the divinity of Christ. Of what mere man —of what angel, could it be used?

10. *And ye are complete in him.* Having no need, for the purposes of salvation, of any aid to be derived from the philosophy of the Greeks, or the traditions of the Jews. All that is necessary to secure your salvation is to be found in the Lord Jesus. There is a *completion*, or a *filling up*, in him, so as to leave nothing wanting. This is true in respect (1.) to the *wisdom* which is needful to guide us; (2.) the *atonement* to be made for sin; (3.) the *merit* by which a sinner can be justified; and (4.) the *grace* which is needful to sustain us in the trials, and to aid us in the duties, of life. Comp. Notes on 1 Cor. i. 30. There is no necessity, therefore, that we should look to the aid of philosophy, as if there was a defect in the teachings of the Saviour; or to human strength, as if he were unable to save us; or to the merits of the saints, as if those of the Redeemer were not sufficient to meet all our wants. The sentiment advanced in this verse would overthrow the whole papal doctrine of the merits of the saints, and, of course, the whole doctrine of papal 'indulgences.' ¶ *Which is the head.* See Notes on Eph. i. 21, 22.

11 In whom also ye are circumcised with the circumcision [a] made without hands, in putting off the body of the sins of the flesh by the circumcision of Christ;

12 Buried [b] with him in baptism, wherein also ye are risen with *him* through the faith of the operation [c] of God, who hath raised him from the dead.

13 And [d] you, being dead in your sins and the uncircumcision

a Je. 4. 4. Ph. 3. 3. b Ro. 6. 4, 5. c Ep. 1. 19. d Ep. 2. 1, 5, 11.

11. *In whom.* In connection with whom, or in virtue of whose religion. ¶ *Ye are circumcised.* You have received that which was designed to be represented by circumcision—the putting away of sin. Notes, Phil. iii. 3. ¶ *With the circumcision made without hands.* That made in the heart by the renunciation of all sin. The Jewish teachers insisted on the necessity of the literal circumcision in order to salvation (comp. Eph. ii. 11); and hence this subject is so often introduced into the writings of Paul, and he is at so much pains to show that, by believing in Christ, all was obtained which was required in order to salvation. Circumcision was an ordinance by which it was denoted that all sin was to be cut off or renounced, and that he who was circumcised was to be devoted to God and to a holy life. All this, the apostle says, was obtained by the gospel; and, consequently, they had all that was denoted by the ancient rite of circumcision. What Christians had obtained, moreover, related *to the heart;* it was not a mere ordinance pertaining *to the flesh.* ¶ *In putting off the body of the sins of the flesh.* That is, in renouncing the deeds of the flesh, or becoming holy. The word '*body,*' here, seems to be used with reference to circumcision. In that ordinance, the *body of the* FLESH was subjected to the rite; with Christians, it is the *body of* SIN that is cut off. ¶ *By the circumcision of Christ.* Not by the fact that Christ was circumcised, but that we have that kind of circumcision which Christ established, to wit, *the renouncing of sin.* The idea of the apostle here seems to be, that since we have thus been enabled by Christ to renounce sin, and to devote ourselves to God, we should not be induced by any plausible arguments to return to an ordinance pertaining to the flesh, as if that were needful for salvation.

12. *Buried with him in baptism.* See Notes on Rom. vi. 4. ¶ *Wherein also.* In which ordinance, or by virtue of that which is signified by the ordinance. ¶ *Ye are risen with* him. From the death of sin to the life of religion. Notes, Rom. vi. 4, 5. Comp. Notes, Eph. ii. 5, 6. ¶ *Through the faith of the operation of God.* By a firm belief on the agency of God in raising him up; that is, a belief of the fact that God has raised him from the dead. The resurrection of Christ is often represented as the foundation of all our hopes; and, as he was raised from the grave to die no more, so, in virtue of that, *we* are raised from the death of sin to eternal spiritual life. The *belief* of this is shown by our baptism, whatever be *the mode* in which that ordinance is performed, and as *well* shown in one mode as another.

13. *And you, being dead in your sins.* Notes, Eph. ii. 1. ¶ *And the uncircumcision of your flesh.* That is, Gentiles, and giving unrestrained indulgence to the desires of the flesh. They lived as those who had not by any religious rite or covenant brought themselves under obligations to lead holy lives. ¶ *Hath he quickened.* Notes, Eph. ii. 1 ¶ *Together with*

of your flesh, hath he quickened together with him, having forgiven you all trespasses;

14 Blotting [a] out the handwriting of ordinances that was against us, which was contrary to

a Ep. 2. 15, 16.

him. In virtue of his being restored to life. That is, the resurrection of the Lord Jesus was the means of imparting to us spiritual life.

14. *Blotting out the handwriting.* The word rendered *handwriting* means something written by the hand, a manuscript; and here, probably, the *writings* of the Mosaic law, or the law appointing many ordinances or observances in religion. The allusion is probably to a written contract, in which we bind ourselves to do any work, or to make a payment, and which remains in force against us until the bond is cancelled. That might be done, either by blotting out the names, or by drawing lines through it, or, as appears to have been practised in the East, by driving a nail through it. The Jewish ceremonial law is here represented as such a contract, binding those under it to its observance, until it was nailed to the cross. The meaning here is, that the burdensome requirements of the Mosaic law are abolished, and that its necessity is superseded, by the death of Christ. His death had the same effect, in reference to those ordinances, *as if* they had been blotted from the statute-book. This it did by fulfilling them, by introducing a more perfect system, and by rendering their observance no longer necessary, since all that they were designed to typify had been now accomplished in a better way. Comp. Notes, Eph. ii. 15. ¶ *Of ordinances.* Prescribing the numerous rites and ceremonies of the Jewish religion. ¶ *That was against us.* That is, against our peace, happiness, comfort; or, in other words, which was oppressive and burdensome. Comp. Notes, Acts xv. 10. Those ordinances bound and fettered the soul, restrained the expansive spirit of true piety which seeks the salvation of all alike, and thus operated as a *hindrance* to the enlarged spirit of true religion. Thus they really operated *against* the truly pious *Jew*, whose religion would lead him to seek the salvation of the world; and to the *Gentile*, since he was not in a situation to avail himself of them, and since they would be burdensome if he could. It is in this sense, probably, that the apostle uses the word '*us*,' as referring to all, and as cramping and restraining the true nature of religion. ¶ *Which was contrary to us.* Operated as a hindrance, or obstruction, in the matter of religion. The ordinances of the Mosaic law were *necessary*, in order to introduce the gospel; but they were always burdensome. They were to be confined to one people; and, if they were continued, they would operate to prevent the spread of the true religion around the world. Comp. Notes on 2 Cor. iii. 7. 9. Hence the exulting language of the apostle in view of the fact that they were now taken away, and that the benefits of religion might be diffused all over the world. The gospel contains nothing which is '*against*,' or '*contrary to*,' the true interest and happiness of any nation or any class of men ¶ *And took it out of the way.* Gr., 'Out of the midst;' that is, he wholly removed it. He has removed the obstruction, so that it no longer prevents union and harmony between the Jews and the Gentiles. ¶ *Nailing it to his cross.* *As if* he had nailed it to his cross, so that it would be entirely removed out of our way. The death of Jesus had the same effect, in regard to the rites and institutions of the Mosaic religion, *as*

us, and took it out of the way, nailing it to his cross;

15 *And* having [a] spoiled principalities and powers, he made a

[a] Ps. 68. 18. Is. 53. 12. Lu. 10. 18. 11. 22. Jno. 12. 31. He. 2. 14.

if they had been affixed to his cross. It is said that there is an allusion here to the ancient method by which a bond or obligation was cancelled, by driving a nail through it, and affixing it to a post. This was practised, says Grotius, in Asia. In a somewhat similar manner, in our banks now, a sharp instrument, like the blade of a knife, is driven through a check, making a hole through it, and furnishing to the teller of the bank a sign or evidence that it has been paid. If this be the meaning, then the expression here denotes that the obligation of the Jewish institutions ceased on the death of Jesus, *as if* he had taken them and nailed them to his own cross, in the manner in which a bond was cancelled.

15. And *having spoiled.* Plundered; as a victorious army does a conquered country. Notes on ver. 8. The terms used in this verse are all military, and the idea is, that Christ has completely subdued our enemies by his death. A complete victory was achieved by his death, so that everything is now in subjection to him, and we have nothing to fear. ¶ *Principalities and powers.* Notes, Eph. i. 21; vi. 12. The 'principalities and powers' here referred to, are the formidable enemies that had held man in subjection, and prevented his serving God. There can be no doubt, I think, that the apostle refers to the ranks of fallen, evil spirits which had usurped a dominion over the world. Notes, John xii. 31. Eph. ii. 2. The Saviour, by his death, wrested the dominion from them, and seized upon what they had captured as a conqueror seizes upon his prey. Satan and his legions had invaded the earth and drawn its inhabitants into captivity, and subjected them to their evil reign. Christ, by his death, subdues the invaders and recaptures those whom they had subdued. ¶ *He made a show of them openly.* As a conqueror, returning from a victory, displays in a triumphal procession the kings and princes whom he has taken, and the spoils of victory. This was commonly done when a 'triumph' was decreed for a conqueror. On such occasions, it sometimes happened that a considerable number of prisoners were led along amidst the scenes of triumph. See Notes on 2 Cor. ii. 14. Paul says that this was now done '*openly*'—that is, it was in the face of the whole universe—a grand victory; a glorious triumph over all the powers of hell. It does not refer to any public procession or display on the earth; but to the grand victory as achieved in view of the universe, by which Christ, as a conqueror, dragged Satan and his legions at his triumphal car. Comp. Rom. xvi. 20. ¶ *Triumphing over them in it.* Marg., 'or, *himself.*' Either 'by the cross,' or 'by himself.' Or, it may mean, as Rosenmüller suggests, that 'God (ver. 12) triumphed over these foes in *him;* i. e., *in Christ.*' The sense is substantially the same, that this triumph was effected by the atonement made for sin by the Redeemer. See the word *triumph* explained in the Notes on 2 Cor. ii. 14. The meaning of all this is, that since Christ has achieved for us such a victory, and has subdued all the foes of man, we should not be led captive, but should regard ourselves as freemen. We should not be made again the slaves of custom, or habit, or ritual observances, or superstitious

shew of them openly, triumphing over them in [1] it.

16 Let no man therefore judge [a] you in [2] meat, or in drink, or in [3] respect of an holy day, or of the new moon, or of the sabbath *days*;

[1] or, *himself*. [a] Ro. 14. 10, 13. [2] or, *for eating and drinking*. [3] or, *part*.

rites, or anything whatever that has its origin in the kingdom of darkness. We are bound to assert and to use our freedom, and should not allow any hostile power in the form of philosophy or false teaching of any kind, to *plunder* or '*spoil*' us. Ver. 8. The Christian is a freeman. His great Captain has subdued all his enemies, and we should not allow them again to set up their dark empire over our souls. The *argument* of the apostle in these verses (13—15) is derived from what Christ has done for us. He mentions *four* things. (1.) He has given us spiritual life; (2.) he has forgiven all our trespasses; (3.) he has blotted out or abolished the 'ordinances' that were against us; and (4.) he has triumphed over all our foes. From all this he infers (vs. 16, seq.) that we should not be made captive or subdued by any of the rites of superstition, or any of the influences of the kingdom of darkness.

16. *Let no man, therefore, judge you.* Comp. Notes on Rom. xiv. 10. 13. The word *judge* here is used in the sense of pronouncing a sentence. The meaning is, 'since you have thus been delivered by Christ from the evils which surrounded you; since you have been freed from the observances of the law, let no one sit in judgment on you, or claim the right to decide for you in those matters. You are not responsible to *man* for your conduct, but to Christ; and no man has a right to impose that on you as a burden from which he has made you free.' ¶ *In meat.* Marg., *for eating and drinking.* The meaning is, 'in respect to the various articles of food and drink.' There is reference here, undoubtedly, to the distinctions which the Jews made on this subject, implying that an effort had been made by Jewish teachers to show them that the Mosaic laws were binding on all. ¶ *Or in respect of a holy day.* Marg., *part.* The meaning is, 'in the part, or the *particular* of a holy day; that is, in respect to it.' The word rendered 'holy-day'—ἑορτή—means properly *a feast or festival;* and the allusion here is to the festivals of the Jews. The sense is, that no one had a right to impose their observance on Christians, or to condemn them if they did not keep them. They had been delivered from that obligation by the death of Christ. Ver. 14. ¶ *Or of the new moon.* On the appearance of the new moon, among the Hebrews, in addition to the daily sacrifices, two bullocks, a ram, and seven sheep, with a meat-offering, were required to be presented to God. Num. x. 10; xxviii. 11—14. The new moon in the beginning of the month Tisri (October) was the beginning of their civil year, and was commanded to be observed as a festival. Lev. xxiii. 24, 25. ¶ *Or of the Sabbath* days. Gr., 'of the Sabbaths.' The word *Sabbath* in the Old Testament is applied not only to the seventh day, but to all the days of holy rest that were observed by the Hebrews, and particularly to the beginning and close of their great festivals. There is, doubtless, reference to those days in this place, as the word is used in the plural number, and the apostle does not refer particularly to *the* Sabbath properly so called. There is no evidence from this passage that he would teach that there was no obligation to observe *any* holy time, for there is not the slightest reason to believe that he meant to teach that one of

17 Which are a shadow [a] of things to come; but the body *is* of Christ.

18 Let [b] no man [1] beguile you of your reward, [2] in a voluntary humility and worshipping of an-

a He. 8. 5.

b Re. 3. 11. [1] or, *judge against you.* [2] *being a voluntary in humility.*

the ten commandments had ceased to be binding on mankind. If he had used the word in the singular number—'THE *Sabbath*,' it would then, of course, have been clear that he meant to teach that that commandment had ceased to be binding, and that a Sabbath was no longer to be observed. But the use of the term in the plural number, and the connection, show that he had his eye on the great number of days which were observed by the Hebrews as festivals, as a part of their ceremonial and typical law, and not to the *moral* law, or the ten commandments. No part of the moral law—no one of the ten commandments could be spoken of as '*a shadow* of good things to come.' These commandments are, from the nature of moral law, of perpetual and universal obligation.

17. *Which are a shadow of things to come.* See Notes on Heb. viii. 5; x. 1. They were only a dim outline of future things, not the reality. ¶ *But the body* is *of Christ.* The reality, the substance. All that they signified is *of* or *in* Christ. Between those things themselves which are in Christ, and those which only represented or prefigured them, there is as much difference as there is between a body and a shadow; a solid substance and a mere outline. Having now, therefore, the *thing itself*, the shadow can be to us of no value; and that having come which was prefigured, that which was designed merely to represent it, is no longer binding.

18. *Let no man beguile you of your reward.* Marg., *judge against you.* The word here used—καταβραβευέτω—occurs nowhere else in the New Testament. It is a word which was employed with reference to the distribution of prizes at the Grecian games, and means, *to give the prize against any one, to deprive of the palm.* Hence it means *to deprive of a due reward;* and the sense here is, that they were to be on their guard lest the 'reward'—the crown of victory to which they looked forward—should be wrested from them by the arts of others. That would be done if they should be persuaded to turn back, or to falter in the race. The only way to secure the prize was to hold on in the race which they were then running; but if they yielded to the philosophy of the Greeks, and the teachings of the Jews, they would be defrauded of this reward as certainly as a racer at the games would if the crown of victory should be unjustly awarded to another. In this case, too, as real injustice would be done, though the apostle does not say it would be in the same manner. Here it would be by art; in the case of the racer it would be by a wrong decision—*but in either case the crown was lost.* This exhortation has the more force from this consideration. Against an unjust *judge* we could have no power; but we may take care that the reward be not wrested from us by *fraud.* ¶ *In a voluntary humility.* Marg., '*being a voluntary in humility.*' Tindal renders this, 'Let no man make you shoot at a wrong mark, which, after his own imagination, walketh in the humbleness of angels.' The word used here (ταπεινοφροσύνη) means *lowliness of mind, modesty, humbleness of deportment;* and the apostle refers, doubtless, to the spirit assumed by those against

gels, intruding [a] into those things which he hath not seen, vainly puffed up by his fleshly mind;

a De. 29. 29. Job 38. 2.

whom he would guard the Colossians—the spirit of modesty or of humble inquirers. The meaning is, that they would not announce their opinions with dogmatic certainty, but they would put on the appearance of great modesty. In this way, they would become really more dangerous—for no false teachers are so dangerous as those who assume the aspect of great humility, and who manifest great reverence for divine things. The word rendered 'voluntary' here—θέλων—does not, properly, belong to the word rendered 'humility.' It rather appertains to the subsequent part of the sentence, and means that the persons referred to were *willing*, or had pleasure in attempting, to search into the hidden and abstruse things of religion. They were desirous of appearing to do this with an humble spirit—even with the modesty of an angel—but still they had pleasure in that profound and dangerous kind of inquiry. ¶ *And worshipping of angels.*—θρησκίᾳ τῶν ἀγγέλων. This does not mean, as it seems to me, that they would *themselves worship angels*, or that they would teach others to do it—for there is no reason to believe this. Certainly the Jewish teachers, whom the apostle seems to have had particularly in his eye, would not do it; nor is there any evidence that *any* class of false teachers would deliberately teach that *angels* were to be worshipped. The reference is rather to the profound reverence; the spirit of lowly piety which *the angels evinced*, and to the fact that the teachers referred to *would assume* the same spirit, and were, therefore, the more dangerous. They would come professing profound regard for the great mysteries of religion, and for the incomprehensible perfections of the divinity, and would approach the subject professedly with the awful veneration which the angels have when they 'look into these things.' 1 Pet. i. 12. There was no bold, irreverent, or confident declamation, but the danger in the case arose from the fact that they *assumed* so much the aspect of modest piety; so much the appearance of the lowly devotion of angelic beings. The word here rendered *worship*—θρησκεία—occurs in the New Testament only here, in Acts xxvi. 5; and James i. 26, 27, in each of which places it is rendered *religion*. It means here the religion, or the spirit of humble reverence and devotion which is evinced by the angels; and this accords well with the meaning in James i. 26, 27. ¶ *Intruding into those things which he hath not seen.* Or *inquiring* into them. The word used here (ἐμβατεύων) means to go in, or enter; then to investigate, to inquire. It has not, properly, the meaning of *intruding*, or of impertinent inquiry (see Passow), and I do not see that the apostle meant to characterize the inquiry here as such. He says that it was the object of their investigations to look, with great professed modesty and reverence, into those things which are not visible to the eye of mortals. The 'things' which seem here to be particularly referred to, are the abstruse questions respecting the mode of the divine subsistence; the ranks, orders, and employments of angelic beings; and the obscure doctrines relating to the divine government and plans. These questions comprised most of the subjects of inquiry in the Oriental and Grecian philosophy, and inquiries on these the apostle apprehended would tend to draw away the mind from the 'simplicity that is in Christ.' Of these subjects what *can* be known more than is revealed?

19 And not holding the Head,[a] from which all the body by joints and bands having nourishment ministered, and knit together, increaseth with the increase of God.

20 Wherefore, if ye be dead with Christ from the [1] rudiments of the world, why, as though living in the world, are ye subject to ordinances,

21 (Touch not; taste not; handle not;

a Ep. 4. 15, 16.

1 or, *elements.*

¶ *Vainly puffed up by his fleshly mind.* Notwithstanding the avowed 'humility,' the modesty, the *angelic reverence*, yet the mind was full of vain conceit, and self-confident, carnal wisdom. The two things are by no means incompatible—the men apparently most meek and modest being sometimes the most bold in their speculations, and the most reckless in regard to the great landmarks of truth. It is not so with *true* modesty, and *real* 'angelic veneration,' but all this is sometimes assumed for the purpose of deceiving; and sometimes there is a native appearance of modesty which is by no means an index of the true feelings of the soul. The most meek and modest men in appearance are sometimes the most proud and reckless in their investigations of the doctrines of religion.

19. *And not holding the Head.* Not holding the true doctrine respecting the Great Head of the church, the Lord Jesus Christ. Notes, Eph. i. 22. This is regarded here as essential to the maintenance of all the other doctrines of religion. He who has just views of the Redeemer will not be in much danger of erring respecting the other points of religious belief. ¶ *From which all the body*, &c. This passage is almost word for word the same as in Eph. iv. 15, 16. See it explained in the Notes there.

20. *Wherefore.* In view of all that has been said. If it be true that you are really dead to the world, why do you act *as if* you still lived under the principles of the world? ¶ *If ye be dead with Christ.* If you are dead to the world in virtue of his death. The apostle here, as elsewhere, speaks of a very close union with Christ. We died with him; that is, such was the efficacy of his death, and such is our union with him, that *we* became dead also to the world. Notes, Rom. vi. 2. 4. 8. 11. ¶ *From the rudiments of the world.* Marg., *elements.* The elements or principles which are of a worldly nature, and which reign among worldly men. See Notes on Gal. iv. 3. ¶ *Why, as though living in the world.* Why do you allow them to influence you, as though you were living and acting under those worldly principles? They ought no more to do it, than the things of this world influence those who are in their graves. ¶ *Are ye subject to ordinances.* The rites and ceremonies of the Jewish religion. See Notes, Gal. v. 1—4.

21. *Touch not; taste not; handle not.* These words seem intended as a *specimen* of the kind of ordinances which the apostle refers to, or an *imitation* of the language of the Jewish teachers in regard to various kinds of food and drink. 'Why are ye subject to ordinances of various kinds, *such as* this—Touch not, taste not, handle not?' That is, such as prohibit you from even touching certain kinds of food, or tasting certain kinds of drink, or handling certain prohibited things. The rapid succession of the words here, without any connecting particle, is supposed to denote the *eagerness* of the persons who imposed this injunction,

22 Which all are to perish with the using;) after the commandments and doctrines of men?

and their *earnestness* in warning others from contaminating themselves with the prohibited things. Many injunctions of this kind are found in the writings of the Jewish Rabbins; and the ancient Jewish sect of the Essenes (Notes, Matt. iii. 7) abounded in precepts of this kind. See *Schoetgen*, and *Pict. Bib. in loc.* 'They allowed themselves no food that was pleasant to the taste, but ate dry, coarse bread, and drank only water. Many of them ate nothing until sunset, and, if any one touched them who did not belong to their sect, they washed themselves as if they had been most deeply defiled. Perhaps there was at Colosse a society of this kind, as there were in many other places out of Judea; and, if there was, it is not improbable that many Christians imitated them in the peculiarity of their rules and observances.' Comp. Jenning's Jew. Ant. i. 471, and Ros. Alt. u. neu. Morgenland, *in loc.* If this be the correct interpretation, then these are not the words of the apostle, forbidding Christians to have anything to do with these ordinances, but are introduced as a *specimen* of the manner in which they who enjoined the observance of those ordinances pressed the subject on others. There were certain things which they prohibited, in conformity with what they understood to be the law of Moses; and they were constantly saying, in regard to them, 'do not touch them, taste them, handle them.' These words are often used as a kind of motto in reference to the use of intoxicating drinks. They express very well what is held by the friends of total abstinence; but it is obvious that they had no such reference as used by the apostle, nor should they be alleged as an *authority*, or as an *argument*, in the question about the propriety or impropriety of the use of spirituous liquors. They may as well be employed in reference to anything else as that, and would have no *authority* in either case. Intoxicating drinks should be abstained from; but the obligation to do it should be made to rest on solid arguments, and not on passages of Scripture like this. This passage could with more plausibility be pressed into the service of the enemies of the total abstinence societies, than into their support; but it really has nothing to do with the subject, one way or the other.

22. *Which all are to perish with the using.* This is commonly marked as a part of the parenthesis, or the quotation; and there is considerable difficulty in ascertaining its true meaning. It seems most probable that these are the words of the apostle himself, thrown in in the rapidity of composition, and that they are not to be connected with the phrase 'touch not,' &c. If so, the idea is, that it cannot be of so much consequence as the Jewish teachers supposed, to mark distinctly the difference between meats and drinks. They were all to perish with the use of them. Nothing was permanent about them. It could really then be of no great importance what was eaten, or what was drunk, provided it was not in itself injurious. These ordinances had a value among the Hebrews when it was designed to keep them as a distinct people; but they had no value in themselves, so as to make them binding on all mankind. To suppose this, was the common error of the Jews; and hence the apostle so frequently laboured to show that the Jewish rites had no permanent value. See Notes on Rom. xiv. 1—6. 1 Cor. viii. Comp. Notes on Matt. xv. 17, 18.

23 Which things have indeed a shew of wisdom in will-worship,

According to this interpretation, the 21st verse should be regarded as expressing the common maxim of the Jewish teachers, and the clause before us as the words of the apostle, and should be marked as a parenthesis. So it is marked in Hahn's Ed. of the New Testament. ¶ *After the commandments and doctrines of men.* Many of the ordinances on which the Jews insisted were those which were handed down by tradition. They depended on human authority only, and, of course, should not bind the conscience. Others take the words here to mean, 'All which things tend to the corruption of religion (*Doddridge*), or are cause of destruction or condemnation (*Rob. Lex.*), by the use of these things, according to the commandments and doctrines of these men.'

23. *Which things.* Which scrupulous observance of the numerous precepts enjoining rites and ceremonies, the observance of days, and the distinctions between meats and drinks. ¶ *Have indeed a show of wisdom.* Have a great appearance of piety, and of regard for the will of God. They have a show of 'wisdom,' too, or of a deep acquaintance with divine things. They who insist on them *appear* to be learned in what constitutes religion, and to have a deep insight into its mysteries. Doubtless they who urged the obligation of these things laid claim to uncommon acquaintance with the nature of religion, and urged the observance of these things on the ground of their tendency to promote piety, just as they always do who insist much on the observance of religious rites and ceremonies. ¶ *In will-worship.* Voluntary worship; *i. e.*, worship beyond what God strictly requires—supererogatory service. Probably many of these things they did not urge as being strictly *required*, but as conducing greatly to piety. The plea doubtless was, that piety might be promoted by service rendered *beyond* what was absolutely enjoined, and that thus there would be evinced a spirit of uncommon piety—a readiness not only to obey *all* that God required, but even to go *beyond* this, and to render him *voluntary* service. There is much plausibility in this; and this has been the foundation of the appointment of the fasts and festivals of the church; of penances and self-inflicted tortures; of painful vigils and pilgrimages; of works of supererogation, and of the merits of the 'saints.' A large part of the corruptions of religion have arisen from this plausible, but deceitful argument. God knew best what things it was most conducive to piety for his people to observe; and we are most safe when we adhere most closely to what he has appointed, and observe no more days and ordinances than he has directed. There is much apparent piety about these things; but there is much wickedness of heart at the bottom, and there is nothing that more tends to corrupt pure religion. ¶ *And humility.* Notes on ver. 18. There is a great show of reverence for divine things in the manner in which they pursue their investigations, and in their humble and meek compliance with painful rites and ceremonies; in fastings, abstinence, and penances. Under all this there lurks often the worst kind of pride; for

> "Pride may be pampered while the flesh grows lean."

¶ *And neglecting the body.* Putting on sackcloth and ashes; subjecting it to painful fastings and penances; appearing in a form of squalid poverty, *as if* the body were not worth regarding, and *as if* the attention were so much engrossed by the no-

and humility, and [1] neglecting of the body; not in any honour to the satisfying of the flesh.

[1] or, *punishing;* or, *not sparing.*

oler care of the soul, as to be entirely regardless of the body. Yet, we may observe, (1.) God made the body as well as the soul, and has shown *his* care of it by its "being fearfully and wonderfully made," and by all the provision which he has made for its wants. (2.) Religion pertains to the body as well as the soul, and should teach a man properly to regard it. Man is bound *so* to take care of the body, as to have the most health and the longest life possible in the service of his Creator, and so as to be able to employ it in the best manner. There is no religion in ragged or squalid clothing, in a dirty face, in offensive personal habits, in filth and defilement, and in setting at defiance the decencies of life. (3.) Much affected sanctity may exist where there is a most proud and corrupt heart. A long face, a demure countenance, a studied disregard of the decencies of dress and the courtesies of life, *as if* they were unworthy of notice, may be the *exponent* of the most hateful pride, and of the basest purposes of the soul. A man should be on his guard always against one who, under pretence of extraordinary sanctity, professes to despise the ordinary dress and usages of society. ¶ *Not in any honour.* That is, there is no real honour in these things; there is nothing to ennoble and elevate the soul; nothing that is to be commended. ¶ *To the satisfying of the flesh.* The only effect is, to satisfy or please the flesh; that is, the carnal and corrupt nature, for so the word *flesh* is often used in the Scriptures. The effect of these observances, on which so much stress is laid as if they would promote piety, is merely to gratify pride, self-righteousness, the love of distinction, and the other carnal propensities of our nature. There *seems* to be a great deal of humility and piety in them; there is really little else than pride, selfishness, and ambition.

REMARKS.

1. We should feel a deep interest for the welfare of other Christians, even those whom we have never seen. Vs. 1, 2. All belong to the same family, have the same enemies to contend with, are engaged in the same warfare, are travelling to the same heaven. By our prayers and sympathy, we may often do much good to those whom we shall never see till we meet them in heaven.

2. We should be on our guard against the seductive arts of false teachers. They are often plausible; they can urge arguments which we may not be able to answer; they may have much more learning than we have; and they may put on the appearance of great humility and of real piety. Vs. 3, 4.

3. It is, in general, a safe rule for a Christian to abide by the views which he had on the great subjects of religion when he became converted. Ver. 6. Then the heart was tender and soft — like wax — and received the impression which the Spirit made on it. There are some things in which the *heart* judges better than the *head;* and in which we are quite as likely to go right if we follow the former as we are the latter. In relation to the performance of many of the duties of life—the duties of kindness and charity—the heart is often a more safe guide than the head; and so in many things pertaining more immediately to religion, a man is more likely to judge right if he follows the promptings of his feelings in the happiest moments of piety, than he is to wait for the more cool and cautious course of argument.

The same thing may be true even of many of the *doctrines* of religion. When a poor sinner trembles on the verge of hell, he feels that none but an *Almighty* Saviour can deliver him, and he goes and commits himself to Jesus *as God*—and he is not in much danger of erring in that. He will be more likely to be drawn aside from the truth by the artful reasonings of the advocates of error, than he will by his *feelings* at that moment.

4. Our views of the 'mystery of God'—of the divine nature, and especially of the rank and character of Christ, will determine *all* our views of theology. Ver. 2. This *has* been so in all ages; and however it may be accounted for, the fact is undoubted, that if at any time we can ascertain what are the prevalent views of Christ, we can easily see what is the prevailing character of the theology of that age. The influence of this will be felt on the views which are held of the native character of man; of regeneration, the divine purposes, the nature of holiness, and the retributions beyond the grave. Hence, the reason why the apostle Paul insisted so much on this, and urged so earnestly the importance of adhering to just views of the Saviour.

5. Christ has laid us under the highest obligations to love and serve him. Vs. 11—15. He has enabled us to put off our sins; he has raised us from spiritual death to spiritual life; he has removed the old ordinances that were against us, and has made religion easy and pleasant; he has subdued our enemies, and triumphed over them. He achieved a glorious victory over 'principalities and powers,' and has led our great enemy captive. He met the enemy of man when on earth, and overcame his power of temptation; expelled him from the bodies of men; laid the foundation for a permanent victory over him on the cross, and triumphed over him when he rose and ascended to heaven. Satan is now an humbled foe. His power is broken and limited, and the Lord Jesus will yet completely triumph over him. He will return from heaven; raise *all* the dead; and reascend, in the face of the universe, to his native skies, with all his ransomed hosts—the 'spoils' of victory. We should not then fear what Satan can do to us; nor should we fear that the great enemy of the church will ever be triumphant.

Stand up, my soul, shake off thy fears,
  And gird the gospel armour on;
March to the gates of endless joy,
  Where thy great Captain Saviour's gone

Hell and thy sins resist thy course;
  But hell and sin are vanquish'd foes;
Thy Jesus nail'd them to the cross,
  And sung the triumph when he rose.

Then let my soul march boldly on,
  Press forward to the heavenly gate;
There peace and joy eternal reign,
  And glittering robes for conquerors wait

Then shall I wear a starry crown,
  And triumph in Almighty grace;
While all the armies of the skies
  Join in my glorious Leader's praise.

6. No individual has a right to appoint ceremonies and ordinances in the church to be binding on the consciences of others; nor is this authority intrusted to any body of men. Ver. 16. What *God* has enjoined is to be obeyed. What *man* enjoins beyond that, is of no binding force on the conscience; and it is the solemn and sacred duty of all Christians to resist all such attempts to make ceremonial observances binding on the conscience. Christ has appointed a *few* ordinances of religion—and they are enough. They are simple, easily observed, and all adapted to promote piety. He appointed baptism and the Lord's Supper; but he appointed no stated festivals or fasts; no days in commemoration of the saints, or of his own birth or death; he enjoined no rites

of religion but those which are most simple, and which are easily observed. He well knew how those observances would be abused to the purposes of superstition, and *obscure the great doctrine of justification by faith.* He knew how ready men would be to rely on them rather than on the merits of the great Sacrifice, and hence he appointed no ordinance where that danger could exist.

7. Pride is often united with apparent humility. Ver. 18. It is easy to *assume* the appearance of humility in the outer deportment, but no such assumed appearance reaches the heart. That remains the same, whatever external appearance is assumed, until it is renewed by the grace of God.

8. A meek, modest, and candid demeanour is consistent with great boldness and daring in speculation. Ver. 18. The most daring speculators in religion; they who make the most reckless attacks on the truth, are often, to appearance, eminently candid, and even put on the aspect of angelic devotion. Yet they are bold 'where angels fear to tread;' and they declaim with confidence on subjects which must be for ever beyond the grasp of the human mind.

9. We should not infer, because a man is modest and humble, and because he appears to be endued with uncommon meekness and piety, that, *therefore*, he is a good man or a safe guide. Ver. 18. The teachers in Colosse, against whom Paul warned the Christians there, appear to have been men just of this stamp; and this is commonly *assumed* by those who would lead their fellow-men into error. 'Satan is often transformed into an angel of light.'

10. We should not attempt to penetrate into those things which lie beyond the grasp of the human mind. Ver. 18. We should not 'intrude into those things which are unseen.' There is an outer limit to our investigations on all subjects, and we soon reach it. In life we are to act chiefly on *facts;* not on the *reason* why those facts exist. When we have ascertained or established *a fact*, our feet stand on a solid rock; and there we shall stand securely. We act safely and wisely if we act in view of *that fact;* we do *not* act safely or wisely if we disregard that, and act on theory or imagination.

11. Many real Christians are in danger of being 'beguiled of the reward' which they might obtain. Ver. 18. They are allured by the world; they are drawn into error by the arts of philosophy; they obscure the lustre of their piety by conformity to the world, and thus they lose the high recompense which they might have obtained in heaven. For the rewards of heaven will be strictly in proportion to the measure of our religion here—the zeal, and faith, and love which we evince in the cause of our Master.

12. Many persons are in danger of losing the 'reward' altogether—for the 'reward' of a life of piety is set before all. Ver. 18. Heaven is offered freely to all, and there is no one who might not obtain it. But, alas! how many there are who are drawn aside by the allurements of error and of sin; who are led to defer to a future time the great subject of preparation for death; who spend their lives in disregard of the commands of God and the invitations of mercy, until it is too late to seek salvation, and they sink down to final ruin. Every impenitent sinner is in imminent danger of losing his soul. The great deceiver is endeavouring to blind him and decoy him down to death, and a thousand snares on every side are spread for his feet, into which he is in constant danger of falling. In a world of allurements, where the work of death from the beginning has been carried on chiefly by deception, with what solicitude

CHAPTER III.

IF ye then be risen [a] with Christ, seek those things which are above, where Christ [b] sitteth on the right hand of God.

2 Set your [1] affection on things above, not [c] on things on the earth.

a c. 2. 12.

b Ro. 8. 34. 1 or, *mind*. c 1 Jno. 2. 15.

should man guard himself lest he be 'beguiled of heaven' and sink to a world where heaven will be offered no more!

CHAPTER III.

ANALYSIS OF THE CHAPTER.

In the previous chapter, the apostle had showed what a true Christian ought *not* to follow after. He had warned the Colossians against the dangers of false philosophy, and the doctrines of erroneous teachers. In this chapter, he teaches them what they *ought* to pursue and to seek. He therefore enjoins various duties in the different relations of life, which they ought to perform in such a way as to show that true religion had a controlling influence over their hearts. He specifies the following: (1.) The duty of setting the affections on things above. Vs. 1—4. They were risen with Christ (ch. ii. 12), they were dead to sin (ver. 3); they were soon to be like Christ (ver. 4), and they should, therefore, fix their affections on heavenly things. (2.) The duty of mortifying their corrupt passions and carnal propensities. Vs. 5—8. (3.) The duty of speaking the truth, since they had put off the old man with his deeds. Vs. 9—11. (4.) The duty of kindness, gentleness, charity, and the spirit of peace. Vs. 12—15. (5.) The duty of edifying one another by psalms and songs of praise. Vs. 16, 17. (6.) The duty of wives, ver. 18; (7.) of husbands, ver. 19; (8.) of children, ver. 20; (9.) of fathers, ver. 21; (10.) of servants, vs. 22—25. There is a very striking similarity between this chapter and the fifth and sixth chapters of the Epistle to the Ephesians, and a full exposition of the principal subjects adverted to here may be found in the Notes there.

1. *If ye then be risen with Christ.* The apostle in this place evidently founds the argument on what he had said in ch. ii. 12. See Notes on that passage. The argument is, that there was such an union between Christ and his people, that in virtue of *his* death *they* become dead to sin; that in virtue of *his* resurrection *they* rise to spiritual life, and that, *therefore*, as Christ now lives in heaven, they should live for heaven, and fix their affections there. ¶ *Seek those things which are above.* That is, seek them as the objects of pursuit and affection; strive to secure them. ¶ *Where Christ sitteth on the right hand of God.* Notes, Mark xvi. 19. The argument here is, that since Christ is there, and since he is the object of our supreme attachment, we should fix our affections on heavenly things, and seek to be prepared to dwell with him.

2. *Set your affection.* Marg., 'or *mind*.' Gr., '*think of*' — φρονεῖτε. The thoughts should be occupied about the things where Christ now dwells, where our final home is to be, where our great interests are. Since we are raised from the death of sin, and are made to live anew, the great object of our contemplation should be the heavenly world. ¶ *Not on things on the earth.* Wealth, honour, pleasure. Our affections should not be fixed on houses and lands; on scenes of fashion and gaiety; on low and debasing enjoyments.

3 For [a] ye are dead, and your life is hid with Christ in God.

4 When [b] Christ, *who is* [c] our life, shall appear, then shall ye also appear with him in glory.

a Ro. 6. 2. *b* 1 Jno. 3. 2. *c* Jno. 11. 25. 14. 6.

5 Mortify [d] therefore your members which are upon the earth; fornication, uncleanness, inordinate affection, evil concupiscence, and covetousness, which is idolatry:

d Ro. 8. 13. Ga. 5. 24. Ep. 5. 3-6.

3. *For ye are dead.* Dead to the world; dead to sin; dead to earthly pleasures. On the meaning of the word *dead*, see Notes on Rom. vi. 2. Eph. ii. 1. The idea of the apostle is, that as Christ became literally *dead* in the tomb, so we, in virtue of our connection with him, have become *dead* to sin, to worldly influences, pleasures, and ambition. Or, in other words, we are to be to them *as if* we were dead, and they had no more influence over us than the things of earth had over him in the grave. Notes, Rom. vi. 2. ¶ *And your life.* There is still *life.* Though *dead* to one class of objects, you are *alive* to others. See the sentiment here expressed, explained at large in the Notes on Gal. ii. 20. ¶ *Is hid with Christ in God.* The language here is taken probably from *treasure* which is 'hid' or concealed in a place of security; and the idea is, that eternal life is an invaluable *jewel* or *treasure*, which is laid up with Christ in heaven where God is. There it is safely deposited. It has this security, that it is with the Redeemer, and that he is in the presence of God; and thus nothing can reach it or take it away. It is not left with *us*, or intrusted to *our* keeping—for then it might be lost, as we might lose an invaluable jewel; or it might be wrested from us; or we might be defrauded of it; but it is now laid up far out of our sight, and far from the reach of all our enemies, and with one who can 'keep that which we have committed to him against that day.' 2 Tim. i. 12. Our eternal life, therefore, is as secure as it could possibly be made. The true condition of the Christian is, that he is 'dead' to this world, but that he has immortal *life* in prospect, and that is secure, being in the holy keeping of his Redeemer, now in the presence of God. From this it follows that he should regard himself as living for heaven.

4. *When Christ*, who is *our life.* Notes, John i. 4; xi. 25. ¶ *Shall appear.* In the day when he shall come to judge the world. ¶ *Then shall ye also appear with him in glory.* 1 Thess. iv. 16, 17. Christians shall then be raised from the dead, and ascend with the Redeemer to heaven.

5. *Mortify therefore your members.* Since you are dead to sin and the world, and are to appear with Christ in the glories of his kingdom, subdue every carnal and evil propensity of your nature. The word *mortify* means *to put to death* (Notes, Rom. viii. 13. Gal. v. 24), and the meaning here is, that they were entirely to subdue their evil propensities, so that they would have no remains of life; that is, they were not at all to indulge them. The word '*members*' here, refers to the different members of the body—as the seat of evil desires and passions. Comp. Notes, Rom. vi. 13. They were wholly to extirpate those evil passions which he specifies as having their seat in the various members of the earthly body. ¶ *Fornication.* Notes, Rom. i. 29. ¶ *Uncleanness.* Notes, Rom. i. 24. ¶ *Inordinate affection.* πάθος. Rendered in Rom. i. 26, 'vile *affections.*' See Notes on

6 For which things' sake the wrath of God cometh on the children of disobedience.

7 In[a] the which ye also walked sometime, when ye lived in them.

8 But now ye also put off all these; anger, wrath, malice, blasphemy, filthy communication out of your mouth.

9 Lie not one to another, seeing that ye have put off the old man with his deeds;

10 And have put on the new *man*, which is renewed[b] in knowledge after the image of him that created him:

a Ti. 3. 3.

b Eph. 4. 23, 24.

that verse. In 1 Thess. iv. 5, the word is rendered *lust*—which is its meaning here. ¶ *Evil concupiscence.* Evil desires; licentious passions. Rom. i. 24. *Greek.* ¶ *And covetousness, which is idolatry.* It is remarkable that the apostle always ranks *covetousness* with these base and detestable passions. The meaning here is, (1.) that it is a low and debasing passion, like those which he had specified; and (2.) that it secures the affections which properly belong to God, and is, therefore, idolatry. Of all base passions, this is the one that most dethrones God from the soul. See this whole passage more fully explained in the Notes on Eph. v. 3—5.

6. *For which things' sake*, &c. See Notes, Eph. v. 6, where the same expression occurs.

7. *In the which.* In all which evil passions. ¶ *Ye also walked sometime.* You formerly lived. These were the common vices of the heathen. Notes, Eph. v. 8. 1 Cor. vi. 10, 11. Comp. Notes, Rom. i. 24—32.

8. *But now ye also put off all these.* All these which follow, as being also inconsistent with the Christian calling. ¶ *Anger, wrath.* Notes, Eph. iv. 26. ¶ *Malice.* Notes, Eph. iv. 31. ¶ *Blasphemy.* Notes, Matt. ix. 3. The word *here* seems to mean *all* injurious and calumnious speaking—whether against God or man. ¶ *Filthy communication out of your mouth.* Lewd, indecent, and immodest discourse. Notes, Eph. iv. 29. The conversation of the heathen everywhere abounds with this. A pure method of conversation among men is the fruit of Christianity.

9. *Lie not one to another.* Notes, Eph. iv. 25. ¶ *Seeing that ye have put off the old man with his deeds.* Your former corrupt and evil nature. Notes, Eph. iv. 22. The reason for putting away lying, stated in Eph. iv. 25, is, that we 'are members one of another'—or are brethren. The reason assigned here is, that we have put off the old man with his deeds. The sense is, that *lying* is one of the fruits of sin. It is that which the corrupt nature of man naturally produces; and when that is put off, then all that that nature produces should be also put off with it. The vice of lying is a universal fruit of sin, and seems to exist everywhere where the gospel does not prevail. Comp. Notes on Titus i. 12. There is, perhaps, no single form of sin that reigns so universally in the heathen world.

10. *Which is renewed in knowledge.* In Eph. iv. 24, it is said that the new man is 'created after God in righteousness and true holiness.' In this place it is *added* that to the renewed soul *knowledge* is imparted, and it is made in that respect as man was when he was first created. This passage, in connection with Eph. iv. 24, proves that before man fell he was endowed with 'righteousness,

11 Where [a] there is neither Greek nor Jew, circumcision nor uncircumcision, Barbarian, Scythian, bond *nor* free: but Christ *is* all, and in all.

12 Put on therefore, as the elect of God, holy and beloved, bowels of mercies, kindness, humbleness of mind, meekness, long-suffering;

a Ro. 10. 12.

true holiness, and *knowledge*.' The *knowledge* here referred to, is not the knowledge of *everything*, but the knowledge *of God*. Man was acquainted with his Creator. He resembled him in his capacity for knowledge. He was an intelligent being, and he had an acquaintance with the divine existence and perfections. Comp. Notes on Rom. v. 12. But especially had he that knowledge which is the fear of the Lord; that knowledge of God which is the result of love. Piety, in the Scriptures, is often represented as the 'knowledge' of God. See Notes on John xvii. 3. Comp. Notes on Eph. iii. 19. ¶ *After the image of him that created him*. So as to resemble God. In *knowledge* he was made in the likeness of his Maker.

11. *Where there is neither Greek nor Jew*. See this fully explained in the Notes on Gal. iii. 28. The meaning here is, that all are on a level; that there is no distinction of nation in the church; that all are to be regarded and treated as brethren, and that *therefore* no one should be false to another, or lie to another. ¶ *Circumcision nor uncircumcision*. No one is admitted into that blessed society *because* he is circumcised; no one is excluded *because* he is uncircumcised. That distinction is unknown, and all are on a level. ¶ *Barbarians*. No one is excluded *because* he is a barbarian, or because he lives among those who are uncivilized, and is unpolished in his manners. See the word *barbarian* explained in the Notes on Rom. i. 14. ¶ *Scythian*. This word does not occur elsewhere in the New Testament. The name *Scythian* is applied in ancient geography to the people who lived on the north and north-east of the Black and Caspian Seas, a region stretching indefinitely into the unknown countries of Asia. They occupied the lands now peopled by the Monguls and Tartars. The name was almost synonymous with *barbarian*, for they were regarded as a wild and savage race. The meaning here is, that even such a ferocious and uncivilized people were not excluded from the gospel, but they were as welcome as any other, and were entitled to the same privileges as others. No one was excluded because he belonged to the most rude and uncivilized portion of mankind. ¶ *Bond* nor *free*. See Notes, Gal. iii. 28. ¶ *But Christ* is *all, and in all*. The great thing that constitutes the peculiarity of the church is, that Christ is its Saviour, and that all are his friends and followers. Its members lay aside all other distinctions, and are known only as *his* friends. They are not known as Jews and Gentiles; as of this nation or that; as slaves or freemen, but they are known as Christians; distinguished from *all* the rest of mankind as the united friends of the Redeemer. Comp. Notes on Gal. iii. 28.

12. *Put on, therefore, as the elect of God*. The fact that you thus belong to one and the same church; that you have been redeemed by the same blood, and chosen by the same grace, and that you are all brethren, should lead you to manifest a spirit of kindness, gentleness, and love. ¶ *Bowels of mercies*. Notes, Phil. ii. 1. ¶ *Kindness*, &c. See Notes on Eph. iv. 32. The language here

13 Forbearing [a] one another, and forgiving [b] one another, if any man have a quarrel [1] against any: even as Christ forgave you, so also *do* ye.

14 And above all these things *put on* charity,[c] which is [d] the bond of perfectness.

15 And let the peace [e] of God rule in your hearts, to the which also ye are called in one body; and be ye thankful.

a Mar. 11. 25. Ep. 4. 2. 32.
b Mat. 6. 14, 15. [1] or, *complaint*.
c 1 Pe. 4. 8. *d* 1 Co. 13. 2, 8, 13.
e Ph. 4. 7.

---

is a little different from what it is there, but the sentiment is the same.

13. *Forbearing one another.* Notes, Eph. iv. 2. ¶ *And forgiving one another.* Notes, Matt. vi. 12. 14. ¶ *If any man have a quarrel against any.* Marg., 'or *complaint*.' The word here used—μομφή—occurs nowhere else in the New Testament. It means, *fault found, blame, censure;* and here denotes *occasion of complaint.* The idea is, that if another one has given us *just occasion of complaint*, we are to forgive him; that is, we are (1.) to harbour no malice against him; (2.) we are to be ready to do him good as if he had not given us occasion of complaint; (3.) we are to be willing to *declare* that we forgive him when he asks it; and (4.) we are always afterwards to treat him as kindly as if he had not injured us—*as God treats* us *when he forgives us.* See Notes, Matt. xviii. 21. ¶ *Even as Christ forgave you, so also* do *ye.* Learn here that Christ has power to forgive sin. Comp. Notes, Matt. ix. 6. Acts v. 31. Christ forgave us (1.) *freely*—he did not hesitate or delay when we asked him; (2.) *entirely*—he pardoned *all* our offences; (3.) *for ever*—he did it so as to remember our sins no more, and to treat us ever onward *as if* we had not sinned. So *we* should forgive an offending brother.

14. *And above all these things.* Over, or upon all these things. Comp. Notes, Eph. vi. 16. ¶ *Charity.* Love. Notes, 1 Cor. xiii. 1. ¶ *Which is the bond of perfectness.* The bond of all perfection; the thing which will unite all other things, and make them complete. Comp. the parallel place in Eph. iv. 3. The idea seems to be that love will bind all the other graces fast together, and render the whole system complete. Without love, though there might be other graces and virtues, there would be a want of harmony and compactness in our christian graces, and this was necessary to unite and complete the whole. There is great beauty in the expression, and it contains most important truth. If it were possible to conceive that the other graces could exist among a christian people, yet there would be a sad incompleteness, a painful want of harmony and union, if love were not the reigning principle. Nor faith, nor zeal, nor prophecy, nor the power of speaking with the tongue of angels, would answer the purpose. See this sentiment expressed in 1 Cor. xiii., and the effect of love more fully explained in the Notes on that chapter.

15. *And let the peace of God.* The peace which God gives. Notes. Phil. iv. 7. ¶ *Rule in your hearts.* Preside in your hearts; sit as umpire there (*Doddridge*); govern and control you. The word here rendered *rule*—βραβευέτω—is commonly used in reference to the Olympic and other games. It means, to be a director, or arbiter of the public games; to preside over them and preserve order, and to distribute the prizes to the victors. The meaning here is, that the peace which God gives to

16 Let the word [a] of Christ dwell in you richly in all wisdom; teaching and admonishing one another in psalms [b] and hymns and spiritual songs, singing with grace in your hearts to the Lord.

17 And whatsoever [c] ye do in word or deed, *do* all in the name of the Lord Jesus, giving thanks to God and the Father by him.

a Ps. 119. 11. *b* Ep. 5. 19. *c* 1 Co. 10. 31.

the soul is to be to us what the *brabeutes*, or governor at the games was to those who contended there. It is to preside over and govern the mind; to preserve everything in its place; and to save it from tumult, disorder, and irregularity. The thought is a very beautiful one. The soul is liable to the agitations of passion and excitement—like an assembled multitude of men. It needs something to preside over it, and keep its various faculties in place and order; and nothing is so well fitted to do this as the calm peace which religion gives, a deep sense of the presence of God, the desire and the evidence of his friendship, the hope of his favour, and the belief that he has forgiven all our sins. The 'peace of God' will thus calm down every agitated element of the soul; subdue the tumult of passion, and preserve the mind in healthful action and order—as a ruler sways and controls the passions of assembled multitudes of men. ¶ *To the which ye are also called.* To which peace. ¶ *In one body.* To be one body; or to be united as one. Notes, Eph. iv. 4—6. ¶ *And be ye thankful.* For all mercies, and especially for your privileges and hopes as Christians. A spirit of thankfulness, also, would tend much to promote harmony and peace. An ungrateful people is commonly a tumultuous, agitated, restless, and dissatisfied people. Nothing better tends to promote peace and order than gratitude to God for his mercies.

16. *Let the word of Christ.* The doctrine of Christ. ¶ *Dwell in you richly in all wisdom.* Abundantly, producing the spirit of true wisdom. That doctrine is adapted to make you wise. The meaning is, that they were to lay up the doctrines of the gospel in their hearts; to meditate upon them; to allow them to be their guide, and to endeavour wisely to improve them to the best purpose. ¶ *Teaching and admonishing*, &c. See this explained in the Notes on Eph. v. 19, 20. The only additional thought here is, that their psalms and hymns were to be regarded as a method of '*teaching*' and '*admonishing;*' that is, they were to be imbued with truth, and to be such as to elevate the mind, and withdraw it from error and sin. Dr. Johnson once said, that if he were allowed to make the ballads of a nation, he cared not who made the laws. It is true in a more important sense that he who is permitted to make the *hymns* of a church, need care little who preaches, or who makes the creed. He will more effectually mould the sentiments of a church than they who preach or make creeds and confessions. Hence, it is indispensable, in order to the preservation of the truth, that the sacred songs of a church should be imbued with sound evangelical sentiment.

17. *And whatsoever ye do in word or deed.* Whatever ye say or do—whether relating to temporal affairs or to religion. The command here extends to *all* that we do. ¶ Do *all in the name of the Lord Jesus.* Do it all because he requires and commands it, and with a desire to honour him. His authority should be the warrant; his glory the aim of all

18 Wives, [a] submit yourselves unto your own husbands, as it is fit in the Lord.

19 Husbands, love *your* wives, and be not bitter against them.

20 Children, [b] obey *your* parents in all things: for this is well pleasing unto the Lord.

21 Fathers, provoke not your children *to anger*, lest they be discouraged.

22 Servants, [c] obey in all things *your* masters according to the flesh: not with eye-service, as men-pleasers; but in singleness of heart, fearing God:

23 And whatsoever ye do, do *it* heartily, as to the Lord and not unto men;

24 Knowing, that of the Lord ye shall receive the reward of the inheritance: for ye serve the Lord Christ.

25 But he that doeth wrong shall receive for the wrong which he hath done: and there is no respect of persons.

a Ep. 5. 22, &c. Ti. 2. 4, 5. 1 Pe. 3. 1, &c. *b* Ep. 6. 1, &c. *c* 1 Pe. 2. 18.

---

our actions and words. See the general sentiment here expressed, fully illustrated in the Notes on 1 Cor. x. 31. ¶ *Giving thanks to God and the Father by him.* Through him; or in his name. All our actions are to be accompanied with thanksgiving. Notes, Phil. iv. 6. We are to engage in every duty, not only in the name of Christ, but with thankfulness for strength and reason; for the privilege of acting so that we *may* honour him; and with a grateful remembrance of the mercy of God that gave us such a Saviour to be an example and guide. He is most likely to do his duty well who goes to it with a heart overflowing with gratitude to God for his mercies, and he who is likely to perform his duties with the most cheerful fidelity, is he who has the deepest sense of the divine goodness in providing a Saviour for his lost and ruined soul. See Notes on 2 Cor. v. 14, 15.

18. *Wives, submit yourselves,* &c. Notes on the parallel passage in Eph. v. 21—24.

19. *Husbands, love* your *wives,* &c. Notes on Eph. v. 25—29.

20. *Children, obey* your *parents,* &c. Notes on Eph. vi. 1—4.

21. *Fathers, provoke not,* &c. Notes on Eph. vi. 4. ¶ *Lest they be discouraged.* Lest, by your continually finding fault with them, they should lose all courage, and despair of ever pleasing you. There is much sound sense and practical wisdom in this observation of the apostle. Children should not be *flattered*, but they should be *encouraged.* They should not be so praised as to make them vain and proud, but they should be commended when they do well. The *desire* of praise should not be the principle from which they should be taught to act, but they should feel that the approbation of parents is a desirable thing, and when they act so as to deserve that approbation, no injury is done them by their understanding it. He who always finds fault with a child; who is never satisfied with what he does; who scolds and frets and complains, let him do as he will, breaks his spirit, and soon destroys in the delicate texture of his soul all *desire* of doing well The child in despair soon gives over every effort to please. He becomes sullen, morose, stupid, and indifferent to all the motives that can be presented to him, and becomes to a great extent indifferent as to *what* he does—since all that he does meets with the same reception from the parent.

22—25. *Servants, obey in all things,* &c. See Notes on Eph. vi 5—8.

CHAPTER IV.

MASTERS,[a] give unto *your* servants that which is just and equal; knowing that ye also have a Master in heaven.

a Ep. 6. 9, &c.

CHAPTER IV.

1. *Masters, give unto* your *servants*, &c. See Notes on Eph. vi. 9. ¶ *That which is just and equal.* What they *ought* to have; what is fairly their due. The apostle here, probably, refers to bondmen or slaves, and the propriety of this rule is apparent. Such persons were subject to their masters' control; their time and services were at their disposal, and they could not enforce their just and equal claims by an appeal to the *laws*. They were, therefore, dependent on the equity and kindness of their masters. There can be no doubt that not a few who were converted to the christian faith were held to involuntary servitude (see 1 Cor. vii.); and it is as clear that the apostles did not design to make a violent disruption of these bonds, or to lead the slaves to rise and murder their masters. See Notes, 1 Tim. vi. 1—4. But it is equally clear that they meant to represent slavery as a hard and undesirable condition; that they intended to instruct the slaves to embrace the earliest opportunity to be free which was presented (1 Cor. vii. 21); and that they meant to suggest such considerations, and to lay down such principles as would lead masters to emancipate their slaves, and thus ultimately to abolish it. Among these principles are such as these. (1.) That all men were of one and the same blood. Acts xvii. 26. (2.) That they were all redeemed by the same Saviour, and were brethren. 1 Tim. vi. 2. Philem. 16. If redeemed; if they were 'brethren;' if they were heirs of glory, they were not '*chattels*,' or '*things*;' and how could a Christian conscientiously hold or regard them *as property?* (3.) That they were to 'render them that which was *just* and *equal*.' What would follow from this if fairly applied? What *would* be *just* and *equal* to a man in those circumstances? Would it not be (*a*) to compensate him *fairly* for his labour; to furnish him an adequate remuneration for what he had earned? But this would strike a blow at the root of slavery—for one of the elementary principles of it is, that there *must* be 'unrequited labour;' that is, *the slave must earn as much more than he receives as will do his part in maintaining the master in idleness*, for it is of the very essence of the system that he is to be maintained in indolence by the slaves which he owns—or just so far as he owns a slave. If he were disposed to earn his own living, he would not need the labour of slaves. No man ever yet became the permanent owner of a slave from *benevolence* to him, or because he desired to pay him fully for his work, or because he meant himself to work in order to maintain his slave in indolence. (*b*) If a man should in fact render to his slaves 'that which is just and equal,' would he not restore them to freedom? Have they not been deprived of their liberty by *injustice*, and would not 'justice' restore it? What has the *slave* done to forfeit his liberty? If he should make him 'equal' in rights to himself, or to what he is by nature, would he not emancipate him? Has he not been reduced to his present condition by withholding that which is '*equal?*' Has he 'equal' rights, and 'equal' privileges with other *men?* Has he not been cut off from them by *denying* him the equality to which he is entitled in the arrangements of God's government? Can he be held at all without violating all the just notions of *equality?* Though, therefore, it may

2 Continue [a] in prayer, and watch [b] in the same with thanksgiving;

3 Withal praying also for us, that God would open [c] unto us a door of utterance, to speak the mystery of Christ, for which I am also in bonds:

4 That I may make it manifest, as I ought to speak.

5 Walk in wisdom [d] toward them that are without, redeeming the time.

a Lu. 18. 1. b Mar. 13. 33. c 2 Th. 3. 1. d Ps. 90. 12. Ep. 5. 15, 16.

---

be true that this passage only enjoins the rendering of that which was 'just' and 'equal' *in* their condition as slaves, yet it contains a *principle* which would 'lay the axe at the root' of slavery, and would lead a conscientious Christian to the feeling that his slaves *ought* to be free. These principles actually effected the freedom of slaves in the Roman empire in a few centuries after Christianity was introduced, and they are destined to effect it yet all over the world. ¶ *Knowing that ye also have a Master in heaven.* Notes, Eph. vi. 9.

2. *Continue in prayer.* That is, do not neglect it; observe it at all stated times; maintain the spirit of prayer, and embrace all proper occasions to engage in it. Comp. Notes, Luke xviii. 1. Eph. vi. 18. 1 Thess. iv. 17. ¶ *And watch in the same with thanksgiving.* Watch for favourable opportunities; watch that your mind may be in a right frame *when* you pray; and watch, that when your mind *is* in a right frame you may not neglect to pray. See Notes on Eph. vi. 18. Phil. iv. 6.

3. *Withal.* With all the supplications which you offer for other persons and things; or at the same time that you pray for them. ¶ *Praying also for us.* Notes, Eph. vi. 19, 20. Comp. 2 Cor. i. 11. Phil. i. 19. Heb. xiii. 18, 19. ¶ *That God would open to us a door of utterance.* To preach the gospel. He earnestly desired to have liberty to preach the gospel, and asked them to pray that this might be restored to him. See Notes on Eph. vi. 19. ¶ *To speak the mystery of Christ.* Called in Eph. vi. 19, the 'mystery of the gospel.' See Notes there. ¶ *For which I also am in bonds.* A prisoner at Rome. Notes, Eph. vi. 20.

4. *That I may make it manifest,* &c. Notes, Eph. vi. 20.

5. *Walk in wisdom.* That is, conduct uprightly and honestly. Deal with them on the strictest principles of integrity, so that they may not have occasion to reproach the religion which you profess. ¶ *Toward them that are without.* Without the pale of the church, or who are not professing Christians. See Notes on 1 Cor. v. 12. They were surrounded by heathens, as Christians now are by men of the world. The injunction is one that requires us to act with prudence and propriety (ἐν σοφίᾳ) towards them; and there is perhaps not a more important direction in the New Testament than this. Among the reasons for this are the following: (1.) Men of the world judge of religion, not from the *profession*, but from the *life* of its friends. (2.) They judge of religion, not from preaching, or from books, or from the conduct of its Founder and his apostles, but from what they see in the daily walk and conversation of the members of the church. (3.) They *understand* the nature of religion so well as to know when its friends are or are not consistent with their profession. (4.) They set a much higher value on honesty and integrity than they do on the doctrines and duties

6 Let your speech *be* alway with grace, seasoned [a] with salt, that ye may know how ye ought to answer every man.

a Mar. 9. 50.

of religion; and if the professed friends of religion are destitute of the principles of truth and honesty, they think they have nothing of any value. They may be very devout on the Sabbath; very regular at prayer-meetings; very strict in the observance of rites and ceremonies —but all these are of little worth in the estimation of the world, unless attended with an upright life. (5.) No professing Christian can possibly do good to others who does not live an upright life. If you have cheated a man out of never so small a sum, it is vain that *you* talk to him about the salvation of his soul; if you have failed to pay him a debt when it was due, or to finish a piece of work when you promised it, or to tell him the exact truth in conversation, it is vain for *you* to endeavour to induce him to be a Christian. He will *feel*, if he does not *say*—and he *might* very properly say—that he wants no religion which will not make a man honest. (6.) No man *will attempt* to do much good to others whose own life is not upright. He will be sensible of the inconsistency, and will feel that he *cannot* do it with any sense of propriety; and the honour of religion, therefore, and the salvation of our fellow-men, demand that in all our intercourse with others, we should lead lives of the strictest integrity. ¶ *Redeeming the time.* Notes, Eph. v. 16.

6. *Let your speech.* Your conversation. In the previous verse the apostle had given a *general* direction that our conduct towards those who are not professing Christians should be wise and prudent; he here gives a *particular* direction in regard to our conversation. ¶ Be *alway with grace.* Imbued with the spirit of religion. It should be such as religion is fitted to produce; such as to show that the grace of God is in our hearts. Bloomfield supposes that this means 'courteous and agreeable, not morose and melancholy.' But though this may be included, and though the rule here laid down would lead to that, it cannot be *all* that is intended. It rather means that our conversation should be such as to show that we are governed by the principles of religion, and that there is unfeigned piety in the heart. This will indeed *make* us mild, courteous, agreeable, and urbane in our conversation; but it will do more than this. It will imbue our discourse *with the spirit of religion*, so as to show that the soul is under the influence of love to the Redeemer. ¶ *Seasoned with salt.* Salt, among the Greeks, was the emblem of *wit.* Here the meaning seems to be, that our conversation should be seasoned with piety or grace in a way similar to that in which we employ salt in our food. It makes it wholesome and palatable. So with our conversation. If it be not imbued with the spirit of piety, it is flat, insipid, unprofitable, injurious. The spirit of piety will make it what it should be—useful, agreeable, beneficial to mankind. This does not mean that our conversation is to be always, strictly speaking, *religious*—wherever we may be—any more than our food should be mere salt; but it means that, *whatever* be the topic, the spirit of piety should be diffused through it—as the salt in our food should properly season it all—whatever the article of food may be. ¶ *That ye may know how ye ought to answer every man.* Be imbued with the spirit of piety, that you may not utter anything that would be rash and foolish, but be prepared to answer any one who mav

7 All [a] my state shall Tychicus declare unto you, *who is* a beloved brother, and a faithful minister and fellow-servant in the Lord:

8 Whom I have sent unto you for the same purpose, that he might know your estate, and comfort your hearts;

9 With Onesimus, [b] a faithful and beloved brother, who is *one* of you. They shall make known unto you all things which *are done* here.

a Ep. 6. 21, 22.

b Phi. 10.

---

question you about your religion in a way that will show that you understand its nature, and that will tend to edification. This remark may be extended farther. It may be understood as meaning also, 'be imbued with the spirit of religion, and you will be able to answer any man appropriately on any subject. If he asks you about the evidence or the nature of religion, you will be able to reply to him. If he converses with you on the common topics of the day, you will be able to answer him in a mild, kind, affable spirit. If he asks you of things of which you are ignorant; if he introduces some topic of science with which you are not acquainted, you will not be ashamed to confess your ignorance, and to seek instruction. If he addresses you in a haughty, insolent, and overbearing manner, you will be able to repress the risings of your temper, and to answer him with gentleness and kindness.' Comp. Luke ii. 46.

7, 8. *All my state shall Tychicus declare unto you.* See these verses explained in the Notes, Eph. vi. 21, 22.

9. *With Onesimus.* Who had been formerly a servant of Philemon, an inhabitant of Colosse. See Notes, Philem. 10. Onesimus had probably been recently converted; and Paul felt towards him the warm attachment of a brother. Philem. 16. In what way he became acquainted with him is unknown. A more full account of him will be found in the Notes on the Epistle to Philemon. ¶ *Who is* one *of you.* That is, either who is from your city, or one of your own people and nation. It is clear from this, that Onesimus was from Phrygia, and probably from the city of Colosse itself. It would seem also that he was of a higher rank than is designated by the word '*slave*' now. He was, indeed, a 'servant'—δοῦλος—of Philemon, but would the apostle have addressed the Colossians, and said that he was 'one of *them*,' if he had occupied precisely the condition which is now denoted by the word *slave?* Would a minister of the gospel now in the Northern States, who should send a letter by a runaway slave to a community of masters at the South, say of him that he was '*one of them?*' Would it be kindly received, or produce a good *impression*, if he did? There is reason, therefore, to think that Onesimus was not a *slave* in the proper sense, but that he might have been a respectable youth, who had bound himself to service for a term of years. Comp. Philem. 18. ¶ *They shall make known to you all things which* are done *here.* Relating to Paul himself and the state of the church in Rome. As the epistle which Paul sent was designed not only for them, but to be a part of the volume of revealed truth, he *wrote* only those things which would be of permanent interest. Other matters he left for those who carried the epistle to communicate. It would also serve to give Tychicus and Onesimus more respectability in view of the church at Colosse, if he referred the

10 Aristarchus [a] my fellow-prisoner saluteth you, and Marcus, [b] sister's son to Barnabas (touching whom ye received commandments: if he come unto you, receive him;)

11 And Jesus, which is called Justus; who are of the circumcision. These only *are my* fellow workers unto the kingdom of God, which have been a comfort unto me.

a Ac. 27. 2. *b* Ac. 15. 37. 2 Ti. 4. 11.

church to them for information on important points.

10. *Aristarchus my fellow-prisoner.* Aristarchus was of Thessalonica, and is mentioned in Acts xix. 29; xx. 4, as Paul's companion in his travels. In Acts xxvii. 2, it is said that he accompanied him in his voyage to Rome, and from the passage before us it appears that he was there imprisoned with him. As he held the same sentiments as Paul, and was united with him in his travels and labours, it was natural that he should be treated in the same manner. He, together with Gaius, had been seized in the tumult at Ephesus and treated with violence, but he adhered to the apostle in all his troubles, and attended him in all his perils. Nothing further is certainly known of him, though "the Greeks say that he was bishop of Assamea in Syria, and was beheaded with Paul at Rome, under Nero." *Calmet.* ¶ *And Marcus, sister's son to Barnabas.* John Mark, in relation to whom Paul and Barnabas had formerly disagreed so much as to cause a separation between Barnabas and Paul. The ground of the disagreement was, that Barnabas wished to take him, probably on account of relationship, with them in their travels; Paul was unwilling to take him, because he had, on one occasion, departed from them. Notes, Acts xv. 37—39. They afterwards became reconciled, and Paul mentions Mark here with affection. He sent for him when he sent Tychicus to Ephesus, and it seems that he had come to him in obedience to his request. 2 Tim. iv. 11. Mark had probably become more decided, and Paul did not harbour unkind and unforgiving feelings towards any one. ¶ *Touching whom ye received commandments.* What these directions were, and how they were communicated, whether verbally or by writing, is now unknown. It was, not improbably, on some occasion when Paul was with them. He refers to it here in order that they might know distinctly whom he meant. ¶ *If he come to you, receive him.* In Philem. 24, Mark is mentioned as a 'fellow-labourer' of Paul. It would seem probable, therefore, that he was not a prisoner. Paul here intimates that he was about to leave Rome, and he enjoins it on the Colossians to receive him kindly. This injunction may have been necessary, as the Colossians may have been aware of the breach between him and Paul, and may have been disposed to regard him with suspicion. Paul retained no malice, and now commended, in the warmest manner, one from whom he was formerly constrained to separate.

11. *And Jesus, who is called Justus.* The name Jesus was probably that which he bore among the Jews. Justus is a Roman name, and was probably that by which he was known among the Romans. It was not uncommon thus to assume another name when one went among a foreign people. Comp. Notes, Acts xiii. 9. ¶ *Who are of the circumcision.* Jews, or Jewish Christians. Nothing more is known of Justus. ¶ *These only* are my *fellow-workers*

12 Epaphras, who is *one* of you, a servant of Christ, saluteth you, always labouring [1] fervently [a] for you in prayers, that ye may stand [b] perfect and [2] complete in all the will of God.

13 For I bear him record, that he hath a great zeal for you, and them *that are* in Laodicea and them in Hierapolis.

14 Luke, [c] the beloved physician, and Demas, greet you.

[1] or, *striving*. [a] Ja. 5. 16. [b] Mat. 5. 48. He. 6. 1. [2] or, *filled*. [c] 2 Ti. 4. 10, 11.

unto the kingdom of God. The word '*only*' here, probably refers to the fact that they only of *all the Jews* who were at Rome assisted Paul in his work. Epaphras and Luke were also with him at Rome, and doubtless aided him. ¶ *Which have been a comfort unto me.* The more so because they were Jews. The other Jews in Rome stood aloof, and doubtless endeavoured to augment the trials of the apostle. Comp. Acts xxviii. 23—29.

12. *Epaphras.* Notes, ch. i. 7. ¶ *Always labouring fervently for you in prayers.* Marg., 'or *striving*.' Gr., *agonizing*. The word denotes the *intense desire* which he had for their salvation; his fervent, earnest pleading for their welfare. ¶ *That ye may stand perfect and complete.* Marg., as in Gr., *filled*. The desire was, that they might maintain their christian principles unadulterated by the mixture of philosophy and error, and completely perform the will of God in every respect. This is the expression of a pious *wish* in regard to them, without any affirmation that any had been absolutely perfect, or that they would be perfect in this world. It is, however, a command of God that we should be perfect (see Matt. v. 48), and it is the highest wish of benevolence in reference to any one that he may be complete in moral character, and may do all the will of God. Comp. Notes on 2 Cor. xiii. 9.

13. *For I bear him record.* Paul had had abundant opportunity to know what were his feelings in regard to these churches. ¶ *A great zeal for you.* A great desire to promote your welfare. ¶ *And them that are in Laodicea.* Laodicea was the capital of Phrygia, and not far from Colosse. There was a church there. See the Introduction, and Notes on ver. 16. ¶ *And them in Hierapolis.* This was also a city in Phrygia, and not far from Laodicea and Colosse. It was situated under a hill to the north, and had on the south a large plain about five miles over. On the south of that plain, and opposite to Hierapolis, was Laodicea, with the river Lycus running between them, nearer to Laodicea than to Hierapolis. This place is now called by the Turks *Pambuck-Kulasi*, or the *Cotton-Tower*, on account of the white cliffs which lie round about it. It is now utterly forsaken and desolate, but the ruins are so magnificent as to show that it was once one of the most splendid cities in the East. It was celebrated for the hot springs in its vicinity, and on account of the numerous temples erected there, it received the name of *Hierapolis*, or the *holy city*. The principal deity worshipped there was Apollo. See Travels by T. Smith, B. D., 1678. Comp. Notes on ver. 16. From the allusion to it here, it would seem that there were Christians there in the time of Paul, though there is no mention of a *church* there. It is nowhere else mentioned in the New Testament.

14. *Luke, the beloved physician.* This was undoubtedly the author of the gospel which bears his name, and of the Acts of the Apostles. He is mentioned as the travelling com-

15 Salute the brethren which are in Laodicea, and Nymphas, and the [a] church which is in his house.

16 And when [b] this epistle is read among you, cause that it be read also in the church of the Laodiceans; and that ye likewise read the *epistle* from Laodicea.

a Ro. 16. 5. 1 Co. 16. 19. b 1 Th 5. 27.

panion of Paul in Acts xvii. 10, and appears to have accompanied him afterwards until his imprisonment at Rome. See 2 Tim. iv. 11. From ver. 11 of this chapter, it is evident that he was not by birth a Jew, but was probably a proselyte. He is supposed to have been a native of Cyrene, and to have died in Achaia, soon after the martyrdom of Paul, at the advanced age of eighty-four. See Rob. Cal. Art. *Luke.* He is here mentioned as a *physician*, and in his Gospel, and in the Acts, there are incidental evidences that he was acquainted with the science of medicine, and that he observed the events which he has recorded with the eye of one who practised the healing art. It is easy to imagine that the presence of a physician might have been of important service to the apostle Paul in his travels, and that his acquaintance with the art of healing may have aided not a little in the furtherance of the gospel. The miraculous power of healing, possessed by the Saviour and his apostles, contributed much to the success of their preaching; for the power of alleviating pain of body—of restoring to health by miracles, would not only be an evidence of the divine origin of their mission—a credential that they were sent from God, but would dispose those who had received such important benefits to listen attentively to the message of salvation. One of the best qualifications in missionaries in modern times, in order to gain access to the heathen, is an acquaintance with the healing art. ¶ *And Demas.* Demas is mentioned in two other places, Philem. 24, and 2 Tim. iv. 10. He is here spoken of with commendation as one in whom the apostle had confidence. Afterwards, when troubles thickened, he was not found proof to the trials which threatened him in Rome, and forsook the apostle and went to Thessalonica. He did this under the influence of the 'love of this present world,' or of life, evidently unwilling to lay down his life in the cause for which Paul suffered. See Notes on 2 Tim. iv. 10. His departure, and that of the others on whom Paul relied in Rome, was one of the severest trials which he was called there to endure. See Notes on 2 Tim. iv. 16.

15. *Salute the brethren which are in Laodicea.* Notes, ch. ii. 1. ¶ *And Nymphas.* This person is nowhere else mentioned, and nothing more is known of him. ¶ *And the church which is in his house.* Notes, Rom. xvi. 5.

16. *And when this epistle is read among you, cause that it be read also in the church of the Laodiceans.* Laodicea was near to Colosse, and the church there was evidently exposed to the same dangers from philosophy and false teachers as that at Colosse. The counsels in this epistle, therefore, would be equally applicable to both. In 1 Thess. v. 27, the apostle also charges those to whom that epistle was addressed to see that it be "read unto all the holy brethren." It is evident that the apostles designed that the letters which they addressed to the churches should be read also by others, and should become the permanent source of instruction to the friends of Christ.

17 And say to Archippus, [a] Take [b] heed to the ministry which thou hast received in the Lord, that thou fulfil it.

a Phi. 2. *b* 1 Ti. 4. 17.

Laodicea, here referred to, was the seat of one of the 'Seven churches' of Asia (Rev. iii. 14); was a city of Phrygia, and was its capital. It was situated on the river Lycus (hence called λαοδίκεια ἐπὶ λύκῳ—*Laodicea on the Lycus*), and stood at the southwestern angle of Phrygia. Its early name appears to have been Diospolis, changed subsequently to Rhoas. The name Laodicea was given to it by Antiochus Theos, in honour of his wife Laodice. Under the Romans it became a very flourishing commercial city. It was often damaged by earthquakes, but was restored by the Roman emperors. It is supposed to have been destroyed during the inroad of Timur Leng, A. D., 1402. The ruins are called by the Turks *Eski Hissar*. These ruins, and the ruins of Hierapolis, were visited by Mr. Riggs, an American missionary, in 1842, who thus speaks of them: "These spots, so interesting to the Christian, are now utterly desolate. The threatening expressed in Rev. iii. 10, has been fulfilled, and Laodicea is but a name. In the midst of one of the finest plains of Asia Minor, it is entirely without inhabitant. Sardis, in like manner, whose church had a name to live, but was dead, is now an utter desolation. Its soil is turned up by the plough, or overgrown by rank weeds; while in Philadelphia, since the day when our Saviour commended those who had there 'kept the word of his patience,' there has never ceased to be a nominally christian church. The ruins of Laodicea and Hierapolis are very extensive. The stadium of the former city, and the gymnasia and theatres of both, are the most complete which I have anywhere seen. Hierapolis is remarkable also for the so-called frozen cascades, a natural curiosity, in its kind probably not surpassed for beauty and extent in the world. It consists of a deposit of carbonate of lime, white as the driven snow, assuming, when closely examined, various forms, and covering nearly the whole southern and western declivities of the elevation on which the city was built. It is visible for many miles, and has procured for the place the name by which alone Hierapolis is known among the Turks, of the Cotton Castle." The cut on the following page will illustrate the ruins of Laodicea. ¶ *And that ye likewise read the* epistle *from Laodicea.* In regard to this epistle, see Introduction, § 6.

17. *And say to Archippus.* Archippus is mentioned also in Philem. 2. He is not elsewhere referred to in the New Testament, and nothing further is known of him. ¶ *Take heed to the ministry*, &c. The Greek here is, τὴν διακονίαν—meaning the office of ministering in divine things; but it is not certain precisely what office he held there. It seems probable, from the language which the apostle applies to him—'the ministry'—(comp. Acts i. 17. 25; vi. 4; xx. 24; xxi. 19. Rom. xi. 13. 1 Cor. xii. 5. 2 Cor. iii. 7, 8, 9; iv. 1; v. 18; vi. 3. Eph. iv. 12), that he was not *a deacon*, properly so called, but that he was a preacher of the word. In Philem. 2, he is mentioned by Paul as his 'fellow-soldier,' and it is evident that the apostle meant to speak of him with honour. There is no evidence, as has been supposed by some, that he intended to imply, by what he said, that he had been remiss in the performance of his duties, but the apostle doubtless meant to encourage him, and to excite him to increased ardour and zeal in the

LAODICEA.—From Macfarlane's "Seven Apocalyptic Churches."

18 The salutation [a] by the hand of me Paul. Remember [b] my bonds. Grace *be* with you. Amen.

Written from Rome to the Colossians, by Tychicus and Onesimus.

a 2 Th. 3. 17. *b* He. 13. 3, 25.

work of the Lord. Comp. Notes Acts xx. 28. It is always proper to caution even the most faithful and self-denying servants of the Lord to 'take heed,' or see to it, that they perform their duties with fidelity. The office of the ministry is such, and the temptations to unfaithfulness are so great, that we need constant watchfulness. ¶ *That thou fulfil it.* That there be nothing wanting, or lacking, in any of the departments of labour which you are called to perform.

18. *The salutation by the hand of me Paul.* Probably the rest of the epistle was written by an amanuensis. As was his custom, Paul affixed his own hand to it in the form of a salutation. Comp. Notes, 1 Cor. xvi. 21. 2 Thess. iii. 17. ¶ *Remember my bonds.* Also evidently written by his own hand, to make the injunction more impressive. Comp. Notes, Heb. xiii. 3. The meaning is, that they should not forget him in his confinement. They should remember that he was suffering on their account (Notes, ch. i. 24), and that he was entitled to every expression of sympathy and love. ¶ *Grace be with you.* Notes, Rom. xvi. 20.

The subscription to this epistle is undoubtedly correct. See the Introduction.

THE END.

CPSIA information can be obtained at www.ICGtesting.com
227074LV00004B/73/P
9 781163 322611